T0238629

Communications
in Computer and Information Science 335

Sabu M. Thampi   Albert Y. Zomaya
Thorsten Strufe   Jose M. Alcaraz Calero
Tony Thomas (Eds.)

Recent Trends in Computer Networks and Distributed Systems Security

International Conference, SNDS 2012
Trivandrum, India, October 11-12, 2012
Proceedings

 Springer

Volume Editors

Sabu M. Thampi
Tony Thomas
Indian Institute of Information Technology and Management
Technopark Campus, Trivandrum, 695581, Kerala, India
E-mail: smthampi@ieee.org; tony.thomas@iiitmk.ac.in

Albert Y. Zomaya
The University of Sydney, School of Information Technologies
Building J12, Sydney, NSW 2006, Australia
E-mail: albert.zomaya@sydney.edu.au

Thorsten Strufe
TU Darmstadt - FB 20, FG Peer-to-Peer-Netzwerke
Hochschulstr. 10, 64289 Darmstadt, Germany
E-mail: strufe@cs.tu-darmstadt.de

Jose M. Alcaraz Calero
Hewlett-Packard Laboratories
Stoke Gifford, BS34 8QZ, Bristol, UK
E-mail: jose-maria.alcaraz-calero@hp.com

Last, but surely not the least, we express
mann of Springer for his excellent support in
time.

October 2012

ISSN 1865-0929   e-ISSN 1865-0937
ISBN 978-3-642-34134-2   e-ISBN 978-3-642-34135-9
DOI 10.1007/978-3-642-34135-9
Springer Heidelberg Dordrecht London New York

Library of Congress Control Number: 2012948545

CR Subject Classification (1998): C.2.0, E.3, C.2.4, K.6.5, E.4, F.2.1

Typesetting: Camera-ready by author, data conversion by Scientific Publishing Services, Chennai, India

Printed on acid-free paper

Springer is part of Springer Science+Business Media (www.springer.com)

Organization

Honorary Chair

Albert Y. Zomaya   The University of Sydney, Australia

Steering Committee

Bharat Bhargava	Purdue University, USA (Chair)
Bharat Jayaraman	University at Buffalo, The State University of New York, USA
Ajith Abraham	MIR Labs, USA
M. Ponnavaikko	(Executive Vice Chair, IEEE India Council), SRM University, India
Satish Babu	(President-Computer Society of India), ICFOSS, India
Deepak Garg	(Chair, IEEE Computer Society Chapter, IEEE India Council), Thapar University, India
John F. Buford	Avaya Labs Research, USA
Axel Sikora	University of Applied Sciences Offenburg, Germany
Subir Biswas	Michigan State University, USA
K. Chandra Sekaran	National Institute of Technology Karnataka, India
El-Sayed El-Alfy	King Fahd University of Petroleum and Minerals, Saudi Arabia
Jaime Lloret Mauri	Polytechnic University of Valencia, Spain
Zhili Sun	University of Surrey, UK
Xavier Fernando	Ryerson University, Canada
Mohan S. Kankanhalli	National University of Singapore, Singapore
Lisimachos Kondi	University of Ioannina, Greece
Sabu Emmanuel	Nanyang Technological University, Singapore
Michele Pagano	University of Pisa, Italy
Debabrata Das	International Institute of Information Technology, Bangalore (IIIT-B), India
Binod Vaidya	University of Ottawa, Canada
Siani Pearson	HP Labs, UK
Pradeep Atrey	University of Winnipeg, Canada
Pascal Lorenz	University of Haute Alsace, France

General Chairs

Shambhu Upadhyaya   University at Buffalo, The State University
                                  of New York, USA
Sudip Misra   Indian Institute of Technology, Kharagpur,
                                  India
Jiankun Hu   University of New South Wales, Australia

Conference Chair

Sabu M. Thampi   Indian Institute of Information Technology
                                  and Management - Kerala, India

Program Chairs

Thorsten Strufe   Darmstadt University of Technology, Germany
Jose M. Alcaraz Calero   Cloud and Security Lab, Hewlett-Packard
                                  Laboratories, UK
Raj Sharman   University at Buffalo, USA

Workshop and Special Session Chairs

Tony Thomas   Indian Institute of Information Technology
                                  and Management - Kerala, India
Wael M. El-Medany   University of Bahrain, Bahrain

Tutorial Chairs

Dilip Krishnaswamy   Qualcomm Research Center, San Diego CA,
                                  USA
Punam Bedi   University of Delhi, India

Poster/Demo Chair

Ryan Ko   Cloud and Security Lab, Hewlett-Packard
                                  Laboratories, Singapore

Technical Program Committee

Ahmed Serhrouchni   ENST, France
Albena Mihovska   University of Aalborg, Denmark
Alexis Olivereau   CEA LIST, France
Alf Zugenmaier   Munich University of Applied Sciences,
                                  Germany

Sabu M. Thampi   Albert Y. Zomaya
Thorsten Strufe   Jose M. Alcaraz Calero
Tony Thomas (Eds.)

Recent Trends in Computer Networks and Distributed Systems Security

International Conference, SNDS 2012
Trivandrum, India, October 11-12, 2012
Proceedings

 Springer

Volume Editors

Sabu M. Thampi
Tony Thomas
Indian Institute of Information Technology and Management
Technopark Campus, Trivandrum, 695581, Kerala, India
E-mail: smthampi@ieee.org; tony.thomas@iiitmk.ac.in

Albert Y. Zomaya
The University of Sydney, School of Information Technologies
Building J12, Sydney, NSW 2006, Australia
E-mail: albert.zomaya@sydney.edu.au

Thorsten Strufe
TU Darmstadt - FB 20, FG Peer-to-Peer-Netzwerke
Hochschulstr. 10, 64289 Darmstadt, Germany
E-mail: strufe@cs.tu-darmstadt.de

Jose M. Alcaraz Calero
Hewlett-Packard Laboratories
Stoke Gifford, BS34 8QZ, Bristol, UK
E-mail: jose-maria.alcaraz-calero@hp.com

ISSN 1865-0929   e-ISSN 1865-0937
ISBN 978-3-642-34134-2   e-ISBN 978-3-642-34135-9
DOI 10.1007/978-3-642-34135-9
Springer Heidelberg Dordrecht London New York

Library of Congress Control Number: 2012948545

CR Subject Classification (1998): C.2.0, E.3, C.2.4, K.6.5, E.4, F.2.1

Typesetting: Camera-ready by author, data conversion by Scientific Publishing Services, Chennai, India

Printed on acid-free paper

Springer is part of Springer Science+Business Media (www.springer.com)

Preface

Networking and distributed systems provide the infrastructure for computation, communication, and storage linking of heterogeneous and possibly a great number of people, hardware devices, and software processes. Security has become more complicated with the expanded use and networking of personal computers. Nowadays, distributed systems are very popular and extensively used throughout the world. With the widespread adoption of distributed systems, there are several security issues that can hurt the enterprises and user communities greatly. To provide tolerable protection for these systems, the security technologies must respond to more and more multifaceted issues and malicious behaviors. However, finding effective ways to guard these systems is challenging even with state-of-the-art technology and trained professionals.

The International Conference on Security in Computer Networks and Distributed Systems (SNDS) aims to provide the most relevant opportunity to bring together students, researchers, and practitioners from both academia and industry to present their research results and development activities in the field of security in computer networks and distributed systems. SNDS 2012 was technically co-sponsored by the IEEE Kerala Section and Computer Society of India. The conference was held in October 2012 at the Indian Institute of Information Technology and Management-Kerala (IIITM-K), Trivandrum, India.

There were 112 paper submissions to SNDS 2012 from 17 countries. From these submissions, 34 papers were selected by the Program Committee for oral presentations and eight papers for poster presentations. All papers were rigorously and independently peer-reviewed by the TPC members and reviewers. The authors of accepted papers made a considerable effort to take into account the comments in the version submitted to these proceedings. In addition to the main track of presentations of accepted papers, two workshops were also hosted.

The final technical program of SNDS 2012 was the result of the dedication and hard work of numerous people. We would like to extend our sincere thanks to all the authors who submitted their work, the conference Chairs/Co-chairs, TPC members, and additional reviewers, who greatly contributed to the success of the SNDS 2012 paper-review process under a tight schedule. Our deepest thanks to the Steering Committee members for their timely help and supervision. Our most sincere thanks go to all keynote speakers who shared with us their expertise and knowledge.

We greatly thank the Organizing Committee members for taking care of the registration, logistics, and local arrangements. It is due to their hard work that the conference was made possible. We are truly grateful to the co-sponsoring societies including the IEEE and Computer Society of India. We would also like to express our sincere thanks to all those who contributed to the success of SNDS 2012 but whose names cannot be listed.

Last, but surely not the least, we express our sincere thanks to Alfred Hofmann of Springer for his excellent support in publishing these proceedings on time.

October 2012

Sabu M. Thampi
Albert Y. Zomaya
Thorsten Strufe
Jose M. Alcaraz Calero
Tony Thomas

Al-Sakib Khan Pathan	International Islamic University Malaysia (IIUM), Malaysia
Amit Sachan	Institute for Infocomm Research, Singapore
Andrea Forte	AT&T, USA
Anitha Varghese	ABB Research, Bangalore, India
Antonio Pescape	University of Napoli Federico II, Italy
Antonio Ruiz-Martinez	University of Murcia, Spain
Arjan Durresi	Indiana University Purdue University Indianapolis, USA
Ashok Das	IIIT Hyderabad, India
Bernd Becker	University of Freiburg, Germany
Bheemarjuna Reddy Tamma	IIT Hyderabad, India
Bogdan Carbunar	Florida International University, USA
Bruhadeshwar Bezawada	International Institute of Information Technology, India
Bruno Crispo	Università di Trento, Italy
Carole Bassil	Lebanese University, Lebanon
Cheng-Kang Chu	Institute for Infocomm Research, Singapore
Ching-Mu Chen	Chung Chou Institute of Technology, Taiwan
Debojyoti Bhattacharya	ABB, India
Debu Nayak	Huawei, India
Di Jin	General Motors, USA
Edward Dawson	Queensland University of Technology, Australia
Efthimia Aivaloglou	University of the Aegean, Greece
Eric Renault	TELECOM & Management SudParis, France
Fangguo Zhang	Sun Yat-sen University, P.R. China
G. Santhosh Kumar	Cochin University of Science and Technology, India
Gaurang Mehta	USC/ISI, USA
Geong-Sen Poh	MIMOS, Malaysia
Geyong Min	University of Bradford, UK
Ghassan Karame	NEC Laboratories Europe, Germany
Giannis Marias	Athens University of Economics and Business, Greece
Gina Kounga	EADS Innovation Works, UK
Hamid Sharif	University of Nebraska-Lincoln, USA
Hao Yang	Nokia Research Center, USA
Helmut Essen	Maxonic GmbH, Germany
Hsiao-Ying Lin	National Chiao Tung University, Taiwan
Igor Bisio	University of Genoa, Italy
Jaydip Sen	Innovation lab, Tata Consultancy Services Ltd., India
Jeffrey Voas	NIST, USA

Jiangtao Li	Intel, USA
Jianhong Zhang	North China University of Technology, P.R. China
Jiannong Cao	Hong Kong Polytechnic University, Hong Kong
Jie Li	University of Tsukuba, Japan
Joni Da Silva Fraga	UFSC, Brazil
Jordi Forne	Technical University of Catalonia, Spain
Jorge Sai Silva	University of Coimbra, Portugal
Ju Wang	Virginia State University, USA
Jun Bi	Tsinghua University, P.R. China
Karima Boudaoud	University of Nice Sophia Antipolis, France
Karthik Srinivasan	Infosys Limited, India
Kaustubh Sinkar	Applied Communication Sciences, USA
Khushboo Shah	Altusystems Corp, USA
Kishore Kothapalli	International Institute of Information Technology, India
Knarig Arabshian	Alcatel-Lucent Bell Labs, USA
Koji Nuida	National Institute of Advanced Industrial Science and Technology, Japan
Kouichi Sakurai	Kyushu University, Japan
Kyriakos Manousakis	Telcordia Technologies, USA
Lau Lung	UFSC, Brazil
Leela Rengaraj	National Institute of Technology Tiruchirappalli India, India
Lei Shu	Osaka University, Japan
Lisimachos Kondi	University of Ioannina, Greece
Luigi Lo Iacono	Cologne University of Applied Science, Germany
Mahesh Tripunitara	University of Waterloo, Canada
Manimaran Govindarasu	Iowa State University, USA
Manu Malek	Stevens Institute of Technology, USA
Maode Ma	Nanyang Technological University, Singapore
Marco Roccetti	University of Bologna, Italy
Marcus Wong	Huawei Technologies, USA
Marius Marcu	Politehnica University of Timisoara, Romania
Markus Ullmann	Federal Office for Information Security, Germany
Matthias Wahlisch	Freie Universität Berlin, Germany
Michele Pagano	University of Pisa, Italy
Mini Ulanat	Cochin University, India
Mohamed Hamdi	Carthage University, Tunisia
Mostafa El-Said	Grand Valley State University, USA
Nidhal Bouaynaya	University of Arkansas at Little Rock, USA
Ning Zhang	University of Manchester, UK
Oliver Friedrich	T-Systems, Germany

Peng Zhang   Northwestern Polytechnical University, India
Periklis Chatzimisios   Alexander TEI of Thessaloniki, Greece
Ping Yang   Binghamton University, USA
Pritam Shah   DSI Bangalore, India
Rafa Marin Lopez   University of Murcia, Spain
Rajarathnam Nallusamy   Infosys Limited, India
Ramasubramanian Natarajan   National Institute of Technology, Trichy, India
Ramesh Hansdah   Indian Institute of Science, Bangalore, India
Rongxing Lu   University of Waterloo, Canada
Ruidong Li   National Institute of Information and
                                  Communications Technology (NICT), Japan
Sabrina Sicari   University of Insubria, Italy
Sachin Agrawal   Samsung, India
Samir Saklikar   RSA, Security Division of EMC, India
Santhi Thilagam P.   National Institute of Technology Karnataka,
                                  Surathkal, India
Sara Foresti   Università degli Studi di Milano, Italy
Saurabh Mukherjee   Banasthali University, India
Sattar Sadkhan   University of Babylon, Iraq
Sherif Rashad   Morehead State University, USA
Shrisha Rao   International Institute of Information
                                  Technology, Bangalore, India
Shu-Ching Chen   Florida International University, USA
Sjouke Mauw   University of Luxembourg, Luxemburg
Skanda Muthaiah   Hewlett Packard India Software Operations,
                                  India
Stefanos Gritzalis   University of the Aegean, Greece
Stephen Groat   Virginia Tech, USA
Sudha Sadhasivam   PSG COllege of Technology, India
Sudhanshu Joshi   Doon University, India
Sudhir Aggarwal   Florida State University, USA
Suzanne McIntosh   IBM T.J. Watson Research Center, USA
Theodore Stergiou   Intracom Telecom, Greece
Thomas Chen   Swansea University, UK
Thomas Little   Boston University, USA
Tim Strayer   BBN Technologies, USA
Vaclav Snasel   VSB-Technical University of Ostrava, FEECS,
                                  Czech Republic
Vasileios Karyotis   National Technical University of Athens,
                                  Greece
Vikas Saxena   Jaypee Institute of Information Technology,
                                  India
Winnie Cheng   IBM Research, USA
Xiangjian He   University of Technology, Sydney, Australia

Xinyi Huang	Institute for Infocomm Research (I2R), Singapore
Yassine Lakhnech	Joseph Fourier University, France
Ye Zhu	Cleveland State University, USA
Young-Long Chen	National Taichung University of Science and Technology, Taiwan
Yu Chen	State University of New York - Binghamton, USA
Yuan-Cheng Lai	Information Management, NTUST, Taiwan
Yung-Fa Huang	ChaoYang University of Technology, Taiwan
Yves Roudier	EURECOM, France
Zhenfu Cao	Shanghai Jiao Tong University, P.R. China
Zhili Sun	University of Surrey, UK
Zouheir Trabelsi	UAE University, UAE

Additional Reviewers

Adetunji Adebiyi	University of East London, UK
Ajay Jangra	KUK University, Kurukshetra, Haryana, India
Amine Abidi	ENSI National School of Computer Science, Tunisia
Amita Sharma	I.I.S. University, India
Angelina Geetha	B.S. Abdur Rahman University, India
Anitha Pillai	HITS, India
Aravind Ashok	Amrita Vishwa Vidyapeetham, India
Baljeet Kaur	Bharati Vidyapeeth Deemed University, India
Bhagyalekshmy N. Thampi	Xlim, France
Bharat Amberker	National Institute of Technology, Warangal, India
Bhawna Singla	NCCE, India
Daphne Lopez	VIT University, India
Deepak Choudhary	LPU, India
Dheerendra Mishra	Indian Institute of Technology, Kharagpur, India
Ed Wilson Ferreira	Federal Institute of Mato Grosso, Brazil
Enrico Cambiaso	IEIIT, Italy
Esshan Gupta	University of Petroleum and Energy Studies, India
Gianluca Papaleo	IEIIT, Italy
Gopal Patra	CSIR Centre for Mathematical Modelling and Computer Simulation, India
Guillaume Bouffard	Xlim, France
Haythem Zorkta	University of Aleppo, Syria
Jerzy Konorski	Gdansk University of Technology, Poland
Komal Balasubramanian Priya Iyer	Sathyabama University, India

Krishen Kandwal	Tata Consultancy Services, India
Kunwar Singh	NIT Trichy, India
Lalit Kumar	NIT Hamirpur, India
Madhumita Chatterjee	IIT Bombay, India
Manjunath Mattam	International Institute of Information Technology, India
Maurizio Aiello	National Research Council, Italy
Mohammad Rasmi	Universiti Sains Malaysia (USM), Malaysia
Monika Darji	Gujarat Technological University, India
Nandan S.	University of Kerala, India
Nilanjan Dey	West Bengal University of Technology, India
Nitin Goel	Decimal Technologies Pvt. Ltd., India
Odelu Vanga	Rajiv Gandhi University of Knowledge Technologies, Hyderabad, India
Praneet Saurabh	Technocrats Institute of Technology, India
Prashant Mishra	National Institute of Technology Trichy, India
Prashant Singh	SRM University, India
Ram Raw	Ambedkar Institute of Advanced Communication Technologies and Research, India
Ramalingam Anitha	PSG College of Technology, India
Rizwan Ahmed	G.H. Raisoni College of Engineering, Nagpur, India
S. Santhanalakshmi	Amrita School of Engineering, India
Sachin Mehta	Infosys Limited, India
Sankararaman Viginesh	Anna University, India
Saurabh Mukherjee	Banasthali University, India
Seema Khanna	National Informatics Center, India
Siddharth Sahu	BITS Pilani K.K. Birla Goa Campus, India
Somanath Tripathy	IIT Patna, India
Somayaji Siva Rama Krishnan	VIT University, India
Suchitra Balasubramanyam	Infosys Limited, India
Taraka Nishitha	JNTU, India
Tataram Adapa	National Institute of Technology, Surathkal, India
Tejaswi Agarwal	Vellore Institute of Technology-Chennai, India
Thilagavathi Manoharan	VIT University, India
Tiana Razafindralambo	Université de Limoges, France
V. Shanthi	St. Joseph College of Engineering, India
Varghese Paul	CUSAT, India
Veerasamy Senthil	Thiagarajar School of Management, India
Vijayaraghavan Varadharajan	Infosys Limited, India
Yatendra Sharma	Banasthali University, India
Zbigniew Kotulski	Warsaw University of Technology, Poland

International Workshop on Security in Self-Organizing Networks (SelfNet 2012)

Sabu M. Thampi	IIITM-K, India (Chair)
Abdelouahid Derhab	CERIST, Algeria
Adel. Ali	University Technology Malaysia, Malaysia
Bing Zhang	National Institute of Information and Communications Technology, Japan
C-F Cheng	National Chiao Tung University, Taiwan
Chun-Chuan Yang	National Chi-Nan University, Taiwan
George Karagiannidis	Aristotle University of Thessaloniki, Greece
Giannis Marias	Athens University of Economics and Business, Greece
Giuseppe Ruggeri	University "Mediterranea" of Reggio Calabria, Italy
Houcem Gazzah	University of Sharjah, UAE
Ibrahim Korpeoglu	Bilkent University, Turkey
Junichi Suzuki	University of Massachusetts, Boston, USA
Kamran Arshad	University of Greenwich, UK
Kyoung-Don Kang	State University of New York, Binghamton, USA
Liza A. Latiff	University Technology Malaysia, Malaysia
Maytham Safar	Kuwait University, Kuwait
Michael Lauer	Vanille-Media, Germany
Mohamed El-Tarhuni	American University of Sharjah, UAE
Mohammad Banat	Jordan University of Science and Technology, Jordan
Nakjung Choi	Bell-Labs, Alcatel-Lucent, Korea
Periklis Chatzimisios	Alexander TEI of Thessaloniki, Greece
Ruay-Shiung Chang	National Dong Hwa University, Taiwan
Sameer Tilak	University of California at San Diego, USA
Sghaier Guizani	Alfaisal University, Saudi Arabia
Yurong Xu	Dartmouth College, USA
Zhenzhen Ye	IBM, USA

International Workshop on Intelligence and Security Informatics for International Security (IIS 2012)

Adam Stewart Cumming	DSTL, UK
Bernd Becker	University of Freiburg, Germany
Fabio Massacci	University of Trento, Italy
Jiannong Cao	Hong Kong Polytechnic University, Hong Kong
Jie Li	University of Tsukuba, Japan
Ju Wang	Virginia State University, USA
Karsten Heidrich	Deutsche Bank AG, Germany
Thomas Chen	Swansea University, UK

Organizing Committee (IIITM-K)

Chief Patron

S. Gopalakrishnan   Executive Co-chair, Board of Directors-IIITM-K
                             and Chair, Executive Council,
                             Infosys Technologies, India

Patron

Elizabeth Sherly   Director, IIITM-K

Advisory Committee

Abdul Rahiman, AICTE   R. Jaishanker, IIITM-K
Alex Pappachen James, IIITM-K   Rajasree M.S., College of Engineering,
Joseph Suresh Paul, IIITM-K   Trivandrum
K. Pradeep Kumar, IIITM-K   T. Radhakrishnan, IIITM-K
Meraj Uddin, IIITM-K   T.K. Manoj Kumar, IIITM-K
R. Ajith Kumar, IIITM-K   Vinod Chandra S.S., Kerala University

Finance Chair

P.C. Daviz, IIITM-K

Web Chair

David Mathews, IIITM-K

Table of Contents

Regular Papers

A Novel Key Management Mechanism for Dynamic Hierarchical Access
Control Based on Linear Polynomials.................................. 1
    Vanga Odelu, Ashok Kumar Das, and Adrijit Goswami

Publicly Auditable Provable Data Possession Scheme for Outsourced
Data in the Public Cloud Using Polynomial Interpolation 11
    B.R. Purushothama and B.B. Amberker

Performance Evaluation of the Fuzzy ARTMAP for Network Intrusion
Detection 23
    *Nelcileno Araújo, Ruy de Oliveira, Ed' Wilson Tavares Ferreira,
    Valtemir Nascimento, Ailton Shinoda Akira, and Bharat Bhargava*

ID-Based Threshold Signcryption and Group Unsigncryption 35
    Prashant Kumar Mishra, Kunwar Singh, and Sudhanshu Baruntar

Protocol for Secure Submissions into Learning Management Systems ... 45
    Manjunath Mattam

Secure Leader Election Algorithm Optimized for Power Saving
Using Mobile Agents for Intrusion Detection in MANET 54
    Monika Darji and Bhushan Trivedi

WAKE: Authentication and Key Establishment for Wireless Mesh
Network 64
    Somanath Tripathy and Debasish Sahoo

Effective Implementation of DES Algorithm for Voice Scrambling 75
    *Jinu Elizabeth John, A.S. Remya Ajai, and
    Prabaharan Poornachandran*

Towards Constructing a Trustworthy Internet: Privacy-Aware Transfer
of Digital Identity Document in Content Centric Internetworking 85
    Amine Abidi, Ghazi Ben Ayed, and Farouk Kamoun

Security Analysis of CAPTCHA 97
    Anjali Avinash Chandavale and A. Sapkal

Imperceptible Image Indexing Using Digital Watermarking 110
    Jobin Abraham and Varghese Paul

A New Deterministic Algorithm for Testing Primality Based on a New
Property of Prime Numbers 117
   Srikumar Manghat

Multilingual Speaker Identification with the Constraint of Limited
Data Using Multitaper MFCC 127
   B.G. Nagaraja and H.S. Jayanna

Secure Group Key Management Scheme for Simultaneous Multiple
Groups with Overlapped Memberships Using Binomial Key Tree 135
   B.R. Purushothama, Kusuma Shirisha, and B.B. Amberker

An Analytical Approach to Position-Based Routing Protocol
for Vehicular Ad Hoc Networks 147
   Ram Shringar Raw, Daya Krishan Lobiyal, and Sanjoy Das

Simulation and Evaluation of Different Mobility Models in Ad-Hoc
Sensor Network over DSR Protocol Using Bonnmotion Tool 157
   V. Vasanthi and M. Hemalatha

Secure Authentication in Multimodal Biometric Systems Using
Cryptographic Hash Functions 168
   Aravind Ashok, Prabaharan Poornachandran, and
   Krishnasree Achuthan

Data Protection and Privacy Preservation Using Searchable Encryption
on Outsourced Databases 178
   Lucas Rodrigo Raso Mattos, Vijayaraghavan Varadharajan, and
   Rajarathnam Nallusamy

A Dynamic Syntax Interpretation for Java Based Smart Card
to Mitigate Logical Attacks 185
   Tiana Razafindralambo, Guillaume Bouffard,
   Bhagyalekshmy N. Thampi, and Jean-Louis Lanet

Taxonomy of Slow DoS Attacks to Web Applications 195
   Enrico Cambiaso, Gianluca Papaleo, and Maurizio Aiello

Crypto-Precision: Testing Tool for Hash Function 205
   Harshvardhan Tiwari, Ankit Luthra, Himanshu Goel,
   Sambhav Sharma, and Krishna Asawa

Performance Analysis and Improvement Using LFSR in the Pipelined
Key Scheduling Section of DES 215
   P.V. Sruthi, Prabaharan Poornachandran, and A.S. Remya Ajai

Towards Retrieving Live Forensic Artifacts in Offline Forensics......... 225
   S. Dija, T.R. Deepthi, C. Balan, and K.L. Thomas

Carving of Bitmap Files from Digital Evidences by Contiguous File
Filtering   234
    Balan Chelliah, Divya S. Vidyadharan, P. Shabana, and
    K.L. Thomas

Lightweight Cryptographic Primitives for Mobile Ad Hoc Networks   240
    Adarsh Kumar and Alok Aggarwal

Intrusion Protection against SQL Injection and Cross Site Scripting
Attacks Using a Reverse Proxy   252
    S. Fouzul Hidhaya and Angelina Geetha

Three-Way Handshake-Based OTP Using Random Host-Side Keys
for Effective Key Transfer in Symmetric Cryptosystems   264
    P.R. Mahalingam

Identity Based Privacy Preserving Dynamic Broadcast Encryption
for Multi-privileged Groups   272
    Angamuthu Muthulakshmi, Ramalingam Anitha, S. Rohini, and
    Krishnan Princy

A Virtualization-Level Future Internet Defense-in-Depth
Architecture   283
    Jerzy Konorski, Piotr Pacyna, Grzegorz Kolaczek,
    Zbigniew Kotulski, Krzysztof Cabaj, and Pawel Szalachowski

Experimental DRM Model Using Mobile Code and White-Box
Encryption   293
    Stefan-Vladimir Ghita, Victor-Valeriu Patriciu, and Ion Bica

Towards a Secure, Transparent and Privacy-Preserving DRM System . . .   304
    Dheerendra Mishra and Sourav Mukhopadhyay

Time Based Constrained Object Identification in a Dynamic Social
Network   314
    M.T. Chitra, R. Priya, and Elizabeth Sherly

A New Approach towards Segmentation for Breaking CAPTCHA   323
    Anjali Avinash Chandavale and A. Sapkal

A Similarity Model to Estimate Attack Strategy Based on Intentions
Analysis for Network Forensics   336
    Aman Jantan, Mohammad Rasmi, Mohd Izham Ibrahim, and
    Azri H.A. Rahman

International Workshop on Security in Self-Organising Networks (SelfNet'12)

Stationary Wavelet Transformation Based Self-recovery of
Blind-Watermark from Electrocardiogram Signal in Wireless
Telecardiology   347
   Nilanjan Dey, Anamitra Bardhan Roy, Achintya Das, and
   Sheli Sinha Chaudhuri

eCloudIDS – Design Roadmap for the Architecture of Next-Generation
Hybrid Two-Tier Expert Engine-Based IDS for Cloud Computing
Environment   358
   Madhan Kumar Srinivasan, K. Sarukesi, Ashima Keshava, and
   P. Revathy

A Comparative Study on Wormhole Attack Prevention Schemes
in Mobile Ad-Hoc Network   372
   Subhashis Banerjee and Koushik Majumder

Management of Routed Wireless M-Bus Networks for Sparsely
Populated Large-Scale Smart-Metering Installations   385
   Philipp Digeser, Marco Tubolino, Martin Klemm, and Axel Sikora

A Survey of Blackhole Attacks and Countermeasures in Wireless Mobile
Ad-hoc Networks   396
   Subhashis Banerjee and Koushik Majumder

International Workshop on Intelligence and Security Informatics for International Security (IIS'12)

iReSign-Implementation of Next-Generation Two-Tier Identity
Classifier-Based Traffic Sign Recognition System Architecture Using
Hybrid Region-Based Shape Representation Techniques   408
   Keerthi Balasundaram, Madhan Kumar Srinivasan, and K. Sarukesi

Work-in-Progress

Neural Synchronization by Mutual Learning Using Genetic Approach
for Secure Key Generation   422
   S. Santhanalakshmi, T.S.B. Sudarshan, and Gopal K. Patra

eCloudIDS Tier-1 uX-Engine Subsystem Design and Implementation
Using Self-Organizing Map (SOM) for Secure Cloud Computing
Environment   432
   Madhan Kumar Srinivasan, K. Sarukesi, Ashima Keshava, and
   P. Revathy

Implementation of MD6 444
    Ananya Chowdhury and Utpal Kumar Ray

Location Estimation of Mobile in GSM and CDMA Networks.......... 456
    Adapa Tataram and Alwyn Roshan Pais

An Adaptive Distributed Intrusion Detection System for Cloud
Computing Framework 466
    Deepa Krishnan and Madhumita Chatterjee

Biologically Inspired Computer Security System: The Way Ahead 474
    Praneet Saurabh, Bhupendra Verma, and Sanjeev Sharma

A Comparative Analysis of the Ant Based Systems for QoS Routing
in MANET... 485
    Debajit Sensarma and Koushik Majumder

Efficient Weighted Innovative Routing Protocol (EWiRP) to Balance
Load in Mobile Ad Hoc Networks (MANETs): Simulation and
Feasibility Analysis... 497
    Nitin Goel, Shruti Sangwan, and Ajay Jangra

Author Index 507

A Novel Key Management Mechanism for Dynamic Hierarchical Access Control Based on Linear Polynomials

Vanga Odelu[1], Ashok Kumar Das[2], and Adrijit Goswami[3]

[1] Department of Mathematics
Rajiv Gandhi University of Knowledge Technologies, Hyderabad 500 032, India
odelu.vanga@gmail.com
[2] Center for Security, Theory and Algorithmic Research
International Institute of Information Technology, Hyderabad 500 032, India
iitkgp.akdas@gmail.com, ashok.das@iiit.ac.in
[3] Department of Mathematics
Indian Institute of Technology, Kharagpur 721 302, India
goswami@maths.iitkgp.ernet.in

Abstract. Several key management schemes for dynamic access control in a user hierarchy are proposed in the literature based on elliptic curve cryptosystem (ECC) and polynomial interpolation. Since the elliptic curve scalar multiplication and construction of interpolating polynomials are time-consuming operations, most of the proposed schemes require high storage and computational complexity. Further, most of the proposed schemes are vulnerable to different attacks including the man-in-the-middle attacks. In this paper, we propose a novel key management scheme for hierarchical access control based on linear polynomials only. We show that our scheme is secure against different attacks including the man-in-the-middle attack, which are required for an idle access control scheme. Moreover, the computational cost and the storage space are significantly reduced in our scheme while compared to the recently proposed related schemes.

1 Introduction

In a user hierarchy, the users and their own information items are divided into a group of disjoint security classes. Each user is then assigned to a security class. Let SC be a set of such N disjoint security classes, say $SC = \{SC_1, SC_2, \ldots, SC_N\}$ which forms a partially ordered set (poset, in short) with a binary relation "$\leq$". In a poset $\langle SC, \leq \rangle$, if SC_i and SC_j be two security classes with the relationship $SC_j \leq SC_i$, then the security level of SC_i is higher than or equal to that for SC_j. We call SC_i as predecessor of SC_j, and SC_j as successor of SC_i. We denote such a relationship by $(SC_i, SC_j) \in R_{i,j}$, which means that $SC_j \leq SC_i$. Hierarchical access control is an important research area in computer science, which has numerous applications including schools, military,

S.M. Thampi et al. (Eds.): SNDS 2012, CCIS 335, pp. 1–10, 2012.

governments, corporations, database management systems, computer network systems, e-medicine systems, etc.

In a hierarchical access control, a trusted central authority (CA) distributes keys to each security class in the hierarchy such that any predecessor of a successor class can easily derive its successor's secret key. Using that derived secret key, the predecessor class can decrypt the information encrypted by its successor. However, the reverse is not true in such access control, that is, no successor class of any predecessor will be able to derive the secret keys of its predecessors. Consider a simple example of a poset in a user hierarchy in Fig. 1. In this figure, we have the following relationships: $SC_2 \leq SC_1$, $SC_3 \leq SC_1$, $SC_4 \leq SC_1$, $SC_5 \leq SC_1$, $SC_6 \leq SC_1$, $SC_7 \leq SC_1$; $SC_5 \leq SC_2$; $SC_5 \leq SC_3$, $SC_6 \leq SC_3$; $SC_7 \leq SC_4$.

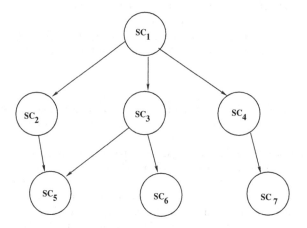

Fig. 1. An example of a poset in a user hierarchy

1.1   Related Work

Akl and Talor [2] first introduced the cryptographic key assignment scheme in an arbitrary poset hierarchy. Since then several different solutions to solve access control problem have been proposed in the literature. Chung et al. [5] proposed an efficient key management scheme for solving dynamic access control problem in a user hierarchy based on polynomial interpolation and elliptic curve cryptography (ECC). However, Das et al. in [6] showed that when a new security class is added into the hierarchy, any external attacker who is not a user in any security class can easily derive the secret key of a security class using the root finding algorithm. In order to withstand this security flaw found in Chung et al.'s scheme, they proposed an improved dynamic access control solution. Jeng-Wang's scheme [7] is based on ECC and it requires to regenerate keys for all the security classes when a security class is inserted into or removed from the existing hierarchy. Lin and Hsu [8] later showed that Jeng-Wang's scheme is insecure against a compromised attack in which the secret key of some security classes can be compromised by an attacker if some public information are modified. In order to remedy this security flaw, Lin and Hsu [8] proposed a key management scheme for dynamic hierarchical access control based on polynomial interpolation and ECC. However, their scheme requires high storage and computational complexity. Wu and Chen [13] proposed a key management scheme to solve dynamic access control problems in a user hierarchy based on hybrid cryptosystem in e-medicine system. Though their scheme improves computational efficiency over Nikooghadam et al.'s scheme [11], it still suffers from large storage space for public parameters in public domain and computational inefficiency due to costly elliptic curve point multiplication operations. Recently, Nikooghadam and Zakerolhosseini [10] showed that Wu-Chen's scheme is vulnerable to the man-in-the-middle attack. In order to remedy this security weakness in Wu-Chen's scheme, they further proposed a secure access control scheme using mobile agent, which is again based on ECC. However, their scheme requires huge computational cost for providing verification of public information in the public domain as their scheme uses ECC digital signature for verifying the public information by the security classes. Atallah et al. proposed a dynamic efficient access control scheme [3], [4] based on one-way hash functions. However, as pointed out in [9], their scheme is not suitable for a deep tree hierarchy or in a situation where a tree contains complex relationships.

1.2   Motivation

Symmetric key cryptosystem is more efficient than public key cryptosystem. Though several key management schemes for dynamic access control in a user hierarchy are proposed in the literature, most schemes are based on elliptic curve cryptosystem (ECC) and polynomial interpolation. Due to time-consuming operations of elliptic curve scalar multiplication and construction of interpolating polynomials, most of the proposed schemes require high storage and computational complexity. Moreover, majority of such schemes are vulnerable to different attacks including active attack called the man-in-the-middle attack. In this paper, we aim to propose a novel key management scheme for hierarchical access control based on linear polynomials. Our scheme does not require any polynomial interpolation and ECC operations. We make use of symmetric key cryptosystem along with efficient hash function so that our scheme will require minimum storage and computational complexity. We further show that our idle access control scheme is secure against different attacks including the man-in-the-middle attack.

1.3   Organization of the Paper

The rest of the paper is organized as follows. In Section 2, we describe our proposed scheme. In Section 3, we discuss dynamic access control problems of our scheme. Security analysis of our scheme is provided in Section 4. We compare the performance of our scheme with other related schemes in Section 5. Finally, we conclude the paper in Section 6.

2   Our Proposed Scheme

We assume that there are N security classes in the hierarchy which form a set $SC = \{SC_1, SC_2, ..., SC_N\}$. We use the following notations for describing our scheme. $H(\cdot)$ is a secure one-way hash function (for example, SHA-1 hash function [12]), Ω a symmetric key cryptosystem (for example, AES symmetric-key block cipher [1]), $E_k(\cdot)/D_k(\cdot)$ the symmetric-key encryption/decryption using key k, ID_{CA} the identity of CA, and $||$ the bit concatenation operator. Our scheme consists the following three phases, namely the relationship building phase, key generation phase, and key derivation phase.

2.1   Relationship Building Phase

CA builds the hierarchical structure for controlling access according to the given relationships among the security classes in the hierarchy. Assume that $SC_i \in SC$ and $SC_j \in SC$ be two security classes such that $SC_j \le SC_i$, that is, SC_i has a higher security clearance than that for SC_j. We say that a legitimate relationship $(SC_i, SC_j) \in R_{i,j}$ between SC_i and SC_j exists if SC_i can access SC_j.

2.2   Key Generation Phase

CA executes the following steps in order to complete this phase:

Step 1. CA chooses a secure hash function $H(\cdot)$, a finite field $GF(m)$ with m is either odd prime or prime power, and a symmetric key cryptosystem Ω.

Step 2. CA randomly selects its own secret key k_{CA}. CA then selects randomly the secret key sk_i and sub-secret key d_i for each security class SC_i ($1 \le i \le N$) in the hierarchy.

Step 3. For each security class SC_i, CA computes the signature $Sign_i$ on sk_i as $Sign_i = H(ID_{CA}||sk_i)$ for the purpose of signature verification of the secret key sk_i. CA then publicly declares them.

Step 4. For each SC_i such that $(SC_i, SC_j) \in R_{i,j}$, CA constructs the linear polynomials $f_{i,j}(x) = (x - H(ID_{CA}||Sign_j||d_i)) + sk_j \pmod{m}$, and declares them publicly.

Step 5. Finally, CA sends d_i to SC_i via a secure channel.

At the end of this phase, CA encrypts d_i of SC_i as $S_i = E_{k_{CA}}(d_i)$, computes its signature Sd_i as $Sd_i = H(ID_{CA}||d_i)$ for the signature verification of d_i and stores the pair (S_i, Sd_i) in the public domain. CA then deletes all the secret keys sk_i and d_i. Note that whenever CA wants to update the secret keys sk_i's, CA first obtains d_i's from public parameters S_i's by decrypting them with its secret key k_{CA} and then verifies signatures by calculating the hash values as $Sd_i' = H(ID_{CA}||d_i)$, and checks if $Sd_i' = Sd_i$. If it matches, CA confirms that derived secret key d_i is legitimate.

2.3   Key Derivation Phase

If the security class SC_i wants to derive the secret key sk_j of its successor SC_j with $(SC_i, SC_j) \in R_{i,j}$, SC_i needs to proceed the following steps:

Step 1. SC_i first computes the hash value $H(ID_{CA}||Sign_j||d_i)$ using its own sub-secret key d_i, signature $Sign_j$ and ID_{CA} publicly available in the public domain.

Step 2. SC_i obtains secret key sk_j of SC_j's (including SC_i) as $sk_j = f_{i,j}(H(ID_{CA}||Sign_j||d_i))$. CA then verifies signature of sk_j as follows. CA computes $Sign'_j = H(ID_{CA}||sk_j)$ and checks if $Sign'_j = Sign_j$. If it holds, SC_i assures that the derived secret key sk_j is correct.

3   Solution to Dynamic Key Management

The solution to dynamic access problem in user hierarchy for our scheme such as adding a new security class into hierarchy, deleting an existing security class from the hierarchy, modifying the relationships among the security classes and updating secret keys are given below.

3.1   Adding a New Security Class

Suppose a security class SC_l with $SC_j \leq SC_l \leq SC_i$ be added into the hierarchy. CA needs the following steps to manage the accessibility of SC_l:

Step 1. CA randomly needs to select the secret key sk_l and the sub-secret key d_l for SC_l.

Step 2. For SC_l, CA needs to compute the signature $Sign_l$ on sk_l as $Sign_l = H(ID_{CA}||sk_l)$ for signature verification of sk_l and publicly declares it.

Step 3. For each SC_i such that $(SC_i, SC_l) \in R_{i,l}$ in the hierarchy, CA will construct the linear polynomials $f_{i,l}(x) = (x - H(ID_{CA}||Sign_l||d_i)) + sk_l$ (mod m), and declares them publicly.

Step 4. For each SC_j such that $(SC_l, SC_j) \in R_{l,j}$, CA will construct the linear polynomials $f_{l,j}(x) = (x - H(ID_{CA}||Sign_j||d_l)) + sk_j$ (mod m), and declares them publicly.

Step 5. CA finally sends d_l to SC_l via a secure channel.

At the end of this phase, CA encrypts d_l of SC_l as $S_l = E_{k_{CA}}(d_l)$, computes signature Sd_l as $Sd_l = H(ID_{CA}||d_l)$ for signature verification of d_l and stores the pair (S_l, Sd_l) in the public domain, and then deletes secret keys sk_l and d_l for security reasons.

3.2   Deleting an Existing Security Class

Suppose the security class SC_l with $SC_j \leq SC_l \leq SC_i$ be removed from the hierarchy. CA needs the following steps to remove SC_l so that the forward security is preserved.

Step 1. CA needs to remove all parameters corresponding to SC_l.

Step 2. After that CA renews secret keys sk_j's of successors SC_j's of SC_l as sk_j^*, and signatures $Sign_j$'s as $Sign_j^* = H(ID_{CA}||sk_j^*)$ and replaces $Sign_j$ with $Sign_j^*$ in the public domain.

Step 3. For each SC_i such that $SC_j \leq SC_i$ ($\neq SC_l$) in the hierarchy, CA constructs the linear polynomials $f_{i,j}^*(x) = (x - H(ID_{CA}||Sign_j^*||d_i)) + sk_j^*$ $(\bmod\, m)$ and declares them publicly.

3.3   Creating a New Relationship

Assume that $SC_j \leq SC_i$ represents a new relationship between two immediate security classes SC_j and SC_i. Further, assume $SC_i \leq SC_l$ and $SC_y \leq SC_j$ (SC_y is not successor of SC_l before creating relationship). CA needs to compute linear polynomials $f_{l,y}(x) = (x - H(ID_{CA}||Sign_y||d_l)) + sk_y$ $(\bmod\, m)$ and publicly declares them.

3.4   Revoking an Existing Relationship

Suppose the relationship between two immediate security classes SC_j and SC_i with $SC_j \leq SC_i$ be deleted from the hierarchy. Let $SC_j \leq SC_l$ ($\neq SC_i$) and $SC_y \leq SC_j$. CA then removes all parameters corresponding to the keys sk_y (including sk_j). CA also renews secret keys sk_y as sk_y^* and updates signatures $Sign_y$ as $Sign_y^* = H(ID_{CA}||sk_y^*)$ in the public domain. Finally, CA constructs public polynomials $f_{l,y}^*(x) = (x - H(ID_{CA}||Sign_y^*||d_l)) + sk_y^*$ $(\bmod\, m)$.

3.5   Changing Secret Keys

Suppose we want to change the secret key sk_j of SC_j, where $SC_j \leq SC_i$. CA needs to renew the secret key sk_j as sk_j^* and update the signature $Sign_j$ as $Sign_j^* = H(ID_{CA}||sk_j^*)$, compute the corresponding polynomials $f_{i,j}^*(x) = (x - H(ID_{CA}||Sign_j^*||d_i)) + sk_j^*$ $(\bmod\, m)$ and declare them publicly.

4   Security Analysis

In this section, we show that our scheme is secure against the following attacks.

4.1   Contrary Attack

Suppose $SC_j \leq SC_i$ and the successor class SC_j tries to derive the secret key sk_i of its predecessor class SC_i from the available public parameters $f_{i,i}(x) = (x - H(ID_{CA}||Sign_i||d_i)) + sk_i$ (mod m) and $f_{i,j}$'s. However, without knowledge of the sub-secret key d_i of SC_i, SC_j cannot compute $H(ID_{CA}||Sign_i||d_i)$ and as a result, the secret key sk_i. One important observation is that the pairs $(Sign_j, d_i)$ used in the construction of linear polynomials are distinct for two different polynomials. Even from the public parameter $S_i = E_{k_{CA}}(d_i)$, SC_j or any other user (except CA) cannot retrieve d_i without knowing CA's private key k_{CA}. Therefore, our scheme is secure against this attack.

4.2   Exterior Collecting Attack

This potential attack is from an external adversary. The question is that whether an external intruder can derive the secret key from lower level security classes through the accessible public parameters? However, to compute the secret key of a security class is computationally infeasible due to collision-resistant property of the one-way hash function $H(\cdot)$. Thus, no external intruder can retrieve the secret key of any security class. Our scheme is thus secure against such an attack.

4.3   Collaborative Attack

In this attack, several users in a hierarchy try to collaborate to launch an attack in order to compute their predecessor's secret key. Let SC_j and SC_l be two immediate successor classes of a predecessor class SC_i and they try to hack the secret key sk_i of SC_i. First, they can exchange secret keys with each other and derive the sub-secret key d_i of SC_i in order to derive the secret key sk_i of SC_i through the public linear polynomials $f_{i,j}(x) = (x - H(ID_{CA}||Sign_j||d_i)) + sk_j$ $(\mod m)$ and $f_{i,l}(x) = (x - H(ID_{CA}||Sign_l||d_i)) + sk_l$ $(\mod m)$. However, d_i is masked with one-way hash function $H(\cdot)$, and thus, determination of d_i is a computational infeasible problem due to hash function properties. Hence, no successor class can obtain the secret key of a predecessor class by collaborating each other and then our method is secure under this attack.

4.4   Equation Attack

Suppose a security class SC_j has common predecessors SC_i and SC_l, where SC_i does not have an accessibility relationship with SC_l. Let SC_i try to access the secret key sk_l of SC_l through the public linear polynomials $f_{i,j}(x) = (x - H(ID_{CA}||Sign_j||d_l)) + sk_j$ $(\mod m)$ and $f_{l,l}(x) = (x - H(ID_{CA}||Sign_l||d_l)) + sk_l$ $(\mod m)$. SC_i can compute $H(ID_{CA}||Sign_j||d_l)$ from $f_{i,j}(x)$ by using the derived secret key sk_j of SC_j, but SC_i cannot compute the sk_l from $f_{l,l}(x)$, since the hash values $H(ID_{CA}||Sign_j||d_l)$ and $H(ID_{CA}||Sign_l||d_l)$ are different. Therefore, the polynomials corresponding to one security class cannot be solvable by other security classes. As a result, our scheme is also secure against this attack.

4.5   Forward Security of Successors While Changing $SC_j \leq SC_k \leq SC_i$ to $SC_j \leq SC_i$

Assume that the relationship $SC_j \leq SC_k \leq SC_i$ is modified to another relationship $SC_j \leq SC_i$ after removing the security class SC_k from an existing hierarchy. Then CA not only deletes the accessibility relationship $SC_j \leq SC_k$, it also updates the accessibility-link relationship between SC_i and SC_j. CA further renews the secret keys sk_j's of SC_j's and the corresponding linear polynomials as $f_{i,j}^* = (x - H(ID_{CA}||Sign_j^*||d_i)) + sk_j^*$ $(\mod m)$. Since the hash values $H(ID_{CA}||Sign_j^*||d_i)$ can be computed only by the security class SC_i, the security class SC_k cannot hack the updated key sk_j^* of SC_j later. Therefore, the authority of SC_k over SC_j is terminated, and our scheme preserves the forward security property.

4.6   Man-in-the-Middle Attack

As in [10], we refer the "man-in-the-middle" attack as the masquerade attack. Suppose an attacker wants to be represented as an authorized central authority. Though the public domain is write-protected, we assume that the attacker can update somehow the information in the public domain. Let the attacker change the public linear polynomials $f_{i,j}(x)$'s in the public domain. The derivation of the secret key sk_j of a security class SC_j becomes a computationally infeasible problem since the sub-secret key d_j is only known to SC_j. As a result, the attacker does not have any ability to change properly the signatures $Sign_j = H(ID_{CA}\|sk_j)$ and $Sd_j = H(ID_{CA}\|d_j)$ in the public domain. Hence, our scheme protects against such an potential attack.

5   Performance Comparison with Other Schemes

Let T_{MUL}, T_{ADD} and T_{INV} denote the time complexity of executing modular multiplication, modular addition and modular inversion in $GF(2^{163})$, respectively. We denote $T_{EC_{MUL}}$ and $T_{EC_{ADD}}$ for time complexity of executing a point multiplication and a point addition in elliptic curve over $GF(2^{163})$. T_{SHA1} denotes the time complexity of hashing 512-bit message block using hash function, SHA-1 and T_{AES} for the time complexity of encrypting/decrypting 128-bit message block using AES with a 128-bit key.

From the analysis provided in Table 1 [13], it is noted that T_{INV}, $T_{EC_{MUL}}$, $T_{EC_{ADD}}$, T_{SHA1} and T_{AES} require approximately 3, 1200, 5, 0.36 and 0.15 field multiplications in $GF(2^{163})$, respectively, whereas T_{ADD} is negligible.

Table 1. Time complexity of various operations in terms of T_{MUL}

$T_{INV} \approx 3T_{MUL}$	$T_{EC_{MUL}} \approx 1,200T_{MUL}$
$T_{EC_{ADD}} \approx 5T_{MUL}$	$T_{SHA1} \approx 0.36T_{MUL}$
$T_{AES} \approx 0.15T_{MUL}$	T_{ADD} is negligible

We consider a hierarchy with N security classes SC_1, SC_2, ..., SC_N. Each security class SC_i has v_i predecessors. Comparison of storage complexity among various schemes is shown in Table 2. In our scheme, each key length is 128-bit since we have used AES algorithm. We see that the storage space of our scheme is reduced significantly compared with other schemes. In Table 3, we have compared the computational complexity and rough estimation in terms of field multiplications of our scheme with other schemes. In our scheme, key generation phase requires $NT_{SHA1} + \sum_{i=1}^{N}(v_i+1)(T_{ADD}+T_{SHA1})$ and $N(T_{SHA1}+TAES)$ operations for computing signature, constructing linear polynomials and the pairs (S_i, Sd_i), whereas key derivation phase requires $\sum_{i=1}^{N}(v_i+1)(T_{ADD}+T_{SHA1})$ operations. Thus, the total computational cost for our scheme is $\sum_{i=1}^{N}(v_i+1)(2T_{ADD}+3T_{SHA1})+3NT_{SHA1}+NT_{AES}$. It is also clear to observe the

Table 2. Comparison of storage space among various schemes

Schemes	CA's private domain	SC_i's private domain	Public domain
[7]	$163(2N+1)$	163	$163(\sum_{i=1}^{N}(v_i+1)+6N+2)$
[5]	$163(2N+1)$	163	$163(\sum_{i=1}^{N}(v_i+1)+6N+2)$
[11]	$163N$	163	$163(2\sum_{i=1}^{N}(v_i+1)+2N)$
[13]	$128+163$	163	$128(\sum_{i=1}^{N}(v_i+1)+N)+$ $163(2N+2)$
[10]	$163(N+1)$	163	$163(\sum_{i=1}^{N}v_i+(5N+2))$
[8]	163	163	$163(\sum_{i=1}^{N}v_i+3N+4)$
Ours	128	128	$128(\sum_{i=1}^{N}(v_i+1)+3N+1)$

Table 3. Comparison of computational costs among different schemes for key generation and key derivation phases

Scheme	Time complexity	Rough estimation
[7]	$\sum_{i=1}^{N}2(v_i^2+v_i).T_{MUL}+2N.T_{EC_{ADD}}$ $+(4N+2\sum_{i=1}^{N}(v_i+1)).T_{EC_{MUL}}$ $+2\sum_{i=1}^{N}(v_i+1).T_{SHA1}$	$(\sum_{i=1}^{N}(2v_i^2+2,402v_i)$ $+7,210N).T_{MUL}$
[5]	$\sum_{i=1}^{N}2(v_i^2+v_i).T_{MUL}+2N.T_{EC_{ADD}}$ $+(3N+2\sum_{i=1}^{N}(v_i+1)).T_{EC_{MUL}}+$ $2\sum_{i=1}^{N}(v_i+1).T_{SHA1}$	$(\sum_{i=1}^{N}(2v_i^2+2,402v_i)$ $+6,010N).T_{MUL}$
[11]	$N.T_{INV}+(N+2\sum_{i=1}^{N}(v_i+1))$ $.T_{EC_{MUL}}+(N+\sum_{i=1}^{N}(v_i+1)).T_{SHA1}$	$(\sum_{i=1}^{N}2,400v_i+3,603N).T_{MUL}$
[13]	$(2N+1).T_{EC_{MUL}}+$ $2(N+\sum_{i=1}^{N}(v_i+1)).T_{AES}+2N.T_{SHA1}$	$(\sum_{i=1}^{N}0.3v_i+2,401N$ $+1,200).T_{MUL}$
[10]	$(2\sum_{i=1}^{N}v_i).T_{XOR}+(N+\sum_{i=1}^{N}v_i)$ $.T_{ADD}+(2N+\sum_{i=1}^{N}v_i).T_{MUL}$ $+((2N+1)+4\sum_{i=1}^{N}v_i).T_{EC_{MUL}}$ $+(N+2\sum_{i=1}^{N}v_i).T_{SHA1}$	$(\sum_{i=1}^{N}4800.72v_i+2402.36N+$ $1200).T_{MUL}$
[8]	$N(3T_{EC_{MUL}}+2T_{MUL}+3T_{SHA1}+$ $T_{INV}+\sum_{i=1}^{N}v_i(T_{MUL}+2T_{SHA1}))+$ $v_iT_{MUL}+T_{SHA1}$	$(N\sum_{i=1}^{N}1.72v_i+v_i+$ $3606.08N+0.72)T_{MUL}$
Ours	$\sum_{i=1}^{N}(v_i+1)(2T_{ADD}+3T_{SHA1})+$ $3NT_{SHA1}+NT_{AES}$	$(\sum_{i=1}^{N}1.08v_i+1.95N)T_{MUL}$

the computational complexity of our scheme is reduced significantly compared to other schemes proposed recently. Further, our scheme, [8] and [10] are secure against possible attacks as compared to other schemes [5], [7], [11], [13]. However, [8] and [10] require very high storage and computational overheads compared to our scheme. Moreover, dynamic access control problems in our scheme are solved efficiently as compared to other schemes. Considering security and low storage and computational complexity, our scheme is significantly better than all other schemes [5], [7], [8], [10], [11], [13].

6 Conclusion

In this paper, we have proposed a novel efficient key management method to solve dynamic access control problems in a user hierarchy. We have utilized the linear polynomials along with symmetric-key cryptosystem to achieve the required goals for an idle access control scheme with low computational cost and small storage space. Further, our scheme is also secure against known attacks including the man-in-the-middle attack. Hence, our approach is more effective than previously proposed methods for practical applications.

References

1. Advanced Encryption Standard: FIPS PUB 197, National Institute of Standards and Technology (NIST), U.S. Department of Commerce (November 2001), http://csrc.nist.gov/publications/fips/fips197/fips-197.pdf
2. Akl, S.G., Taylor, P.D.: Cryptographic solution to a problem of access control in a hierarchy. ACM Transactions on Computer Systems (TOCS) 1(3), 239–248 (1983)
3. Atallah, M., Blanton, M., Fazio, N., Frikken, K.: Dynamic and Efficient Key Management for Access Hierarchies. ACM Trans. Inf. Syst. Secur. 12(3), Article 18, 198–208 (2009)
4. Atallah, M., Frikken, K., Blanton, M.: Dynamic and efficient key management for access hierarchies. In: ACM Conference on Computer and Communications Security (CCS 2005), pp. 190–202 (2005)
5. Chung, Y.F., Lee, H.H., Lai, F., Chen, T.S.: Access control in user hierarchy based on elliptic curve cryptosystem. Information Sciences 178(1), 230–243 (2008)
6. Das, A.K., Paul, N.R., Tripathy, L.: Cryptanalysis and improvement of an access control in user hierarchy based on elliptic curve cryptosystem. Information Sciences 209, 80–92 (2012)
7. Jeng, F.G., Wang, C.M.: An efficient key-management scheme for hierarchical access control based on elliptic curve cryptosystem. Journal of Systems and Software 79(8), 1161–1167 (2006)
8. Lin, Y.L., Hsu, C.L.: Secure key management scheme for dynamic hierarchical access control based on ECC. Journal of Systems and Software 84(4), 679–685 (2011)
9. Lo, J.W., Hwang, M.S., Liu, C.H.: An efficient key assignment scheme for access control in a large leaf class hierarchy. Information Sciences 181(4), 917–925 (2011)
10. Nikooghadam, M., Zakerolhosseini, A.: Secure Communication of Medical Information Using Mobile Agents. Journal of Medical Systems (2012), doi:10.1007/s10916-012-9857-8
11. Nikooghadam, M., Zakerolhosseini, A., Moghaddam, M.E.: Efficient utilization of elliptic curve cryptosystem for hierarchical access control. Journal of Systems and Software 83(10), 1917–1929 (2010)
12. Secure Hash Standard: FIPS PUB 180-1, National Institute of Standards and Technology (NIST), U.S. Department of Commerce (April 1995)
13. Wu, S., Chen, K.: An Efficient Key-Management Scheme for Hierarchical Access Control in E-Medicine System. Journal of Medical Systems (2011), doi:10.1007/s10916-011-9700-7

Publicly Auditable Provable Data Possession Scheme for Outsourced Data in the Public Cloud Using Polynomial Interpolation

B.R. Purushothama and B.B. Amberker

Department of Computer Science and Engineering
National Institute of Technology Warangal
Andhra Pradesh-506004, India
{puru,bba}@nitw.ac.in

Abstract. Cloud computing paradigm provides computing and storage infrastructure for the clients to outsource their data and computation. This new computing paradigm poses several security challenges. We focus on the problem of checking the possession of data by the untrusted cloud storage server. We design publicly auditable provable data possession scheme using polynomial interpolation technique. In our scheme, the client can delegate the task of verification to the Third Party Auditor. Interestingly, the client will not use any secret to compute the public metadata and client or Third Party Auditor need not to maintain any metadata for the verification of the proof. The verifier can verify the proof using public metadata and a random key kept secret for the challenge. We have focused on reducing the size of the proof returned by the cloud server to save the network bandwidth. We have defined the security and proved the security of the scheme under the group satisfying Computational Diffie Hellman assumption against a cheating cloud server. In the proposed scheme, the verifier can make unlimited number of data possession challenges to the server.

Keywords: Provable Data Possession, Polynomial interpolation, Public Auditability, CDH, DLP, Public Cloud.

1 Introduction

Increasing demand of the computing resources and the advancement in the network technology has made the organizations to outsource their storage and computing needs. This new computing paradigm which offers several benefits is termed as Cloud Computing. Various definitions of cloud can be found in [1]. Cloud Computing being economic offers various types of services.

- **Infrastructure as a Service (IaaS)**: The customer makes use of the cloud service provider's storage, computing and networking infrastructure. A good example of IaaS is Amazon's Elastic Cloud (Amazon EC2) [2].

S.M. Thampi et al. (Eds.): SNDS 2012, CCIS 335, pp. 11–22, 2012.

- **Platform as a Service (PaaS)**: Platform comprises of development tools and runtime environment. The cloud customer leverages the provider's development tools to run the custom applications. Examples include Microsoft Azure [3] and Google Apps.
- **Software as a Service (PaaS)**: Customers use application softwares that are hosted on the provider's infrastructure. Examples include Google docs and web mail services.

There are two categories of cloud infrastructure.

1. **Private Cloud Infrastructure**: In this category, the infrastructure is owned and managed by the customer (organization) and located on-premise (in the customer's region of control). The access to the data is controlled by the customer and the access is granted to the trusted parties. We hope, the use of users, customers, data owners, service providers will be clear from the context.

2. **Public Cloud Infrastructure**: In this category, the cloud service provider owns and manages the infrastructure and the data is located off-premise (in the service provider's region of control). The access to the data could be potentially granted to the untrusted parties as the data is not controlled by the customer but the service provider.

1.1   Data Outsourcing and Data Possession Guarantee

There is increase in cost for building the in-house storage and there is need for managing the huge amount of sensitive information. This requires both storage capacity and the skilled personnel. Data outsourcing reduces management cost and more effective disaster protection than the in-house disaster protection operations. The confidentiality and integrity of the owner's data will be at risk as the data on the public cloud will be under the control of the untrusted service provider.

Archival storage servers retain large amounts of data, little of which is accessed frequently. The servers store the data for long periods of time, during which there may be exposure to data loss. Archival storage requires guarantees about the authenticity of data on storage, namely that storage servers possess data. *The provable data possession guarantee that a client that has stored data at an untrusted storage server can verify that the server possesses the original data without retrieving it. A storage server can generate a valid proof if and only if it really stores the data. This proof can be verified without retrieving back the data from the storage server.*

Based on the role of the verifier , the Provable Data Possession (PDP) schemes can be categorized as follows:

1. **Private Auditable PDP Schemes**: Only the client (data owner) can verify the proof of data possession returned by the cloud storage server.

2. **Public Auditable PDP Schemes**: In public auditable schemes, the client (data owner) can delegate the task of verification to the third party. In these schemes, clients need not devote computational resources for the verification. So, the computation can also be outsourced to the Third Party Auditor (TPA).

1.2 Our Contribution

We design a provable data possession scheme with public auditability based on the polynomial interpolation technique. In the proposed method, the data owner wont use any secret information in computing the metadata that helps in verifying the proof returned by the cloud storage server. The data owner wont store any metadata information for verification. Any TPA can verify the proof of data possession. The data owner need not to give any secret to the third party auditor to carry out the verification process. The scheme is elegant in a way that using some random challenge and public data, the third party can verify the proof returned by the cloud storage server. The proof size returned by the cloud storage in the proposed scheme is less than the scheme proposed in [9]. The verifier can make unlimited number of data possession challenges. We define the security and prove the security of the proposed scheme.

2 Related Work

The recent work on the outsourced data has focused on the verification of the integrity and possession of the data by the untrusted cloud [4][5][6][7] under different security models. The symmetric key PDP scheme in [8] suffers from limited number of possession checkings. Wang et. al [5] proposed the public auditing for data storage security in cloud computing. They use the blinding technique to hide the information about stored data in proof. Ateneise et al. [9] have proposed a provable data possession model for ensuring possession of data on untrusted storage. They have left open the problem of reducing the size of the proof returned by the server. This work focuses in that direction to reduce the size of the proof in schemes supporting public verifiability. In their scheme, to make it public auditable, client has to delegate the secret to the third party auditor which is not the case in our proposed scheme.

3 System Model

The cloud data storage model comprises of the following entities.

- **Client/Data Owner (C)**: It is an entity that possesses large data files to be stored on the cloud data storage. Client relies on the cloud for the computation and maintenance of the data.

- **Cloud Storage Server (CSS or S)**: Cloud Storage Provider (CSP) manages the CSS. The CSS has "large" storage space and computation resources to maintain and manage the client's data. **The Cloud Storage Server is untrusted.**
- **Third Party Auditor, (TPA)**: It is an entity with computational resources and capabilities trusted to assess and expose the untrusted CSS for cheating. This entity carries out the process of challenging and verification of proof of data possession.

The client C stores data on the untrusted cloud server CSS. C deletes the data from its local storage. C is relieved of the burden of computation and storage. As client no longer possesses the data in local, it is of much importance to the client to check that the data is indeed correctly stored and maintained by CSS. The client C or TPA will be able to verify the proof returned by CSS for the requested data items possession guarantee without downloading the data items.

3.1   Cloud Storage Server as Adversary

- The server S is not trusted to store the data items.
- The server might discard some portion of the client's data which is rarely accessed to get financial benefit by reselling the storage.
- The server might hide the data loss incidents to maintain its reputation
- The server might try to convince the verifier (TPA/C) it possesses (store) the data item, even if the data item is totally or partially corrupted or even without possessing the data item.

4   The Proposed Scheme

4.1   Notations and Preliminaries

- $\pi = \{0,1\}^k \times \{0,1\}^{\log_2 n} \to \{0,1\}^{\log_2 n}$ be the Pseudo-Random Permutation (PRP).
- $F = \{b_1, \ldots, b_n\}$ be the set of data blocks/items.
- $x \xleftarrow{\$} X$ denotes uniformly and randomly chosing x from X.

Definition 1 (Discrete Logarithm Assumption, DLP). *Consider a multiplicative cyclic group G of prime order p, with generator g [10]. The DLP problem is, given g, g^x, return x. The DLP assumption is that there exists no probabilistic polynomial time algorithm to solve an instance of DLP problem with non-negligible probability [11]. Simply it says, DLP problem is hard.*

Definition 2 (Computational Diffie Hellman Assumption, CDH). *Consider a multiplicative cyclic group G of prime order p, with generator g. The CDH problem is, given g, g^x, g^y, compute g^{xy}. The CDH assumption says that there exists no probabilistic polynomial time algorithm to solve an instance of CDH problem with non-negligible probability [11]. Simply it says, CDH problem is hard.*

Definition 3 (Standard Signature Scheme (SigScheme)). *A signature scheme is a tuple of possibly probabilistic polynomial time algorithms (Keygen, Sign, Verify), Where:*

- *KeyGen(1^k): which takes as input the security parameter k and outputs a public key PK and a private key SK.*
- *Sign(m, SK): which takes as input a message m and a private key SK and produces a signature σ for the message m.*
- *Verify(m, PK, σ): which takes as input a message m, a public key PK and a signature σ, and outputs either accept or reject.*

Definition 4 (Assumption on Standard Signature Scheme: SigScheme). *Any standard signature scheme SigScheme, which satisfies the notion of strong existential unforgeability under adaptive chosen-message attack (where an adversary cannot create a new signature even for a previously signed message) should be used in our constuction of the scheme.*

Definition 5 (Provable Data Possession Scheme (PDP)). *The Provable Data Possession scheme is a tuple of four polynomial time algorithms (KeyGen, OutsourceAndPublish, ChalGen, GenProof, VerifyProof) defined as below.*

- *KeyGen(1^k) $\rightarrow$ (pk, sk): The Key Generation algorithm takes security parameter k as input and outputs the public key, pk and the secret key, sk for the data owner or the client.*
- *OutsourceAndPublish(sk, F) $\rightarrow$ P_{pub}: This algorithm is run by the client to generate the public data that helps in verification of the proof. The algorithm takes as input the secret key sk, the set of data items to be outsourced F and outputs the public information P_{pub}.*
- *ChalGen(1^k) $\rightarrow$ \{chal, S_{chal}\}: Challenge Generation algorithm is run by the TPA (client can also be verifier) to query for possession proof of data items. Algorithm returns chal that contains the number of data items and the corresponding data items indices that are queried for the proof. Also, it returns S_{chal}, the secret corresponding to chal which is kept secret by TPA.*
- *GenProof(F, chal) $\rightarrow$ V : The Generate Proof algorithm is run by the cloud storage server to generate the proof of possession for the data items requested by the TPA. This algorithm takes as input, the set of data items F, the challenge chal received by the client and returns the proof of possession V.*
- *VerifyProof(S_{chal}, chal, V) $\rightarrow$ \{ "success", "failure"\}: The Verify Proof algorithm is run by the TPA (client can also be verifier) to verify the proof of possession received from the cloud server for the requested data items. This algorithm takes as input the secret S_{chal}, challenge chal and the proof V and returns whether V is a correct proof of possession of data items as specified by chal.*

The PDP system is constructed using the PDP scheme by the following two phases.

- **Setup:** The client C possesses the set of data items F to be outsourced on to the server. Client runs $(pk, sk) \leftarrow KeyGen(1^l)$ to obtain the public and secret keys. Then, C runs $P_{pub} \leftarrow OutsourcePublish(sk, F)$. C stores F on the server S and P_{pub} in the *public directory*. Client C deletes F from the storage.
- **Challenge:** The client C or any TPA generates the challenge *chal* containing information about the specific data items for which the proof of possession is sought and sends chal to S and keeps secret S_{chal} from S. S runs $V \leftarrow GenProof(F, chal)$ and sends V to C or TPA. C or TPA checks the validity of the proof by running $VerifyProof(S_{chal}, chal, V)$.

4.2 Security of the Proposed PPDP Scheme

We define the security model of the proposed PDP scheme as a "game" between adversary and a challenger (client/TPA). In this game, adversary has full access to the information stored in the server which means the the adversary can play the part of prover (CSS). The goal of the adversary is to cheat the verifier successfully. The adversary tries to generate the valid responses without possessing the data items and the pass the data verification without being detected.

Definition 6 (Security of the Proposed PDP Scheme: Data Possession Game). *The following game is played between Challenger C (Client/TPA) and the Adversary A, (Cloud Storage Server, CSS). There are three phases in the game. Setup, Outsourse and Publish, Challenge and Forge Phases.*

- *Setup Phase: The challenger C, runs Key generation algorithm to get key pair $(pk, sk) \leftarrow KeyGen(1^l)$. pk is sent to A and keeps sk secret.*
- *Outsource and Publish Phase: A chooses $m_1, m_2, \ldots, m_n$ and sends to C. C runs $P_{pub} \leftarrow OutsourceAndPublish(sk, F)$, sends P_{pub} to A.*
- *Challenge Phase: Challenger runs $ChalGen(1^k) \rightarrow \{chal, S_{chal}\}$, sends chal to A which specifies the data items $m_{i_1}, m_{i_2}, \ldots, m_{i_t}$ such that $1 \leq i_j \leq n$, $1 \leq j \leq t$, $1 \leq t \leq n$. Challenger keeps S_{chal} secret.*
- *Forge Phase: A computes the proof of possession V for the data items specified in chal and sends V to C.*
- *If "Success" $\leftarrow VerifyProof(S_{chal}, V)$, then the adversary wins the Data Possession Game.*

5 Publicly Auditable Data Possession Scheme Based on Polynomial Interpolation

5.1 Construction of the Proposed Scheme

The Client C runs **Algorithm 1** where it chooses the multiplicative cyclic group G where *Computational Diffie Hellman problem* (Definition 2) is hard (Note that in G, DLP is also hard as CDH hard implies DLP is also hard). C will have its set of data items F to be outsourced.

Algorithm 1. Setup

Input   : Security Parameter, k

1 Choose large prime p such that *Computational Diffie Hellman Problem* is hard in multiplicative cyclic group $G = Z_p^*$;

2 Let $\alpha : \{0,1\}^k \times \{0,1\}^{\log_2 n} \to Z_p^*$;

3 Let $F = \{m_1, m_2, \ldots, m_n\}$, where $m_i \in Z_p^*$;

4 Choose the generator $g \in Z_p^*$;

5 $(pk, sk) \leftarrow KeyGen(1^k)$. `// It is the KeyGen of SigScheme (Definition 3)`

C runs **Algorithm 2** with F as input. C stores the data items F on to the Cloud Storage Server S and deletes data items from the local storage. For each data item it computes the *public data* and signs each public data using the standard signature algorithm as per **Definition 3** which satisfies the security notion as per **Definition 4**. Readers should note that this signature scheme is used to ensure that the public data is indeed correctly published by C corresponding to F. This can be verified by S in obvious way using *Verify* algorithm of the *SigScheme*. *SigScheme* can be replaced by any construction which satisfies the security notion given in Definition 4.

Algorithm 2. Outsource and Publish: OutsourceAndPublish

Input   :
- Security Parameter, k
- Secret Key, sk for signature only.
- The set of data items to be outsourced, $F = \{m_1, m_2, \ldots, m_n\}$, where $m_i \in Z_p^*$

Output: The data to be published to the public directory, P_{pub}

1 $P_{pub} = \emptyset$;

2 **for** $i = 1$ *to* n **do**

- Compute : g^{m_i}
- Compute : $\sigma(g^{m_i}) \leftarrow Sign(sk, h(g^{m_i}))$ `// ` $\sigma(g^{m_i})$ ` is signature of ` g^{m_i}
- $P_{pub} = P_{pub} \cup \{(g^{m_i}, \sigma(g^{m_i}))\}$;

end

3 **return** P_{pub};

C or TPA runs **Algorithm 3** to query S for the proof of possession of data items. The challenge comprises of the number of data items for which the proof is sought, and keys that help in computing the proof.

S receives the challenge and runs **Algorithm 4** to generate the proof and sends the same to C. The time taken to compute the proof is $O(t(\log t)^2)$.

C or TPA runs **Algorithm 5** to verify the proof of possession received from S. It outputs whether the proof is correct or not.

Algorithm 3. Challenge Generation: ChalGen

Input : Security Parameter, k

Output: Challenge , chal

1 $d \xleftarrow{\$} \mathbb{Z}_p^*$;

2 Compute g^d;

3 Choose $t \xleftarrow{\$} [1, n]$;   // Number of data items challenged;

4 Choose $k_c^1 \xleftarrow{\$} \{0, 1\}^k$;

5 Choose $k_c^2 \xleftarrow{\$} \{0, 1\}^k$ such that
  for $j \leftarrow 1$ **to** t **do**

$\quad$ $a_j \xleftarrow{\$} \alpha_{k_c^2}(j)$ is distinct from previous values.   // These are the set of
$\quad$ co-efficients such that no two a_i, i= 1 to t is same

  end

6 Let $chal = \{t, g^d, k_c^1, k_c^2\}$;

7 Return $chal$.

Algorithm 4. Generation of Proof of Possession : ProofGen

Input :
  − Challenge , $chal = \{t, g^d, k_c^1, k_c^2\}$
  − $F = \{m_1, m_2, \dots, m_n\}$

Output: The Data Possession Proof, V

1 **for** $j \leftarrow 1$ **to** t **do**
$\quad$ $i_j = \pi_{k_c^1}(j)$ // These are the indices of the data items for which
$\quad$ the proof of possession to be generated
  end

2 **for** $j \leftarrow 1$ **to** t **do**

$\quad$ $a_j \xleftarrow{\$} \alpha_{k_c^2}(j)$.   // These are the set of co-efficients such that no
$\quad$ two a_i, i= 1 to t is same i.e., all are distinct.

  end

3 Construct a polynomial $P_d(x)$ by using the Principle of Lagrange's interpolation
  given by Equation 1 (Section 8) with the points
  $\{(a_1, m_{i_1}), (a_2, m_{i_2}), \dots, (a_t, m_{i_t})\}$;

4 Compute $S_d = P_d(0)$;

5 Compute $V = g^{dS_d}$;

6 Return V;

---

6   Security Analysis

Definition 7 (Cheating Cloud Storage Server). *A Cheating Cloud Storage Server is the CSS which tries to pass the data possession proof verification stage without possessing the data items requested in the challenge by the verifier.*

Algorithm 5. Verifying the Proof of Data Possession : VerifyProof

---

Input :
- Challenge , $chal = \{t, g^d, k_c^1, k_c^2\}$
- The proof of possession V and Secret of the challenge, d
- Public metadata, P_{pub}

Output: Correctness of the proof, Success or Failure.

1 **for** $j \leftarrow 1$ **to** t **do**

   $i_j = \pi_{k_c^1}(j)$ // These are the indices of the data items for which the proof of possession to be generated·

  end

2 Let $T = \emptyset$;

3 **for** $j \leftarrow 1$ **to** t **do**

   $a_j \xleftarrow{\$} \alpha_{k_c^2}(j)$

   $T = T \bigcup a_j$; // These are the set of co-efficients such that no two a_i, i= 1 to t is same. All the a_j are distinct.

  end

4 **for** $j \leftarrow 1$ **to** t **do**

   Compute $l_j(0)$ with $T = \{a_1, \ldots, a_t\}$ using Equation 2 (See Section 8).

        // $l_j(0)$ is the lagrange's coefficient wrt a_j evaluated at 0

  end

5 Compute $g^u = \prod_{j=1}^t g^{m_{i_j} l_j(0)}$;   // It has access to P_{pub}, $\{g^{m_{i_1}} \ldots g^{m_{i_t}}\}$;

6 **if** $(g^u)^d = V$ **then**

   Return "Success"

  else

   Return "Failure"

  end

Proposition 1. *Under Computational Diffie Hellman Assumption, a cheating Cloud Storage Server can provide the correct proof of possession for the data items specified in the challenge with negligible probability.*

Proof. Consider the data possession game of *Definition* 6. Let A be an adversary (a cheating CSS). Challenger (TPA) runs Algorithm 1, sends pk to A and keeps sk secret. *We assume that in the group G chosen Computational Diffie Hellman (hence DLP assumption holds as CDH implies DLP) assumption holds.* A chooses $m_1, m_2, \ldots, m_n$ and sends to C. C runs Algorithm 2 with $\{m_1, m_2, \ldots, m_n\}$ as input and gives $\{(g^{m_i}, \sigma(g^{m_i}))\}$, for $1 \leq i \leq n$ to A.

Challenger runs Algorithm 3 and sends $chal = \{t, g^d, k_1, k_2\}$ to A and keeps d secret. The parameter t, where $1 \leq t \leq n$ specifies the number of data items for which the proof is sought. k_1 specifies indices of t data items. Let $\{i_1, i_2, \ldots, i_t\}$ be the set of indices determined by the PRP with key k_1. Let $m_{i_1}, m_{i_2}, \ldots, m_{i_t}$ be the corresponding data items. Adversary A generates the set of coefficients $\{a_1, \ldots, a_t\}$ using k_2 and the function α. We consider the following two cases:

1. *Adversary A possesses all challenged data items*: If adversary A possesses $m_{i_1}, m_{i_2}, \ldots, m_{i_t}$ then it constructs the polynomial $P(x)$ passing through

(a_j, m_{i_j}), for $1 \leq j \leq t$ and sends $g^{dP(0)}$ to challenger (See Algorithm 4). TPA computes $l_j(0), j = 1, \ldots, n$ using Lagranges polynomial Equation 2 (Section 8). Using public data $g^{m_{ij}}$, for $j = 1$ to t, it computes $g^u = \prod_{j=1}^{t} g^{m_{ij} l_j(0)}$. TPA uses secret d to compute $(g^u)^d$. It accepts as success as $(g^u)^d = g^{dP(0)}$ (See Algorithm 5).

2. *Adversary A is missing some/all challenged data items*: Suppose adversary is not in possession of say l, where $1 \leq l \leq t$ data items among requested t data items. W.l.o.g let these missing l blocks be $\{m_{i_1}, m_{i_2}, \ldots, m_{i_l}\}$. Now A want to construct the proof of possession so that it passes the verification. We give the following attempts that A can make.

   Case 1: With the set of coefficients $\{a_1, \ldots, a_t\}$ generated using k_2, A can compute $l_j(0)$, for $j = 1, \ldots, t$ using equation 2 (Section 8). Using the public data $g^{m_{ij}}$, for $j = 1$ to t, it computes $g^u = \prod_{j=1}^{t} g^{m_{ij} l_j(0)}$. This is similar to what challenger computes in step 5 of Algorithm 5. To pass thorugh the *step 6*, now A should get d. Now adversary has to solve the instance of Discrete Logarithm Problem: Given (g, g^d) A should compute d. According to Discrete Logarithm Assumption (Definition 1), the probability that A can solve this is negligible. Hence, a cheating CSS cannot pass the verification without solving an instance of Discrete Logarithm problem. A fails to pass the verification.

   Case 2: Adversary A might try to guess the missing l blocks. The probability with which A can guess a data item is $\frac{1}{p}$. The probability that the adversary can guess all l blocks is $\frac{1}{p^l}$. For larger p and l this is negligible (close to 0).

   Case 3: With the set of coefficients $\{a_1, \ldots, a_t\}$ generated using k_2, A can compute $l_j(0)$, for $j = 1, \ldots, t$ using equation 2 (Section 8). Using the public data $g^{m_{ij}}, j = 1$ to t, it computes $g^u = \prod_{j=1}^{t} g^{m_{ij} l_j(0)}$. If A computes g^{du} from g^u and g^d, it can pass the verification. Under the Computational Diffie Hellman assumption (Definition 2), given g^u and g^d, A cannot compute g^{du}. So, A fails to pass the verification.

So, a cheating CSS without possessing data items requested can pass the verification phase with negligible probability.

6.1 Performance

We analyze the performance of our proposed scheme for the computation cost of each algorithm (Table 1), the storage cost of each entity (Table 2) and the communication cost of each phase (Table 3). In Table 1, Table 2 and Table 3, k is the security parameter, $|p|$ is the size of an element (in bits) in the group G considered in our scheme, t is the number of data items for which the proof of possession is sought, n is the number of number of data items outsourced on to the CSS and $|t|$ is the required number of bits to specify t.

It should be noted that, the computation cost to generate the proof requires one exponentiation. It means CSS should carry out only one exponentiation per request. Client need to store only its primary secret key used for signature generation. The proof size is essentially an element of the group under consideration.

Table 1. Computation Cost of each Algorithm in Proposed PDP Scheme

Algorithm	Addition	Multiplication	Exponentiation
Setup	0	0	0
OutSourcePublish	0	0	n
ChalGen	0	0	0
ProofGen	2(t-1)	2(t-1)	1
VerifyProof	t-1	2(t-1)	t

Table 2. Storage Cost of each Entity of the PDP Scheme

Entity	Storage Cost (Bits)
Client	k (Secret key for SigScheme)
Cloud Storage Server	$n|p|$
Verifier	$|p| + 2k + |t|$
Public Directory	$n|p|$

Table 3. Communication Cost at each Phase of the PDP system

Phase	Communication Cost (Bits)
Challenge	$2k + |p| + |t|$
Response (Proof Size)	$|p|$

7 Comparison

We compare our proposed scheme with the scheme by Ateneise et. al in [9]. Suppose the size of the modulus in [9] and p in our scheme is of l bits. Then client should store $3l$ bits and 128 bits (AES key size) and delegate the same to TPA for public auditability. The challenge has four values of about l *bits* + 40 *bytes*. The proof from server contains two values which total l *bits* + 20 *bytes*.

In the proposed scheme, client need not to store any information except its secret key of signature scheme. Client need not to give any secrets to TPA. Challenge has four values similar to [9]. The TPA should keep only one secret till the completion of the proof verification (in our scheme it is the value of d). The proof from server contains only one value total of l bits.

8 The Lagrange Form of the Interpolation Polynomial

Let $\{(x_1, y_1), \ldots, (x_j, y_j), \ldots, (x_k, y_k)\}$ be the set of k points, where no two $x'_j s$ are same. The *interpolation polynomial in the Lagrange form* is the linear combination,

$$P(x) = \sum_{j=1}^{k} y_j l_j(x) \quad (1) \quad \text{of} \quad l_j(x) = \prod_{1 \le i \le k, i \ne j} \frac{x - x_i}{x_j - x_i} \quad (2)$$

The degree of the polynomial $P(x)$ is less than or equal to $k - 1$.

9   Conclusion

We have designed a publicly auditable provable data possession scheme for the outsourced data in the public cloud. We have defined the security of the scheme and proved the security of the scheme under the group satisfying CDH (hence DLP) assumption against a cheating cloud storage server. Any TPA including the client can check the proof of verification. In the proposed scheme, there is no secret key involved in computing the metadata (except for signature) that helps in verification of the proof of possession. Client or TPA need not to store any secrets related to public metadata. The size of the proof is less compared to the size of the proof generated in [9]. The cloud storage server needs only one exponentiation operation to generate the proof which is desirable. As a future work, we focus on reducing the size of the proof.

Acknowledgements. This work was supported by Information Security Education and Awareness - ISEA Fellowship, Department of Information Technology, Ministry of Communications and Information Technology and Ministry of Human Resource Development, Government of INDIA.

References

1. Vaquero, L.M., Rodero-Merino, L., Caceres, J., Lindner, M.: A break in the clouds: towards a cloud definition. ACM SIGCOMM Computer Communication Review 39, 50–55 (2009)
2. Amazon Elastic Compute Cloud (Amazon EC2), http://aws.amazon.com/ec2/
3. Microsoft Windows Azure Platform, http://www.microsoft.com/windowsazure
4. Chang, E.-C., Xu, J.: Remote Integrity Check with Dishonest Storage Server. In: Jajodia, S., Lopez, J. (eds.) ESORICS 2008. LNCS, vol. 5283, pp. 223–237. Springer, Heidelberg (2008)
5. Wang, C., Wang, Q., Ren, K., Lou, W.: Privacy preserving public auditing for data storage security in cloud computing. In: 29th Conference on Information Communications, pp. 525–533 (2010)
6. Juels, A., Kaliski, B.S.: POR: Proofs of Retrievability for Large Files. In: 14th ACM Conference on Computer and Communication Security, pp. 584–597 (2007)
7. Bowers, K.D., Juels, A., Oprea, A.: Proofs of Retrievability: Theory and Implementation: Report 2008/175, Cryptology ePrint Archive (2008)
8. Ateniese, G., Di Piotro, R., Mancini, L.F., Tsudik, G.: Scalable and efficient provable data possession. In: 4th International Conference on Security and Privacy in Communication Networks, pp. 1–10 (2008)
9. Ateniese, G., Burns, R., Curtmola, R., Herring, J., Kissner, L., Peterson, Z., Song, D.: Provable data possession at untrusted stores. In: 14th ACM Conference on Computer and Communications Security, pp. 598–609 (2007)
10. Lidl, R., Niederreiter, H.: Introduction to finite fields and their applications. Press Syndicate of the University of Cambridge, Cambridge Britain (1986)
11. Delfs, H., Knebl, H.: Introduction to Cryptography, Principles and Applications. Springer, Heidelberg (2007)

Performance Evaluation of the Fuzzy ARTMAP for Network Intrusion Detection

Nelcileno Araújo[1], Ruy de Oliveira[2], Ed' Wilson Tavares Ferreira[2],
Valtemir Nascimento[2], Ailton Shinoda Akira[3], and Bharat Bhargava[4]

[1] Universidade Federal de Mato Grosso - UFMT, Cuiabá, MT, Brasil
[2] Instituto Federal de Educação, Ciência e Tecnologia do Estado de Mato Grosso - IFMT,
Cuiabá, MT, Brasil
[3] Universidade Estadual Júlio de Mesquita Filho - UNESP, Ilha Solteira, SP, Brasil
[4] Purdue University, West Lafayette, IN, USA
`nelcileno@yahoo.com.br`,
`{ruy,ed,valtemir.nascimento}@cba.ifmt.edu.br`,
`shinoda@dee.feis.unesp.br`, `bb@cs.purdue.edu`

Abstract. Recently, considerable research work have been conducted towards finding fast and accurate pattern classifiers for training Intrusion Detection Systems (IDSs). This paper proposes using the so called Fuzzy ARTMAT classifier to detect intrusions in computer network. Our investigation shows, through simulations, how efficient such a classifier can be when used as the learning mechanism of a typical IDS. The promising evaluation results in terms of both detection accuracy and training duration indicate that the Fuzzy ARTMAP is indeed viable for this sort of application.

Keywords: Fuzzy ARTMAP, security, intrusion detection.

1 Introduction

The non-authorized access into a computer network represents one of the most dangerous threats to the computer's security in such networks. Because of that, it is crucial to have mechanisms that inform system administrators of potential threats so proper actions can be taken, preventing the attacked system from further damage. These mechanisms are commonly called Intrusion Detection System (IDS).

In general, An IDS works based on one of two principles. It can either match suspicious patterns to previously known intrusion rules or recognize abnormal activities in the network [1]. The former approach is called *signature detection*, while the latter is the *anomaly detection*.

The drawback of signature-based IDSs is that they are limited to previously known attacks, i.e., these IDSs are not able to detect new forms of attacks that may arise. Because of that, new approaches, based on learning machine techniques, for anomaly detection are of paramount importance these days. Additionally, such techniques should not be too computationally intensive [2]. In this sense, we focus on the learning machine paradigm in this work.

S.M. Thampi et al. (Eds.): SNDS 2012, CCIS 335, pp. 23–34, 2012.

We investigate here the effectiveness of using the neural network called fuzzy ARTMAP in training an IDS. This classifier provides a unique solution known as stability-plasticity dilemma since it both preserves the previously acquired knowledge over the evaluated data (stability) and self-adapts to new patterns of classification (plasticity) [3]. Firstly, we evaluated the IDS training duration, global detection rate, and accuracy by using the well-known KDD99 training dataset. We used this dataset because it has been widely and successfully used for IDSs calibration [4]. Subsequently, we evaluated the IDS on a real wireless network (WLAN). In these experiments, four types of attacks were evaluated and the results were compared to three distinct IDS of the literature. The results are encouraging.

The remainder of this paper is organized as follows. In section 2 we present related work. Section 3 explains the fuzzy ARTMAP. In section 4 we introduce our proposed approach for training IDSs on the basis of the fuzzy ARTMAP, and also present the performance evaluations related to both the KDD99 dataset and the real WLAN. Finally in the last section we conclude our evaluations and outline potential future work.

2   Related Work

There exist various learning approaches for training and classifying IDS. The proposal presented in [5] shows that the Fuzzy ARTMAP classifier renders low performance in detecting intrusion. Nevertheless, their experiments were conducted in wired networks only and they did not use any optimizing mechanism to improve the right classification rate.

On the other hand, the proposal in [2] uses a genetic algorithm based technique, as optimizing mechanism, for computing setup parameters that enhance the effectiveness of the Fuzzy ARTMAP classifier toward 100% of correct detection rate. The disadvantage here is that the dataset used does not represent a wireless network either.

The work in [6] uses a Fuzzy ARTMAP neural network to detect intrusion in heterogeneous wireless networks. Their approach attempts to reduce error in classifying the attacks by using an access control security service based on the context aware role paradigm. As the proposal focuses on access control modeling, it does not fit Wireless LAN (WLAN) attacks.

Finally, in this work we propose a Fuzzy ARTMAP neural network as a classifier of features to recognize attacks in the MAC sub layer of a WLAN.

3   Fuzzy ARTMAP Neural Networks

Neural networks have been used extensively for detecting intrusions in computer networks [2], which confirms that the paradigm of learning by sampling in training IDSs are becoming more and more popular these days. In particular, the fuzzy ARTMAP neural network represents a valuable supervisioned learning system that classifies input data into stable categories to respond to random input patterns [3].

Fig. 1 depicts the architecture of the fuzzy ARTMAP neural network. It comprises two modules: fuzzy ART_a and fuzzy ART_b. Both modules use the same structure of the neural network ART1 (not shown in the figure) that uses the logical operations of the fuzzy logic theory [7].

These two modules are interconnected by a third module called inter-ART which controls the training of the mapping of ART_a recognition categories onto ART_b recognition categories. The inter-ART associates the input parameters (ART_a) with the output parameters (ART_b) using the *match tracking* mechanism, aiming at maximizing the generalization of the recognition categories and minimizing the network errors [3].

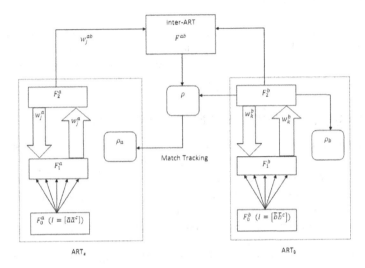

Fig. 1. Architecture of the fuzzy ARTMAP neural network [3]

The algorithm of such a neural network works based on the following steps [3]:

- **Step 1**: If needed, normalize the ART_a (input vector) and ART_b (output vector). Initially, all neuron values should be normalized to guarantee that they are in the range 0-1;
- **Step 2**: Encode the vectors of ART_a and ART_b modules: a new input pattern should go through a preliminary complement coding in order to preserve the information amplitude;
- **Step 3**: Initialize the weights and parameters of ART_a, ART_b and Inter-ART. First initialize the weights (when set to 1, means that all the categories are deactivated), then the training rate (β between 0 and 1), followed by the choice parameter ($\alpha > 0$) and finally the vigilance parameter (ρ_a, ρ_b and ρ_{ab} between 0 and 1);
- **Step 4**: Choose the category for ART_a and ART_b. If more than one module is active, take the one that has the highest ordering index;
- **Step 5**: Test the vigilance of ART_a and ART_b. If the vigilance criterion is met, then the resonance (match) takes place. Otherwise a new index is chosen restarting from phase 4. The searching process repeats until an index value, that meets the vigilance test, is found;

- **Step 6**: *Match tracking* between ART_a and ART_b: check if there was matching between the input and output. If not, search another index that satisfies it;
- **Step 7** Adaptation of the weights: the vector (layer F_2) of the ART_a, ART_b and Inter-ART are updated with the new weights;
- **Step 8**: Repeat steps 4 through 7 for every pair of vectors to be trained.

4   Investigating the Performance of the Fuzzy ARTMAP in Detecting Intrusions

In this section we will initially detail the use of the fuzzy ARTMAP classifier being used for training an IDS. In these evaluations, we used the well-known KDD99 training dataset. Subsequently, we will compare our approach with existing work in terms of its accuracy to detect attacks in real wireless LAN.

4.1   Applying Fuzzy ARTMAP Classifier on KDD99 Dataset

Despite being relatively old and encompasses just little attacks against UNIX based systems and Cisco routers, KDD99 [8] is a well-known dataset widely used in training and testing IDSs in the literature. Many researchers still adopt such a dataset for evaluating both intrusion detection and machine learning algorithms [4]. By using KDD99, we intended mainly to facilitate comparisons to similar work [1,2,9]. In fact, in order to reduce the amount of samples to be processed, we used here the so called training dataset (10% KDD99) only.

The input vector receives the registers of the KDD99 training dataset. However, we used the optimized dataset proposed in [9], in which only the most relevant features of the original dataset are taken. As a result, the input vector is shortened to a dimension of 14.

The output vector, which contains the classes of detections by the IDS, is defined through a binary coding of two bits, as illustrated in Table 1.

Table 1. Output Vectors (binary) corresponding of the classes of intrusions

Detection type	Class	Output vector b
Normal	S1	01
Anomaly	S2	10

To evaluate the performance of the IDS trained with the fuzzy ARTMAP classifier, we worked with three scenarios as shown in Table 2. Scenario 2 has half of the samples for effective training, and the other half for testing the Fuzzy ARTMAP. Scenarios 1 and 3 vary the amount of such samples. The idea here is to see how much such the variation of the number of samples impact the proposed approach performance. The whole dataset used in these evaluations contains 125.793 instances.

The parameters setup used in the fuzzy ARTMAP classifier for training the IDS are the same as the one in [10]. The reasoning here is that although the work in [10]

Table 2. Configuration of the simulated scenarios

Scenario	Total registers of the KDD99 training dataset in each phase	
	Training	Test
1	33%	67%
2	50%	50%
3	66%	34%

uses a neuro-fuzzy-wavelet network to detect voltage anomalies in electric power systems, the final goal is pretty similar to the one in our work. That is, both researches pursue to detect anomalies using data from a given dataset. Hence, we used as parameters setup for the fuzzy ARTMAP the values shown in Table 3.

Table 3. Configuration parameters for the Fuzzy ARTMAP classifier

Parameter	Value
Choice Parameter (α)	0,001
Training rate (β)	1
Network vigilance Parameter ARTa(ρ_a)	0,99
Network vigilance Parameter ART$_b$(ρ_b)	0,9
Vigilance Parameter of the inter-ART(ρ_{ab})	0,99

The efficiency of the IDS were assessed through the following parameters: training duration, global detection rate, accuracy rate.

The simulations were conducted using the WEKA programing tool [11], which had been used in [9] and turned out being very efficient in the implementation of patterns classifiers.

The results in Table 4 indicate that for the training duration parameter the three scenarios provided similarly small values, i.e., duration of about 2 minutes long. This happens mainly due to the stability-plasticity dilemma property of the classifier, which causes it to employ an incremental learning. This means it only trains new activity patterns, as it keeps the former learned activities (sort of retentive memory).

Based on that, as long as the new samples inserted into the dataset do not represent new activity patterns, no further training is needed. As a consequence, shorter training periods are achieved.

Another important observation to be highlighted in Table 4 is that the slight reduction in the training duration for the scenario 2 was not maintained for scenario 3. In other words, despite the gradual increase in the number of training data from scenario 1 to scenario 3, there was not a sensible plasticity in the learning achievement since the training duration reduction was not linear.

Table 4. Results of the Simulated Scenarios

Scenario	Performance	
	IDS training duration (sec)	Global detection rate (%)
1	122,97	72,85
2	118,81	87,20
3	121,54	88,91

Concerning the global detection rate parameter, one can see in Table 4 that from scenario 2 onwards the value of this parameter seems to converge to a value around 88%. This happens because of the reduction in the number of new activity patterns. It means that even though the number of samples in the training dataset have been increased, the sample contains no new learning categories.

The results depicted in Fig. 2 indicate that when the IDS input data includes a large diversity of values, it is possible to achieve higher accuracy rates. This is confirmed by the results for scenarios 2 and 3, in which at least 50% of the dataset are used for training the IDS, and an accuracy of approximately 90% is achieved. This is definitely an encouraging result given the short duration of the involved training.

In addition to the parameters addressed above, it is also very important to evaluate the false positive rate, since it might assist us in finding situations in which a classifier enhances detection rate at the expense of the accuracy [9].

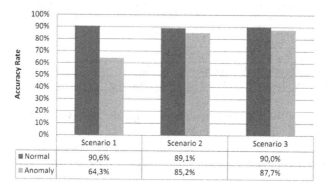

Fig. 2. Results of the accuracy rate for the simulated scenarios

As shown in Fig. 3, the neuro-fuzzy classifier did not perform satisfactorily for scenario 1 in which the training dataset used was limited to only 33% of the whole training dataset. In this case, almost half of the evaluated "normal data" were labeled as being anomalous data. On the other hand, as the number of samples in the training dataset increased the false positive rate reduced and established around 10%. Hence, it is proper to say that the accuracy of the classifier depends strongly on the threshold established for the minimal number of samples in the training.

The main advantage of the evaluated classifier shown in our evaluations is the fast processing in the training phase of the IDS. Even when a large number of samples were used (about 85.000 samples) the training duration was really short. Once again, this is possible because the fuzzy ARTMAP classifier keeps its former learned knowledge and only retrain the IDS when a new activity pattern comes in.

This property is key here since most classifiers have to train the whole training data whenever new samples are inserted in the dataset. The only problem here is that such a retraining may be complicated since changes can occur while the data are being retrained. Besides, when a new pattern is learned, there is no guarantee that the network topology and the previous learning parameter continue representing a good

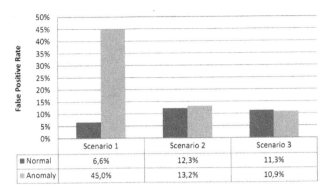

Fig. 3. Results of the false positive rate for the simulated scenarios

solution. As a consequence, the training duration increases because new decision regions are needed, the network will have more hidden layers, and the size of the neural network input matrix will be greater.

4.2   Applying Fuzzy ARTMAP Classifier on a WLAN

In order to validate our Wireless IDS (WIDS), we conducted evaluations in a controlled environment, whose topology is illustrated in Fig. 4, to generate data set to be used in training, validating and test of the WIDS. The evaluated network was composed of three wireless station and one access point (AP). Station 1 injected normal traffic into the network (HTTP, FTP). Airplay tool was executed in station 2 to launch simultaneously the four predefined attacks (chopchop, duration, deauthentication e fragmentation). In station 3 was run the wireshark to capture the passing-by (normal and intrusion) traffic. The predefined attacks are as follows:

- Chopchop – attacker intercept a cryptography frame and uses the base station to guess the clear text of the frame by brute force that is repeated until all intercepted frames are deciphered [12].
- Deauthentication - attacker transmits to the client stations a false deauthentication frame to render the network unavailable [13].
- Duration - attacker sends a frame with the high value of NAV (Network Allocation Vector) field to prevent any client station from using the shared medium to transmit [13].
- Fragmentation - attacker uses a fragmentation/assembly technique running in the base station to discover a flow key used to encrypt frames in a WLAN [12].

Next, the captured data were pre-processed to extract only the MAC header out of the control frames of the MAC sub layer (*protocol version, type, subtype, to DS, from DS, more fragment, retry, power management, more data*, WEP, *order, duration, address1, address2, address3* e *sequence control*). This was necessary because we intended to determine the impact of such frames in specifying the signatures of attacks against wireless LANs.

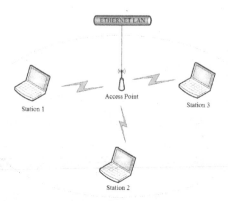

Fig. 4. Topology of the WLAN used for generating data

Subsequently, it was included in each sample a field with its type of attack so the classifier could distinct among training, validation and test frames. This way, it was simple to compare the detection by our algorithm against the actual cause of attack associated to that frame.

The generated data set collected in the experiments was divided in three subsets: training, validation and test. Table 5 shows how the samples were divided into both the three subsets and the recognition categories (type de traffic) evaluated in the experiments.

The generated data set collected in the experiments was divided in three subsets: training, validation and test. Table 5 shows how the samples were divided into both the three subsets and the recognition categories (type de traffic) evaluated in the experiments.

The training subset, as shown in Table 5, comprises 9600 samples: 6000 samples of normal traffic and 3600 samples of intrusion traffic. This subset is used to train the Fuzzy ARTMAP neural network to recognize these classification standards by adjusting dynamically the network parameters (vigilance, choose and training), mitigating the error rate between the expected output and the output computed by the network. The training is stopped once the error rate reaches a given limit.

Table 5. Distribution of the samples collected from the WLAN into datasets

			Datasets		
			Training	Validation	Test
Intrusion Categories of WIDS		Normal	6000	4000	5000
	Intrusion	ChopChop	900	600	800
		Deauthentication	900	600	800
		Duration	900	600	800
		Fragmentation	900	600	800
Total Number of Samples			9600	6400	8200

The validation of the Fuzzy ARTMAP neural network occurs by using validation data set composed of 6400 samples, being 4000 samples of normal traffic and 2400 samples of intrusion traffic, as shown in Table 5. The validation phase is needed to prevent that, in some cases, the classifier presents a good performance with the samples from the training subset, but keeps a poor performance with samples from the test subset.

Once the network is trained and validated, we get the parameters of the Fuzzy ARTMAP neural network, which are: choose parameter (α) = 0.01, vigilance parameter of the network ARTa (ρ_a) = 0.7, vigilance parameter of the network ARTb (ρ_b) = 1, vigilance parameter of the associative map (ρ_{ab}) = 0.99 and training rate (β) = 1. After this, the test subset is computed by the classifier which computes its outputs. From Table 5, the test subset has 8200 new samples divided in 5000 samples of normal traffic and 3200 samples of intrusion traffic.

In the evaluation of our approach, we compared our results with the ones of other three classifiers: Support Vector Machine (SVM), Multilayer Perceptron with Backpropagation (MPBP) and Radial Basis Function (RBF). We used here the test subset presented in Table 5. These classifiers were chosen because of their large use in machine learning based IDS [5].

The following metrics can be used to evaluate a pattern classifier for intrusion detection systems: True Positive (TP), an intrusive activity is identified correclty; True Negative (TN), a non-intrusive activity is identified correctly; False Positive (FP), a non-intrusive activity is identified as an intrusive one; False Negative (FN), a intrusive activity is identified as an non-intrusive one.

In general, however, the detection rate and false alarm rate metrics are the most common ones in evaluating IDSs [4]. The detection rate is is computed as TP/(TP+FN) and false alarm rate is computed as FP)TN+FP). An efficient classifier should get a high detection rate and a low false alarm rate [4]. We present next the results from the performance evaluation we have conducted.

To evaluate the performance of the classifier of standard used in the proposed WIDS, 8200 samples of the test subset were used in the two comparison scenarios below.

The result for the first scenario, shown in Fig 5, we have the training time spent by the classifier in constructing its learning data set. It is clear that our approach renders much shorter training time than the others the classifiers. This is due mainly the stability-plasticity property [3] that causes the Fuzzy ARTMAP neural network to use incremental learning (training only the new standards of activities), without forgetting the standards of activities previously learned.

Fig. 6 shows the result of the second evaluated scenario, in which the detection rate of the classifiers are evaluated based on the categories above mentioned. Note that for the normal category, although our classifier gets a representative detection rate of roughly 80%, it performs poorer than the other classifiers.

Regarding the categories related to attacks, we have two clearly distinct situations. The four classifiers provided high detection rate of approximately 100% for the duration and deauthentication attacks. This means these categories of attacks have traffic characterization of easy recognition by the classifiers evaluated in this work.

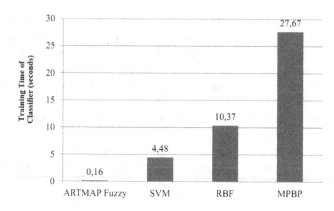

Fig. 5. Training time for the classifiers

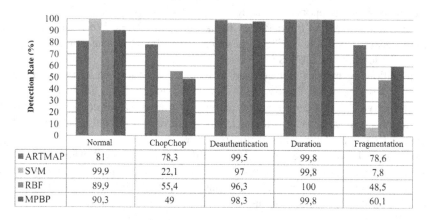

	Normal	ChopChop	Deauthentication	Duration	Fragmentation
■ARTMAP	81	78,3	99,5	99,8	78,6
▦SVM	99,9	22,1	97	99,8	7,8
■RBF	89,9	55,4	96,3	100	48,5
■MPBP	90,3	49	98,3	99,8	60,1

Fig. 6. Detection rate for the classifiers

On the other hand, ChopChop attacks and Fragmentation are harder to detect, since their signature are too similar to the normal category. Even so, the Fuzzy ARTMAP outperformed the other three classifiers, as it provided detection rate near 80%, while the other classifiers managed rates in the range 7.8% to 60%.

4.3   Discussions

From the results obtained in this work, it is sensible to say that there are rooms for improvements in this application of the fuzzy ARTMAP. The evaluation of the proposed WIDS along with the other three approaches indicates that Fuzzy ARTMAP neural network helps reducing training time and additionally provides high detection rate. The main issue to be addressed is to find a fine balance between high accuracy rate and low false positive rate. We believe this can be reached by using the neuro-fuzzy classifier evaluated here in conjunction with other low computational processing schemes like wavelet, rough sets or genetic algorithms.

5   Conclusions and Outlook

We have evaluated the efficiency of the fuzzy ARTMAP classifier in assisting an IDS. The achieved results suggest that this classifier is viable to be implemented in anomaly-based IDSs. Using short period of training resulted in high detection and accurate rates. In the preliminary evaluations conducted here, by comparing our proposal with the existing ones, our approach performed really well.

As future work, we intend to investigate the use of the fuzzy ARTMAP classifier in hybrid training architectures. This means to combine this classifier with other lightweight classification techniques. Another interesting task to be conducted is to apply new feature selection techniques towards further reducing the vectorial space of the samples used in the IDS training. The challenges ahead regard achieving these enhancements without compromising accuracy and/or the computational processing.

Acknowledgments. This material is based on a research project funded by the Foundation for Research Support of Mato Grosso (FAPEMAT) on the supervision of the Network and Security Research Group (GPRS). GPRS is managed by the Federal Institute of Mato Grosso (IFMT) in conjunction with the Federal University of Mato Grosso (UFMT), State University Júlio de Mesquita Filho (UNESP) and Federal University of Uberlandia (UFU). The authors acknowledge the facilities provided by IFMT for the development of this work.

References

1. Souza, P.: Study about anomaly based intrusion detection systems: an approach using neural networks. M.Sc. Thesis, Salvador University/Salvador (2008)
2. Vilakazi, C.B., Marwala, T.: Application of feature selection and fuzzy ARTMAP to intrusion detection. In: Proceedings of 2006 IEEE International Conference on Systems, Man and Cybernetics, pp. 4880–4885 (2006)
3. Carpenter, G.A., Grossberg, S., Markuzon, N., Reynold, J.H., Rosen, D.B.: Fuzzy ARTMAP: A neural network for incremental supervised learning of analog multidimensional maps. IEEE Transactions on Neural Network 3(5), 689–713 (1992)
4. Wu, S., Banzhaf, W.: The Use of Computational Intelligence in Intrusion Detection Systems: A Review. Applied Soft Computing 10, 1–35 (2010)
5. Ahmad, I., Abdullah, A., Alghamdi, A.: Towards the selection of best neural network system for intrusion detection. International Journal of the Physical Sciences 5(12), 1830–1839 (2010)
6. Santra, A.K., Nagarajan, S., Jinesh, V.N.: Intrusion Detection in Wireless Networks using FUZZY Nerural Networks adn Dynamic Context-Aware Role based Access Control Security (DCARBAC). Int. Journal of Computer Application 39(4), 23–31 (2012)
7. Carpenter, G.A., Grossberg, S., Rosen, D.B.: Fuzzy ART: fast stable learning and categorization of analog patterns by an adaptive resonance system. Neural Networks 4(1), 759–771 (1991)
8. Lippmann, R., Haines, J.W., Fried, D., Korba, J., Das, K.: The 1999 DARPA off-line intrusion detection evaluation. Computer Networks 34(4), 579–595 (2000)

9. Araújo, N., Shinoda, A.A., de Oliveira, R., Ferreira, E.T.: Identifying important characteristics in the KDD99 intrusion detection dataset by feature selection using a hybrid approach. In: Proceedings of 2010 IEEE International Conference on Telecommunications, pp. 552–558 (2010)

10. Malange, F.C.V.: A neuro-fuzzy-wavelet network to detect voltage anomalies in electric power systems. D.Sc. Thesis. Universidade Estadual Júlio de Mesquita Filho/Ilha Solteira (2010)

11. Bouckaert, R.R., et al.: WEKA manual for version 3-7-0, http://www.cs.waikato.ac.nz/ml/weka/ (last access: August 2009)

12. Bellardo, J., Savage, S.: 802.11 Denial-of-Service Attacks: Real Vulnerabilities and Practical Solutions. In: Proceedings of the 12th Conference on USENIX Security Symposium, vol. 12, pp. 15–28 (2003)

13. Bittau, A., Handley, M., Lackey, J.: The Final Nail in WEP's Coffin. In: Proceedings of the 2006 IEEE Symposium on Security and Privacy, pp. 386–400 (2006)

ID-Based Threshold Signcryption
and Group Unsigncryption

Prashant Kumar Mishra, Kunwar Singh, and Sudhanshu Baruntar

Department of Computer Science Engineering,
National Institute of Technology, Trichy, India
{206110019,kunwar.singh,206110009}@nitt.edu
http://www.nitt.edu

Abstract. Xiaoyu et. al. [1] presented efficient identity based (K, n) threshold signcryption scheme. In this paper, we present variant of [1] with group shared unsigncryption, which is based on discrete logarithm problem in finite field. For unsigncryption to recover the message the cooperation of group members of the receivers group is required. The proposed scheme has additional advantage against malicious verifiers.

Keywords: signcryption, group unsigncryption, identity-based cryptography, threshold signcryption.

1   Introduction

Confidentiality, integrity, non-repudiation and authentication are the important requirements for many cryptographic applications. A traditional approach to achieve these requirements is to *sign-then-encrypt* the message. Signcryption, first proposed by Zheng [2] in 1997, is a new cryptographic primitive that performs signature and encryption simultaneously, at much lower computational and communication overhead than the *sign-then-encrypt* approach. This idea is widely accepted today.

Identity-based (ID-based) cryptosystem was introduced by Shamir [3]. The unique property of ID-based cryptosystem is that a users public key can be any binary string, such as an email address that can identify the user. This removes the need for senders to look up the recipients public key before sending out an encrypted message. These systems involve a trusted authority called private key generators (PKGs) whose job is to compute users private key from his/her identity information. Although Shamir constructed an identity-based signature scheme using RSA function but he could not construct an identity-based encryption and this became a long-lasting open problem. Only in 2001, Shamir's open problem was independently solved by Boneh and Franklin [4] and Cocks [5].

First ID-based signcryption scheme was proposed by Malone-Lee [6]. Libert and Quisquater [7], pointed out that [6] scheme was not semantically secure and proposed a provably secure ID-based signcryption schemes from pairings. However, the properties of public verifiability and forward security are mutually

S.M. Thampi et al. (Eds.): SNDS 2012, CCIS 335, pp. 35–44, 2012.

exclusive in their scheme. Chow et al. [8] proposed ID-based signcryption schemes that provide both public verifiability and forward security.

The idea of threshold cryptography is to protect information (or computation) by fault-tolerantly distributing it among a cluster of cooperating computers. The fundamental problem of threshold cryptography is problem of securely sharing of a secret(key or information). A secret sharing scheme allows one to distribute a piece of secret information among several servers in a way that meets the following requirements:

- No group of corrupt servers (smaller than a given threshold) can figure out what the secret is, even if they cooperate.
- When it becomes necessary that the secret information be reconstructed, a large enough number of servers (a number larger than the above threshold) can always do it.

Duan et al. [9] proposed an identity based threshold signcryption scheme by combining the concept of ID-based threshold signature and signcryption together. However, in [9], the master key of the PKG is distributed to a number of PKGs, which creates a bottleneck on the PKGs. Peng et al. [10] proposed an ID- based threshold signcryption scheme based on [7] (Kudo [11]). However, [10] scheme does not provide the forward security, which means anyone who obtains the senders private key can recover the original message of a signcrypted text. Ma et al. [12] also proposed a threshold signcryption scheme using the bilinear pairing. However, [12] is not ID-based. Fagen Li et al. [13] proposed an ID-based threshold signcryption scheme based on bilinear pairing and proved the confidentialiy under DBDH assumption in the random oracle model.

Above all identity-based signcryption schemes are based on bilinear pair ing. To our best knowledge Xiaoyu et al.[1] is the latest work in identity-based threshold signcryption without bilinear pairing.

1. The receiver of the signcryption in the presented scheme is now a group of users rather than an individual.
2. The scheme presented here has taken measures to make sure that verifiers even if they become malicious are identified.

2 Preliminaries

2.1 Computational Complexity Assumptions

Definition: Discrete Logarithm Problem(DLP) is defined for a given a finite field Z_p, a generator g of a multiplicative group Z_p, and $y \in Z_p$, compute the least positive integer $x \in Z_p$, such that $y = g^x \ mod \ p$.

Complexity Assumptions: We assume that the DLP is intractable, which means there is no polynomial time algorithm to solve any of them with non-negligible probability.

2.2   Threshold Cryptography

Threshold cryptography aims at enhancing the availability and security of decryption and signature schemes by splitting private keys into several (say n) shares (typically, each of size comparable to the original secret key). In these schemes, a quorum of at least $t(\leq n)$ servers needs to act upon a message to produce the result (decrypted value or signature), while corrupting less than t servers maintains the schemes security.

   Threshold cryptography [14] [15] [16] avoids single points of failure by splitting cryptographic keys into $n > 1$ shares which are stored by servers in distinct locations.

2.3   Shamir's (t,n) Threshold Signcryption

In order to share a private key D_{ID}, we need the Shamir's (t, n) threshold scheme. Suppose that we have chosen integers t(a threshold) and n satisfying $1 \leq t \leq n \leq q$. First, we pick $R_1, R_2, \ldots R_{t-1}$ at random from G^*. Then we construct a function

$$F(u) = D_{ID} + \sum_{j=1}^{t-1} u^j R_j$$

Finally, we compute $D_{ID_i} = F(i)$ for $1 \leq i \leq n$ and send D_{ID_I} to the ith member of the message recipient group. When the number of shares reaches the threshold t, the function $F(u)$ can be reconstructed by computing,

$$F(u) = \sum_{j=1}^{t} D_{ID_j} N_j$$

where

$$N_j = \sum_{i=1, j\neq i}^{t} \frac{u - i}{j - i} \ mod \ q$$

The private key D_{ID} can be recovered by computing $D_{ID} = F(0)$.

3   Overview of the Proposed Scheme

Let $G = \{U_1, U_2, \ldots, U_n\}$ represents a signer group. This sheme has 4 stages: *setup, key distributing-extract, signcrypt* and *unsigncrypt*.

1. *Setup*: For a security parameter k, outputs the public parameters $\{p, q, g, H_1, H_2\}$. These parameters are used in latter phases of the scheme.
2. *Key distributing-extract*: Here the keys are registered to the users based on their ID_i in the Key Management Center(KMC). Using published public parameters the KMC, outputs a group key pair (y, v) for the group manager and a key pair (y_i, v_i) for ID_i

3. *Signcrypt*: On input the key pair (y_i, v_i) and ID_i of every user $U_i(i = 1, 2, \ldots, n)$, message m and the public key Y_{BG} of the designated receiver group, outputs a threshold signcryption σ
4. *Unsigncrypt*: In this step each member of the recieving group $U_i \in BG$ contributes in unsigncryption. On input the key pair (Y_{BG}, v_{BG}) of the designated verifiers, the public key of the signer group y, and signature σ outputs a verification decision, $\perp$, if the member rejects else the message is accepted by the receiver group. This additionally provides mechanism against malicious verifiers, via partial signature scheme.

4 Details of Our Scheme

The following will show the detailed modeling of the scheme

4.1 Setup

Let p and q be two large primes where $p = 2q + 1$. Let $\alpha \in Z_p$ be an element of order q. Then let $1 \le a \le q - 1$ and let $\beta = \alpha^a \bmod p$. We then let G denote the multiplicative subgroup of Z_p of order q where G consists of the quadratic residues $\bmod \ p$. Finally we let the set of possible messages be equal to the set of possible signatures be equal to G. Choose $g \in G$, a generator of the group G. We also define cryptographic functions $H_1 \colon \{0, 1\}^* \to Z_q^*$ and $H_2 \colon Z_p \to \{0, 1\}^*$. The public parameters are declared as $\{p, q, g, H_1, H_2\}$

4.2 Key Distributing-Extract

There are two different types of services provided in this phase: *sender side key management* and *receiver side key management*.

For sender side, let $G = \{U_1, U_2, \ldots, U_n\}$ represents a signer group. Signer Group Manager(SGM) can be viewed as a group manager who can be trusted in this group.

1. KMC chooses a random polynomial of degree $t - 1 \colon f(x) = a_0 + a_1 x + a_2 x^2 + \cdots + a_{t-1} x^{t-1} \bmod q$, computes $y = g^{f(0)}$ as group public key and $v = f(0)$ is group secret key.
2. On receiving private key extraction query ID_i (such as an email address) from any $Ui(i = 1, 2, \ldots, n)$, KMC computes $v_i = f(ID_i) \bmod q$ and $yi = g^{v_i} \bmod p$. Then KMC sends the private key v_i to U_i in a secure way. y_i is user's public key.
3. KMC publishes y, y_i and $ID_i(i = 1, 2, \ldots, n)$, then sends the private key $v = f(0)$ to SGM in a secure way.

Every receiver $B_i \in BG$ (receiver group) performs the following steps to obtain the public key for the group:

1. Chooses private key, uniformly randomly $x_i \in Z_q$
2. Compute public key, $y_i = g$

3. Choose $\alpha_i \in Z_{q/p}$
4. Compute $\beta_i = \alpha_i^{x_i} \ mod \ p$
5. Broadcast y_i, α_i and β_i

On receiving y_i from other members of the group if RGM finds two or more members having same values for y_i then those members are to redo the previous steps. Otherwise each B_i computes the following

$$Y_{BG} = \prod_{i=1}^{n} y_i$$

The Receiver Group Manager(RGM) of the group BG then publishes the Y_{BG}

4.3 Signcrypt

1. U_i performs the following:
   (a) Choose k_i uniformly at random Z_q^*
   (b) Compute $r_i = g^{k_i} \ mod \ p$
   (c) Send $r_i(i = 1, 2, \ldots, t)$ to SGM
2. SGM performs the following:
   (a) Check whether $r_i = r_j$, if it returns YES, then ask $U_i(or U_j)$ to send a new r_i(or r_j)
   (b) Otherwise, SGM broadcast $r_i(i = 1, 2, \ldots, t)$ in the group.
3. When all the collaborative users receive $r_i(i = 1, 2, \ldots, t)$, U_i performs the following:
   (a) Compute $r = \sum_{i=1}^{t} r_i \ mod \ p$
   (b) Choose l_i uniformly at random from Z_q^* and compute $L_i = g^{l_i} \ mod \ p$
   (c) Compute $s_i = v_i \left[\prod_{i=1}^{t} \frac{ID_j}{ID_j - ID_i} \right] - k_i r + l_i H_1(m) \ mod \ q$
   (d) Set $\sigma_i = (m, r_i, s_i, L_i)$ as a signature fragment and send it to SGM.
4. On receiving $\sigma_i = (m, r_i, s_i, L_i)$, SGM accept σ_i if and only if the following equation holds:

$$r_i^r g^{s_i} = y_i^{\prod_{i=1}^{t} \frac{ID_j}{ID_j - ID_i}} L_i^{H_1(m)} \tag{1}$$

5. If all the $\sigma_i = (m, r_i, s_i, L_i)$ is efficient, SGM performs the following:
   (a) Compute $S = \sum_{i=1}^{t} s_i$
   (b) Compute $R = \left(\prod_{i=1}^{t} r_i \right)^r \ mod \ p$
   (c) Compute $W = \prod_{i=1}^{t} L_i \ mod \ p$
   (d) Compute $C = m \oplus H_2(Y_{BG}^{f(0)})$
   Set $\sigma = (C, R, W, S)$ as the threshold signcryption and send to members of BG.

4.4   Unsigncrypt

On receiving $\sigma = (C, R, W, S)$, each verifier $B_i \in BG$ performs the following:

1. Compute $z_i = y^{x_i}$
2. Send z_i to RGM

On receiving $z_j (j = 1, 2, \ldots, n | j \neq i)$ from all the members of the group, RGM then does the following for each member:

1. RGM chooses at random $e_1, e_2 \in Z_q$
2. RGM then computes $d_i = z_i^{e_1} \beta_i^{e_2} \bmod p$ and send it to $B_i \in BG$.

One receiving d_i from RGM, each B_i then computes and send back to RGM the following:

$$t_i = d_i^{x_i \bmod q} \bmod p$$

RGM accepts z_i as a valid partial signature on y if and only if

$$t_i \equiv y^{e_1} \alpha_i^{e_2} \bmod p \tag{2}$$

After verifying all the z_i, RGM broadcasts them to all the members of BG. Then each member does the following:

1. Compute $z = \prod_{i=1}^{n} z_i$
2. Compute $m = C \oplus H_2(z)$
3. Accept σ if and only if the following equation holds

$$yR^{-1}W^{H_1(m)} = g^S \bmod p \tag{3}$$

5   Correctness

Theorem 1: If $\sigma_i = (m, r_i, s_i, L_i)$ is effective, then (1) holds.

Proof: The proof of this is same as given in (1). If $\sigma_i = (m, r_i, s_i, L_i)$ is indeed signed by the user U_i, then

1. $y_i = g^{v_i} \bmod p$
2. $L_i = g^{l_i} \bmod p$
3. $s_i = v_i \left[\prod_{i=1}^{t} \frac{ID_j}{ID_j - ID_i} \right] - k_i r + l_i H_1(m) \bmod q$

Now it can be shown,

$$r_i^r g^{s_i} = g^{k_i r} \cdot g^{v_i \left[\prod_{i=1}^{t} \frac{ID_j}{ID_j - ID_i} \right] - k_i r + l_i H_1(m)}$$

$$= g^{v_i \left[\prod_{i=1}^{t} \frac{ID_j}{ID_j - ID_i} \right]} \cdot g^{l_i H_1(m)}$$

$$= y_i^{\prod_{i=1}^{t} \frac{ID_j}{ID_j - ID_i}} \cdot L_i^{H_1(m)}$$

Hence (1) will always hold.

Theorem 2: If z_i is effective, then (2) holds.

Proof: RGM accepts z_i as a valid partial signature for y if and only if (2) holds. The full proof can be found in [17]. Let us assume that z_i is a valid partial signature for y from B_i and then show that RGM will accept it. We begin by looking at the response t_i RGM receives from B_i. From the definition we directly get

$$t_i \equiv d_i^{x_i^{-1}} \ mod \ p$$
$$\equiv z_i^{e_1 x_i^{-1}} \beta^{e_2 x_i^{-1}} \ mod \ p \qquad (4)$$

Where all exponents are as usual reduced modulo the group order q. Now let us look at how z_i and β_i are defined

$$z_i \equiv y^{x_i} \ mod \ p$$
$$z_i^{-x_i} \equiv y \ mod \ p \qquad (5)$$

and

$$\beta_i \equiv \alpha^{x_i} \ mod \ p$$
$$\beta_i^{-x_i} \equiv \alpha \ mod \ p \qquad (6)$$

By substituting from (5) and (6), in (4) we get

$$t_i \equiv y^{e_1} \alpha_i^{e_2} \ mod \ p$$

Thus (2) will hold.

Theorem 3: If $\sigma = (C, R, W, S)$ is effective then (3) holds.

Proof: The proof is same as given in [2]. From the given below:

1. $L_i = g^{l_i} \ mod \ p$
2. $W = \prod\limits_{i=1}^{t} L_i \ mod \ p$
3. $R = \left(\prod\limits_{i=1}^{t} r_i \right)^r \ mod \ p$
4. $S = \sum\limits_{i=1}^{t} s_i$

Now using Lagrange Interpolation Formula, we have:

$$\prod_{i=1}^{t} y_i^{\prod\limits_{i=1, j \neq i}^{t} \frac{ID_j}{ID_j - ID_i}} = g^{\sum\limits_{i=1}^{t} v_i \cdot \prod\limits_{i=1, j \neq i}^{t} \frac{ID_j}{ID_j - ID_i}} \ mod \ p$$

$$= g^{f(0)}$$

$$= y \qquad (7)$$

Also

$$R^{-1} = \left(\prod_{i=1}^{t} r_i\right)^{-r} \bmod p$$

$$= \left(\prod_{i=1}^{t} g^{k_i}\right)^{-r} \bmod p$$

$$= g^{\sum_{i=1}^{t} -k_i r} \bmod p \qquad (8)$$

and,

$$R^{-1} W^{H_1(m)} = g^{\sum_{i=1}^{t} -k_i r} \cdot g^{\sum_{i=1}^{t} l_i H_1(m)}$$

$$= g^{\sum_{i=1}^{t} [-k_i r + l_i H_1(m)]} \qquad (9)$$

From (7), (8) and (9),

$$y R^{-1} W^{H_1(m)} = g^{\sum_{i=1}^{t} \left[v_i \cdot \left[\prod_{i=1, j \neq i}^{t} \frac{ID_j}{ID_j - ID_i} \right] - k_i r + l_i H_1(m) \right]}$$

$$= g^{\sum_{i=1}^{t} s_i}$$

$$= g^{S} \bmod p$$

Thus (3) will hold.

6 Security Analysis of Scheme

Our scheme has the properties of authentication, secrecy, data integrity, privacy of signers, privacy of verifier's and security against malicious verifier.

6.1 Authentication

From **Theorem 1** and **Theorem 3**, we have shown that the signature are indeed produced by legitimate users, and (1) and (3) guarantees their verifiability by verifiers.

6.2 Secrecy

In section 4.4, we can see that the message can only be extracted if all the members secret key x_i, are known for calculation of z_i.

6.3 Data Integrity

Hash function H_1 will ensure the data integrity. If message m is changed by an adversary, then $H_1(m)$ will not be the same and (3) will no longer hold.

6.4   Privacy of Signers

From section 4.3, we can see that in computation si no information about the secret key v_i is revealed to SGM as finding k_i and l_i is DLP.

6.5   Privacy of Verifiers

From section 4.4, we can see that in computation z_i no information about the secret key x_i is revealed to RGM or any other user as finding x_i is DLP.

6.6   Security against Malicious Verifiers

In **Theorem 2** we have shown that if any of the verifiers become malicious then they will be caught immediately.

7   Conclusion

We have proposed a secure identity-based (t, n)threshold signcryption and group unsigncryption with extension to security against malicious verifiers. This scheme is the first of its kind to incorporate group unsigncryption without using bilinear pairing.

References

1. Zhang, X., Zhang, R.: A new id-based (t,n) threshold signcryption scheme. In: Progress in Informatics and Computing (PIC), vol. 1, pp. 589–592. IEEE (2010)
2. Zheng, Y.: Digital Signcryption or How to Achieve Cost (Signature & Encryption) << Cost(Signature) + Cost(Encryption). In: Kaliski Jr., B.S. (ed.) CRYPTO 1997. LNCS, vol. 1294, pp. 165–179. Springer, Heidelberg (1997)
3. Shamir, A.: Identity-Based Cryptosystems and Signature Schemes. In: Blakely, G.R., Chaum, D. (eds.) CRYPTO 1984. LNCS, vol. 196, pp. 47–53. Springer, Heidelberg (1985)
4. Boneh, D., Franklin, M.K.: Identity based encryption from the weil pairing. IACR Cryptology ePrint Archive 2001, 90 (2001)
5. Cocks, C.: An Identity Based Encryption Scheme Based on Quadratic Residues. In: Honary, B. (ed.) Cryptography and Coding 2001. LNCS, vol. 2260, pp. 360–363. Springer, Heidelberg (2001)
6. Chen, L., Malone-Lee, J.: Improved Identity-Based Signcryption. In: Vaudenay, S. (ed.) PKC 2005. LNCS, vol. 3386, pp. 362–379. Springer, Heidelberg (2005)
7. Libert, B., Quisquater, J.-J.: New identity based signcryption schemes from pairings. IACR Cryptology ePrint Archive 2003, 23 (2003)
8. Chow, S.S.M., Yiu, S.M., Hui, L.C.K., Chow, K.P.: Efficient Forward and Provably Secure ID-Based Signcryption Scheme with Public Verifiability and Public Ciphertext Authenticity. In: Lim, J.I., Lee, D.H. (eds.) ICISC 2003. LNCS, vol. 2971, pp. 352–369. Springer, Heidelberg (2004)

9. Duan, S., Cao, Z., Lu, R.: Robust id-based threshold signcryption scheme from pairings. In: Proceedings of the 3rd International Conference on Information Security, InfoSecu 2004, pp. 33–37. ACM, New York (2004), http://doi.acm.org/10.1145/1046290.1046298

10. Peng, C., Li, X.: An Identity-Based Threshold Signcryption Scheme with Semantic Security. In: Hao, Y., Liu, J., Wang, Y.-P., Cheung, Y.-M., Yin, H., Jiao, L., Ma, J., Jiao, Y.-C. (eds.) CIS 2005, Part II. LNCS (LNAI), vol. 3802, pp. 173–179. Springer, Heidelberg (2005), http://dx.doi.org/10.1007/11596981_26

11. Kudo, M.: Secured electronic sealed-bid auction protocol with public key cryptography. IEICE Transactions on Fundamentals

12. Ma, C., Chen, K., Zheng, D., Liu, S.: Efficient and Proactive Threshold Signcryption. In: Zhou, J., López, J., Deng, R.H., Bao, F. (eds.) ISC 2005. LNCS, vol. 3650, pp. 233–243. Springer, Heidelberg (2005)

13. Li, F., Yu, Y.: An efficient and provably secure id-based threshold signcryption scheme. In: Communications, Circuits and Systems, ICCCAS 2008, pp. 488–499 (2008)

14. Boyd, C.:

15. Desmedt, Y., Frankel, Y.: Threshold Cryptosystems. In: Brassard, G. (ed.) CRYPTO 1989. LNCS, vol. 435, pp. 307–315. Springer, Heidelberg (1990)

16. Desmedt, Y.: Society and Group Oriented Cryptography: A New Concept. In: Pomerance, C. (ed.) CRYPTO 1987. LNCS, vol. 293, pp. 120–127. Springer, Heidelberg (1988)

17. Stinson, D.R.: Cryptography Theory and Practice. Chapman and Hall/CRC (2006)

Protocol for Secure Submissions into Learning Management Systems

Manjunath Mattam

MSIT Division, International Institute of Information Technology,
Gachibowli, Hyderabad 500 032, Andhra pradesh, India
manjunath.m@iiit.ac.in

Abstract. This paper proposes a model (architecture and protocol) that will help in securing assignment submissions into learning management systems. A client server architecture that uses cryptography is proposed to transform a regular assignment deliverable into a secure deliverable. A protocol is devised between client and server such that faculty and students can securely obtain symmetric keys to either encrypt or decrypt an assignment deliverable.

Keywords: application specific protocols, learning management systems, secure protocol, symmetric key exchange mechanism, client server architecture, plagiarism check, confidentiality in transit, confidentiality in storage, integrity of deliverables.

1 Introduction

Information and communication technologies have transformed the way we teach and way we learn. These technologies opened avenues for remote learning, digital learning (e-learning) and automation of processes in conventional education systems. In this context, deliverables (worked out assignment answers that are submitted after completion) play major role in student assessments. For managing the deliverables and course content most universities use learning management systems (example Moodle, other university specific applications). Learning management systems (LMS) provide users with options to upload the deliverables. Majority of the learning management systems operate on HTTP (web based - plain text).

Plagiarism is one of the primary concerns in student assessment, although most universities operate tools to detect copied deliverables majority of these cases go undetected. My assumption here is reputed universities give assignments that are designed specifically for enrolled students and therefore solutions are not available on the internet. Copied deliverables can be classified based on whether student deliberately shared his work output, or the deliverable is copied without authors notice.

Consider two given scenarios: (1) A student shares his worked out deliverable after uploading it in LMS, by giving away his login details. Ultimately claiming my account is hacked, if he gets caught. (2) Other students can use network traffic sniffers (like wireshark, libcap) to read ongoing traffic, and pick up deliverables without authors

S.M. Thampi et al. (Eds.): SNDS 2012, CCIS 335, pp. 45–53, 2012.

consent. Because most LMS are not HTTPS enabled (reasons being certificates are expensive, and performance intense). It is possible to pick up deliverables that are transferred in regular HTTP traffic (plain text). In scenario 2 students gets punishment without his/her fault, if he/she gets caught.

This paper proposes an approach, which minimizes problems created by above mentioned two scenarios. Over all goals are, if an assignment deliverable is copied then it is due to willful sharing of students (not on transit or at server), making students accountable. A client server architectural approach & application specific protocol is proposed that will ensure secure deliverable submissions (capable of confidentiality, integrity, authentication, and non repudiation of each deliverable).

2   Crypto Primitives

This application uses cryptographic primitives to achieve secure deliverable submissions. Each (secure) deliverable submitted by a student is encrypted with industry adopted symmetric key crypto algorithms that have received substantial public review and have been proven to work effectively like AES with substantial key size (256 bits). When encrypted deliverable is submitted to LMS over open network, it is hard for packet sniffers to retrieve plain text (high level crypto with large key size makes it almost impossible).

Managing the symmetric key is the challenging part of these kinds of applications. Alternative approaches with asymmetric key cryptography are available using public key infrastructure (proven with other electronic commerce applications), which is not recommended in this scenario because (1) it involves issuing certificates to all the users including students (2) public key algorithms need funding and they are expensive (3) computationally performance intense, and consume lot of time.

To open the decrypt deliverables faculty will need same symmetric key used by students for encryption. Transferring the symmetric key unprotected is almost equivalent to no encryption. Stand alone client server program is proposed for secure key transfer and key management. Server acts as trusted third party for all the users (in this case students and faculty). Server generates, issues, stores, and manages symmetric keys. All communication between server and client software is protected by protocol designed specifically for this kind of applications.

The proposed model does not involve asymmetric key cryptography hence the computation required for encrypting or decrypting a deliverable is relatively lower. Client program is not responsible for creation of symmetric keys hence at user computer this computation is saved.

3   Client Server Program

Client server programming model is most appropriate for managing keys; socket programming is best suited for sending/receiving messages between client and server. All communication is encapsulated in application layer, rest of the internet layers are constructed by network sockets. Server waits for client's request on a designated port number. Server program is capable of understanding application specific pre-defined codes that corresponds to type of client requests (for example: request for creation of symmetric key, request for using existing symmetric key, change of user password etc. all are pre-defined constants). Server is also capable of performing role based operations, (for example: if client software is logged-in by student it generates symmetric key and if client software is logged-in by faculty it retrieves already generated symmetric key).

Given below is an image that illustrates (at high level) how client and server program is used for this process. Server interface in client program does the socket communication. Client interface in client program is responsible for encrypting and decrypting the deliverables. Server program is responsible for key management.

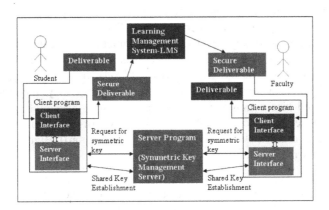

Fig. 1. Model architecture for secure assignments submission. Assignment submission in LMS is as usual. Client server program will help convert regular derliverable into secure deliverable.

3.1   The Server Program

Server is programmed to store, search, retrieve, respond based on user request type. Server is programmed to concurrently handle multiple client programs connected at one point in time. Server stores application details with-in, this storage can be made either in database or inside regular text files (additional security measures are required for data that is stored inside flat files implementation). Users of this application are registered with the server therefore login details like user id, password, role in organization, login status etc. are stored and maintained by the server. Passwords used for authenticating a user must adhere with server specified size, usage of alpha numerals etc.

All communications between clients and server are encrypted, symmetric key that is required to encrypt or decrypt communication is called shared key between client and server. Server stores all the shared keys along with time stamp, corresponding user identification in its data store, as represented in table 1 below. Server will need to

Table 1. Example data structure at the server to store user shared keys

User Identifier	Time Stamp	Shared key between client and server

define time threshold, indicating how long a shared key is valid. If this time threshold expires, client will need to request for a new shared key.

Apart from above mentioned details, server will also store all the symmetric keys required to encrypt assignment deliverables. These symmetric keys are generated by the server upon request from user with a student role on client program. These symmetric keys are used by client programs to encrypt a deliverable. Because there is no time limitation for how long a deliverable is maintained in LMS, server may have to stored these keys for longer period of time like till the end of academic year. For faster retrieval of these keys, each of these symmetric keys is uniquely identified with an ID number. Server maintains key details corresponding to each user, that is User id, message digest of the file, IP/MAC address from which deliverable is uploaded, unique id given for the key, the symmetric key required for the deliverable. Fixed size symmetric keys are generated using simple programming logic for faster execution (for example: Message Digest of (Random Number ‖ User ID ‖ File message digest ‖ Unique file identifier ‖ Time stamp)). Higher the key sizes better the security measures.

Table 2. Example data structure at the server to store symmetric keys to encrypt or decrypt deliverables

Symmetric key unique identifier	Symmetric key	User identifier	Message Digest	MAC address

If the unique identifier for symmetric key are sequential in nature then data is stored in sorted order, hence it is faster to retrieve specific symmetric key using key identifier with search algorithms. If all the values are stored inside data base management systems, then symmetric keys can be retrieved even faster as values are indexed by DBMS software that can scale up to billions of deliverable symmetric keys.

Connection time required for client server communication is low, as maximum number of message exchanges is 4. This way server wait queue is processed quickly. With help of socket programming concurrency techniques like threads server can scale up to thousands of users or more.

3.2   The Client Program

Client program must be installed by all the users (faculty and students). Client program always initiates the connection, this request starts with a user log-in. Client program provides interface for login with username and password. Client software is configured to accept a strong password that includes alpha numeral characters and special symbols with minimum number of letters for password. Client programs can also be configured to bring users to assigned/specific work stations, such that a student can upload deliverables from his/her designated computer only (however this functionality is optional). Client program can send workstation specific information like IP address or MAC address to know location from where user is uploading the deliverable. Client program provides interface to browse and select a file from the resident computer. Once a file is selected client program is capable of encrypting or decrypting that file using symmetric key assigned by server. Based on the user role like (1) students will use client software for encrypting deliverables. (2) Faculty will use client software for decrypting deliverables.

For a student after selecting the deliverable that is choosing the file from local computer he will need to use encryption options, output of the program is saved in same directory with server sent symmetric key unique identifier as file extension (for example: rollno2_program3_dotc.2342313, here 2342313 is symmetric key identifier). This is the output file, and it can be uploaded in learning management systems (LMS), as deliverable. Uploading into the LMS is out of scope for the proposed system, this is the usual procedure a student follows to submit their assignments / deliverables.

Faculty can download student's deliverable from LMS with the usual procedure. Faculty also uses client program because he needs to evaluate the encrypted deliverable. After login a faculty can select downloaded deliverable using client program browse interface. To obtain the plain text (un-encrypted) original file (in our previous example: rollno2_program3_dotc) faculty end client program must send symmetric key identifier to the server. If symmetric key identifier is not present on the deliverable file name, offline communication is needed to obtain the key ID from the student. Client program at faculty must recognize key ID from the deliverable or provide interface for the user to input. Faculty end client program receives symmetric key to decrypt secure deliverable from the server that is symmetric key corresponding to unique key identifier of the deliverable.

Client software must be capable of calculating message digests or hash functions before and after cryptographic process. Deliverable integrity checks are done by comparing (string compare) fixed length hash function output strings.

4   The Protocol

Client and server exchange messages based on rules and formats mentioned below. Application specific protocol messages are explained here using formal methods as specified in reference [1]. First step in this protocol is shared key establishment; in this phase client and server arrive upon a shared key which is used as encryption key for all subsequent communication.

4.1   Shared Key Establishment

Given here is the formal method, please note enclosed in curly brackets { } means encrypted, with a key that is mentioned outside brackets, T means time stamp, N represents nonce, MAC represents media access control address used for identifying a network interface, U represents username.

C --> S: U, {U, Mac Address$_C$, Nc, T}$_{Password}$
S --> C: {U,Mac Address$_S$,Nc,Ns, Kcs, T}$_{Password}$
C --> S: {U, Ns, Nc^1, T}$_{Kcs}$
S --> C: {Nc^1}$_{Kcs}$

Client initiates the connection by sending username (in plain text), encrypted authentication information, the user id, client MAC address, a random number (nonce), and time stamp, all this information is encrypted with user password. Here password is used as encryption key. Server decrypts received information with password corresponding to username. This is an attempt to authenticate user without actually having to transfer password (on wire) in plain text. Decryption can only happen when user password stored in server is equal to password client program used for encryption, if server can decrypt information it only mean username password are correct. If user password stored in server data store does not match with password used as key, generated output will have all garbage values. Server can respond authentication failure and close the connection.

Once authenticated, server responds to client with Username, server MAC address, nonce sent by client, server random number (nonce), shared key, server time stamp all this information is again encrypted by user password. Client software can decrypt this communication with user password. Nonce is a random number used for freshness of message and for verification. By observing these nonce, client and server can be sure the messages are corresponding to current session, not the once stored from previous client and server communications (this ensures protection against replay attacks). After this step client has the shared key sent by the server therefore all further client server messages are encrypted with the shared key.

Next two messages are used for confirmation, which is agreeing upon the shared key. Client sends to the server username, server nonce, a new client nonce, time stamp all this information encrypted with the shared key. This is confirmation that client has agreed to use server given shared key. Server sends back the new client nonce (encrypted with shared key) indicating successful establishment of shared key.

If client or server nonce does not match then shared key establishment is failure or incomplete. Similarly if client program does not demonstrate the knowledge of share key then server does not engage / communicate with the client. Server also returns pre defined code for in correct shared key usage.

4.2   Symmetric Key Management

Learning management systems (LMS) usually provide students option for uploading single or multiple files. Where ever necessary, students will have to zip (compress or combine) all files before uploading into one submit-able file, the deliverable. These deliverables are encrypted with symmetric key algorithms. In cryptography, symmetric key means same (one) key for both encryption and decryption process.

4.2.1 At Student, the Symmetric Key Is Requested for Encrypting

Client program requests server for symmetric key and server program responds with unique identifier and the symmetric key. Given here is a formal method for clients requesting symmetric key to encrypt a deliverable:

Message 1   C --> S: U, $\{CODE, U, H(X), T\}_{Kcs}$
Message 2   S --> C :$\{ Id, K, \{Ns\}_{K,T} \}_{Kcs}$
Message 3   C --> S :$\{ Ns \}_{Kcs}$

Here U represents user id, CODE is pre-defined number indicating client is requesting for symmetric key (for example: 511525), H(X) represents hash function output of given deliverable, T represents timestamp, K represents symmetric key, N represents nonce, and Kcs is shared key between client and server.

In message 1, Client communicates with the server by sending user name in plain text, and remaining sent information is encrypted with the shared key, that is request code for symmetric key, user name, message digest of deliverable, time stamp. Server can decrypt this client communication with user's corresponding shared key. In message 2, server generates the fixed length symmetric key, unique symmetric key identifier, a nonce (encrypted with symmetric key for verification), and time stamp. All this information is encrypted with shared key before sending to client. In message 3, client obtains the symmetric key, stores key identifier and decrypts server nonce (that was previously encrypted and sent in message 2). This decrypted nonce is sent back to server, which is now verified (if Ns match - client has got the right symmetric key).

4.2.2 At Faculty, the Symmetric Key Is Requested for Decrypting

Server is programmed to retrieve symmetric key only if key identifier is provided. Server responds to key requests based on user name, and its role. Request for decryption key (with key identifier) is possible only for owner of the deliverable and users with faculty role. Given here is a formal method for clients requesting symmetric key to decrypt a deliverable:

Message 1   C --> S: U, $\{CODE, U, Id, T\}_{Kcs}$
Message 2   S --> C: $\{Id, K, \{Ns\}_{K}, T\}_{Kcs}$
Message 3   C --> S: $\{Ns\}_{Kcs}$

Here U represents user id, CODE is pre-defined number indicating client is requesting for symmetric key (for example: 411525), Id is the identifier of symmetric key, T represents timestamp, K represents symmetric key, N represents nonce, and Kcs is shared key between client and server.

In message 1, client (at faculty end) requests to server by sending user name in plain text, and remaining sent information is encrypted with shared key, that is request code for symmetric key, user name, unique id of the symmetric key, time stamp.

Server can decrypt this client communication with corresponding shared key. In message 2, server retrieves symmetric key corresponding to unique key identifier. Server sends to client identifier, key, a nonce (encrypted with this symmetric key for verification), and time stamp. All this information is encrypted with shared key before sending to client. In message 3, client obtains the symmetric key, stores key identifier and decrypts server nonce (that was previously encrypted and sent in message 2). This decrypted nonce is sent back to server, which is now verified (if Ns match - client has got the right symmetric key).

Faculty can now use this symmetric key to decrypt student's deliverables.

5   The Integrity Check

Message integrity checks are required to verify completeness and consistency. Many hash functions like message digest are used to generate message integrity codes. Client software will verify if the intended communication is complete. It is important for the faculty to know, that a deliverable is not altered during communication or storage.

Client software applies hash function before a deliverable goes through encryption process. A deliverable, and its message digest are part of the plain text. After decryption, the deliverables and message digest are saved in the faculty computer. Client software verifies file message digest with decrypted message digest. If they are exactly same this means deliverable is not altered in transit or storage.

6   Other Applications

Security modules in existing learning management systems are either SSL/TLS based or LMS specific proprietary security (lock-in) mechanisms. With SSL / TLS based encryptions all educational institutions need digital certificates for assignments purpose (and will need effective certificates management) which is expensive as specified in section 2 (crypto primitives). Learning management system specific security solutions work only in that LMS environment and may be difficult to migrate (to other LMS) later on.

Architecture discussed in this paper will work in assignment submissions scenario and can be applied to all group (1 to many) based circulation of confidential information like securing digital notice boards, securing office documents where one party acts at encryption end while other party obtains key using role based authentication at decryption end. For the submissions that do not require secure transfer, proposed model can be bypassed and users can continue with the usual / regular mode of submissions.

7   Conclusion

Secure assignment (deliverables) submission architecture & protocol will help in achieving confidentiality of student deliverables on wire & LMS storage through cryptography, authentication is achieved through passwords and machine specific information like MAC address, integrity of the deliverable is achieved using hash functions and non repudiation is achieved using shared keys & client software. This process will rule out chances of copying deliverables on wire and from learning management systems.

Long passwords must be used to avoid dictionary attacks before establishing shared key. Hashing is used by student client program while uploading the deliverable this is used in avoiding corrupted files occasionally created by network transfers. This is because network protocols verify packet level integrity not at file/deliverable level.

Existing learning management systems need not be changed or modified to incorporate this solution. This solution can also avoid writing numerous plug-ins for different kinds of Learning Management Systems, secure transfers. Simple applications like these can enhance universities deterrence toward plagiarism check.

References

1. Abadi, M., Needham, R.: Prudent Engineering Practice for Cryptographic Protocols. In: IEEE Computer Society Symposium on Research in Security and Privacy (1994)
2. Anderson, R., Needham, R.: Programming Satan's Computer. Cambridge University Computer Laboratory
3. Bellovin, S.M., Merrit, M.: Encrypted Key Exchange: Password-Based Protocols Secure Against Dictionary Attacks. In: 1992 IEEE Computer Society Symposium on Research in Security and Privacy (1992)
4. Richard Stevens, W.: UNIX Network Programming: Networking APIs: Sockets and XTI, 2nd edn., vol. 1. Prentice Hall (1998) ISBN 0-13-490012-X
5. Bellare, M., Canetti, R., Krawczyk, H.: A Modular Approach to the Design and Analysis of Authentication and Key Exchange Protocols. In: Proc. of the 30th STOC. ACM Press, New York (1998)
6. Bellare, M., Pointcheval, D., Rogaway, P.: Authenticated Key Exchange Secure against Dictionary Attacks. In: Preneel, B. (ed.) EUROCRYPT 2000. LNCS, vol. 1807, pp. 139–155. Springer, Heidelberg (2000)
7. Morris, R., Thompson, K.: Password security: a case history. Communications of the ACM 22, 594–597 (1979)
8. Glass, E.: The NTLM authentication protocol (2003)

Secure Leader Election Algorithm Optimized for Power Saving Using Mobile Agents for Intrusion Detection in MANET

Monika Darji[1] and Bhushan Trivedi[2]

[1] L.J Institute of Computer Application, Ahmedabad, India
monikadarji79@gmail.com
[2] GLS Institute of Computer Technology, Ahmedabad, India
bhtrivedi@yahoo.com

Abstract. In this paper we reduce the communication and computation overhead involved in Leader Election for running Intrusion Detection System (IDS) for a cluster of nodes in mobile ad hoc networks using Mobile Agents. To reduce the performance overhead of IDS, a leader node is elected to handle intrusion detection service for the whole cluster. If the cluster head selection is random, it might be possible that resource consumption of the leader is higher and it might just lose all its power. Thus overall lifetime of cluster reduces to lesser than useful lifetime. It is clear that such methods have no guarantee to work. The solution requires balancing the resource consumption among all the nodes and thus increase the overall lifetime of a cluster by electing the most cost- efficient node. We will call it leader-IDS. Our contribution to the election scheme is to design an algorithm which uses mobile agents to gather resource information from all the cluster nodes and use it to elect leader in optimum and secure manner.

Keywords: MANET security, Intrusion detection system, Mobile Agents, Cluster Head Election.

1 Introduction

Mobile Ad hoc NETwork (MANET) [1] is a set of mobile devices like laptops, PDAs, smart phones which communicate with each other over wireless links without a predefined infrastructure or a central authority. The member nodes are themselves responsible for the creation, operation and maintenance of the network using single hop or multi hop communication. The characteristics of MANET includes dynamic topology, lack of fixed infrastructure, vulnerability of nodes and communication channel, lack of traffic concentration points, limited power, less and varying computational capacity, less memory, and limited bandwidth which makes the task of achieving a secure and reliable communication more difficult.

MANETS have no centralized checkpoint where Intrusion Detection System can be deployed. Earlier proposed solutions had each node run IDS to perform local intrusion detection and cooperate with other nodes to perform global intrusion

S.M. Thampi et al. (Eds.): SNDS 2012, CCIS 335, pp. 54–63, 2012.

detection [2]. This scheme was inefficient in terms of resource consumption therefore cluster-based detection scheme were proposed [3][4].For Clustering, the nodes in MANET are divided into a set of 1-hop clusters where each node belongs to at least one cluster and a leader node (Cluster Head) is elected to run the IDS for the entire cluster. The leader-IDS election process can be random [3] or decided on the connectivity [4]. The resource availability of different nodes is different which must be considered by an election scheme otherwise some node's batteries dip will faster than others, leading to a loss in connectivity and reduction in overall lifetime of a cluster when these nodes become unavailable due to lack of power. Moreover if a shellfish node is elected then it may impede to run IDS and put the entire cluster at risk. To balance the resource consumption of IDSs among nodes and increase lifetime of a cluster, nodes with the most remaining resources should be elected as the leaders [5][6][7]. But resource information being private information, shellfish nodes may not reveal their remaining resources, during an election of the leader node to conserve their resource and vent other's. To balance the resource consumption among all the nodes and increase the overall lifetime of a cluster a mechanism is given using Vickrey, Clarke, and Groves (VCG) [8] and mechanism design theory in [5][6] for leader election.

While these schemes provide a solution for election of leader-IDS in presence of shellfish nodes, [5] and [7] do not deal with security issues, [6] provides a secure communication using public key infrastructure but all the nodes need to sign their information before sending and also needs to verify other nodes signature before computing costs which increases overhead. Moreover all the above schemes require broadcasts by all the nodes. We propose to use mobile agents to elect leader-IDS. Mobile agents are light weight; computationally efficient, flexible autonomous program agents can halt and ship themselves to another node on the network, and continue execution at the new node. An agent doesn't restart execution from the beginning at the new node; it continues where it left off.

For communication MANET over wireless links, mobile agents can be used for their efficiency in lightweight computation and suitability in cooperative Cluster Head computation. Mobile agents have been used in several techniques for intrusion detection systems in MANETs [10]. Due to its capability to travel through the large network, they can interact and cooperate with nodes, collect information, and perform tasks assigned to them. Opposed to traditional approaches where large amounts of data are transported towards the computation location, mobile agents allows the analysis programs to move closer to the audit data. Mobile agents can reduce the amount of communication through the network and is extensively used for distributed applications.

We have designed new algorithm that uses mobile agents to gather resource information from all the cluster nodes and use it to elect leader-IDS in optimum manner. Our scheme is inspired from Ajanta Systems [11] to design mechanisms that allow a mobile agent's owner to ensure security of an agent using three techniques: read only state, append only logs and selective revealing of the state. This work will be able to reduce the battery and bandwidth consumption for leader-IDS election and will be greatly useful for scenarios where mobility of nodes is higher. We justify the correctness of our proposed scheme through analysis.

The rest of this paper is organized as follows: Section 2 reviews related work. Section 3 illustrates our approach. Section 4 illustrates the Leader election scheme without Mobile Agents. Section 5 devises the Leader Election Process with Mobile Agents. Finally, Section 6 concludes the paper and discusses future work.

2   Related Works

The first distributed and cooperative IDS was proposed in [2] which used statistical anomaly detection, this model was extended in [3] where the job of intrusion detection was carried out by a Cluster Head selected in random fashion where each node is equally likely to be elected regardless of its remaining resources. In [4], elects a node with a high degree of connectivity even though the node may have little resources left.

In [5] a unified framework is proposed for balancing the resource consumption among all the nodes and for electing the most cost-efficient node known as leader-IDS. A mechanism is designed using Vickrey, Clarke, and Groves (VCG) to achieve the desired goal. To monitor the behavior of the leader and to catch and punish a misbehaving leader, they have made use of checkers that interact among each other using cooperative game-theoretic model to reduce the false-positive rate. A multi-stage catch mechanism is also introduced to reduce the performance overhead of checkers.

In [7] leader election scheme is proposed for electing most energy remaining node using QA-VCG mechanism by simplifying it to increase the survival time of nodes and to motivate the nodes to behave honestly and reveal their true cost of analysis by giving them incentives. The mechanism derives from QA-VCG an efficient multi-attributes procurement combinatorial auction model.

In [6] which is an extension to [5] leader election in presence of shellfish nodes. To address the selfish behavior, incentives are given in the form of reputation to encourage nodes to honestly participate in the election scheme by revealing of their available resources. The design of incentives is based on a classical mechanism design model, namely, Vickrey, Clarke, and Groves (VCG) [8] which guarantees that truth-telling is always the dominant strategy for every node during each election phase. They propose a series of local election algorithm that can lead to globally optimal election results with low cost. This scheme uses public key infrastructure for secure communication.

Limitation of existing scheme is the number of broadcasts and signature verifications that needs to be performed on all the nodes for gathering resource information to ensure secure communication. We propose a scheme where Mobile agents are used to gather the resource information from the nodes to avoid the broadcasts and signature verifications by each individual node. Instead of all the nodes broadcasting their resource information and vote, one of the nodes creates mobile agent to perform the task in an efficient manner by reducing the battery and bandwidth consumption.

Whenever the agent moves to a node, the node should not be allowed to steal the agent's information. Also the agent should be protected against modifications. The agent also requires protection against attacks from a hostile host which can be maliciously destroying an agent or tempering with an agent such that it may attack its own initiator. Unfortunately fully protecting an agent against all kind of attacks is impossible (Farmer et al., 1996) and alternative approach is to organize the agents in a way that modifications can be detected. This approach has been followed in Ajanta Systems [11]. Ajanta provides three mechanisms that allow an agent's owner to detect that an agent has been tampered with: read only state, append only logs and selective revealing of the state. These three mechanisms has inspired us to device a scheme for secure Cluster Head Election in MANET.

In our work for leader-IDS election, we propose to modify the algorithms in [6] by introducing mobile agents that will be used for gathering resource information and votes in a secure manner and thus reduce the overall battery and bandwidth consumption leading to efficiency and power saving.

3   Our Approach

MANET can modeled as undirected graph G = (N, L) where N is the set of mobile nodes and L is the set of bidirectional links. Using Cluster-first approach [12] clusters are formed in a network, and then, the nodes belonging to that cluster elect a leader node. Every cluster has a set of nodes n   N and a set of links l   L. One-hop neighbor nodes form a cluster and nodes might belong to more than one cluster. It is assumed that each node has an IDS and a unique identity. Nodes can overhear each other using omnidirectional antenna.

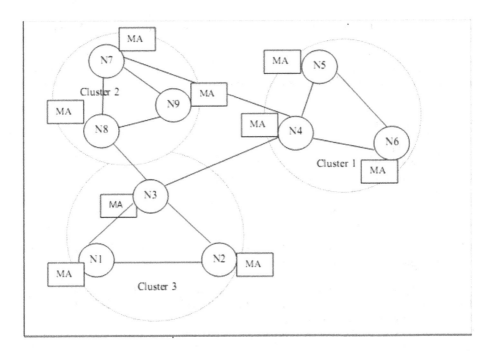

Fig. 1. An example scenario of leader election in MANET

Cluster head election is time consuming and resource intensive and requires broadcast and signature verification by every participating node; we propose to optimize it using mobile agents using our algorithm for leader election which is described below. We have extended the algorithm described in [6] with the introduction of mobile agents. Figure 1 shows a MANET composed of 9 nodes labeled from N1 to N9. These nodes are located in three 1-hop cluster nodes with varying resource and energy level. We assume the nodes N3 and N4 have low energy level. With Random Election Model [3], each node will have equal probability of being elected as leader to run the IDS, if nodes N3 and N4 are elected, they will die faster leading to partitioning in the network. Under Connectivity Index based approach [4], N3 and N4 will score higher and get elected leading to similar circumstances. Moreover, if shellfish nodes are elected as leaders, they will decline to do their job of running IDS. The scheme presented in [6] balances the resource consumption of IDS among all nodes and also prevents shellfish behavior by giving incentives in the form of reputation. We extend the scheme presented in [6] by using Mobile Agents which will move from one node to another in the cluster for gathering resource information and vote information and Cluster Head computation.

4   Leader Election Scheme without Mobile Agent

Leader election scheme without using mobile agents is presented in [5], [6] and [7].

4.1   Requirements of Designing Leader Election Algorithm as Described in [6]

1) To protect all the nodes in a network, every node should be monitored by a leader
2) To balance the resource consumption of IDS service, the overall cost of analysis for protecting the whole network should be minimized.

4.2   Assumptions

1) Every node knows its (2-hop) neighbors
2) Loosely synchronized clocks are available between nodes.
3) Each node has a key (public and private) pair for establishing a secure communication between nodes.
4) Each node is aware of the presence of a new node or removal of a node.

4.3   To Start a New Election, the Election Algorithm Uses Four Types of Messages Which Are as Follows

Hello: used by any node k to initiate the election process, Hello $(ID_k, Hash(cost_k))$
Begin-Election: used to announce the cost of a node Begin-Election, $(ID_k, cost_k)$
Vote: sent by every node to elect a leader, $Vote(ID_k)$
Acknowledge: sent by the leader to broadcast its payment, and also as a confirmation of its leadership.

4.4   For Describing the Algorithm, Following Notations Are Used [6]

service-table(k): The list of all ordinary nodes, those voted for the leader node k.
reputation-table(k): The reputation table of node k. Each node keeps the record of reputation of all other nodes.
neighbors(k): The set of node k's neighbors.
leadernode(k): The ID of node k's leader. If node k is running its own IDS, then the variable contains k.
leader(k): A boolean variable that sets to TRUE if node k is a leader and FALSE otherwise.

Our election scheme is similar to that given in [6] but we are using mobile agents.

5   Leader Election Using Mobile Agent

Any node k which belongs to a cluster, initiates the election process by creating a Hello Agent contains Hello Message table whose format is shown in Table 1:

Table 1. Hello Message Table

Node Unique ID	Hash of Nodes Cost*	Signed MD	Checksum
ID_k	$Hash(cost_k)$	$E(PR_k, ID_k + Hash(cost_k))$	C_{init}

Explanation of Hello Massage Table of Table 1 is given below:
*Cost implies a node's cost of analysis
ID_k: node k's unique identifier
$Hash(cost_k)$: hash value of the node k's cost of analysis
Hash is needed to ensure non-repudiation (avoid cheating) as all the nodes before knowing others cost values will have to declare their hash of cost and later on cannot change it.
$E(PR_k, ID_k + Hash(cost_k))$: The $ID_k + Hash(cost_k)$ is the message digest signed by node k.
This provides read-only state, authentication and integrity. When the agent arrives at another node, the node can easily detect whether read only state has been tampered with.
Cinit $= E(PU_k, N)$: PU_k is the public key of the agent's owner node k and N is the secret nonce known only to the node k.

When the agent arrives at a node l, it appends its ID and hash value of cost and new checksum in the Hello Message table as shown in Table 2.

Table 2. Hello Message Table with node k and l's data

Node Unique ID	Hash of Nodes Cost	Signed MD	Checksum
IDk	$Hash(cost_k)$	$E(PR_k, ID_k + Hash(cost_k))$	C_{init}
ID_l	$Hash(cost_l)$	$E(PR_l, ID_l + Hash(cost_l))$	C_{new}

Explanation of Hello Massage Table of Table 2 is given below:

ID_l: nodes unique identifier

$Hash(cost_l)$: hash value of the node's cost of analysis

$E(PR_l, ID_l + Hash(cost_l))$: The ID_l+$Hash(cost_l)$ is the message digest signed by node l.

C_{new} : New checksum calculated by node l. $C_{new} = E(PUk, (C_{old} + Signed MD + PU_l))$

To allow an agent to collect information while moving between hosts, we provide secure append only table. This table is characterized by the fact that data can only be appended to the log; there is no way that data can be removed or modified without the owner being able to detect this. Initially the table and has only an associated checksum C_{init} When the agent moves to a node l, it appends its ID, hash of its cost and Signed MD, and the new checksum.

When the agent comes back to its owner, owner can verify if the table has been tampered with. The owner starts reading the table at the end by successively computing $D(PR_k, C_{new})$, on the checksum C_{new}. Each iteration will return a checksum C_{next} for the next iteration, along with Signed MD and public key, PU_l for some node l. The agent owner can then verify if the last element in the table matches signed MD, for each node in each iteration step. The iteration stops when the initial checksum is reached or when a there is a signature mismatch. If the agent is not back after T1 expires, a new agent is launched.

Algorithm 1 (Executed by Hello Agent owner node k)

/*On receiving Hello Agent, all nodes append their data in Hello Message table*/

1. if (Hello Agent returns after visiting all neighbors) then

2. Perform verification of ID and Hash of Node Cost against Signed MD

3. Validate the checksum to ensure integrity of table data

4. Send Begin-Election Agent only to the nodes who have placed data in Hello Message table;

/* Begin-Election agent contains Begin-Election Message table which allows each node to put their costs of analysis*/

4. else if(neighbors(k)=) then

5. Launch IDS.

6. end if

When hello Agent returns, node k checks whether it has received all the hash values from its neighbors. Nodes from whom the entries are not received are excluded from the election. On receiving the entries from all neighbors, node k creates Begin-Election Agent containing Begin-Election table as shown in Table 3, in which allows nodes to enter their cost of analysis, and then, starts timer T2. If node k is the only node in the network or it does not have any neighbors, then it launches its own IDS.

Table 3. Begin-Election Table

Node Unique ID	Nodes Cost	Signed MD	Checksum
ID_k	$cost_k$	$E(PR_k, ID_k + costk)$	C_{init}

When Begin-Election agent returns, the node k compares the hash value of Hello Message table to the value received in the Begin-Election Message table to verify the cost of analysis for all the nodes.

Algorithm 2 (Executed by Begin-Election Agent owner node k)
/*On receiving Begin-Election Agent, all nodes append their actual cost in Begin-Election table*/
1. if (Begin-Election Agent returns after visiting all neighbors) then
2. Perform verification of ID and Node Cost against Signed MD
3. Validate the checksum to ensure integrity of table data
4. Calculate Hash of Nodes Cost and compare to Hash of Nodes Cost from Hello Message table
4. Send Vote Agent to the nodes;
/* Vote Agent contains read only Vote Message table which allows each node to find nodes with least costs of analysis and cast their votes*/

Node k then creates a read only Vote Agent containing Vote Message table containing ID, hash of cost, actual cost of analysis that it has obtained from each node as shown in Table 4. Vote Agent is used by a node to view cost of analysis of other nodes and cast their vote for any one neighboring node and start a timer. Note that cost of analysis is lesser if a node has higher energy level. Reputation value of all neighbouring nodes is maintained by each node

Table 4. Read Only Vote Message Table

Node Unique ID	Hash of Nodes Cost	Nodes Cost
ID_1	$Hash(cost_1)$	$Cost_1$
ID_i	$Hash(cost_i)$	$Cost_i$

Algorithm 3 (Executed by every node)
/*Each node votes for one node among the neighbors*/
if (cost of neighbor node i is less than cost of node l) then
send Vote $PR_l(ID_l,ID_i)$;
leadernode(l) :=i;
endif

On receiving Vote Agent containing Vote Message table, the node l checks cost of analysis for the neighboring nodes to calculate the least-cost value and sends Vote for node i as in Algorithm 3. Vote message contains digitally signed ID_l of the source node and the ID_i of the proposed leader. Then, node l sets node i as its leader in order to update later on its reputation. The second least cost of analysis is needed by the leader node to calculate the payment [6]. If node l has the least cost among all its neighbors, then it votes for itself and starts a timer.

Algorithm 4 (Executed by Elected leader-IDS node)[6]
/*Send Acknowledge message to the neighbor nodes*/
1. Leader(i) := TRUE;
2. Compute Payment, P_i;
3. update service-table(i);
4. update reputation-table(i);
5. Acknowledge = P_i + all the votes;
6. Send Acknowledge(i);
7. Launch IDS.

When the timer expires, elected nodes calculate their payment. The elected node i calculates its payment P_i given in the form of reputation where truth telling is dominant strategy as given in [6].Updates the service table and reputation table for the voting nodes, sends an Acknowledge message to all the voting nodes as in Algorithm 3. The Acknowledge message contains the payment and all the votes the leader received. The leader then launches its IDS.

As described in [6] each node verifies the payment received from leader node and updates its reputation table. Leader nodes run the IDS for inspecting packets, during an interval T_{ELECT} after which election process is carried out again to choose new leader-IDS.

6   Conclusions

A mobile agent framework is deployed for communication among the nodes for Cluster Head Election related information. In our proposed algorithm, we use the autonomy and mobility associated with mobile agent technology to present an efficient and flexible and secure system, to deal with weak connectivity and inadequate bandwidth in MANETs and device a method to effectively and efficiently elect a cluster head. The above algorithm is cost efficient and secure leader election drastically reduces the computation overhead specially in case of high mobility networks where the frequency of elections is more.

In the original algorithm [6], each normal node signs three messages and verifies 3•Ngi•+ 1 messages, where Ngi is the number of neighboring nodes. On the other hand, the leader node signs four messages and verifies 3•Ngi•messages. Each node must find the least cost node which requires $O(\log(Ngi))$. Therefore, each node approximately performs $O(Ngi)$ verifications, $O(1)$ signatures, and $O(\log(Ngi))$ to calculate the least-cost node. Thus, the computation overhead for each node is approximately $O(Ngi)$.

In our algorithm each normal node signs three messages but verification is done only by mobile agent owner therefore the computation overhead of all normal nodes is less than $O(Ngi)$.Communication overhead of each node broadcasting message in the first three steps is reduced using mobile agents and only leader node needs to broadcast a final Acknowledge message.

Thus by modifying the algorithm in [6] to introduce mobile agents we can achieve reduction in communication and computation overhead leading to lesser power consumption. This technique of Secure Leader Election can be useful in Wireless Sensor Networks. As a future direction we would like to extend this model to provide efficient Intrusion Detection using Secure Mobile Agents.

References

1. Murthy, C.S.R., Manoj, B.S.: Ad Hoc Wireless Networks. Pearson Education (2008)
2. Zhang, Y., Lee, W.: Intrusion Detection in Wireless Ad-Hoc Networks. In: Proc. MOBICOM 2000, pp. 275–283. ACM Press, Boston (2000)
3. Huang, Y.-A., Lee, W.: A Cooperative Intrusion Detection System for Ad Hoc Networks. In: Proceedings of the 1st ACM Workshop on Security of Ad Hoc and Sensor Networks, SASN 2003, pp. 135–147. ACM, NY (2003)
4. Kachirski, O., Guha, R.: Efficient Intrusion Detection Using Multiple Sensors in Wireless Ad Hoc Networks. In: Proc. IEEE Hawaii Int'l Conf. System Sciences, HICSS (2003)
5. Otrok, H., Mohammed, N., Wang, L., Debbabi, M., Bhattacharya, P.: A game-theoretic intrusion detection model for mobile ad hoc networks. Comput. Commun. 31(4), 708–721 (2008)
6. Mohammed, N., Otrok, H., Wang, L., Debbabi, M., Bhattacharya, P.: Mechanism Design-Based Secure Leader Election Model for Intrusion Detection in MANET. IEEE Transactions on Dependable and Secure Computing 8(1) (2011)
7. Zeng, Chen, Z.: A Cluster Header Election Scheme Based on Auction Mechanism for Intrusion Detection in MANET. In: International Conference on Network Computing and Information Security (2011)
8. Anderegg, L., Eidenbenz, S.: Ad Hoc-VCG: A Truthful and Cost-Efficient Routing Protocol for Mobile Ad Hoc Networks with Selfish Agents. In: Proc. ACM MobiCom (2003)
9. Agents, http://www.java2s.com/Article/Java/SOAservices/ The_Architecture_of_Aglets_IBMs_Mobile_Java_Agents_Under_the _Hood.html
10. Albers, P., Camp, O., Percher, J.-M., Jouga, B., Ludovic, M., Puttini, R.: Security in ad hoc networks: a general intrusion detection architecture enhancing trust based approaches. In: Proc. of the First International Workshop on Wireless Information Systems, WIS 2002, pp. 1–12 (2002)
11. Tripathi, A.R.: A Security Architecture for Mobile Agents in Ajanta. In: Proceedings of the 20th International Conference on Distributed Computing Systems, ICDCS 2000, pp. 402–409. IEEE Computer Society, Washington, DC (2000)
12. Krishna, P., Vaidya, N.H., Chatterjee, M., Pradhan, D.K.: A Cluster-Based Approach for Routing in Dynamic Networks. Proc. ACM SIGCOMM Computer Comm. Rev. (1997)

WAKE: Authentication and Key Establishment for Wireless Mesh Network

Somanath Tripathy and Debasish Sahoo

Indian Institute of Technology Patna, India
{som,d.sahoo}@iitp.ac.in

Abstract. Wireless mesh network (WMN) is an effective means to provide internet services at cheaper cost. Authentication and key management is a challenging issue in WMN due to the wireless media, multi-hop communication and dynamic environment. On the other hand, neither the pre-shared key nor the IEEE 802.1x based authentication mechanisms are suitable for WMN. This paper proposes an effective authentication mechanism named *WAKE*, to provide access control for mesh clients. WAKE uses identity based cryptography and is non trivially secure.

Keywords: Wireless mesh network, security, authentication, denial of services attacks, identity based cryptography.

1   Introduction

Wireless mesh network has become more popular as it provides fast, simple, reliable and less-expensive network deployment [1]. On the other hand, security has become an important concern due to the wireless links in WMN which makes it prone to several malicious attacks. Above all, the multi-hop communication and self configuring features make the security issues more challenging.

Assume a typical wireless mesh network as shown in Figure. 1, in which, all networking devices communicate each other through wireless communications. The mesh routers (MRs) form the backbone, while a mesh client (MC) can access the network services through MR, we refer those mesh access points (MA) synonymously in this paper.

Authentication and key establishment between the MC and nearest MA is most important to access control. Unfortunately, authentication and key agreement is not within the scope of the $IEEE$802.11 networks. $IEEE$802.11s standard is an amendment towards meeting the requirement of WMN security. The 802.11s standard uses efficient mesh security association (EMSA) to prevent unauthorized party from receiving or sending the information in WMN. EMSA extends the security frameworks from 802.11i and 802.1x to fit into WMN for establishing key between the MC and MR [10]. As per the recent draft standard of 802.11s [9], RSNA establishment is based on 3 different approaches: (i) using 802.1x, (ii) PSK and (iii) password based. The password-based is recently updated referred as simultaneous authentication for equals (SAE) [12].

S.M. Thampi et al. (Eds.): SNDS 2012, CCIS 335, pp. 64–74, 2012.

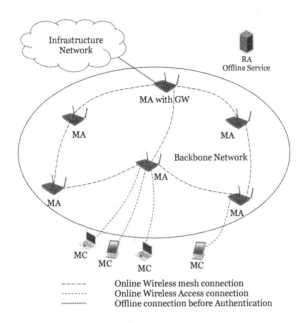

Fig. 1. A Typical Wireless Mesh Network

SAE seems to be an efficient authentication framework which, provides secure alternative when, central authority is not available. It supports fast establishing of shared key between two peers. On the other hand, the new mesh node willing to join into the WMN may not have the shared Password or PSK. Therefore, fails to establish security association (SA) and tries to establish security association based on 802.1x. However, 802.1x is not suitable for multi-hop networks like WMN, since an attacker can exploit this opportunity to flood the network by sending multiple SA requests leading to DoS attacks.

To address the above issue, this paper proposes an effective authentication and key establishment for WMN called *WAKE*. WAKE provides mutual authentication to get rid from the rogue servers attacks. Apart from that, any MR can execute WAKE without forwarding the packets to Authentication server (through multi-hop), to avoid DoS attacks. The proposed-scheme is based on identity based cryptography but does not use the complex bilinear mapping operations, so easily implementable.

This paper is organized as follows. Next section discusses briefly about the existing schemes. The proposed key establishment mechanism is discussed in Section 4. In Section 5 we evaluate our scheme against security as well as performance, and the proposal is concluded in Section 6. Rest of the paper uses the symbols given in Table 1.

2 Related Works

Many security proposals for WMN have focused on client authentication to provide access control. MobiSEC [7] uses 802.11i for authentication and key agreement between MC and the MR (acts as access point to the MC). Zhang et.al [14] proposed a ticket based universal pass (UPASS) technique in a novel user-broker-operator trust model. This universal pass is given by a trusted broker. Zhu et.al [15] adapted the UPASS approach without the role of the broker. To improve the security Zhu et.al [16] proposed a secure localized authentication and billing for multihop WMN.

Lee et.al [6] proposed a distributed authentication mechanism aiming at reducing authentication delay. Their model uses multiple trusted nodes which are distributed over WMN acting as authentication server. Consequently, the performance decreases, if multiple clients fires authentication requests at the same time. He et.al [4] proposed a lightweight AKE scheme based on hierarchical multivariable symmetric functions. Li et.al [17] proposed a Ticket based fast authentication protocol for mobile nodes in wireless mesh networks. The solution in [2] aims to mitigate the high computation and communication overheads due to certificates in PKCS. Authentication server (AS) acts as the PKG which shares a password with the authenticating STA. After the successful initial authentication, the STA will have its private key. Subsequently the STA uses IBC signature mechanism to authenticate other STAs. During initial authentication, the authenticator mesh node acts as the forwarding node between the new STA and AS, therefore flooding attack is feasible as on the 802.1x. Moreover, AS needs to be on-line which would be a bottleneck.

Table 1. Notation

Symbol	Meaning
AS	Authentication server
PKG	Private Key Generator
RA	Registration Authority
ID_x	Identity of x
S_x	Secret of node x given by RA
N_x	Random nonce of x
$H(.)$	One way hash function
x	a mesh node $x \in \{MC, MR\}$
T_{exp_x}	Expire time for node x
K_{xy}	PMK between x and y
e	public key of RA
d	private key of RA
PSK	Pre-shared key between MC and MR
MAC	Message Authentication Code

3   Network Assumptions

As shown in Fig.1, there are three major components in a typical wireless mesh network.

Registration Authority RA: The registration authority server is used for initialization of system parameters and providing the secret keys to each authorized node (MCs, MAs) to participate in WMN.

Mesh Access Point MA: WMN comprises of certain number of MAs forming backbones by wireless mesh connection. These MAs provide the distribution service to MCs and forward/ route the information so we call them MR (mesh router) also.

Mesh Client MC: The mesh client nodes MCs are mobile and obtain the WMN service through a MA.

The operator controls and manages all the MAs and MCs in his domain. Therefore, all the MAs are registered with the RA before the deployment and to prevent unauthorized access MCs are registered before accessing for the services. Each MC and MA get their secrets from RA during the registration phase.

4   *WAKE:* Authenticated Key Establishment for WMN

The proposed authentication mechanism *WAKE*, is to provide authentication and key establishment between MC and MA. The scheme comprises with the following 4 operational phases.

1. **System Initialization Phase:** Before the network starts its operation, the (off-line) RA chooses a large 1024-bit prime numbers p and q randomly, and a small number to be used as public key e. The corresponding secret key d is determined to be $e * d \equiv 1 \ mod \ (p - 1)(q - 1)$. Let g be the generator of that group and n is the product of primes p and q. RA makes $\langle e, H, n, g \rangle$ publicly available (each registered party will store these to use in future), while keeps d a secret, where H is a strong one-way hash function.

2. **Registration Phase:** Before joining or accessing into the WMN, each mesh client and access point need to be registered with the registration authority (RA). The Registration process for each entity executes for once only and can be performed through any of the existing secure registration process like interacting with the RA directly/ physically.

   The mesh client (c) with identity ID_c sends a registration request to the registration authority RA. As a response, RA computes the secret S_c as

$$S_c = g^{g_c \cdot d} \ mod \ n \tag{1}$$

$$where, g_c = H(ID_c || T_{exp_c}).$$

Finally, RA sends $\langle S_c, T_{exp_c} \rangle$ to the registered MC along with the public parameters (e, H, p, g) . The mesh client c stores S_c in secret.

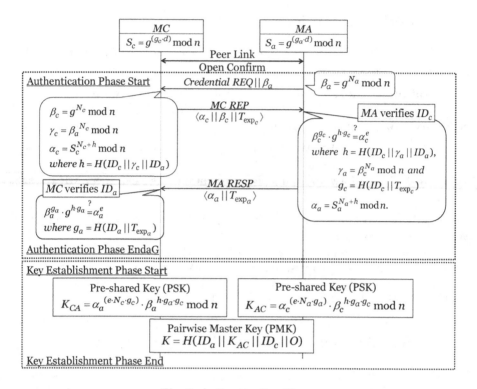

Fig. 2. Authentication Phase

In the similar fashion each access point MA also registers with the RA before participating into the network. Consequently, upon receiving the request of MA, RA sends $\langle S_a, T_{exp_a} \rangle$ along with the the public parameters (e, H, p, g) to the registered MA where RA computes secret S_a as

$$S_a = g^{g_a \cdot d} \mod n \qquad (2)$$
$$where, g_a = H(ID_a || T_{exp_a}).$$

3. **Authentication and Key agreement Phase:** In this phase, the mesh client (MC) acts as supplicant associated with an existing MR which acts as authenticator (MA). WAKE authentication techniques is depicted in Figure 2, which executes through the following steps.

S3.1: After the successful execution of peer link open and confirmation process, the mesh router MA, generates random nonce N_a and computes

$$\beta_a = g^{N_a} \mod n. \qquad (3)$$

MA requests for credential to client peer MC along with β_a. MA keeps N_a in its buffer and invalidates the nonce after a specified time.

S3.2: As a response, MC generates a random nonce N_c and computes $\gamma_c, \alpha_c,$ as

$$\beta_c = g^{N_c} \bmod n, \tag{4}$$

$$\gamma_c = \beta_a{}^{N_c} \bmod n \text{ and} \tag{5}$$

$$\alpha_c = S_c{}^{(N_c+h)} \bmod n \tag{6}$$

$$\text{where } h = H(ID_c||\gamma_c||ID_a).$$

MC sends $\langle \alpha_c, \beta_c, T_{exp_c} \rangle$ to MA.

S3.3: Upon receiving $\langle \alpha_c, \beta_c, T_{exp_c} \rangle$, MA checks that she owns an active session.// MA assures the ID and T_{exp} of MC, if

$$\beta_c{}^{g_c} \cdot g^{h \cdot g_c} = \alpha_c{}^e \tag{7}$$

$$\text{where } h = H(ID_c||\gamma_a||ID_a),$$

$$\gamma_a = \beta_c{}^{N_a} \bmod n \text{ and}$$

$$g_c = H(ID_c||T_{exp_c}).$$

If the above verification fails MA stops communication, otherwise it computes

$$\alpha_a = S_a{}^{(N_a+h)} \bmod n. \tag{8}$$

Then, MA sends $\langle \alpha_a, T_{exp_a} \rangle$ to MC. MA computes the pairwise session key (PSK) as

$$K_{AC} = \alpha_c{}^{(e \cdot N_a \cdot g_a)} \cdot \beta_c{}^{(h \cdot g_a \cdot g_c)} \bmod n. \tag{9}$$

MA computes PMK as $K = H(ID_a||K_{AC}||ID_c||O)$.

S3.4: Upon receiving $\langle \alpha_a, T_{exp_a} \rangle$, MC verifies the legitimacy of MA. // MC assures the ID and T_{exp} of MA, if

$$\beta_a{}^{g_a} \cdot g^{h \cdot g_a} = \alpha_a{}^e \tag{10}$$

$$\text{where } g_a = H(ID_a||T_{exp_a}).$$

If the verification fails MC stops communication, otherwise it compute the PSK as

$$K_{CA} = \alpha_a{}^{(e \cdot N_c \cdot g_c)} \cdot \beta_a{}^{(h \cdot g_a \cdot g_c)} \bmod n. \tag{11}$$

MC computes PMK as $K = H(ID_a||K_{CA}||ID_c||O)$.

4. Handover Authentication Phase:

S4.1: When a mesh client (MC) wants to move from one mesh access point MA (with which it is associated) to another mesh access point MA', it sends a request along with a nonce $N_{A'}$ for a roaming token. Subsequently, MA sends the roaming token $RT_{AA'}$ as follows.

$$\eta = \{N_{A'} + 1, ID_c\}_{K_{AA'}}$$

$$RT_{AA'} = \{N_{A'} + 1, \eta\}_{K_{AC}}$$

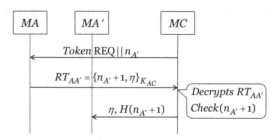

Fig. 3. Handover Authentication Phase

S4.2: MC decrypts the token $RT_{AA'}$ and assures the token to be authentic by checking $N_{A'} + 1$.

Finally, MC sends the request for association along with η and $H(N_{A'} + 1)$ to MA'.

S4.3: MA' decrypts the response and verifies if the obtained hash value matches with that computed and the Identity ID_c. If so MA' assures MC to be authentic.

4.1   Correctness of AKE Protocol

(a) *Equality of* γ_a *and* γ_c:

$$\gamma_a = \beta_c^{N_a} \bmod n = (g^{N_c})^{N_a} \bmod n$$
$$= (g^{N_a})^{N_c} \bmod n = \beta_a^{N_c} \bmod n = \gamma_c.$$

$$(12)$$

(b) *Verification of* ID_c *at* MA:

$$\alpha_c{}^e = (S_c^{N_c+h})^e \bmod n$$
$$= (g^{g_c \cdot d})^{(N_c+h) \cdot e} \bmod n$$
$$= g^{(N_c+h) \cdot g_c} \bmod n$$
$$= (g^{N_c})^{g_c} \cdot g^{h \cdot g_c} \bmod n$$
$$= \beta_c^{g_c} \cdot g^{h \cdot g_c}.$$

$$(13)$$

(c) *Verification of* ID_a *at* MC:

$$\alpha_a{}^e = (S_a^{N_a+h})^e \bmod n$$
$$= (g^{g_a \cdot d})^{(N_a+h) \cdot e} \bmod n$$
$$= g^{(N_a+h) \cdot g_a} \bmod n$$
$$= (g^{N_a})^{g_a} \cdot g^{h \cdot g_a} \bmod n$$
$$= \beta_a^{g_a} \cdot g^{h \cdot g_a}.$$

(d) *Equality of PSKs (K_{AC} and K_{CA}):*

$$
\begin{aligned}
K_{AC} &= \alpha_c^{(e \cdot N_a \cdot g_a)} \cdot \beta_c^{(h \cdot g_a \cdot g_c)} \bmod n \\
&= S_c^{(N_c+h) \cdot (e \cdot N_a \cdot g_a)} \cdot g^{N_c \cdot (h \cdot g_a \cdot g_c)} \bmod n \\
&= g^{g_c \cdot d \cdot (N_c+h) \cdot (e \cdot N_a \cdot g_a)} \cdot g^{N_c \cdot (h \cdot g_a \cdot g_c)} \bmod n \\
&= g^{g_c \cdot (N_c+h) \cdot N_a \cdot g_a} \cdot g^{N_c \cdot (h \cdot g_a \cdot g_c)} \bmod n \\
&= g^{g_c \cdot N_c \cdot N_a \cdot g_a} \cdot g^{g_c \cdot h \cdot N_a \cdot g_a} \cdot g^{N_c \cdot h \cdot g_a \cdot g_c} \bmod n
\end{aligned}
$$

$$(14)$$

Similarly,

$$
\begin{aligned}
K_{CA} &= \alpha_a^{(e \cdot N_c \cdot g_c)} \cdot \beta_a^{(h \cdot g_a \cdot g_c)} \bmod n \\
&= S_a^{(N_a+h) \cdot (e \cdot N_c \cdot g_c)} \cdot g^{N_a \cdot (h \cdot g_a \cdot g_c)} \bmod n \\
&= g^{g_a \cdot d \cdot (N_a+h) \cdot (e \cdot N_c \cdot g_c)} \cdot g^{N_a \cdot (h \cdot g_a \cdot g_c)} \bmod n \\
&= g^{g_a \cdot (N_a+h) \cdot N_c \cdot g_c} \cdot g^{N_a \cdot (h \cdot g_a \cdot g_c)} \bmod n \\
&= g^{g_a \cdot N_a \cdot N_c \cdot g_c} \cdot g^{g_a \cdot h \cdot N_c \cdot g_c} \cdot g^{N_a \cdot h \cdot g_a \cdot g_c} \bmod n
\end{aligned}
$$

$$(15)$$

From equations (14) and (15), $K_{AC} = K_{CA}$.

5   Evaluation of *WAKE*

In this section we evaluate the proposed scheme *WAKE* in terms of both security and performance features.

5.1   Security Features

- *Non trivially Secure:* The key establishment scheme is said to be non trivially secure if, it results a shared secret when run by the two parties and no third party can generate the same shared secret. As verified in the earlier section that both MC and MA compute the same PSK and there after same PMK can be computed.
  On the other hand, no other party can compute the same PSK due to the computational Diffie-Hellman problem, without knowing N_c and N_a.
- *Mutual Authentication:* Both the MC and MA verifies the legitimacy of the other party respectively during Steps *S3.4 and S3.3*.
- *Full Forward Secrecy:* A key establishment protocol is said to provide full forward secrecy, if the compromised session key does not result in previously established session keys. In the proposed scheme no further session key can be computed from the compromised previous session key due to the one way property of hash function and discrete logarithm. Also, if the secret S_x is leaked, no one can determine the previous session key because of lack of the random numbers N_a and N_c.

- *Physical capture:* Physical capturing is a serious threat, in which an adversary captures one station and extracts the secret information stored on it to compromise the other nodes in the networks. In *WSA-AKA* the mesh point MC holds only its pairwise master key and pairwise shared keys. So compromising of MC could become a threat for the communication between MC and its neighbors, but it does not effect to the other secure channels of the networks.
- *Man-in-the-Middle (MIM) Attack:* WSA provides mutual authentication and therefore, resistant against MIM attacks. Moreover, the use of secret (S_c and S_a) in equations (8 and 6) makes the message forgery infeasible.
- *Denial of Services Attack:* An attacker attempts for a DoS attack, by flooding a large amount of 'request for joining (start authentication)' message into the network, the genuineness of client is verified at the MR. A genuine MC can prove his credential to any MR (acts as a MA) of the network. Thus WAKE is DoS resistant.
- *Replay Attack:* The nonces N_c, N_a are used to withstand against replay attacks. We assume that the length of these nonce are 128- bit, so that the probability of the same nonce in two consecutive authentication could be 2^{-128}. Moreover N_c is invalidated after a small time.
- *Known Session Key Attack:* Since the ephemeral parameters N_a, N_c in each PSK are random and independent, therefore, knowing previous PSK does not help in deriving the current PSK.

5.2   Performance Evaluation

Authentication delay is the most important parameter in a network security architecture for quality of services. Authentication delay is the time period between the instant the MC gives its credential and receives the authentication success reply. Thus

$$T_{auth\_delay} = T_{comm} + T_{comp}. \tag{16}$$

Where, T_{comm}, T_{comp} respectively denotes for delay arise due to communication overhead and computation overhead, during authentication.

- *Communication overhead:* The communication latency in WSA-AKA phase arises from the authentication message exchange between MA and MC, is a 3-way handshake. Our mechanism needs about 4160-bits of communication overheads due to both the ends during their execution, assuming that T_{exp_x} is of 32-bits while, α_x, β_x are of 1024-bits. This requires extra 0.0735 ms if the wireless network supports 54Mbps as per 802.11g standard.
- *Computation Overhead:* It is required to put lesser computational burden into the authenticator (MA) to withstand against the attacker attempts to drain energy from MA making it computation burden. Therefore, WSA does not use any complex pairing based cryptographic operations. In WSA-AKA, MA needs only to compute 5 modular exponentiation and two hash operation to authenticate an MC.

6   Conclusion

We proposed an efficient authentication and key establishment mechanism named *WAKE*, tailored to WMN for providing access control. WAKE does neither use certificate based public key cryptography nor the on-line TTP server to authenticate mesh clients. Moreover, no MR forwards any packet without authenticating them, therefore DoS attcks are avoided. We are working on formal security analysis and to expand the scheme for implementing in a real network.

References

1. Akyildiz, I.F., Wang, X., Wang, W.: Wireless Mesh Networks: A Survey. Computer Networks and ISDN Systems 47(4), 445–487 (2005)
2. Boudguiga, A., Laurent, M.: An ID-based Authentication Scheme For the IEEE 802.11s Mesh Network. In: IEEE 6th International Conference on Wireless and Mobile Computing, Networking and Communications, pp. 256–263 (2010)
3. Glass, S., Portmann, M., Muthukkumarasamy, V.: Securing Wireless Mesh Networks. IEEE Internet Computing, 30–36 (2008)
4. He, B., Joshi, S., Agrawal, D., Sun, D.: An efficient authenticated key establishment scheme for wireless mesh networks. In: 2010 IEEE Global Telecommunications Conference (GLOBECOM 2010), pp. 1–5 (2010)
5. Kohl, J.T., Neuman, B.C.: The Kerberos Network Authentication Service (Version 5). Technical report, IETF Network Working Group, Internet Request for Comments RFC-1510 (1993)
6. Lee, I., Lee, J., Arbaugh, W., Kim, D.: Dynamic Distributed Authentication Scheme for Wireless LAN-Based Mesh Networks. In: Vazão, T., Freire, M.M., Chong, I. (eds.) ICOIN 2007. LNCS, vol. 5200, pp. 649–658. Springer, Heidelberg (2008)
7. Martignon, F., Paris, S., Capone, A.: MobiSEC: A novel security architecture for wireless mesh networks. In: 4th ACM Symposium on QoS and Security for Wireless and Mobile Networks, pp. 35–42 (2008)
8. IEEE Draft Amendment to Standard for Information Technology Telecommunications and Information Exchange Between Systems - LAN/MAN Specific Requirements - Part 11: Wireless Medium Access Control (MAC) and physical layer (PHY) specifications: Amendment: ESS Mesh Networking(S), IEEE P802.11s (March 2007)
9. IEEE Draft Amendment to Standard for Information Technology Telecommunications and Information Exchange Between Systems -LAN/MAN Specific Requirements - Part 11: Wireless Medium Access Control (MAC) and physical layer (PHY) specifications: Amendment: 10 Mesh Networking(S), IEEE P802.11s/D5.0 (April 2010)
10. IEEE Standard 802.11i-2004: Standard for Information Technology - Telecommunication and Information Exchange between Systems - Local and Metropolitan Area Networks-Specific Requirements (July 2004)
11. Shamir, A.: Identity-Based Cryptosystems and Signature Schemes. In: Blakely, G.R., Chaum, D. (eds.) CRYPTO 1984. LNCS, vol. 196, pp. 47–53. Springer, Heidelberg (1985)

12. Harkins, D.: Simultaneous Authentication of Equals: A Secure, Password-Based Key Exchange for Mesh Networks. In: Proc. of Sensorcomm 2008, pp. 839–844 (2008)
13. Internet Engineering Task Force, The TLS protocol version 1.2 RFC5246, http://tools.ietf.org/html/rfc5246
14. Zhang, Y., Fang, Y.: ARSA: An Attack-Resilient Security Architecture for Multihop Wireless Mesh Networks. IEEE Journal on Selected Areas in Communications 24(10), 1916–1928 (2006)
15. Zhu, X., Fang, Y., Wang, Y.: How to secure multi-domain wireless mesh networks. Wireless Networks 16, 1215–1222 (2010)
16. Zhu, H., Lin, X., Lu, R., Ho, P.-H., Shen, X.(S.): Slab: Secure localized authentication and billing scheme for wireless mesh networks. IEEE Trans. Wireless Communication, 3858–3868 (2008)
17. Li, C., Nguyen, U.T.: Fast Authentication for Mobility Support in Wireless Mesh Networks. In: 2011 IEEE Wireless Communications and Networking Conference, WCNC, pp. 1185–1190 (2011)

Effective Implementation of DES Algorithm
for Voice Scrambling

Jinu Elizabeth John[1], A.S. Remya Ajai[1], and Prabaharan Poornachandran[2]

[1] Department of ECE, Amrita Vishwavidyapeetham, India
[2] Center for Cyber Security, Amrita Vishwavidyapeetham, India
{amritianjinu,remya.amrita}@gmail.com, praba@amrita.edu

Abstract. This paper presents a high performance reconfigurable hardware implementation of speech scrambling–descrambling system which can be used for military and high security environments. The scrambling algorithm is based on DES algorithm with a novel skew core key scheduling. The scrambled speech signal is not intelligible to the listener, but the recovered audio is very clear. This type of encryption can be used in applications where we need to discourage eavesdropping from co-channel users or RF scanners. The DES design is implemented on Virtex 5 XC5VLX110T Field Programming Gate Arrays (FPGA) technology. Final 16-stage pipelined design is achieved with encryption rate of 35.5 Gbit/s and 2140 number of Configurable logic blocks (CLBs).

Keywords: Scrambling, Skew core, Key scheduling, Pipelining.

1   Introduction

Speech or man's spoken word is the most fundamental form of communication. If highly confidential information is being discussed among the communicators, they must use some form of scrambling device to make the transmitted signal unintelligible to an unauthorized interceptor. Voice Scramblers are the most inevitable module in secure speech transmission as they serve as a powerful measure against eavesdropping and are needed to ensure privacy in speech transmission in radio communication, telephone networks and in emerging cellular mobile radio systems. In a typical speech scrambler , the clear speech is digitized and the digital sequence is scrambled into an unintelligible signal in order to avoid eavesdropping.The scrambled sequence is converted back to analog form for transmission.The microphone audio is recorded by the scrambling module for a required time slot.The recorded slot is then subdivided into smaller blocks of 64 bit. A 64 bit novel DES encryption algorithm is used to rearrange blocks within each segment .For transmission the rearranged blocks are played back. The use of different keys in every clock cycle, make the scrambled voice seem unintelligible and very tough to break making time slot based voice scrambling suitable for the most sensitive strategic communications.

S.M. Thampi et al. (Eds.): SNDS 2012, CCIS 335, pp. 75–84, 2012.

The scrambling is based on a 16 –stage pipelined DES algorithm with a novel skew core key scheduling. It allows simultaneous processing of 16 data blocks, resulting in an impressing gain in speed. This the overall security of the speech scrambling improved since it uses different keys every clock cycle and therefore the users are not restricted to the use of same key at any time of data transfer.This design is implemented on Virtex 5 FPGA.

2   Voice Security Systems

In voice scrambling systems, the recorded voice is modified by a known scrambling algorithm so as to make the scrambled voice unintelligible does not convey any information of the original signal. This voice scrambling algorithm is governed by a specific code or "key".Different scrambled signals can be obtained if different keys are used. The voice that is thus scrambled is transmitted. At the receiver the scrambled signal is again modified by a descrambling algorithm under the control of a specific key. This ultimately results in a voice, which resembles the original voice exactly. In a correctly operating system, the Scrambling Key and Descrambling Key are identical, and the descrambling algorithm is the inverse of the scrambling algorithm. Therefore, whatever the scrambling algorithm does, the descrambling algorithm undoes. If the Scrambling Key and Descrambling Key are different, then the descrambling algorithm will not recover the original signal properly. This paper uses a pipelined DES algorithm with a novel key scheduling to scramble communications.

Fig. 1. Voice Security System

3   Background

In this project the scrambling and descrambling is done by means of DES algorithm. The data encryption standard (DES) is the best known and most widely used private key encryption algorithm developed by IBM in 1977 as a modification of an earlier system known as Lucifer[1].The overall scheme of DES algorithm is illustrated in Fig.2.DES is a Feistel cipher which operates on two inputs: the 64 bit plain text to be encrypted and 56-bit secret key. Precisely, the input key is specified as 64 bits, 8 bits of which is used for parity checking. With a key length of 56 bits 2^56 combinations

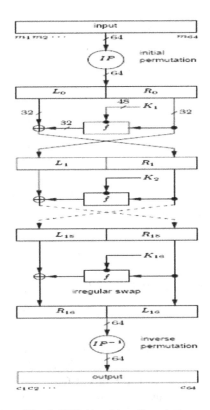

Fig. 2. DES Algorithm Description

are possible, and therefore the cryptanalytic works seem very tough. The encryption proceeds in 16 stages or rounds. From the input key K, sixteen 48-bit sub keys K_i are generated, one for each round[1]. Within each round, 8 fixed, carefully selected 6-to-4 bit substitution mappings (S-boxes) S_i, collectively denoted S, are used. The 64-bit plaintext is divided into 32-bit halves L0 and R0. Each round is functionally equivalent, taking 32-bit inputs L_i-1 and R_i-1 from the previous round and producing 32-bit outputs L_i and R_i for $1 \leq i \leq 16$

3.1   f Function

The f function of DES algorithm is made up of four functions: Expansion, Xor , Substitution, Permutation. The right half of each round carries out a key-dependent substitution on each of 8 characters, then uses a fixed bit transposition to redistribute the bits of the resulting characters to produce 32 output bits.

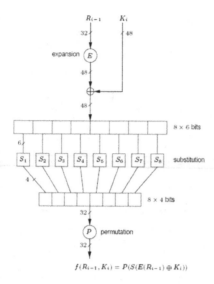

$$f(R_{i-1}, K_i) = P(S(E(R_{i-1}) \oplus K_i))$$

Fig. 3. f Box

3.2   Key Scheduling

In DES algorithm 16 different sub keys each of 48 bit wide is developed from a single 56 bit key. These operations make use of tables PC1 and PC2 which are permuted choice 1 and permuted choice 2 [6].The 8 bits of 64 bits is discarded by PC1 . The remaining 56 bits are permuted and assigned to two 28-bit variables C and D; and then a cyclic shift operation is carried out on each half. That is, for 16 iterations, both C and D are rotated either 1 or 2 bits, and 48 bits (K_i) are selected from the concatenated result. This process is repeated for each stage of 16 stage pipeline. In rounds, 1, 2, 9 and 16 of DES algorithm the halves are shifted one position to left and for all other rounds it is shifted to left by two positions.

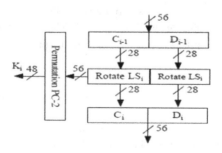

Fig. 4. Key Scheduling

3.3   Pipelined Implementation

The ECB mode of DES algorithm is implemented in this paper as it can be easily pipelined[8].This pipelined DES design increases the speed and throughput of DES significantly[6]. If a combinational digital circuit can be divided into stages, we can insert buffers (registers) at proper places and convert the circuit into a pipelined design [2]. Adding pipeline into a combinational design can only increase a system's throughput. Such an approach does not reduce the delay in an individual task. Actually, because of the overhead introduced by the registers and non-ideal stage division, the delay will be worse than that of the non-pipelined design [2].

3.4   Skew Core Implementation of DES

For the 16-stage pipelined DES design, the sub keys are precomputed and it is necessary to control the time at which the sub keys are available to each function f block[6]. This is accomplished by addition of an array of D flip flops that delays the individual sub-keys by required amount[6,9].

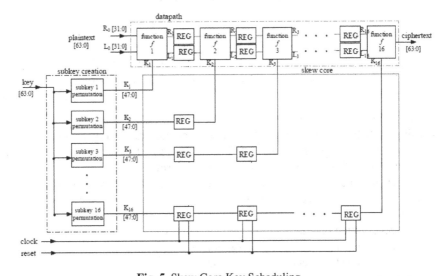

Fig. 5. Skew Core Key Scheduling

4   Speech Scrambling and Descrambling Principles

Speech scrambler described in this paper actually digitizes the conversation at telephone and applies a cryptographic technique to the resulting bit stream. The original voice signal, m, is first digitized to another sequence of bits, m(k).This m(k) is then digitally scrambled into a different sequence of bits, y(k) by a novel implementation of pipelined DES, and finally converted to analog and transmitted. The digital scrambling techniques offer very high degree of security. This type of technique can be used in existing analog telephone systems, since the scrambled signal is analog, with similar bandwidth and characteristics to the original speech signal.The scrambling and descrambling devices must process exactlly the same block of bits. The scrambling technique presented in this paper offers high speed and throughput alongside improved levels of security.

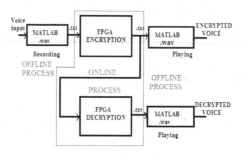

Fig. 6. Voice Scrambling-Descrambling

4.1   Offline Process

The offline simulation process does not include any hardware implementation but is used for self-testing of decryption/encryption algorithm. The following steps were required:

☐ In the recording process, first a voice source input is taken. Then, the voice input is read using Matlab, as a wave (.wav) file. The voice duration and its bit rate were the parameters that were given during creation of the .wav file. Matlab codes for the conversion of voice(.wav file) to text (.txt) file was written .
☐ Just after text file creation, a test bench in Verilog HDL is written read the voice text file character-by-character as a block of 64 bit each and then these values were mapped for the
decryption/encryption operation.
☐ After performing the encryption/decryption operation, a test bench again created, but this one contains the encrypted form of the original voice that is recorded.
☐ Then, Matlab code is written again to read the encrypted version of the text file and it is played at the previously specified bit rate.

4.2   Online Process

Both the hardware and software implementation are included in the online process.Verilog HDL code written at the voice scrambling end performs mainly two functions:

☐ The voice input is scrambled using a cryptographic algorithm.

☐ The encrypted values are displayed to the world outside

Verilog HDL code written at the voice descrambling end performs mainly two functions:

☐ Descrambling using a decryption algorithm; and

☐ Digital-to-analog conversion and the decrypted values are sent to the outside world.

This is a real-time process. Input comes continuously from a microphone and is given to the Virtex 5 FPGA after digitizing it. The symmetric-key cryptography for scrambling because here the same code can be used for both scrambling and descrambling. Symmetric key cryptography means both sender and recipient uses the same key. The same key is used at the sender and receiver side . The algorithm used for descrambling is the reverse of the scrambling algorithm.The only thing is that the key must be kept secret. A novel implementation of DES (Data Encryption Standard) with skew core scheduling is used here.

5   Implementation Result

FPGA implementation of DES algorithm was accomplished on Virtex 5 FPGA,Xilinx as synthesis tool and Modelsim 6.2c as simulation tool. The design was coded using Verilog HDL language.It occupied 2140 (45%) CLB slices, 1808 (19%) slice Flip Flops and 187 (80%) I/Os. It takes 16 clock cycles latency first time only then encrypts one data block (64-bits) per clock cycle. Therefore, the achieved throughput is 35.5 Gbits/s. Full design schematic and simulation window are shown.

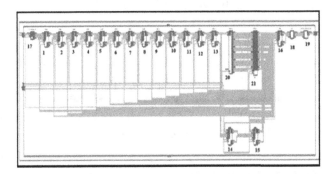

Fig. 7. Full DES design schematic generated by Xilinx ISE tool

BLOCKS:1 to 16 (Round Function),17(Initial Permutation),18(Swap),19(Inverse initial Permutation),20(Key Top),21(Skew Core)

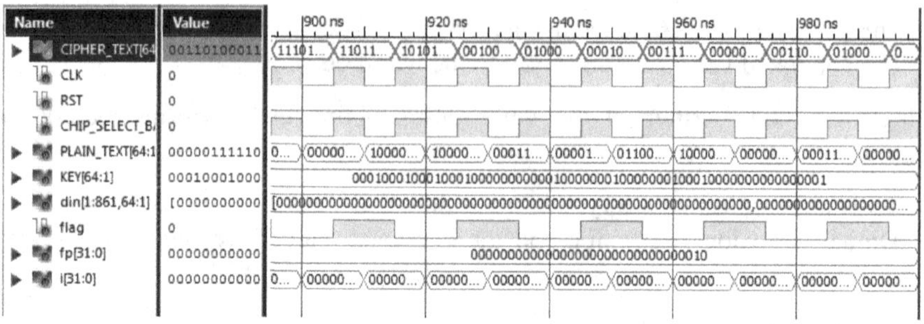

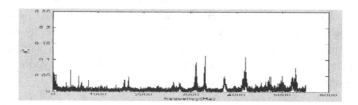

Fig. 8. Simulation Window of DES design

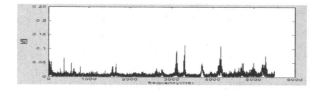

Fig. 9. Original Speech Signal

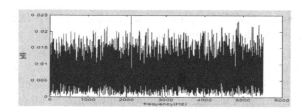

Fig. 10. Encrypted Speech Signal

Fig. 11. Decrypted Speech Signal Output

6   Performance Comparison

The fastest DES software implementation achieves a throughput of 127 Mbit/s on a 300MHz Alpha 8400 processor[4]. A VLSI implementation of DES on static 0.6 micron CMOS technology at [7] is the fastest implementation of DES reported in the literature. The voice scrambling scheme was implemented in design with skew and also without skew core key scheduling and the device utilization details are shown in

COMPARISON OF SPECIFICATIONS FOR DES HARDWARE AND
SOFTWARE IMPLEMENTATIONS:

DEVICE USED	SYSTEM CLOCK (MHz)	DATA RATE (Giga bits/second)
XC4020E	10	0.0267
Alpha 8400	300	0.127
XC4028EX	25.18	0.4027
XCV400	47.7	3.052
XCV1000(McLoone,McCanny)	59.5	3.808
ASIC	--	9.280
XCV150	168	10.752
*XE3S500E (SPARTAN 3E)	50	3.2
*XC5VLX110T (VIRTEX 5)	550	35.5
*NET FPGA	400	25.58

* AS PER OUR IMPLEMENTATION RESULTS

Fig. 12. Various Implementation Results

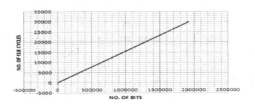

Fig. 13. No. of Bits vs No. of Clock Cycles

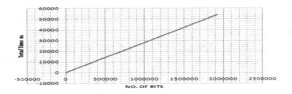

Fig. 14. No. of Bits vs Time

figure. And it is found that pipelined DES has high speed, high data throughput and less CLB utilization. The performance analysis in terms of area ,timing and power was obtained using Synopsys tool.

7   Conclusion

This paper describes a high speed, high throughput voice scrambling system. A 16-stage pipelined novel implementation of DES algorithm design is presented here for scrambling. The input voice is split into blocks of 64 bits and it allows the processing of 16 data blocks simultaneously. Voice data blocks can be loaded every clock cycle and after an initial delay of 16 clock cycles the corresponding encrypted/decrypted voice data blocks will appear on consecutive clock cycles. Different keys can be loaded every clock cycle allowing the possibility of using multiple keys in any one session of data transfer. In general, hardware implementations of encryption algorithms and their associated keys are physically secure, as they cannot easily be modified by an outside attacker. The 16-stage pipelined design can encrypt or decrypt data blocks at a rate of 35.5Gbit/sec.

References

1. Alani, M.M.: DES96-improved DES security. In: 7th International Multi-Conference on Systems Signals and Devices, SSD (2010)
2. Wilcox, D.C., Pierson, L.G., Robertson, P.J., Witzke, E.L., Gass, K.: A DES ASIC Suitable for Network Encryption at 10 Gbps and Beyond. In: Koç, Ç.K., Paar, C. (eds.) CHES 1999. LNCS, vol. 1717, pp. 37–48. Springer, Heidelberg (1999)
3. Patterson, C.: High performance DES encryption in virtex FPGAs using Jbits. In: Proc. IEEE Symp. on Fieldprogrammable Custom Computing Machines, FCCM 2000, Napa Valley, CA, USA, pp. 113–121. IEEE Comput. Soc., CA (2000)
4. Kaps, J.-P., Paar, C.: Fast DES Implementations for FPGAs and Its Application to a Universal Key-Search Machine. In: Tavares, S., Meijer, H. (eds.) SAC 1998. LNCS, vol. 1556, pp. 234–247. Springer, Heidelberg (1999)
5. Free-DES Core (2000), http://www.free-ip.com/DES/
6. McLoone, M., McCanny, J.: High-performance FPGA implementation of DES using a novel method for implementing the key schedule. IEE Proc.: Circuits, Devices & Systems 150, 373–378 (2003)
7. Biham, E.: A Fast New DES Implementation in Software. In: Biham, E. (ed.) FSE 1997. LNCS, vol. 1267, pp. 260–272. Springer, Heidelberg (1997); Van Der Lubbe, J.C.A.: Basic methods of cryptography. Cambridge University Press (1998); In: Proceedings of TENCO 1997. IEEE (December 1997)
8. Patel, V., Joshi, C., Saxena, A.K.: FPGA implementation of DES using pipelining concept with skew core key scheduling. Journal of Theoritical and Applied Information Technology (2005-2009)

Towards Constructing a Trustworthy Internet: Privacy-Aware Transfer of Digital Identity Document in Content Centric Internetworking

Amine Abidi[1], Ghazi Ben Ayed[2], and Farouk Kamoun[3]

[1] CRISTAL Lab, ENSI School of Engineering, University of Manouba, Tunisia
[2] Department of Information Systems, Faculty of Business and Economics,
University of Lausanne, CH-1015, Lausanne, Switzerland
[3] SESAME University, Tunis, Tunisia
amine.elabidi@cristal.rnu.tn, ghazi.benayed@unil.ch,
frk.kamoun@planet.tn

Abstract. Managing digital identity documents with a proper privacy protection is of pivotal importance to construct trustworthy Internet. As far as the amount of digital identities is expanding at an accelerating rate, content-centric model provides administration capabilities of data transfer. We propose an innovative approach and implementation of privacy-aware Content-Centric Internetworking (CCN)-based of federated digital identity. Privacy requirements related to identity are translated with user-centric federated digital identity parlance into a set of eleven rules. CCN has been enforced by respecting a set of rules, designing a data packet and creating an identity contract. We provide an implementation of privacy-aware CCN data packet that is bound to XML-based digital identity document. We explain that the forwarding engine verifies the validity of digital identity document transmission on the basis of identity contract terms. Three use cases are presented to detail the proposed approach with the corresponding UML sequence diagrams.

Keywords: Federated digital identity, content-centric internetworking, privacy contract, data packet.

1 Introduction

Internet is qualified as 'trustworthy' when users depend on and trust it; otherwise the cost of the distrust would be high. Trustworthy Internet promises security, reliability and resilience to attacks and operational failures that fit into mechanisms, architectures and networking infrastructures. In addition to quality of service, protecting user's data, ensuring privacy and providing usable and trusted tools to support users in their security management are guaranteed [1]. Thus, managing digital identity with proper privacy protection is of pivotal importance for creating the necessary trust for the Internet.

Data-centric architecture has proven to be a promising model to accommodate in and drive the Internet of the future. Wired and wireless communication networks are

S.M. Thampi et al. (Eds.): SNDS 2012, CCIS 335, pp. 85–96, 2012.

making data collection and transmission cheap and widespread. Data-centric architecture is a paradigm for creating loosely coupled information-driven systems and designing such architecture is based on separating between data and behavior. Data and data-transfer contracts then become the primary organizing constructs and data changes drive the interactions between system's components. The data bus connects data producers to consumers and enforces data-handling contracts over data transfers [2].

In this article, we aim to deal with the question: how privacy could protect digital identities within data-centric model to construct the Trustworthy Internet? The reminder of the paper is organized as follows. In section 2, we introduce digital identity and privacy and we provide a description of privacy rules related to identity. Such rules are drawn from the translation of privacy requirements related to identity with user-centric federated digital identity technical model foundations. . In section 3, we introduce data centric paradigm and discuss major data centric approaches, while in section 4, we detail the description of the Content Centric Networking (CCN) approach. In section 5, we explain privacy-aware transfer mechanism of digital identities in CCN. Three use cases are presented to detail the approach with the corresponding UML sequence diagrams. We end up this section by providing an implementation of the mechanism. Finally, we conclude in section 6 and highlight future work that can be conducted to enhance the proposed solution.

2   Digital Identity and Privacy

Digital identity becomes an asset and valuable and protecting it becomes one of today's urgent needs. Digitalization is allowing several digital representation of reality, including that of identity. Digital identity is seen as an intersection of identity and technology in the digital age. It has evolved from being a simple assigned identifier to an identifier of a 'profile' that represents a collection of various attributes and entitlements in digital form such as personal characteristics, special interests, favorite activities, and hair color. Attributes could represent context-specific attributes that are assigned to a person by others in the sake of identifying him temporarily within that context and based on some kind of relationship. Driver's license, credit card, health insurance card, library card are examples. Currently, individuals are having greater choice for interaction in different social circles and more possibilities of exercising freedom by maintaining multiple digital identities. Thus having identities distributed over multiple environments brings new security risks [3-5]. We assume that different formats of a digital identity are convertible into XML complaint documents (DigIdDocs).

Privacy is a right and could be adopted as an efficient mean to protect identity in digital world. Privacy becomes more important in today's society in which "for very little cost, anybody can learn anything about anybody", a quote by Robert Ellis Smith, editor of the Washington (DC) newsletter Privacy Journal. Privacy's importance is reflected in the fact that fundamental documents that define human rights all include reference to privacy or related ideas, such as the Universal Declaration of Human

Rights [6] (UDHR, Article 12), the International Covenant on Civil and Political Rights [7] (ICCPR 1966, Article 17), the 1950's European Convention on Human Rights, Article 8 and the 2000's Charter of Fundamental Rights of the European Union, articles 7 and 8 [8]. When identity attributes control and protection is compromised, security of the individual, the organization or the country could be threatened. Thus, giving protection to and control over digital identity could contribute to prevent from identity theft and avoid damages related to it such as unauthorized access, frauds, cyber crimes and cyber terrorism [5].

2.1   Privacy Rules

Technology and technical solutions would never be enough to protect digital identities, laws and organizational policies should be considered. Identity-related privacy requirements are drawn from three types of privacy policies: 1) Global Privacy Policies: CDT's 2007 Privacy Principles for Identity in the Digital Age [9], OECD's 1980 Guidelines on the Protection of Privacy and Transborder Flows of Personal Data [10], OECD's 2008 Data Protection and User Control for Identity Management Systems [11], and (95/46/EC1) European Union Data Protection Directive; 2) Regional Privacy Policies: The United States Privacy Act of 1974, CSA Model Code for the Protection of Personal Information of 1996, the Canadian Personal Information Protection and Electronic Document Act of 2000, the Canadian Privacy Act of 1983, the Japanese Act on the Protection of Personal Information of 2003, and the Australian Privacy Act of 1998 (Private Sector), the Swiss Federal Law on Personal Data Protection (1992), and the French Data Protection and Freedoms Act (DPA); and 3) Domain-Specific Privacy Policies represent industry or domain-specific requirement such as health, finance, education, and transportation sectors. Here, we cover the 1996 Health Insurance Portability and Accountability Act and the 1999 -Bliley Financial Services Modernization Act.

We limit our study only on policies that are related to personal information and digital identity. The outcome of this study is a set of requirements that we consider as a starting point of any identity-related privacy implementation initiatives. The requirements are identified in [12] and they are translated, with basic concepts of user-centric [13]: IdP (Identity Provider), SP (Service Provider), Subject, and Circle-of-Trust (CoT) into a set of eleven rules: 1) when identity attributes are needed either for creating credentials or for providing a specific service, both IdP and SP should specify and clearly articulate the purpose for which identity information will be collected and used; 2) identity attributes collection should be in the restriction and consistency with the purpose. The amount, sensitivity and type of identity attributes that are collected from the subject should be proportional to the collection's purpose; 3) SP and IdP should use identity attributes solely for the specified purpose(s). Secondary use, sharing, and sale of identity attributes should be permitted only when necessary and within the purpose of collection's; 4) identity attributes, identity aggregation, and identity linkage should be used, shared and stored by SPs only until the fulfillment of the initial identity collection's purpose; 5) SPs and IdPs should be transparent by notifying subjects and, to the extent possible, seeking the subject's consent regarding collection, use, disclosure, and maintenance of identity attributes; 6) subjects should also be able to challenge gathered identity conclusion that SP draw from digital identity aggregation. Indeed, the subject could negotiate the accuracy, credibility, correctness, and reliability of the SP's in-hold conclusion; 7) subjects should be allowed to have an easy identity access, edition, and update; 8) subjects should have a reasonable, granular control and choice over which identity attributes are necessary to successfully enroll, authenticate or use of either identity or linked information; 9) IdP should, insofar as possible, ensure that identity attributes are accurate, relevant, up-to-date, secure and complete; 10) subject's enrollment or authentication should be with different identities for different purposes. Subjects should be allowed to choose the appropriate enrollment/authentication mean to satisfy a specific need; and 11) identity attributes should be protected by both IdP and SP through appropriate security safeguards against risks such as loss, unauthorized access or use, destruction, modification, or unintended or inappropriate disclosure. IdP and SP have to be accountable for complying with security policies.

3   Data-Centric Internetworking

In contrast to the application-centric paradigm, which is no longer fully up to the task of implementing the ubiquitous and pervasive computing, data-centric model becomes a crucial computing need as far as data is driving everything [14]. In this section, we present a literature review of Data Centric Internetworking basic concepts and its different approaches: DONA, PSIRP, NetInf, DHT based solutions, and CCN.

3.1   Data Centric Paradigm

In recent years, the use of the internet has changed from machine interconnection to data or service oriented communication. This new purpose has increased the number of Internet users and the variety of applications leading to the emergence of many limitations in term of mobility, security, routing and content delivery scalability. To overcome these problems, new infrastructure propositions are mostly data centric. They change radically the internetworking concept from simple host to host communication to data delivery. This new vision has made data or services a "first class citizen". That's why any new infrastructure proposition is made around data manipulation [15-18].

The current Internet communication model is based on IP number usage to identify hosts (naming) and to find their location (routing). Thus, after locating the data provider, data exchange will be processed. This communication model has made difficult the overcoming of the challenges related to Internet's limitations. In addition, most of the proposed solutions are presented as an external add-ins to the Internet rather than enhancing the TCP/IP architecture itself. IP address is no longer a key identifier; however, every piece of data is identified by a unique key, called a content name. New data delivery mechanism is based on two elements: 1) data naming is the content name attribution process; and 2) name resolution is a locating process to find the appropriate host that holds a valid copy of the requested data [15-18]. Below, we present the different data centric internetworking approaches

3.2   Overview of Data Centric Approaches

DONA. Data Oriented and Beyond Network Architecture [19] is a hierarchical approach for data centric internetworking. It's based on hierarchically organized routers called Resolution Handlers (RH) and two primitives REGISTER and FIND. For the data naming process, DONA uses cryptographic names. Any data provider has its own public-private key pair which is used to generate data names. Names are of the form (P: L) where P is the cryptographic hash of the principal public key and L is the label generated to name the data. The cryptographic feature guaranties both uniqueness and authenticity of names. Unfortunately, the built names are still not understandable by users. The resolution mechanism uses the two primitives.   As illustrated in figure 1, data providers forward the REGISTER request to announce their position and to register in the RH the owned data. The request will be forwarded through the hierarchy and every RH that receives this request tracks data name and location and forwards the request to the next level. Seeking the desired data, the client sends FIND request to the nearest RH which will forward it through the network until reaching the data location [19].

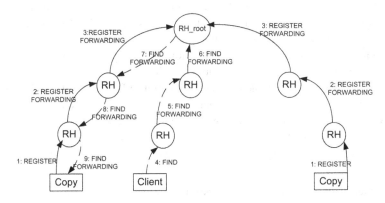

Fig. 1. DONA name resolution approach

PSIRP. Publish Subscribe Internet Routing Paradigm is a mechanism that is based on temporal and spatial decoupling of the relation between data source (the publisher) and the client (subscriber). Client request and data forwarding are no longer related. As a consequence, a data provider can share data in the rendezvous points before any client who expresses interest to acquire data. PSIRP name resolution, figure 2, is reduced to a search request sent by the client to any known rendezvous point, which communicates with other peers to locate the requested data [20].

NetInf. The Network of Information project [21] is an attempt to adapt actual Internet to the data centric paradigm. Each data provider registers owned data in a Name Resolution Service (NRS). Resolution mechanism is the same as the one of the Internet since NRS plays the same role as a domain name system (DNS). When a client needs data, its request is routed through NRS system until it reaches data registrar. Data requestor gets back location information by which, he will be able to contact the data provider.

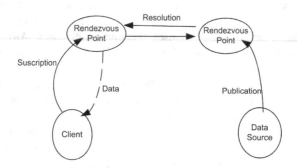

Fig. 2. Rendezvous point-based name resolution approach

DHT-Based Solutions. Distributed Hash Table based systems have been successfully used and made their big name in P2P networks. For this reason, researchers have introduced these solutions in the data centric internetworking. DHT are decentralized, highly scalable, and self-organized. Without any need of administrative entities, nodes are cooperating to guarantee name resolution. The key property is an ordered namespace that is used to identify in the same time: nodes and data entities. Each node maintains a local hash table and stores location information about data having identifier's values lower than its own one. So, when trying to resolve a data name, nodes will forward the request to the node having the closest identifier's value compared to the requested data one. We should note that any request is solved at most in (LogN) steps, where N is the number of nodes [22].

CCN. Content Centric Networking is one of the recent projects on the data centric internetworking field. It gives new naming and resolution mechanisms. CCN names are built hierarchically from specified components. The name is composed from at least: a globally routable name and organizational name. In opposition to DONA's flat names which are considered incomprehensible and complex, hierarchical CCN names are more suitable for data retrieval and the resolution process [23]. CCN relies on two packets, as shown in figure 3, to perform name resolution and data delivery: 1) interest packet is broadcasted by a consumer over all the possible and available connectivity to express his interest in a specific content; and 2) data packet responds to requests [23].

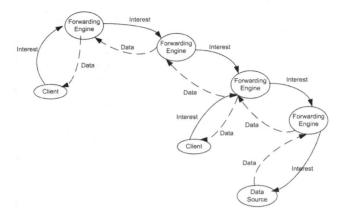

Fig. 3. CCN communication model

4   Digital Identity Data Packet within CCN

We choose a content centric internetworking infrastructure because it improves the availability of data and it simplifies ensuring the integrity of content. More details about CCN adoption motivations and implementation of federated digital identity in CCN are already presented in [24].

4.1   CCN and Privacy: Related Work

Few ongoing research efforts are undertaken in privacy within CCN such as [25], in which the authors propose a technical approach in order to hide user's content requests in CCN. We believe that tackling privacy issues over CCN must be within a multi-disciplinary approach, which dictates that privacy issues should be resolved and to be seen from multiple perspectives such as user's needs, policies, laws, and business-specific requirements. Here, we consider privacy as a set of rules that should be drawn from laws and policies as presented in section 2.1. Privacy is more than insuring un-linkability, confidentiality or anonymity. In opposition to earlier work [24] where we implemented 'expiration date' in CCN DigIdDoc Packet in order to provide more user's control over digital identity documents; in this article, we propose to implement privacy rules in a federated digital identity conversation between subject, SP, and IdP within a CoT. Narrowly, we propose the inclusion of the 'privacy contract', which will be detailed in section 4.2.

4.2   DigIdData Packet

In a previous work [24], we introduced two fields: 1) content type refers to the multiple types of data that CCN infrastructure could support; and 2) expiration date.

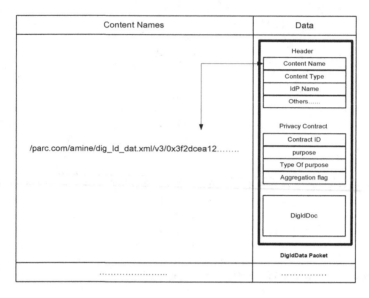

Fig. 4. CCN Content store and DigIdData packet

Here, as in figure 4, the later filed is changed with a new field: the IdPname, which refers to the Identity Provider that stores privacy contract.

The privacy contract section has been introduced in DigIdData Packet to include privacy attributes in response to privacy rules: 1) the contract Id is used to identify privacy contract; 2) the purpose describes which purpose identity information are either collected, disclosed, transmitted to a secondary party, or processed. These alternatives represent the 3) type of purpose; and 4) the aggregation flag indicates whether these identity information can be subject to aggregation process.

5   DigIdData Packet for Privacy-Aware CCN

In figure 5, 6, and 7, we present and explain the collaboration between participants over CCN core. Three use cases are considered in order to fully explain the mechanism of privacy-aware transfer of DigIdDocs over CCN.

5.1   Enrollment Use Case

In figure 5, the subject asks IdP(s) to enroll then IdP in its turn asks for DigIdDoc. The subject conveys to IdP DigIdDoc coupled with DigIdContract. IdP saves the information and sends back an enrollment confirmation bounded with IdPname.

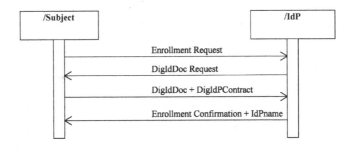

Fig. 5. Enrollment Sequence Diagram.

5.2   Service Request Use Case

In figure 6, we present and explain that subject sends a service request to SP, which sends back DigIdDoc Request.

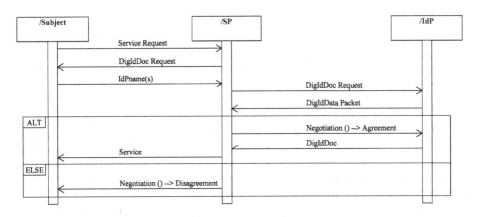

Fig. 6. Sequence Diagram of Service Request

The subject sends IdP(s) identifiers to SP through which it locates the associated IdP(s). SP sends DigIdDoc request to IdP, which sends back DigIdData packet that comprises the privacy contract. Either the SP agrees or initiates a negotiation process until reaching an agreement then the IdP(s) release(s) DigIdDoc to SP; or SP does not agree and after a negotiation, a disagreement is not resolved, the SP does not receive DigIdDoc and therefore no service is send to the subject.

5.3   Privacy-Aware DigIdDoc Transfer Use Case

Any party, which means an SP, official authority, or opportunistic SP, could contact another SP to request DigIdDoc. SP sends DigIdDoc and DigIdData packet through forwarding engine to a specific IdP requesting a verification. IdPname provides

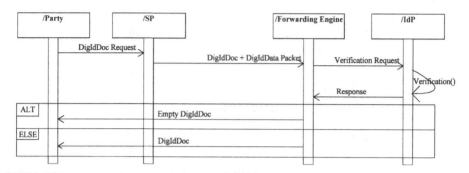

Fig. 7. Privacy-aware DigIdDoc Transfer Sequence Diagram

details of recipient IdP. IdP proceeds to a verification and provides the response. If privacy contract does not permit DigIdDoc transfer, an empty document is sent back to the party; otherwise the DigIdDoc is sent, as in figure 7.

5.4   Implementation of Privacy-Aware CCN

The implementation of the stop dissemination mechanism is integrated in the open source code of the CCN project [26]. The implementation consists of two steps: 1) updating content object packet header; and 2) introducing DigIdDoc's contract verification functions.

Header Update. The CCN core uses *enum ccn_content_type* enumeration to define a list of content type. We propose to add a new pair (alias, value): *CCN_CONTENT_DIGIDDOC = 0x34008B* in order to refer to DigIdDoc type. We add two new Offset Ids to identify the contract Id in the enumeration *enum ccn_parsed_content_object_offsetid*:   *CCN_PCO_B_Contract_ID*   and *CCN_PCO_E_Contract_ID* In fact, such enumeration is used to delimit different fields in the content packet structure. The beginning Offset Id is marked with "_B_" and the ending one with "_E_". The two offsets define the position and the size of the content packet field in the content's buffer.

```
enum ccn_content_type {CCN_CONTENT_DATA = 0x0C04C0, …
CCN_CONTENT_DIGIDDOC = 0x34008B};

enum ccn_parsed_content_object_offsetid {
CCN_PCO_B_Signature, CCN_PCO_B_DigestAlgorithm, … ,
CCN_PCO_B_Contract_ID, CCN_PCO_E_Contract_ID, CCN_PCO_E};
```

DigIdDoc_Verification Functions. The CCN forwarding engine validates DigIdDocs transmission between SPs based Identity contract verification, which is generated by an IdP. The contract verification function is lunched if any DigIdData packet is received by the engine. As mentioned in the following C codes, the IdPname verification request will be sent to the appropriate IdP.

```
Void DigIdDoc_verification (Contentpacket Dig_packet) {
      String IdPname=Get_IdPname_function (Dig_packet);
      Send (IdPname) ;}
```

After receiving the IdP response, the forwarding engine decides whether the DigIdDoc transmission is valid or not and it will react by invoking the following function.

```
Void IdP_response_process(String IdP_Response) {
If (IdP_response=="valid") then
      Perform_DigIdDoc_transmission();
  Else
      Send_Empty_DigIdDoc();}
```

6 Conclusion and Outlooks

Digital identity protection becomes one of the key tracks to be studied in Web Science. Nigel Shadbolt and Tim Berners-Lee [27] explain, in their own words that "studying the Web will reveal better ways to exploit information, prevent identity theft, revolutionize industry and manage our ever growing online lives". Technology and technical solutions would never be enough to protect DigIdDoc. A multi-disciplinary approach is adopted in order to figure out privacy rules. Data-centric architecture is a paradigm for creating loosely coupled information-driven systems. So, In this paper, we presented an innovative approach to enforce privacy over DigIdDoc transfer within CCN. The forwarding engine checks privacy conformity of the DigIdDoc to-be transmitted. It verifies privacy contract and notifies noncompliance to any of its terms. In the near future, we intend to look in, more details about the negotiation process between SP and IdP; and at what level an agreement or disagreement should be set?

References

1. Blefari-Melazzi, N., et al. (eds.): Trustworthy Internet (2011)
2. Joshi, R.: Data-Centric Architecture: A Model for the Era of Big Data (2011)
3. Palfrey, J., Gasser, U.: Born Digital: Understanding the first generation of digital natives. Basic Books (2008)
4. Benantar, M.: Access Control Systems: Security, Identity Management and Trust Models. Springer Science + Business Media (2006)
5. Ben Ayed, G., Sifi, S., Becha Kaanich, M.: Towards Building Weak Links between Persistent Digital Identity Documents: MetaEngine and Distance to Make Identity Less Visible. In: Ariwa, E., El-Qawasmeh, E. (eds.) DEIS 2011. CCIS, vol. 194, pp. 676–690. Springer, Heidelberg (2011)
6. U. Nations. The Universal Declaration of Human Rights (1948)
7. The Office of the United Nations High Commissioner for Human Rights. International Covenant on Civil and Political Rights (1966)

8. European Union. The Charter of Fundamental Rights of the European Union (2000)
9. Center for Democracy & Technology. Privacy Principles for Identity in the Digital Age (2007)
10. Organization for Economic Co-operation and Development (OECD). Guidelines on the Protection of Privacy and Transborder Flows of Personal Data (1980)
11. Organization for Economic Co-operation and Development (OECD). At Crossroads: Personhood and Digital Identity in the Information Society. The Working Paper series of the OECD Directorate for Science, Technology and Industry (2008)
12. Ben Ayed, G., Ghernaouti-Hélie, S.: Privacy Requirements Specification for Digital Identity Management Systems Implementation: Towards a digital society of privacy. In: 6th International Conference for Internet Technology and Secured Transactions, ICITST 2011, Abu Dhabi, UAE (2011)
13. Organisation for Economic Co-operation and Development. The Role of Digital Identity Management in the Internet Economy: A primer for policy makers (2009)
14. Norfolk, D.: The Data-Centric World, ed: Bloor (2011)
15. Meyer, D., et al.: Report from the IAB Workshop on Routing and Addressing (RFC 4984) (2007)
16. Clark, D., et al.: Addressing Reality: An architectural response to real world demands on the evolving internet. In: ACM SIGCOMM Conference - Workshop on Future Directions in Network Architecture, FDNA 2003, Germany (2003)
17. Handley, M., Greenhalgh, A.: Steps Towards a Dos-Resistant Internet Architecture. In: ACM SIGCOMM Conference - Workshop on Future Directions in Network Architecture, FDNA 2003, USA (2004)
18. Jacobson, V.: If a Clean Slate is the Solution What Was the Problem. In: Stanford Clean Slate Seminar (2006)
19. Koponen, T., et al.: A Data-Oriented (and beyond) Network Architecture. In: 2007 ACM SIGCOMM Conference on Applications, Technologies, Architectures, and Protocols for Computer Communications, Kyoto, Japan (2007)
20. Jokela, P., et al.: LIPSIN: Line Speeds Publish/Subscribe Inter-Networking. In: ACM SIGCOMM Conference on Data Communication, USA (2009)
21. Ahlgren, B., et al.: 4WARD EU FP7 Project (Deliverable D-6.2 v2.0) (2010)
22. Stoica, I., et al.: CHORD: A Scalable Peer-to-Peer Lookup Protocol for Internet Applications. In: 2001 Conference on Applications, Technologies, Architectures, and Protocols for Computer Communications, USA (2001)
23. Jacobson, V., et al.: Networking Named Content. In: The 5th International Conference on Emerging Networking Experiments and Technologies, ACM CoNEXT 2009, pp. 1–12 (2009)
24. Elabidi, A., et al.: Towards Hiding Federated Digital Identity: Stop-Dissemination Mechanism in Content-Centric Networking. In: The 4th International Conference on Security of Information and Networks, SIN 2011, Sydney, Australia (2011)
25. Arianfar, S., et al.: On Preserving Privacy in Content-Oriented Networks. In: ACM SIGCOMM Workshop on Information-Centric Networking, ICN 2011, Toronto, Ontario, Canada (2011)
26. PARC (Xeros). CCNx Project (relase 0.3.0) (2010)
27. Shadbolt, N., Berners-Lee, T.: Web Science Emerges Scientific Amercican Magazine, 76–81 (2008)

Security Analysis of CAPTCHA

Anjali Avinash Chandavale[1] and A. Sapkal[2]

[1] Member IEEE
[2] LMIETE
anjali.chandavale@mitpune.edu.in,
ams.extc@coep.ac.in

Abstract. CAPTCHA stands for Completely Automated Public Turing test to distinguish Computers and Humans apart. CAPTCHA is a program which can generate and grade the tests that it itself cannot pass. The security aspect of CAPTCHA should be such that none of the computer program should be able to pass the tests generated by it even if the knowledge of the exact working of the CAPTCHA is known. The effectiveness of CAPTCHA of a given strength is determined by how frequently the guesses of CAPTCHA can be tested by an attacker. This paper proposes a simple and uniform framework for the assessment of security and usability of CAPTCHA that arbitrary compositions of security measures can provide". In this sentence instead of "a simple and uniform framework", use "parameters". This paper proposes parameters for the assessment of security and usability of CAPTCHA that arbitrary compositions of security measures can provide.The pre-processing attack on targeted CAPTCHA is demonstrated having success rate of approximately 97% which in turn helps to build more robust and human friendly CAPTCHA. The universal structure for segmentation attack is framed to analyze security of CAPTCHA.

Keywords: Security, Strength, CAPTCHA.

1 Introduction

In general the security may be defined as the sense of protection from hostile actions. Another way of defining security can be the degree of protection against danger, damage, loss, and crime. In modern day world traditional approach towards security fails to muddle through the ever increasing complexity of security breaches. As we enter into digital world we can no more rely completely on physical aspect of security. Like, if a computer system connected to a network, gets infected with some malicious code. It can cause serious damage to data on memory or might monitor the system user even when perpetrator(s) has no physical access to machine. Also a copyrighted material can get stolen even though original copy is still intact, with nothing actually stolen, and just got copied. Such kind of security breaches cause loss of billions of dollars, identity theft etc. A single isolated computer is less susceptible to be victim of malicious activities in comparison to systems connected to a network such as intranet or internet. In today's age of WEB, more and more people are relying on internet for online information exchange, e- commerce and hence the network security becomes very important. Some of the key issues of network security are

- Privacy
- Authentication

S.M. Thampi et al. (Eds.): SNDS 2012, CCIS 335, pp. 97–109, 2012.
© Springer-Verlag Berlin Heidelberg 2012

- Authorization

Encryption and Decryption of information

To protect from network threats, security measures are exercised at various levels of computer. Network security starts with authenticating the user, commonly with a username and a password. Since this requires an elaboration authenticating the user name i.e. the password, which is something the user has the knowledge of. This is sometimes termed one-factor authentication. With two-factor authentication, something the user possess is also used (e.g. a security token or 'dongle', an ATM card, or a mobile phone); and with three-factor authentication, a biometric feature of the user is used (e.g. a fingerprint or retinal scan). CAPTCHA systems are widely used to protect various Internet services or applications from unauthorized access of robots or other types of automatic attacks. CAPTCHA stands for Completely Automated Public Turing test to distinguish Computers and Humans apart. CAPTCHA is a program which can generate and grade the tests that it itself cannot pass [3]. The security aspect of CAPTCHA should be such that no computer program should be able to pass the tests generated by it even if the knowledge of the exact working of the CAPTCHA is known. This type of security systems are also called "reverse Turing tests" and used extensively, such as in blogs to prevent spam comments, in forums to stop multiple postings, in email service registration to prevent multiple accounts creation and so on. The role of a CAPTCHA is to make the difference between a bot and a human, through the validation test which can be easily be understood by humans, and nearly impossible to understand by robots. This principle of working of a CAPTCHA is a theoretical view towards understanding the capabilities of robots (artificial intelligence). In practice, many CAPTCHA systems, without having the test generation algorithm, were made public and were broken by researchers as mentioned in [5] [6]. Most of the CAPTCHA systems require the user to type some letters or numbers dynamically generated as a picture by the server. Depending on the directives used in the generation of an algorithm, the letters are rendered in various ways with different types of clutters in background, having the role to make the optical character recognition more difficult for robots. To quote an example, the characters could be rotated, distorted and scaled with different types of background clutters such as Crisscrossing straight lines and arcs, background textures, and meshes in foreground and background colors. Over the past few years, there have been some researches on character recognition dealing with CAPTCHA characters [1]. They emphasized on creating different techniques for different aspects of the problem. Some of the researches on CAPTCHA characters focused on segmentation. Also, most of the methods presented were specific to their own set of problems, but cannot be generalized for common usage. In our research, we use different kinds of CAPTCHA as our subject of experiment and try to analyze security aspect of CAPTCHA. The said paper is organized as follows. Section 2 mentions our simple framework. This includes the parameters to measure the strength of a CAPTCHA for different social web sites. Section 3 focuses on architecture overview to analyze CAPTCHA. Section 4 gives experimental results and section 5 gives the conclusion of the research paper.

2   The Parameters to Measure Strength of CAPTCHA

The strength of CAPTCHA is its effectiveness in resisting and guessing the attacks of BOTS. [10] Specifically, it estimates how many trials an attacker, who does not have direct access to the CAPTCHA, would need on an average to correctly guess it. The security aspect of CAPTCHA should be such that no computer program should be able to pass the tests generated by it even if the knowledge of the exact working of the CAPTCHA is known. The main constraints encountered by most of the CAPTCHAs are:

1. Readable: The CAPTCHA must be easily legible and should be possible to be decoded by humans.
2. Ungues sable: The CAPTCHA message cannot be guessed at random with any real confidence.
3. Order-able: Characters are read left to right, top to bottom (exceptions could include Hebrew or Arabic CAPTCHAs). If a CAPTCHA is readable, its character ordering should be apparent.

These constraints are important because difficult CAPTCHAs can dissuade potential customers, which is not the intent of using CAPTCHAs. Typically, the basic task that a CAPTCHA imposes to users is intuitive, easy to understand and easy to remember. Thus, CAPTCHA has a relatively good learning ability. The nature of CAPTCHAs determines the parameters applicable to address the level of efficiency, errors and satisfaction:

1. Accuracy: How accurately can a user pass a CAPTCHA challenge? For example, how many times he/she has to try in order to pass a test.
2. Response time: How long does it take for a user to pass the test?
3. Perceived difficulty/satisfaction of using a scheme: How difficult to use do people perceive a CAPTCHA is. Are users subjectively satisfied and would they be willing to use such a scheme?

This set of parameters can be a key for quantitatively evaluating the strength of CAPTCHAs. However, this set offers partial guidance on how to improve accuracy, response time or difficulty/satisfaction. Instead, we propose the following parameters for measuring the strength of CAPTCHA which in turn will be helpful to analyze its security.

1. Noise: This examines the form and amount of noise employed in CAPTCHA.
2. Characters: This dimension examines contents embedded in CAPTCHA challenges (or tests) and their impact on its strength. For example, how should the content be organized, and whether the content is appropriate?
3. Response Time/Speed: Duration it take for a user to pass the test. With these parameters strength of CAPTCHA can be measured and thus in turn will help to build more robust CAPTCHA, which is resistant to attack. [11].

2.1   Noise

Noise is an important parameter from security aspect of CAPTCHAs, since it is difficult or impossible for human users to recognize over distorted characters. To cope with this problems caused by distortion, a system will have to allow multiple attempts for each user. Typically a new challenge is used for each attempt. This will not only annoy the users, but also lowers the security of the system by a factor of the number of allowed attempts. The following section describes variations in amount and type of Noise observed in different social web sites like MSN, Google, Badongo, Government services such as Indian Railways etc.

2.1.1 The Use of Color

Badongo uses colored lines to distort the image, and Youtube uses colored blocks; whereas RapidShare uses smaller colored characters as image noise to increase the security. Generally in user interfaces color is extensively used. Using color has also been common in CAPTCHAs, mainly for the following reasons [8]

- Color is a strong attention-getting mechanism.
- Color can provide variation to fit different user preferences [12].
- Color is appealing and can make CAPTCHA challenges interesting.
- Color can facilitate recognition, comprehension and positive effect.
- Color can make CAPTCHA images compatible with the color of web pages and make them look less intrusive [12].

In addition, color schemes might also be expected to work as an additional defense against OCR software attacks in some schemes. Since typically OCR software performs poorly in recognizing texts in color images, particularly they do not do well in segmenting color images. However, we have seen many CAPTCHAs, (refer to Fig. 1) in which the use of color is not effective in context of the concerned security. It has caused negative impact on security, or is problematic in terms of both usability and security. To make challenge images appear to be interesting; some CAPTCHAs generate images in which adjacent characters have distinct colors.

(a)   (b)

Fig. 1. a) Google CAPTCHA b) Hollow CAPTCHA (CAPTCHA images where color is used as noise)

2.1.2 Clutters

Crisscrossing straight lines and arcs, background textures, and meshes in foreground and background colors are common examples of clutter used in CAPTCHAs. The representatives of them are the MSN and Yahoo systems, which are used as the basis for the main discussion as shown in Fig. 2

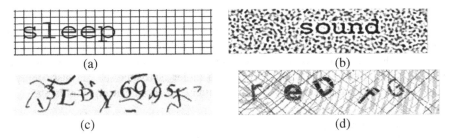

Fig. 2. a) Ez-Gimpy (i.e. mesh) CAPTCHA b) Dotted CAPTCHA c) MSN Hotmail d)Digg CAPTCHA

2.1.3 Unwanted/Confused Characters:

Distortion often creates ambiguous characters, which results the inability of users to recognize such characters. In certain cases of characters this distortion may lead to confusion in recognition of characters. Enlisted below are few characters which we studied and found to be resulting into confusion among readers.

Letter vs digits: hard to tell distorted O from 0, 6 from G and b, 5 from S/s, 2 from Z/z, 1 from l.

- Letter vs letters: Under some distortion, "vv" can resemble "w"; "cl" can resemble "d"; "nn" can could resemble "m"; "rn" can resemble "m" ; "rm" can resemble "nn"; "cm" can resemble "an". Fig. 3b shows some such confusing example that we observed in the Google CAPTCHA (used for its Gmail service). We observed that about 6% of challenges generated by this Google scheme contained such characters.
- Characters vs clutters: In CAPTCHAs such as the MSN schemes, random arcs are introduced as clutters. Confusion between arcs and characters is often observed in this Microsoft scheme. For example, it is difficult to tell an arc from characters such as 'J', '7' and 'L'. In particular, the confusion between an arc and 'J' was observed regularly in this scheme.
- Check board characters: The characters are organized in chess board form (as shown in Fig. 3a) which annoys the user.
- Note: characters that look similar in one typeface can look differently in another typeface.

Fig. 3. a) BOTdetect (Chess board) CAPTCHA b) Confusing characters (starting character is cl or d)

2.2   Characters Used in CAPTCHA

The choice of content materials used in each CAPTCHA challenge can also have significant impact on security.

2.2.1 Character Set

The size of the character set used in a CAPTCHA matters for security. It specifies whether TBC image contains only digits, only alphabets or combination of both. Typically, the larger the character set, the higher resistance to random guessing attacks each challenge can have. However, a larger character set can also imply a higher number of characters that look similar after distortion, causing confusion.

2.2.2 String Length

If both the character set size and the string length are small, random guessing would have a high chance of passing the CAPTCHA. Typically, the longer the string is used in a challenge, the more secure is the result. For example, assume that the state of the art techniques can achieve an individual character recognition rate of r (<1), the chance of recognizing the whole challenge of n characters can be $r*n$, which decreases as n grows. Whether the length of strings used in a scheme is predictable or not, is again a design issue. Some schemes choose to use a fixed length. For example, in the MSN scheme, each challenge uses eight characters. In some other schemes such as Google's CAPTCHA, the string length is variable, i.e. each challenge uses a different number of characters and the string length for each challenge is unpredictable. This design issue turns out to have implications on both security and usability. For example, the use of a fixed string length in the MSN scheme has a negative impact on its security. The knowledge as to how many characters can be expected in a challenge, can be used for locating connected characters and estimating the number of such characters in the challenge, which is a crucial step in segmentation attack on the MSN scheme [7].

2.2.3 Recognition Rate

The number of characters recognized by bot (automated software program)/system correctly.

2.3 Response Time

How long does it take for a bot to pass the test? One way to judge the strength of a CAPTCHA is to estimate the time and computing power required for its cracking.

3   Attack on CAPTCHA to Determine Strength Measurement Parameters

While focusing towards the task of attacking a CAPTCHA, we observed three procedures namely preprocessing, segmentation and recognition as shown in fig. 4. The preprocessing procedure removes different types of noise (mentioned in section 2), and thus determines the type and amount of noise present in an image. The length of characters in CAPTCHA image is determined by the segmentation procedure which requires identification of the correct positions for each character where as recognition rate is determined by character recognition technique. The recognition procedure identifies which character is in each position. Lastly once the CAPTCHA is broken in the sense the system gets success in correctly guessing the characters embedded in CAPTCHA image, response time is calculated. In recent research, [9] shows "segmentation" is a much more difficult problem than "recognition" since machine learning algorithms can efficiently solve the recognition problem, but currently we do not have any effective general algorithm to solve the segmentation problem caused by these added clutters. Therefore, this paper proposes an efficient preprocessing algorithm for attacking CAPTCHAs which cleans image to enable the OCR to recognize.

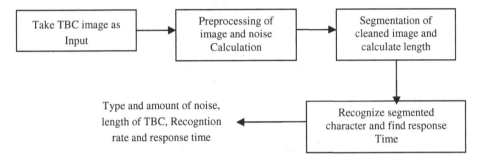

Fig. 4. Procedure for attacking CAPTCHAs

3.1   Implementing Preprocessing Attack

The preprocessing attack implemented in this paper is based on flow chart shown in Fig. 6. CAPTCHA image contains many colors and to work on each of them is quite difficult, so initially it is converted into grey scale using eqn 1 which helps only to work on 256 intensity values. Binary images are often produced by thresholding a grey scale or color image, in order to separate an object in the image from the background. The color of the object (usually white) is referred to as the foreground color.

$$\text{Grey Color} = (0.299*R+0.58*G+0.114*B) \tag{1}$$

The rest (usually black) is referred to as the background color. By analyzing the various color of CAPTCHA images, we found that:

1. Number of pixels of same or similar color in background always dominates number of pixels of characters to be recognized.
2. There is usually color difference of at least 35-40 pixel levels between foreground colors and background colors, considering readability factor of human being to identify characters from background.

In static threshold method of binarization process, pixels having value below predefined threshold are converted into black and the pixels having value above predefined threshold are converted into white. Generally it is observed that static threshold method doesn't give satisfactory results for images having variations in color. It is possible that sometimes it may erode the characters as shown in Fig.5. The binarization process in our preprocessing attack calculates threshold value during run time, depending on dominating color intensity value.

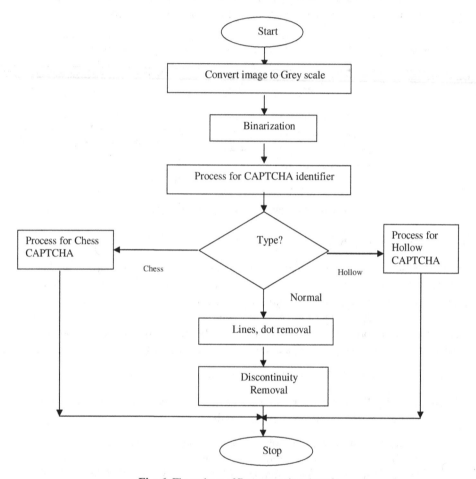

Fig. 5. a)Color image b)Grey scale image c) binarized image with static threshold=127

Fig. 6. Flow chart of Preprocessing Attack

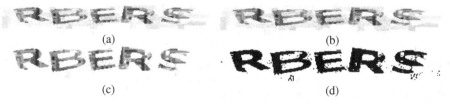

Fig. 7. a) Color Image (b) Grey scale image (c) Color 255 replaced with white (d) Color 133 replaced with black

Dominating color is a color of maximum number of pixels has. First it scans the image and searches for such dominating color. If color difference between this dominating color and previous color is less than 35-40 pixel level then replace dominating color and similar color (similar color is calculated as ± 8 % of dominating color) with white and again scan the image otherwise replace with black. The binarization process is illustrated with example in Fig. 7.

Once image is converted into binary, it is passed through CAPTCHA identifier which identifies type of CAPTCHA and accordingly passes through particular processing algorithm. We have concentrated mainly on three types of CAPTCHA namely Chessboard i.e. Bot detect, Hallow and CAPTCHA with various kinds of clutter as noise such as Yahoo, MSN Hotmail, Digg CAPTCHA etc. Chess board CAPTCHA is determined using following algorithm:

1. Calculate width and height of alternating color sections.
2. Calculate average measure using eqn. 2

$$avg = \frac{\sum_{i=1}^{k} width[i]}{k} \quad , \tag{2}$$

Where K = no. of width sample taken.

3. Calculate deviation of each measure from the average measure using eqn.3

$$Deviation = \frac{\sum_{i=1}^{k} |avg - width[i]|}{k} \tag{3}$$

4. Finally, obtain ratio of Deviation and avg as shown in eqn.4

$$ratio = \frac{Deviation}{avg} \tag{4}$$

5. If the ratio obtained lies between 0.9 to 1.1, then dimensions are considered equal or nearly equal.
6. Repeat steps 2-5 for height. If it is successful for width as well as height then it can be concluded that these measures are of fairly equal sized cells and hence this CAPTCHA is Botdetect CAPTCHA else test fails and algorithm proceeds with hollow CAPTCHA check.

To process Botdetect CAPTCHA, the algorithm first detects each chess box. If the majority of pixels in a box are black, all the pixels that are originally black are changed to white, and the pixels that are originally white, if any, are changed to black. If the majority of pixels in the box are white, then no color change is done. The result of Botdetect/Chess CAPTCHA process algorithm is shown in fig. 8.

Hollow CAPTCHA is determined based on observation that the contour of characters is formed by black pixels in such a way that number of black pixel count is always 25%-35% less than white pixel count. To determine Hollow CAPTCHA, ratio of total number of black pixels to total number of white pixels is calculated. If ratio is less than 0.35 then, algorithm proceeds with further check or else this check fails. The algorithm for Hollow CAPTCHA identification is as follows:

1. The background of image is filled with black color using boundary fill algorithm.
2. Calculate no. of pixels inside the characters using eqn.5

$$No. of\ pixels\ inside\ characters = (total\ no.\ of\ pixels\ in\ image) - (x + y) \tag{5}$$

Where total no. of pixels in image = height * width of image in pixels.

X is no. of pixels filled during boundary fill.

Y is no. black pixels initially in the binary image.

3. Calculate ratio of pixels inside the characters and total no. of pixels in the image as indicated in eqn.6

$$ratio = \frac{no.\ of\ pixels\ inside\ the\ characters}{total\ no.\ of\ pixels\ in\ the\ image} \tag{6}$$

4. If calculated ratio satisfies the observation then the CAPTCHA is considered as Hollow, or else check fails and CAPTCHA is considered as CAPTCHA with clutter.

Most of the social web sites like Yahoo, hotmail uses straight lines, slanting lines, wavy lines and arcs as clutter to confuse bots but at the same time maintaining human friendliness. The width of such type of clutter is less than width of characters so taking into consideration clutter width, our preprocessing attack easily cleans up the image for character recognition. The breaks in characters are removed using discontinuity algorithm which reconnects background pixel if any of its four neighbors in the direction of East, West, North and South pixels are of fore color.

(a)   (b)

Fig. 8. a) Botdetect CAPTCHA b) Result of Botdetect CAPTCHA processing algorithm

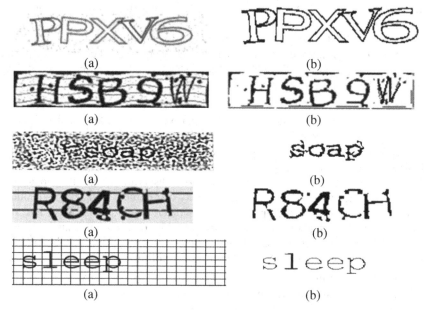

(a)   (b)

(a)   (b)

(a)   (b)

(a)   (b)

(a)   (b)

Fig. 9. a) Original image b) image cleaned by preprocessing attack

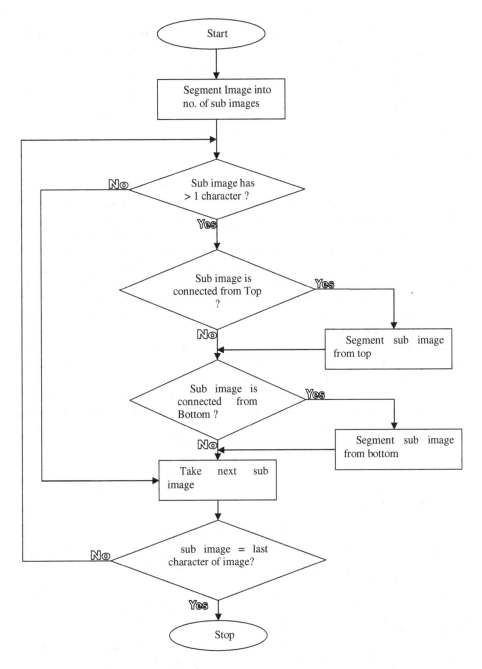

Fig. 10. Segmentation attack

3.2   Segmentation Attack

Segmentation attack extracts characters from image along with its position in image. We have developed universal structured flow chart for segmentation attack (shown in Fig.10) applicable to most of characters (i.e. connected, overlapped and disconnected characters) present in CAPTCHA image. Our future work will concentrate on implementation of structure which will be based on projection value of characters and vertical slicing process.

4   Results

In this section we present quantitative analysis of our preprocessed attack on various samples of standard database (approximately 200 images) obtained from social websites such as yahoo, Google etc. To show the effectiveness of our algorithm, we added various colors and random noise to images to generate distorted images and tested our algorithm on these images along with standard database obtained from social websites. The success rate is calculated depending on number of images cleaned. For example, if total number of images are 10 with each image having 6 characters and number of images converted to two valued color are 8 then success rate for binarization is calculated as (8*6)/ (10*6) = 80%. Similarly, the success rate for CAPTCHA identifier is calculated when type of CAPTCHA is identified correctly. The binarization gives approximately 95% success rate where as CAPTCHA identifier, Chess board and hollow CAPTCHA processing algorithm gives 94% result. The CAPTCHA with various types of clutter such as arcs, wavy and straight lines and dots are removed in 98% images of sample set. In all these experiments, we use same parameters specifically standard deviation between foreground and background in process of binarization .Fig.9 shows preprocessing attack is implemented successfully on targeted CAPTCHAs giving overall success rate as 97%.

5   Conclusion

There are two main explanations towards the shortcomings of security in the CAPTCHAs we analyzed. First, their design was almost exclusively based on research in computer vision, document recognition, and machine learning. However, our attacks did not rely on sophisticated, specialized algorithms. Instead, we applied our training in security engineering to identify critical vulnerabilities in each of the schemes, especially invariants at the pixel levels, and then design simple but novel methods to exploit those flaws. Second, a good CAPTCHA requires striking the right balance between robustness and usability, which often have subtle influences on each other. Our preprocessing attack has shown that a key strategy involved in preventing automated attacks is to incorporate random distortions in such a way that width of characters and distortion should not be noticeable. The experimental result proves that use of color doesn't enhance the security features but sometimes it annoys users leading to usability issues. This paper has mentioned the effect of noise (one of the parameters of framework to measure strength of CAPTCHA) causing security as well as usability issues of CAPTCHA. Our future work will concentrate on next set of parameter used to measure strength of CAPTCHA through segmentation attack and hence to analyze its security. We don't claim the list of parameters we have discussed for security analysis of CAPTCHA is complete and encourage the researchers to identify more parameters using our framework.

Acknowledgements. The authors wish to thank the anonymous reviewers for their useful suggestions that helped in improving the quality of this paper. This work was supported in part by MAEERs MIT, Pune in association with University of Pune.

References

[1] Kato, N., Suzuki, M., Omachi, S., Aso, H., Nemoto, Y.: A handwritten character recognition system using directional element feature and asymmetric Mahalanobis distance. IEEE Trans. on Pattern Analysis and Machine Intelligence 21(3), 258–262 (1999)

[2] Lu, Y.: Machine Printed Character Segmentation-An Overview. Pattern Recognition 28(1), 67–80 (1995)

[3] von Ahn, L., Blum, M., Langford, J.: Telling humans and computers apart (automatically), CMU Tech. Report CMUCS-02-117 (2002)

[4] von Ahn, L., Blum, M., Hopper, N.J.: CAPTCHA: Using Hard AI Problems for Security. In: Biham, E. (ed.) EUROCRYPT 2003. LNCS, vol. 2656, pp. 294–311. Springer, Heidelberg (2003)

[5] Mori, G., Malik, J.: Recognizing Objects in Adversarial Clutter: Breaking a Visual CAPTCHA. In: Proc. IEEE Conf. Computer Vision and Pattern Recognition, vol. 1, pp. 134–141 (2003)

[6] Moy, G., Jones, N., Harkless, C., Potter, R.: Distortion Estimation Techniques in Solving Visual CAPTCHAs. In: IEEE Computer Society Conference on Computer Vision and Pattern Recognition (CVPR 2004), vol. 2, pp. 23–28 (2004)

[7] Chellapilla, K., Larson, K., Simard, P.Y., Czerwinski, M.: Building Segmentation Based Human-Friendly Human Interaction Proofs (HIPs). In: Baird, H.S., Lopresti, D.P. (eds.) HIP 2005. LNCS, vol. 3517, pp. 1–26. Springer, Heidelberg (2005)

[8] Yan, J., Ahmad, A.E.: A Low-cost Attack on a Microsoft CAPTCHA. Technical report, School of Computing Science, Newcastle University, UK (2008)

[9] Rabkin, A.: Personal knowledge questions for fallback authentication: Security questions in the era of Face book. In: IEEE Symposium on Usable Privacy and Security, SOUPS 2008 (July 2008)

[10] Chandavale, A.A., Sapkal, A.M., Jalnekar, R.M.: A framework to analyze security of Text based CAPTCHA. International Journal of Forensics and Computer Application (February 2010)

[11] Converse, T.: CAPTCHA Generation as a Web Service. In: Baird, H.S., Lopresti, D.P. (eds.) HIP 2005. LNCS, vol. 3517, pp. 82–96. Springer, Heidelberg (2005)

[12] Ahmad, A.E., Yan, J.: Colour, Usability and Security: A Case Study. Tech. report CS-TR 1203, School of Computing Science, Newcastle Univ. (May 2010),
http://www.cs.ncl.ac.uk/publications/trs/papers/1203.pdf

Imperceptible Image Indexing
Using Digital Watermarking

Jobin Abraham[1] and Varghese Paul[2]

[1] M.G University, Kerala
[2] CUSAT, Kochin, Kerala, India
{jnabpc,vp.itcusat}@gmail.com

Abstract. Proposed image watermarking scheme embeds identification watermark in certain selected regions where modifications introduced during the process of watermarking is less sensitive to HVS (Human Visual System). Edge detectors are used to estimate regions in the image where intensity changes rapidly. Modifications to such pixel will not attract the attention of human eyes. Watermark is thus integrated imperceptibly into the digital images. The proposed is a scheme for embedding a unique index number as watermark for content tracking and identification.

Keywords: Digital watermarking, DCT based, edge detection, watermark embedding, extraction, psnr.

1 Introduction

Today, Internet is popular and widely used for communication and commercial purposes. Any digital resources such as image, music, video or multimedia data can be transferred to a buyer via Internet. Commercial vendors may market and sell their contents to potential buyers. Online business transactions are dependable only if powerful tools exist for controlling unauthorized replication and misuse of costly contents transferred. Watermarking is proposed as a powerful security mechanism that has immense applications as a tool for copyright protection, authentication, fingerprinting and many more [1]. Watermarking can also be used to restrict content misuse and illegal tampering.

Digital watermarking is the process of integrating identification information such as the owner name or his logo imperceptibly in the digital media. The identification watermark can be a text or logo image for uniquely identifying the content owner [2]. Two common approaches for watermark selection can be seen in the literature. One is the use of a pseudo random sequence [3] and the other is the use of an image as watermark [4]. The watermark image can be a logo or initials of the company or owner. In most methods, one dimensional array of binary digits is formed by preprocessing the watermark and these bits are then integrated with the original image during the process of watermarking.

Method proposed in [5], uses a binary image as watermark data. Non-overlapping 2x2 blocks from host image is taken and one pixel of watermark is embedded. Some

S.M. Thampi et al. (Eds.): SNDS 2012, CCIS 335, pp. 110–116, 2012.

proposed watermarking schemes embed a PN sequence in the LSB of host data. Though these spatial domain methods are simple and easy to implement, they are highly sensitive to signal processing operations that corrupt the embedded watermark.

Watermarking is still in evolutionary stage. Watermarking techniques has generated great interest as more and more vendors opt to sell their works through Internet. Watermarks should be able to withstand all intentional and unintentional attacks targeted to remove the identification mark. Creating robust watermarking methods is still a challenging problem for researchers as some methods withstand some attacks, but is broken by others. Current research is concentrated mainly on methods to suit to the specific application in hand and effectively address that issue.

A watermarking scheme that uses edge detection is proposed in [6]. The method use Gaussian noise of zero mean and unit variance as watermark. Though the method can address copyright issues, it is not pragmatic for sequentially ordering the digital resources using a numeric identifier.

[7] describes another method that can embed a watermark comprising eight symbols. Every element in the watermark is coded using a {+1, -1} to deduce a 64 bit ID. This is then embedded in host image.

The paper is organized as follows: section 2 introduces the aim and features of the proposed scheme. Section 3 outlines watermark embedding and extraction algorithm. Section 4 describes the experimental analysis and quality metrics used for assessing the proposed scheme. Finally, section 5 concludes the work.

2   Features of the Proposed Method

The proposed is a novel scheme for embedding a unique identification number as watermark for content tracking and identification. This may be used for sequentially numbering documents in a content archival system. The proposed method can also be used for fingerprinting digital contents with buyers ID. The seller can use this hidden information for identifying the owner and tracing the traitor in cases of illegal content replications.

Vidyasagar et al. [8] describe content archiving as a potential application for watermarking. The integrated watermark here acts as an object identifier. This has several advantages over conventional archiving that uses file names. Documents when archived using the file names, accidental changes in file names will create unpredictable issues in file access that may even lead to the non availability of contents.

Edges in images are areas with sharp variation in pixel intensity. There will be noticeable changes or abrupt discontinuities in pixel intensity in the vicinity of edges. These regions are detected using an edge detector and are effectively used in the proposed method for hiding an external watermark signal without distracting the eyes of the viewer.

Robustness is a measure of immunity of embedded watermark to attacks targeted to weaken them. Normally when images are cropped part of the embedded watermark is lost, making extraction of identification watermark cumbersome and unsuccessful. However, the method assures watermark retrieval even if the image is reduced to one-by-fourth of the actual size.

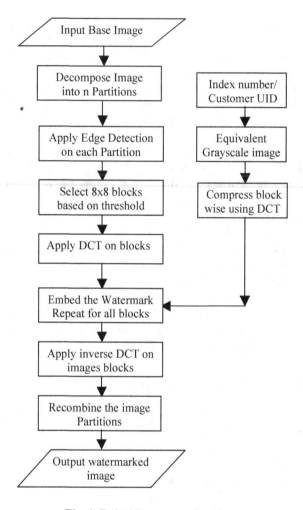

Fig. 1. Embedding process flowchart

3   The Algorithm

The algorithm has two phases. First is the watermark embedding phase and second the watermark extraction phase. General steps in watermarking are:

1) Preprocess the numeric watermark
2) Decompose the image I into n equal sized regions and estimate the edge detection threshold.
3) Construct non-overlapping 8x8 blocks and apply DCT.
4) Select blocks for watermark embedding based on the edge detection threshold.

5) Alter the coefficients in selected blocks to hide the watermark
6) Apply inverse DCT on blocks and recombine the sub-sections.

3.1   Embedding Algorithm

The watermark phase algorithm has two stages. First stage is the preprocessing and compressing of watermark image using DCT. Most significant coefficients are chosen for embedding in the base image. The second stage, adds the preprocessed watermark signal to selected mid-frequency locations in the regions selected using edge detector. Flowchart of the embedding process is shown in figure.1

Stage 1: Preprocess the watermark

Input: Unique ID, UID
Output: Equivalent grayscale watermark image, W
- Assign an equivalent grayscale values for each decimal digits in the number, d = {0, 1, 2, 3....9} from the set of grayscale values, egv = {25, 50, 75, ...225}.
- Construct a 4x4 block for every digit by repeating the selected equivalent grayscale value from the above list.
- Convert every digit in the UID in the same fashion above, to obtain a watermark image. For instance, a sixteen digit UID will result in a 16x16 grayscale image.

Stage 2: Watermark embedding

Input: Base image, I and watermark image, W
Output: Watermarked image, I_w
- Compress W by applying DCT on 4x4 non-overlapping blocks. Built an array, $wmk(q) = f_i(1,1)$. Here, i is the block number of a digit in the watermark.
- Split I into n regions. If n=4, results in four quadrants, each of size N/2 X N/2.
- Embed the watermark in each quadrant, considering one at a time.
- Use Sobel Edge detection for finding the threshold, t
- Consider 8x8 blocks and compute their threshold, t_b.
- Select the blocks with in a range of threshold. Say, $((t_b > 2t) \ \&\& \ (t_b < 3t))$
- Embed the watermark in a mid-frequency coefficient, $f(i,j) = f(i,j) + sf*wmk(q)$ where sf is the strength factor and f is the DCT of an 8x8 block from I.
- Repeat the above three steps to mark all eligible block in a region.
- Apply inverse DCT and recombine the sub-regions to output the watermarked copy, I_w.

3.2   The Extraction Algorithm

The proposed is a non-blind technique and requires the original image for extracting the hidden watermark signal. DCT of base image I and the watermarked copy I_w are found and the difference between the chosen mid-frequency coefficient is computed for decoding the embedded watermark information.

The watermark extraction algorithm is discussed below:

Input: Base image, I and Watermarked image, I$_w$
Output: Watermark, W
- First step is to decompose the image I and I$_w$ into sub-regions, as done during watermark embedding.
- Determine the edge detection threshold t for the sub-region and t$_b$ for each 8x8 block in consideration from I
- Extract embedded watermark information from I$_w$ whenever threshold for the block is within the range employed during the watermarking process.

    wmk (k) = (f'w$_i$(p, q) - f$_i$(p, q))/sf.

    Here, i is the block number, sf is the strength factor, fw is DCT of an 8x8 block from I$_w$ and f is DCT of the corresponding 8x8 block from I.
- Extract all watermark coefficients by considering the subsequent set of blocks from I$_w$ and I.
- Reconstruct the watermark image by taking inverse DCT of each extracted element to generate the 4x4 grayscale blocks per digit.
- Use the proposed grayscale lookup table for finding the equivalent digit and repeat the above steps for extracting all the digits in the numeric watermark.
- Output the extracted watermark , *w*

4   Experimental Analysis

For evaluating the performance of the proposed scheme we watermarked various images. Figure.2 shows the results for two test cases, where images are watermarked using a sixteen digit number. Two important requirements to be met by any watermarking scheme is visual appeal ness and robustness to watermark removal attacks. PSNR (Peak Signal to Noise Ratio) ratio is computed to estimate the visual quality of the watermarked image. Higher the PSNR lesser the distortion and hence better the image quality. The measured PSNR values are tabulated in table.1. The robustness of the watermarked image is tested by subjecting to certain common signal processing attacks. The method is found to be dependable as the watermark is still decodable and recognizable. NCC (Non-correlation coefficient) is used to measure the similarity of the extracted the watermark with the original embedded watermark. NCC value ranges from 0 to 1. Any value close to 1 indicates that the extracted signal is closely similar to the original embedded watermark. Table.2 gives the NCC values for the extracted watermarks, supposing that there are four watermarked regions, I to IV, in a watermarked Lena image.

Table 1. Sinal to Noise Ratios

Image	PSNR	MSE
Lena	45.28	1.92
Deer	44.11	2.52
Boat	44.65	2.28

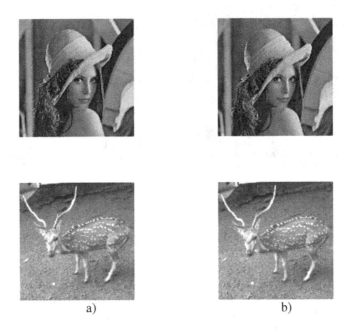

a)   b)

Fig. 2. Watermarking images. a) Base images b) Watermarked images

Figure.3 shows the pixels that were altered during the process of watermark insertion. The significant edges are alone carefully selected from the base image discarding the monotonous areas in the image. As there is a sharp change in intensity near the edges distortions are not observable to the human eyes. Hence it may be inferred that the proposed watermarking method do not significantly degrade the visual qualities of the output watermarked image. Figure 3.a shows the binary difference image of the base Lena image and its watermarked copy. And in figure 3.b, the watermark hidden areas in base image are highlighted.

Table 2. Correlation Measurements after attacks for watermarks from regions I to IV

Types of Attack	NCC			
	I	II	III	IV
No Attack	0.99	0.99	0.99	0.99
Salt & Pepper	0.95	0.99	0.97	0.94
Gaussian	0.92	0.93	0.87	0.82
Speckle	0.88	0.97	0.91	0.98

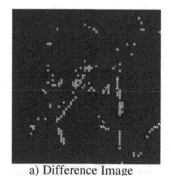   

a) Difference Image   b) Watermarked Positions

Fig. 3. Watermark embedded positions in lena image

5   Conclusion

A method for imperceptibly indexing digital resources using watermarking is discussed here. The embedded index number could be used effectively for archiving multimedia digital documents in databases. It also helps in locating the resources in case of causalities like unintentional alterations. To ensure that watermark is embedded imperceptibly, the watermark is compressed using DCT and only significant coefficients are selected for insertion in base image. The algorithm is then implemented on various test image and the results for various quality metrics is found. It is observed that the embedding process does not degrade the quality of the base image and at the same is robust against various image processing attacks.

References

1. Cox, I.J., Miller, M.L.: The First 50 years of Electronic Watermarking. J. of Applied Signal Processing, 126–132 (2002)
2. Lian, S., Kanellopoulos, D., Ruffo, G.: Recent Advances in Multimedia Information System Security. Informatics 33, 3–24 (2009)
3. Al Haj, A.: Combined DWT-DCT Digital Image Watermarking. Journal of Computer Science 3(9), 740–746 (2007)
4. Sharkas, M., Elshafie, D., Hamdy, N.: A Dual Digital Image Watermarking Technique. World Academy of Science, Engineering and Technology (2005)
5. Dorairangaswamy, M.A.: A Novel Invisible and Blind Watermarking Scheme for Copyright Protection of Digital Images. IJCNS 9 (2009)
6. Ellinas, J.N.: A Robust Wavelet based Watermarking Algorithm Using Edge Detection. World Academy of Science, Engineering and Technology 34 (2007)
7. Kim, W.-G., Seo, Y.-S., Jung, H.-W., Lee, S.-H., Oh, W.-G.: Wavelet Based Multi-bit Fingerprinting Against Geometric Distortions. Key Engineering, 1301–1305 (2006)
8. Potdar, V.M., Han, S., Chang, E.: A Survey of Digital Image Watermarking Techniques. In: IEEE International Conference on Industrial Informatics (2005)

A New Deterministic Algorithm for Testing Primality Based on a New Property of Prime Numbers

Srikumar Manghat

Indira Vihar, Hemambika Nagar, Kallekulangara.P.O;
Palakkad-678009, Kerala, India
msrikumar1981@rediffmail.com

Abstract. Although they have been being intensely studied, there remain numerous open questions around prime numbers. For example, no known formula exists that yields all of the prime numbers and no composites. Due to this uncertainty surrounding the theory of prime numbers, popular algorithms proposed in literature till date, rely heavily on probabilistic methods to determine primality. The paper proposes a new theory on the nature of prime numbers. In particular the paper proposes new theorems by which any prime number can be calculated from the knowledge of any other prime number of lower value in a simple way. It is shown in the paper that, in so doing, the theorems prove to be a common thread through which all the prime numbers of a number system can be related. Based on the theorems, a new prime number generating algorithm and a new purely deterministic method to test primality is explained and illustrated with the help of examples.

Keywords: Prime numbers, prime number generating algorithm, primality test.

1 Introduction

A prime number (or a prime) is a natural number such that it has exactly two distinct natural number divisors: 1 and itself. An infinite number of prime numbers exists and this fact has been demonstrated as early as 300 BC by Euclid [1]. Any nonzero natural number **n** can be factored into primes; that is; these can be written as a product of primes or powers of different primes. This factorization is unique except for a possible reordering of the factors.

Although they have been intensely studied, there remain numerous open questions around prime numbers. For example, no known formula exists that yields all of the prime numbers and no composites. For more than a century, the Goldbach's conjecture which asserts that any even natural number bigger than two is the sum of two primes, or the twin prime conjecture which says that there are infinitely many twin primes (pairs of primes whose difference is two), have remained unresolved, notwithstanding the simplicity of their statements. However, it has been demonstrated by mathematicians that the distribution of primes or in other words the statistical behaviour of primes in the large can be modelled. For instance, the prime number theorem, says that the probability that a given, randomly chosen number **n** is prime is

S.M. Thampi et al. (Eds.): SNDS 2012, CCIS 335, pp. 117–126, 2012.

inversely proportional to the logarithm of **n**. The unproven Riemann hypothesis [2] implies a refined statement concerning the distribution of primes and though it has been unproven since its inception in 1859.

Primes have been applied in several fields in information technology, such as public-key cryptography, which makes use of the difficulty of factoring large numbers into their prime factors. Searching for big primes, often using distributed computing, has stimulated studying special types of primes, chiefly Mersenne primes whose primality is comparably quick to decide. As of 2011, the largest known prime number has about 13 million decimal digits [3].

The property of being prime is called primality. The simplest method for verifying the primality of a given number **n** can be done by trial division. The method tests whether **n** is a multiple of an integer **m** between 2 and $\sqrt{n}$. If **n** is a multiple of any of these integers then it is a composite number, and so not prime; if it is not a multiple of any of these integers then it is prime. As this method requires up to $\sqrt{n}$ trial divisions, it is only suitable for relatively small values of **n**. More sophisticated algorithms, which are much more efficient than trial division, have been devised to test the primality of large numbers.

Different methods have been proposed in literature to test primality, for example the latest methods by Shafi Goldwasser & Joe Kilian [4]; M.Aggrawal & S.Biswas [5]; Rene Shoof [6]; etc. A common feature of all these latest algorithms, is that they rely primarily on probabilistic methods to determine primality and use deterministic methods only as a secondary instrument.

The paper proposes a new theory on the nature of prime numbers. In particular the paper proposes new theorems by which any prime number can be calculated from the knowledge of any other prime number of lower value in a simple way. It is shown in the paper that, in so doing, the theorems prove to be a common thread through which all the prime numbers of a number system can be related. Based on the theorems, a new prime number generating algorithm and a new purely deterministic method to test primality is explained and illustrated with the help of examples.

Section 1 has provided the introduction. The proposed theorem and its proof are given in Section 2. The proposed algorithms for generating prime numbers and for testing primality are described in Section 3. Examples illustrating the operation of the proposed algorithms are shown in Section 4. Section 5 provides the concluding remarks.

2   Proofs

Our objective is to first prove a theorem by which any prime number can be calculated from the knowledge of any other prime number of lower value. Let us begin by proving some smaller theorems and see how these theorems lead us to our final objective.

Theorem 1:
A number **P** of the form

$$P = 3a,$$

is an odd number, for any odd number **a**.

Proof 1:

We know that any odd number O can be expressed in the form:

$$O = 2n + b, \tag{1}$$

where n is any integer and b is an odd integer.

Now, a number of the form $P = 3a$, where a is an odd number, can be written as

$$P = 3a,$$
$$= 2a + a$$

Since P is a number expressible in the form given by equation (1), we can say that $P = 3a$ is an odd number.

Hence the theorem is proved.

Corollary to theorem 1:

Theorem 1 implies that non-prime numbers of any other form are interspersed between non-prime odd numbers of the form $P = 3a$, a being an odd number. It is, therefore, easy to see that a non-prime number Q of the form

$$Q = C^2,$$

where C is a prime number, occurs in between two non-prime odd numbers, say, $3a_1$ and $3a_2$, where a_1 and a_2 are two consecutive odd numbers.

These facts are illustrated below in Table 1, where a set of contiguous non-primes are listed out along with their factors

Table 1. A set of contiguous non-primes and their factors

Odd non-primes	Factors
9	3×3
15	3×5
21	3×7
→ 25	5×5
27	3×9
33	3×11
35	5×7
39	3×13
45	3×15
→ 49	7×7
51	3×17
55	5×11
57	3×19

→ : indicates odd non-prime numbers of the form $P = C^2$, where C is a prime number.

Another fact that emerges (which can be easily verified) is that between two non-prime odd numbers of the form $3a$, say, $3a_1$ and $3a_2$, where a_1 and a_2 are two consecutive odd numbers, there can occur just two other odd numbers, both of which will, obviously, be of some other form. For example, between 3×17 and 3×19, the two odd numbers are 53 and 55. Therefore, between $3a_1$ and $3a_2$ there can occur just one number Q of the form

$$Q = C^2, \text{ where } C \text{ is prime,} \tag{2}$$

because $Q \pm 2$ which can be the only other odd number that can occur between $3a_1$ and $3a_2$ is obviously not of the form given by equation (2). In other words, two 'square of prime' numbers cannot occur between $3a_1$ and $3a_2$, where a_1 and a_2 are two consecutive odd numbers.

Recapitulating, the two facts that emerge are:
a) Non-prime odd numbers of the form
$$Q = C^2, \text{ where } C \text{ is prime}$$
occur between non-prime odd numbers of the form $3a$,say, $3a_1$ and $3a_2$, where a_1 and a_2 are two consecutive odd numbers.
b) Between two non-prime odd numbers of the form $3a$,say, $3a_1$ and $3a_2$, where a_1 and a_2 are two consecutive odd numbers, there can occur just one odd number of the form
$$Q = C^2, \text{ where } C \text{ is prime.}$$

Theorem 2:
If a non-prime odd number Q of the form
$$Q = P^2,$$
where P is a prime number greater than or equal to 5, is such that it occurs between two non-prime odd numbers of the form $3a$, say, $3a_1$ and $3a_2$, where a_1 and a_2 are two consecutive odd numbers with $a_2 > a_1$; and two integers x_1 and x_2 are such that
$$x_1 = Q - 3a_1,$$
$$x_2 = 3a_2 - Q,$$
then,
$$x_1 = 2x_2$$

Proof 2:
Any odd number $N > 1$ can be expressed as
$$N = (2n + 1),$$
where n is any integer greater than 0.

Now, prime numbers are all odd and the square of any prime number $P > N$ can be expressed in terms of N as follows:
$$Q = P^2 = (2(n+k) + 1), \text{ where } k \text{ is some integer greater than 0.}$$
$$= 2n + 1 + 2k$$
$$= N + 2k$$

Suppose N is of the form $3a$ (where a is odd). Now, let us consider two odd numbers of the form $3a$ (where a is odd) in terms of k such that they are closest to $Q = P^2$ and one number is greater than Q and the other is lesser than Q. It is easy to verify that the smaller number is
$$A = N \quad \text{(of the form } 3a, \text{ where } a \text{ is odd)}$$
And the greater number is
$$B = N + 3k \quad \text{(of the form } 3a, \text{ where } a \text{ is odd)}$$
Now, when $k = 2$; A and B are equal to, say, $3a_1$ and $3a_2$ respectively such that a_1 and a_2 are two consecutive odd numbers with $a_2 > a_1$. Also, it follows from theorem 1and its corollary that only one number of the form
$$Q = P^2$$

can exist between them. Therefore, the value of $\mathbf{k} = 2$ is the only value of $\mathbf{k}$ that concerns us.

Let us define the differences

$$x_1 = Q - A$$

And
$$x_2 = B - Q$$

From the foregoing statements regarding the values of $\mathbf{k}$, $\mathbf{A}$ and $\mathbf{B}$; replacing the values of these in the above two equations we have:

$$x_1 = Q - 3a_1 = 2k = 2$$

And
$$x_2 = 3a_2 - Q = k = 1$$

Therefore the ratio

$$x_1 : x_2 = 2 : 1$$

Hence the theorem is proved.

Theorem 3:

The difference between the square of two prime numbers that are each greater than or equal to 5 is always divisible by 3. Or, if a number $\mathbf{T}$ is such that

$$T = abs(N_1^2 - N_2^2)$$

then $\mathbf{T}$ is always divisible by 3 if both $\mathbf{N_1}$ and $\mathbf{N_2}$ are dissimilar prime numbers and have values greater than or equal to 5.

Proof 3:

Let us consider two odd non-primes N_1^2 and N_2^2 such that N_1 and N_2 are both prime numbers. By theorem 1 and its corollary, N_1^2 and N_2^2 are located amidst non-prime odd numbers of the form $3a$, a being odd. Let us assume that N_1^2 is located between numbers $3a_1$ and $3a_2$; and N_2^2 is located between numbers $3a_3$ and $3a_4$ such that $a_1 < a_2 < a_3 < a_4$ and; (a_1, a_2) and (a_3, a_4) are consecutive odd number pairs.

Let us define numbers x_1, x_2, x_3, x_4 such that

$$x_1 = 3a_1 - N_1^2$$
$$x_2 = N_1^2 - 3a_2$$
$$x_3 = 3a_3 - N_2^2$$
$$x_4 = N_2^2 - 3a_4$$

This is graphically shown below in Fig. 1:

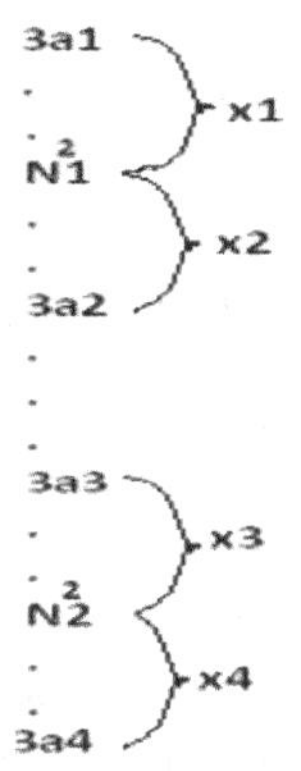

Fig. 1. Graphical illustration

Theorem 2 states that for $N_1, N_2 \geq 5$,

$$x_1 = 2x_2$$
$$\text{and} \quad x_3 = 2x_4$$

Thus,

$$x_2 = (1/3)(x_1 + x_2)$$
$$= (1/3)(3a_2 - 3a_1)$$
$$= (a_2 - a_1)$$

Similarly,

$$x_3 = (2/3)(x_3 + x_4)$$
$$= (1/3)(3a_4 - 3a_3)$$
$$= 2(a_4 - a_3)$$

Since (a_1, a_2) and (a_3, a_4) are consecutive odd number pairs,

$$a_2 - a_1 = a_4 - a_3 = 2$$

Therefore,

$$x_2 = 2$$
$$\text{and} \quad x_3 = 2 \times 2 = 4$$

Now, (making use of the figure 1 above)

$$T = \text{abs}(N_1{}^2 - N_2{}^2) = \text{abs}(x_2 + (3a_2 - 3a_3) + x_3)$$
$$= \text{abs}(3a_2 - 3a_3 + x_3 + x_2)$$

Or, replacing the values of x_2 and x_3,

$$= \text{abs}(3a_2 - 3a_3 + 6)$$

$T = \text{abs}(N_1{}^2 - N_2{}^2)$ is thus always divisible by 3.
Hence the theorem is proved.

Theorem 4:
If P is a prime number greater than or equal to 5, and if P^2 is expressed as

$$P^2 = (a5^{2t} + \ldots + b5^{2n} + \ldots + c5^2 + 3d)$$

where a, b, c, etc; are integers such that each of them has a value less than 3×5^2 and d is an integer with value less than 5^2, and t, n, etc; are integers such that $t > \ldots > n > \ldots > 2$; then the coefficient of 5^2, c, is a non-zero integer that is never divisible by 3.

Proof 4:
Using theorem 3, a prime number P greater than or equal to 5, can be written as

$$P^2 = (P_1{}^2 + 3i_1)$$

where i_1 is an integer and P_1 is some prime number.
    Let us choose P_1 as the least prime number for which theorem 3 is applicable, i.e., let $P_1 = 5$. Then,

$$P^2 = (5^2 + 3i_1)$$
$$= (3s5^{2t} + \ldots + 3r5^{2n} + \ldots + (3k+1)5^2 + 3i)$$

because $3i_1$ can be expressed as: $3i_1 = 3s5^{2t} + \ldots + 3r5^{2n} + \ldots + 3k5^2 + 3i$, where i, s, r, k, etc; are integers such that each of them has a value less than 5^2 and t, n, etc; are integers such that $t > \ldots > n > \ldots > 2$. Thus, P^2 can be written as:

$$P^2 = (a5^{2t} + \ldots + b5^{2n} + \ldots + c5^2 + 3d)$$

where a, b, c, etc; are integers such that each of them has a value less than 3×5^2 and d is an integer with value less than 5^2, and the coefficient of 5^2, c, is never divisible by 3. Hence the theorem is proved.

Theorem 5:
If C is an odd composite number such that it is a product of two or more prime numbers with values other than 3 and 5, and if C^2 is expressed as

$$C^2 = (a5^{2t} + ... + b5^{2n} + ... + c5^2 + 3d)$$

where a, b, c, etc; are integers such that each of them has a value less than 3×5^2 and d is an integer with value less than 5^2, and t, n, etc; are integers such that $t > ... > n > ... > 2$; then the coefficient of 5^2, c, is always either 0 or divisible by 3.

Proof 5:
Using theorem 3, the square of an odd composite number C that is a product of two or more prime numbers with values other than 3 and 5, can be written in the general form as

$$C^2 = (P^2 + 3i_1)^l(P^2 + 3i_2)^m ....$$

where i_1, i_2, l, m, ...etc; are all integers and P is some prime number.

Let us choose P as the least prime number for which theorem 3 is applicable, i.e., let $P = 5$. Then,

$$C^2 = (5^2 + 3i_1)^l(5^2 + 3i_2)^m ....$$
$$= 5^{2n} + 3i_e$$
$$= (3s5^{2t} + ... + (3r + 1)5^{2n} + ... + 3k5^2 + 3i)$$

because $3i_e$ can be expressed as: $3i_e = 3s5^{2t} + ... + 3r5^{2n} + ... + 3k5^2 + 3i$ where i_e is an integer and i, s, r, k, etc; are integers such that each of them has a value less than 5^2 and t, n, etc; are integers such that $t > ... > n > ... > 2$. Thus, C^2 can be written as:

$$P^2 = (a5^{2t} + ... + b5^{2n} + ... + c5^2 + 3d)$$

where a, b, c, etc; are integers such that each of them has a value less than 3×5^2 and d is an integer with value less than 5^2, and the coefficient of 5^2, c, is always either 0 or divisible by 3.
Hence the theorem is proved.

Thus, since numbers in a number system are either prime or are a product of two or more prime numbers with one or more of them having values equal to 3 or 5 or are a product of two or more prime numbers with values other than 3 and 5; the following corollary to theorems 4 & 5:

Corollary to theorems 4 & 5:
Theorems 4 & 5, thus, imply that if a number Q is an odd number and Q is not divisible by 3 and 5 and if Q^2 is expressed as

$$Q^2 = (a5^{2t} + ... + b5^{2n} + ... + c5^2 + 3d)$$

where a, b, c, etc; are integers such that each of them has a value less than 3×5^2 and d is an integer with value less than 5^2 and t, n, etc; are integers such that $t > ... > n > ... > 2$, then Q is a prime number if the coefficient of 5^2, c, is a non-zero integer that is never divisible by 3.

This corollary is the basis for developing the primality algorithms that follow.

3   Algorithms

By theorems 4 & 5, it is possible to calculate the next prime number in the sequence from a prime number whose value is known.

The algorithm to calculate the next prime number from a previously known prime number is as follows:

Algorithm 1:

1. Let **M** is a known prime number.
2. Find the value of **k(i)** from the formulae
$$k(i) = (O(i\text{-}1) + 2),$$
using the value of **O(i-1)** as
$$O(i\text{-}1) = M.$$
3. If **k(i)** is divisible by 3 or 5, then **O(i)** is non-prime. Proceed to step 6.
4. If **k(i)** is not divisible by 3 and 5, express **k(i)** ^{2} as
$$k(i)^2 = (a5^{2t} + \ldots + b5^{2n} + \ldots + c5^2 + 3d)$$
where **a, b, c**, etc; are integers such that each of them has a value less than $3{\times}5^2$ and **d** is an integer with value less than 5^2 and **t, n**, etc; are integers such that **t** $>\ldots>$ **n** $>\ldots>2$.
5. The current value of **O(i)** which is
$$O(i) = O(i\text{-}1) + 2$$
is a prime number if the coefficient of 5^2, **c**, is a non-zero integer that is not divisible by 3, by theorems 4 & 5. Output **O(i)** as the result and stop. If **c** is 0 or divisible by 3, then **O(i)** is non-prime by theorems 4 & 5. Proceed to step 6.
6. Calculate the new value of **k(i)** using
$$k(i) = (O(i\text{-}1) + 2),$$
the new value of **O(i-1)** being
$$O(i\text{-}1) = O(i).$$
7. Go to step 3.

From the nature of the algorithm, it is clear that, starting from a prime number of lowest value, any prime number of any desired value can be calculated with the help of theorems 4 & 5. Therefore, theorems 4 & 5 serve as a link by which all prime numbers in a number system can be related. Prime numbers, which were hitherto considered to be distributed throughout the number system following no particular rule, seem to follow the rules set by theorems 4 & 5.

Theorems 4 & 5 can also be used to formulate a simple procedure to check the primality of any odd number. Suppose **X** is the odd number whose primality needs to be checked. The procedure is as follows:

Algorithm 2:

1. If **X** is divisible by 3 or 5, then **X** is non-prime.
2. If **X** is not divisible by 3 and 5, express X^2 as
$$X^2 = (a5^{2t} + ... + b5^{2n} + ... + c5^2 + 3d)$$
   where **a**, **b**, **c**, etc; are integers such that each of them has a value less than 3×5^2 and **d** is an integer with value less than 5^2 and **t**, **n**, etc; are integers such that **t** >...> **n** >...>2.
3. **X** is a prime number if the coefficient of 5^2, **c**, is a non-zero integer that is not divisible by 3, by theorems 4 & 5.

4   Examples

Suppose a prime number 79 is given and it is required to find the value of the next highest prime number. Following Algorithm 1 of the previous section we have:

1. **M** = 79
2. Putting the value of **O(i-1)** = **M** in equation
$$k(i) = (O(i-1) + 2)$$
   we have
$$k(i)^2 = 81^2 = 6561$$
3. Value of **k(i)** = 81 is divisible by 3. So,
$$O(i) = O(i-1) + 2 = 81$$
   is not prime.
4. The new value of **k(i)** is obtained by putting **O(i-1)** = **O(i)** in the equation
$$k(i) = (O(i-1) + 2) = 83$$
   Or,
$$k(i)^2 = 83^2 = 6889$$
5. **k(i)** is not divisible by 3 and 5 and $k(i)^2$ can be expressed as
$$k(i)^2 = 83^2 = 3 \times 3 \times 5^4 + (3 \times 16 + 1) \times 5^2 + 3 \times 13,$$
   which is of the form,
$$k(i)^2 = (a5^{2t} + ... + b5^{2n} + ... + c5^2 + 3d)$$
   where **a**, **b**, **c**, etc; are integers such that each of them has a value less than 3×5^2 and **d** is an integer with value less than 5^2 and **t**, **n**, etc; are integers such that **t** >...> **n** >...>2, as required by theorems 4 & 5.
6. Since the coefficient of 5^2, **c** = $(3 \times 16 + 1)$, is a non-zero integer that is not divisible by 3, hence, by theorems 4 & 5,
$$O(i) = O(i-1) + 2 = 83,$$
   is the next highest prime number.

In order to test the primality of an odd number, say, **X** = 187, following algorithm 2, we have:

1. $\mathbf{X}$ is not divisible by 3 and 5 and $\mathbf{X}^2$ can be expressed as
    $$\mathbf{X}^2 = 187^2 = (3{\times}18 + 1){\times}5^4 + 3{\times}7{\times}5^2 + 3{\times}23,$$
    which is of the form,
    $$\mathbf{X}^2 = (\mathbf{a}5^{2t} + \ldots + \mathbf{b}5^{2n} + \ldots + \mathbf{c}5^2 + 3\mathbf{d})$$
    where $\mathbf{a}$, $\mathbf{b}$, $\mathbf{c}$, etc; are integers such that each of them has a value less than $3{\times}5^2$ and $\mathbf{d}$ is an integer with value less than 5^2 and $\mathbf{t}$, $\mathbf{n}$, etc; are integers such that $\mathbf{t} > \ldots > \mathbf{n} > \ldots > 2$, as required by theorems 4 & 5.
2. Since the coefficient of 5^2, $\mathbf{c} = 3{\times}7$, is divisible by 3, hence, by theorems 4 & 5, $\mathbf{X}$ is not a prime number.

5   Conclusion

The paper proposes a new theory on the nature of prime numbers. In particular the paper proposes new theorems by which any prime number can be calculated from the knowledge of any other prime number of lower value in a simple way. It is shown in the paper that, in so doing, the theorems prove to be a common thread through which all the prime numbers of a number system can be related. Based on the theorems, a new prime number generating algorithm and a new method to test primality is explained and illustrated with the help of examples.

References

1. Euclid's 'Elements', Book 9, Proposition 10
2. Peter, B., Choi, S., Rooney, B., et al. (eds.): The Riemann Hypothesis: A Resource for the Afficionado and Virtuoso Alike. CMS Books in Mathematics. Springer, New York (2008)
3. Great Internet Mersenne Prime Search Home, http://www.mersenne.org/
4. Goldwasser, S., Kilian, J.: Primality testing using elliptic curves. Journal of the ACM (JACM) 46(4), 450–472 (1999)
5. Aggrawal, M., Biswas, S.: Primality and identity testing via Chinese remaindering. In: 40th Annual Symposium on Foundations of Computer Science, pp. 202–208 (1999)
6. Schoof, R.: Four Primality testing algorithms; arXiv.org > math > arXiv:0801.3840 (2004)

Multilingual Speaker Identification with the Constraint of Limited Data Using Multitaper MFCC

B.G. Nagaraja and H.S. Jayanna

Department of Information Science and Engineering
Siddaganga Institute of Technology, Tumkur-572103, India
{nagarajbg,jayannahs}@gmail.com

Abstract. Feature extraction has the ability to improve the performance of speaker identification systems. This paper studies the significance of low-variance multitaper Mel-frequency cepstral coefficient (multitaper MFCC) features for Multilingual speaker identification with the constraint of limited data. The speaker identification study is conducted using 30 speakers of our own database. Sine-weighted cepstrum estimator (SWCE) taper MFCC features are extracted and modeled using Gaussian Mixture Model (GMM)-Universal Background Model (UBM). The results show that the multitaper MFCC approach performs better than the conventional Hamming window MFCC technique in all the speaker identification experiments.

Keywords: Speaker identification, MFCC, multitaper MFCC and Confusion matrix.

1 Introduction

Automatic Speaker Identification (ASI) and Automatic Speaker Verification (ASV) systems have always been demanding in terms of robustness and accuracy for the modern state-of-the-art security applications [1]. Depending on the mode of operation, speaker identification system can be either text-dependent (constraint on what is spoken) or text-independent (no constraint on what is spoken) [2]. Speaker identification can be classified into Closed-set and Open-set identification. In closed-set speaker identification, the unknown speaker to be identified is a member of the set of N enrolled speakers whereas in an open-set speaker identification, a reference model for the unknown speaker may not exist [3,4]. This paper concentrates on closed-set text-independent speaker identification.

Speaker identification system can be performed in Monolingual, Crosslingual and Multilingual mode. In Monolingual speaker identification, training and testing languages for a speaker are the same whereas in Crosslingual speaker identification, training is done in one language (say A) and testing is done in another language (say B). In Multilingual speaker identification, some speakers in database are trained and tested in language A, some speakers in language B

S.M. Thampi et al. (Eds.): SNDS 2012, CCIS 335, pp. 127–134, 2012.

and so on [4], i.e., Speaker Models are trained in one language and tested with multiple languages of different speakers.

Speaker identification in limited data conditions refers to the task of recognizing speakers where both the training and test speech available only for few seconds. In this work, sufficient and limited data notionally denote the case of more than one minute and less than or equal to 15 seconds [5]. Most of state-of-the-art speaker identification systems work on Monolingual (preferably English) using sufficient data. The use of speaker identification system in Multilingual context is a requirement in a country like India where there is a coexistence of large number of languages.

Tomi kinnunen et al. [6] promoted to use multitaper MFCC feature extraction for speaker verification. Results indicate that multitapers outperform conventional single-window technique. A novel Multilingual text-independent based speaker identification algorithm was proposed by Geoffrey Duron in [7] and investigated 2 facets of speaker recognition: cross-language speaker identification and the same language non-native text independent speaker identification. The results indicated that how Speaker identification performance will be affected when the population is composed of native speakers or when speakers do not use the same language during the training and testing sessions. Bipul Pandey et al. [8] proposed a Multilingual speaker recognition scheme using adaptive neuro fuzzy inference scheme (ANFIS) for the identification of the speaker and the words spoken. The experimental results show the system to be amply efficient and successful in the recognition of the tasks that are involved.

In our previous work [9], we have compared the performance of GMM-UBM-Not Including Evaluation set (NIE) and GMM-UBM-Including Evaluation set (IE) for Mono, Cross and Multilingual speaker identification with the constraint of limited data. The speaker independent UBM was trained by IE and NIE. The results indicate that GMM-UBM can be used for improving speaker identification performance (%) with the Constraint of limited data in Multilingual scenario.

The state-of-the-art speaker recognition system uses MFCC as a feature for identifying speakers [1]. Squared magnitude of the Fourier transform of the windowed estimate, termed as Periodogram is used for the estimation of the spectrum for MFCC computation [10]. The convolution of the signal and window function spectra results in the spectral leakage. This spectral leakage is reduced by the Hamming-type of time-domain window. Therefore the windowing reduces the bias but the variance remains high [6]. The variance of the spectral estimates is reduced by the multitaper methods which uses multiple time-domain window functions [11]. The basic idea in multitapering is to pass the analysis frame through the multiple window functions and then estimate the weighted average of individual sub-spectra to obtain the final spectrum [6]. Designing of the tapers is to give approximately uncorrelated spectrum estimates so that averaging them reduces the variance [12].

The rest of the paper is organized as follows: Section 2 describes the database used for the experiments. Feature extraction using multitaper MFCC and speaker modeling using GMM-UBM technique are presented in Section 3. Section 4 gives experimental results. Finally, Summary and conclusions of this study and scope for the future work are mentioned in Section 5.

2 Speech Database for the Study

Since the standard Multilingual database is not available, experiments are carried out on an our own created database of 30 speakers who can speak the three different languages. The database includes 17-male and 13-female speakers. The voice recording was done in the Engineering college laboratory. The speakers were undergraduate students and faculties in an engineering college. The age of the speakers varied from 18-35 years. The speakers were asked to read small stories in three different languages. The training and testing data were recorded in different sessions with a minimum gap of two days. The approximate training and testing data length is two minutes. Recording was done using free downloadable wave surfer 1.8.8p3 software and Beetel Head phone-250 with a frequency range 20-20 kHz. The speech files are stored in .wav format.

3 Feature Extraction and Modeling

Feature extraction is the most important part of speaker recognition. Speech recordings were sampled at the rate of 8 kHz and pre-emphasized (factor 0.97). Frame duration of 20 msec and a 10 msec of overlapping durations are considered. Let $F = [f(0)\ f(1)\ ...\ f(N-1)]^T$ denote one frame of speech of N samples. Windowed discrete Fourier transform spectrum estimate is given by [12] [13] [14] & [15].

$$\hat{S}(f) = \left| \sum_{t=0}^{N-1} w(t)f(t)e^{-i2\pi ft/N} \right|^2 \tag{1}$$

where $W = [w(0)\ w(1)\ ...\ w(N-1)]^T$ is the time-domain window (Hamming) function. Fig. 1 shows the block diagram representation of the multitaper MFCC method. The use of windowing (hamming) technique, on average reduces the bias of the spectrum estimate i.e., amount by which the estimated spectrum value differs from the actual value but the variance of the estimated spectrum remains still high [12]. To reduce the variance, multitaper spectrum estimator can be used [12].

$$\hat{S}(f) = \sum_{j=1}^{K} \lambda(j) \left| \sum_{t=0}^{N-1} w_j(t)f(t)e^{-i2\pi ft/N} \right|^2 \tag{2}$$

Here K represents the number of multitapers used. $W_j = [w_j(0)\ w_j(1)\ ...\ w_j(N-1)]^T$ is the multitaper weights and j = 1, 2, ..., K, are used with corresponding weights $\lambda(j)$. A number of different tapers have been proposed for spectrum estimation. In [12], it was mentioned that the choice of multitaper type was

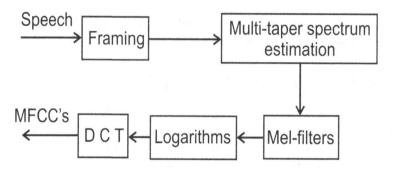

Fig. 1. Block Diagram of multitaper MFCC technique

found less important than the choice of the number of tapers, K ($3 \leq k \leq 8$). In this work, SWCE multitaper is used with K=6 windows. A mel-warping is then performed using 35 triangular band pass filters followed by Discrete Cosine Transform (DCT). A 13-dimensional MFCC feature vectors are finally obtained. The 0th coefficient is discarded since it is average of the input signal and carries less speaker specific information.

The GMM is the most commonly used probabilistic modeling technique in speaker identification. The complete Gaussian mixture density is parameterized by the mean vector, the covariance matrix and the mixture weight from all component densities. These parameters are collectively represented by $\lambda = \{w_i, \mu_i, \Sigma_i\}$; i = 1, 2, ..., M. where M is the number of speakers. In limited data speaker recognition systems, speech is pooled from many speakers to train a single independent model, known as UBM [16]. Individual speakers are then adapted from the UBM using the maximum a posterior (MAP) adaptation algorithm [16]. The parameters of the GMM models were estimated using expectation maximization (EM) algorithm. The k-means algorithm was used to obtain the initial estimate for each cluster [17]. Speech data collected from large number of speakers is pooled and the UBM is trained via EM algorithm. UBM acts as a speaker independent model in GMM-UBM system. The speaker dependent model (GMM) can be created by performing MAP adaptation technique from the UBM using speaker-specific training speech. In [5] and [18], it was mentioned that there are no criteria to select number of speakers and amount of data to train the UBM. We trained UBM using 30 speakers with roughly one hour of speech data.

4 Experiments

The Monolingual experimental results for the 30 speakers for 15 sec of training and testing data and for different Gaussian mixtures are given in Table 1. Note: A/B indicates training with language A and testing with language B. The speaker identification system trained and tested with English language (E/E) gives the highest performance of 90% and 93.33% for 256 Gaussian Mixtures for

Table 1. Monolingual Speaker identification performance (%). P_i represents the maximum identification performance among the number of Gaussian mixtures.

Train/Test language	Technique	Gaussian mixtures					P_i
		16	32	64	128	256	
E/E	MFCC	76.66	76.66	83.33	86.66	90.00	**90.00**
	multitaper MFCC	80.00	80.00	83.33	90.00	93.33	**93.33**
H/H	MFCC	76.66	86.66	86.66	90.00	86.66	**90.00**
	multitaper MFCC	73.33	80.00	86.66	93.33	93.33	**93.33**
K/K	MFCC	80.00	83.33	83.33	86.66	83.33	**86.66**
	multitaper MFCC	76.66	80.00	86.66	90.00	90.00	**90.00**

Table 2. Crosslingual Speaker identification performance (%). P_i represents the maximum identification performance among the number of Gaussian mixtures.

Train/Test language	Technique	Gaussian mixtures					P_i
		16	32	64	128	256	
H/E	MFCC	73.33	80.00	83.33	86.66	90.00	**90.00**
	multitaper MFCC	83.33	80.00	86.66	93.33	86.66	**93.33**
K/E	MFCC	63.33	76.66	80.00	80.00	86.66	**86.66**
	multitaper MFCC	73.33	83.33	86.66	86.66	90.00	**90.00**
E/H	MFCC	66.66	66.66	76.66	80.00	76.66	**80.00**
	multitaper MFCC	76.66	73.33	83.33	86.66	83.33	**86.66**
K/H	MFCC	66.66	66.66	76.66	76.66	80.00	**80.00**
	multitaper MFCC	70.00	76.66	83.33	83.33	83.33	**83.33**
E/K	MFCC	60.00	70.00	70.00	66.66	83.33	**83.33**
	multitaper MFCC	60.00	76.66	73.33	76.66	86.66	**86.66**
H/K	MFCC	63.33	73.33	73.33	76.66	80.00	**80.00**
	multitaper MFCC	63.33	73.33	83.33	86.66	80.00	**86.66**

MFCC and multitaper MFCC, respectively. The highest performance may be due to the speakers considered for the study. The speaker identification system trained and tested with Hindi language (H/H) gives the highest performance of 90% and 93.33% for 128 and 256 Gaussian Mixtures for MFCC and multitaper MFCC, respectively. The performance of speaker identification system trained and tested with Kannada language (K/K) is 86.66% and 90% for 128 and 256 Gaussian Mixtures for MFCC and multitaper MFCC, respectively.

The Crosslingual experimental results for the 30 speakers for 15 sec of training and testing data and for different Gaussian mixtures are given in Table 2. The speaker identification system trained with Hindi and tested with English language (H/E) yields a highest performance of 90% and 93.33% for 256 and 128 Gaussian Mixtures for MFCC and multitaper MFCC, respectively. For English as a testing language, no much difference in identification performance was observed in comparison with Hindi and Kannada as training languages.

Table 3. Multilingual Speaker identification performance (%). P_i represents the maximum identification performance among the number of Gaussian Mixtures.

Technique	Gaussian mixtures					P_i
	16	32	64	128	256	
MFCC	80.00	83.33	90.00	90.00	86.66	**90.00**
multitaper MFCC	80.00	86.66	90.00	93.33	96.66	**96.66**

The Multilingual experimental results for the 30 speakers for 15 sec of training and testing data and for different Gaussian mixtures are given in Table 3. The Multilingual speaker identification system yields a highest performance of 90% and 96.66% for 128 and 256 Gaussian Mixtures for MFCC and multitaper MFCC, respectively.

Table 4 and 5 shows Confusion matrices for the Multilingual speaker identification using MFCC and multitaper MFCC features, respectively for 256 Gaussian mixture. Correct identification (%) in a particular linguistic group is indicated by the main diagonal elements and off-diagonal elements show the misidentification [4]. Confusion matrices for MFCC and multitaper MFCC are having all off-diagonal elements as zeros, meaning that all the speakers in a particular linguistic group are identified or misidentified in their respective language only [4].

Some of the observations can be made from the results are as follows: (i) The multitaper (SWCE) MFCC perform better than the conventional hamming window MFCC in all the speaker identification experiments. This may be due to, use of multitapers reduce the variance of the MFCC features and thus making the spectrum less sensitive to the noise compared to the conventional single-window (hamming) method [6]. (ii) In comparison with the Monolingual speaker identification, Crosslingual speaker identification performance decreases drastically. This may be due to the variation in fluency and word stress when same speaker speaks different languages and also due to different phonetic and prosodic patterns of the languages [7]. (iii) The Multilingual results are better than the Mono and Crosslingual speaker identification experiments. This may be due to the better discrimination between the trained and testing models (multiple languages) in Multilingual scenario. (iv) Confusion matrix for multitaper MFCC is better than the conventional Hamming window MFCC technique.

Table 4. Confusion matrix for the Multilingual Speaker identification using MFCC features

	Eng	Hin	Kan
Eng	90	0	10
Hin	0	90	10
Kan	20	0	80

Table 5. Confusion matrix for the Multilingual Speaker identification using multitaper MFCC features

	Eng	Hin	Kan
Eng	100	0	0
Hin	0	100	0
Kan	0	10	90

5   Conclusion

This work presented the task of Mono, Cross and Multilingual speaker identification with the constraint of limited data condition using multitaper (SWCE with K=6) MFCC features. By replacing the windowed (hamming) DFT with multitaper spectrum estimate (SWCE), we found systematic improvements in all the speaker identification experiments. The results indicate that multitaper MFCC can be used for improving the speaker identification performance in Multilingual with the Constraint of limited data. A number of different tapers (Thomson, sine and multipeak etc.) have been proposed in literature for spectrum estimation needs to be verified for robustness of the speaker identification system.

Acknowledgement. This work is supported by Visvesvraya Technological University (VTU), Belgaum-590018, Karnataka, India.

References

1. Salman, A., Muhammad, E., Khurshid, K.: Speaker Verification using Boosted Cepstral Features with Gaussian Distributions. In: Proc. IEEE, INMIC 2007, pp. 1–5 (2007)
2. Reynolds, D.A., Rose, R.C.: Robust Text-Independent Speaker Identification Using Gaussian Mixture Speaker Models. IEEE Trans. Speech and Audio Processing 3, 72–83 (1995)
3. Jayanna, H.S., Mahadeva Prasanna, S.R.: Analysis, Feature Extraction, Modeling and Testing techniques for Speaker Recognition. IETE Technical Review 26, 181–190 (2009)
4. Arjun, P.H.: Speaker Recognition in Indian Languages: A Feature Based Approach. Ph.D. dissertation, Indian Institute of Technology Kharagpur, INDIA (July 2005)
5. Jayanna, H.S.: Limited data Speaker Recognition. Ph.D. dissertation, Indian Institute of Technology, Guwahati, INDIA (November 2009)
6. Kinnunen, T., Saeidi, R., Sandberg, J., Hansson-Sandsten, M.: What Else is New Than the HammingWindow? Robust MFCCs for Speaker Recognition via Multitapering. In: Proc. Interspeech 2010, pp. 2734–2737 (September 2010)
7. Durou, G.: Multilingual text-independent speaker identification. In: Proc. MIST 1999 Workshop, Leusden, Netherlands, pp. 115–118 (1999)
8. Pandey, B., Ranjan, A., Kumar, R., Shukla, A.: Multilingual Speaker Recognition Using ANFIS. In: Proc. IEEE, ICSPS, vol. 3, pp. 714–718 (2010)
9. Nagaraja, B.G., Jayanna, H.S.: Multi-lingual Speaker Identification with the constraint of Limited data. Accepted for publication in Proc. ICAdC 2012, MSRIT, Bengaluru. Springer (July 2012)
10. Sandberg, J., Hansson-Sandsten, M., Kinnunen, T., Saeidi, R., Flandrin, P., Borgnat, P.: Multitaper Estimation of Frequency-Warped Cepstra With Application to Speaker Verification. IEEE Signal Processing Letters 17, 343–346 (2010)
11. Alam, M.J., Kinnunen, T., Kenny, P., Ouellet, P., O'Shaughnessy, D.: Multi-taper MFCC Features for Speaker Verification using I-vectors. In: Proc. IEEE, ASRU 2011, pp. 547–552 (December 2011)

12. Kinnunen, T., Saeidi, R., Sedlák, F., Lee, K.A., Sandberg, J., Hansson-Sandsten, M., Li, H.: Low-Variance Multitaper MFCC Features: A Case Study in Robust Speaker Verification. IEEE Transaction on Audio, Speech and Language Processing 20, 1990–2001 (2012)
13. Percival, D.B., Walden, A.T.: Spectral Analysis for Physical Applications. Cambridge Univ. Press, Cambridge (1993)
14. Thomson, D.J.: Spectrum estimation and harmonic analysis. Proc. IEEE 70, 1055–1096 (1982)
15. Riedel, K.S., Sidorenko, A.: Minimum bias multiple taper spectral estimation. IEEE Trans. Signal Process. 43, 188–195 (1995)
16. Ku, J.M.K., Ambikairajan, E., Epps, J., Togneri, R.: Speaker Verification Using Sparse Representation Classification. In: Proc. IEEE, ICASSP, pp. 4548–4551 (2011)
17. Hosseinzadeh, D., Krishnan, S.: Combining Vocal Source and MFCC Features for Enhanced Speaker Recognition Performance Using GMMs. In: Proc. IEEE, MMSP 2007, pp. 365–368 (October 2007)
18. Reynolds, D.: Universal Background Models. Encyclopedia of Biometric Recognition, Journal Article (February 2008)

Secure Group Key Management Scheme for Simultaneous Multiple Groups with Overlapped Memberships Using Binomial Key Tree

B.R. Purushothama, Kusuma Shirisha, and B.B. Amberker

Department of Computer Science and Engineering
National Institute of Technology Warangal
Andhra Pradesh-506004, India
{puru,bba}@nitw.ac.in, shirisha.kusuma@gmail.com

Abstract. The rich literature available for key management schemes for Secure Group Communication focuses on operating only a single group. We consider the operation of simultaneous/concurrent multiple groups in the Secure Group Communication model with overlapping memberships. Designing a secure key management scheme with efficient rekeying process in this scenario is a challenging task. We design an efficient secure group key management scheme for simultaneous multiple groups with overlapping memberships. We propose a new key structure called Binomial Key Tree Queue to manage the keys. Our scheme scales well as the overlapping memberships across the multiple groups increases. We compare the schemes with two schemes which have recently focused on key management protocol design for simultaneous multiple groups. The proposed scheme achieves significant reduction in rekeying cost, storage compared to these schemes. Interestingly, we achieve this efficiency in the rekeying cost without much increase in storage at user.

Keywords: Simultaneous multiple groups, Binomial Key Tree Queue, Overlapping memberships, Rekeying, Group Key Management.

1 Introduction

Secure Group Communication (SGC) refers to a scenario in which the group of users communicate securely among themselves such that confidentiality of the message is maintained among the group users in a way that outsiders are unable to get any information even when they are able to intercept the messages. Several applications like distributed interactive simulation, video conferences, collaborative work, teleconferences, white-boards, tele-medicine, real-time information services take advantage of the SGC model. The confidentiality of group communications is provided by encrypting group messages with a common shared secret, called *group key* among the group members in group communication.The confidentiality of the messages within the secure group are provided using encryption methods. The encryption of the message within the group is carried out using the common key called *group key*. The users possessing this *group key*

S.M. Thampi et al. (Eds.): SNDS 2012, CCIS 335, pp. 135–146, 2012.

can participate in the group communication securely. The group messages are shielded from the non-members of the group, as these users wont have access to the *group key*.

So, key management is a challenge in the SGC which is about methodology that enables distributing the *group key* securely among the group users. Often the groups are dynamic in which the users join and leave the group during the lifetime of the group. Whenever a member join/leaves a group the *group key* needs to be changed as the newly joining member should not be able to access the past communication (**backward access control**) and the leaving user should not be able to access the future communication (**forward access control**) of the continuing group communication. So, how to change the key, both efficiently and scalably, is a challenge.

The group key management schemes proposed in the literature follow different approaches. Centralized group key management schemes or protocol employ a trusted centralized entity called *Key Distribution Center (KDC)* for key management [1][2][3]. In decentralized group key management schemes the responsibility of managing the large group is divided among subgroup managers [4]. The group key is generated by all group members contribution in Distributed or Contributory group key management schemes [5][6] and the group members carry out the task of access control. Sandro et.al in [7] provide the classical survey on *group key management schemes*.

The rich literature focuses on key management in a single operating group. Recently, we have focused our research on group key management in the simultanoeous (concurrent) multiple groups with overlapping membership. The challenge in this scenario is to make a user of a group to participate in multiple groups with less keys storage and rekeying cost.

1.1   Our Contribution

We have designed a SGC scheme for simultaneous multiple groups with overlapping membership using Binomial Key Tree Queue.

- We propose new key structure called Binomial Key Tree Queue for managing the simultaneous multiple groups with overlapping membership.
- We compare the proposed scheme with the schemes proposed in [8] and [9] for rekeying cost including number of encryptions, key changes and rekeying messages during membership change. We show that our proposed scheme is much efficient than the schemes in [8] and [9].
- Our keying scheme has the property that a user of a group can be in other multiple group communication sessions with only two keys per group apart from the keys which he has to hold for his own group and number of encryption and key changes are also significantly less upon group join and leave activities.
- In the proposed scheme, the efficiency in rekeying cost is achieved due to the non computation of auxiliary keys for a user when a user does have overlapping membership in other groups.

2   Simultaneous Secure Multiple Groups and Overlapping Membership in SGC Model

A secure group is the set of users communicating securely among themselves. The members of the secure group will have a *group key* using which they communicate securely. Secure multiple group is the collection of secure subgroups which are secure groups on their own. Each secure subgroup comprises of set of distinct users. The users of the subgroup communicate among themselves using their corresponding *group key*.

Definition 1 (Overlapping Membership in SMG). *Let $G_1, G_2, \ldots, G_m$ be the groups operating simultaneously. The members of the parent group G_i, for $i \in [1, m]$ want to communicate with the other groups G_j for $j \neq i$, $j < m$. Then, these members are said to have overlapping membership with the groups G_j.*

In simultaneous multiple groups with overlapping membership, the groups and the users of the groups are categorized as following. Let G_i be the group with users $\{u_1^i, u_2^i, \ldots, u_n^i\}$ and G_j be the group with users $\{u_1^j, u_2^j, \ldots, u_n^j\}$. Suppose k users of G_j have overlapping membership with group G_i. W.l.o.g let these users be $\{u_1^j, u_2^j, \ldots, u_k^j\}, k < n$. We categorize the users of the group G_i as

- **Parent Group and Parent Group Users**: For the users in $\{u_1^i, u_2^i, \ldots, u_n^i\}$, G_i is the parent group and these users are the parent group users of G_i. For the users $\{u_1^j, u_2^j, \ldots, u_n^j\}$, G_j is the parent group and these users are the parent group users of G_j.
- **Non-Parent Group and Non-Parent Group Users**: For the users in $\{u_1^j, u_2^j, \ldots, u_k^j\}$, for $k \leq n$, G_i is the non-parent group and these users are the non-parent group users of $G_{i,}$.

2.1   Example Illustrating the Overlapping Memberships in Simultaneous Multiple Groups

Consider Fig 1. There are three groups *Group A*, *Group B*, and *Group C*. For distinguishing the users of the various groups , members of the groups are colored red, green and blue for *Group A*, *Group B*, and *Group C* respectively. In Fig 1 there are 9 users colored red in *Group A*. For these users *Group A* is the **parent group**. Likewise, there are 10 and 8 users respectively in **parent group** *Group B* and **parent group** *Group C* colored green and blue respectively. The secure groups *Group A*, *Group B*, and *Group C* operate simultaneously. Therefore, these are termed as *simultaneous multiple groups*.

Overlapping membership is defined as the members of *Group i* for whom the *Group i* is the *parent group* and want to communicate with members of other groups *Group j*, where $i \neq j$ and $i, j = 1, 2, 3$ in Fig 1.

In Fig 1 , the overlapping memberships can be interpreted as described below.

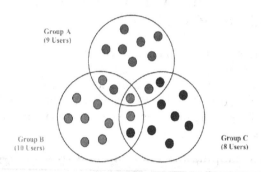

Fig. 1. Multiple Groups and Overlapping membership

1. The overlapping memberships of the group members of *parent group A*,
   - One of the member of *Group A* (colored red) wants to communicate with (Group B). This can be seen in the area $A \cap B$ of Fig 1. So, that user is said to have a overlapping membership with the *Group C*.
   - Likewise, a member of *Group A* in $A \cap C$ has overlapping membership with the *Group C*.
2. The overlapping membership of the group members of *parent Group B*,
   - A member of *Group B* in $(B \cap A) - (A \cap B \cap C)$ has a overlapping membership with *Group A*.
   - A member of *Group B* in $B \cap C - (A \cap B \cap C)$ has a overlapping membership with *Group C*.
   - A member of *Group B* in $B \cap A \cap C$ has a overlapping memberships with both the groups *Group A* and *Group C*.
3. Likewise, the overlapping membership of the group members of *parent Group C* can be interpreted.

The same illustration can be found in our previous work [8].

3   Notations and Definitions

- Let $U = \{u_1, u_2, \ldots, u_n\}$ be the set of users.
- $G_1, G_2, \ldots, G_m$ be the m groups with $n_1, n_2, \ldots, n_m$ distinct users respectively. No two users are same in the groups G_i, for $i = 1$ *to* m. In other words, $G_1, G_2, \ldots, G_m$ are disjoint.
- $\{M\}_K$: Encrypt the message M with key K. If $M = m_1, m_2, \ldots, m_n$, then encrypt each m_i, for $i, \ldots, n$ and send as one message or encrypt $m_1, \ldots, m_n$ and send. In the latter case, the receiver is assumed to know how to segregate the decrypted message.
- $Userset(K)$: Set of users possessing the key K.
- $u_j \rightarrow KDC : (J, G_i)$, Join request to KDC from a user u_j to join the group G_i. When the context is clear the single user u_j can be replaced with set of users $\{u_1, \ldots, u_l\}$.

Definition 2 (Binomial Tree). *The binomial tree S_h of height h is defined recursively [10]. The binomial tree S_0 has only one node. The binomial tree S_h has two binomial trees S_{h-1} that are connected as a one single tree. The root of one subtree is the leftmost child of the root of the other subtree. The Binomial tree satisfies the following properties. Let n be the number of nodes in a binomial tree.*

1. *If $n = 2^h$, the binomial key tree will be with*
   - *One binomial tree S_h and the degree of the root is h*
   - *Height h and 2^h nodes*
   - *Exactly $\binom{h}{i}$ nodes at depth i, such that $i = 0, 1, \ldots, h$*
2. *If n is not a power of 2 and $2^h + 1 \le n \le 2^h - 1$. Then,*

   - *The Binomial is a forest of binomial subtrees.*
   - *Consists atmost $h + 1$ binomial subtrees whose height range from 0 to h.*
   - *There will be surely a binomial subtree S_h with height h and depending on n, there exists binomial subtrees with heights ranging from 0 to $h-1$.*
   - *If it exists, there will be only one binomial subtree S_i, for some $i \in [0, h]$*

Definition 3 (Binomial Key Tree). *Binomial Key Tree is essentially a binomial tree consisting of nodes representing the users $\{u_1, \ldots, u_n\}$ in U. Each node (user node) also represents the keys held by the corresponding user.*

Definition 4 (Binomial Key Tree Queue (BKTQ)). *It is a Queue of Binomial Key Trees or forest of Binomial Key Trees.*

- *$BKTQ_G$:* This denotes the representation of a secure group G using $BKTQ$.
- *$BKTQ_G[h]$:* It is a BKT with height h of the group G.
- *$BKTQ_G[h,1]$:* BKT of height h of the parent group users in $BKTQ_G$
- *$BKTQ_G[h,2]$:* BKT of height h of the non-parent group users in $BKTQ_G$
- *$BKTQ_{PGU(G)}$:* This denotes the representation of a secure group consisting of parent group users of G using $BKTQ$
- *$BKTQ_{NPU(G)}$:* This denotes the representation of a secure group consisting of non-parent group users of G using $BKTQ$

4   Proposed Binomial Key Tree Queue Structure for Secure Group

In this section, we define the *Binomial Key Tree Queue (BKTQ)* that is constructed by the KDC for managing the group keys in the scenario of multiple secure group communication with overlapping membership. For each secure group G the KDC constructs a $BKTQ_G$.

KDC constructs set of $BKT's$ for the parent group users in G as in [11]. W.l.o.g let these set of BKT's be $\{S_h, S_{h-1}, \ldots, S_0\}$ whose height is respectively $h, h-1, \ldots, 0$. It should be noted that h depends on the number of parent group users. The BKT $S_i, i \in [0, h]$ will have 2^i user nodes along with their corresponding keys. The KDC Constructs the $BKTQ_{PGU(G)}$ for parent group

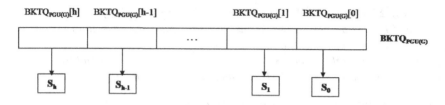

Fig. 2. Binomial Key Tree Queue Representation for Parent Group Users of Group G

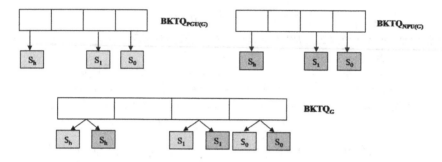

Fig. 3. Lazy Merge of BKTQ of Parent and Non-Parent Group Users of Group G

users in G as shown in Fig 2. As a notational convenience if any of the BKT S_i is empty we denote it as $BKTQ_{PGU(G)}[i] = \emptyset$.

KDC constructs the set of $BKT's$ for the non-parent group users of G followed by the $BKTQ_{NPU(G)}$ as shown in Fig 2. KDC will run the **Algorithm 1** to construct the final BKTQ of group G, $BKTQ_G$ by lazily merging $BKTQ_{PGU(G)}$ and $BKTQ_{NPU(G)}$. Finally, the BKTQ of group G as a result of execution of **Algorithm 1** looks as in Fig 3.

5   Secure Group Key Management Scheme Using $BKTQ$

In this section, we elaborate the group set up , join of parent and non-parent group users and leave of parent and non-parent group users. Readers should note that due to space limitations we are unable to give examples. We elaborate in detail the protocol and the ideas that helps in analysis of the protocols for rekeying cost. For binomial key tree basic join and leave operations one can refer [11][1]. We focus on the non-parent group user join and leave operations and show that our proposed scheme is efficient n comparison with the existing schemes.

Our scheme employs KDC to manage the simultaneous groups. Initially, the groups are empty. We assume that each user who joins the group will have a shared secret key with the KDC. We assume that the KDC authenticates the user before sending securely the shared key to the user.(Initially we assume the existence of the secure channel to give the shared key to user).

For every group G_i for $i = 1$ to m KDC forms the $BKTQ$ as explained in section 4. Each group will have a group key K_{G_i}.

Algorithm 1. Lazy Merge of Binomial Key Tree Queues: LazyMerge-BKTQ

Input :
- $BKTQ_{PGU(G)}$, Binomial Key Tree Queue of Parent Group users of G
- $BKTQ_{NPU(G)}$, Binomial Key Tree Queue of Non-Parental Group users of G

Output: $BKTQ_G$, Binomial Key Tree Queue of G

1 Let h_1 be the height of the leftmost BKT in $BKTQ_{PGU(G)}$;
2 Let h_2 be the height of the leftmost BKT in $BKTQ_{NPU(G)}$;
3 **for** $i \leftarrow 0$ to $min(h_1, h_2)$ **do**
  if $BKTQ_{PGU(G)}[i] \neq \emptyset$ and $BKTQ_{NPU(G)[i]} \neq \emptyset$ **then**

   - $BKTQ_G[i, 1] = BKTQ_{PGU(G)}[i]$;
   - $BKTQ_G[i, 2] = BKTQ_{NPU(G)}[i]$;

  end
  if $BKTQ_{PGU(G)}[i] = \emptyset$ **then**

   - $BKTQ_G[i, 1] = \emptyset$;
   - $BKTQ_G[i, 2] = BKTQ_{NPU(G)}[i]$;

  end
  if $BKTQ_{NPU(G)}[i] = \emptyset$ **then**

   - $BKTQ_G[i, 1] = BKTQ_{PGU(G)}[i]$;
   - $BKTQ_G[i, 2] = \emptyset$;

  end
end

5.1   Join of Parent Group User

When a new user u wants to join the parent group $G_i, i \in [1, m]$, KDC runs **Protocol 2**. The joining point for the new user is in the subtree corresponding to the parent group users of the corresponding group's BKTQ. The group key, the subtree key of the subtree corresponding to the joining point needs to be changed and communicated to the appropriate users.

5.2   Leave of Parent Group User

Suppose a parent group user u wants to leave parent group G_i, for $i \in [1, m]$. KDC runs **Protocol 3**. The leaving point is in the subtree of the parent group users corresponding to the leaving group's BKTQ. The group key, the subtree keys of the subtree of which the leaving user is part should be changed. The changed keys should be communicated to appropriate users. For the non-parent group users the KDC encrypts the changed group key using the subtree keys of the BKTQ corresponding to the non-parent group users.

Protocol 2. Join Protocol for the Parent Group

Input :
- Security parameter, k

1 Let K_{G_j} be the current group key of G_j represented by $BKTQ_{G_j}$;
2 Let n be the number of users in G_j;
3 $u \to KDC : (J, G_j)$;
4 $KDC \Longleftrightarrow u$: KDC Authenticate the user u and distribute K_u;
           // K_u is the shared private key of the user u with KDC;
5 KDC generates randomly a new group key K'_{G_j}.;
6 Refer Join protocol in [1] or steps $4 - 14$ of Algorithm 1 in [11] ;
7 $KDC \to userset(K_{G_i}) : \{K'_{G_j}\}_{K_{G_j}}$;
8 $KDC \to u : \{K'_{G_j}\}_{K_u}$;

Protocol 3. Leave Protocol for the Parent Group

---

1 Follow the leave protocol in [11] and execute the next step.;
2 Send the new group key K' to the non-parent group users using their respective subtree keys.;

---

6 Join and Leave of Non-parent Group Users

Consider $G_1, G_2, \ldots, G_m$ groups represented as $BKTQ_{G_i}$, for $i = 1, \ldots, m$ such that $BKTQ_{G_i}[j, 1]$, for $j = 1, \ldots, h$ as the parent group users BKT's and $BKTQ_{G_i}[j, 2]$, for $j = 1, \ldots, h$ as non-parent group user BKT's. To achive efficiency in the rekeying process in the user join and leave operation we exploit the structure of Binomial Key Subtrees.

Suppose the users of G_i want to have overlapping membership with users of G_j. We propose the following process.

- We know that KDC has to rearrange the $BKTQ_{G_j}$ when a new user joins. KDC is assumed to make the users of G_i who wants to have overlapping membership with G_j as a part of one subtree. The users in this new subtree are non-parent group users of G_j.
- All the users who belongs to a subtree will have a common key (each subtree will have a common key). When these users join as non-parent group users to G_j there is no need to generate the intermediate/auxiliary keys for these users in G_j.
- These users are given only a single key of the new subtree that is formed by the KDC as part of G_j and the group key of G_j.
- With these the storage at the non-parent group user will be 2 keys apart from what he holds for his parent group.

The process of joining of a non-parent group user is given in Protocol 4.

Protocol 4. Join Protocol for the Non-Parent Group

---

1 Let $BKTQ_{G_i}$, for $i = 1, \ldots, m$ be the BKTQ's that contains the set of BKT's from G_i, for $i = 1, \ldots, m$ that wants to have overlapping memberships with G;

2 **for** $i=1$ to m **do**

$\quad BKTQ_{NPU(G)} = MergeBKTQ(BKTQ_{G_i}, BKTQ_{NPU(G)})$ // Refer

$\quad$ Algorithm 6 for MergeBKTQ

end

3 KDC generates keys for $BKTQ_{NPU(G)}[i]$, for $i = 0$ to h;

$\quad\quad\quad\quad$ // These are the keys for the subtrees constructed;

4 KDC generates new group key K';

5 $KDC \rightarrow Userset(K) : \{K'\}_K$;

$\quad$ // K is the old group key. The existing non-parent group users of G will also get this new group key;

6 **for** $i=0$ to h **do**

$\quad KDC \rightarrow Userset(K_{BKTQ_{NPU(G)}[i]}) : \{K'\}_{K_{BKTQ_{NPU(G)}[i]}}$;

end

$\quad$ // This distributes the keys for the newly joined non-parent group users.

Algorithm 5. Combine Binomial Key Subtree: CombineBKT

Input : S_i, S_j, Binomial Key Trees of same height h

Output: Binomial Key Tree of height, h or $h+1$

1 **if** $S_i \neq \emptyset$ and $S_j \neq \emptyset$ **then**

$\quad$ **return** $< S_{i+1}, i+1 >$;   // See Definition 2

end

2 **if** $S_i = \emptyset$ **then**

$\quad$ **return** $< S_j, j >$

end

3 **if** $S_j = \emptyset$ **then**

$\quad$ **return** $< S_i, i >$

end

6.1   Leave of a Non-parent Group User

Protocol 7 gives the protocol wherein the users of a non-parent group leave. A new group key needs to be generated and the subtree keys should be changed for the subtree of which the leaving user is a part and the same should be communicated to appropriate users. The parent group users are distributed with the changed keys as in [11]. The non-parent group users are given the changed group keys using the new subtree keys generated.

7   Storage Cost Estimation

Suppose a user u is part of a group G_i with n users. Suppose the user is a part of BKT subtree $S_{\log_2 n}$. Then u will have $\log_2 n$ keys and the shared secret with

---

Algorithm 6. Merge of Binomial Key Tree Queues: MergeBKTQ

Input : $BKTQ_{G_i}$, $BKTQ_{G_j}$, Binomial Key Tree Queues of groups G_i and G_j

Output: $BKTQ_{G_{ij}}$, Merged Binomial Key Tree Queue

1 Let h_1 be the height of the leftmost BKT in $BKTQ_{G_i}$;
2 Let h_2 be the height of the leftmost BKT in $BKTQ_{G_j}$;
3 **for** $k \leftarrow 0$ *to* $min(h_1, h_2)$ **do**
   $< S, l >= CombineBKT(BKTQ_{G_i}[k], BKTQ_{G_j}[k]);$ // Refer
   Algorithm 5 for CombineBKT

   if $l=k$ **then**
      $< S, p >= CombineBKT(BKTQ_{G_{ij}}[l], S;); BKTQ_{G_{ij}}[p] = S$
   else
      $BKTQ_{G_{ij}}[l] = S;$
   end
end
for $k = min(h_1, h_2) \leftarrow$ *to* $max(h_1, h_2)$ **do**
   if $h_1 < h_2$ **then**
      $BKTQ_{G_{ij}}[k] = BKTQ_{G_j}[k];$
   else
      $BKTQ_{G_{ij}}[k] = BKTQ_{G_i}[k];$
   end
end

Protocol 7. Leave Protocol for the Non-Parent Group

---

1 Let S_i, for $i \in [0, h]$ be the subtree that contains the users who want to leave.;
2 Split S_i till the subtree of the users who leave is obtained.;
3 Remove the subtree containing leaving users;
4 Combine the remaining subtrees S_j, for $j \in [0, h]$ using Algorithm 5;
5 KDC will generate new keys for subtrees formed after combine. Also KDC generates the new group key;
6 Identify the subtrees in the combined tree where old subtrees before removal of the users are part.;
7 Distribute the new subtree keys and changed group key with their old subtree common keys.;
8 Distribute the changed group key to parent group users by following the leave protocol in [11].

KDC. Suppose u joins the group G_j, then he will be given the group key of G_j and the subtree key of the new BKT subtree of which he is part. So he will have additional 2 keys per overlapping membership. New intermediate keys need not be generated in G_j. When we make users of a group to have a overlapping membership as a subtree, the join and leave become efficient.

8   Comparison with the Existing Schemes

In this section, we analyze the proposed BKTQ based key managagement scheme for the simultaneous multiple groups with the schemes in [8] (given in Table 1)

Table 1. Comparison of the scheme in [8] and our proposed $BKTQ$ based scheme

	Scheme in [8]		Our Proposed Scheme	
	# Encryptions	# Key Changes	# Encryptions	# Key Changes
Join of a PGU	$2\lceil \log_2 n \rceil + 1$	$\lceil log_2 n \rceil$	2	1
Join of a NPGU	2	1	2	1
Leave of a PGU	$2\lceil \log_2 n \rceil + m - 2$	$\lceil log_2 n \rceil$	$\leq \log_2 n$	$\log_2 n + 1$
Leave of a NPGU	$\leq (m + 2^{\frac{log_2 n - 1}{2}})$	1	$\leq \log_2 m + \log_2 n - 1$	2

and [9] (not given in Table 1) please refer comparison section in [8]). Consider $m = 2^k, k > 0$ groups with each group having $n = 2^t, t > 0$ *parent group users*. In these m groups, every *parent group members* of every group has a overlapping membership with every other group. So in a group, there are $(m-1)n$ *non-parent group members* and n *parent group members*. The results of comparison based on this scenario are provided in Table 1. In Table 1, PGU is Parent Group User and NPGU is Non Parent Group User. As it is depicted in Table 1, our proposed $BKTQ$ based scheme out performs the scheme in [8] and [9].

9   Conclusion

We have proposed an efficient secure group key management scheme for managing the keys in simultaneous multiple groups with overlapping membership. We have proposed a new tree structure, Binomial Key Tree Queue. We have compared our scheme with the schemes in [8] and [9] for rekeying cost. Our results show that, the proposed scheme is efficient. The significant observation is that this efficiency achieved without much increase in storage at the user and KDC. In this scheme a group user will have to only store additional two keys per group for the groups with which he has overlapping membership. In complete paper, we will provide the protocol details with examples and provide the detailed analysis of the protocols for the rekeying cost.

Acknowledgments. This work was supported by Information Security Education and Awareness - ISEA Fellowship, Department of Information Technology, Ministry of Communications and Information Technology and Ministry of Human Resource Development, Government of INDIA.

References

1. Aparna, A., Amberker, B.B.: Secure group communication using binomial trees. In: Third International Symposium on Advanced Networks and Telecommunication Systems, IEEE ANTS (2009)
2. Blundo, C., De Santis, A., Herzberg, A., Kutten, S., Vaccaro, U., Yung, M.: Perfectly-Secure Key Distribution for Dynamic Conferences. In: Brickell, E.F. (ed.) CRYPTO 1992. LNCS, vol. 740, pp. 471–486. Springer, Heidelberg (1993)

3. Wong, C.K., Gouda, M., Lam, S.S.: Secure Group Communication Using key Graphs. IEEE/ACM Transactions on Networking 8, 16–30 (2000)
4. Mittra, S.: Iolus: A framework for Scalable Secure Multicasting. In: ACM SIG-COMM 1997 Conference on Applications, Technologies, Architectures, and Protocols for Computer Communication, vol. 27, pp. 277–288 (1997)
5. Amir, Y., Kim, Y., Nita-Rotaru, C., Schultz, J., Stanton, J., Tsudik, G.: Secure Group Communication using Robust Contributory Key Agreement. IEEE Transactions on Parallel and Distributed System 15, 468–480 (2004)
6. Burmester, M., Desmedt, Y.: A Secure and Efficient Conference Key Distribution System. In: De Santis, A. (ed.) EUROCRYPT 1994. LNCS, vol. 950, pp. 275–286. Springer, Heidelberg (1995)
7. Rafaeli, S., Hutchison, D.: A Survey of Key Management for Secure Group Communication. ACM Computing Surveys 35, 309–329 (2003)
8. Purushothama, B.R., Amberker, B.B.: Group key management scheme for simultaneous multiple groups with overlapped membership. In: Third International Conference on Communication Systems and Networks, COMSNETS, pp. 1–10 (2011)
9. Aparna, A., Amberker, B.B.: Key Management Scheme for Multiple Simultaneous Secure Group Communication. In: IEEE International Conference on Internet Multimedia Systems Architecture and Applications, IMSAA 2009, pp. 1–6 (2009)
10. Cormen, T.H., Leiserson, C.E., Rivest, R.L., Stein, C.: Introduction to Algorithms. PHI Publishers, New Delhi (2006)
11. Aparna, A., Amberker, B.B.: A key management scheme for secure group communication using binomial key trees. International Journal of Network Management 20, 383–418 (2010)

An Analytical Approach to Position-Based Routing Protocol for Vehicular Ad Hoc Networks

Ram Shringar Raw[1], Daya Krishan Lobiyal[2], and Sanjoy Das[2]

[1] Ambedkar Institute of Advanced Communication Techologies & Research, Delhi, India
[2] School of Computer and Systems Sciences, Jawaharlal Nehru University, New Delhi, India
rsrao08@yahoo.in, {lobiyal,sdas.jnu}@gmail.com

Abstract. Position-based routing protocols have been proposed to utilize the geographical position information of nodes to supports efficient routing in ad hoc networks. In this paper we examined the significance of position-based routing with border-node based forwarding for Vehicular Ad hoc Network (VANET) to optimize path length and minimize end-to-end delay between vehicles. This proposed protocol is called Border-node based Most Forward progress within Radius (B-MFR) since it uses border nodes with Most Forward progress within Radius (MFR). In our work, results clearly show that using the border-node is an advantage to maximize the performance of routing protocol in terms of average number of hops with minimum delay. We have simulated the proposed protocol in MATLAB and compared the result with existing protocol MFR. `

Keywords: VANET, Routing Protocol, Position-based Routing, MFR, B-MFR.

1   Introduction

The automotive industries are strongly deploying communication based public safety applications that save lives and improve traffic flow. The manufacturing of wireless device enabled vehicles is increased recently. These vehicles can include wireless communication devices such as phones, Bluetooth, and onboard communication units. These devices can communicate among themselves while vehicles are on move. Therefore, these vehicles form temporary network that keeps on changing its topology dynamically and frequently. Such a network is called Vehicular Ad hoc Network (VANET) [1]. This network is useful to reduce large number of vehicular traffic accidents, improve safety, and manage city traffic control system with high and reliable efficiency.

Vehicular communications has significant advantages but also has some challenging issues such as error prone links, bandwidth constraints, node density, highly dynamic topology, authentication, repudiation, and scalability. However, highly dynamic topology makes routing a challenging issue. But, some of the traditional ad hoc routing protocols can be used in VANET [2]. However, due to the frequently changing network topology caused by fast mobility and regular change in vehicle density, these routing protocols perform poorly in VANET. A number of

S.M. Thampi et al. (Eds.): SNDS 2012, CCIS 335, pp. 147–156, 2012.

routing protocols have been proposed for VANET and most of these protocols use different data dissemination methods over multiple paths for reliable data transmission. In this paper, we present the significant role of routing protocols especially position-based routing protocols for VANETs. Our contribution in this paper is folded as two:

- For city scenario, we introduce a novel position-based routing protocol for VANETs that is called Border-node based Most Forward within Radius routing (B-MFR) protocol that takes advantage of Most Forward within Radius (MFR) routing protocol. B-MFR considers the characteristics of VANETs while at the same time takes into account the limitations of the existing routing protocols.
- We do the mathematical analysis of the protocol.

B-MFR improves data delivery in various scenarios of VANETs. Especially, B-MFR is designed to efficiently route the packets with small number of hops and therefore, small delay. It uses the concepts of border-node of the sender's communication range to minimize the number of hops between source and destination.

Our paper is organized as follows. We present the work related to our research in section 2. In section 3, we introduce the design of B-MFR routing protocol. Section 4 presents the mathematical analysis of B-MFR routing protocol. In section 5, simulation results for performance analysis of the proposed protocol are presented. Finally, we conclude the work presented in this paper in section 6.

2   Related Work

In all the position-based routing protocols, the minimum information a node must have to make useful routing decisions is to our knowledge, assumed to be its position, position of its neighbors, and the final destination's location. Position-based routing protocols exploit the availability of accurate position information. In VANET, each vehicle wishes to know its own position through GPS receiver as well as position of its neighbors by exchanging Hello (beacon) packet periodically. Position-based routing protocols are based on greedy forwarding scheme. In the greedy forwarding scheme, a source node finds the position information of its direct neighbor nodes and selects that direct neighbor node which is nearest to the destination node as the next-hop node. Position-based routing protocols are more suited to dense networks and to frequent network disconnections. Recently, some position based routing protocols such as DIR (Compass Routing) and MFR, specific to VANETs have been proposed.

A DIrectional Routing (DIR) [3] (referred as the Compass Routing) is based on the greedy forwarding method in which the source node uses the position information of the destination node to calculate its direction. Then the message is forwarded to the nearest neighbor having direction closest to the destination. Therefore, a message is forwarded to the neighboring node minimizing the angle between itself, the previous node, and the destination node. Most Forward within Radius (MFR) [3] is a well-known method for finding a route in a network by utilizing position information of nodes. The neighbor with the greatest progress towards the destination is chosen as next-hop node for sending packets further. Therefore, MFR forwards the packet to the node that is closest to the destination node to minimize the number of hops. In MFR, next-hop neighbor node is decided through unicast forwarding by using the position information of the sender node, its next neighbor nodes, and the packet destination node.

These routing protocols outperform previous routing protocols in terms of packet delivery ratio and end-to-end delay in highway scenarios. But they also suffer due to large end-to-end delay and decreased packet delivery ratio when network size is large as there are obstacles such as building and trees in the region.

3   Proposed Work

In this work, we have designed a routing protocol that is B-MFR to deliver a message for the city traffic scenario in a fully distributed manner. We have developed a mathematical model for B-MFR to determine average number of hop counts using Poisson distribution for node deployment in the next section. Further a mathematical model for this protocol has been designed to determine expected distance to the next-hop node, and expected distance between source and destination. Also, performance of the protocol has been compared with the existing MFR routing protocol.

3.1   Border-Node Based MFR (B-MFR)

Next-hop forwarding method like greedy forwarding scheme for linear network does not support well in highly MANET such as VANET. Therefore, other position-based protocols such as MFR, GEDIR, DIR, etc. have been used for VANET to improve its performance for non-linear network in a high vehicular density environment. These protocols can be further improved by utilizing farthest one-hop node in a dense and highly mobile network. In this work, we have proposed a routing protocol that uses border-nodes with maximum projection as next-hop node [4]. This protocol is a modified version of MFR routing protocol.

In this protocol, only nodes at the border of the sender's transmission range are considered for forwarding the packets in a dense network. Since the nodes closer to the border cover more distance and therefore, may reduce the number of hop counts. A node at the border of the transmission radius with maximum projection is selected as a next-hop node. It may not be possible to find even a single node at the extreme end of the transmission range. Therefore, we have considered a region around the extreme end of the transmission radius.

3.2   Selecting Next-Hop Node in B-MFR

The B-MFR utilizes the border-node to avoid using interior nodes within the transmission range for further transmitting the packet. This method selects the border-node as a next-hop node for forwarding packet from source to destination.

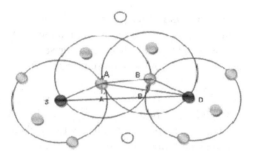

Fig. 1. B-MFR forwarding method

In this method, a packet is sent to the border-node with the greatest progress that is defined as the projected distance of the border-node on the line joining source and destination. In Fig. 1, node A is a border-node of source node S, since node A is positioned at maximum transmission range. It has maximum progress distance SA' where A' is projection of A on line SD. Therefore, node A is selected as the next-hop forwarding node. Node A when receives the message from S uses the same method to find the next-hop forwarding node with greatest projected distance towards destination. In this way, node B is selected as a border node of A for forwarding packets to the destination. Finally node B directly delivers the message to destination node D.

4   Mathematical Analysis of B-MFR Routing Protocol

In this work, we have mathematically analyzed the performance of the proposed routing protocol. We have discussed the probabilistic analysis of finding at least one node in a given area. Further, we have evaluated the average number of hops and expected distance between a source and a destination. Due to the randomness and high mobility, estimating the average number of hops becomes very essential in multi-hop vehicular ad hoc networks. A mathematical model has been developed for the protocol for selecting a border node towards destination node.

4.1   The Probability of Finding at Least One Node in a Border Region

We assume that the neighbor nodes are distributed in a circular region of radius R. R is the maximum transmission range of a node. Given the area of the transmission range (circular region) is A, λ is the vehicle density, and $N = \lambda \pi R^2$ is the number of nodes in the transmission range. The nodes may be inside the circular region as well as on the border of the circular region. However, at times there may not be any node on the border. Therefore, we consider some area along with the boundary of the circular region. We will refer to this region as border region. Fig. 2 shows, this region as a border region (shaded area) and the neighbor nodes (which we refer to as border nodes) placed in this region can be selected as a next-hop node. The border region can be calculated as follows:

Border Region (A$_s$) = Area of the half circle – Area of the triangle

$$A_s = \frac{\pi R^2 - 2R^2}{2} \tag{1}$$

Further, we assume that nodes are placed following Poisson distribution. If X is the random variable representing the number of nodes in the border region, the probability of n nodes present in border region is given by

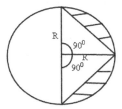

Fig. 2. Border region

$$P_{As}(X = n) = \frac{(\lambda A_s)^n \cdot e^{-\lambda A_s}}{n!} \tag{2}$$

Where λ is the node density. The probability of selecting k nodes out of n nodes is given by

$$P(Y = k) = \binom{n}{k}(p)^k(1-p)^{n-k} \tag{3}$$

Where p is probability of selecting a node and q (=1-p) is the probability of not selecting a node. Now probability of selecting exactly k nodes in the given border region is [5], [6], [7]

$$P(k) = \sum_{n=k}^{\infty} \binom{n}{k}(p)^k(1-p)^{n-k} \cdot \frac{(\lambda A_s)^n}{n!} e^{-\lambda A_s}$$

$$= \frac{(p\lambda A_s)^k}{k!} \cdot e^{-p\lambda A_s} \tag{4}$$

Now, we put the value of A_s from equation (1) into equation (4). The probability of selecting exactly k nodes is

$$P(k) = \frac{\left(\frac{p\lambda(\pi R^2 - 2R^2)}{2}\right)^k}{k!} \cdot e^{-\frac{p\lambda(\pi R^2 - 2R^2)}{2}} \tag{5}$$

Therefore, the probability to select at least k nodes in the border region is given by

$$P(at\ least\ k\ node) \quad = 1 - \sum_{i=0}^{k-1} \frac{(p\lambda A_s)^i}{i!} \cdot e^{-p\lambda A_s} \tag{6}$$

After putting the value of A_s from equation (1) into equation (6), the probability to select at least k nodes is given by

$$P(at\ least\ k\ node) = 1 - \sum_{i=0}^{k-1} \frac{\left(\frac{p\lambda(\pi R^2 - 2R^2)}{2}\right)^i}{i!} \cdot e^{-\frac{p\lambda(\pi R^2 - 2R^2)}{2}} \tag{7}$$

From the equation (7), we can easily obtain the probability of having at least one node within the border region as

$$P = 1 - P(X = 0) = 1 - e^{-\frac{p\lambda(\pi R^2 - 2R^2)}{2}} \tag{8}$$

Similarly, the probability of not having any node in a border region is given by

$$P^\circ = e^{-\frac{p\lambda(\pi R^2 - 2R^2)}{2}} \tag{9}$$

4.2   Average Number of Hops between Source and Destination Node

To determine the average number of hop counts, nodes within the transmission range R follow the Poisson distributed model. We also assume that the destination is present in the transmission range of the source node. Therefore, the probability of destination node can be defined as the probability of next-hop node. Let D_l is the link distance between the source and next-hop node (shown in Fig. 3). The probability density function of the link distance D_l between source and next-hop node is defined as [8], [9]

$$f(D_1) = 2\pi\lambda D_1 \cdot e^{-\pi\lambda D_1^2}$$

The probability of one-hop count can be calculated as follows:

$$P(1) = \int_0^R f(D_1)\,dD_1 \quad = 1 - e^{-\pi\lambda R^2} \tag{10}$$

Now, assume that the destination node is placed outside the transmission range of the source node. We need to calculate two-hop counts, three-hop counts, and so on. The distance between source node and two-hop node is greater than the transmission range R but less than or equal to the $2R$. There will be at least one intermediate node between source and two-hop node. The position of forwarding node must lie within the intersection of two circles. Therefore, the probability of a two-hop counts can be calculated as follows:

$$P(2) \quad = \left[e^{-\pi\lambda R^2} - e^{-4\pi\lambda R^2}\right] \times \left[1 - e^{-\frac{p\lambda(\pi R^2 - 2R^2)}{2}}\right] \tag{11}$$

Similarly, the probability of three-hop count is

$$P(3) \quad = \left[e^{-4\pi\lambda R^2} - e^{-9\pi\lambda R^2} \right] \times \left[1 - e^{-\frac{p\lambda(\pi R^2 - 2R^2)}{2}} \right]^2 \tag{12}$$

And consequently, the probability of j-hop counts can be defined as

$$P(j) \quad = \left[e^{-(j-1)^2\pi\lambda R^2} - e^{-j^2\pi\lambda R^2} \right] \times \left[1 - e^{-\frac{p\lambda(\pi R^2 - 2R^2)}{2}} \right]^{j-1} \tag{13}$$

Now, by using equations 10, 11, 12, and 13, we can calculate the expected number of hops $E(H)$ between source and destination as follows:

$$E(H) = \sum_{H=1}^{j} H \left[e^{-(H-1)^2\pi\lambda R^2} - e^{-H^2\pi\lambda R^2} \right] \times \left[1 - e^{-\frac{p\lambda(\pi R^2 - 2R^2)}{2}} \right]^{H-1} \tag{14}$$

4.3   Expected Distance between Source and Next-Hop Node

Assume a source node S has n neighbors in the direction of destination. Let A be the border node in the transmission range R of source node S (shown in Fig. 3).

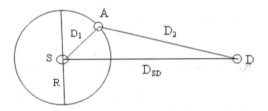

Fig. 3. Selection of border node A as a next-hop node

Let $d_1, d_2, d_3..., d_n$ denotes the distances between source node and its neighbors [10]. D_l is the distance between source node and its border node (next-hop node), and it is expressed as

$$D_1 = Max_{i=1}^{n} d_i$$

We can calculate the expected value of distance D_l as follows:
    Let $F(D_l)$ and $f(D_l)$ be the CDF and PDF of D_l, respectively. Then,

$$F(D_1) = P[d_1 \leq D_1, d_2 \leq D_1, ..., d_n \leq D_1] = \prod_{i=1}^{n} P[d_i \leq D_1] = \left(\frac{D_1}{R} \right)^n$$

Similarly,

$$f(D_1) = \frac{d}{dD_1} F(D_1) \quad = \frac{n}{R} \left(\frac{D_1}{R} \right)^{n-1}$$

The expected value of D_l is,

$$E(D_1) = \int_{\frac{R}{\sqrt{2}}}^{R} D_1 f(D_1)\, dD_1 \;=\; \int_{\frac{R}{\sqrt{2}}}^{R} D_1\, d\, F(D_1) = \frac{nR}{(n+1)}\left[1 - \frac{1}{2^{\left(\frac{n+1}{2}\right)}}\right] \quad (15)$$

4.4   Expected Distance between Source and Destination

In this section, we estimate the expected distance between source and destination node. In equation (14), we have calculated the expected number of hops $E(H)$ between source and destination node. In equation (15), we have calculated the expected distance $E(D_1)$ between source and next-hop node. By using these two equations, we can determine the expected distance between source and destination as follows:

$$E(D_{sd}) = E(D_1) \times E(H)$$

$$= \frac{nR}{(n+1)}\left[1 - \frac{1}{2^{\left(\frac{n+1}{2}\right)}}\right] \times \sum_{H=1}^{j} H\left[e^{-(H-1)^2 \pi \lambda R^2} - e^{-H^2 \pi \lambda R^2}\right] \times$$

$$\left[1 - e^{-\frac{p\lambda(\pi R^2 - 2R^2)}{2}}\right]^{H-1} \quad (16)$$

This is the expected distance a packet has to travel during transmission from source to destination.

5   Numerical Results and Performance Analysis

In real city traffic environment, there are many junctions with traffic signs. To communicate with other vehicles, a packet is passed from one junction to another junction. In this section, we evaluate the performance of our proposed routing protocol using results obtained through simulation. To simulate an unbounded area, only nodes located at a distance larger than the transmission range R are considered for packet transmission. In the simulations, results have been computed in terms of average number of hops between source and destination. The results have been also compared with existing MFR routing protocol.

5.1   Average Number of Hops between Source and Destination

Fig. 4 shows the effect of transmission range on average number of hops. As the transmission range increases, the average number of hops decreases for given number of nodes. Fig.4 also shows that the network with less number of nodes (e.g. 10 nodes) has relatively large average number of hops compared to the network with large number of nodes (e.g. 15 nodes). This characteristic of the network is observed because in a network to provide the connectivity, nodes should be at more distance if they are lesser in numbers.

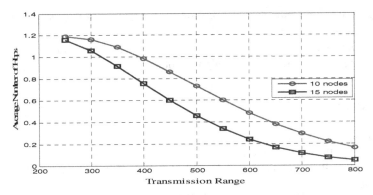

Fig. 4. Average number of hops

Fig. 5 shows the comparison of MFR and B-MFR routing protocols in terms of average number of hops for different network size (number of nodes). In both the cases, as the number of nodes increases, the average number of hops decreases. Compared to MFR routing protocol, B-MFR gives better result. The Fig. 5 shows average number of hops for varying transmission range. From the figure, we can see that average number of hop counts for B-MFR is comparatively smaller than MFR due to selection of border nodes as next-hop nodes.

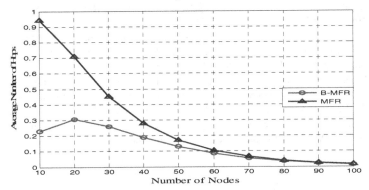

Fig. 5. Average number of hops comparison in MFR and B-MFR

Fig. 5 also shows that as the number of nodes increases, the node density of the network also increases. It means the performance of B-MFR would grow with the higher density of nodes.

6   Conclusion

In this work, we have introduced the working of proposed protocol B-MFR that uses border node to route a data packet in VANETs. The average number of hops has been used as the key metric for performance comparison between B-MFR and MFR in multi-hop vehicular network. We have developed a mathematical model for calculation of average number of hop counts in B-MFR using Poisson distribution for node deployment in the network. B-MFR protocol is designed to find paths with small average number of hop counts to forward packets. B-MFR gives better performance than existing protocol MFR even in highly mobile VANET.

References

1. Moustafa, H., Zhang, Y.: Vehicular networks: techniques, standards, and applications, pp. 1–28. CRC Press, Taylor & Francis Group, Boca Raton, London (2009)
2. Mohapatra, P., Krishnamurthy, S.V.: Ad Hoc Networks: Technologies and Protocols. Springer (2009)
3. Stojmenovic, I., Ruhil, A.P., Lobiyal, D.K.: Voronoi diagram and convex hull based Geocasting and routing in wireless networks. Wireless Communications and Mobile Computing Special Issue on Ad Hoc Wireless Networks 6(2), 247–258 (2006)
4. Raw, R.S., Lobiyal, D.K.: B-MFR Routing Protocol for Vehicular Ad hoc Networks. In: IEEE, ICNIT 2010, Manila, Philippines, June 11-12, pp. 420–423 (2010)
5. Xi, S., Xia-miao, L.: Study of the Feasibility of VANET and its Routing Protocols. In: The Proceeding of 4th IEEE International Conference on Wireless Communications, Networking and Mobile Computing, WiCOM 2008, Dalian, pp. 1–4 (2008)
6. Ukkusuri, S., Du, L.: Geometric connectivity of vehicular ad hoc networks: Analytical characterization. Transportation Research Part C 16(5), 615–634 (2008)
7. Heissenbuttel, M.: A Novel Position-Based and Beacon-less Routing Algorithm for Mobile Ad-Hoc Networks. In: NCCR-MICS (2004)
8. Harb, S.M., McNair, J.: Analytical Study of the Expected Number of Hops in Wireless Ad Hoc Network. In: Li, Y., Huynh, D.T., Das, S.K., Du, D.-Z. (eds.) WASA 2008. LNCS, vol. 5258, pp. 63–71. Springer, Heidelberg (2008)
9. Miller, L.E.: Probability of a Two-Hop Connection in a Random Mobile Network. In: 31st Conference on Information Science and Systems. Johns Hopkins University (March 2001)
10. Yi, C., Chuang, Y., Yeh, H., Tseng, Y., Liu, P.: Streetcast: An Urban Broadcast Protocol for Vehicular Ad-Hoc Networks. In: The Proceeding of 71st IEEE Vehicular Technology Conference (VTC 2010 - Spring), Taipei, Taiwan, May 16-19, 2010, pp. 1–5 (2009)

Simulation and Evaluation of Different Mobility Models in Ad-Hoc Sensor Network over DSR Protocol Using Bonnmotion Tool

V. Vasanthi and M. Hemalatha[*]

Department of Computer Science
Karpagam University, Coimbatore
{vasarthika,hema.bioinf}@gmail.com

Abstract. With the current advances like wireless networks is becoming more useful technology and also increasing popularity. Simulation is the technique which is used for evaluation of wireless networks. WSN is Multi-hop Self-configuring and consists of sensor nodes. The movements of nodes are like the patterns which can be classified into different mobility models and each of them have been characterized by its own distinctive features and also plays an important role in the connectivity of these nodes. There is numerous number of Network Simulator's available. Here we are using the NS2 simulation tool is used to find that which mobility model is best for real-life Scenarios. The simulator is a usage of Open System Interconnections (OSI) layers utilized in wireless simulation. In this paper, we analyze the realistic mobility models likewise entity models (Manhattan model and Gauss Markov model) and group mobility model (Reference Point Group Model) and Random Waypoint mobility model. The performance study of AWSN that uses Dynamic Source Routing (DSR) as the routing protocol. Network simulation uses Randomwaypoint in the mobility model. The high-level contribution of this paper is based on simulation analysis of Existing Mobility Models are discussed on a variety of the simulation settings and parameters to find these results are as follows Packet-Delivery Ratio (PDR), End-to-End Delay (ED),Dropped Packets (DP) and Generated Packets (GP) are studied in detailed.

Keywords: Performance, NS2, Bonnmotionv.1, MHN, RWP, GM, RPGM.

1 Introduction

Ad-hoc Wireless Sensor Networks have recently emerging trends as a premier research topic. They have a great long-term economic potential, ability to transform our lives, and pose many new systems-building challenges. In Ad-hoc Sensor networks consist of a number of new concepts and optimization problems. Some are, such as location, deployment, and tracking, are fundamental issues, in that many applications rely on them for required information [8].

---

[*] Corresponding author.

S.M. Thampi et al. (Eds.): SNDS 2012, CCIS 335, pp. 157–167, 2012.
© Springer-Verlag Berlin Heidelberg 2012

Important characteristics of AWSN are:

- Mobility of nodes
- Node failures
- Scalability
- Dynamic network topology
- Communication failures
- Random and Group models
- Heterogeneity of nodes
- Large scale of deployment

The rest of the paper's sections are: Section 2 describes related work of performance study of different mobility models using routing protocols. Section 3 Contribution Section 4 an overview of the DSR routing protocol and discuss about existing mobility models which is about the Random Way Point (RWP), Reference Point Group Mobility Model (RPGM), and Manhattan model (MHN) and the Gauss-Markov mobility model (GM). Section 4 illustrates the simulation results and compares the mobility models with respect to the results obtained for Packet-Delivery Ratio (PDR), End-End Delay (ED) and Generated Packets (GP), Dropped Packets (DP) Section 5 summarizes the results observed and Section 6 conclusions and Future work of this paper.

2   Related Works

A brief survey of performance metrics, Different mobility models with metrics and routing in WSNs is presented [14,13]. WSN has been an extensively studied area of research, [13] examines the area in detail giving a review of the architecture ranging from management, communication, coordination, and current and potential applications. Ariyakhajorn et al., [1] Evaluates that RWP and GM models evaluates with on-demand protocol (AODV) Routing Protocol RWP performs well in throughput and End to End Delay in low delay. Bai et al., [5] it examines the usage of metrics of relative motion and average degree of spatial dependence to characterize the different mobility models used in their study. Certain random mobility models can be considered harmful to the mobile application and [8] investigates the deterioration in velocity under the random waypoint model. In [8] the author compares such as DSDV, DSR and AODV perform better than table-driven ones such as Destination Sequenced Distance Vector (DSDV) routing protocol at high mobility rates, while DSDV perform quite well at low mobility rates. WSN recently explored their effects on the network operation and high mobility.

Guolong Lin et al., [8] analyzed the steady state distribution function of the random way point model. In addition to confirming the drawbacks of the random waypoint model and theoretical solution for the speed decay problem was determined and provides a general framework for analyzing other mobility models. In [11], the author compares the performance of proactive Destination Sequenced Distance Vector (DSDV) Protocols under the Different Mobility Models. Random mobility has been studied to improve data capacity [13], [12] and networking performance and created a routing protocol [8]. In such cases the latency of data transfer cannot be bounded deterministically, and the delivery itself is in jeopardy if the data is cleared from the sensor node buffer.Vasanthi et al.,[15] it examines the use of metrics of control overhead and Received Packets is to characterize the performance of different mobility models using DSR protocol.

3   Overview of DSR

Dynamic Source Routing (DSR) protocol is specifically designed for multi-hop ad hoc networks. The difference in DSR and other routing protocols is that it uses source routing supplied by packet's originator to determine its packet's path through the network instead of independent hop-by-hop routing decisions made by each node [3,4].

The packet will pass through the root header by the source routing is going to be routed through the network which carries the complete ordered list of nodes. Fresh routing information [5] is not needed to be maintained in intermediate nodes in design of source routing, since all the routing decisions are contained in the packet by themselves. DSR protocol is divided into two mechanisms which show the basic operation of DSR.

The two mechanisms are:
- **Route Discovery**
- **Route Maintenance**.

For Eg: when a node called S wants to send a packet to destination node D, the route to destination node D is obtained by route discovery mechanism.

The route maintenance by which source node S detects if the topology of the network has changed so that it can no longer use its route to destination node D.

4   About Existing Mobility Models

In this Section is to discuss about the mobility models. These models are built-in the Bonn motion tool.

Random Waypoint Model (RWP): In the simulation area nodes are randomly assumed and placed. The movement of each node is independent with another node [11]. The nodes are moved randomly to the target location .Nodes are distributed randomly over a convex Area [16].

Manhattan Model (MHN): In this Simulation area the region is divided into a grid after that the regions are like the square blocks of identical block length. The node movement is decided from one street at one time [13,14]. Equal chances are given to this movement. After a node is selected in its initial location, a node begins to move in the same direction then it passed to the intersection of the other street to reach it's probable.

Reference Point Group Model (RPGM): It is group mobility model and Spatial Dependencies mobility model. The RPGM mobility model works as follows: Nodes move in a group with the group leader (a logical center for the group) to determine the group's mobility pattern [14].

Gauss-Markov Mobility Model (GM): Nodes are placed as randomly and works independently. It is a Temporal Dependencies mobility model. Nodes are placed initially at random locations in the network. The movement of a node is independent to another node in the network [13, 14]. Each node has been assigned as i and mean speed, i S, and mean direction, i of movement. For every constant time period, the speed and direction of movement based on the speed and direction during the previous time period on a node, along with a certain degree of randomness incorporated in the calculation.

5   Experimental Results

To assess the performance of the DSR protocol with different mobility model, we have implemented them within the version 2.24 of the ns2 [7] network simulator. The gateway selection function uses in all types of cases, the minimum distance is the criteria to the gateway, in order to get a fair comparison of these approaches.movement patterns have been generated using the Bonn Motion [16] tool, creating scenarios with the Random Waypoint, Gauss–Markov and Manhattan mobility models, Reference point group mobility model. Random Waypoint is the most widely used mobility models in MANET research because of its simplicity. Nodes are selected in random speed and destination around the simulation area and move toward that destination, then they stop for a given pause time and repeat the process. The Gauss–Markov model makes node's movements to be based on previous ones, so that there are no changes of speed and direction. Finally, Manhattan Grid models the simulation area as a city section which is only crossed by vertical and horizontal streets. Nodes are only allowed to move through these streets.

All simulations have been run during 300seconds, with speeds randomly chosen between 0 m/s and (2, 4, 6, 8, 10) m/s as a Speed Variations in all mobility models. In this subsection we focus on the following as a Packet Delivery Ratio (PDR), Generated packets (GP), End to End delay (ED), Dropped Packets (DP) as a metric during the simulation in order to evaluate the performance of the different mobility models.

Simulation Parameters: The network designed consists of basic network entities the Table 1 below describes the list of parameters used for simulation.

Table 1. Parameter values for Simulation scenarios

Parameter	Sets
No. of Nodes	50,100,150,200,250
Area Size	1000 X 1000
Mac	802.11
Simulation time	300 sec
Traffic Source	CBR
Transmission Range	300
Speed	0,2,4,6,8,10
Routing Protocol	DSR
Mobility models	RWP, Gauss-Markov, Manhattan, RPGM

1.   **Generated Packets (GP):** here all the mobility models have packets generated as follows

Table 2. Generated packets Vs Speed

Nodes	50	100	150	200	250
No. of. Packets	3480	5798	9272	11586	13898

Here all mobility models at speed 0 to 10ms the 50,100,150..250 nodes using a different mobility model with different Speed (maximum speed = 10 m/s with the interval of 2ms). The Generated Packets (GP) is remains same even in the change of number of Speed varies.

2. **Packet Delivery Ratio (PDR):** This is the ratio of total number of packets successfully received by the destination nodes to the number of packets sent by the source nodes throughout the simulation.

PDR =   Total number of data packets successfully delivered x100%
                        Total number of data packets sent

This estimate gives us an idea about how successful the protocol is in delivering packets to the application layer. A high value of PDF indicates that the packets are delivered to the higher layers and it dictates the protocol performance.

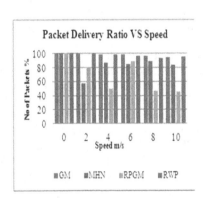

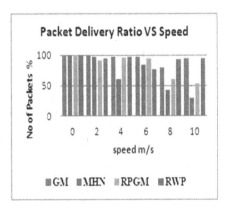

Fig. 1. PDR Vs Speed for Nodes 50   **Fig. 2.** PDR Vs Speed for Nodes 100

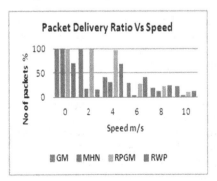

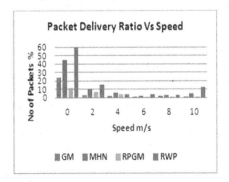

Fig. 3. PDR Vs Speed for Nodes 150   **Fig. 4.** PDR Vs Speed for Nodes 200

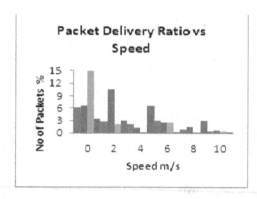

Fig. 5. PDR Vs Speed for Nodes 250

In Packet Delivery Ratio (PDR) in the nodes like 50 to 250 with the interval nodes of 50 using a different mobility model with different Speed (maximum speed = 10 m/s). In Fig 1 represents the Packet Delivery Ratio in accordance with Speed. By using 50 nodes, the performance of the GM model gives better PDR results. At 0 Speed PDR is 100% for Speed 2, 4, 6, 8, 10 and also it differs with other models, but RPGM model is low giving high transmission of packets successfully and also it differs with other models. In Fig 2, 100 nodes are used to represent the **packet delivery ratio (PDR)**, in which Random-Waypoint model and Gauss-Markov model outperforms than other models. At speed 8, 10 Manhattan model and RPGM packets deliver very low performance of PDR.

In fig 3, 150 nodes are used to represent **packet delivery ratio (PDR)**, in which at speed 0, Gauss-Markov, Manhattan model and RPGM model outperforms than RWP model. At speed 2, Manhattan and RWP model is very in delivers the packets and Gauss-Markov and RPGM gives better PDR as 99 and 98 respectively. At speed 4, RPGM gives better PDR than other models. At speed 6,8,10 Manhattan gives PDR is lower than other models. At speed 6, 8 RWP gives PDR is high with 41.2 and 24.9 respectively. At speed 10, Gauss-Markov model is giving better PDR than other models. In Fig 5, 200 nodes are used to represent **packet delivery ratio (PDR)**, in which at speed 0,2 RWP model gives 99.8 %and 15.55% Respectively as PDR which is better than other models. At speed 4, 8 MHN model gives better PDR as 6.4 and 3.25% respectively than other models. At speed 6, 10, RWP model delivering the packets as a higher value than other models. Overall at nodes 200 RPGM model is very low in the PDR.

In Fig 5, 250 nodes are used to represent **packet delivery ratio (PDR)**, in which at speed 0, RPGM model gives 15.56 % as PDR which is better than other models. At speed 2 MHN model gives better PDR as 10.6% than other models. At speed 6, 10, RWP model delivering the packets as a higher value than other models. Overall at nodes 200 RPGM model is very low in the PDR.

3. **End-to-End delay (ED):** The average delay in transmission of a packet between two nodes and is calculated. A higher value of end-to-end delay means that the network is congested and it dictates that the routing protocol does not perform well. The upper bound on the values of end-to-end delay is determined by the application [2].

An End to End Delay (ED) in the nodes like 50 to 250 with the interval nodes of 50 using a different mobility model with different Speed (maximum speed = 10 m/s).

In Fig 7, 50 nodes are used to represent the **End to End Delay (ED)** in accordance with Speed. By using 50 nodes, a congestion packet of RWP model shows high delay but RPGM group mobility model outperforms than other models. At speed 0 2, 4, 6 Manhattan and at speed 8, 10 RWP models involves high Delay.

In Fig 8, 100 nodes the congestion of packets in RPGM shows low delay and overall performance of Gauss-Markov and Manhattan model has high delay and this model is better for the medium size network.In Fig 9, 150 nodes are used to represent **End to End delay(ED)** at speed 0, Gauss-Markov models show lower delay than other models and RWP models shows high delay. At speed 2, RWP model shows high delay that follows Manhattan and other two models. At speed 4, 6, 8 Manhattan models show high delay than others. At speed 10, RPGM and Gauss-Markov models show high delay and Manhattan delay shows low delay.

In Fig 10, 200 nodes are used to represent **End to End delay (ED)** at speed 0,2 RWP model shows lower delay than other models and GM models shows high delay with 540.961 and 352.245 respectively. At speed 2, MHN model shows lower delay than other models. At speed 4, 6, 8 GM models high delay and Manhattan models show high delay than others. At speed 10, RPGM models shows high delay and Manhattan delay shows low delay.

In Fig 11, 250 nodes are used to represent **End to End delay (ED)** at speed 0, RWP model shows high delay than other models and GM models shows low delay. At speed 2, MHN model shows high delay than other models. At speed 4, GM models high delay and at speed 6, Manhattan models shows high delay than others. At speed 8, RPGM models shows high delay and RWP model delay shows low delay. At speed 10, RWP models shows high delay and MHN model delay shows low delay.

By this End to End Delay for 50,100,150 nodes end delay is high with RWP model and at 200,250 nodes GM models shows high delay.

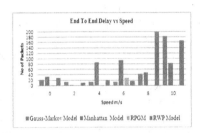

Fig. 6. End to End Delay for nodes 50

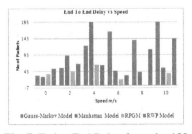

Fig. 7. End to End Delay for nodes 100

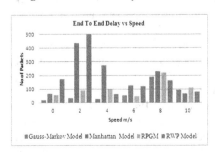

Fig. 8. End to End Delay for nodes 150

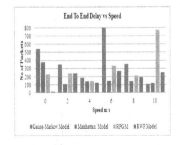

Fig. 9. End to End Delay for nodes 200

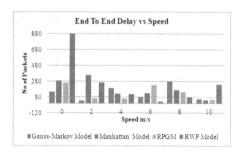

Fig. 10. End to End Delay for nodes 250

4. **Dropped Packets (DP):** This is calculated as the ratio between the numbers of routing packets transmitted to the number of packets actually received

Dropped packets (DP) = No. Of Routing Packets send / No of Data Packets Received.

In Dropped Packets (DP) in the nodes like 50 to 250 with the interval nodes of 50 using a different mobility model with different Speed (maximum speed = 10 m/s). In Dropped Packets (DP) in the 50 nodes using a different mobility model with different Speed maximum speed = 10 m/s). In fig11, 50 nodes are used to represent **Dropped Packets (DP)** in accordance with Speed. At Speed 0, there is no dropped packet in all models. At Speed 2, the dropped packet is very lower in GM models than other models. MHN models give high Dropped packets. At Speed 4, GM and RWP models give same dropped Packets which are lower than other models, MHN model returned packets are high with the packet of 427, RPGM models is very high dropped packets. At speed 6, GM model is dropped packet of 51 and MHN model gives high dropped packets of 534. At speed 8, RPGM model gives high dropped packets of 1828 and at the same time low dropped packets GM model. At Speed 10, RWP model gives low dropped packets and RPGM model gives high dropped packets.

In fig 12, 100 nodes are used to represent **Dropped Packets (DP)** in accordance with Speed. At Speed 0, the dropped packet MHN models there are no dropped packets. RWP models which are highly dropped the packets. At Speed 2, the dropped packet is very lower in GM models than other models. MHN models give high Dropped packets. At Speed 4, GM and RWP models gives same dropped Packets which is low than other models, MHN model returned packets are high with the packet of 427, RPGM models is very high dropped packets of 1719.At speed 6, GM model is dropped packet of 51 and MHN model gives high dropped packets of 534. At speed 8, RPGM model gives high dropped packets of 1828 and at the same time low dropped packets GM model. At Speed 10, RWP model gives low dropped packets and RPGM model gives high dropped packets.

In Fig 13, 150 nodes are used to represent **Dropped Packets (DP)** in accordance with Speed. At Speed 0, the dropped packet GM models gives lower than other models. RWP models which are highly dropped the packets. At Speed 2, the dropped packet is very lower in GM models than other models. RWP models give high Dropped packets. At Speed 4, RPGM models gives lower than other models, MHN model returned packets are high with the packet of 6293.At speed 6,8 RWP model is dropped packet of 5214 and 6871 respectively and MHN model gives high dropped packets of 8627and 8030 respectively. At speed 10, GM model gives low dropped packets of 7004 and MHNmodel gives high dropped packets of 8587.

In Fig 14, 200 nodes are used to represent **Dropped Packets (DP)** in accordance with Speed. At Speed 0, the dropped packet RWP models gives lower than other models. RPGM models which are highly dropped the packets. At Speed 2, the dropped packet is very lower in RWP models than other models. GM models give high Dropped packets. At Speed 4, MHN models gives lower than other models, GM model returned packets are high with the packet of 11136.At speed 6,8 RWP model is dropped packet of 10716 and 10788 respectively and GM models gives high dropped packets of 11091. At Speed 8, RPGM model gives high dropped packet of 10891.At speed 10, RWP model gives low dropped packets of 10020 and RPGM model gives high dropped packets of 10921.

In fig 15, 250 nodes are used to represent dropped packets in accordance with Speed. At Speed 0, the dropped packet RPGM models gives lower than other models. RWP models which are highly dropped the packets. At Speed 2, the dropped packet is very lower in MHN models than other models. GM models give high Dropped packets. At Speed 4, RWP models gives lower than other models, MHN model returned packets are high with the packet of 11136.At speed 6,8,10 MHN model is dropped packet of 12814,12847 and 12885 respectively and GM model gives high dropped packets of 13143. At Speed 8, RPGM model gives high dropped packet of 13162.At speed 10, RWP model gives high dropped packets of 13292.

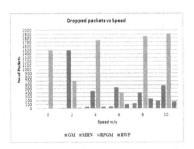

Fig. 11. Dropped Packets for nodes 50

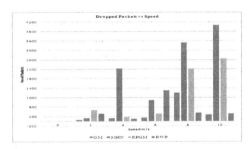

Fig. 12. Dropped packets for nodes 100

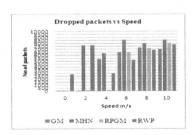

Fig. 13. Dropped Packets for nodes 150

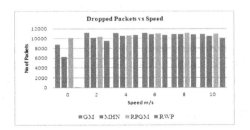

Fig. 14. Dropped packets for nodes 200

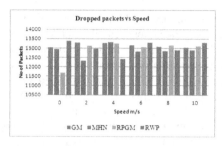

Fig. 15. Dropped packets for nodes 250

6   Conclusion and Future Work

The main aim is to prove the mobility model extremely affects the performance results of a Routing protocol in a realistic environment. NS-2 simulation was used to evaluate the performance of different mobility models over DSR protocols using the performance metrics like Generated Packets (GP), Packet Delivery Ratio (PDR) and End-to-End Delay (ED). Based on the performance analysis of the different models, the Generated Packets (GP) remain same even in the change of number of Speed varies but when we consider the PDR, DP and ED there is a high variance in the result. In particular, certain ad hoc routing metrics at speed 0 the number of nodes is 50,100,150 the packet Delivery Ratio (PDR) the models give 90% and above and at Speed 2, 4, 6, 8, 10 the PDR the models gives very low.

The overall performance of End to End Delay (ED) is when the number of nodes is 50,100,150 the models give low and the number of nodes is 200,250 the models gives very high delay. The overall performance of the dropped Packets (DP) is when the number of nodes is 50,100,150 the models gives low dropped packets whereas the nodes like 200,250 the dropped packets is high packets. With this result our study has shown that the simulation results are highly dependent on the movement behaviors of a mobile node and simulation environment.

By this study we are going to give the Obstruction Avoidance Generously Mobility Model (OAGM) mobility model under geographic restriction and the presence of obstacles and how to avoid the obstacles using graph-theory with GUI Environment to reduce the dropped packets and increase the Packet Delivery Ratio (PDR). The Existing model might not show the accuracy that represents any scenario in the world, simply because real MN's must travel around obstacles and along pre-defined paths. So, the future work is to avoid obstacles using graph theory based mobility model which suited for the current environment.

Acknowledgement. I thank expert members of mobility model for providing the necessary information. I thank Karpagam University for the motivation and Encouragement to make this Research work as a successful one.

References

[1] Ariyakhajorn, J., Wannawilai, P., Sathitwiriyawong, C.: A Comparative Study of Random Waypoint and Gauss-Markov Mobility Models in the Performance Evaluation of MANET. In: International Symposium on Communications and Information Technologies, ISCIT 2006, April 2 (2007)

[2] Divecha, Abraham, A., Grosan, C., Sanyal, S.: Impact of Node Mobility on MANET Routing Protocols Models. Journal of Digital Information Management 4(1), 19–23 (2007)

[3] Johnson, D.B., Maltz, D.A., Broch, J.: DSR: The Dynamic Source Routing Protocol for Multi-hop Wireless Ad hoc Networks. In: Perkins, C.E. (ed.) Ad Hoc-Networking, ch. 5, pp. 139–172. Addison-Wesley (2001)

[4] Maltz, D.: The Dynamic Source Routing Protocol for Multi-Hop Ad Hoc Networks (November 5, 1999)

[5] Bai, F., Sadagopan, N., Helmy, A.: IMPORTANT: A Framework to Systematically Analyze the Impact of Mobility on Performance of Routing Protocols for Ad hoc Networks. In: Proceedings of the IEEE International Conference on Computer Communications, pp. 825–835 (March-April 2003)

[6] Lin, G., Noubir, G., Raja-maran, R.: Mobility Models for Ad-hoc Network Simulation. In: Proceedings of INFOCOM (2004)

[7] http://www.isi.edu/nsnam/ns/

[8] Lego, K., et al.: Comparative Study of Ad-hoc Routing Protocol AODV, DSR and DSDV in Mobile Adhoc NETwork. Indian Journal of Computer Science and Engineering 1(4), 364–371 (2010)

[9] Latiff, L.A., Fisal, N.: Routing Protocols in Wireless Mobile Ad Hoc Network – A Review. In: The 9th Asia-Pasific Conference on Communication, APCC 2003, vol. 2, pp. 600–604 (2003)

[10] Saad, M.I.M., Zukarnain, Z.A.: Performance Analysis of Random-based Mobility Models in MANET Routing Protocol. European Journal of Scientific Research 32(4), 444–454 (2009)

[11] Meghanathan, N., Farago, A.: On the Stability of Paths, Steiner Trees and Connected Dominating Sets in Mobile Ad Hoc Networks. Elsevier Ad Hoc Networks 6(5), 744–769 (2008)

[12] Naski, S.: Performance of Ad Hoc Routing Protocols: Characteristics and Comparison. Seminar on Internetworking. Helsinki University of Technology, Finland (2004)

[13] Camp, T., Boleng, J., Davies, V.: A Survey of Mobility Models for Ad Hoc Network Research. Wireless Communication & Mobile Computing (WCMC): Special Issue on Mobile Ad Hoc Networking: Research, Trends and Applications 2(5), 483–502 (2002)

[14] Vasanthi, V., Ajith Singh, N., Romen Kumar, M., Hemalatha, M.: A Detailed study of Mobility model in sensor network. Int. Journal of Theoretical and Applied Information Technology 33(1), 7–14 (2011)

[15] Vasanthi, V., Hemalatha, M.: A Proportional Analysis of Dissimilar Mobility Models in Ad-Hoc Sensor Network over DSR Protocol. Int. J. Computer Applications 42(15), 26–32 (2012)

[16] https://net.cs.unibonn.de/fileadmin/ag/martini/projekte/Bonn Motion/src/BonnMotion_Docu.pdf

Secure Authentication in Multimodal Biometric Systems Using Cryptographic Hash Functions

Aravind Ashok, Prabaharan Poornachandran, and Krishnasree Achuthan

Amrita Center for Cyber Security, Amrita University, Amritapuri Campus, Kollam, India
aravindashok@am.amrita.edu,
{praba,krishnashree}@amrita.edu

Abstract. In this Information Age, security of personal data is one of the biggest issues faced by most of the nations. Biometrics provides substantial help in guarding against attempts to establish fraudulent multiple identities or prevent identity fraud. The greatest advantage that the biometric data of an individual remains constant acts as its biggest liability. Once the attacker gets biometric password of an individual then security of his data becomes a big problem. This paper comes with a unique solution which will allow people to change their biometric password and helps to overcome some of the present issues in biometric systems. The biometric password is created by hashing the biometric data of the user. Merging of biometrics and cryptography proves to be more secure and helps to provide a better authentication system for the society.

Keywords: Biometrics, Multimodal Biometrics, Authentication, Biometric Set, Hashing, SHA-1 Algorithm, Database.

1 Introduction

Due to rapid increase in cyber-crimes it has become extremely important for all nations to safeguard their confidential data. A biometric system is essentially a pattern- recognition system that recognizes person based on a feature vector derived from a specific physiological or behavioral characteristic that a person possesses [1]. Automated biometric systems have only been available over the last few decades due to significant advancement in the field of computing. Many of these techniques are however based on the ideas that were originally conceived centuries ago. Some of the various biometric recognition methods are face, iris, voice, fingerprint, palm geometry etc. Biometric data cannot be borrowed or forgotten but at the same time it cannot be changed as well. Though it provides better security than the traditional passwords, it has a lot of vulnerabilities which are being exploited by various attackers.

A simple biometric system consists of five basic components or modules [2]:

1. **Sensor**: Module which takes the biometric data as an input.
2. **Feature Extractor**: Module where the data taken from the sensor is converted into vector form.
3. **Template Database**: Module where the vectors regarding biometric data were already stored during enrollment.
4. **Matching Module**: Here the vectors obtained from feature extraction module are compared with the vectors present in the database.

S.M. Thampi et al. (Eds.): SNDS 2012, CCIS 335, pp. 168–177, 2012.
© Springer-Verlag Berlin Heidelberg 2012

5. **Decision Making Module**: Based on the result of the matching module the claimer's identity is accepted or rejected.

An attack can be done in any of these five modules. There are eight main areas where attacks may occur in a biometric system:

As we can see not only the modules but also the channels connecting the modules are being attacked. In order to make the attacking procedure complex and ensure better security measures multimodal biometric systems were introduced.

In certain situations, the user might find one form of biometric identification is not exact enough for identification. According to a report [3] by the National Institute of Standards and Technology (NIST) to the United States Congress concluded that approximately two percent of the population does not have a legible fingerprint and therefore cannot be enrolled into a fingerprint biometrics system.

Experimental result shows that multimodal biometric systems for small-scale populations perform better than single- mode biometric systems [4]. Multimodal biometric technology uses more than one biometric identifier fused together to compare the identity of the person.

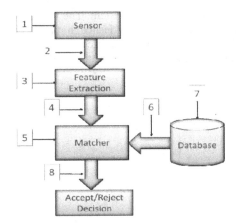

Fig. 1. Places where attack can occur in a biometric system

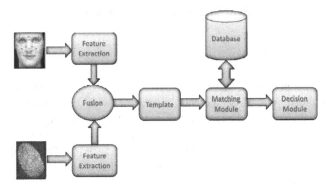

Fig. 2. Working of a basic multimodal biometric system

Though the limitations of uni-modal biometric systems can be overcome by multimodal systems, the later fails to provide solution to the following issues:

1. **Security of personal identity:** Though comparatively complex, the attacker can perform same type of attacks on the multimodal biometric system as well and once the biometric data is stolen the whole effort to construct the multimodal technology seems useless.
2. **Security of Database:** Cases has been found out where reconstruction of biometric data has been done even from the fused templates stored in the database.
3. **Providing identity to the disabled:** Some systems fail to retrieve biometric data from handicapped or disabled people [3]. Even though the percentage of such users is very less, when this technology comes out for mass identification projects like UIDAI [14] in India, this shortcomings really matter.
4. **Balance between FAR and FRR error:** False Acceptance Rate[FAR] is the probability that a random impostor is accepted as one of randomly selected user by the system [5] whereas False Rejection Rate[FRR] is the probability of a user being rejected by the system. The two error rates FAR and FRR are complementary to each other. Hence a proper balance has to be made between these errors. Generally a threshold value is calculated which decides whether the user's claim should accepted or not.

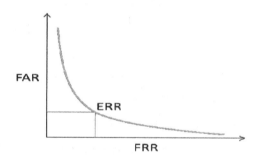

Fig. 3. Estimation of threshold value from error rates

2   Proposed System

In this paper we propose a solution to overcome some of the limitations of present biometric systems. We have merged biometrics with cryptography using Hash functions to produce a changeable biometric password for a user. A strong combination of biometrics and cryptography has the potential to link a user with a digital signature she created with a high level of assurance [6]. Though there are many biometric cryptosystems in existence, the idea of changeable biometric password is unique and more secure.

2.1   System Features

This system has inbuilt five different biometric algorithms:

1. **Face**: One of the oldest and most basic examples of a characteristic that is used for recognition by humans is the face. Face recognition is non-intrusive and cheap as well [7]. This technique uses 3D sensors to capture information about the face. 3D sensors vastly improve the precision of facial recognition and can also identify a face from various angles.
2. **Iris**: Iris recognition is known for its accuracy and use in high level security systems. Compared to other biometric features (such as DNA, face, Voice etc.), iris is more stable and reliable feature [8]. Statistical analysis reveals that irises have an exceptionally high degree-of-freedom up to 266 (fingerprints show about78) [9], and thus are the most mathematically unique feature of the human body; more unique than fingerprints. Hence, the human iris promises to deliver a high level of uniqueness to   authentication applications that other biometrics cannot match.
3. **Fingerprint**: Fingerprint recognition is the most developed and economical biometric feature. Also very small storage space is required to store fingerprint templates, thus reducing the size of the database.
4. **Palmprint**: A palm print refers to an image acquired of the palm region of the hand. Like fingerprint, palms of human hands contain unique pattern of ridges and valleys. Since palm is larger than the finger it is expected to be more reliable than fingerprint [2].
5. **Tongue**: Like fingerprint and palm print even human tongue print is unique. The tongue is a unique organ in that it can be stuck out of mouth for inspection, in this act offering a proof of life, and yet it is otherwise well protected in the mouth and is difficult to forge [10].

For biometric identification, it is comparatively difficult as it is a smooth member with different shapes. But the research is interesting since it is very difficult to forge and because of its uniqueness.

This system can be best explained by dividing it into three main parts:

1. **Enrollment**: First the user has to enroll by providing his biometric data and creating a biometric password in the system.
2. **Database**: Both the biometric data and password are stored in the database which can be used for matching during authentication.
3. **Authentication**: The user has to enter his biometric set by which a biometric password will be created. This password is then matched with the one in the database to accept/reject the user's claim.

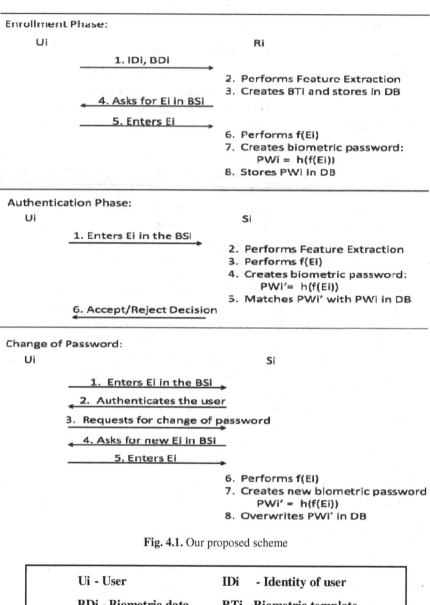

Fig. 4.1. Our proposed scheme

Ui - User	**IDi - Identity of user**
BDi - Biometric data	**BTi - Biometric template**
BSi - Biometric set	**Si - System**
Ei - Elements in BSi	**DB - Database**
h(.) - Hash function	**f(.) - Fusion function**
Ri- Registration center	**PWi - Biometric Password**

Fig. 4.2. Notations used in the proposed scheme

2.2   Enrollment

As mentioned earlier this system has inbuilt five different biometric algorithms and hence the user will have to provide the biometric data of each biometric part during enrollment.

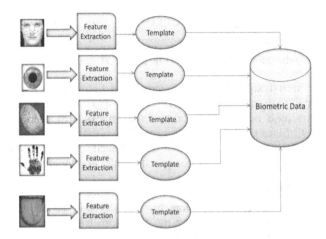

Fig. 5. Enrollment process by providing biometric data

The data enters the feature extraction module where it is converted into vector forms. These vector forms are then stored in templates which finally goes to the database.

2.2.1   Secure Hash Algorithm (SHA-1)

A Hash function is a one-way encryption algorithm which creates a unique fixed length output for a variable length unique input. A hash function is more complex and irreversible in nature when compared with encryption algorithms. Even if 1 bit is flipped in the input string, at least half of the bits in the hash value will flip as a result. SHA and MD-5 are some of the most secure hashing algorithms. For any given message **m** its hash value **h** remains unique. It is difficult for two different messages **m** and **m'** to have the same hash value. Also it is very difficult to get the original message from its hash value [15].

$$\text{hash (m)} = \text{hash (m')} \text{ only if } m = m'$$

The elements inside the biometric set are hashed to produce a biometric password. The elements are none other than the biometric data of the user. For our proposal we have used SHA-1 hash algorithm. SHA-1 is the most widely used of the existing SHA hash functions, and is employed in several widely used security applications and protocols. SHA-1 produces a 160-bit message digest based on principles similar to MD4 and MD5 message digest algorithms, but has a more conservative design [11]. SHA-1 requires the operation of 80 rounds which can be grouped into 4 groups, 20 rounds each [12]. The four different functions are as follows:

$$f(B,C,D) = \begin{cases} \text{Ch } (B, C, D) = (B \bullet C) \wedge (\neg B \bullet D) & , 0 \leq t \leq 19 \\ \text{Parity } (B, C, D) = B \oplus C \oplus D & , 20 \leq t \leq 39 \\ \text{M } (B, C, D) = (B \bullet C) \wedge (B \bullet D) \wedge (C \bullet D), 40 \leq t \leq 59 \\ \text{Parity } (B, C, D) = B \oplus C \oplus D & , 20 \leq t \leq 39 \end{cases}$$

$\oplus, \bullet, \wedge, \neg$ denote the XOR, AND, OR and NOT operations respectively.

The working of SHA-1 algorithm can be understood by the link in [16]. However, weak and normal hash passwords can be cracked [17] i.e. the plain text can be obtained from its hash output using brute force attacks [18], rainbow tables and lookup tables [19]. Since the biometric characteristic is extremely large and complex, it is nearly impossible to reverse it [17] and we will need to utilize multiple rounds of a hash algorithm, and that adds to the complexity of the cryptanalysis [20].

2.2.2   Password Creation Module

Biometric password is made from the biometric data stored in the database. The system asks the user to select at least two out of the five biometric parts in any sequence to create the password. For e.g. {Face, Iris, Finger} can be a biometric set. Even repetition of biometric parts is allowed. Hence even sets like {Face, Iris, Face} or {Iris, Iris, Tongue} can be used to make the password. The minimum number of elements required inside the set is 2, whereas there are no restrictions to the maximum number of elements to be included in the biometric set.

The biometric password thus formed will be stored in the database. As there will be minimum of two elements in a biometric set, doing all permutations and combinations a user can have a total of:

$$\sum_{i=2}^{n} 5^i = 5^2 + 5^3 + 5^4 + \cdots + 5^n = \infty$$

Thus a user can have **infinite** number of different biometric sets and thus **infinite different biometric passwords**. Whenever the user wants to change his password he will just have to login into the system and select a new biometric set. The new password automatically gets updated to the system database.

Algorithm:
1. Read the entered Biometric Set.
2. Fetch the feature extracted template of the first element in the biometric set stored in database.
3. Search whether another element is present in the entered set.
   3.1. If yes, fetch the biometric template of that element. The templates are fused and the contents are then hashed to form a 160bit key. This 160 bit key cipher text is then stored inside a sample template. Goto step 3.
   3.2. If no, the data stored in the previous template acts as the biometric password.
4. Save the biometric password into the database.

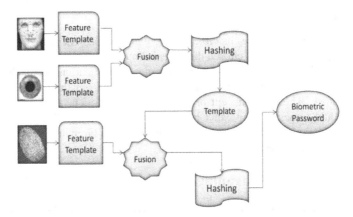

Fig. 6. Biometric password creation process

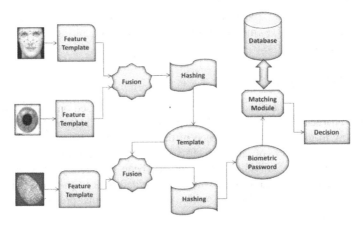

Fig. 7. Detailed view of Authentication of the User

2.3   Database

For the proper functioning and performance evaluation of biometric recognition systems large multimodal databases are required under real working conditions [21]. In this section we describe the characteristics and uses of the database system. Database of this system consists of two parts:

1. **<u>Biometric data</u>**: It consists of templates which has the vector form of five biometric parts of the user.
2. **<u>Biometric Password</u>**: Some of the biometric data templates are chosen by the user in a sequence and encrypted to create the biometric password.

Even if the attacker gets the biometric data of an individual, authentication will not be verified until the proper biometric set is entered. Moreover, finding out biometric set from the biometric password is tough.

2.4   Authentication

During authentication the user has to enter the elements present in his biometric set in the exact sequence as he had chosen during enrollment.

The biometric password thus formed during authentication is matched with the one in the database. According to the result obtained from the matching module a decision is made whether to accept or reject user's claim. The only constraint is that the user should remember the exact biometric set by which he had enrolled into the system. Any change in the sequence of elements in the biometric set will reject the authentication of the user.

3   Strengths and Advantages

- People can change their biometric password according to their wish.
- Even if attacker gets the biometric data he won't be able to login unless he knows the sequence in which it has to be used.
- Extremely tough to reconstruct biometric set from the biometric password.
- Provides alternative measures of identification for physically challenged or handicapped persons.

4   Conclusion

Biometrics refers to an automatic recognition of a person based on his physiological or behavioral characteristics. Many applications will in future rely on biometrics as it is the only way to guarantee the presence of the owner when a transaction is made [2]. The common drawback of all biometric systems is that they fail to provide an alternative even if an individual's account has been hacked by an attacker. In this paper we have put forward an idea which will actually allow an individual to change his biometric password and solve some of the problems present in the modern biometric systems.

References

[1] Prabhakar, S., Pankanti, S., Jain, A.K.: Biometirc Recognition: Security and Privacy Concerns. IEEE Security & Privacy, 33–44 (March/April 2003)

[2] Delac, K., Grgic, M.: A Survey of Biometric Recognition Methods. In: 46th International Symposium Electronics in Marine, Zadar, Croatia (June 2004)

[3] NIST report to United State Congress. Summary of NIST Standards for Biometric Accuracy, Tamper Resistance, and Interoperability (November 13, 2000), http://www.itl.nist.gov/iad/894.03/NISTAPP_Nov02.pdf

[4] Snelick, R., Indovina, M., Yen, J., Mink, A.: Multimodal Biometrics: Issues in Design and Testing. In: International Conference on Multimodal Interfaces (ICMI), Vancouver, British Columbia, Canada. ACM (November 2003) 1-58113-621-8/03/0011

[5] Korte, U., Krawczak, M., Martini, U., Merkle, J., Plaga, R., Niesing, M., Tiemann, C., Vinck, H.: A cryptographic biometric authentication system based on genetic fingerprints. LNI, vol. P-128, pp. 263–276. Springer (2008)

[6] Hao, F., Anderson, R., Daugman, J.: Combining Crypto with Biometrics Effectively. IEEE Trans. on Computers 55(9) (September 2009)

[7] Jain, A.K., Ross, A., Prabhakar, S.: An Introduction to Biometric Recognition. IEEE Trans. on Circuits and Systems for Video Technology 14(1), 4–19 (2004)

[8] Zhang, Z.B., Ma, S.L., Zuo, P., Ma, J.: Fast Iris Detection and Localization Algorithm Based on AdaBoost Algorithm and Neural Networks. In: International Conference on Neural Networks and Brain (ICNN), vol. 2, pp. 1009–1014 (October 2005)

[9] Chen, W.-S., Chih, K.-H., Shih, S.-W., Hsieh, C.-M.: Personal Identification Technique based on Human Iris Recognition with Wavelet Transform. In: International Conference on Acoustics, Speech and Signal Processing (ICASSP), vol. 2, pp. 949–952 (March 2005)

[10] Liu, Z., Yan, J.-Q., Zhang, D., Tang, Q.-L.: A Tongue-Print Image Database for Recognition. In: Procedings of the Sixth International Conference on Cybernetics, Hong Kong (August 2007)

[11] SHA-1 Hash function, http://en.wikipedia.org/wiki/SHA-1

[12] Pongyupinpanich, S., Choomchuay, S.: An Architecture for a SHA-1 Applied for DSA. In: 3rd Asian International Mobile Computing Conference, AMOC 2004, Thailand, May 26-28 (2004)

[13] National Institute of Standards and Technology (NIST), "Secure Hash Standard", Federal Information Processing Standards Publication 180-2 (August 2002)

[14] Unique Identification Authority of India, Planning Commission, Government of India, http://uidai.gov.in/

[15] Cryptographic hash function, http://en.wikipedia.org/wiki/Cryptographic_hash_function

[16] Alderson, N.: Increasing Security Expertise in Aviation- oriented Computing Education: A Modular Approach, part of Cryptography module, Embry-Riddle Aeronautical University in Prescott, Arizona, http://nsfsecurity.pr.erau.edu/crypto/sha1.html

[17] Kisasondi, T., Baca, M., Lovrencic, A.: Biometric Cryptography and Network Authentication. Journal of Information and Organizational Sciences 31(1) (2007)

[18] How hashes are cracked, http://crackstation.net/hashing-security.html

[19] How Crackstation cracks hashes, http://crackstation.net/

[20] Hellman, M.E.: A cryptanalytical time-memory trade off. IEEE Transactions on Information Theory IT-26 (1980)

[21] Ortega-Garcia, J., Fierrez-Aguilar, J., Simon, D., Gonzalez, J., Faundez-Zanuy, M., Espinosa, V., Satue, A., Hernaez, I., Igarza, J.-J., Vivaracho, C., Escudero, D., Moro, Q.-I.: MCYT baseline corpus: a bimodal biometric database. IEE Proc.-Vis. Image Signal Process. 150(6), 391–401 (2003)

Data Protection and Privacy Preservation Using Searchable Encryption on Outsourced Databases

Lucas Rodrigo Raso Mattos*, Vijayaraghavan Varadharajan,
and Rajarathnam Nallusamy

Infosys Labs, Infosys Limited, Bangalore, India
lmattos@dcc.ufmg.br, {vijayaraghavan_v01,rajarathnam_n}@infosys.com

Abstract. With the increasing popularity of social networks in the globalized environment, the process of sharing data and information from anywhere at anytime has become easier and faster. Furthermore, cloud based computing and storage services have become mainstream. Unfortunately, if the information is on the Internet, it is susceptible to attacks leading to leakage and hence needs to be encrypted. Searchable encryption is a way to obtain efficient access to a large encrypted database, improving the data security even when it is stored on untrusted servers. We present few applications which can use and benefit from searchable encryption and explain how secrecy of the data is maintained without compromising usability.

Keywords: Cloud Security, Searchable Encryption, Outsourced Databases.

1 Introduction

In the current global context, with more and more users, devices, and applications joining the Internet, we have reached the next stage where the global network is not used just for disseminating information from a server. Applications are being run from the cloud and vast amount of data uploaded and stored on the cloud. With all this technological growth, malicious attacks with the intention to steal or damage data have also become increasingly common. Unfortunately, the world has already seen the damage caused to big organizations as well as individuals by the leak of confidential information.

Ristenpart, Tromer, Shacham and Savage [7] have shown how the cloud can be insecure by exploring some weaknesses on the Amazon's cloud service, the Amazon EC2. In addition, there are also other famous leaks as the one to Heartland Payment in 2009 and to TK Maxx in 2007, as reported in *The Guardian* [6].

The attack to the Play Station Network [PSN], the Sony's network where users can play and download games and movies, which happened in April, 2011, is one of the best examples of how a security breach can turn into a crisis, with

---

* This work was done when Lucas was an Intern at Infosys Labs.

S.M. Thampi et al. (Eds.): SNDS 2012, CCIS 335, pp. 178–184, 2012.
© Springer-Verlag Berlin Heidelberg 2012

77 million users having their personal information leaked, including credit card numbers, and the company had their services down for more than two weeks. On PlayStation's Blog [1], Sony has said that "The entire credit card table was encrypted and we have no evidence that credit card data was taken" but has confirmed that "The personal data table, which was a separate data set, was not encrypted". This means that unauthorized persons have illegal access to the plain text data of 77 million users, which can potentially be detrimental to the security and privacy of those users.

Another interesting case of leak was released by ComputerWorld.com [8], when a "non-profit organization that administers student loans announced that an outside contractor had lost an unspecified piece of equipment containing the names and Social Security Numbers of approximately 1.3 million borrowers". This harm to the privacy of the users brings big responsibility to the data owner and with it a lot of troubles and costs. For the users, there is the worry in how the data will be used and to whom it will be given or sold.

The reason why big companies maintain non-encrypted information on their database is that they need to perform queries on this data, and if it is encrypted, it will be much more complicated to match and find the search results and the search will also make the response slower. In this paper, we give some examples of applications in different areas which would need the data to be stored on the Cloud, but also want to guarantee the security of the information, and present searchable encryption as a solution to overcome the limitation of search over encrypted data.

The organization of the rest of the paper is as follows: Section 2 gives an overview of searchable encryption. Section 3 presents example applications that could use searchable encryption as a solution for protecting data even when they are stored on the outsourced databases and Section 4 presents conclusions of the paper.

2   Searchable Encryption

Searchable encryption is a method that allows performing queries in databases where even the names of the tables and attributes are encrypted. It also permits to control users' access by just creating and validating users' keys without the need to encrypt all the data again with a new key whenever users join or leave the group. There are many literature available on searchable encryption, such as those from Boneh, Ostrovsky, Persiano and Crescenzo [2], and Gu and Zhu [4]. This paper is based on the proxy based searchable encryption scheme presented by Dong, Russello and Dulay [3].

Searchable encryption can be implemented and used in various ways, but it basically consists of a RSA encryption key and a RSA decryption key, both divided into two pieces. The user would have his piece of each of the encryption and decryption keys and a proxy would have the other two pieces. When it is needed to add a new user, the manager of the RSA keys (can be the system, depending upon the case) can just make different splits, adding the proxy's keys to the system. To revoke the access of a user, the proxy's keys can be deleted from the system, and the user will not be able to perform queries.

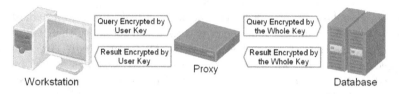

Fig. 1. Data flow for searchable encryption

Figure 1 shows the flow of a search using searchable encryption. The servers on the cloud, the proxy, and the communication channels can all be untrusted, and hence the data traversing through them shall always be encrypted. When a query arrives at the database, the parameters are encrypted with the whole key, as the database is also encrypted with the same key, it is possible to match and compare the cells of the database table.

The key is split in such a way that the split key of the proxy is relatively small as compared to the split key of the user. This ensures that the encryption and decryption overhead is less on the proxy. Also, the queries made by the user and the results are usually small amount of data. As the encryption and decryption is over the small amount of data, this method is computationally efficient.

3   Applications

With the increasing adoption of cloud computing, more and more companies are migrating their data to the cloud. Unless protected adequately, this data is exposed to additional risks due to malicious attacks. In this section we present some applications that need to store sensitive data on the Cloud.

3.1   Healthcare

E-Health is a fast growing area, where patients look for a fast and easy way to contact their doctors and doctors look for an efficient system to attend and monitor their patients. In addition, there are the hospitals looking for a way to control all their information about material, surgeries, personnel, patients, medicines and even financial. Also, there are other entities like students, universities, pharmacists, Health Ministry, etc. that need to consume these information for analysis and research purposes.

It would be possible to unify all the data in one database, and with all the advantages offered (as cost reduction, easy management, backup, quality of servers, etc) it should be on the Cloud. But, since there are many sensitive data such as financial or users' personal information, some encryption is required to protect users' privacy.

In Figure 2, we show a simplified scheme of how searchable encryption could be adapted to an e-Health application. Note that the key splitter application will manage the RSA keys; so in this case the key splitter should be trusted. The proxy would also handle the users' authentication and authorization, which

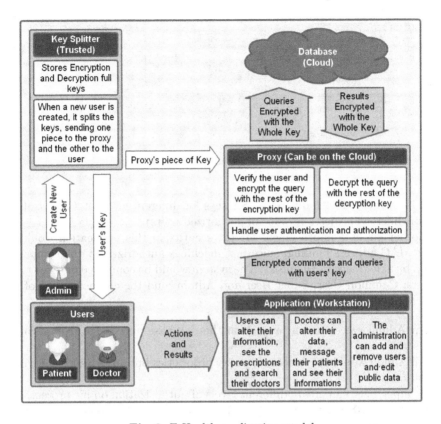

Fig. 2. E-Health application model

means that it would release information just for users authorized by the system to see them.

In this case, the security would be a combination of the user's authentication (login and password) with the user's part of the key given when he is added to the system. Even in the case of a malicious user getting access to the proxy, the user will not be authenticated and hence will not be able to get any information. So the privacy of user's data is guaranteed.

3.2 Secure Data Exchange in Outsourcing Model

In the outsourcing model, lot of sensitive data travels over the Internet. Companies need to share logs, files, messages, and even clients' information with other companies or between offices in different locations. These are confidential data that could have great value on Internet's black-market, so they are more likely to be targeted in malicious attacks. The need for data security here is very clear.

With this in mind, we designed an application as safe as possible, where all the data transiting and stored on the Internet would be encrypted and the only place where the data could be decrypted is the workstation. Even more, the data

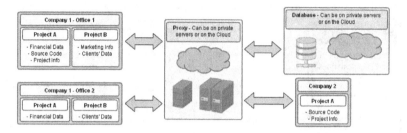

Fig. 3. eBusiness application as an example

could be encrypted with different RSA keys for different levels of authorization, and for different projects (groups of authorized users).

Another possible improvement for the security in this application would be to use MAC address binding, since just machines authorized by the companies should be able to access the proxy. The system would be composed of three types of users: Common User, Super User and Admin, and the characteristics of the application would be

1. An Admin can create a project on the database and assign to it a Super User.
2. An Admin would have access to proxy proprieties but no access to encrypted data.
3. A Super User can create different levels of authorization on his project, and can assign RSA keys to each one (the whole RSA key should never transit on the Internet, and just the Super User would have access to it)
4. A Super User can add new users to his project, choosing which levels of authorization the user would have, splitting the project's RSA keys and sending one part to the proxy and the other to the user.
5. A Super User can do everything that a Common User can do.
6. A Common User cans add/remove/edit files in the systems, which are part of his authorization level.

Figure 3 shows an example of access to both proxy and database, from two different companies in three different locations which can be in different parts of the world. In this example, there are two companies who share data using the same system, and for company 1 there are two offices that have different authorization levels of access to the projects' data.

Besides Company 2 having access to Company 1's data on Project A, it will not have access to Project B, since it does not have Project B's keys. Even if they are able to discover the keys, their users will not be allowed by the proxy to see the restricted information. So, searchable encryption is applied here to authenticate and authorize users to perform queries and searches on encrypted outsourced databases.

Let us consider an example of how a user's query flows through the system. A user from Company 2 wants to download a file from "Project A" related to

Project Information. He has a field in his application where he writes the name of the file. The application sends a message to the proxy with the command and query, but all the attributes and columns are encrypted by user's key. The proxy sees that the user has authorization to perform this query, encrypt it with the rest of the key and pass it to the database. The database searches by matching the encrypted file name and return the encrypted file data to the proxy, which decrypts it with part of the key and sends it to the user, who can finish the decryption and download the file.

This application is not limited to eBusiness or outsourcing; the same model can also satisfy many eScience requirements. eGovernment can also make use of this system in some Government – Business, Government – Government and Government – Employees interactions. For operations of Government – Citizen type, where the number of users are in millions, it is preferred to use a different model.

3.3   Social Networking

With major social networking services having hundreds of millions of active users, the discussions about users' privacy on the Internet have become a worldwide frenzy. Users of social networking sites fill their pages with data about themselves and upload it to the social networks. This information can be leaked through malicious attacks or accessed by the server administrator (if the data is stored on the cloud, for example), or by the social network's staff.

According to the research published by Irany, Webb, Pu and Li [5], the attribute set Birth date, Gender, Zip in the US Census data poses the risk of personal identification as these attributes can uniquely identify 87% of the US population. The study also points out that the combination of birth date, gender and location would be enough to uniquely identify 53% of the US population.

A leak of this kind of information is a very sensitive issue. The use of the data can be just for surveys (market surveys, for example), or it can be used to approach the users in many ways to gain more information, such as financial, passwords, confidential data, etc. If such data are in the wrong hands, it can be even dangerous to the user's safety. The victims can have their identity wrongly used, can suffer blackmailing and be target for thieves and kidnappers.

Encrypting the data would solve many of these problems, and the searchable encryption could be used to guarantee fast access to the database and also the privacy of the user is preserved, as even the social networking hosts are not allowed to see restricted information. Searchable encryption can also be easily adopted by many other portals on the Internet, like job portals, matrimony sites, forums and other web services where users' profiles are stored.

4   Conclusions

In this Internet era, as there is valuable data transiting the global network, there are many advanced techniques used by hackers and other malicious agents trying to obtain the data. There are enough instances, some of which are highlighted in this paper, to prove that no data on the Internet is secure enough against attacks by malicious users. We have shown in this paper how data can be protected and privacy preserved in outsourced databases using searchable encryption. We have presented application scenarios in the areas of healthcare, outsourcing, and social networking services.

References

1. Playstation's blog (2011),
   http://blog.eu.playstation.com/2011/04/28/
   playstation-network-and-qriocity-outage-faq/
2. Boneh, D., Di Crescenzo, G., Ostrovsky, R., Persiano, G.: Public Key Encryption with Keyword Search. In: Cachin, C., Camenisch, J. (eds.) EUROCRYPT 2004. LNCS, vol. 3027, pp. 506–522. Springer, Heidelberg (2004),
   http://dx.doi.org/10.1007/978-3-540-24676-3_30
3. Dong, C., Russello, G., Dulay, N.: Shared and searchable encrypted data for untrusted servers. Journal of Computer Security 19, 367–397 (2011),
   http://iospress.metapress.com/content/5400312680314865
4. Gu, C., Zhu, Y.: New efficient searchable encryption schemes from bilinear pairings. International Journal of Network Security 10, 25–31 (2010)
5. Irani, D., Webb, S., Pu, C., Li, K.: Modeling unintended personal-information leakage from multiple online social networks. IEEE Internet Computing 15(3), 13–19 (2011)
6. Quinn, B., Arthur, C.: Playstation network hackers access data of 77 million users (2011), http://www.guardian.co.uk/technology/2011/apr/26/
   playstation-network-hackers-data
7. Ristenpart, T., Tromer, E., Shacham, H., Savage, S.: Hey, you, get off of my cloud: exploring information leakage in third-party compute clouds. In: Proceedings of the 16th ACM Conference on Computer and Communications Security, CCS 2009, pp. 199–212. ACM, New York (2009),
   http://doi.acm.org/10.1145/1653662.1653687
8. Vijayan, J.: Two more organizations report data breaches (2006),
   http://www.computerworld.com/s/article/9000878/
   Two_more_organizations_report_data_breaches_?taxonomyId=17/

A Dynamic Syntax Interpretation for Java Based Smart Card to Mitigate Logical Attacks

Tiana Razafindralambo, Guillaume Bouffard,
Bhagyalekshmy N Thampi, and Jean-Louis Lanet

Smart Secure Devices (SSD) Team
XLIM/Université de Limoges – 123 Avenue Albert Thomas, 87060 Limoges, France
`aina.razafindralambo@etu.unilim.fr`,
{`guillaume.bouffard,bhagyalekshmy.narayanan-thampi,`
`jean-louis.lanet`}`@xlim.fr`

Abstract. Off late security problems related to smart cards have seen a significant rise and the risks of the attack are of deep concern for the industries. In this context, smart card industries try to overcome the anomaly by implementing various countermeasures. In this paper we discuss and present a powerful attack based on the vulnerability of the linker which could change the correct byte code into malicious one. During the attack, the linker interprets the instructions as tokens and are able to resolve them. Later we propose a countermeasure which scrambles the instructions of the method byte code with the Java Card Program Counter (`jpc`). Without the knowledge of `jpc` used to decrypt the byte code, an attacker cannot execute any malicious byte code. By this way we propose security interoperability for different Java Card platforms.

Keywords: Smart card, Java Card, Logical Attack, Countermeasure.

1 Introduction

A smart card is a secure, efficient and cost effective embedded system device comprising of a microcontroller, memory modules (RAM, ROM, EEPROM) serial input/output interfaces and data bus. On chip operating system is contained in ROM and the applications are stored in the EEPROM. A smart card can also be viewed as an intelligent data carrier which can store data in a secured manner and ensure data security during transactions. Security issues are one major area of hindrance in smart card development and the level of threat imposed by malicious attacks on the integrated software is of high concern. To overcome this, industries and academia are trying to develop countermeasures which will protect the smart card from such attacks and render secure transactions [4]. Size constraints restrict the amount of on chip memory and a majority of smart cards on the market have at most 5 KB of RAM, 256 KB of ROM, and 256 KB of EEPROM which has a deep impact on software design. The first tier safety relates to the underlying hardware. To resist an internal bus probing, all components (memory, CPU, crypto-processor, *etc.*) are on the same chip which

S.M. Thampi et al. (Eds.): SNDS 2012, CCIS 335, pp. 185–194, 2012.
© Springer-Verlag Berlin Heidelberg 2012

is embedded with sensors covered by a resin. Such sensors (light sensors, heat sensors, voltage sensors, *etc.*) are used to disable the card when it is physically attacked. The software is the second security barrier. The embedded programs are usually designed neither for returning nor for modifying sensitive information without guaranty that the operation is authorized.

All applications stored in the smart card should be resistant to attacks. It is important to analyze all the possible attack paths and find a way to mitigate them through adequate software countermeasures. In this paper we are talking about logical attacks where we are abusing the linker to change the correct byte code instruction of a given method into a malicious one. It occurs when a smart card is operating under normal physical conditions, but sensitive information is gained by examining the bytes going to and from the smart card [13].

Developing Java Card application remains a challenge for security purpose. Smart card manufacturers are differentiated from one another by the way they implement security features. An application proved secure on a platform can be prone to hardware attacks on another platform. This difference in security implementation raises serious problems for the certification process like Common Criteria [11]. One of the challenges is to define a common behavior in term of security. For that purpose it has been proposed to define an API or annotation process [4] that could standardize the security behavior of the platform. Within this approach it becomes possible to have a common security behavior of Java Card applications.

This paper is organized as follows: the first section is about Java Card security. The second section provides a brief state of the art on Java Card attacks. In the third section we introduce the new logical attack. The countermeasure which we proposed is suitable for security interoperability and is described in the fourth section. Finally we conclude our work with the future perspectives.

2   Literature Survey

2.1   Java Card security

Java Card is a kind of smart card that implements the standard Java Card 3.0 [12] in one of the two editions *Classic Edition* or *Connected Edition*. Such a smart card embeds a virtual machine, which interprets codes already romized with the operating system or downloaded after issuance. Due to security reasons, the ability to download code into the card is controlled by a protocol defined by Global Platform [7]. Java Cards have shown an improved robustness compared to native applications with respect to many attacks. They are designed to resist numerous attacks using both physical and logical techniques. To resist such attacks several mechanisms have been added while others have been removed from the Java Card specification.

Java Card is quite similar to any other Java edition, it only differs (at least for the *Classic Edition*) from standard Java in three aspects: i) restriction of the language, ii) run time environment and iii) the applet life cycle. Due to resource constraints the virtual machine in the *Classic Edition* must be split into two parts:

the byte code verifier (invoked by a converter) is executed off-card; while the interpreter, the API and the Java Card Run time Environment (JCRE) are executed *on-card*. The byte code verifier is the offensive security process of the Java Card. It performs the static code verifications required by the virtual machine specification. The verifier guarantees the validity of the code being loaded into the card. The byte code converter converts the Java class files and verified by a byte code verifier into a CAP file format which is more suitable for smart cards. An *on-card* loader installs the classes into the card memory. The conversion and the loading steps are not executed consecutively (a lot of time can separate them). In order to avoid it, the Global Platform Security Domain checks the integrity and authenticates the package before its registration in the card. Through out this paper, discussion on Java Card refers to the *Classic Edition*.

Element of the Security. The Java Card platform is a multi-application environment in which an applet's critical data must be protected against malicious access from the other applets. To enforce protection between applets, traditional Java technology uses type verification, class loaders and security managers to create private name spaces for applets. In a smart card, it is not possible to comply with the traditional enforcement process. Firstly, the type verification is executed outside the card due to memory constraints. Secondly, class loaders and security managers are replaced by the Java Card firewall.

CAP File. The CAP (`Converted APplet`) file format is based on the notion of interdependent components that contain specific information from the Java Card package. For example, the `Method` component contains the methods byte code, and the `Class` component has information on classes such as references to their super-classes or declared methods. In order to manipulate the instructions of a given method we need to use the `Method` component, which provides all the methods used in the applet and each one contains set of instructions. One optional component (`custom` component) can be used to define proprietary properties on the application like annotation.

Byte code verification. Allowing code to be loaded into the card after post-issuance raises the same issues as with web applets. An applet that has not been compiled by a compiler (hand made byte code) or that has been modified after compilation can break the Java sandbox model. Thus the client must check that the Java typing rules are preserved at the byte code level. The absence of pointers reduces the number of programming errors. But it does not stop attempts to break security protections by disloyal use of pointers. Byte Code Verifier (BCV) is a crucial security component in the Java sandbox model: any bug in the verifier causing an ill-typed applet to be accepted can potentially enable a security attack. At the same time, byte code verification is a complex process involving elaborate program analysis. Moreover such an algorithm is very costly in terms of time consumption and memory usage. For these reasons, many cards do not implement such a component and rely on the fact that it is the responsibility of the organization that signs the code of the applet to ensure that the code is well typed.

The Linking step. The linking step is defined by the Java Card Specification [12] and has been done during the loading of a CAP file. When the software is loaded into the card, the JCVM provides the way to link the CAP file with the installed Java Card API, thanks to the token link resolution referred in the `Constant Pool` component. Indeed the `Reference Location` component keeps a list of offsets in order to easily retrieve each token placed in the `Method` component.

The Firewall. The separation between different applets is enforced by the firewall which is based on the package structure of Java Card and the notion of contexts. When an applet is created, the JCRE uses a unique applet identifier (AID). If two applets are instances of classes coming from the same Java Card package, they are considered to be in the same context. Every object is assigned to a unique owner context which is the context of the applet that created the object. It is this context that decides whether the access to another object is allowed or not. The firewall isolates the contexts in such a way that a method executing in one context cannot access any attributes or methods of objects belonging to another context.

2.2   Attacks against Java Card platform

There are three main types of attacks on a smart card. First one is the the logical attack, which provides a cheap solution to access sensitive information from the targeted cards. Next is the side channel attack, by which the attacker can obtain the cryptographic secrets [6] with some electromagnetic curves or can find the executed byte code as explained in [1]. The third is the physical attack, which can provide information about the target, optical or laser faults. This sort of physical modification may create a logical fault which is used to attack a card and is called combined attack [3,5]. In this paper, our focus is limited to logical attacks.

First Logical Attacks. E. Hubbers *et al.* presented in [9] a quick overview of the classical attacks available and suggested some countermeasures.

First, a manipulated program is sent to the card. Then it is modified to bypass the BCV after the compilation step. The efficient way to block this attack is an *on-card* BCV. Another solution to have a type confusion without the modification of the applet files is the Shareable interfaces mechanism. The authors created two applets which exchange information, thanks to the Shareable interface mechanism. To create a type confusion, each applet uses a different type of array to exchange data. During compilation or on the loading step, the BCV cannot detect an incoherence. This attack is no more applicable on the new cards. Finally, the last attack is about the transaction mechanism. The aim of a Java Card transaction is to make atomic operations with a rollback mechanism which should deallocate any allocated objects during the aborted transaction and clear the references. On some card, the authors found a way to keep the reference to objects allocated during transaction even after a rollback.

The First Trojan in a Smart Card. In [10], J. Iguchi-Cartigny *et al.* described the way to install a Trojan in a smart card. This Trojan will read and modify the smart card memory. The firewall mechanism is abused to build this attack, thanks to the unchecked instructions on static. These instructions without checks during the installation step, define a way to call a malicious byte code which is presented in a Java Card array. They achieved this through the following steps. The first step obtains the array address and this reference address of the applet instance to be modified. In the second step, the `getstatic` and `putstatic` instructions are used to read and write the smart card memory. Finally, a modification of the `invokestatic` parameter provides the redirection of the install program's Control Flow Graph (CFG). When the `invokestatic` instruction is called, the Java Card Program Counter (`jpc`) jumps to the malicious byte code contained in the Java Card array.

A Java Card Stack Overflow. G. Bouffard *et al.* described in [5], two methods to change the Java Card CFG. The first one, EMAN 2 provides the way to change the return address of the current function. This information is stored in the Java Card stack header. When the malicious function exits on correct execution, the program counter returns to the instruction which addresses it. The address of the `jpc` is stored on the Java Card Stack header. An overflow attack has succeeded to change the return address by the address of our malicious byte code.

Our malicious method has one local variable which received the return of `getMyAddress` function. The function return increased by the size of the Java Card array header (here 6), corresponding to the address of the shell code.

After the characterization of the Java Card stack, the return address was located. In order to modify this address the parameter of the `sstore` instruction was changed. As there is no runtime checking on the parameter it allows a standard buffer overflow attack.

How to find the Java Card API. The main difficulty to use this attack in the previous case is that, there is no access to the linked Java Card API. Hamadouche *et al.* described in [8] a way to abuse the Java Card linker in order to obtain the Java Card API. Some instructions are followed by tokens. These tokens are referred in the constant pool component of the unlinked applet. Speed of the linking process can be increased by using the reference location. The aim of their attack was to resolve the tokens which were preceded by instruction that pushes a short[1] on the stack. So it is easy to send this value into the APDU buffer or update a shell code contained in a Java Card array.

3   Building a New Attack

Assume that there is no embedded *on-card* BCV. In order to characterize this card, it is necessary to abuse the previously explained linking mechanism.

To perform this attack, there are set of instructions which are to be modified by using an abuse linking mechanism as shown in the listing 1.1. We used a

---

[1] On the targeted card, each address are stored into 2-byte value

tool developed by our team: the Cap Map [14], for CAP File Manipulator. It provides a friendly environment to modify the CAP file by respecting the inter-dependencies between the affected components.

Each instruction is referred by an offset in the current method in the Method component.

```
/*0020*/    [0x00]           nop
/*0021*/    [0x02]           sconst_m1
/*0022*/    [0x02]           sconst_m1
/*0023*/    [0x3C]           pop2
/*0024*/    [0x04]           sconst_1
/*0025*/    [0x3B]           pop
```

Listing 1.1. Set of instruction to attack with the link mechanism abuse technic

As we have previously seen in the section 2.1, it is the Reference Location component that helps to link between a token used in the Method component and the Constant Pool.

By using the linking mechanism abuse, described in the section 2.2, the linker uses the instructions nop and sconst_m1 (0x0002) as a token.

```
.ConstantPoolComponent {
    [...]
    /* 0008, 2 */CONSTANT_StaticMethodRef:
                        external: 0x80, 0x8, 0xD
    [...]
}

.ReferenceLocationComponent {
[...]
    offsets_to_byte2_indices = {
        [...] @0020 [...]
    }
}
```

Listing 1.2. Reference Location modification with CAPMAP

To perform the previous manipulation as seen in the listing 1.2, we modify the Reference Location by adding a new link. The offset value 0x0020 is referred to the token 0x0002 in the Method component. In the Constant Pool component, we see that this token is associated to a static method reference. By looking to our first linker attack presented in the section 2.2, the token method 0x0002 is linked by the value 0x8E03 into the targeted card.

Once the Java Card linker finished linking as shown in the listing 1.3, it mutates the method byte code. The link resolution needed two bytes, and the instructions from the offset 0x0021 to 0x0024 became the invokeinterface operands.

/* 0020 */	[0x8E]	invokeinterface
/* 0021 */	[0x03]	// nargs
/* 0022 */	[0x02]	// indexByte1
/* 0023 */	[0x3C]	// indexByte2
/* 0024 */	[0x04]	// method
/* 0025 */	[0x3B]	pop

Listing 1.3. Set of instruction after link resolution

In this case abusing the token resolution mechanism leads to the call of a method referred in the **Constant Pool** by the index composed of two bytes 0x02, 0x3C. This index corresponds to the method **getKey** which gives us the ability to return the key data *via* the APDU buffer. Most of the attack in the literature tried to retrieve the secret key thanks to physical means. Here it is possible to force the virtual machine to send back clear text value of the key to the attacker. Of course, this attack works well due to the absence of the byte code verifier which could have detect the ill formed CAP file. But as demonstrated by G. Barbu in [2] a laser fault can allow logical attack with or without the presence of the byte code verifier. Therefore the shell code do not access any objects of the security context and it will never detect the attack.

4   The Newly Proposed Countermeasure

G. Barbu in [2] proposed a countermeasure which prevents the malicious byte code from being executed. His idea was to scramble each instruction during the installation step. For that each Java Card instruction *ins* performs a xor with the $K_{bytecode}$ key. Thus the hidden instructions are computed as follows:

$$ins_{hidden} = ins \oplus K_{bytecode} \tag{1}$$

If an attack as EMAN 2 succeeds described in the section 2.2, the attacker cannot execute his malicious byte code without the knowledge of the $K_{bytecode}$ key. Thus to find the xor key he should just change the CFG of the program to a **return** instruction. As defined by the Java Card specification [12], the associated opcode is 0x7A. With a 1-byte xor key, this instruction may have 256 possibles values. A brute force attack offers the way to find the xor key.

To improve his countermeasure we add a **jpc** value to perform the hidden instruction and it can be written as:

$$ins_{hidden} = ins \oplus K_{bytecode} \oplus jpc \tag{2}$$

By using the previous example described in the section 2.1, we scramble the byte code in the installed method to prevent a modification of the original byte code from an attacker. For that, we have a $K_{bytecode}$ set to $0x42$. So in the installed applet, we have the following byte code as given in the listings 1.4 and 1.5 given below.

```
/*0x8068*/  0x42  nop
/*0x8069*/  0x40  sconst_m1
/*0x806A*/  0x40  sconst_m1
/*0x806B*/  0x7E  pop2
/*0x806C*/  0x46  sconst_1
/*0x806D*/  0x79  pop
```

Listing 1.4. Scrambling Byte Code with the equation 1

```
/*0x8068*/  0x2a  nop
/*0x8069*/  0x29  sconst_m1
/*0x806A*/  0x2a  sconst_m1
/*0x806B*/  0x15  pop2
/*0x806C*/  0x2d  sconst_1
/*0x806D*/  0x12  pop
```

Listing 1.5. Scrambling Byte Code with the equation 2

In the listing 1.4, the scrambling was done without the jpc value. If you have many times the same instruction sconst_m1 in the example will always have the same value. Thus it becomes easy for an attacker to find this constant key value (to find it, an attacker has a constant complexity in $O(256)$). To improve that, we added the jpc value. As described in the listing 1.5, each similar instruction has a different byte code value.

This countermeasure can be enabled by the developer during the compilation step. For that he has to set each enabled countermeasure flag on CAP file custom component. It is only parsed if the targeted JCVM can parse it. The way to enable or not this countermeasure on specific applet provides an additional complexity for the attacker. An special key for each security context may be used to improve this protection. For the Java Card runtime this countermeasure is not expensive. Indeed, just a double xor should be done at the beginning of the main loop. A native implementation is provided in the listing 1.6.

```
while (true) {
    if (scrambled) ins = ins_array[jpc] ^ Key ^ (jpc & 0x00FF
        )
    else           ins = ins_array[jpc]
    switch (ins) {
        case ...
        /* a case for each Java Card instruction to execute it
           in which is incremented */
    }
}
```

Listing 1.6. A countermeasure implementation

Depends on the jpc value, each instruction is stored in the smart card memory. Without the knowledge of where each instruction is stored in the EEPROM, an attacker will not have the possibility to execute some malicious byte code by the attacked JCVM.

If an attacker succeeded to change the return address, he can jump to the shell code to read Java Card memory as described in the section 2.2. For that, he use the unscrambled shell code as given in the listing 1.7. This shell code is stored in the EEPROM at the address 0xAB80. The information in the array should not be masked by the Java Card loader like the executed instructions.

```
/*0xAB80*/ 0x8D getstatic 8000
/*0xAB83*/ 0x78 sreturn
```

Listing 1.7. Unscrambling shell code

```
/*0xAB80*/ 0x4F  sshl
/*0xAB81*/ 0x43  ssub
/*0xAB82*/ 0xC0  //
          Undefined
/*0xAB83*/ 0xB9  //
          Undefined
```

Listing 1.8. Unscrambling shell code

During the execution of our shell code, the runtime unmasks each instruction to obtain the code shown in the listing 1.8. Of course the code is detected invalid by the interpreter because 0xC0 is undefined by virtual machine. Moreover the sshl and ssub byte codes need two parameters on the top of the stack. Thus the interpreter will detect an empty stack.

5 Conclusion and Future Work

This paper contributes a way to protect the Java Card from logical attacks. We introduced a powerful logical attack based on the linker vulnerability. This attack allows one to execute a buffer overflow attack on a smart card and it succeeds well with several products which demonstrates the need of an efficient countermeasure. We proposed a cost effective countermeasure to mitigate this attack. This countermeasure scrambles the binary code. Within this process the syntax of the stored code varies according to a variable. Reverse engineering the executable code becomes impossible if the scrambled memory is dumped. Attacker cannot execute the malicious byte code without knowing where the application instructions are stored in EEPROM. Our future work involves reverse engineering process using the electromagnetic side channel attack [15] and evaluate the ability to bypass the proposed countermeasure.

Acknolwledgements. The work was partly funded by the French project IN-OSSEM (PIA-FSN2 - Technologie de la Sécurité et Résilience des Réseaux) and the Région Limousin.

References

1. Aranda, F.X., Lanet, J.L.: Smart Card Reverse-Engineering Code Execution Using Side-Channel Analysis. NTCCS, Théorie des Nombres, Codes, Cryptographie et Systèmes de Communication, Oujda, Marocco (April 2012)
2. Barbu, G.: On the security of Java Card platforms against hardware attacks. Ph.D. thesis, TÉLÉCOM ParisTech (2012)
3. Barbu, G., Thiebeauld, H., Guerin, V.: Attacks on Java Card 3.0 Combining Fault and Logical Attacks. In: Gollmann, D., Lanet, J.-L., Iguchi-Cartigny, J. (eds.) CARDIS 2010. LNCS, vol. 6035, pp. 148–163. Springer, Heidelberg (2010)

4. Bouffard, G., Lanet, J.-L., Machemie, J.-B., Poichotte, J.-Y., Wary, J.-P.: Evaluation of the Ability to Transform SIM Applications into Hostile Applications. In: Prouff, E. (ed.) CARDIS 2011. LNCS, vol. 7079, pp. 1–17. Springer, Heidelberg (2011)

5. Bouffard, G., Iguchi-Cartigny, J., Lanet, J.-L.: Combined Software and Hardware Attacks on the Java Card Control Flow. In: Prouff, E. (ed.) CARDIS 2011. LNCS, vol. 7079, pp. 283–296. Springer, Heidelberg (2011)

6. Clavier, C.: De la sécurité physique des crypto-systèmes embarqués. Ph.D. thesis, Université de Versailles Saint-Quentin-en-Yvelines (2007)

7. Global Platform: Card Specification v2.2 (2006)

8. Hamadouche, S.: Étude de la sécurité d'un vérifieur de Byte Code et génération de tests de vulnérabilité. Master's thesis, Université de Boumerdés (2012)

9. Hubbers, E., Poll, E.: Transactions and non-atomic API calls in Java Card: specification ambiguity and strange implementation behaviours. Dept. of Computer Science NIII-R0438, Radboud University Nijmegen (2004)

10. Iguchi-Cartigny, J., Lanet, J.: Developing a Trojan applet in a Smart Card. Journal in Computer Virology (2010)

11. ISO/IEC: Common Criteria v3.0. Tech. rep., ISO/IEC 15408:2005 Information technology - Security techniques - Evaluation criteria for IT security (2005)

12. Oracle: Java Card Platform Specification

13. Petri, S.: An introduction to smart cards. Secure Service Provider TM (2002), http://www.artofconfusion.org/smartcards/docs/intro.pdf

14. Smart Secure Devices (SSD) Team – XLIM, Université de Limoges: The CAP file manipulator, http://secinfo.msi.unilim.fr/

15. Vermoen, D., Witteman, M., Gaydadjiev, G.N.: Reverse Engineering Java Card Applets Using Power Analysis. In: Sauveron, D., Markantonakis, K., Bilas, A., Quisquater, J.-J. (eds.) WISTP 2007. LNCS, vol. 4462, pp. 138–149. Springer, Heidelberg (2007)

Taxonomy of Slow DoS Attacks
to Web Applications

Enrico Cambiaso[1,2], Gianluca Papaleo[2], and Maurizio Aiello[2]

[1] Dipartimento di Informatica e Scienze dell'Informazione
(DISI), Univesity of Genova, via Dodecaneso, 35, 16146, Genova, Italy
s2869539@studenti.unige.it
[2] Istituto di Elettronica ed Ingegneria dell'Informazione e delle Telecomunicazioni
(IEIIT-CNR), via De Marini, 6, 16142, Genova, Italy
{papaleo,aiello}@ieiit.cnr.it

Abstract. In the last years, Denial of Service (DoS) attacks have been widely spreaded becoming a more than ever relevant threat to network security.

DoS attacks evolved from flood to low bandwidth rate based, making a host unreachable through the usage of a small amount of bandwidth and eluding an Intrusion Detection System more easily.

In this paper, we analyze the 'most common slow Denial of Service attacks to web applications, proposing a taxonomy to categorize such attacks. The proposal of our work is to make an overview and to classify slow DoS attacks for a better understanding of their action strategy, thus helping developers and network administrators to design proper defense methodologies.

Keywords: Taxonomy, Denial of Service, Web Applications.

1 Introduction

The Internet is the most used communication medium of the modern society as it connects million of computers around the world, providing personal and professional services to users and corporations. This widespread connectivity among computers enables malicious users to misuse resources and attacks against the services.

In this context, Denial of Service (DoS) attacks are one of the most dangerous threats as they aim to deprive legitimate users from the service offered by a generic system [1, 2].

A variation of DoS are Distributed Denial of Service (DDoS) attacks, which involve more machines, sometimes also without they are aware (botnet), in assaulting the same victim. As a consequence, the attack is enhanced and it is harder to mitigate [3, 4].

There are many implementations of DDoS attacks [5], such as the smurf, the SYN flooding [6] or the UDP flooding attacks.

DoS attacks were originally classified in two categories: (i) flooding based attacks, which send a large amount of packets to the victim, exhausting its

S.M. Thampi et al. (Eds.): SNDS 2012, CCIS 335, pp. 195–204, 2012.
© Springer-Verlag Berlin Heidelberg 2012

resources and (ii) vulnerability attacks, characterized by sending a specially crafted message to the attacked host, denying the offered service [7].

DoS attacks have been evolved to a third mixed category, which combines both flooding and vulnerability based attacks. This approach reduces the needed traffic rate to be effective [8] and it makes more difficult to distinguish malevolent traffic from the legitimate one [9, 10, 8, 11]. Moreover, the attack can also be launched from a non-performing host, such as a mobile phone [10]: accordingly, a new *slow DoS* attacks category has been defined.

In 2009, cyber attacks to Iran have shown that this kind of attacks are a real and serious menace not only for internet services but also for governments.

In this paper, we analyze slow DoS attacks (SDAs in the following) to web applications, which use low bandwidth rate (LBR in the following) to hit a web service, by providing a proper taxonomy.

The paper is organized as follows: in Sec. 2, we will report related works to DoS attacks and detection techniques. We then describe SDAs (Sec. 3) and in Sec. 4 we build a taxonomy of them, describing the most relevant threats. Due to space limitations, we don't provide a detailed description of the presented attacks, but we limit to a brief summary of them. Finally, in Sec. 5 we report the conclusions of our work.

2   Related Work

The study of the Internet attacks includes the analysis of menaces, detection strategies and reaction and mitigation methods.

Regarding the early attack techniques which have been replaced by SDAs, some researches are related to SYN flooding, where a lot of incomplete connections are able to fill the server's listen queue, causing a denial of service for legitimate users [12]. Hussain et al. try to define a new framework for classifying DoS [13]: they build a taxonomy, distinguishing software exploits from flooding based attacks and analyzing in detail these latter approaches, ignoring SDAs. Chen et al. propose a DDoS taxonomy of defense techniques [14], categorizing both the defense and the reaction systems in function of the adopted approach. Since nowadays the attacks have evolved, the taxonomy should be adapted to slow DoS attacks. Mirkovic et al. define an exhaustive taxonomy of DDoS attacks and defense mechanisms [15]; Tariq et al. categorize only network/transport level attacks [16], whereas Douligeris et al. classify both DoS and DDoS attacks, deeply analyzing defense techniques [7].

Regarding the slow DoS attacks, the first research work related to LBR DoS attacks is the *shrew attack* against TCP flows, in particular acting against the TCP retransmission mechanism [11]. In this attack TCP flaws are reduced to a small fraction of their ideal rate.

An effective taxonomy related to slow DoS attacks is still missing and it's needed to address the research to efficient detection methods. Relatively to the detection techniques of slow attacks, there are studies about the reduction of quality (RoQ) attacks, which are able to reduce the performance of the victim by sending a small amount of data. These studies analyze the SDAs on various scenarios [17, 18, 19, 20], without providing a proper taxonomy neither of the attacks nor of the defenses.

3   Slow DoS Attacks Description

The strategy followed during a DoS attack consists in moving the victim host to the saturation state, which is reached by the attacker seizing all the available resources of the server. The attacker's purpose is to force the victim to process only the malicious requests. Indeed, if the victim's service queue has no free positions, any new legitimate connection to the server will be ineffective, therefore causing a DoS. In order to minimize the resources needed for the attack itself and to bypass security systems based on statistical detection of high-rate traffic [21, 22, 23], a LBR mechanism is chosen. In fact, while in a flooding DoS attack most of the packets sent to the target could be useless, in a low-rate one almost all the packets play a role for the success of the action.

A SDA may also exhibit an ON-OFF nature, which characterizes the attack execution by a succession of activity and inactivity periods [10]. This behavior resembles the typical user interaction, giving the menace an increased degree of hazard.

A SDA slows down the connections *from* or *to* the target machine by exploiting the HTTP protocol or the application software (i.e. PHP, SOAP), thus maintaining the network channel active as long as possible, with minimum data transfer.

4   Taxonomy

We now define the taxonomy of the slow DoS attacks.

SDAs to web applications have been categorized in two types: (i) *pending requests DoS*, which act by sending incomplete (pending) requests and (ii) *long responses DoS*, characterized by sending legitimate requests which slow down the responses of the server.

We have decided to insert into the taxonomy a third type of attacks, the *multi-layer DoS* attacks: they don't purely act at application level, nevertheless they use LBR traffic to induce a DoS on the target machine.

Moreover, as those categories can be mixed, we have also reported the mixed category with an example of the Slow Read mixed attack.

Another classification is based on feasibility; in this categorization, we consider two features: (i) *practical attacks*, which exploit a specific vulnerability relative to a particular environment and they have also been implemented and deployed; (ii) *meta-attacks*, defined at a higher level, which are able to abstract the attack operation without specifying a single vulnerability to exploit, specific for the target system. Therefore, the latter may have different implementations for the same kind of attack.

A scheme of our taxonomy is reported on Fig. 1.

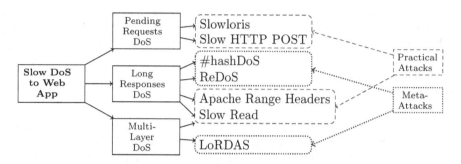

Fig. 1. Taxonomy of slow DoS attacks to web applications

4.1 Pending Requests DoS

These attacks are characterized by sending incomplete requests to the victim host, in order to saturate its resources, while the server is waiting for the end of the requests. This is the same policy adopted by the SYN flood attack where the 3-way handshake is not completed, but in this case the attack is launched at the application layer instead of the transport one. Typically in SYN flood attacker's IP address changes continuously (spoofed IP) to avoid detection and reaction from IDS. A practical implementation consists in selecting IP addresses randomly, but the side effect of this approach is that a high percentage of the attacker's packets are wasted, due to the TCP reset sent by *active spoofed IP* to the victim. These reset packets are a large number, due to a limited IPv4 address space [24]. Instead, in the SDAs, since the socket has really to be established and IP spoofing is therefore not usable, fewer packets are sent.

Any complete HTTP request ends with a line identified as \r\n, followed by a empty line, which denotes the end of the request itself. If this final line is not sent by the client, the server would wait the end of the request for a specific timeout before closing the connection. The timeout would restart as the client sends some data. A pending requests DoS will never send this final line, in order to keep the connection active as long as possible. Usually web servers use a threshold to limit the active connections number, so the attacker opens a lot of connections with the victim host, in order to seize all the available positions on the server, reaching the saturation state. Then, the attacker's purpose is letting the connections idle, by slowly sending data to the target host, thus denying the offered service of the victim host.

Any request belonging to a pending requests DoS attack is sent in two different phases. The first part of the request is shown in Example 1, which reports the beginning of a standard HTTP request. Some implementations may add the Keep-Alive parameter or edit the requested URI, the user-agent or the content length, as these may improve the result for a specific attack.

Example 1.

```
GET / HTTP/1.1\r\n
Host: [...] \r\n
User-Agent: [...] \r\n
Content-Length: [...] \r\n
```

The next part of the request is sent slowly, by repeatedly sending a small amount of data to the server and waiting a specific timeout before the next sending. This action allows the client to maintain the connection with the server opened, by sending a small amount of data, thus preventing an expiration of the server timeout.

We have decided to identify the first part of the request as the *preparing phase*, since it has been sent to prepare the connection for the next step. The core phase of the attack has been called the *slow sending phase*, as the attacker maintains the connection with the victim by slowly sending data through the established channel. We have also decided to identify the timeout used during the slow sending phase as the *wait timeout parameter*, since it's used to switch the ON-OFF status of the attack. The wait timeout value has to be properly chosen from the attacker, in order to prevent a connection close from the target host. Moreover, this timeout is directly related to the amount of data used during the attack.

For a better understanding, we now briefly describe two pending requests DoS attacks, which are distinguished by the data type sent during the slow sending phase. Since they use the technique reported above, which exploits a vulnerability of the HTTP protocol, the attacks belong to the *practical attacks* typology.

Slowloris. The slowloris attack, also known as *Slow Headers* or *Slow HTTP GET*, has been designed by Robert "RSnake" Hansen, which has also released a Perl script implementing it. Slowloris purpose is to fill the listen queue of the victim and to maintain it occupied by sending a small amount of data.

While the preparing phase is pretty similar to the one described above, the slow sending phase is accomplished by repeatedly transmitting a specific string: `X-a: b\r\n`.

Slowloris has many implementations and some of them vary the HTTP parameters sent during the attack, in order to bypass a security system. For instance, some variants randomly generate part of the string sent during the slow sending phase.

Slow HTTP POST. This attack, also known as *slow body*, is pretty similar to the slowloris explained above, except the fact that it uses HTTP POST requests (instead of HTTP GET ones) to simulate a request coming from an HTML form element. In this case the `Content-Length` value becomes relevant, as it specifies the size of the message body to the server forcing the web server to wait for the end of the body.

During the preparing phase, the attacker sends the first part of a POST request to the target host, according to Example 1. Then he appends one POST parameter name and its relative value, without reaching the `Content-Length` value.

The slow sending phase is accomplished by repeatedly waiting for the *wait timeout* and sending another randomly generated POST parameter name and its relative value.

4.2   Long Responses DoS

This section describes attacks characterized as above by the LBR, but using different techniques. In fact, legitimate and complete requests are sent, although these are customized in a way to slow down the response of the server. Because of this, we have decided to group all this kind of attacks and call them *long responses DoS*.

These attacks may be difficult to identify, since the sent requests appear to be regular and it can be difficult to distinguish between an appropriate request and a suspicious one.

We now briefly describe three implementations of long responses DoS attacks.

Apache Range Headers. During 2011 a Perl script known as `killapache.pl` has been released on the web from a user known as Kingcope, offering the potential to attack a web server powered by Apache.

The attack is based on the *byte range* parameter of the HTTP protocol, which is typically used to request a resource portion. For instance, this functionality could be effective for requesting a large file or to resume an interrupted download.

Apache Range Headers sends a request (see Example 2) specifying a large amount of portions of the resource.

Example 2.

```
HEAD / HTTP/1.1
Host: [...]
Range: bytes=0-,5-0,5-1,5-2,[...],5-1296,5-1297,5-1298,5-1299
Accept-Encoding: gzip
Connection: close
```

The request may force the Apache web server to make a wide number of copies (in memory) of the requested file, in order to prepare them for sending. In many cases, this operation can exhaust the resources of the server.

Although this attack has been a serious threat to Apache, nowadays it isn't effective anymore, as the developer team released a patch able to mitigate this flaw, appropriately checking the request[1].

Apache Range Headers belongs to the *practical attacks* typology, since it is specific for the HTTP protocol and it has already been implemented.

---

[1] If the requests contains the byte range parameter, the sum of all ranges is calculated: if it's larger than the requested file, the request is ignored and the entire file content is sent.

#hashDoS. This attack has been presented by Julian Wälde and Alexander Klink during the 28C3 conference in 2011.

#hashDoS exploits a vulnerability of hash tables, which are frequently used by web applications for data storing. Hash tables are data structures which store key-value pairs very efficiently, since insert, retrieve and delete operations are executed with constant complexity, both in the best and average case. Instead, hash tables operations are not efficient in the worst case, as they work with exponential complexity. Many hash tables implementations use a deterministic hash function to map a key to a 32 bit or 64 bit value, which is used as an integer index to access the table. Moreover, the values are stored using a linked list and in case of multiple collisions for the hash function, the performance are slowed down.

The attack takes advantage of the above knowledge using low bandwidth rate to generate a large amount of collisions, thus generating a degradation of server performance, as the victim would saturate its resources during the response building, leading to a denial of service.

Since the #hashDoS attack is not bound to a specific hash function, it belongs to the *meta-attacks* type.

ReDoS. The ReDos, or Regex DoS, takes advantage of a vulnerability specific to the most common implementations of regular expressions. In such algorithms, the computational time needed for the verification is exponential to the input size.

One of the most common regex algorithms builds a Nondeterministic Finite Automaton: a finite state machine which may relate each pair of state and input symbol to a set of possible next states. Since various possible next states could be found, a deterministic algorithm is chosen, in order to visit each state until a match is found, if any.

Some regexes, known as *evil regexes*, force the server to check among 2^{n-1} possible paths, with n the input size; this weakness is exploited by the attacker to cause the program enter in this extreme situation, where a long time is required to check for the expression. The attacker could send a well-crafted input able to slow down the system exploiting the regex used by the web application. In other cases, if the system allows users to specify a custom regex, the attacker could inject an evil regex too, thus making the system vulnerable. Since the attack could be different for each targeted system, ReDoS belong to the *meta-attacks* type.

4.3   Multi-layer DoS

This kind of attacks usually operate non properly at application level, even if they share with the above categories a typical low transmission rate. Furthermore, these attacks use network or transport functionalities in conjunction with application ones to attack the web server.

We now summarily describe a multi-layer DoS attack named LoRDAS [8, 25].

LoRDAS. LoRDAS is the acronym of Low-Rate DoS Attack against Application Servers and it has been proposed by Maciá-Fernández et al. [25].

In a LoRDAS attack, the attacker purpose is to estimate the instants in which resources will be freed by the server, in order to occupy them. Limiting the active phase only to those instants, the attack rate is reduced, as the possibility of being revealed by an Intrusion Detection System.

The forecasting of the time period when the busy resource become available again is not based on a common and general vulnerability which affect any application server; instead, it depends on the specific server implementation. Therefore, this attack belongs to the *meta-attacks* category. In the likely case that the server exhibits a deterministic behavior, the estimation could be forecasted by the aggressor [25]: for example, a web server which implements the persistent connections feature could be vulnerable [8]. In this case, the attacker may send a probing request to the victim in order to get information about the timeout used by the server to close pending connections. In this way, when the resource is freed, the malicious host could launch a short burst of packets with the aim of occupying it again. The same approach is used when any connection is shut down for any reason (graceful or reset connection close).

4.4   Mixed Attacks

The above methodologies can also be mixed. We now describe an example of attack where long responses DoS and multi-layer DoS are involved.

Slow Read. This attack has been designed by Sergey Shekyan of Qualys Security Labs: it sends a legitimate HTTP request to the server, demanding the core part to lower layers (TCP in this case). Slow Read aims to take up all the available connections of the server, forcing the victim to reply slowly. Therefore, this menace belongs to the category of *long responses DoS* attacks.

In a standard communication most of the received packets are sized 1448 bytes, which is the TCP *Maximum Segment Size* encapsulated in a Ethernet frame. The key point of the attack is that the server is forced to use a window size of 28 bytes, by specifying this limit when sending the initial SYN packet to the victim host. This action would lead the server to reply very slowly; due to the high number of connections, it may cause a denial of service. Therefore, this is classified like a *practical attack*. Furthermore, as Slow Read acts at transport level by specifying a custom window size, it is also categorized like a *multi-layer DoS*.

5   Conclusions

In the slow DoS field, there are a multitude of attacks and defense methodologies, although accurate classifications and taxonomies of these attacks are still missing.

In this paper we gather known slow DoS attacks, trying to structure the knowledge in this field. The taxonomy we report is intended to help both (i) network administrators, helping them for a better understanding of the vulnerabilities exploited by the attacks and (ii) the research community, facilitating the cooperation among researchers and giving a common language for discussions related to this topic.

Our work has to be considered a report related to the actual threats: as new attacks and techniques are continuously discovered, taxonomies have to adapt themselves to the growing field and they have to be refined.

As we have reported a taxonomy of slow DoS attacks, a similar work could also be done for detection and.mitigation techniques, in order to clarify the methodologies used to protect systems from such attacks. Indeed, this paper is the beginning of a study about SDAs and it will be expanded into a more detailed paper.

References

[1] Kumar, S., Singh, M., Sachdeva, M., Kumar, K.: Flooding Based DDoS Attacks and Their Influence on Web Services. (IJCSIT) International Journal of Computer Science and Information Technologies 2(3), 1131–1136 (2011)

[2] Sachdeva, M., Singh, G., Kumar, K., Singh, K.: DDoS Incidents and their Impact: A Review. International Arab Journal of Information Technology 7(1), 14–20 (2010)

[3] Paxson, V.: An analysis of using reflectors for distributed denial-of-service attacks. Computer Communication Review 31(3), 38–47 (2001)

[4] Keromytis, A.D., Misra, V., Rubenstein, D.: SOS: An architecture for mitigating DDoS attacks. IEEE Journal on Selected Areas in Communications 22(1), 176–188 (2004)

[5] Northcutt, S., Novak, J.: Network intrusion detection, 3rd edn. New Riders, Indianapolis (2002)

[6] Schuba, C.L., Krsul, I.V., Kuhn, M.G., Spafford, E.H., Sundaram, A., Zamboni, D.: Analysis of a denial of service attack on TCP. In: 1997 IEEE Symposium on Security and Privacy - Proceedings, pp. 208–223 (1997)

[7] Douligeris, C., Mitrokotsa, A.: DDoS attacks and defense mechanisms: classification and state-of-the-art. Computer Networks 44(5), 643–666 (2004)

[8] Macia-Fernandez, G., Rodriguez-Gomez, R.A., Diaz-Verdejo, J.E.: Defense techniques for low-rate DoS attacks against application servers. Computer Networks 54(15), 2711–2727 (2010)

[9] Macia-Fernandez, G., Diaz-Verdejo, J.E., Garcia-Teodoro, P.: Evaluation of a low-rate DoS attack against iterative servers. Computer Networks 51(4), 1013–1030 (2007)

[10] Macia-Fernandez, G., Diaz-Verdejo, J.E., Garcia-Teodoro, P.: Evaluation of a low-rate DoS attack against application servers. Computers & Security 27(7-8), 335–354 (2008)

[11] Kuzmanovic, A., Knightly, E.W.: Low-rate TCP-targeted denial of service attacks and counter strategies. IEEE-ACM Transactions on Networking 14(4), 683–696 (2006)

[12] Safa, H., Chouman, M., Artail, H., Karam, M.: A collaborative defense mechanism against SYN flooding attacks in IP networks. Journal of Network and Computer Applications 31(4), 509–534 (2008)

[13] Hussain, A., Heidemann, J., Papadopoulos, C.: A framework for classifying denial of service attacks. Computer Communication Review 33(4), 99–110 (2003)

[14] Chen, L.C., Longstaff, T.A., Carley, K.M.: Characterization of defense mechanisms against distributed denial of service attacks. Computers & Security 23(8), 665–678 (2004)

[15] Mirkovic, J., Reiher, P.: A taxonomy of DDoS attack and DDoS Defense mechanisms. Computer Communication Review 34(2), 39–53 (2004)

[16] Tariq, U., Hong, M.-P., Lhee, K.-S.: A Comprehensive Categorization of DDoS Attack and DDoS Defense Techniques. In: Li, X., Zaïane, O.R., Li, Z. (eds.) ADMA 2006. LNCS (LNAI), vol. 4093, pp. 1025–1036. Springer, Heidelberg (2006)

[17] Guirguis, M., Bestavros, A., Matta, I.: Exploiting the transients of adaptation for RoQ attacks on Internet resources. In: 12th IEEE International Conference on Network Protocols - Proceedings, pp. 184–195 (2004)

[18] Guirguis, M., Bestavros, A., Matta, I., Zhang, Y.T.: Reduction of Quality (RoQ) attacks on Internet end-systems. In: Proceedings of the IEEE Infocom 2005: The Conference on Computer Communications, vol. 1-4, pp. 1362–1372 (2005)

[19] Guirguis, M., Bestavros, A., Matta, I., Zhang, Y.T.: Reduction of quality (RoQ) attacks on dynamic load balancers: Vulnerability assessment and design tradeoffs. In: Infocom 2007, vol. 1-5, pp. 857–865 (2007)

[20] Guirguis, M., Bestavros, A., Matta, I., Zhang, Y.T.: Adversarial exploits of end-systems adaptation dynamics. Journal of Parallel and Distributed Computing 67(3), 318–335 (2007)

[21] Siris, V.A., Papagalou, F.: Application of anomaly detection algorithms for detecting SYN flooding attacks. Computer Communications 29(9), 1433–1442 (2006)

[22] Huang, Y., Pullen, J.M.: Countering denial-of-service attacks using congestion triggered packet sampling and filtering. In: Proceedings of the Tenth International Conference on Computer Communications and Networks, pp. 490–494 (2001)

[23] Gil, T.M., Poletto, M.: MULTOPS: A data-structure for bandwidth attack detection. In: Usenix Association Proceedings of the 10th Usenix Security Symposium, pp. 23–34 (2001)

[24] Stallings, W.: IPv6: The new Internet protocol. IEEE Communications Magazine 34(7), 96–108 (1996)

[25] Maciá-Fernández, G., Díaz-Verdejo, J.E., García-Teodoro, P., de Toro-Negro, F.: LoRDAS: A Low-Rate DoS Attack against Application Servers. In: Lopez, J., Hämmerli, B.M. (eds.) CRITIS 2007. LNCS, vol. 5141, pp. 197–209. Springer, Heidelberg (2008)

Crypto-Precision: Testing Tool for Hash Function

Harshvardhan Tiwari, Ankit Luthra, Himanshu Goel, Sambhav Sharma,
and Krishna Asawa

Computer Science and Engineering Department,
Jaypee Institute of Information Technology, Noida, India

Abstract. In this paper, we present a new generic cryptographic hash function testing tool called Crypto-Precision. It is designed to be adaptable to various Cryptographic Hash Function algorithms and different hash function constructions. We have tested three hash functions; SHA-1, FORK-256 and NewFORK-256.The current version of the tool dynamically generates code for a Hash Function and then tests that Hash Function on the basis of its speed, collision resistance and randomness.

Keywords: Hash function, Merkle-Damgard, Message digest, SHA-1, FORK-256, NewFORK-256, Collision.

1 Introduction

Our World is getting smaller. The Internet has removed all boundaries and people have come closer to each other. But this has also led to an unfortunate development. Hacking has become a serious threat to people who use the Internet. With the introduction of E-commerce and sharing of confidential data over the Internet, the need for data protection is at its strongest. One way of protecting data is through Cryptographic Hash Functions.

A Hash Function converts a variable length message into a fixed length key known as a Message Digest. This is determined by using various methods that make up the Hash Function Algorithm. These Algorithms are applied on different Hash Function Constructions to provide more complexity to the Hash Function. Higher the complexity lesser is the chance to decipher the actual message from its Message Digest.

Over the years, many Algorithms have been proposed for Hashing which are based on a certain set of rules known as Construction of that particular algorithm. Some of the known Hash Function algorithms are MD4, MD5, SHA-1, FORK and most of these are based on Merkle-Damgard Construction. Some new types of constructions, that have come up to give more complexity to the Hash Functions, are Merkle-Damgard with Permutation, Dither and HAIFA.

Most of these Algorithms have been defined only on a certain type of construction and hence their functionality has not been tested with other types of constructions. So we need a tool that can combine different Algorithms to different constructions and then analyze them on the basis of different standard test cases like Collision Test, Bit Variance Test, Speed Test, etc. This is where our Tool **Crypto-Precision** comes in.

S.M. Thampi et al. (Eds.): SNDS 2012, CCIS 335, pp. 205–214, 2012.

Crypto-Precision allows its user to dynamically generate code for these hash functions by trying every possible combination of different algorithm and construction. The user after generating the code is able to run the code through the Testing phase where their efficiency, collision rate and randomness are tested using different test cases. In this paper we explore how we went about designing this tool and the challenges that were faced during the development of this tool.

In the current version of Crypto-Precision, we have implemented three different algorithms: SHA-1, FORK-256 and NEW FORK-256. These algorithms have can be implemented on five different constructions: Merkle-Damgard with Permutation (MDP), Dither, HAIFA, Dither with Permutation and HAIFA with Permutation. This gives us the user fifteen different Hash Functions to choose from.

2   Requirements

The first step involved in making Crypto-Precision was to specify the requirements of the tool.

- The Interface Should be User-Friendly
- Primary Requirement of the Tool is to take the user input regarding combination of Hash Function Algorithm and Hash Function Construction and then dynamically generate the code for that Hash Function
- The Hash Function Generated should be able to encodes messages, text files, images, videos, etc
- The Tool should be compatible with other Java based Applications to be able to provide the Hash Function Functionality to that application
- The Tool should be able to Test the Hash Function on the basis of different Test Cases
- The Tool should be able to differentiate between the Test Cases according to parameters entered for Testing
- The Tool should provide Statistical Analysis of Hash Function
- Test cases that should be supported: Collision Test, Bit Variance Test, ASCII Test, Entropy Test, Speed Test

3   Review of Literature

3.1   Hash Function Methodology

The Steps involved in computing hash value from an input message in any basic Hash Algorithm are:

1. Padding: The input message is broken up into chunks of 512-bit blocks; the message is padded so that its length is divisible by 512. The basic padding works as follows: first a single bit, 1, is appended to the end of the message. This is followed by as many zeros as are required.[5]
2. The algorithms use state variables, each of which is a 32 bit integer (an unsigned long on most systems). These variables are sliced and diced and are (eventually) the message digest.[5]

3. Now on to the actual meet of the algorithm: The hash functions, using the state variables and the message as input, are used to transform the state variables from their initial state into what will become the message digest. For each 512 bits, rounds are performed and the hashed value is calculated.[5]

3.2   Algorithms and Constructions

In this section, the Algorithms that are supported by Crypto-Precision are secure hash algorithm (SHA)[2] , FORK-256 and NEW FORK-256[1].

All of these algorithms are based on Merkle-Damgard [3] Construction. MDP is a variant of the Merkle-Damgård construction with a permutation to provide more complexity to the Hash Function. Next is the Dither construction with Dither Sequence [6] generated using a Pseudo random sequence   or an abelian square free sequence. The HAIFA [4] construction is taken from Hash Iterative Framework. Dither with permutation and HAIFA with permutation constructions are similar to Dither and HAIFA respectively but (like in MDP) a permutation is applied right before the processing of the last message block in both cases to increase the complexity of these constructions.[4]

3.3   Description of Test Cases

The different test cases that we have considered are the Speed Test [8], Collision Test[8], Randomness Test[9], Bit Variance Test[9] and the statistical analysis of the Hash Function created by any given combination of the user.

-    In the speed Test, we calculate the average amount of time each Hash Function takes to compute the hash value of a given message or file. This tells us the efficiency of the Hash Function and how quickly it is able to encrypt data.
-    The Randomness Test   checks the randomness of the generated hash function. This is done by taking the message entered by the user and calculating its Hash Value. Then flipping one bit of the message and calculating the Hash Value again. Now we take these two Hash Values and XOR them. Then we count the number of one's that we get in the result. If this value is close to 50% then there is quite a less probability for collision   to occur for two similar messages. This means that the Hash Function has provided enough randomness. The bit variance test   consists of measuring the impact of change in input message bits on the digest bits. More specifically, given an input message, all the small changes as well as the large changes of this input message bits are taken and the bits in the corresponding digest are evaluated for each such change. Afterwards, for each digest bit the probabilities of taking on the values of 1 and 0 are measured considering all the digests produced by applying input message bit changes.
-    In the Collision test, we generate 2048 random messages and check for collision (number of hits) in them. We also calculate minimum absolute difference, maximum absolute difference and the mean absolute difference   for these messages according to the collision values.

- In statistical analysis of the Hash Function, a paragraph of message is randomly chosen, and the corresponding Hash value is generated. Then a bit in the message is randomly selected and toggled, and a new Hash value is obtained. Finally, two Hash values are compared, and the number of hanged bits is counted as Bi. We use four different statistics: Mean changed bit Number, Mean changed Probability, Standard Deviation of the changed bit number and the Standard Deviation of Probability [8, 9].

3.4   Related Work

According to the research done in the literature, none of the work is related to our approach. We came across many existing encryption and testing tools, such as OpenSSL[10] for C and Crypto++[11] for C++. These are open source class libraries of cryptographic algorithms that allow us to access performance of built-in hash functions but do not allow us to test how these hash functions perform against specific test cases. Theses libraries also do not have any provision for customizing the hash functions.

JCATT (Japan Cryptographic Algorithm implementation Testing Tool) [12]and CAVP (Cryptographic Algorithm Validation Program) [13]test the conformance to the cryptographic algorithm specifications and each function of the cryptographic algorithm. These tools work only on the certified hash functions and not on the customized hash functions and moreover they only check the implementation of the hash functions but fail to test them.

Another one is PEARL (Performance Evaluator of Cryptographic Algorithms) [14]. This tool collects and analyzes information related to the execution of the cryptographic algorithms in mobile devices. PEARL also allows evaluating the performance of symmetrical and asymmetrical cryptographic algorithms and hash functions for J2ME platform[14]. It computes the performance on the basis of time, message size and virtual machine used. Based on the evaluation, it suggests the best suited algorithm for the particular task. This tool also lacks the ability to customize the code and to test the hash functions against more test cases.

TSIK (VeriSign's Trusted Services Integration Kit)[15] is a java based tool focuses on the secure transactions in the web services; this toolkit evaluates the performance on account of execution time and compares the result with respect to Java's Cryptography Extensions (JCE[18]). Some more tools like Salvasoft HashCalc[16] and HASH TAB[17] are stand-alone programs. They compute hashes and compare file hash value with another file but do not compare a hash value computed by different hash functions of single file.

Most of the tools mentioned above evaluate the performance of existing hash functions on the basis of execution time and other system dependent parameters. None of the tools have a provision for customizing the algorithm by basing them on different construction, generating code in a programming language and testing them on the basis of system dependent parameters and their performance against specific test cases like Collision Test, Bit Variance Test, Speed Test, etc. Thus **Crypto-Precision** has an advantage over all these tools.

4   Design

4.1   Design Issues

The Design Issues with respect to this tool were many as a result of the complex requirements. The requirement of combining the algorithms with the constructions dynamically was the primary concern while designing the tool. The tool's architecture needed to be such that it would be easy to dynamically generate code and add new algorithms or constructions to the Tool without too much of effort. For this we needed to make sure that the atomicity of the tool was quite high so that different blocks of the Hash Function could be combined together at runtime instead of coding the Hash Functions separately. We needed to design a database consisting of these different blocks so that the tool can use this database to generate the Hash Function code dynamically. This database also needed to be portable and easily linkable to the part of the tool that would be responsible for dynamic Hash Function generation. The other issue was of executing the test cases on the generated Hash Function. The Testing Class needed to be part of the Architecture at a point where it could the run the different test cases on the dynamically generated code. These issues were kept in mind while deciding on the Design of Crypto-Precision.

4.2   Identifying Basic Blocks

A Hash Function is made up of some basic blocks that are common to all Hash Functions. Before designing the tool, these basic blocks were needed to be identified so that we can edit them for different constructions and algorithms. These basic blocks increase the *atomicity* of Crypto-Precision and improve the way in which the code will be generated dynamically.

The Basic Blocks that we identified and implemented in our database were:

- Padding: changing with the number of inputs that are required for padding the initial message. This depends on the construction that is being used.
- Compression Function: depends on the algorithm being used. It is the main building block of the hash function as the its complexity depends on it
- Chaining Variables Used by Algorithm: the values that are used as inputs to the compression function should be complex and distinct
- Abelian Square Free Sequence: random sequence being used in the FORK algorithms
- Pseudo Random Sequence: random sequence being used in the SHA-1 Algorithm

4.3   Tool Design

Adapting a Hash function algorithm to a new Hash Function construction requires a trade-off between generality and user friendliness. The objective of **Crypto-Precision** is to provide as much support for adapting the tool to a new target code, a new Hash Function algorithm and a new Hash Function construction.

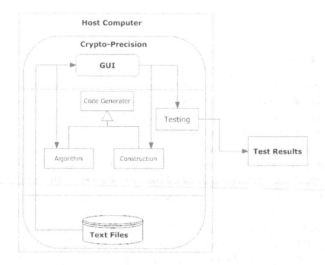

Fig. 1. Three Layered Architecture of Crypto-Precision

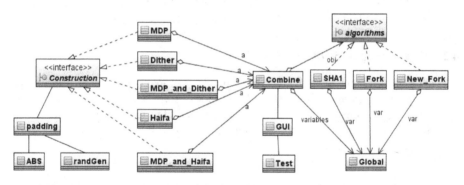

Fig. 2. Class Diagram

The architecture of **Crypto-Precision** can be divided in to a three layers. At the top layer is the graphical user interface (GUI). From the interface, the user can choose different combinations of Hash Function Construction and Hash Function Algorithm to generate a unique code for that specific combination. This code would be then dynamically generated at runtime.

The middle layer is the one responsible for the dynamic generation of code. It consists of a number of classes that describe the different Hash Function algorithm and construction, the dynamic code generation class, the classes that describe the basic blocks and the testing class that would test the generated hash function. The generating class will use the information provided by the user to the tool to fetch data from database to create the algorithm and construction class. These classes would then be linked with the basic blocks classes (padding, Pseudo Random, Abelian Sqaure Free) to complete the hash function code. This dynamically generated code can then be tested by the Test class based on a number of different test cases.

The bottom layer consists of the database that consists of the text files containing the different methods that are required in order to generate the code dynamically based on the user's choice. The atomicity of the different methods is quite high considering we have created separate text files for all the basic blocks of the Hash Function.

4.4   Interface Design

The Interface forms the top layer of Crypto-Precision. It is an important part of the tool as the user interacts with the tool through this user interface only. The interface design has been made in such a way that the user has complete control over the hash function that will be generated through the tool.

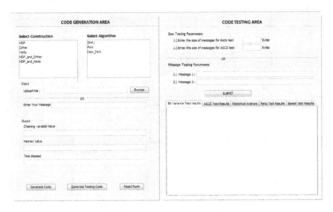

Fig. 3. Screenshot of interface

The interface consists of two parts: the Code Generation Window and the Testing Window. In the Code Generation Window, it displays options for the Hash Function Algorithm and Hash Function Construction. Below these options, it displays text boxes that are required to enter the file path or the string for which the hashed value needs to be calculated and in which the calculated hashed value will be displayed later on. The buttons in this window are used to generate the codes dynamically for calculating hashed value and for testing.

The Testing window consists of text boxes for entering the parameters for testing of the dynamically generated hash Function and also a large Text Area that will display the results of the different Tests that are conducted.

5   Working of Tool

When the user starts up Crypto-Precision, the interface will ask the user to choose the Hash Function Algorithm and the Hash Function Construction on which the Hash Function should be based.

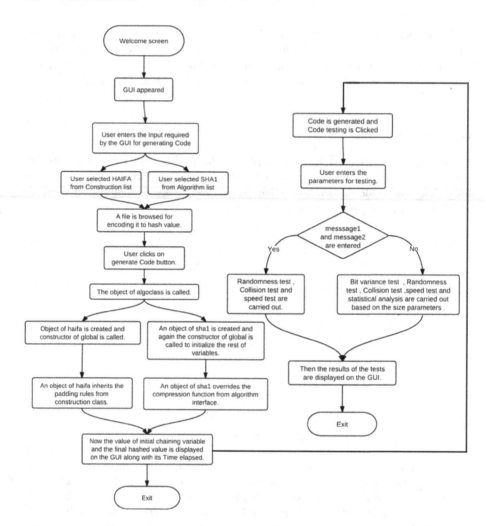

Fig. 4. Flow diagram of *Crypto-precision* for generating the *Hash function* and testing them

Once the user has chosen the combination, the user can either enter a file path in the given box or enter a string for which the hashed value is to be calculated.

Now when the user will click on 'Generate Code' Button, using the database, the code for the given combination of algorithm and construction will be generated and the Hashed value for the file or the string will be calculated. This will be displayed in the box marked as 'Hashed Value Generated'.

Now we come to the testing part. To test the generated code, the user will click on 'Generate Test Code' button which will generate the code again for Testing. The right hand side of the interface deals with the Testing Functionality of Crypto-Precision.

The tool will require the user to either enter two sample messages in the Testing window or the number of bytes for which the testing has to take place. Once the values are entered, the testing process will start by clicking on the Test Button. The results of the test will be displayed in the large box below. The user can now look through each of the test results easily by clicking on the different tests that are done on the code.

6   Conclusion

This paper described the Cryptanalyst Tool Crypto-Precision. The tool is implemented in the Java language to support maintainability and portability between different host platforms. All data used by the tool is stored in a portable text files based database. An object-oriented approach was used to minimize the programming effort needed for combining different Hash Function algorithms and Hash Function Constructions and generate Hash Function Code dynamically. Three Hash Function Algorithms and Five Hash Function Constructions have been implemented in the current version of Crypto-Precision. This tool is extremely helpful for testing different Hash Functions for Speed, Randomness, Collisions, etc and for customizing algorithms to different constructions dynamically.

References

1. Hong, D., Chang, D., Sung, J., Lee, S., Hong, S., Lee, J., Moon, D., Chee, S.: New FORK-256. IACR Cryptology ePrint Archive (2007)
2. Chatterjee, R., Saifee, M.A., Chowdhury, D.R.: Modifications of SHA-0 to Prevent Attacks. IIT Kharagpur (2005)
3. Hirose, S., Park, J.H., Yun, A.: A Simple Variant of the Merkle–Damgård Scheme with a Permutation. J. Cryptology 25(2), 271–309 (2012)
4. Biham, E., Dunkelman, O.: A Framework for Iterative Hash Functions — HAIFA. IACR
5. Cryptology ePrint Archive 2007: 278 (2007)
6. Rivest, R.L.: Abelian square-free dithering for iterated hash functions, http://theory.lcs.mit.edu/rivest/RivestAbelianSquareFreeDithering ForIteratedHashFunctions.pdf (accessed)
7. Piechowiak, S., Kolski, C.: Towards a Generic Object Oriented Decision Support System for University Timetabling: An Interactive Approach. International Journal of Information Technology and Decision Making 3, 179–208 (2003)
8. Hu, M., Wang, Y.: The Collision Rate Tests of Two Known Message Digest Algorithms
9. Kaur, G., Nayak, V.S.: Analysis of the Hash Function – Modified Grøstl
10. OpenSSL, http://www.openssl.org/
11. Crypto++, http://www.cryptopp.com//
12. Specifications of Cryptographic Algorithm Implementation Testing - Hash Functions: Information-Technology Promotion Agency, Japan (2009)
13. Pattinson, F.: Assurance in Implementation Correctness of Cryptographic Algorithms Gained Through the NIST Cryptographic Algorithm Validation Program

14. Filho, B., Viana, W., Andrade, R., Monteiro, A.J.: PEARL: a PErformance evaluAtor of cRyptographic aLgorithms for mobile devices
15. Lamprecht, C., van Moorsel, A., Tomlinson, P., Thomas, N.: Investigating the efficiency of Cryptographic Algorithms in online transactions
16. SlavaSoft HashCalc, `http://www.slavasoft.com/hashcalc/index.html`
17. HashTab: `http://implbits.com/HashTab/HashTabWindows.aspx`
18. Java™ Cryptography Extension (JCE),
`http://docs.oracle.com/javase/1.4.2/docs/guide/security/jce/JCERefGuide.html`

Performance Analysis and Improvement Using LFSR in the Pipelined Key Scheduling Section of DES

P.V. Sruthi[1], Prabaharan Poornachandran[2], and A.S. Remya Ajai[3]

[1] Dept of ECE, Amritapuri, Amrita University, India
[2] Amrita Centre for Cyber Security, Amritapuri, Amrita University, India
[3] Dept of ECE, Amritapuri, Amrita university, India
sruthipv141@gmail.com,
{praba,remya}@amrita.edu

Abstract. In this paper, DES algorithm is implemented by applying pipelining concept to the key scheduling part. Using this implementation, it is possible to have the key length equal to data length; which further improves the security of the system, at the same time decaying the performance. This scenario is similar to that of one time pad. i.e, here key storage and transmission is going to occupy more area and power, degrading the performance of the system. The security vs performance trade off is analyzed for the circuit. Another solution is also introduced in this paper, i.e, the Linear Feedback Shift Registers(LFSRs). Using LFSR, it is possible to have different keys generated every clock cycles, improving the security of the system, at the same time we need to store or transmit the single seed of LFSR only. The design is implemented in Virtex 5 FPGA device using Xilinx 12.1 platform. An encryption rate of 35.5 gbits/S is obtained, which is almost the fastest among all other current implementations. The performance of the system in terms of area, power and timing is analyzed using the Synopsys tool.

Keywords: DES, Skew, key scheduling, security, performance, LFSR.

1   Introduction

Nowadays each and every sensitive data is stored digitally. Bank accounts, medical records, and personal emails are some such examples in which data must be kept secure. The science of cryptography tries to encounter the lack of security. Data confidentiality, authentication, non-reputation and data integrity are some of the main parts of cryptography. The evolution of cryptography drove in very complex cryptographic models which they could not be implemented before some years. The revolution of computers and especially CMOS technology permit the design and the implementation of with characteristics as limited area resources, low power consumption and high speed. Secure communications systems often require the capacity to encrypt messages with several different algorithms in addition to the need to change keys regularly[1].

S.M. Thampi et al. (Eds.): SNDS 2012, CCIS 335, pp. 215–224, 2012.

The DES algorithm is a private-key encryption algorithm, which was developed by IBM and has been a federal standard since 1977 [2]. DES has subsequently enjoyed widespread use internationally. Data Encryption Standard is a block cipher – an algorithm that takes a fixed length string of plaintext bits and transforms it through a series of complicated operations into another cipher text string of the same length. The inputs to the data encryption block include a 64 bit data input, 64 bit key input along with the other essential I/O control lines. The basic block diagram for DES is given in figure 1.

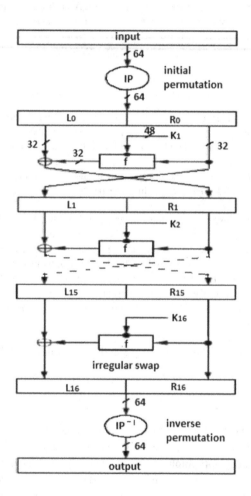

Fig. 1. DES algorithm block diagram

The 64 bit key is given as input to the key scheduler within the DES engine, which generates 16 distinct keys of 48 bit width each. Each of these 48 bit keys is then given as input to each of 16 feistel function operations that takes place during encryption.

The 64-bit data is given as input which is then processed as defined by the algorithm to form the 64-bit encrypted data. This process mainly includes an initial permutation of the data , 16 feistel function operations and a final permutation. The actual encryption within DES takes place as the data is continually replaced by pre defined cipher texts within the 'S-blocks' that are executed during each of the feistel operations.

In this paper, pipelining concept is applied to the key scheduling part of DES algorithm by introducing registers in between each stage. Registers are used to delay the sub keys so that the key distribution to each stage is made easy. An encryption rate of 35.5 Gbps is obtained by using virtex 5 FPGA technology, giving a fastest hardware implementation. Here we can have different keys for each 64 bit data block making cryptanalysis a tough job. But at the same time it becomes similar to one time pad; i.e, for more security we use key with same length as that of data input, so key storage becomes a problem. An analysis of security v/s storage(performance) is done to find out the tradeoff between these quantities. Another solution to solve this problem is to introduce LFSRs to generate keys. A single LFSR seed is used to generate different keys every clock cycles, which in turn makes cryptanalysis rather tough. So we need to transmit or store that single LFSR seed only instead of the key with same length as that of the data block.

2   Pipelining the Des Algorithm

The iterative nature of the DES algorithm makes it ideally suited to pipelining. The DES algorithm implementation presented in this paper is based on the ECB mode. Although the ECB mode is less secure than other modes of operation, it is commonly used and its operation can be pipelined [5]. The fully pipelined DES implementation will also operate in counter mode. Counter mode is a simplification of output feedback (OFB) mode and involves updating the input plaintext block as a counter, $Ij+1¼Ij+1$, rather than using feedback. Hence, the cipher text block i is not required in order to encrypt plaintext block i+1 [4]. Counter mode provides more security than ECB mode and operation of either mode involves trading security for high throughput. In order to pipeline the algorithm, the function f block must be instantiated 16 times. Registers are then placed at the left and right outputs of each function f block to allow the data to be sequenced.[5]

3   Key Scheduling Procedure

In the implementation of the DES algorithm key schedule [4] employed here, the sub-keys are pre-computed and hence, for a 16-stage pipelined DES design, it is necessary to control the time at which the sub-keys are available to each feistel function, f block.

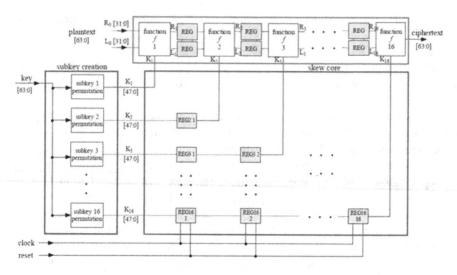

Fig. 2. DES with skew core key scheduling [4]

This is accomplished by the addition of a skew that delays the individual sub-keys by the required amount [5]. This design comprises of two blocks, a sub-key generation block and a skew core. The block diagram for this block is shown in figure 2.

3.1   Sub-key Generation Block

The conventional key scheduling procedure is introduced here, which is shown in figure 2. The 64 bit key is given to the permutation block, which after permutation

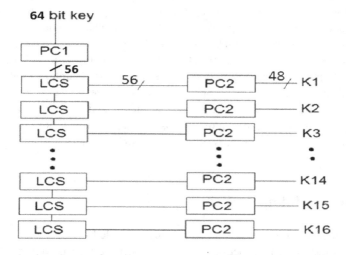

Fig. 3. Sub key generation in DES

produces a 56 bit key. This 56 bit key after a left circular shift, goes through another permutation to produce the first sub key, k1. This process isrepeated 16 times to generate the 16 sub keys as shown in figure 3.

3.2   Skew Core

For the 16-stage pipelined des design it is necessary to control the time at which the sub-keys are available to each function f block. This is accomplished by the addition of a skew that delays the individual sub-keys by the required amount. The skew is introduced by introducing d flip flop (register) arrays.Since the des algorithm consists of 16 rounds, the skew core is set to loop 15 times since a register is not required to delay the first sub key.[3].

4   Key Generation Problems

Here different keys are used every clock cycle. So the key length becomes same as that of data block, creating a scenario similar to one time pad, i.e. larger key length will create complexities in transmission and storage of the key, at the same time it improves the security. So here we have a trade off between security and performance (security and storage) of the cryptographic system. There are two ways to analyse this situation, firstly a single key can be chosen to repeat for 'n' number of data blocks so that a value can be found out for 'n', where security and performance are equally satisfied. The second way is to use LFSRs (Linear Feedback Shift Registers) to generate the keys for every clock cycle. LFSR generates random patterns every clock cycles and hence the security of the system is maintained as such. Again in order to generate the same key pattern at the decryption side, we need to transmit or store only the specific primitive polynomial (the basic LFSR seed) which in turn overcomes the problem with key storage and transmission.

5   Security vs. Performance Trade Off

In this implementation it is possible to have the key length equal to that of the data length. This is very helpful to improve the security of the system, but the key storage becomes a problem in such a situation. So there arises a trade off between security and performance. 3000 data blocks are taken as input to analyse this situation. If 3000 keys are used to process 3000 data blocks, we have 100 percent security, but we need to store or transmit 3000 bytes of data. Now if we reduce the number of keys to 1500, security percentage reduces to 50 percent. This process continued and a graph is obtained (see figure 4).

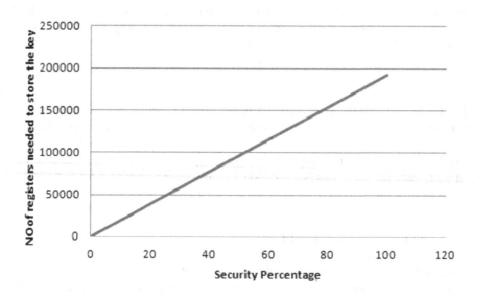

Fig. 4. Security vs performance trade off

6   Linear Feed Back Shift Registers (LFSRs)

A linear feedback shift register (LFSR) is a shift register whose input bit is a linear function of its previous state. The most commonly used linear function of single bits is XOR. Thus, an LFSR is most often a shift register whose input bit is driven by the exclusive-or (XOR) of some bits of the overall shift register value. The initial value of the LFSR is called the seed, and because the operation of the register is deterministic, the stream of values produced by the register is completely determined by its current

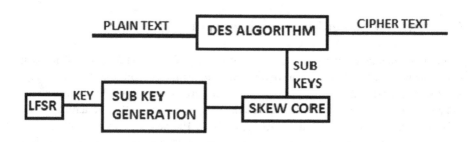

Fig. 5. LFSR Key generation

(or previous) state. Likewise, because the register has a finite number of possible states, it must eventually enter a repeating cycle. However, an LFSR with a well-chosen feedback function can produce a sequence of bits which appears random and which has a very long cycle (see figure 5).

Applications of LFSRs include generating pseudo-random numbers, pseudo-noise sequences, fast digital counters, and whitening sequences. Both hardware and software implementations of LFSRs are common. The mathematics of a cyclic redundancy check, used to provide a quick check against transmission errors, are closely related to those of an LFSR.

In this scenario LFSR with primitive polynomial $X^{64}+X^4+X^3+X^2+1$ is used. In every clock cycle, a new key is generated here as given figure 6.

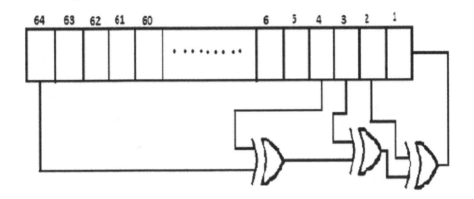

Fig. 6. LFSR with primitive polynomial $X^{64}+X^4+X^3+X^2+1$

7   Implementation Summary

FPGA implementation of des algorithm using skew core key scheduling and key generation using lfsr was accomplished on a virtex 5 – xc5vlx110t-3ff1100 device using xilinx foundation series 12.1 as synthesis and modelsim se6.5f as simulation tool. The design was coded using verilog language. It occupied 1808 slice registers out of available 69120 (2%), and 1870 (2%) slice luts. The design achieves a throughput of 35.5 gbits/s. This result is very much advanced compared to other existing designs since the operating frequency of virtex 5 fpga is very high (550 mhz) compared to other devices used in earlier cases. i.e, In [12] using Spartan 3E, the throughput obtained is 7.160 Gbits/s.

Full design schematic and simulation window shown in figure 7 and 8.

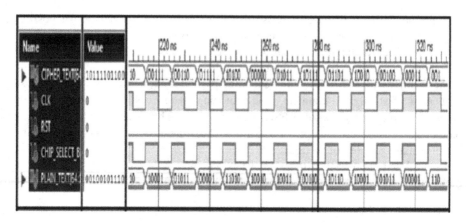

Fig. 7. Simulation window of DES design with skew core key scheduling and LFSR key generation

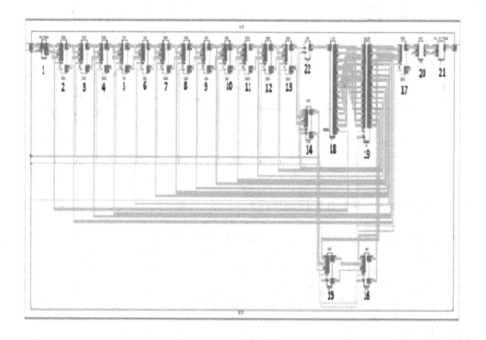

Fig. 8.

RTL design schematic;   Blocks: 1-initial permutation,
2 to 17- the 16 rounds of operation,   18- Key Scheduling
19- Skew Core,   20-Swappling,
21- Final permutation   22- LFSR

8   Performance Comparison

The design is implemented and compared with previously implemented designs (See Table 1).

Table 1. Performance Comparison

Manufacturer	Device used	System clock (MHz)	Data rate (Gbit/s)
Wong *et al.* [6]	XC4020E	10	0.0267
Biham [7] (software)	Alpha 8400	300	0.127
Kaps and Paar [8]	XC4028EX	25.18	0.402
Free-DES [9]	XCV400	47.7	3.052
McLoone, McCanny [4]	XCV1000	59.5	3.808
Sandia Laboratories [10]	ASIC	---	9.280
Patterson (Jbits) [11]	XCV150	168	10.752
Proposed Design	XC5VLX110T	550	35.5

The performance of the system is analysed using Synopsys and the area, timing and power reports are obtained. The design with LFSR occupied an area of 73387units, consuming a total dynamic power of 2.4272 mW and the data arrival time was found to be 1.37nS.

9   Conclusion

The key scheduling concept in DES algorithm is modified by introducing the concept of pipelining. The security vs performance trade off of the system is analysed. LFSR is introduced for key generation as a solution to the security vs performance trade off that occurs while pipelining. The design is implemented in virtex 5 - xc5vlx110t-3ff1100 FPGA device and Xilinx platform. The performance of the design is analysed using Synopsys tool.

References

[1] Leonard, J., Mangione-Smith, W.H.: A Case Study of Partially Evaluated Hardware Circuits: Key-Specific DES. In: Glesner, M., Luk, W. (eds.) FPL 1997. LNCS, vol. 1304, pp. 151–160. Springer, Heidelberg (1997)

[2] Van Der Lubbe, J.C.A.: Basic methods of cryptography. Cambridge University Press (1998)

[3] Menezes, A., Oorschot, P., Vanstone, S.: Handbook of applied cryptography. CRC Press (1117)

[4] McLoone, M., McCanny, J.: High-performance FPGA implementation of DES using a novel method for implementing the key schedule. IEE Proc.: Circuits, Devices & Systems 150, 373–378 (2003)

[5] McLoone, M., McCanny, J.V.: Data encryption apparatus. UK Patent Application 0023409.6 (October 2000)

[6] Wong, K., Wark, M., Dawson, E.: A single-chip FPGA implementation of the data encryption standard (DES) algorithm. In: Proc. IEEE Globecom Communications Conf., Sydney, Australia, pp. 827–832 (November 1998)

[7] Biham, E.: A Fast New DES Implementation in Software. In: Biham, E. (ed.) FSE 1997. LNCS, vol. 1267, pp. 260–272. Springer, Heidelberg (1997)

[8] Kaps, J.-P., Paar, C.: Fast DES Implementations for FPGAs and Its Application to a Universal Key-Search Machine. In: Tavares, S., Meijer, H. (eds.) SAC 1998. LNCS, vol. 1556, pp. 234–247. Springer, Heidelberg (1999)

[9] Free-DES Core (March 2000), http://www.free-ip.com/DES/

[10] Wilcox, D.C., Pierson, L.G., Robertson, P.J., Witzke, E.L., Gass, K.: A DES ASIC Suitable for Network Encryption at 10 Gbps and Beyond. In: Koç, Ç.K., Paar, C. (eds.) CHES 1999. LNCS, vol. 1717, pp. 37–48. Springer, Heidelberg (1999)

[11] Patterson, C.: High performance DES encryption in virtex FPGAs using Jbits. In: Proc. IEEE Symp. on Field-Programmable Custom Computing Machines, FC 2000, Napa Valley, CA, USA, pp. 113–121. IEEE Comput. Soc., CA (2000)

[12] Patel, V., Joshi, R.C., Saxena, A.K.: FPGA implementation of DES using pipelining Concept with skew core key-scheduling

Towards Retrieving Live Forensic Artifacts in Offline Forensics

S. Dija, T.R. Deepthi, C. Balan, and K.L. Thomas

Centre for Development of Advanced Computing, Thiruvananthapuram, Kerala, India
{dija,deepthitr,cbalan,thomaskl}@cdac.in

Abstract. Live Forensics is the process of collecting forensically sound evidence from the suspect's computer system when it is in running state. But, this process is not widely accepted as a cyber forensic procedure in most of the countries. Instead of starting with a live forensic procedure, usually a traditional offline forensics is adopted according to the accepted cyber forensic procedure. This involves pulling the power plug of the suspect's system and imaging the storage media. The crucial evidence available in the running system is lost forever when turning off the system. The most important information that can be collected in live forensics is the evidence available in the Random Access Memory of a system. Since a Windows operating system adds footprints of each of its current activity in RAM, analyzing its content is indispensable in a cyber forensic analysis. And, this may provide information that can be crucial in carrying out further investigation. Since RAM content is highly volatile, its complete content is lost when turning off the system. In this paper a methodology to retrieve memory forensic artifacts while adopting a traditional offline forensics is explained. This is done by analyzing the hibernation file available in windows directory partition inside the hard disk of the suspect's system.

Keywords: Random Access Memory, Hibernation File, Live Forensics.

1 Introduction

Cyber Forensics is the identification, acquisition, authentication, analysis, presentation and preservation of cyber crime evidence. Physical Memory or Random Access Memory (RAM) is an important source of evidence for cyber forensic investigators. This is because memory contains details of all the recent activities in a computer system. Whenever a user initiates an activity, it makes changes in the RAM content. So, each activity inside a system is reflected in the physical memory. Memory Forensics is the process of RAM content acquisition, its analysis and report generation. However, RAM acquisition is possible only in a running machine because of its volatile nature. So, Memory Forensics is not possible when adopting an offline forensic procedure. But, Windows operating system copies the content of memory to a file when it goes to hibernation mode. This file, named hiberfil.sys, is available in the partition containing windows directory inside the hard disk of a system.

S.M. Thampi et al. (Eds.): SNDS 2012, CCIS 335, pp. 225–233, 2012.

By analyzing this file, an investigator can collect all the activities happened in the system just before turning off the system. Hence, it makes all the artifacts that can be retrieved only in Live Forensics through Memory analysis available in Offline Forensics also. Thus, analysis of hibernation file is indispensible in Offline Forensics.

2   Hibernation File

Based on system settings, a computer system goes to a new state called hibernation mode when it is standby in order to save power. During this hibernation mode, the system saves the entire content of the RAM to a file, hiberfil.sys, present in the window directory partition of the hard disk. The content of the RAM is saved into this hibernation file as a number of compressed blocks. In Offline Forensics, the entire list of files and folders of the hard disk is recreated from the bit-stream image of the hard disk taken by a disk forensic imaging tool. By this, the hibernation file available in windows directory partition becomes available for forensic analysis. This hibernation file holds everything available in RAM as a set of compressed memory blocks. A hibernation file can contain a great deal of very valuable historic information, including processes and network connections from some pint in the past [9]. By analyzing this file, similar results as in Memory Forensics can be extracted as part of Offline Forensics also. Since it contains the content of the RAM in an encoded and compressed form, decoding and decompression should be done before starting evidence collection as performed in usual Memory Forensics. The following section describes the structure of a hibernation file.

2.1   Hibernation File Structure

The hibernation file is organized such that the physical memory is stored in the form of compressed memory blocks in it. It consists of several pages of 4096 bytes [1]. The first page is hibernation file header, which starts with a 4 byte file signature that specifies the type of hibernation file. In windows XP, this case sensitive file signature uses small case but in Vista it is in upper case letters. In both cases, 'hibr' indicates an active hibernation file and 'wake' indicates an inactive one. Different file signatures in a hibernation file are explained by P. Kleissner in [1]. But, this hibernation file header is usually cleared out on successful restoration of the hibernation file. The next two pages in a hibernation file consist of reserved spaces for initializing and reloading memory and memory tables [14]. They are followed by a number of memory tables. Table1 shows the structure of a memory table.

Each Memory Table consists of a header, a number of Memory Table entries and Xpress Images. Each Memory Table entry defines a portion of physical memory. Xpress Images are compressed memory blocks. Memory blocks copied from a particular portion of RAM are compressed to get these Xpress Images. There will be multiple Xpress images inside a memory table. The total number of entries in a memory table is 255 except for the last memory table. The structure of memory table header, table entry and an Xpress image header are shown in table 2, table 3 and table 4 respectively.

Table 1. Structure of a Memory Table

Table Header
Table Entries
Xpress Images

Table 2. Structure of a Memory Table Header

Byte Offset	Field Length	Field Name	Sample Value
0x00	DWORD	PointerSystemTable	//Invalid
0x04	UINT32	NextTablePage	0xA287
0x08	DWORD	CheckSum	//Always 0
0x0C	UINT32	EntryCount	255

Table 3. Structure of a Memory Table Entry

Byte Offset	Field Length	Field Name	Sample Value
0x00	UINT32	PageCompressedData	// Invalid
0x04	UINT32	PhysicalStartPage	0x34849
0x08	UINT32	PhysicalEndPage	0x3484A
0x0C	DWORD	CheckSum	//Always 0

Table 4. Structure of an Image Xpress Header

Byte Offset	Field Length	Field Name	Sample Value
0x00	CHAR[8]	Signature	81h 81h xpress
0x08	BYTE	UncompressedPages	0x0f
0x09	UINT32	CompressedSize	0x01cac0
0x0D	BYTE[19]	Reserved	0

In the memory table header, NextTablePage field points to the next memory table. Its value is zero in the last memory table. The value of Checksum is always zero. The count of memory table entries is stored in the EntryCount field. It is 255 except for the last table. The values of PhysicalStartPage and PhysicalEndPage fields in the memory table specify the start and end offsets of a particular memory block. While writing the hibernation file, this portion of memory is compressed in the form of xpress image inside a memory table. The corresponding memory table entry is also written to the same memory table. An Xpress image consists of an image header followed by the compressed data. Each Xpress image is identified by a signature '81h 81h xpress' [5].The LZ77 and DIRECT2 algorithms are used simultaneously to compress a physical memory block as an Xpress image.

2.2   Physical Memory Structure

Physical memory of a windows system stores information related to its current activities in different data structures. The most important structure present in memory is an EProcess structure. EProcess structure is very important forensically because it provides a link to the details of all the running processes inside a system. This is because the EProcess structures of different processes are interconnected in a doubly linked list. Thus, by traversing through this doubly linked list entire list of processes can be retrieved [11]. Figure 1 shows some important fields related to a process in the EProcess structure of Windows 7, Windows XP SP2 and Windows 2000. Here, the _LIST_ENTRY field is called ActiveProcessLink which contain a forward link and a backward link to the next and previous processes respectively [11].

An EProcess structure has a field named PEBPointer, which is a link to PEB (Process Environment Block) structure. This structure is linked to LDR (Loader) module through PEB_LDR_DATA structure as shown in figure 3. This LDR module [8] gives details of Dlls used by that process. An EProcess structure has a pointer to the Handle Table which holds the details of open files accessed by that process. The LoadedModuleList pointed by pSLoadedModuleList in KDEBUGGER32 structure provides a link to TCB (Transmission Control Block) table structure [3] as shown in figure 4. This TCB table gives details of TCP/IP modules used by that process.

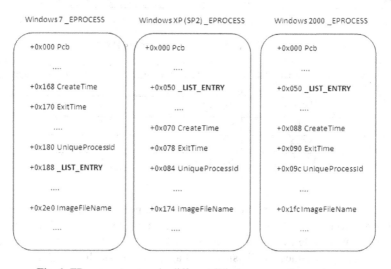

Fig. 1. EProcess structure in different Windows operating systems

3   Collecting Hibernation File

Traditional Forensics involves imaging the entire hard disk content into a binary file. From this bit-stream image file, all the files and folders inside a hard disk can be recreated using disk forensic analysis tools like EnCase-Forensic[7] or CyberCheck[6] etc. From the recovered files, the hibernation file can be exported to a storage media location. Then, this hibernation file can be analyzed to retrieve the Memory Forensics artifacts. Here, memory dump is generated from the hibernation file which can be further analyzed to explore different memory forensic artifacts as extracted in Live Forensics.

4   Analysis of Hibernation File

The memory blocks are compressed and stored in the random order inside a hibernation file. So analyzing the hibernation file and generating the corresponding memory dump is a challenging task in Offline Forensics. The compressed memory blocks are saved as Xpress images inside the hibernation file. These compressed memory blocks are stored in different memory tables. The first memory table starts in the fourth page of a hibernation file. The different memory tables inside a hibernation file are traversed by using NextTablePage field in the current memory table. A memory table consists of a number of Xpress images as described in section 2.1. The decompression module takes an Xpress image as input and generates a decompressed block containing raw memory data. The size of an Xpress image is not a constant.

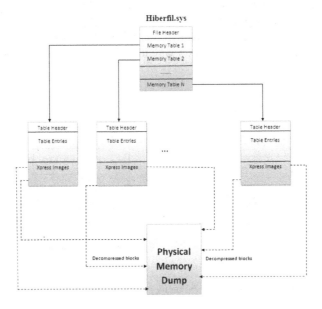

Fig. 2. Generation of a memory dump from a hibernation file

The total count of memory table entries is not same as Xpress images i.e. each memory table entry does not have a corresponding xpress image. So, it is difficult to find the correct offset while writing a raw memory block to the memory dump file. Figure2 describes the creation of a memory dump file from a hibernation file.

PhysicalStartPage and PhysicalEndPage fields in a memory table entry specify the location where the decompressed block is to be written in the memory dump file. The decompressed blocks are written to the memory dump file in the order followed in the memory table entries. Here, the number of bytes to be written to the memory dump file from a decompressed block is equal to the difference of PhysicalStartPage and PhysicalEndPage in the corresponding memory table entry. The remaining bytes in the decompressed block, if any, are written to the offset specified by next memory table entry. The same procedure is followed for the other xpress images also. The dump thus generated is similar to memory dump acquired from the running system in Live Forensics. Thus, this file can be analyzed in the same way as that of a memory analysis conducted in Live Forensics.

4.1   Memory Dump Analysis

Valuable evidence can be extracted from the data structures present in the memory dump file created from the hibernation file. Memory analysis reveals details of running processes, open documents, network connections etc. It also reveals the details of hidden malwares running inside a system. Nowadays, memory resident malwares are used as rootkits. Usually, these rootkits may not leave any footprints in the hard disk. An example of a memory resident malware is the W32.Witty.Worm worm [2]. In addition to this, RAM may contain many recovery keys. Different encryption programs store recovery keys in RAM in different ways [4]. So, through memory analysis, encrypted data available in the Hard Disk can be decrypted with these recovered keys. Thus, it opens a way to recover data encrypted with Bitlocker Drive Encryption.

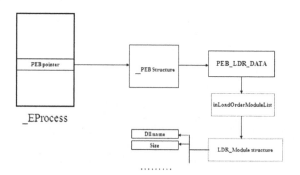

Fig. 3. Structures in physical memory for storing details of open dlls

Since RAM data structures used by an operating system is different change from one version to another, new versions of memory analysis software are needed each time as mentioned by J.Okolica and G.L.Peterson[3]. The difference in structure depends whether the OS is PAE (Page Address Extension) enabled or disabled when it is 32-bit. It also varies in 64-bit operating systems. Memory analysis in Windows 7 is explained in [10]. In order to read different structures from memory, virtual address to physical address translation is needed. This translation is different depending on the operating system. The structures of virtual address in different operating systems are described in [4, 9]. Some important fields in the EProcess structure related to a process in different OS are shown in Figure 1. One of the main techniques implemented in rootkits is the facility to hide itself. In order to make it hidden, these rootkits access kernel space. Usually, rootkits are developed in such a way that it can access kernel space. By properly modifying different data structures in the kernel space, these rootkits hide itself. This process is called DKOM (Direct Kernel Object Manipulation).

Each running process uses or accesses some files in the system. By finding the list of files accessed by a process, its behavior can be identified partially. Sometimes, by retrieving the list of accessed files, the malicious activities indented by a process can also be identified. A memory analysis tool is capable of doing this by exploring the handle tables pointed by an EProcess structure. Dlls are dynamic link libraries and usually a running process uses one or more dlls. In order to explore the complete behavior of a running process, the behavior of dlls is also to be examined. The information of Dynamic Link Libraries accessed by a process is very important especially in malware analysis. Here, from PEB_LDR_DATA structure inside the _PEB (Process Environment Block) structure, all the details of dlls can be retrieved. It is available in the LDR_Module structure pointed by PEB_LDR_DATA. Sometimes, only by checking the dlls accessed by a process, some malicious activities intended by it can be identified. Block diagram for retrieving dll names from _EProcess structure is shown in figure 3.

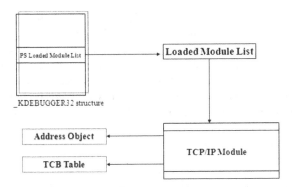

Fig. 4. Structures in physical memory for storing details of open sockets and network connections

In addition to open files and dlls, each running process may use some sockets and it is very important to identify those sockets to extract the nature of that running process. Identifying network connections used by a process is very important in finding the suspicious nature of a process. Here, TCP/IP connections can be identified from the TCP/IP module in LoadedModuleList pointed by PSLoadedModuleList in _KDEBUGGER32 structure available in memory. Method for retrieving TCB table from _KDEBUGGER32 structure is shown in figure 4. In this way, a clear picture of all the activities inside a system can be extracted by Memory Forensics. Here, first step is to read the ImageFileName in the EProcess structure to find the name of a process. Next, by traversing through the forward link and backward link pointers in LIST_ENTRY, the entire list of processes can be retrieved. Then, the list of dlls, open files, network connections used by a process can also be explored as explained in this paper.

But, the most important information that can be collected from a memory dump file is the process memory. Here, the executable file corresponding to a process is recovered from the memory dump file by collecting its process memory in PE (Portable Executable) format. For this, first read the starting address of the executable from the PEB structure. Then, from this address, read PE header to determine the location and the size of various sections of the executable. Then, the pages associated with each section referenced in the PE header can be extracted. Finally, combine all these pages into a single file to form the executable. The executable file extracted in this way can be analyzed using reverse engineering programs such as IDA[12] or OllyDbg[13]. By this, the entire content in the executable can be analyzed and corresponding assembly language code can be generated. This assembly language code reveals the logic behind the application. From this, an in-depth idea regarding the intentioned malicious activity behind the executable, if any, can be traced. This provides crucial information to the cyber forensic investigators in Offline Forensics.

5   Challenges

But, this hibernation file will be generated only when the system enters into a standby mode. Usually, this hibernation mode is enabled by default only in laptops and in some windows operations systems. In all other cases, this hibernation file will be created only when the user enables the hibernation mode by modifying system settings. But in all these cases, a valid hibernation file is created only when the system goes to a standby mode. Thus, this type of an analysis is not possible if there is no valid hibernation file available inside the hard disks.

6   Conclusion

Thus, it is possible to get the information available in physical memory in Offline Forensics through hibernation file analysis. It provides crucial information to the cyber forensic investigator, which is usually obtained while conducting a live forensic analysis. And, this information provides the cyber forensic investigator a clear picture of last activities in the suspect's system. So, hibernation file analysis plays a significant role in a cyber crime investigation. But, this type of analysis can be done only if the user enters to a hibernation mode. In most of the cases, the system goes to a hibernation mode when the system is not used for a long time period. Thus hibernation file analysis should be recommended in an offline cyber forensic analysis.

References

1. Kleissner, P.: Hibernation File Attack, Spain (2010)
2. W32.Witty.Worm, http://www.securityresponse.symantec.com/avcenter/venc/data/w32.witty.worm.html
3. Okolica, J., Peterson, G.L.: Windows operating systems agnostic memory analysis. Digital Investigation, S48–S56 (2010)
4. Hejazi, S.M., Talhi, C., Debbabi, M.: Extraction of forensically sensitive information from windows physical memory. Computer Security Laboratory, Concordia Institute for Information Systems Engineering, Concordia University, Montreal, Quebec, Canada (2009)
5. Matthieu, S.: Exploiting Windows Hibernation. Den Haag, NL, Europol High Tech Crime Expert Meeting (2008)
6. CyberCheck 4.0, http://www.cyberforensics.in/Products/Cybercheck.aspx
7. EnCase Forensic, http://www.guidancesoftware.com
8. Walters, A.: FATKit: detecting malicious library injection and upping the "anti", Technical report. 4TFResearch Laboratories (July 2006)
9. Carvey, H.: Windows Forensic Analysis Toolkit (2012)
10. Shuhui, Z., Lianhai, W., Ruichao, Z., Qiuxiang, G.: Exploratory Study on Memory Analysis of Windows 7 Operating System. In: 3rd International Conference on Advanced Computer Theory and Engineering, ICACTE (2010)
11. Butler, J., Undercoffer, J.L., Pinkston, J.: Hidden Processes: The Implication for Intrusion Detection. In: IEEE Workshop on Information Assurance, NY (2003)
12. IDA, http://www.hex-rays.com/products/ida/index.shtml
13. OllyDbg, http://www.ollydbg.de/
14. Hibernation File Format, http://web17.webbpro.de/downloads/Hibernation%20File%20Attack/Hibernation%20File%20Format.pdf

Carving of Bitmap Files from Digital Evidences by Contiguous File Filtering

Balan Chelliah, Divya S. Vidyadharan, P. Shabana, and K.L. Thomas

Center for Development of Advanced Computing,Trivandrum
Ministry of Communications and Information Technology, Government of India
{cbalan,divyasv,shabana,thomaskl}@cdac.in

Abstract. An evidence file is a bit-stream copy of any digital storage media or a hard disk partition. Retrieving files from these evidence files without the intervention of file system is quite challenging as the storage locations where file contents are stored are unknown or the contents of files are unavailable in contiguous storage locations. In addition to this, portion of some of the deleted files might have been overwritten by new files. In this paper, we propose a method to carve bitmap files from evidence files by making use of the presence of slack area in the evidence file. The contiguous file filtering technique proposed in this paper makes the carving of fragmented files easier.

Keywords: Cyber Forensics, File Carving, Slack Area, Bitmap files.

1 Introduction

Cyber forensics is the process of acquisition, authentication, analysis and documentation of digital evidences from any digital media. Cybercrime investigators look for proof indicating that a particular crime has been carried out or not. Most of the time, culprits remove such evidences from the storage media. For example, criminals may purposefully delete or hide files or corrupt file system metadata or format/delete partitions so as to make evidence collection nearly impossible. So it becomes a very difficult task for investigators to retrieve all the files including those deleted files.

A computer user creates/modifies/accesses a file through the operating system. The file system management module of the operating system is responsible for managing storage and access of file. For this purpose, different data structures are used depending on the file system selected by the user at the time of formatting the hard disk partition.

Files may be stored at contiguous storage locations or at different storage locations depending on the availability of free storage area. The addresses of the storage locations occupied by a file are kept inside the data structures of file system. But, if this data structure becomes corrupted or overwritten with information of a new file, the location information will be lost. In this scenario, the file has to be retrieved by analyzing the contents of storage locations in the media. The process of

S.M. Thampi et al. (Eds.): SNDS 2012, CCIS 335, pp. 234–239, 2012.

extracting files from raw data area without the use of any file system metadata is known as carving.

Different applications use different types of files with different file signatures. Picture files in JPEG format contain header and footer and the data between this header and footer constitutes file contents. Another set of files will have the file size specified in the header but no footer. Due to the dissimilarities in the way file contents are organized within the file, different carving techniques have been devised for different types of files.

Garfinkel et al. have proposed a file carving taxonomy [1]. Pal et al. recorded the evolution of file carving techniques in [2]. The file carver, Foremost, developed by US Air Force Office of Special Investigations makes use of header-footer based and file size based carving[3]. Shanmugasundaram et al. proposed a model for automatic reassembly of document files using statistical modeling tools [4].

In this paper, we propose a novel method of carving Windows bitmap files (bmp) from evidence file. In the following sections, the storage media is assumed to be a hard disk partition containing bitmap picture files.

1.1   Basics of Storage Allocation by File System

A file system is the collection of data structures and software required for managing and maintaining files and folders in a digital storage media. Usually file system management module is part of the operating system. Excluding the presence of a file system, a partition can be considered as a collection of sectors. A sector is the smallest addressable storage location in the hard disk. When the user formats the partition with a file system, these sectors are grouped to form clusters or blocks. A cluster is the basic storage allocation unit addressed by the file system. The number of sectors constituting a cluster will be according to the cluster size specified by the user at the time of formatting.

Whenever user creates a file, the file system allocates free clusters to the file depending on the file size. To make file access easier and efficient, the file system driver will always try to allocate contiguous clusters. But, as the partition gets filled up by lot of files, enough contiguous space may not be available. So the file system will be forced to store portions of file contents at different locations, thereby making the file fragmented.

The locations where file contents are stored will be mentioned inside the data structures used by the file system. For example, in FAT32, the data structures containing metadata are directory entries and File Allocation Tables (FAT) [5]. In New Technology File System (NTFS), the cluster locations are stored inside the Master File Table (MFT) entries representing the file [5].   So recovery of files is possible if file system metadata is available or known. In the case of deleted files, recovery is possible only to an extent depending on the file system and if the clusters are not overwritten.

If file system metadata is corrupted or unavailable then files have to be recovered directly from the clusters. This requires data carving techniques. Before explaining the proposed carving method, a special kind of unused storage area within the clusters is explained in section 1.2.

1.2   Slack Area

The number of clusters required for a file is calculated using the file size. Since partial allocation of cluster is impossible, there would be some free unused area after the end of the file, in the last cluster, if the file size is not completely divisible by cluster size. This unused area is known as file slack. The slack area within the sector where file ends is known as RAM slack, as this area contained contents of RAM when data is moved to hard disk from Random Access Memory. But newer operating systems fill this area with zeroes.

2   Proposed Method for BMP File Carving

File contents begin with application specific header containing a unique signature or magic number indicating the file type. File signature for Windows bmp files is 'BM' or 42 4D in Hexadecimal notation [9]. Since clusters are the basic allocation unit, files will always begin at the beginning of clusters. So for identifying the total number of files in the evidence file, we have to look at locations where a cluster starts. Normally, carving is attempted when either file system information is unavailable/corrupted/deleted or the file is deleted or when file system no longer points to the clusters occupied by the file. In both cases, the original cluster size used by the file system is unknown. Three options for file signature searching can be considered here. First, assume a cluster size and search at the beginning of all clusters. If no files are found, change the cluster size and repeat the process. The second option is to search at the beginning of all the sectors. But for identifying embedded files, each byte has to be searched for file signature [6]. Obviously, the third option is very slow and the first option is the fastest and the second option is a midway solution. Searching the beginning of sectors or clusters is less time consuming than search through all the bytes for the file signature. If a byte by byte search is the selected option then Boyre-Moore string search algorithm [7] is used.

An initial search for all the bmp file signatures will give the total number of bitmap images stored in the evidence file. At this point, a search for the known file types can be done so that those clusters can be omitted while searching for fragments of bmp files. This step optimizes carving algorithm substantially [2]. Once all the bmp files are identified, carving process begins. In the proposed method, carving is performed only for fragmented files. This is ensured by recovering the entire contiguous files within the evidence in a novel way as explained in section 2.1.

2.1   Recovery of Contiguous Files

File size is specified in the bmp file header. So, the number of clusters occupied by this file can be calculated. Here, it is assumed that if the file was allocated contiguous clusters then there would be slack after the expected area allocated for storing file contents. The slack contents will be different from the file contents. This fact is exploited to identify contiguous files. The data within the file is compared with data in the RAM slack area. If there is a significant difference between the file contents and the assumed slack area, it indicates that the file was contiguous and ends there. An exception for the above slack area assumption occurs when the file size is exactly divisible by cluster size. In this case, though there is no slack area, the contents in the immediately following location will be different from the contents of the current file.

Image width, available in the bmp file header is used to get the number of pixels in a row of the image. Each pixel will be represented by RGB value storing Red, Green and Blue components separately. In an image, the color changes are gradual and so adjacent rows exhibits only a slight variation in color. So, if we compare the last line of RGB values of the image and same number of values taken from the RAM slack area, there would be a substantial difference.

There are several methods for checking consecutive image rows [8] like pixel matching, sum of differences and median adaptive prediction. Poh Kok Loo et. al have proposed a color distance function that can be used to calculate the closeness of two colors [10]. In our experiments, Median Adaptive Prediction (MAP) method as devised by Stephen A. Martucci in [11] is used. In MAP, the current row of pixels is used to predict the next row. If we have to predict pixel 'x' where 'a' is the left pixel of x, 'b' is the top pixel of 'x' and 'c' the diagonal left pixel of x in the previous row, then three values for x will be predicted as follows,

$$x\_pred1 = a . \tag{1}$$

$$x\_pred2 = b . \tag{2}$$

$$x\_pred3 = a + b - c . \tag{3}$$

$$\text{Predicted value of 'x'} = (x\_pred1 + x\_pred2 + x\_pred3) / 3 . \tag{4}$$

Then sum of errors will be calculated using the sum of differences of actual value and predicted value. If the sum of differences is a low value then it indicates a match.

2.2   Recovery of Fragmented Files

When a file fails in the contiguous file checking, it becomes clear that the file is fragmented. Now, the file fragment at hand is the first fragment of the file containing bitmap header. The last row of image present in the first fragment has to be checked with all the clusters for identifying the next fragment. Here, it is assumed that within a picture file, the contents change gradually such that adjacent rows are highly related. The matching criteria for selecting a cluster as the successor to the current fragment is the MAP error explained in section 2.1.

MAP error is calculated for all clusters and a fragment with minimum error is selected as the next fragment of the current file [8]. Fragments get added to a file until it exceeds the file size specified in the file header. Once a file is recovered then the next file in the BMP list is taken for carving. The process continues until all the BMP files in the evidence are processed.

3   Experimental Results

Carving of fragmented BMP files is tested on different evidence files. All the evidence files contained a variety of file types including document files and picture files in formats other than bmp. Different evidence files of sizes 2 GB and 1 GB were tested. An average 71.4% of files where recovered successfully by identifying contiguous files. But in the rest of the cases, contiguous file filtering failed, and the files were treated as fragmented files. This happened, because MAP error failed to identify the slack area. When a contiguous file is not identified as contiguous, it will make the carving process slower as the MAP error with all the clusters have to be calculated. The level to which the entire carving process gets impeded depends on the total number of clusters occupied by the contiguous file. A properly identified contiguous file makes the carving process faster by eliminating all the clusters belonging to the contiguous file from fragment search area. Results are tabulated in the following Table 1.

Table 1. Results

Sl.No	Test image	Size (GB)	No. of bmp files	No. of contiguous files	No.of contiguous files correctly identified (Threshold>100)
1	H_01.000	1	1858	1855	1301
2	Image1.000	1	88	83	73
3	Image2.000	1	120	117	83
4	Image4.000	1	909	907	625
5	Image5.000	2	8	6	2
6	Image6.000	3	914	912	626

4   Conclusion

Though the proposed method has been successful in identifying all the files, it has to be made sure that all the contiguous files be identified properly. More experiments need to be conducted to fix the threshold for accepting the presence of slack area. Also, the proposed method has been applied only in the case of bitmap files. The contiguous file recovery has to be extended to other known file types containing file size in header, so that a large number of clusters can be excluded while searching for fragments. Instead of MAP error, other closeness criteria can be devised or adopted for identifying the exact successor fragment. Contiguous file filtering is very promising as it reduces the computation required for fragmented bmp file carving.

References

1. http://www.forensicswiki.org/wiki/Carving
2. Pal, A., Memon, N.: The Evolution of File Carving. IEEE Signal Processing Magazine 26, 59–71 (2009)
3. Foremost 1.5.7, http://foremost.sourceforge.net/
4. Shanmugasundaram, K., Memon, N.: Automatic reassembly of document fragments via data compression. Presented at the 2nd Digital Forensics Research Workshop, Syracuse, NY (July 2002)
5. Carrier, B.: File System Forensic Analysis. Pearson Education, Addison-Wesley Professional, Boston, MA (2005)
6. Povar, D., Bhadran, V.K.: Forensic Data Carving. In: Baggili, I. (ed.) ICDF2C 2010. LNICST, vol. 53, pp. 137–148. Springer, Heidelberg (2011)
7. Boyre, R.S., Moore, J.S.: A Fast String Searching Algorithm. Communications of the ACM 20(10), 762–772 (1977)
8. Pal, A.: Automated Reassembly of File Fragmented Images using Greedy Algorithms, Master of Science Thesis, Polytechnic University, Brooklyn, New York (August 2005)
9. http://en.wikipedia.org/wiki/
   BMP_file_format#Example_of_a_2.C3.972_Pixel.2C_24-
   Bit_Bitmap_.28Windows_DIB_Header_BITMAPINFOHEADER.29
10. Loo, P.K., Tan, C.L.: Adaptive Region Growing Color Segmentation for Text Using Irregular Pyramid. In: IEEE Proc. Document Analysis Systems, pp. 264–275 (2004)
11. Martucci, S.A.: Reversible compression of HDTV images using median adaptive prediction and arithmetic coding. In: IEEE International Symposium on Circuits and Systems, vol. 2, pp. 1310–1313 (1990)

Lightweight Cryptographic Primitives
for Mobile Ad Hoc Networks

Adarsh Kumar and Alok Aggarwal

Computer Science Engineering and Information Technology Department,
Jaypee Institute of Information Technology, Noida, India
{adarsh.kumar,alok.aggarwal}@jiit.ac.in

Abstract. The tight computing constraints of low capacity mobile devices require lightweight cryptographic implementations. A software and hardware based performance analysis of cryptographic primitives: lightweight encryption/decryption, lightweight key exchange and lightweight authentication using hashing mechanism are conducted in this work. The parameters taken for software comparison are: high throughput, minimum delay and for hardware are: minimum gate equivalents (GE) and minimum power consumption. Cryptographic primitives are combined using two scenarios: (i) authentication to plaintext and confidentiality to message_to_send and (ii) confidentiality to plaintext and authentication to message_to_send. Two combinations are having similar results comparisons but authentication to plaintext and confidentiality to message_to_send is more meaningful. Furthermore, these two combinations provide implementation of cryptographic primitives with 30% of total GE at 52 μW. Thus, these are two complete cryptographic solutions with ultra-lightweight features which are suitable for extremely resource constraint environments such as mobile sensor devices.

Keywords: lightweight, cipher, hashing, authentication, key management.

1 Introduction

Mobility, Ad Hoc connectivity and infrastructure less nature are increasing the applications of Mobile Ad Hoc Networks (MANETs). Some of the major application areas of MANET are: military purpose, household security appliances, road traffic management system, Vehicular Ad Hoc Networks (VANETs), mobile cloud clusters etc. Ad Hoc connectivity increases the chances to threat the secured information. In particular much research attention has been recently drawn to the security issues of MANETs. The ubiquitous computing on tiny mobile devices could bring security risks. Implementing multiple security primitives on resource constraint devices is almost impossible or even impractical. In order to secure the information, various lightweight cryptographic aspects are taken into consideration. For example, lightweight encryption/decryption, lightweight key management protocols, lightweight hashing mechanism, lightweight authentication & authorization mechanism etc.

Encryption/Decryption mechanism can be classified broadly on two major categories: (i) Symmetric and (ii) Asymmetric. Examples of encryption/decryption

S.M. Thampi et al. (Eds.): SNDS 2012, CCIS 335, pp. 240–251, 2012.

mechanisms are: Data Encryption Standard (DES), Advanced Encryption Standard (AES), Elliptic Curve Cryptography (ECC), Hyper Elliptic Curve Cryptography (HECC) etc. [7], [8]. Symmetric encryption/ decryption mechanisms are much faster than asymmetric mechanism thus preferred in MANETs. Key management approach is a combination of (i) key agreement and key transport/distribution or (ii) symmetric, asymmetric and hybrid key management protocols. Example of key management protocols are: Blom's key pre-distribution, Janson-Tsudik protocols, Basic Diffie Hellman (DH) etc [1], [9]-[13]. Another category of key management protocol is group based key management protocols. Group key management can be classified as: general, Tree based, re-keying based and ID-based [1],[15]. Steiner et. al. proposed Group Diffie Hellman (GDH) protocols: GDH.1, GDH.2, GDH.3, Authenticated-GDH (A-GDH), Secure Association-GDH (SA-GDH) from 1996 to 2000 [16]-[19]. In 1994, Burmester and Desmedt (BD) proposed less computational and two rounds efficient protocol [14], [20]-[25]. Tree-Based Group Diffie Hellman (TGDH), Lee-Kim, MARKS, Yu and Tang, Deng, Mukherjee and Aggarwal etc[1] . Most of these protocols are high computational protocols and thus inappropriate for low power mobile devices. In order to maintain the integrity of message two mechanisms are taken into consideration are: (i) Message Authentication Code (MAC) and (ii) Digital Signature (DS). For example, MAC based protocols are: Data Authentication Algorithm (DAA), Hash MAC (HMAC)[2], Ultra-lightweight Mutual Authentication Protocols (UMAP, PUMAP, FLMAP, M2AP, EMAP, LMAP, SASI) etc. Other lightweight cryptography hash functions are: Quark, PHOTON family protocols etc.

This paper is organized as follows: Section 2 presents the lightweight encryption/decryption, lightweight key exchange and lightweight authentications using hashing with their comparisons. In section 3 two approaches of providing the complete solution for cryptographic services are presented. In section 4 various lightweight components from each category are paired to evaluate the performance of algorithms designed in section 3. Lastly section 5 shows the conclusion based on implementations and results.

2   Review of Protocols

About restricted devices, it is often quoted consensus that 200-3000 GE out of a total available 1000-10,000 GE are available for security purposes [43], [44]. According to Moore's Law [45], for next four to five years this figure is expected around three to four times at lesser cost. Three major cryptographic components are needed to be adjusted among these 200 to 3000 GE: lightweight encryption/decryption, lightweight key exchange and lightweight authentication using hashing. In this work, lightweight cryptographic components are taken into consideration (<1000 GE).

2.1   Lightweight Encryption/Decryption

Various lightweight ciphers having less than 1000 gates are: A2U2, LED-64, LED-128 [40], Piccolo-80[29], PRINTCIPHER-48, PRINTCIPHER-96 [41], KTANTAN64 [26] and SEA. A2U2 is a stream cipher and others are block ciphers. Block ciphers are often preferred over stream ciphers because of its simplicity. Otherwise stream ciphers are much faster than block ciphers, require less number of equivalents and suitable for low end devices. Now a day, lightweight block ciphers are designed that are equally efficient as of stream ciphers. In this section, efficient block ciphers having less than 1000 gates are discussed and compared with their characteristics.

2.1.1   LED

Light Encryption Device (LED) is a lightweight block cipher designed in 2011[40]. Strengths of this algorithm are: (i) it is of compact size, ultra-light cipher and provide security against related key attacks, (ii) it is more hardware efficient but software efficiency is also taken into consideration to a great extent. One major weakness of this cipher is larger security margins because of equivalent encryption time (EET)[51].

2.1.2   Piccolo

It is a lightweight 64-bits block cipher developed in 2011 [29]. Major strengths are: (i) power and energy efficient as compared to other feistel based ciphers, (ii) protected against linear and differential attacks due to minimum number of active F-functions with least probability (2^{-64}) so far. Weaknesses of this cipher are: (i) due to feistel structure, it is still open to weak key attacks, (ii) storage of keys increases the complexity of hardware implementation and (iii) not strong against side channel attack.

2.1.3   Other Protocols

(i) PRINTCIPHER is another lightweight block cipher for resource constraint devices designed in 2010 [41]. Strengths of this algorithm is: designed to exploit properties of integrated circuits. Weakness of this cipher is: silent against side-channel attacks, for example: equivalent encryption time [42]. (ii) KATAN & KTANTAN are two families of lightweight block cipher developed in 2009[26]. Major strengths of this cipher is: use of flip flop technology reduces the gates and power consumption. (iii) Scalable Encryption Algorithm (SEA) is a block cipher designed in 2006 [46]. Strengths of this cipher is: designed for devices having limited processing and memory resources, limited instruction sets etc. Weakness is: increase in number of rounds increases the hardware cost and thus not suitable for small devices. Various other lightweight cryptographic block and stream ciphers are: mCrypton, DES, HIGHT, CLEFIA, Camellia, PUFFIN etc [27], [28], [31], [32], [36]-[39].

2.1.4   Comparison

Figure 1 show that SEA is having minimum gates (449 GE) as compared to Piccolo-80 (683 GE), LED-64 (688 GE), KTANTAN64 (688GE), KTANTAN64 (688 GE), LED-128(700 GE), PRINTCipher-80 (726GE) and Piccolo-128(818) with maximum throughput but these GE increases exponentially with number of encryption rounds and thus it cannot be considered good for resource constraint devices. Other block ciphers like: Piccolo-80, LED-64, KTANTAN-64, LED-128 are having almost similar GE but KTANTAN-64 and Piccolo-80 provide high throughput with minimum initial setup time, encryption/decryption time and processing time. Lesser throughput and more delay (initial setup, encryption/decryption and processing) make Piccolo-128 less interesting as compared to Piccolo-80 and KTANTAN-64. In our implementation two ciphers are referred: KTANTAN-64 and Piccolo-80.

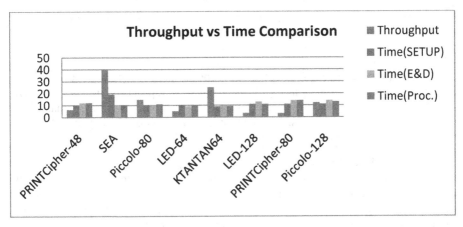

Fig. 1. Throughput vs Time comparison of block ciphers

2.2   Lightweight Key Exchange Protocol

2.2.1   WLH Protocol

This is hybrid key protocol developed in 2005 [33], [34]. The protocol runs as:

Protocol: WLH Protocol

Premises: Let ID_C, ID_S, K_{MC} , K_{PBS}, K_{PRS}, $E_{K_{PBS}}(M)$, $D_{K_{PRS}}(M)$, r_c , r_s, f(), H() are the identifications of client & server, master key stores at client, server's public key, server's private key, encryption of message 'M' with server's public key, decryption of message 'M' with server's private key, random numbers selected at client and server ends, two one way hash functions.

Goal: Shared a common session key K_S with least overall computation.

Phase I: Pre-computation

    Step 1: Client: Select random number $r_c \in \{ 0,1 \}^K$.

    Step 2: Client: Compute $C(ciphertext) = E_{K_{PBS}}(ID_C, K_M, r_c)$.

Phase II: Protocol Execution

    Step 1: Client → Server: C

    Step 2: a.   Server: $(ID'_C, K'_M, r'_c) = D_{K_{PRS}}(C)$

          b.   Server: Match f(ID'_C, K'_M) with stored data.

          c.   Server: If results does not match then exit

          d.   Server: if result matches then continue.

          e.   Server: compute server's authentication function:
               $A_S = H (H(C, r_c, r_s), 2)$

          f.   Server→Client: r_s, A_S

    Step 3: Client→Server: $A_C = H (H(C, r_c, r_s),1)$

    Step 4: Server: $K_S = H (H(C, r_c, r_s),0)$

    Step 5: Client: $K_S = H (H(C, r_c, r_s),0)$

Strengths of this protocol are: (i) lighter computational overhead for message integrity, (ii) one way hashing and identification check prevent key compromise. One major weakness of this mechanism is that it is weak in providing forward secrecy and integration of Diffie Hellman for secrecy increases the overhead [34].

2.2.2   Tseng's Protocol

Y. M. Tseng proposed key agreement protocol for resource constraint devices in 2005 [3].Consequently, two extensions of this mechanism were proposed in 2005 and 2007 [4]-[6]. Major strengths of this protocol is: small size conference key management with less number of key rounds. Major weakness of this protocol is that it does not provide secrecy against linear or differential attacks [6].

2.2.3   Teo & Tan's Protocol

J. C. M. Teo and C. H. Tan proposed energy efficient key agreement proposed for low capacity mobile devices in 2005 [35]. Major strengths of this protocol is: provable security against symmetric key exchange [14]. Weaknesses of this protocol are: (i) no strong signature mechanism and (ii) prone to impersonation attack.

2.2.4   Comparison

Figure 2 and figure 3 show the comparative analysis of throughput and end-to-end delay for (i) WLH and (ii) Tseng and (iii) Teo and Tan. End-to-end delay includes processing, propagation and transmission delays. Ad hoc On-demand Distance Vector (AODV), Destination Sequenced Distance Vector (DSDV) and Dynamic Source Routing (DSR) are three basic MANET's routing protocols used for comparison for 1000 mobile nodes

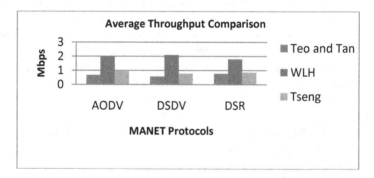

Fig. 2. Throughput comparison for 1000 nodes

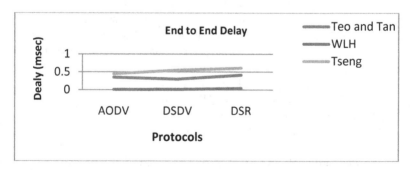

Fig. 3. Delay comparison for 1000 nodes

on NS-3 platform[47]. The results show that WLH is having the minimum end-to-end delay and maximum throughput with DSDV protocol. Although it lacks in forward and backward secrecy but it reduces the hardware and software overheads [34]. Thus WLH is considered to be the efficient protocol for lighter key agreement.

2.3   Lightweight Hash Protocols

Table 1 shows various lightweight hash algorithms developed in recent years. ARMADILLO02-E provides the highest security against attacks but also have highest GEs. If we keep the criteria of 33% (1000) GE then three algorithms qualify the criteria are: SPONGENT-88, SPONGENT-128 and PHOTON -80. In this section SPONGENT and PHOTON protocols are briefly discussed with their characteristics.

Table 1. Comparison of lightweight Hash Algorithms

Hash Algorithm	GE	Power (μW)	Throughput (kbps)	Collision Resistant	Preimage	Second Preimage
PHOTON-80	865	1.59	2.82	2^{40}	2^{64}	2^{40}
PHOTON-128	1122	2.29	1.61	2^{64}	2^{112}	2^{64}
PHOTON-160	1396	2.74	2.70	2^{80}	2^{124}	2^{80}
PHOTON-224	1735	4.01	1.84	2^{112}	2^{192}	2^{112}
PHOTON-256	2177	4.55	3.21	2^{128}	2^{224}	2^{128}
U-Quark[30]	1379	2.44	1.47	2^{64}	2^{120}	2^{64}
D-Quark[30]	1702	3.10	2.27	2^{80}	2^{144}	2^{80}
S-Quark[30]	2296	4.35	3.13	2^{112}	2^{192}	2^{112}
H-PRESENT-128	2330	6.44	11.45	2^{64}	2^{128}	2^{64}
DM-PRESENT-80	1600	1.83	14.63	2^{32}	2^{64}	2^{64}
DM-PRESENT-128	1886	2.94	22.90	2^{32}	2^{64}	2^{64}
C-PRESENT-192	4600	NA	1.9	2^{96}	2^{192}	2^{192}
SPONGENT-88	738	1.57	0.81	2^{40}	2^{80}	2^{40}
SPONGENT-128	1060	2.20	0.34	2^{64}	2^{120}	2^{64}
SPONGENT-160	1329	2.85	0.40	2^{80}	2^{144}	2^{80}
SPONGENT-224	1728	3.73	0.22	2^{112}	2^{208}	2^{112}
SPONGENT-256	1950	4.21	0.17	2^{128}	2^{240}	2^{128}
KECCAK-f[400]	5090	11.50	14.40	2^{80}	2^{160}	2^{160}
KECCAK-f[200]	2520	5.60	8.00	2^{64}	2^{128}	2^{128}
ARMADILLO2-A	2923	44	27	2^{40}	2^{80}	2^{40}
ARMADILLO2-B	4353	65	250	2^{64}	2^{128}	2^{64}
ARMADILLO02-C	5406	83	250	2^{80}	2^{160}	2^{80}
ARMADILLO2-D	6554	102	25.0	2^{96}	2^{192}	2^{96}
ARMADILLO02-E	8653	137	25.0	2^{128}	2^{256}	2^{128}

2.3.1   PHOTON

It is a lightweight cryptographic hash function for resource constraint devices developed in 2011 [49]. Major strengths of this hash mechanism are: (i) internal memory size is low as compare to other hashes, (ii) sponge like extension protects from structural flaws and collisions, (iii) protected from linear or differential attacks. One major weakness of this hash mechanism is the use of S-boxes decreases the hardware efficiency.

2.3.2   SPONGENT

It is a lightweight block cipher developed in 2011 [50]. Strengths of this hash algorithm are: (i) truncated differential characteristics decreases the probability to find a path for collision attacks, (ii) provide protection from pre-image attack in pre-computational stage only. Weaknesses are: (i) silent on side channel attacks and (ii) for higher security implementation, larger block size and more number of rounds increases the GE and thus not suitable for low capacity devices.

2.3.3   Comparison

Figure 4 and table 1 shows that SPONGENT-128 provides maximum security from collision, pre-image and second pre-image attacks out of three selected hash algorithms with minimum GEs. SPONGENT-128 is also having minimum initial setup time and processing delay with comparable power consumption. These characteristics make SPONGENT-128 suitable for analysis.

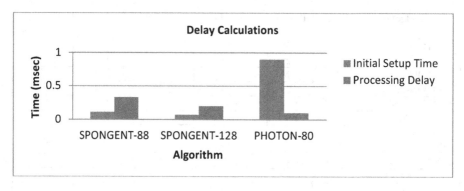

Fig. 4. Delay Comparison of selected Hashing Mechanisms

3   Work Done

In this work, three cryptographic primitives discussed in previous section are combined to implement and analyze the performance on MANET devices using ns-3 simulator [47]. In case 1 and case 2, cryptographic primitives are integrated using: (i) WLH protocol for key exchange and (ii) Lightweight Message Authentication Code (LMAC) [48] using SPONGENT-128 for hashing mechanism and (iii) KTANTAN-64 or Piccolo-80 for encryption. Two combinations of integrating encryption/decryption are possible. Either authentication can be attached to message_to_send and confidentiality to plaintext (case 1) or authentication can be attached to plaintext and confidentiality to message_to_send (case 2). Later is meaningful and preferred.

Case 1: Message authentication and confidentiality, when authentication is attached with ciphertext and confidentiality to plaintext.

Premises: Same as WLH protocol. In addition, M and C are used to denote plaintext and ciphertext.

Goals: (i)   Securely share the symmetric keys K_s^1, K_s^2 between two ends.

(ii)   Using 'K_S', authenticate 'M' between two ends.

(iii)   Secure the authenticated message using encryption.

Protocol:

(a) Share the keys K_s^1 and K_s^2 between source and destination using WLH protocol discussed in section 2.

(b) Source: Encryption Process [Source: Encrypted_Messsage $= E_{K_S^2}(M)$.]

(c) Generate HMAC over Encrypted_Message. Same as Case 1's (b)(I) but on Encrypted_Message and using key K_s^1.

(d) Concatenate Encrypted_Message and HMAC.

Source: message_to_send = Encrypted_Message ‖ HMAC

(e) Destination: Separate Encrypted_Message and HMAC at destination.

(f) Destination: Verification of HMAC at destination using step 1 to step 5 of Case 1 (b)(II) over Encrypted_Message $E_{K_S^2}$ and 'M'. If HMAC equals HMAC' then continue else discard the message and exit.

(g) if HMAC equals HMAC' then   Decryption: Message$= D_{K_S^2}$(Encrypted_Message).

Strengths are: (i) added confidentiality of message as compared to case 1, (ii) good for applications that require secure transmission. For example: password exchange and (iii) for non-authenticated messages it saves the decryption computation at destination. Weaknesses are: (i) if message contains sequence number then it starts problematic at initial stage of routing rather than later as in case 3 and (ii) it is preferable to attach authentication over plaintext thus case 3 is more preferred in use.

Case 2: Message authentication and confidentiality, when authentication is attached with plaintext and confidentiality to message_to_send.

Premises: Same as Case I in section 3.

Goals: (i)   Securely share the symmetric keys K_s^1, K_s^2 between two ends.

(ii)   Secure the message using encryption.

(iii)   Using 'K_S', authenticate 'M' between two ends.

Protocol:

(a) Share the keys K_s^1 and K_s^2 between source and destination using WLH protocol discussed in section 2.

(b) Source: Generate HMAC over message 'M': Same as Case 1(b)(I)'s step 1 to step 3 using key K_s^1. (Result: HMAC is generated).

(c) Source: Encryption Process [Source: messsage_to_send $= E_{K_S^2}(M||HMAC)$]

(d) Destination: Decryption Process

Destination: Message_to_receive = message_to_send

Destination: (M‖HMAC) $= D_{K_S^2}(Message\_to\_receive)$.

(e) Verification of HMAC at destination.Same as Case I(b)(II)'s step 1 to step 5.

Strengths are: (i) added confidentiality of message as compared to case 1, (ii) good for applications that require secure transmission. For example: password exchange and (iii) it is good for case, where confidentiality is prolonged until transmission but authentication is required at local system level. Weaknesses are: (i) overhead increases and throughput decreases because of encryption process and (ii) if we start encrypting the message_to_send then to identifying the route from packet there will be need of decryption at intermediate level, which will be much costlier.

4   Results and Analysis

Result 1: Message authentication and confidentiality, when authentication is attached with ciphertext and confidentiality to plaintext.

This mechanism include: (i) KTANTAN-64 or Piccolo-80 for encryption & decryption, (ii) WLH protocol for key exchange with 700 GE and (iii) LMAC with 500 GE using SPONGENT-128 for hashing mechanism with 1060 GE. Thus a total of 2948 GE with 50µW using KTANTAN-64 or 2943 GE with 52 µW using Piccolo-80 are required to implement cryptographic primitives. Figure 5 and figure 6 shows the throughput and delay comparison of this scenario as case 1. This mechanism provides confidentiality which is important for all secret messages.

Result 2: Message authentication and confidentiality, when authentication is attached with plaintext and confidentiality to message_to_send.

This mechanism is having similar characteristics and results as of case 1 with similar primitives. As authentication is meant for plaintext thus case 1 is more preferred over case 2.

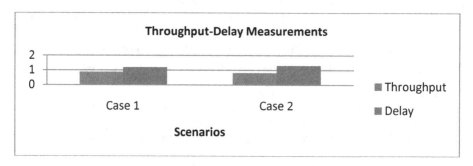

Fig. 5. Throughput-Delay Measurements for KTANTAN64

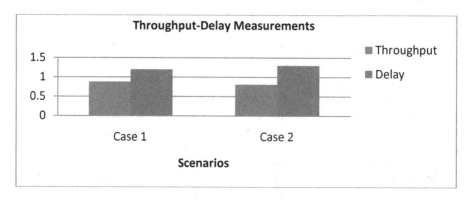

Fig. 6. Throughput-Delay Measurements for Piccolo-80

5   Conclusion

In this work, lightweight cryptographic primitives with high throughput and minimum delay are selected to implement complete security solution for resource constraint mobile ad hoc devices. Software and hardware analysis shows that KTANTAN-64 and Piccolo-80 are lightest ciphers, WLH is the lightest key exchange mechanism and SPONGENT-128 is the lightest hash function. The proposed mechanism shows that two combinations of lightweight cryptographic primitives are possible. Since authentication is assumed to be tied with plaintext thus authentication to plaintext and confidentiality to message_to_send is preferred. Furthermore, combination of lightweight primitives shows that it can be implemented with the complexity of about 2948 GE with power consumption of 52 μW, depending on protocols and capabilities (authentication only, authentication with confidentiality). It can be expected that stream cipher techniques can considerably reduce the complexity. As another possible future work, we could perform reusability of gates for hardware and software efficiency.

References

1. Boyd, C., Mathuria, A.: Protocols for Authentication and Key Establishment, 1st edn. Springer (2003)
2. van Tilborg, H.C.A.: Encyclopedia of Cryptography and Security. Springer (2005)
3. Tseng, Y.M.: Efficient authenticated key agreement protocols resistant to a denial of service attack. International Journal of Network Management 15, 193–202 (2005)
4. Tseng, Y.M.: An improved conference key agreement protocol with forward secrecy. Informatica 16(2), 275–284 (2005)
5. Tseng, Y.M.: A communication efficient and fault tolerant conference key agreement protocol with forward secrecy. Journal of Systems and Software 80, 1091–1101 (2007)
6. Lee, S., Kim, J., Hong, S.J.: Security weakness of Tseng's fault tolerant conference key agreement protocol. Journal of Systems and Software 82, 1163–1167 (2009)
7. Perkins, C.E.: Ad hoc Networking. Addison-Wesley, New York (2001)
8. Stallings, W.: Cryptography and Network Security: Principles and Practice, 5th edn. Prentice Hall (2010)
9. Mao, W.: Modern Cryptography: Theory and Practice. Prentice Hall PTR (2004)
10. Krawczyk, H.: SKEME: A Versatile Secure Key Exchange Mechanism for Internet. In: Proc. of the Symposium on Network and Distributed System Security, pp. 114–127 (1996)
11. Harkins, D., Carrel, D.: The Internet Key Exchange, Internet Request for Comments 2409 (November 1998)
12. Kaufman, C., Hoffman, P., Nir, Y., Eronen, P.: Internet Key Exchange Protocol version 2 (IKEv2), Internet Request for Comments 5996 (September 2010)
13. Arkko, J., Haverinen, H.: Extensible Authentication Protocol Method for 3rd Generation Authentication and Key Agreement (EAP-AKA), Internet Request for Comments 4187 (2006)
14. Katz, J., Yung, M.: Scalable Protocols for Authenticated Group Key Exchange. In: Boneh, D. (ed.) CRYPTO 2003. LNCS, vol. 2729, pp. 110–125. Springer, Heidelberg (2003)

15. Ingemarsson, I., Tang, D.T., Wong, C.K.: A Conference key distribution system. IEEE Transactions on Information Theory 28(5), 714–720 (1982)
16. Steiner, M., Tsudik, G., Waidner, M.: Diffie-Hellman Key Distribution Extended to Group Communication. In: ACM Conference on Computer and Communication Security, pp. 31–37 (1996)
17. Ateniese, G., Michael, Tsudik, G.: Authenticated Group Key Agreement and Friends. In: International Conference on Computer and Communication Security, pp. 17–26 (1998)
18. Steiner, M., Tsudik, G., Waidner, M.: CLIQUES: A new approach to group key agreement. In: Proc. of the 18th International Conference on Distributed Computing Systems, pp. 380–387 (1998)
19. Steiner, M., Tsudik, G., Waidner, M.: Key agreement in dynamic peer groups. IEEE Transactions on Parallel and Distributed Systems 11(8), 769–780 (2000)
20. Burmester, M., Desmedt, Y.: A Secure and Efficient Conference Key Distribution System. In: De Santis, A. (ed.) EUROCRYPT 1994. LNCS, vol. 950, pp. 275–286. Springer, Heidelberg (1995)
21. Harney, H., Muckenhirn, C.: Group Key Management Protocol Architecture. Internet Request for Comments 2094 (July 1997)
22. Harney, H., Muckenhirn, C.: Group Key Management Protocol Specification. Internet Request for Comments 2093 (July 1997)
23. Harney, H., Meth, U., Colegrove, A.: Group Secure Association Key Management Protocol. Internet Request for Comments 4535 (June 2006)
24. Weis, B., Rowles, S., Hardjono, T.: The Group Domain of Interpretation. Internet Request for Comments 6407 (October 2011)
25. Baugher, M., Weis, B., Hardjono, J., Harney, H.: The Group Domain of Interpretation. Internet Request for Comments 3547 (July 2003)
26. De Cannière, C., Dunkelman, O., Knežević, M.: KATAN and KTANTAN — A Family of Small and Efficient Hardware-Oriented Block Ciphers. In: Clavier, C., Gaj, K. (eds.) CHES 2009. LNCS, vol. 5747, pp. 272–288. Springer, Heidelberg (2009)
27. Lim, C.H., Korkishko, T.: mCrypton – A Lightweight Block Cipher for Security of Low-Cost RFID Tags and Sensors. In: Song, J.-S., Kwon, T., Yung, M. (eds.) WISA 2005. LNCS, vol. 3786, pp. 243–258. Springer, Heidelberg (2006)
28. Leander, G., Paar, C., Poschmann, A., Schramm, K.: New Lightweight DES Variants. In: Biryukov, A. (ed.) FSE 2007. LNCS, vol. 4593, pp. 196–210. Springer, Heidelberg (2007)
29. Shibutani, K., Isobe, T., Hiwatari, H., Mitsuda, A., Akishita, T., Shirai, T.: *Piccolo*: An Ultra-Lightweight Blockcipher. In: Preneel, B., Takagi, T. (eds.) CHES 2011. LNCS, vol. 6917, pp. 342–357. Springer, Heidelberg (2011)
30. Aumasson, J.-P., Henzen, L., Meier, W., Naya-Plasencia, M.: QUARK: A Lightweight Hash. In: Mangard, S., Standaert, F.-X. (eds.) CHES 2010. LNCS, vol. 6225, pp. 1–15. Springer, Heidelberg (2010)
31. Hong, D., Sung, J., Hong, S., Lim, J., Lee, S., Koo, B.-S., Lee, C., Chang, D., Lee, J., Jeong, K., Kim, H., Kim, J., Chee, S.: HIGHT: A New Block Cipher Suitable for Low-Resource Device. In: Goubin, L., Matsui, M. (eds.) CHES 2006. LNCS, vol. 4249, pp. 46–59. Springer, Heidelberg (2006)
32. Shirai, T., Shibutani, K., Akishita, T., Moriai, S., Iwata, T.: The 128-Bit Blockcipher CLEFIA (Extended Abstract). In: Biryukov, A. (ed.) FSE 2007. LNCS, vol. 4593, pp. 181–195. Springer, Heidelberg (2007)
33. Wen, H.A., Lin, C.L., Hwang, T.: Provably secure authenticated key exchange protocols for low power computing clients. Computers and Security 25, 106–113 (2006)

34. Vesteras, B.: Analysis of Key Agreement Protocols. Master's Thesis Report, Department of Computer Science and Media Technology, Gjovik University College (2006)

35. Teo, J.C.M., Tan, C.H.: Energy-Efficient and Scalable Group Key Agreement for Large Ad Hoc Networks. In: PE-WASUN's 2005, October 10-13, pp. 114–121 (2005)

36. Feldhofer, M., Dominikus, S., Wolkerstorfer, J.: Strong Authentication for RFID Systems Using the AES Algorithm. In: Joye, M., Quisquater, J.-J. (eds.) CHES 2004. LNCS, vol. 3156, pp. 357–370. Springer, Heidelberg (2004)

37. Aoki, K., Ichikawa, T., Kanda, M., Matsui, M., Moriai, S., Nakajima, J., Tokita, T.: *Camellia*: A 128-Bit Block Cipher Suitable for Multiple Platforms - Design and Analysis. In: Stinson, D.R., Tavares, S. (eds.) SAC 2000. LNCS, vol. 2012, pp. 39–56. Springer, Heidelberg (2001)

38. Good, T., Chelton, W., Benaissa, M.: Hardware Results for Selected Stream Cipher Candidates. Presented at SASC (2007), http://www.ecrypt.eu.org/stream/

39. Cheng, H., Heys, H.M., Wang, C.: PUFFIN: A Novel Compact Block Cipher Targeted to Embedded Digital Systems. In: Euromicro Conference on Digital System Design (DSD 2008), Parma, Italy, pp. 383–390 (2008)

40. Guo, J., Peyrin, T., Poschmann, A., Robshaw, M.: The LED Block Cipher. In: Preneel, B., Takagi, T. (eds.) CHES 2011. LNCS, vol. 6917, pp. 326–341. Springer, Heidelberg (2011)

41. Knudsen, L., Leander, G., Poschmann, A., Robshaw, M.J.B.: PRINTCIPHER: A Block Cipher for IC-Printing. In: Mangard, S., Standaert, F.-X. (eds.) CHES 2010. LNCS, vol. 6225, pp. 16–32. Springer, Heidelberg (2010)

42. Leander, G., Abdelraheem, M.A., AlKhzaimi, H., Zenner, E.: A Cryptanalysis of PRINTCIPHER: The Invariant Subspace Attack. In: Rogaway, P. (ed.) CRYPTO 2011. LNCS, vol. 6841, pp. 206–221. Springer, Heidelberg (2011)

43. Juels, A., Weis, S.A.: Authenticating Pervasive Devices with Human Protocols. In: Shoup, V. (ed.) CRYPTO 2005. LNCS, vol. 3621, pp. 293–308. Springer, Heidelberg (2005)

44. Peris-Lopez, P., Hernandez-Castro, J.C., Estevez-Tapiador, J.M., Ribagorda, A.: RFID Systems: A Survey on Security Threats and Proposed Solutions. In: Cuenca, P., Orozco-Barbosa, L. (eds.) PWC 2006. LNCS, vol. 4217, pp. 159–170. Springer, Heidelberg (2006)

45. Moore, G.E.: Cramming More Components onto Integrated Circuits. Electronics (1965), http://www.intel.com

46. Standaert, F.-X., Piret, G., Gershenfeld, N., Quisquater, J.-J.: SEA: A Scalable Encryption Algorithm for Small Embedded Applications. In: Domingo-Ferrer, J., Posegga, J., Schreckling, D. (eds.) CARDIS 2006. LNCS, vol. 3928, pp. 222–236. Springer, Heidelberg (2006)

47. NS3 Simulator, http://www.nsnam.org

48. Fouda, M.M., Fadlullah, Z.M., Kato, N., Lu, R., Shen, X.: A Lightweight Message Authentication Scheme for Smart Grid Communications. IEEE Transaction on Smart Grid 2(4), 675–685 (2011)

49. Guo, J., Peyrin, T., Poschmann, A.: The PHOTON Family of Lightweight Hash Functions. In: Rogaway, P. (ed.) CRYPTO 2011. LNCS, vol. 6841, pp. 222–239. Springer, Heidelberg (2011)

50. Bogdanov, A., Knežević, M., Leander, G., Toz, D., Varıcı, K., Verbauwhede, I.: SPONGENT: A Lightweight Hash Function. In: Preneel, B., Takagi, T. (eds.) CHES 2011. LNCS, vol. 6917, pp. 312–325. Springer, Heidelberg (2011)

51. Grosso, V., Christina, B., Gerard, B., Standaert, F.X.: A Note on the Empirical Evaluation of Security Margins against Algebraic Attacks (with Application to Low Cost Ciphers LED and Piccolo). In: The Proceedings of the 33rd WIC Symposium on Information Theory in the Benelux, Boekelo, pp. 52–59 (May 2012)

Intrusion Protection against SQL Injection and Cross Site Scripting Attacks Using a Reverse Proxy

S. Fouzul Hidhaya and Angelina Geetha

Department of Computer science,
B.S. Abdur Rahman University,
Chennai, Tamilnadu, India
{fouzul_hameed,anggeetha}@yahoo.com

Abstract. Internet and web applications have grown exponentially and have become an essential part of day-to-day living. But level of security that this Internet provides has not grown as fast as the Internet applications. The drawbacks, such as the intrusions, that are attached with the Internet applications sustain the growth of these applications. Two such vulnerabilities that dominate are the SQL Injection attacks (SQLIA) and the Cross Site Scripting Attack (XSS), contributing to 30% of the total Internet attacks. Much research is being carried out in this area. In this paper we propose a system that uses MD5 algorithm and grammar expression rules, manipulated in a reverse proxy, to mitigate SQL injection and Cross Site Scripting Attacks. This system provides a server side solution for XSS attack. The system has been tested on standard test bed applications and our work has shown significant improvement detecting and curbing the SQLIA and primary XSS attacks.

Keywords. SQL Injection, XSS attacks, Cross Site Scripting Attacks, SQL attack, Security threats, Web application vulnerability.

1 Introduction

The glory of Internet and its merits are being highly masked by the drawback associated with it. Of them the prime issue is Internet vulnerability, leading to data modification and data thefts. Many Web applications store the data in the data base and retrieve and update information as needed. These applications are highly vulnerable to many types of attacks and the most predominant among them are the SQL injection Attacks (SQLIA) and the Cross Site Scripting (XSS) attacks.

A SQL injection attack occurs when an attacker causes the web application to generate SQL queries that are functionally different from what the user interface programmer intended. For example, consider an application dealing with author details. A typical SQL statement looks like this:

select id, firstname, lastname from authors;

This statement will retrieve the 'id', 'forename' and 'surname' columns from the 'authors' table, returning all rows in the table. The 'result set' could be restricted to a specific 'author' using 'where' clause.

S.M. Thampi et al. (Eds.): SNDS 2012, CCIS 335, pp. 252–263, 2012.
© Springer-Verlag Berlin Heidelberg 2012

select id, firstname, lastname from authors where firstname = 'James' and lastname = 'Baker' ;

An important point to note here is that the string literals 'James' and 'Baker' are delimited with single quotes. Here the literals are given by the user and so they could be modified. They become the vulnerable area in the application. Now, to drop the table called 'authors', a vulnerable literal can be injected into the statement as given below.

Firstname: Jam'; drop table authors--

lastname:

Now the statement becomes, *select id, firstname, lastname from authors where firstname = 'Jam; drop table authors-- and lastname = ' ';* and this is executed. Since the first name ends with delimiter ' and - - is given at the end of the input, all other command following the - - is neglected. The output of this command is the deletion of the table named 'authors', which is not the intended result from a server database.

The XSS attack mainly happens when the validation on the input and the output from the user is insufficient. The hacker can write a script, most commonly a JavaScript, and submit it to the server. If the server does not validate the input from the user then this script gets included as a part of the main code. This malicious script could contain code that would trap a user's session ID or a cookie and send it to the hacker. So, once a genuine user requests for this infected page, the server responses to this request by sending the malicious script which in turn traps the user's information.

The objective of this work is to handle SQLIA in any form and to curb primitive XSS attacks. SQLIA can be done either using the input form or the URL, taking into account all the new techniques used for evading signatures. XSS attacks are mainly carried out in feedback forms and comments form. Providing Client side solution for the XSS attack needs the involvement of the client which is not always reliable. So, we have provided a server side solution.

2   Related Work

SQL language being a very rich language, paves way for a number of attacks. The first real existence of SQL injection was explored 1998 in a magazine Phrack [1]. Attacks that could be done using SQL injection were explained by RFP (Rain forest puppy) in an article of the magazine. But this article did not use the term SQL injection.

David Litchfield [1], in his paper classifies the attacks into 3 types: in-band, out-of-band, inference attack. In this paper, he discusses how data could be collected using inference. The black box testing methodology used in WAVES [2], is a web crawler tool to identify all points in web application that can be used to inject SQLIAs and to verify if the code contains XSS. It uses machine learning approaches to guide its testing. Static code checkers like the JDBC-checker [3] is a technique for statically checking the type correctness of dynamically generated SQL queries. This will be able to detect only one type of SQL vulnerability caused by improper type checking of input.

Combined static and dynamic analysis like the AMNESIA [4] is a model based technique that combines static analysis and runtime monitoring. In its static part, this technique uses program analysis to automatically build a model of the legitimate queries that could be generated by the application. In its dynamic part, the technique monitors the dynamically generated queries at runtime and checks them for compliance with the statically-generated model.

SQLGuard [5] and SQLCheck [6] also check queries at runtime to see if they conform to a model of expected queries. Taint based approaches like the WebSSARI [7] detects input-validation-related errors using information flow analysis. In this approach, static analysis is used to check taint flows against preconditions for sensitive functions. Livshits and Lam [8] use information flow technique to detect when tainted input has been used to construct a SQL query. It gets the vulnerability specifications from the user and uses this as static analyzer point. This technique detects SQLIA, XSS and HTTP splitting attacks.

Security gateway [9] is a proxy filtering system that enforces input validation rules on the data flowing to a web application to detect and prevent SQLIA and XSS Attacks. SQLRand [10] is an approach based on instruction-set randomization. It allows developers to create queries using randomized instruction instead of normal SQL keywords. A proxy-filter intercepts queries to the database and de-randomizes the keywords.

Kenneth et.al [11] describes how Deterministic Finite Automata (DFA) induction can be used to detect malicious web request. Used in combination with rules for reducing variability among request and uses heuristics for filtering. Konstantinos Kemalis and Theodoros Tzouramanis [12] developed a prototype SQL injection detection system (SQLIDS). The system monitors Java-based applications and detects SQL injection attacks in real time. The detection technique is based on the assumption that injected SQL commands have differences in their structure with regard to the expected SQL commands that are built by the scripts of the web application. Ben Smith et al. [13] in their work examine two input validation vulnerabilities, SQL injection vulnerability and error message vulnerability in four open source applications. They assessed the effectiveness of system and unit level testing of web applications to reveal both the type of vulnerabilities when used with iterative test automation.

SWAP [14] uses proxy layer and provides a server-side solution to detect and prevent XSS attack. Noxes [15] is a client side solution for XSS attacks. It creates a personal firewall on the client side and checks every outgoing request and incoming response. It uses both manual and automatically generated rules to prevent XSS attacks on the client side.

Ulfar Erlingsson et al. [16] propose a client side solution. It proposes a Mutation-event transforms system which defines policies to be enforced in the client side browser. It defines security policies based on monitoring client behavior. Noncespaces [17] sets rules and in each document it randomizes the XML Namespace prefix. These prefixes are identifiable by the user and so the user will be able to identify the trusted content by the web application and un-trusted content provided by the attacker. Anh Nguyen et al. [18] proposes a system that works on PHP scripts. This system uses a modified interpreter along with the PHP interpreter to identify un-trusted sites.

In this paper we have used MD5 hashing to curb SQLIA using the input give through the login form and used regular expression to curb SQLIA attempted through the URL and to detect and prevent the XSS attack in the feedback form or the comment form. The System uses a sanitizing application in proxy server that will sanitize the request before it is being forwarded to the main server and the database.

3   System Architecture

The architecture of the system is illustrated in Fig. 1. In a client server model, a reverse proxy server is placed, in between the client and the server. The presence of the proxy server is not known to the user. The sanitizing application is placed in the Reverse proxy server. A reverse proxy is used to sanitize the request from the user. When the request becomes high, more reverse proxy's can be used to handle the request. This enables the system to maintain a low response time, even at high load.

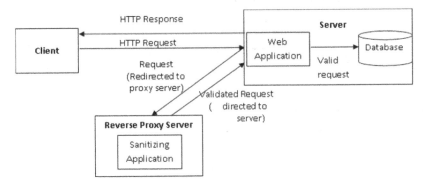

Fig. 1. System Architecture

The general work of the system is as follows:
1. The client sends the request to the server.
2. The request is redirected to the reverse proxy also called as the Intrusion Prevention proxy(IP Proxy).
3. The sanitizing application in the proxy server extracts the URL from the HTTP , the user data from the SQL statement or the user data from the script code.
   a.   The URL is send to the signature check
   b.   The user login data (Extracted using prototype query model) is encrypted using the MD5 hash.
   c.   The user input data (extracted using prototype query model) from script code is send for expression check.
4. The sanitizing application sends the validated URL, validated user input, hashed user login data and the original request to the web application in the server.
5. The filter in the server denies the request if the sanitizing application had marked the URL request malicious or the user input data malicious.

6. If the URL is found to be benign, then the hashed value is send to the database of the web application.
7. If the URL and the user input data is found benign, then the user input data in the feedback / comment form is included in the original code of the web page.
8. If the hashed user data matches the stored hash value in the database, then the data is retrieved and the user gains access to the account.
9. Else the user is denied access. Fig. 2 gives the flowchart of the system.

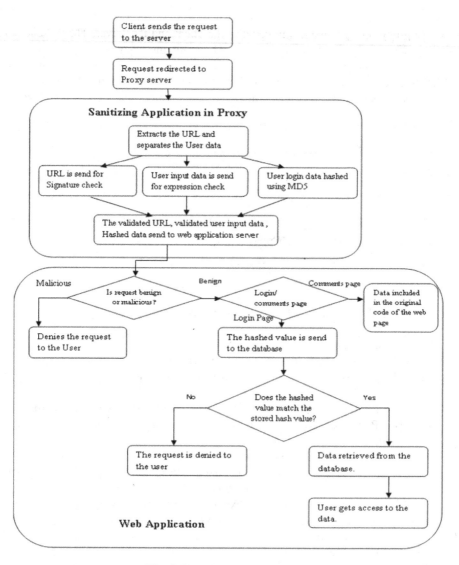

Fig. 2. Flowchart of the system

3.1   The Sanitizing Application

The sanitizing application uses the data cleansing algorithm to sanitize the user input.

Data Cleansing Algorithm (DC algorithm):
Step 1:
    Parse the user login data into Tokens-*tok*;
    While (not empty of *tok*)
      Check if *tok* ≠ reserved SQL Keyword
          Move *tok* to User data Array-*UDA*;
Step 2:
    For (every data in *UDA*)
    Convert to Corresponding MD5 and store in *MD5-UDA*.
Step 3:
    Parse the user input data into Tokens-*token*;
    While (not empty of *token*)
      Check if *token* ≠ reserved JavaScript keyword
          Set the *flag1* to *continue*;
    Else
          Set the *flag1* to *deny*;
Step 4:
    Extract the URL from HTTP;
    Parse the URL into Tokens-*toks;* ·
    While (not empty of *toks*)
      Check if (URL = Benign using the signature check)
          Set the *flag* to *continue*;
    Else
          Set the *flag* to *deny*;
Step 5:
    Send the *MD5-UDA ,flag, flag1* and original web request to Web application
Server;

Data Cleansing Algorithm Details

Extracting user data from SQL statement:
The SQL statement is extracted from the HTTP request and the query is tokenized.
The tokenized query is then compared with the prototype document. A prototype
document consists of all the SQL queries from the Web application. The query tokens
are transformed into XML format. The XSL's pattern matching algorithm is used to
find the prototype model corresponding to the received Query. This method has been
adapted in the previous work COMPVAL [19].

XSL's Pattern Matching
The query is first analyzed and tokenized as elements. The prototype document
contains the query pertained to that particular application.
    For example the input query is,

SELECT * FROM members WHERE login='admin' AND password='XYZ' OR '1=1'

When this query is received this is converted into XML format using a XML schema. The resulting XML would be,

```
<SELECT>
  <*>
  <FROM>
   <members>
    <WHERE login= 'admin'>
     <AND password= XYZ>
      <OR 1=1>
      </OR>
     </AND>
    </WHERE>
   </members>
  </FROM>
  </*>
</SELECT>
```

Using the pattern matching the elements is searched such that the nested elements is similar to query tokens. The corresponding matching XML mapping is,

```
<SELECT>
  <identifier>
  <FROM>
   <identifier>
    <WHERE id_list= 'userip'>
     <AND id_list='userip'>
     </AND>
    </WHERE>
   </identifier>
  </FROM>
  </identifier>
</SELECT>
```

When the match is found, the corresponding prototype query would be,

SELECT identifier FROM identifier WHERE identifier op 'userip' AND identifier op 'userip'

which will be used to identify the user input data . The extra XML tags other than those in the prototype will be considered as user input. This search is less time consuming because the search is based on text and string comparison. The time complexity is $O(n)$. This helps in increasing the effectiveness of the program and reduces the latency time. Similar to the query pattern, a script pattern contains all the valid patterns of script available in the application, to check for user posted data in the feedback form and the comments form.

Encrypting using MD5 hash and Signature check, Script check using regular expressions

The user data extracted from the extraction phase is then encrypted using the MD5 hash function. All the possible forms of SQL injection manipulation are stored in the signature check in the form of regular expressions. The URL is extracted from the HTTP request and the URL is tokenized. These tokens are checked using the regular expressions. If they contain any form of the signature that has been defined as SQL injection then the request is marked as malicious else it is marked as benign. Similarly, The JavaScript keywords are stored in script check in the regular expressions form. The user input data extracted from web page is tokenized and these tokens are then checked against the regular JavaScript keywords. If any JavaScript keyword was found in the process then the post is marked malicious else it is marked benign.

4   Implementation

This system implements the DC algorithm in the automated sanitizing application using Java. We have used 4 systems in the lab setup connected through LAN. One system is considered as the web application server. We set up two systems for the proxy server which has the automated sanitizing application installed. One system acts as the client. On the server an Eclipse integrated development Environment (IDE) runs the open source project.   On the server gateway a filter program is installed. This filter application redirects the request from the user to the proxy server. For each request the server chooses one of the two proxy server alternatively. This is done to minimize the loading on a particular proxy server which might slow down the process.

In each of the proxy server the sanitizing application is executed in the Eclipse IDE. When the redirected request from the server reaches the sanitizing application the DC Algorithm is triggered. As a first step, the SQL query and the URL is extracted from the HTTP. The SQL query is processed using the XSL's pattern matching and the prototype document. The user data is separated from the query. The URL is passed on to the signature check, which uses the regular expression to validate the URL.

The following signature checks are done on the URL's extracted from the HTTP request.

1. Query delimiter (--)
2. White Spaces
3. Comment delimiter (/* */)
4. EXEC keyword
5. UTF coding
6. Scanning for query with signature OR followed same characters before and after '='.
7. Dropping meta characters (and their encoding) like ; ,(,), >, <, %, +,= and @
8. Use of 'IN', 'BETWEEN' after 'OR'.
9. Use of SQL keywords. Just looking into the keywords will bring about a lot of false positives. So the context before and after the keyword is also checked.

The following script checks are done on the user posted data.

1. <script>, </script>
2. Names of the event handlers (Eg. onClick, onLoad, onUnload, onChange, onFocus, onSubmit etc...)

3. Function
4. Document.
5. (,)
6. Javascript:
7. <, >

The user data is converted into its corresponding hash value using the MD5 algorithm. The hash value, the validated URL and validated user posted data are then directed back to the server.

Depending on the validation results the filter on the web application server decides whether to continue with the request or to deny the request. If the URL and the user posted input data is benign then the URL, the original data and the hash value is forwarded to the web application on the server system. The user posted data is included in the original code. The web application sends the hash value to the database and the value are checked. If the values match, then the user gains access. Else the request is denied. The database used with the web application is MySQL.

5   Evaluation

This system was tested on 4 open source projects. The open source projects that was considered for this study, was taken from *gotocode.com*. The four projects that were taken into study were Online Bookstore, Online portal, Employee directory, registration form. We used Burp suite [20] as an attacking tool. Our system was able to detect all the intrusions injected by burp suite and was able to achieve 100% detection rate. The total number of SQL injections by the Burp suite and the total number of detections by our system defining the detection rate is stated in Table 1.

Table 1. Detection Rate

Web Application	No. of Attacks	No. of Detections	Detection Rate
Portal	276	276	100%
Employee Directory	238	238	100%
Book store	197	197	100%
Registration Form	419	419	100%

6   Analysis and Result

We have analyzed our system and other methodologies that are used to curb SQLIA and XSS attacks. The detailed analysis is shown in Table 2.

The system was run under light load condition, medium load condition and heavy load condition. The time taken for the response with our system's reverse proxy also called as the Intrusion Prevention proxy (IP proxy) and without the Intrusion Prevention proxy was noted in Nanoseconds. Under Light and medium load condition 5 and 50 requests from client system was send to the server. The results are as shown in Fig.3. For heavy load 1000 requests was send using client system. The results are as shown in Fig. 4. The time taken did not show much difference for light load and medium load condition. For heavy load condition, there was a slight difference in nanoseconds.

Table 2. Analysis of methodologies used for curbing SQLIA and XSS Attacks

Methodology	Change in source Code	Detection/Prevention of attack	Type of attack addressed
WAVES[2]	Not necessary	Automatized/ report generated	SQLIA, XSS/Client side
JDBC-Checker[3]	Needed for automatic prevention of attack.	Can be automatized.	SQLIA
AMNESIA[4]	Not necessary	Fully automatized	SQLIA
SQLGuard[5]	Necessary	Fully automatized	SQLIA
SQLCheck[6]	Necessary	Partially automatized	SQLIA
WebSSARI[7]	Necessary	Partially Automatized	SQLIA, XSS
Livshits and Lam [8]	Not necessary	Manual assistance needed	SQLIA, XSS, HTTP splitting Attacks.
Security Gateway[9]	Not needed	Manual detection / automatized prevention	SQLIA, XSS/Client Side
SQLRand[10]	Necessary	Fully automatized	SQLIA
SQL-IDS[12]	Not necessary	Fully Automatized	SQLIA
Idea[13]	Not necessary	Only exposes vulnerabilities	SQLIA
SWAP[14]	Necessary	Fully automated	XSS/ Server side
Noxes[15]	Not necessary	Can be automatized	XSS/ Client side
Ulfar Erlingsson et al. [16]	Not necessary	Can be fully automatized	XSS/ Client side
Noncespaces[17]	Necessary	User intervention needed	XSS/ Client side
Proposed DC algorithm	Not necessary	Fully automated	SQLIA, XSS/ Server side

The system using the proxy server protection was responding a little slower than the other system, but had full protection against SQL injection attacks. If we increase the number of proxy server to four then the server was able to handle the request with an increased pace. We have not yet worked on optimization of the system. We believe, after optimization of the system, the performance will   improve.

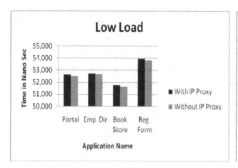
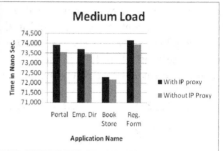

Fig. 3. Low load and the medium load

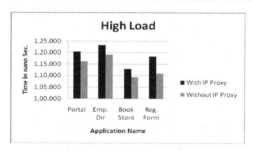

Fig. 4. High Load

7 Conclusion

The novel system with intrusion prevention proxy has proved to be effective in detecting the SQL injection attacks and primitive XSS attacks and preventing these attacks from penetrating the web application. This system does not do any changes in the source code of the application and the system is fully automated. The system provides a server side solution, and thus the user intervention is not needed in mitigation of these attacks. By increasing the number of proxy servers the web application can handle any number of requests without obvious delay in time and still can protect the application from SQL injection and XSS attack. In future work, the focus will be on optimization of the system and removing the vulnerable points in the application itself, in addition to detection and studying alternate techniques for detection and prevention of these attacks.

References

1. Litchfield, D.: Data-mining with SQL Injection and Inference. Next Generation Security software Ltd., White Paper (2005)
2. Huang, Y., Huang, F., Lin, T., Tsai, C.: Web Application Security Assessment by Fault Injection and Behavior Monitoring. In: 12th International World Wide Web Conference 2003, pp. 148–159 (2003)

3. Gould, C., Su, Z., Devanbu, P.: JDBC Checker: A Static Analysis Tool for SQL/JDBC Application. In: 26th International Conference on Software Engineering 2004, pp. 697–698 (2004)
4. Halfond, W.G., Orso, A.: AMNESIA: Analysis and Monitoring for NEutralizing SQL-Injection Attacks. In: 20th IEEE/ACM International Conference on Automated Software Engineering 2005, pp. 174–183 (2005)
5. Buehrer, G., Bruce Weide, W., Paolo Sivilotti, A.G.: Using Parse Tree Validation to Prevent SQL Injection Attacks. In: 5th International Workshop on Software Engineering and Middleware, pp. 106–113 (2005)
6. Su, Z., Wassermann, G.: The Essence of Command Injection Attacks in Web Applications. In: 33rd ACM SIGPLAN-SIGACT Symposium on Principles of Programming Languages 2006, pp. 372–382 (2006)
7. Huang, Y., Yu, F., Hang, C., Tsai, C.H., Lee, D.T., Kuo, S.Y.: Securing Web Application Code by Static Analysis and Runtime Protection. In: 13th International World Wide Web Conference 2004, pp. 40–52 (2004)
8. Livshits, V.B., Lam, M.S.: Finding Security Errors in Java Programs with Static Analysis. In: 14th Usenix Security Symposium 2005, pp. 271–286 (2005)
9. Scott, D., Sharps, R.: Abstracting Application-level Web Security. In: 11th International Conference on the World Wide Web 2002, pp. 396–407 (2002)
10. Boyd, S.W., Keromytis, A.D.: SQLrand: Preventing SQL Injection Attacks. In: Jakobsson, M., Yung, M., Zhou, J. (eds.) ACNS 2004. LNCS, vol. 3089, pp. 292–302. Springer, Heidelberg (2004)
11. Kenneth Ingham, L., Somayaji, A., Burge, J., Forrest, S.: Learning DFA Representations of HTTP for Protecting Web Applications. Computer Networks 51, 1239–1255 (2007)
12. Kemalis, K., Tzouramanis, T.: SQL-IDS: a specification-based approach for SQL-injection detection. In: 2008 ACM Symposium on Applied Computing, pp. 2153–2158 (2008)
13. Smith, B., Williams, L., Austin, A.: Idea: Using System Level Testing for Revealing SQL Injection-Related Error Message Information Leaks. In: Massacci, F., Wallach, D., Zannone, N. (eds.) ESSoS 2010. LNCS, vol. 5965, pp. 192–200. Springer, Heidelberg (2010)
14. Wurzinger, P., Platzer, C., Ludl, C., Kirda, E., Kruegel, C.: SWAP: Mitigating XSS Attacks using a Reverse Proxy. In: ICSE Workshop on Software Engineering for Secure Systems, SESS, pp. 33–39. IEEE Computer Society Press (2009)
15. Kirda, E., Kruegel, C., Vigna, G., Jovanovic, N.: Noxes: A client-side solution for mitigating cross-site scripting attacks. In: 21st ACM Symposium on Applied Computing, SAC 2006, pp. 330–337 (2006)
16. Erlingsson, U., Livshits, B., Xie, Y.: End to End Application Security. In: 11th USENIX Workshop on Hot Topics in Operating Systems, pp. 1–6 (2007)
17. Van Gundy, M., Chen, H.: Noncespaces: Using Randomization to Enforce Information Flow Tracking and Thwart XSS Attacks. In: 16th Annual Network and Distributed System Security Symposium (2009)
18. Nguyen-Tuong, A., Guarnieri, S., Greene, D., Shirley, J., Evans, D.: Automatically Hardening Web Applications Using Precise Tainting. In: Sasaki, R., Qing, S., Okamoto, E., Yoshiura, H. (eds.) Security and Privacy in the Age of Ubiquitous Computing. IFIP, vol. 181, pp. 295–307. Springer, Boston (2005)
19. Fouzul Hidhaya, S., Geetha, A.: COMPVAL – A system to mitigate SQLIA. In: International Conference on Computer, Communication and Intelligence, ICCCI 2010, pp. 337–342 (2010)
20. Burp suite, http://portswigger.net/burp/

Three-Way Handshake-Based OTP Using Random Host-Side Keys for Effective Key Transfer in Symmetric Cryptosystems

P.R. Mahalingam

Department of Computer Science
Rajagiri School of Engineering & Technology, Rajagiri Valley, Cochin, India
prmahalingam@gmail.com

Abstract. Vernam cipher is said to be one of the most secure cipher systems in use, based on the key size. It is derived from the One-Time Pad (OTP) method. One of the main features of the cipher is that it is completely reversible with the use of XOR operation, with no loss of data. It is independently a symmetric cryptosystem, which needs the key to be transmitted to both ends for effective working. The same case applies for all symmetric ciphers. But the main drawback of symmetric ciphers is that the key has to be transmitted from sender to recipient, over the insecure channel. Even if we try to implement maximum security, the key transmission should be secured as much as possible. Here, we use the power of OTP to implement key transmission in symmetric cryptosystems. The concept is based on an age-old principle of securing parcels, by using two separate locks, and not transferring the keys across. But this involves multiple transactions for sending the same parcel, and the same method can be implemented as a 3-way handshake. The keys at the host can be chosen randomly since they are never transmitted across. The method has been shown to have the strength exceeding Vernam cipher itself. But the drawback is that the method becomes inefficient for large data, since the handshakes involve lot of data transfer.

Keywords: Symmetric ciphers, handshake mechanism, One-Time Pad, Vernam cipher, channel security, random keys.

1 Introduction

The increase in influence of networking has made life easier for everyone, especially in data acquisition and processing. But the technology is such that the data has to be sent across a channel, out of the safe bounds of end hosts. A notable feature of the channel is that it is "insecure". It means that the channel by itself provides little help when it comes to getting the data to the destination safely. The built-in mechanisms may monitor the timely delivery and data accuracy, but not whether the data has been tampered with. As long as the channel is insecure, the data will be subject to attacks[8][10], and the possibility of attack goes up with the sensitivity of the contents[11] being transmitted. Attacks can be passive, where the data is simply read and used, or active, where the data is modified.

S.M. Thampi et al. (Eds.): SNDS 2012, CCIS 335, pp. 264–271, 2012.
© Springer-Verlag Berlin Heidelberg 2012

2   Encryption

Encryption is the main method to maintain the confidentiality of the data[6]. By confidentiality, we refer to the non-disclosure of contents of the messages. This primarily deals with the passive attacks like content disclosure, and traffic analysis, since they are hard to detect. One cannot predict whether the message was opened in transit by being at the end points.

Encryption is the method to prevent, or counter the passive attacks. It play with the data in such a way that even if·a passive attack is carried out, the data recovered from that attack is virtually useless. This is since encryption algorithms "mask" or modify the data in a recoverable way. A cryptosystem mainly consists of 5 components:

- Plaintext message (M), Ciphertext message (C), Key (K), Encryption algorithm (E) and Decryption algorithm (D)

When we send the data, we modify it as $C = E (M, K)$. Once the ciphertext is received at the receiver, the data is recovered as $M = D (C, K)$.

So, we can see that the entire process depends on a key K. The algorithm should function depending solely on the value of K, and still make the channel secure. This organization, where the cipher is dependent on a shared key is called **symmetric cipher**. Another method exists, where a pair of keys is generated. In that case, encryption is using one key (called *public key*) and decryption using the other[5] (called *private key*). This is called **asymmetric cipher**.

This paper mainly deals with symmetric cryptosystems.

3   Symmetric Cryptosystems and One-Time Pad (OTP)

Symmetric ciphers rely on a shared key to perform the encryption and decryption. They are simple to implement, but have limited security, since the method normally involves blocks of data, vulnerable to cryptanalysis. But still, they have their importance, since public key cryptosystems have complex mathematical operations associated with them.

One Time Pad - One – Time pad proved to be impossible to break if used correctly[3]. Here the plaintext is XOR'ed with a Pad[1] (which is a random key) which is of the same length as the plaintext. The Pad is used only once and it is discarded after a single use. That is why the name "One-time Pad". The following are the reasons why One – Time pad is not used widely[1]

1. Key length is an important issue. As the plaintext length increases the Key (Pad) length also increases in the same way. Plaintext length ∞ Key length (" ∞ " represents direct proportionality) That is , length of Plaintext is directly proportional to length of the key (Pad).
2. Key Transfer is another issue. The reason is that once the key is compromised, any person with the basic knowledge about XOR operation can decrypt it.
3. Problem with generating a perfect random key.

So, the same key has to be used for encryption and decryption. This means that even for OTP, key transfer is essential.

4   Key Transfer in Symmetric Cryptosystems

As mentioned before, key sharing is very important when it comes to symmetric cryptosystems. But the channel is already insecure, and transferring the key will make it vulnerable, resulting in breaking the entire cryptosystem. So, there should be an efficient method to transfer the keys from source to destination. Some possible methods are:

1. Both sender and recipient can agree on common keys by monitoring the communications[13]. For one session, a key can be maintained, which is scrapped and replaced by the next one in queue for next session. There is no key transfer here, but the key sequence may become predictable, since both key updates have to be synchronized.
2. A third party can transfer the keys[14]. This can be implemented by public key cryptosystems between the source-arbiter pair and arbiter-destination pair. But the involvement of third party can be a weak link in the security.
3. There are specialized algorithms for key exchange using random values. One main example is the "Diffie Helmann Key Exchange Algorithm", which uses random numbers to compute keys at both sender and receiver. It is quite difficult to break, but it poses limitations on the key. The sender may not be able to choose the key himself, since values for computing the key are generated at both ends. Also, a lot of computation is required.

5   Proposed Methodology

The proposed methodology revolves around the following principle, which is represented by an abstract methodology.

The proposal is inspired by a real-world problem which deals with sending a box locked by a padlock. In order for the recipient to open it, the key should also be made available. But sending the key can jeopardize the security. The solution for the problem is by using the method as shown in Figure 1. The method can be summarized as:

1. Sender locks the box with lock1 using key1 and sends it to receiver.
2. Receiver locks the box with lock2 using key2 and sends it back to sender. Now the box is locked using two locks.
3. Sender will then unlock lock1 using key1 and send it to the receiver. Now the box has only one lock which is lock2.
4. Receiver will then unlock lock2 using key2 and thereby opening the box to see the content.

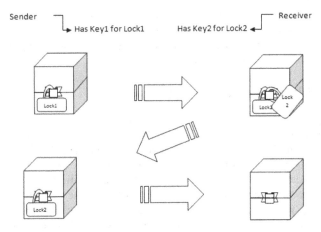

Fig. 1. A real-world schemata of the proposed method

The main advantage of the method is that there is little restriction on the keys. Each side can choose their own keys for locking / unlocking the box. Also, neither of the keys has to be sent across the channel.

When we implement it, the concept is taken as a reversible cipher system for each transaction. One of the first and foremost choices is the OTP itself. In that case, locking and unlocking simply involves XORing with the key.

Key Generation – Since the algorithm puts no restrictions on the key itself, it can be chosen completely at random. Many random number generators are available that can perform this generation. But to speed up the generation and computation, the keys can be generated in such a way that segments are generated, and then merged together to form the single key. This is effective since there are less chances of getting 0s with such merged keys. 0s are critical in the case of OTP since XOR operations with 0 won't change the input bit. Similarly, XORing an input sequence with a stream of 0s will keep the message as such.

Encoding – Since we are using OTP for the individual processes, the process of encryption and decryption are the same, and we can merge it as an "encoding" process. Here, we consider the input data and split it into blocks of fixed size. The size of block is dependent on the size of merged key. ie, if we take a merged key of 128 bits, the input data should also be taken as blocks of 128 bits, applying padding bits wherever needed. Then we directly perform XOR operation, and send the data as streams.

Procedure – The overall procedure can be summarized as follows:

1. Sender generates a key. It splits the data into blocks and XORs the blocks with the key. The encoded data is sent to the receiver.
2. Receiver generates its key, and XORs the data, and sends it back to the sender.
3. Sender performs another XOR with its own key, and sends the data to the receiver.
4. Receiver performs the final XOR of the procedure to retrieve the data.

These steps form part of the "handshake"[2] constituted by OTPs. One possible drawback is that same blocks will be encoded the same way. We can rectify that using a sequence of keys, and XORing the blocks with the keys in sequence. So, a fair amount of traffic analysis is broken[7].

6   Possible Threats and Solutions

Replay Attacks - As mentioned before, the algorithm involves three handshakes and at each handshake data is XORed. This algorithm is prone to replay attack. This means that if a third person comes in between the sender and receiver(Man-in-the-middle) and if he/she acts as the receiver, then it will cause problems. The problem is that if the intruder completes the first handshake and if initiate the second handshake by XORing the data received using his/her own key, the sender thinks that he is communicating with the receiver. Then the sender initiates the third handshake by XORing the data with his key thereby cancelling his part of XOR. If then the intruder gets the data, he/she can easily read the data by XORing it using the same key which was used before.

Same Key Issue - If suppose both sender and receiver uses the same key for XORing, then the data send during the second handshake will be the original plaintext because if a number is XORed with itself, it will cancel off.

Solutions - These problems can be solved using the following supplementing schemes.

- Use of proper authentication scheme before initiating transmission to fend off replay attacks.
- Use of checksum to monitor whether the keys are getting cancelled off.
- Use of session key to further enhance key strength, and avoid "man-in-the-middle".
- Timestamping to avoid conflicts with normal data transfers.

Impact of Size of Data – Even if size of key is flexible, the size of data is a main factor in this method. This is since the whole data is transmitted thrice through the network. So, if we have a data of size 1 MB, just the cryptosystem will create traffic of 3 MB. So, this method is best suited for smaller data items, making it a **secure key transfer algorithm**. But if the data is small enough, the method can be used directly on the data.

7   Simulation and Evaluation of results

A sample simulation was built on Java (another implementation is available [9]), with the following specifications:

- *Key size*   : 128 bits
- *Key sequence*   : 10 keys
- *Key generation*   : 16-bit random numbers, with overlap of 8 bits. A total of 15 random numbers have to be generated.
- *Input data*   : Here, the paper abstract itself is used.

Once the simulation was run, the following output was observed.

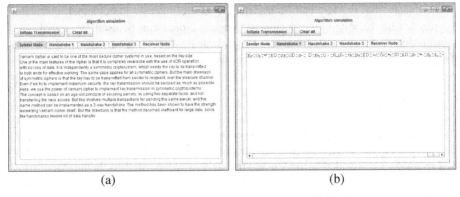

Fig. 2. (a) Actual data, at the sender side, (b) Handshake 1 contents

Fig. 3. (a) Handshake 2 contents, (b) Handshake 3 contents

Fig. 4. Received data

When we perform an analysis, we find that the possibility of traffic analysis has come down to nearly 10%, since only **14% of repetitive characters were encoded to the same ciphertext**.

This means that the key can be transferred securely across the channel. Once the key reaches the recipient, any normal symmetric cipher can be used for actual data transmission (It was observed that this method can be directly used with good amount of efficiency as long as the data is not larger than 30 KB).

8   Conclusion

The algorithm uses a simple concept of using XOR to tackle the complicated task, security. This algorithm involves no key transfer. The usual key transfer in commonly used techniques is avoided here by using the three way handshake scheme. Moreover, it uses XOR operation for encryption and decryption which involves key which a random number. So as a whole, this scheme can be used for securing key transfer ie. this algorithm can be used to complement other faster cryptography algorithms where key transfer is the only issue. So this can be used in symmetric key algorithms to share the private key between sender and receiver. Thus, the fastness of symmetric key algorithm and the security provided by this algorithm paves way for a better encryption algorithm.

9   Future Work

More study can be done on the security of the algorithm, and if some shuffling can be done on the data blocks, the security can be enhanced. An efficient scheme has to be devised for the reordering[4] so that the recoverability isn't affected (the key sequence has to be shuffled alongwith the input[12], and the order shouldn't be transmitted across the channel).

References

1. Dodis, Y., Spencer, J.: On the (non)universality of the one-time pad. In: Proceedings of the 43rd Annual IEEE Symposium on Foundations of Computer Science, pp. 376–385 (2002)
2. Yadav, D., Sardana, A.: Enhanced 3-way handshake protocol for key exchange in IEEE 802.11i. In: 3rd International Conference on Electronics Computer Technology, ICECT, pp. 132–135 (2011)
3. Deng, S.: Compare of New Security Strategy With Several Others in WLAN. In: 2nd International Conference on Computer Engineering and Technology, ICCET (2010)
4. Rittera, T.: Substitution Cipher with pseudorandom Shuffling: The Dynamic Substitution Combiner. Cryptologia 14(4), 289–303 (1990)
5. Zhang, L., Han, W., Zheng, D., Chen, K.: A Security Solution of WLAN Based on Public Key Cryptosystem. In: Proceedings of the 2005 11th International Conference on Parallel and Distributed Systems, ICPADS 2005, pp. 123–127 (2005)
6. Zeynep Gurkas, G., Halim Zaim, A., Ali Aydin, M.: Security Mechanisms and Their Performance Impacts on Wireless Local Area Networks. In: Proceedings of the Seventh IEEE International Symposium on Computer Networks, ISCN 2006, pp. 14–18 (2006)

7. Raub, D., Steinwandt, R., Müller-Quade, J.: On the Security and Composability of the One Time Pad. In: Vojtáš, P., Bieliková, M., Charron-Bost, B., Sýkora, O. (eds.) SOFSEM 2005. LNCS, vol. 3381, pp. 288–297. Springer, Heidelberg (2005)
8. Harris, B., Hunt, R.: TCP/IP security threats and attack methods. Computer Communications 22(10), 885–897 (1999)
9. Lindquist, T.E., Diarra, M., Millard, B.R.: A Java cryptography service provider implementing one-time pad. In: Proceedings of the 37th Annual Hawaii International Conference on System Sciences (2004)
10. Apostolopoulos, G., Peris, V., Saha, D.: Transport layer security: how much does it really cost? In: Proceedings of IEEE Eighteenth Annual Joint Conference of the IEEE Computer and Communications Societies, INFOCOM 1999, vol. 2, pp. 717–725 (1999)
11. Parthasarathy, M.: Analysis of network management of remote network elements. In: International Conference on Systems and International Conference on Mobile Communications and Learning Technologies (2006)
12. Shefi, A.: System and method for synchronizing one time pad encryption keys for secure communication and access control, US Patent 6,445,794 (2002)
13. Glover, J.J.: One-time pad Encryption key Distribution, US Patent 6,868,495 (2005)
14. Hammersmith, W.S.: One-time-pad encryption with central key service and key management, US Patent App. 10/254,754 (2002)

Identity Based Privacy Preserving Dynamic Broadcast Encryption for Multi-privileged Groups

Angamuthu Muthulakshmi, Ramalingam Anitha, S Rohini, and Krishnan Princy

Department of Applied Mathematics and Computational Sciences,
PSG College of Technology Coimbatore, India
anitha_nadarajan@mail.psgtech.ac.in,
{muthulakshmi.a,srohini.psg,princykrishnan65}@gmail.com

Abstract. An identity-based broadcast encryption scheme (IBBE), is the one in which the broadcasting sender combines the public identities of receivers and system parameters and then encrypts a message. Attacks on user privacy may happen as the user identity is not preserved. This paper presents an IBBE scheme for multi-privileged users using Chinese Remainder Theorem and bilinear pairing that preserves the user identities. The proposed scheme is proved secure under random oracle model. The proposed scheme provides a stateless broadcast, is dynamic with ease for revocation of users and also collusion resistant.

Keywords: Chinese Remainder Theorem, Bilinear Paring, Diffie-Hellman problem, Identity Based Encryption, Broadcast Encryption.

1 Introduction

In applications like video conferencing, pay-per-view channels, distance learning, distribution of stock quotes and news, transmitting a single data stream to a set of intended receivers decreases the load on network and bandwidth resources. But in order to ensure confidentiality of the message, these applications need access control mechanisms to be deployed. Usage of broadcast encryption helps a targeted set of users S alone to decrypt the content. But, even if the entire sets of users outside S collude, they cannot obtain information about the broadcast content, which results in a collusion resistant system. In a broadcast encryption scheme the revoked users must not be given access to the messages.

ID-based encryption scheme is a novel type of cryptographic scheme which enables users to communicate securely without exchanging private keys and without keeping any key directories. ID-based encryption (IBE) reduces initialization, intercommunication, computational overhead in encryption, simplifies key management, and eliminates the need for private key database. In conventional group communications, all members in a group have same level of access privileges, whereas in the current globalization scenario, many group applications such as pay–per-view, online teaching, have multiple related data streams and members have different access privileges, which led to the advent of multi-privileged groups. Group users can subscribe to different data streams according to

S.M. Thampi et al. (Eds.): SNDS 2012, CCIS 335, pp. 272–282, 2012.
© Springer-Verlag Berlin Heidelberg 2012

their interest and have multiple access privileges with the support of multi-privileged group communications.

2   Related Work

This section details about related work under broadcast encryption, IBBE, and multi-privileged group communication.

Fiat and Naor have introduced Broadcast Encryption (BE) in [1]. [4] presents a fully collusion secure broadcast encryption based on generically secure computational problem in the standard model. Public key broadcast encryption systems for stateless receivers have been discussed in [7]. Identity based cryptosystem assuming the existence of trusted key generation centers was given in [2]. [6] gives a public key cryptosystem related to the difficulty of solving the quadratic residuosity problem. In [16],[8] identity-based broadcast system whose security rests on the hardness of Diffie-Hellman Exponent problem has been constructed. A completely anonymous identity-based cryptosystem has been presented in [21]. An IBBE scheme based on the q-TBDHE assumption with IND-IDCCA2 security without random oracles has been constructed in [22]. Construction of CCA-secure public-key encryption in the standard model was given in [17]. An efficient and secure anonymous multireceiver IBE scheme and an IBBE with constant size ciphertexts and private keys were proposed in [5] and [3] respectively. A privacy-preserving IBBE scheme, to encrypt messages to some subset S has been given in [11]. An IBE scheme in which revoked users cannot seek help from the non-revoked users was proposed by Boneh and Franklin in [8]. A security definition for Anonymous Broadcast Encryption (ANOBE) has been provided and a slightly modified version of the Kurosawa-Desmedt (KD) PKE scheme has been presented in [13]. The first broadcast encryption scheme with sublinear ciphertexts to attain receiver anonymity was proposed in [9].

Secure broadcasting using a secure lock generated using CRT has been given in [10]. CRT-based secure verifiable secret sharing scheme, with periodically renewed user shares, without changing the long-term secret schemes was presented in [12]. An integrated key graph that maintains keying material for all members with different access privileges in multi-group key management scheme for hierarchical group access control was given by Sun and Liu [18]. A group key management scheme called IDHKGS for secure multi-privileged group communications which employs a key graph was proposed by Wang et al [20]. Group key management for multi-privileged groups was discussed in [14],[15].A Data Group (DG) in a multi-privileged group consists of the users who can access a particular resource and a Service Group (SG) consists of users who are authorized to access exactly the same set of resources.

Motivation: In most of the existing IBBE schemes, the broadcasting sender merges the public identities of receivers and system parameters to encrypt a message, posing threat to user privacy. In Applications like Military field, the list of receivers of a command should be confidential, which otherwise will reveal all the identities when a single node is trapped. In pay-per-view channels and commercial websites, it would be favorable for the competitive service providers for targeted advertisement, if the identities are revealed. Information passed to the account holders of a bank should not reveal the identities of the users. Hence in addition to access control the user identities also need to be confidential in some systems, which is the prime focus of the proposed work. The scheme also aims to provide dynamism, revocation and collusion resistance in an efficient manner.

Contributions of the Proposed Scheme: With the above motivations, an identity based broadcast encryption scheme for multi-privileged groups that preserves the user privacy is proposed using Chinese Remainder Theorem and Bilinear Pairing. The system preserves both forward and backward secrecy, due to the use of session keys. The scheme differs from [11] in the sense that our scheme is dynamic with ease for revocation of users, provides collusion resistant and a stateless broadcast in addition to user privacy. The users have to provide O (1) size memory for private key storage. The receiver number needs to compute only one pairing which is lesser as compared to [3],[11]and[22]. Also the proposed scheme doesn't demand any exponent computation from receiver end. The computational cost of our scheme is one third as compared to [11].

The rest of the paper is organized as follows: Section 3 deals with the preliminaries and notations. Section 4 discusses the proposed scheme. Section 5 deals with the proof of correctness and section 6 gives the analysis of the proposed work and finally section 7 gives the conclusion.

3   Preliminaries and Notations

This section gives the preliminaries needed for discussing the proposed work.

Chinese Remainder Theorem: Suppose $m1, m2, ..., mk$ are positive integers which are pair wise coprime. Let $m = \prod_{i=1}^{k} m_i$ and for any given sequence of integers a1,a2, ..., ak, there exists a unique integer x solving the system of simultaneous congruence equations,

$$x \equiv ai \ (mod \ mi); 1 \le i \le k.$$

BILINEAR PAIRING: Let G and G_T be cyclic groups of prime order p and g be the generator of G. A bilinear map is a function $\hat{e} : G \times G \rightarrow G_T$ which satisfies the following properties:

- Bilinear: $\hat{e}(g^a, g^b) = \hat{e}(g, g)^{ab}$ for all $a, b \in Z_p^*$
- Non-degenerative: The map does not send all pairs in $G \times G$ to the identity in G_T. Since G and G_T are groups of prime order, it implies that if g is a generator of G, then $\hat{e}(g, g)$ is a generator of G_T.
- Computability: There is an efficient algorithm to compute $\hat{e}(g, g) \ \forall g \in G$.

DIFFIE-HELLMAN PROBLEM: The computational Diffie-Hellman problem in a cyclic group G of prime order p is: Given a generator g of G and two elements

$\mathbf{g^a, g^b} \in G$ for a,b random in $\mathbf{Z_p^*}$, compute $\mathbf{g^{ab}}$.Define DH(X, Y) = W, where X = $\mathbf{g^a, Y = g^b}$ and $W = \mathbf{g^{ab}}$. The DH assumption asserts that it is hard to compute DH(X, Y) with random choice X,Y∈G.

BILINEAR DIFFIE-HELLMAN PROBLEM: The Bilinear Diffie-Hellman problem in $\langle G, \mathbf{G_T}, ê\rangle$, where G, $\mathbf{G_T}$ are cyclic groups of equal order p and $ê : G \times G \rightarrow \mathbf{G_T}$ is a bilinear map is: Given a generator g of G and three elements $\mathbf{g^a, g^b, g^c} \in G$ for a,b,c random in $\mathbf{Z_p^*}$, compute $ê(\mathbf{g, g})^{abc}$. An algorithm A is said to solve the BDH problem with an advantage of ϵ if $P[A(\mathbf{g, g^a, g^b, g^c}) = ê(\mathbf{g, g})^{abc}] \geq \epsilon$

4   Proposed Scheme

Consider a group of users with multiple privileges under different service groups . A message broadcast to these users can be done with the proposed scheme, preserving their identities. The message is encrypted for each service group separately. Table 1 presents the notations used in the proposed scheme.

Table 1. Notations

$H_1: \{0, 1\}^* \rightarrow G$	Hash function
$SG_j; 1 \leq j \leq m$	j^{th} service group ; m denotes the number of service groups
$ID_{ij}; 1 \leq i \leq n_j$	i^{th} user of SG_j; n_j denotes the number of users in SG_j
$\{N_l; 1 \leq l \leq N\}$	Pool of relatively prime integers; N denotes the total number of users in all the service groups.

In this scheme, the Key Distribution Center (KDC) runs Setup with security parameter k as input and gives the ouput tuple, $<p, G, G_T, ê, P, H_1 >$. The users authenticate themselves with their ID's and the KDC runs **Extract** to get their corresponding secret keys $S_{ID_{ij}}$ and N_l for the congruence system. The cipher text C is generated from the message M by encrypting it for each service group SG_j. Then the key K_{ij} is computed for each ith user in the jth service group using bilinear pairing. The session key is XORed with K_{ij}, used in CRT to find the solution X and finally the KDC broadcasts the tuple (X, Y, U, C), where $U = E_{SK_j}(SK_j)$. After receiving the tuple (X, Y, U, C), user ID_{ij} computes the key K_{ij} using his secret key $S_{ID_{ij}}$ from the bilinear pairing and recovers R_i from X. By XORing R_i with K_{ij}, user ID_{ij} can recover SK_j. He then verifies if the decryption of U using SK_j is equal to SK_j or not. If they match, he proceeds for decryption of the cipher text C using SK_j to obtain the message M. If not, the receiver knows that this message was not sent to him and stops. The algorithms of the proposed scheme is below

Setup(k)

Construct a bilinear mapping ê: $G \times G \to G_T$ of prime order p, with$|p| = k$.

Select generator, $g \in G$ and $pr \in$ Zp*

Compute $P = g^{pr}$.

The master public, secret key(msk) pair is (P, pr).

Choose a hash function $H_1 : \{0,1\}^* \to G$

Construct a pool of relatively prime integers with N element for the system of congruences.

The public parameters are $< p, G, G_T, ê, P, H_1 >$

Extract(ID_{ij}, msk)

Compute the secret key of user ID_{ij} as $S_{ID_{ij}} = H_1(ID_{ij})^{pr}$

Give each user, an integer N_l from the pool of relatively prime integers, for use in the congruence equation.

Encrypt (M, {IDij })

Step 1: Select random $sk_j \in \mathbb{Z}_p^*$ and compute the session key $SK_j = e(g,g)^{sk_j}$ for jth service group, to encrypt M

Step 2: Computation of the key K_{ij}

Choose random y$\in \mathbb{Z}_p^*$ and compute $Y = g^y$.

Compute key K_{ij} for each user using the master public.

$$K_{ij} = e(H_1(ID_{ij}), P)^y = e(Q_{ij}, g^{pr})^y$$

K_{ij} is the key corresponding to the user with ID_{ij}.

Step 3: Use CRT algorithm to compute the common solution from the following system of congruence equations:

$X \equiv R_i \bmod N_l$ where, $R_i = SK_j \oplus K_{ij}$; $1 \le i \le n_j$.

Step 4: Compute U and encipher M with SK_j.

i.e., $U = E_{SK_j}(SK_j)$ and $C = E_{SK_j}(M)$

Step 5: Broadcast X, Y, U and C to the receivers.

Step 6: End.

Decrypt ($S_{ID_{ij}}$, Y, C, N_l)

Step 1: The receivers compute their respective key K_{ij}

Receivers know their secret key $S_{ID_{ij}}$ and has received Y

Computes K_{ij} as

$$K_{ij} = e(S_{ID_{ij}}, Y)$$

Step 2: Compute SK_j from X using the key K_{ij}.

i.e., compute $SK_j = K_{ij} \oplus (X \bmod N_l) = K_{ij} \oplus R_l$

Step 3: Verify if $decrypt(U, SK_j) = SK_j$; if so $then$ $step$ 4 $else$ $step$ 5

Step 4: Decipher the cipher text C with SK_j.

Step 5: End.

5   Proof of Correctness

The KDC computes the key K_{ij}, using the parameters Q_{ij}, random $y \in \mathbb{Z}_p^*$ and g^{pr}.

$$K_{ij} = e(H_1(ID_{ij}), P) = (Q_{ij}, P)^y = e(g^{h_1}, g^{pr})^y = e(g, g)^{y pr h_1} \qquad (1)$$

Upon receiving the message (X, Y, U, C), the receiver computes the key K_{ij} using the secret key $S_{ID_{ij}}$ and Y.

$$K_{ij} = e\left(S_{ID_{ij}}, Y\right) = e\left(Q_{ij}^{pr}, g^y\right) = e\left(g^{h_1 pr}, g^y\right) = e\left(g, g\right)^{y pr h_1} \tag{2}$$

From (1) and (2), the key K_{ij}, computed in both ways yield the same value. Thus the receiver recovers the key and decrypts the message. The proposed scheme has the following properties:

Revocation: The KDC can select the set of users for broadcasting a message, excluding few others by appropriately modeling the congruence system of equations. Including or deleting users can be done with ease, since, for every session, the KDC models the congruence system and computes the solution. Consider the case where, the users with identities ID_{12} and ID_{32} , leaves SG_2. The system of congruence in this case becomes $X \equiv R_i \bmod N_l$, where, $R_i = SK_2 \oplus K_{i2}$; $1 \leq i \leq n_2$ and $i \neq 1,3$.   Similarly when users ID_{42} and ID_{52} newly joins SG_2 which already has n_2 users, then the congruence system becomes $X \equiv R_i \bmod N_l$, where, $R_i = SK_2 \oplus K_{i2}$; $1 \leq i \leq n_2 + 2$.

Collusion Resistance: The KDC can select the set of users for whom the message has to be sent during that particular broadcast session. Even if the entire excluded users join together they cannot get the correct session key SK_j . The congruence system whose solution X is broadcasted, has not included equations for the excluded users, in which case they can just compute $K_{ij} = e\left(S_{ID_{ij}}, Y\right)$ and $X \bmod N_l$ will not yield the correct $SK_j \oplus K_{ij}$. Hence they cannot recover SK_j. Also a service group completely can be excluded from decrypting the broadcast in the same manner.

Stateless Broadcast: The KDC can broadcast to a selected set of receivers without a need for change in key for the revoked users. If the user belongs to the intended set of receivers, then he can decrypt the message and others cannot decrypt it. The individual user keys serve only partially for encryption and help for decryption. Hence revocation of users doesn't demand change in keys for the remaining users.

Dynamism: The KDC can include an extra equation in the congruence system upon a user join and recompute the solution. Consider the case where users ID_{42} and ID_{52} newly join SG_2 which already has n_2 users and already broadcasted the cipher text to the group. Then the congruence system becomes $X_{new} \equiv X_{old} \bmod lcm(N_l)$; $X_{new} \equiv R_i \bmod N_{l+n_2}$; $1 \leq i \leq n_2 + 2$, where, $R_i = SK_2 \oplus K_{i2}$; $1 \leq i \leq n_2 + 2$.

The new solution will satisfy the existing users and the newly joined users, in which case the existing users need not change their keys. Thus the proposed system provides dynamism for user join.

6   Analysis of the Proposed Scheme

6.1   Security Analysis

If the adversary $\mathcal{A}_{IBE\_BDH\_CRT}$ finds the value of N_l IBE_{BDH_CRT} gets reduced to IBE_{BDH} , which can be done only by brute force attack since $N_l's$ are a collection of pair-wise relatively prime integers. Once this is done then advantage of the adversary is given by $Adv_{A\_IND-CCA2\_IBE_{BDH}}$ and modeled using random oracle as below. Let ϵ be the probability of finding the correct N_l.

Theorem 1: For any IBE-BDH adversary $\mathcal{A}_{IBE_{BDH}}$, in the random oracle model, against CCA-2, with security parameter k which has advantage $Adv_{A\_IND-CCA2\_IBE_{BDH}}$, running in at most time T , making at most Q_{id} , Q_s and Q_d , hash queries, secret key queries and decryption queries respectively , there exists $\mathcal{B}_{BDH}, \mathcal{B}_{SE}$ against Bilinear Diffie Hellman problem and Symmetric key Encryption Scheme which run in at most time. Then the advantage of $\mathcal{A}_{IBE_{BDH}}$ is given by $Adv_{A\_IND-CCA2\_IBE_{BDH}} \leq (1 - \delta)^{Q_s} + \delta^{Q_d} + Adv_{\mathcal{B}\_BDH} + Adv_{\mathcal{B}\_SE}.$

Proof: Suppose H_1 is modeled as random oracle, the DH assumption holds and the symmetric cipher is secure against CCA, then the proposed scheme is secure against CCA. A reductionist argument is presented assuming that there exists a PPT adversary $\mathcal{A}_{IBE\_BDH}$ that has non-negligible advantage against IBE_{BDH}.

Given a CCA adversary $\mathcal{A}_{IBE\_BDH}$ against the IBE_{BDH} it can be used to build another algorithm $\mathcal{B}_{BDH}$ for solving the BDH problem. Let $\mathcal{B}$, be the challenger for $\mathcal{A}_{IBE\_BDH}$ who simulates the results to answer for queries from the adversary by maintaining the hash table H_1T

H_1 *Query* : Given a ID_{ij} query, $\mathcal{B}$ searches for that ID_{ij} in H_1T and ouputs the the corresponding Q_{ij}. Otherwise it selects a random $h_{ij} \in \mathbb{z}_p^*$, computes $Q_{ij} = H_1(ID_{ij}) = g^{h_{ij}}$, for marked cases and $Q_{ij} = H_1(ID_{ij}) = g^{rh_i}$, for unmarked cases, where ID_{ij}'s are marked with $\Pr(mark) = \delta$. Then it gives the result to the adversary and stores the tuple $(ID_{ij}, h_{ij}, H_1(ID_{ij}))$ in H_1T.

Extract Query:On input ID_{ij} , $\mathcal{B}$ checks H_1T if it is marked and then outputs corresponding secret key $S_{ID_{ij}} = P^{h_{ij}}$. Otherwise it aborts.

Decrypt Query: On an input (C, ID_{ij}, Hdr), $\mathcal{B}$ checks if that ID_{ij} is marked in H_1T and aborts. In case the ID_{ij} is from the challenge query, then $\mathcal{B}$ aborts irrespective of marking. Otherwise it uses the corresponding secret key of the user to decrypt the message.

Challenge Query: On an input (ID_{ij}, m_0, m_1), $\mathcal{B}$ randomly chooses $b \in \{0,1\}$ and encrypts the message m_b and returns X, Y, U and C. Challenge query should not include the messages or ID_{ij} that has been queried earlier.

Game 0: Let this be the original IBE chosen cipher text attack game. Challenger selects random $pr \in \mathbb{z}_p^*$, computes $P = g^{pr}$ and gives it to $\mathcal{A}_{IBE\_BDH}$. $\mathcal{A}_{IBE\_BDH}$ makes extract queries and decryption queries to the original system. Once the adversary decides the game is over, it gives the challenge query to , outputs b' and wins if $b' = b$. The advantage winning is $Adv_{A\_IND-CCA2\_IBE_{BDH}} = \left| P(b' = b \text{ in } G = G_0) - \frac{1}{2} \right|.$

Game 1: In this game $\mathcal{A}_{IBE\_BDH}$, in addition to the extract key queries and decryption queries to the original system, can make H_1 *Queries* to $\mathcal{B}$. $\mathcal{B}$ simulates H_1T to answer as given above. If $\mathcal{A}_{IBE\_BDH}$, decides the game is over, it gives the challenge query to $\mathcal{B}$ and then it outputs b' and wins the game if $b' = b$. This doesn't give any additional advantage and therefore, $P(b' = b \text{ in } G = G_1) = P(b' = b \text{ in } G = G_0)$

Game 2: The adversary is given an additional access to the simulated secret key query. The abortion of extract queries for unmarked cases makes the difference of this game from the previous one. Therefore, $|P(b' = b \text{ in } G = G_2) - P(b' = b \text{ in } G = G_1)| \leq (1 - \delta)^{Q_s}$

Game 3: An additional access of simulated decryption query is also given the adversary in this game. The abortion of decryption queries for marked cases makes the difference of this game from the previous one. Hence, $|P(b' = b \text{ in } G = G_3) - P(b' = b \text{ in } G = G_2)| \leq \delta^{Q_d}$

Finally in game 3, $\mathcal{A}_{IBE\_BDH}$ plays CCA2 game against symmetric key encryption scheme or solves the BDH problem and hence $|P(b' = b \text{ in } G = G_3) - 1/2| \leq Adv_{\mathcal{B}\_SE} + Adv_{\mathcal{B}\_BDH}$. Hence the total advantage of the adversary against t IBE_{BDH} is given by $Adv_{\mathcal{A}\_IND-CCA2\_IBE_{BDH}} \leq (1 - \delta)^{Q_s} + \delta^{Q_d} + Adv_{\mathcal{B}\_BDH} + Adv_{\mathcal{B}\_SE}$.

Therefore the advantage of the adversary against the proposed scheme is $Adv_{\mathcal{A}_{IND-CCA2}}{}_{IBE_{BDH_{CRT}}} \leq \epsilon\big((1 - \delta)^{Q_s} + \delta^{Q_d} + Adv_{\mathcal{B}_{BDH}} + Adv_{\mathcal{B}_{SE}}\big)$

6.2   Receiver Anonymity

Every user only knows if he is one of the exact receivers of the cipher text, but he cannot determine the other exact receivers of the cipher.

Theorem 2: The proposed IBBE scheme is $(T, Q_{id}, Q_s, Q_d, \varepsilon + \gamma) - \text{ANON} - \text{sID} - \text{CCA}$ secure under $(T', \varepsilon') - \text{BDH}$ assumption where $\varepsilon' \geq \varepsilon\gamma$ and $T' \approx T + (Q_{id} + Q_s + Q_d)T_1 + Q_d T_2$ where T_1, T_2 denote the computing time for an exponentiation and paring in G.

Proof: Assume an $\text{ANON} - \text{sID} - \text{CCA}$ PPT adversary, $\mathcal{A}$, against the proposed scheme has advantage $Adv_{\mathcal{A}\_ANON-sID-CCA\_IBE_{BDH\_CRT}} \geq \varepsilon\gamma$, where $Adv_{\mathcal{A}\_ANON-sID-CCA\_IBE_{BDH}} \geq \varepsilon$, γ be the probability of finding the correct N_l and running in time T. Then algorithm $\mathcal{B}$, can solve BDH problem with advantage $\varepsilon' \geq \varepsilon$ and running time $T' \approx T + (Q_{id} + Q_s + Q_d)T_1 + Q_d T_2$ using the adversary $\mathcal{A}$. $\mathcal{B}$ with input g^a, g^b, g^c can simulate the challenger of the proposed scheme against $\mathcal{A}$ as given below to find $\hat{e}(g, g)^{abc}$.

Phase 1: $\mathcal{A}$ outputs a target identity pair (ID_0, ID_1) to the challenger.

Setup : $\mathcal{B}$ chooses a random b from $\{0, 1\}$. It also selects random master secret key (msk) pr $\in Z_p^*$, computes the master public key $P = g^{pr}$ and gives the public parameters $< p, G, G_T, \hat{e}, P, H_1 >$ where H_1 is a random oracle controlled by $\mathcal{B}$ as given in theorem 1.

Phase 2: $\mathcal{A}$, runs extract query as given in theorem 1, upon receiving $ID_{ij}; i \notin \{0, 1\}$

Phase 3: $\mathcal{A}$ issues decryption queries from theorem 1 with $(C^*, ID_{ij}); i \in \{0,1\}$ as input.

Challenge : $\mathcal{A}$ outputs a target plain text M for which the challenger returns the target cipher text C for ID_{bj}.

Phase 4: $\mathcal{A}$ issues private key extraction queries and decryption queries, similar to Phase 2 and 3 for target identities where a restriction here is that $C^* \neq C$

Guess: $\mathcal{A}$ outputs b' $\in\{0, 1\}$. If b'=b then $\mathcal{B}$ outputs 1, otherwise 0. If $K_{ij} = \hat{e}(g, g)^{abc}$ then $SK_j = K_{ij} \oplus (X \bmod N_l) = K_{ij} \oplus R_l$

$$P[\mathcal{B}(g, g^a, g^b, g^c) = \hat{e}(g, g)^{abc}) = 1] = P[b' = b], \text{ where } \left| P(b' = b) - \frac{1}{2} \right| \geq \varepsilon\gamma$$

6.3   Performance Analysis

Table 1 gives the notations used for comparison. Table 2 gives the efficiency comparison among IBBE schemes. Table 3 shows the analysis results. For each operation, benchmark timing is included. Each cryptographic operation was implemented using the PBC library ver. 0.4.18 [19] on a 3.0 GHZ processor PC. The public key parameters were selected to provide 80-bit security level. The computational cost is analyzed in terms of the pairing, exponentiation operations in G and G_T. The comparatively negligible hash operations are ignored in the time result.

Table 2. Notations and terminologies

n	number of receivers in S
Sp	bit size of an element in $\mathbb{Z}_p^*$
S_1	bit size of an element in G
S_T	bit size of an element in G_T
S_{ID}	bit size of an identity of a user
S_{RI}	bit size of a relatively prime integer
S_{CRT}	bit size of an integer output from CRT

Table 3. Efficiency comparison among IBBE schemes

	Delerablee [3]	Ren et al. [22]	Hur et al. [11]	Proposed
Public key	$(n + 3)S_1 + S_T$	$7S_1 + Sp$	S_1	S_1
Secret key	Sp	Sp	$S_1 + Sp$	Sp
Storage	S_1	$(n + 2)S_1$	S_1	$S_1 + S_{RI}$
Communication	$2S1 + 3S_T + Sp + nS_{ID}$	$\leq (n + 2)S_1$	$2S_1 + nS_{ID}$	$S_1 + S_T + S_{CRT}$
Privacy	$(n + 3)S_1 + S_T$	$7S_1 + Sp$	S_1	S_1

Table 4. Comparison of computation cost

Operation	Time (ms)	Delerablee [3]		Ren et al. [22]		Hur et al.[11]		Proposed scheme	
		Sender	Receiver	Sender	Receiver	Sender	Receiver	Sender	Receiver
Pairing	2.9	-	2	3	3	n(pre-computations)	3	n(pre-computations)	1
Exp. in G	1.0	2n+2	2n-1	2n+1	n	$\leq n + 2$	1	1	-
Exp. in G_T	0.2	1	2	4	8	1		$\leq n + 1$	-
Computation(ms)		2n + 2.2	2n + 5.2	2n 10.5	+n + 10.3	$\leq n + 2.2$	9.7	$\leq 0.2n + 1.2$	2.9

7   Conclusion

In the current globalization via internet, many broadcast encryptions need protection of receiver privacy. An Identity based broadcast encryption scheme using Chinese Remainder Theorem and Bilinear Diffie-Hellman approach was presented. The proposed system was analyzed for security under random oracle model. It has been compared to be efficient than the existing ones. Using the proposed scheme the key distribution center sends the session keys in an encrypted form along with the cipher text, which overcomes the rekeying overhead, preserving forward and backward secrecy. The scheme also provides dynamism with reference to user join/leave, computation efficiency, collusion resistance and ease in user revocation.

References

1. Fiat, A., Naor, M.: Broadcast Encryption. In: Stinson, D.R. (ed.) CRYPTO 1993. LNCS, vol. 773, pp. 480–491. Springer, Heidelberg (1994)
2. Shamir, A.: Identity-Based Cryptosystems and Signature Schemes. In: Blakely, G.R., Chaum, D. (eds.) CRYPTO 1984. LNCS, vol. 196, pp. 47–53. Springer, Heidelberg (1985)
3. Delerablée, C.: Identity-Based Broadcast Encryption with Constant Size Ciphertexts and Private Keys. In: Kurosawa, K. (ed.) ASIACRYPT 2007. LNCS, vol. 4833, pp. 200–215. Springer, Heidelberg (2007)
4. Delerablée, C., Paillier, P., Pointcheval, D.: Fully Collusion Secure Dynamic Broadcast Encryption with Constant-Size Ciphertexts or Decryption Keys. In: Takagi, T., Okamoto, T., Okamoto, E., Okamoto, T. (eds.) Pairing 2007. LNCS, vol. 4575, pp. 39–59. Springer, Heidelberg (2007)
5. Fan, C., Huang, L., Ho, P.: Anonymous multi-receiver identity-based encryption. IEEE Transactions on Computers 59, 1239–1249 (2010)
6. Cocks, C.: An Identity Based Encryption Scheme Based on Quadratic Residues. In: Honary, B. (ed.) Cryptography and Coding 2001. LNCS, vol. 2260, pp. 360–363. Springer, Heidelberg (2001)
7. Boneh, D., Gentry, C., Waters, B.: Collusion Resistant Broadcast Encryption with Short Ciphertexts and Private Keys. In: Shoup, V. (ed.) CRYPTO 2005. LNCS, vol. 3621, pp. 258–275. Springer, Heidelberg (2005)
8. Boneh, D., Franklin, M.: Identity-Based Encryption from the Weil Pairing. In: Kilian, J. (ed.) CRYPTO 2001. LNCS, vol. 2139, pp. 213–229. Springer, Heidelberg (2001)
9. Fazio, N., Perera, I.M.: Outsider-anonymous broadcast encryption with sublinear ciphertexts. Cryptology ePrint Archive (2012)
10. Chiou, G.-H., Chen, W.-T.: Secure Broadcasting Using the Secure Lock. IEEE Transactions on Software Engineering 15(8), 929–934 (1989)
11. Hur, J., et al.: Privacy-preserving identity-based broadcast encryption. Informat. Fusion (2012), doi:10.1016/j.inffus.2011.03.003
12. Kaya, K., Selçuk, A.A.: Secret Sharing Extensions based on the Chinese Remainder Theorem. IACR Cryptology ePrint Archive (2010)
13. Libert, B., Paterson, K.G., Quaglia, E.A.: Anonymous broadcast encryption. Cryptology ePrint Archive, Report 2011/476 (2011)
14. Angamuthu, M., Ramalingam, A.: Balanced key tree management for multi-privileged groups using (N, T) policy. Security and Communication Networks 5(5), 545–555 (2012)

15. Muthulakshmi, A., Anitha, R., Sumathi, M.: Non-split balancing higher order tree for multi-privileged groups. WTOC 10(10), 308–321 (2011)
16. Wu, Q., Wang, W.: New Identity-based Broadcast Encryption with Constant Ciphertexts in the Standard Model. Journal of Software 6(10), 1929–1936 (2011)
17. Canetti, R., Halevi, S., Katz, J.: Chosen-Ciphertext Security from Identity-Based Encryption. In: Cachin, C., Camenisch, J. (eds.) EUROCRYPT 2004. LNCS, vol. 3027, pp. 207–222. Springer, Heidelberg (2004)
18. Sun, Y., Liu, K.J.: Hierarchical group access control for secure multicast communications. IEEE/ACM Transactions on Networking 15(6), 1514–1526 (2007)
19. The Pairing-Based Cryptography Library, http://crypto.stanford.edu/pbc/ (accessed March 10, 2010)
20. Wang, G., Ouyang, J., Chen, H., Guo, M.: Efficient group key management for multi-privileged groups. Computer Communications 30(11-12), 2497–2509 (2007)
21. Boyen, X., Waters, B.: Anonymous Hierarchical Identity-Based Encryption (Without Random Oracles). In: Dwork, C. (ed.) CRYPTO 2006. LNCS, vol. 4117, pp. 290–307. Springer, Heidelberg (2006)
22. Ren, Y., Gu, D.: Fully CCA2 secure identity-based broadcast encryption without random oracles. Information Processing Letters 109, 527–533 (2009)

A Virtualization-Level Future Internet Defense-in-Depth Architecture

Jerzy Konorski[1], Piotr Pacyna[2], Grzegorz Kolaczek[3],
Zbigniew Kotulski[4], Krzysztof Cabaj[4], and Pawel Szalachowski[4]

[1] Gdansk University of Technology, Poland
jekon@eti.pg.gda.pl
[2] AGH University of Technology, Poland
[3] Wroclaw University of Technology, Poland
[4] Warsaw University of Technology, Poland

Abstract. An EU Future Internet Engineering project currently underway in Poland defines three Parallel Internets (PIs). The emerging IIP System (IIPS, abbreviating the project's Polish name), has a four-level architecture, with Level 2 responsible for creation of virtual resources of the PIs. This paper proposes a three-tier security architecture to address Level 2 threats of alien traffic injection and IIPS traffic manipulation or forging. It is argued that the measures to be taken differ in nature from those ensuring classical security attributes. A combination of hard- and soft-security mechanisms produces node reputation and trust metrics, which permits to eliminate or ostracize misbehaving nodes. Experiments carried out in a small-scale IIPS testbed are briefly discussed.

Keywords: Future Internet, virtualization, security architecture, HMAC, anomaly detection, reputation system.

1 Introduction

The EU Future Internet (FI) Engineering project currently underway in Poland (named IIP, which abbreviates its Polish name) focuses on the idea of a physical communication substrate shared by three Parallel Internets (PI), each running a different protocol stack over a set of virtualized links and nodes [1]. This is in line with existing FI approaches, cf. [2], [3], [4] and Fig. 1a. Two post-IP PIs are named Data Stream Switching (DSS), and Content Aware Network (CAN), and one is IPv6 QoS oriented. A testbed embodiment of this idea, the *IIP System* (IIPS), is physically based on Ethernet links over which IIPS protocol data units (IIPS-PDUs) are transmitted. In each link, virtual links are created to connect virtual nodes adjacent in a PI topology, the task of separation of the PIs' traffic and performance being left to nodal schedulers. IIPS architecture consists of four Levels (Fig. 1b), where Level 1 is the physical infrastructure and Level 2 is responsible for creation of PI virtual links and nodes.

This paper addresses two IIPS Level 2 security concerns. First, an external intruder (*outsider*) might manipulate IIPS traffic or inject alien traffic into IIPS in order to disrupt IIPS functionality. Second, a virtual machine (VM) implementing a virtual IIPS node can be compromised by an internal intruder (*insider*) and so is not a trusted

S.M. Thampi et al. (Eds.): SNDS 2012, CCIS 335, pp. 283–292, 2012.

entity. In particular, it can forge IIPS traffic to instigate harmful actions or states at an IIPS node; an attack upon a single VM in a PI may also affect other PIs. To address these concerns, Level 2 security measures are proposed instead of classical perimeter protection or protocol- and application specific measures. In Section 2 we briefly comment on existing work on FI security. In Section 3 we characterize Level 2 security threats to IIPS and our defense approach. In Section 4 we outline the proposed Level 2 security architecture. We believe this novel approach transcends its project context and applies to any networking environment where multiple virtual protocol stacks are embedded in a common/public physical substrate. The envisaged cooperation of hard- and soft-security mechanisms including local anomaly detection (Section 5) and a reputation system (Section 6) permits to eliminate or ostracize distrusted IIPS nodes. We present these mechanisms with a view of their implementation. Experiments in a small-scale IIPS testbed are discussed in Section 7.

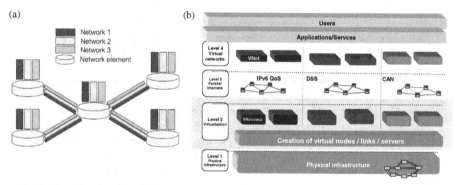

Fig. 1. Virtualization-based FI; a) virtual network infrastructure [3], b) IIPS architecture [1].

2   Current Work on FI Security

In many FI projects, trust and security appear jointly as an important building block. A common perception is the need for addressing trust and security concerns from a project's initial stages [5]. The FI X-ETP Group [6] lists security build-up at design time as a key challenge and presents a concept of a trust architecture. Emerging threats in the FI urge work on FI security before they materialize [7]. The 4WARD project [8] presents a concept of an information-centric architecture with security-aware object identifiers. In the follow-up SAIL project [9], content- rather than channel-oriented security services are developed as part of the NetInf architecture. Effectsplus, an FP7 funded Coordination & Support Action [10], analyses current trust and security work to identify key areas and players. References to trust and security-related pages with a work-in-progress are offered e.g., by EFII [11] and FIA [12], cf. also [13].

Network and resource virtualization is present in several FI projects ([8], [14], [15]). It is also the leading motive of IIPS. In a promising approach of the NetSE project [16], the contemporary Internet migrates towards the FI through the deployment of dedicated software modules called Cognitive Managers. Each of them is responsible for specific virtual resource abstractions and has an in-built Supervisor and Security Module that among others ensures selected security attributes.

3   Level 2 Security Threats and Defense Approach

A *threat* is a possibility of damage arising from a specific IIPS vulnerability, and an *attack* refers to an intruder's activity which exploits this vulnerability. Here we only address IIPS Level 2 security threats and attacks i.e., related to IIPS traffic over virtual links in a PI topology. *External* threats relate to generation of fake IIPS traffic or illegal modification of IIPS traffic outside IIPS. IIPS-PDUs are multiplexed over a common Ethernet infrastructure along with alien traffic, where outsider attacks via VLAN hopping, IIPS-PDU capture or corruption are relatively easy to launch. Their impact depends on the outsiders' capabilities, such as injecting alien PDUs, sensing, buffering and/or modification of IIPS-PDUs; however, with adequate PI perimeter protection, fake or modified IIPS traffic can often be recognized as such. *Internal* threats are posed by compromised VMs. An insider controlling the VM can spoof a virtual node, forge or modify IIPS-PDUs, and append correct security tags to get the traffic past perimeter protection. This may lead to more serious damage than an outsider can inflict, and not necessarily confined to a single PI. Straightforward attacks are traffic *injection, replay/resequencing, ruffling* (disruption of IIPS-PDU spacing via IIPS-PDU capture and hold-up) and *forging* (generation of fake though IIPS-formatted traffic). While the first three mainly induce "quantitative" harm at an IIPS node (e.g., extra processing effort or a perception of poor inter-PI performance isolation), traffic forging has a "qualitative" effect—it may disrupt the core functionality of, or create any undesirable state at an IIPS node.

Contemporary security measures are often *model-based*—they rely on a repository of misuse signatures corresponding to specific vulnerabilities and attacks. In IIPS, these vulnerabilities and defenses are higher-level protocol dependent, thus cannot be addressed by the proposed architecture. On the other hand, symptoms of Level 2 attacks are less specific and so harder to capture without an awareness of higher-level protocol semantics. Within a *policy-based* approach, which we take here, no attempt is made to predict possible attack vectors; instead, anomalous traffic or node behavior is defined and watched for (we especially relate this to IIPS-PDU contents, timing or sequence, as well as IIPS node state). The proposed security measures prevent an outsider from traffic injection or IIPS traffic modification, and reliably detect traffic replay/resequencing, ruffling and forging. Thus they differ substantially from classical measures ensuring data authentication, confidentiality, and non-repudiation.

4   Defense Tiers

The proposed defense-in-depth architecture features three tiers (Fig. 2). It is primarily meant as an integration platform for various state-of-the-art security mechanisms within each tier, enabling easy replacement by more effective ones when they arise.

1st Tier. To block entry of injected, replayed or resequenced traffic, integrity and authentication are assured over a virtual link by appending a hash-based message authentication code (HMAC) [17] to all IIPS-PDUs. Each pair of neighboring virtual nodes share an HMAC key and a IIPS-PDU counter. Both the IIPS-PDU contents (including relevant IIPS headers) and its sequence number are protected, thus any received physical (Level 1) frame can be verified as alien traffic or an in-/out-of-sequence IIPS-PDU. In the former case the frame is dropped and its relevant fields are passed to the 2nd and 3rd tier for further inspection. HMAC constitutes a uniform 1st-tier security measure for the whole IIPS irrespective of the IIPS-PDU format or PI affiliation. Unlike e.g., IPSec or TLS, it is not tied to any protocol stack. To fully utilize the virtual link, both HMAC and IIPS-PDU drop modules are implemented in a four-port netFPGA board [18], with HMAC-SHA-512 message digest employed.

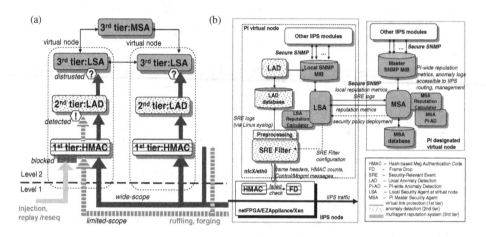

Fig. 2. IIPS Level 2 security architecture; (a) defense tiers (thick arrows visualize attack origin and impact), (b) placement of security modules.

2nd Tier. Ruffling or forging attacks cannot be stopped by HMAC, yet anomalous behavior they cause can be detected as *security-relevant events* (SREs) defined by an SRE Filter e.g., HMAC ordered IIPS-PDU drops, illegal control or management messages, suspicious traffic statistics, abnormal resource usage etc. SREs are stored in a local anomaly detection (LAD) database and subjected to analysis by a LAD module implemented within a virtual node's VM code. Two complementary algorithms are used: times series analysis [19] to detect suspicious traffic and resource usage, and data mining via frequent sets [20] to detect specific patterns in suspicious IIPS-PDUs. Anomalies indicative of attacks are reported to the 3rd tier.

3rd Tier. At a compromised virtual node, LAD cannot be trusted for proper detection and honest reporting of local anomalies. Moreover, certain wide-scope attacks would be missed if local-scope SRE and anomaly logs were only analyzed. This calls for inter-node cooperation. A Local Security Agent (LSA) at an IIPS virtual node translates the detected anomalies into local reputation metrics to derive the current level of trust that node deserves. LSA reports these metrics, along with the SRE logs, to the PI's Master Security Agent (MSA) via a PI-wide multi-agent reputation system using SNMPv3, a cryptographically protected version of the Simple Network Management Protocol. MSA uses a data fusion algorithm to calculate PI-wide reputation and trust metrics of the virtual nodes and its PI-wide anomaly detection (PI-AD) module captures anomalies of a larger scope. Results are made accessible to other IIPS modules, such as routing or management, via an SNMP database. They are also fed back to the nodal LSAs, which can then suitably redefine SRE Filters.

5   Local Anomaly Detection

Suspicious traffic able to penetrate the 1st tier can be detected by LAD through checking the semantics of received traffic against the security policy, or through observation of temporal traffic and virtual node behavior. The former uses data mining methods and is suitable against forging attacks targeting specific management and higher-level functionalities; the latter uses time series analysis and protects against ruffling attacks and all-purpose forging attacks such as malicious redirecting of IIPS traffic between the PIs.

Data Mining. Target specific forging attacks e.g., scanning, DoS or malware/spam outbreaks, produce repetitive patterns in observed sequences of SREs. The allowed sources of SREs are local firewall or HMAC ordered IIPS-PDU drop data and errors reported by the local SNMP agent e.g., unauthorized resource access attempts.

An SRE is represented as a set of relevant SRE features e.g., offending IPv6 address, used protocol or port identifiers. An SRE related to a reported SNMP error can have the form (sourceIPv6 = 2001:db8:201::3, user name = management, SNMP action = denied, OID = 1.3, …), where OID is the SNMP database object identifier. SRE logs are analyzed in successive *time windows* in search of *frequent sets* [20] i.e., subsets of features found abnormally frequent, as dictated by the *minimal support* parameter. E.g., a time window of 10 s and the minimal support of 4 mean that any pattern of features repeated at least four times over 10 s raises an anomaly alarm. If a discovered frequent set contains, say, a source address then a report sent to LSA via a secure SNMP message indicates the culprit node. E.g., the *nmap scanning* attack, used to discover services running on a victim machine, can manifest itself as a frequent set {type = security policy violation, sourceIPv6 = 2001:db8:201::3, destination IPv6 = 2001:db8:201::3, packet length = 1080, used protocol = TCP}. The lack of features related to source and destination ports indicates that in the current time window they have taken diverse values, as expected in a scanning attack. An anomaly has two attributes on a scale from 0 to 1: *severity*, a measure of the anomaly's adverse impact, and *probability*, a measure of conviction that the anomaly indeed indicates a security threat. (Note that the term "probability" is used here in its axiomatic sense.) For preliminary experiments described in Section 7, arbitrary severity and probability values reflect typical threat occurrences e.g., 0.05 and 0.5 for low-impact anomalies, 0.3 and 0.7 for probable software configuration errors, and 1 and 1 for (D)DoS attacks. Future research is expected to fine-tune such assignments.

Time Series Analysis. LAD also checks for anomalies in an IIPS node's behavior regarding memory and CPU usage, per-PI received and transmitted traffic volume etc. Abnormally high CPU usage or received traffic volume are typical of DoS (in particular, traffic injection) or all-purpose forging attacks, whereas traffic ruffling creates abnormal statistics of traffic bursts. First, relevant behavioral features are selected. Next, historical (training) selected feature values are compared with the current ones to learn how indicative the latter are of possible anomalies. Upon iterating the above steps, anomalies are indicated by discrepancies between the statistics of the current feature values and those derived from training data.

The anomaly detection algorithm takes as input the time series of feature values in successive time windows, denoted $x_1,..., x_l,...$ Following [19], the severity of an anomaly accompanying the observation of x_l is calculated as

$$c_l = \min\{1, \sqrt{[|x_l - x_{P,l}|/(3\sigma_{P,l})]^2 + [|x_l - x_{T,P,l}|/(3\sigma_{T,P,l})]^2}\}, \tag{1}$$

where $x_{P,l}$ and $\sigma_{P,l}$ ($x_{T,P,l}$ and $\sigma_{T,P,l}$) are, respectively, the current exponential moving average and standard deviation of the time subseries consisting of arithmetic averages $\sum_{k=0}^{P-1} x_{l-k} / P$ ($\sum_{k=0}^{T-1} x_{l-kP} / T$), P and T being predefined integers. Note that for a current feature value close to both averages the severity is close to 0, whereas deviations treble the corresponding standard deviations indicate a maximum severity. The anomaly probability is the proportion of observations yielding distinctly positive severities. (Note that this time the term "probability" is used in its empirical sense.)

As an illustration, artificially generated received traffic of 5000-byte IIPS-PDUs, with Pareto distributed of interarrival times with mean 15 ms and standard deviation 75 ms, is regarded as typical and produces zero-severity observations. After 20 LAD time windows, an extra stream of 500-byte IIPS-PDUs with normally distributed interarrival times with mean 20 ms and standard deviation 5 ms is superimposed. As a result, the severity and probability values increase (Fig. 3). If the change of the traffic pattern is permanent, LAD eventually learns it and returns to zero severities, as is the case in Fig. 3. Were the extra traffic to vanish after another 30 LAD time windows, modeling a short-term ruffling attack, the period of nonzero severity and probability values would roughly double in length.

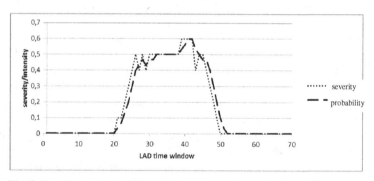

Fig. 3. Severity and probability values during a change in the traffic pattern

6   Proposed Reputation System

The proposed PI-wide multi-agent reputation system has LSAs communicate with MSA in successive *reporting intervals*. Local trust metrics derived by LSAs are reported to MSA, which converts them into global (PI-wide) trust and reputation metrics. These are accessed by other IIPS modules e.g., routing or management, and used to identify and/or ostracize ill-reputed nodes. They are also fed back to LSAs to modify local SRE Filters i.e., update the security policy, and to enable LSAs to act as backup MSA in case the original MSA itself is disrupted by an attack.

In the nth reporting interval, LSA at node i records the severity and probability values, $c_l \in [0, 1]$ and $p_l \in [0, 1]$, of anomalies detected by LAD as caused by node j. The involved *risk* values are taken to be $r_l = c_l p_l$. Then local trust placed in node j is calculated as $T_n^{i,j} = \alpha^h(1 - r_{max})$, where $r_{max} = \max_l c_l p_l$, $h = |\{l \mid r_{max}/2 \le r_l < r_{max}\}|$ is the number of other high-risk anomalies, and $\alpha \in [0, 1]$ is selected experimentally. Thus threats arising from both a single maximum-risk attack and repeated high-risk ones are accounted for. Having collected the $T_n^{i,j}$ from LSAs, MSA calculates the global trust placed in node j as a combination of local trust metrics from other nodes, weighted by their respective reputation metrics

$$T_n^j = \sum_i T_n^{i,j} R_n^i / \sum_i R_n^i , \qquad (2)$$

where $R_n^i \in [0, 1]$ is the current reputation metric of virtual node i (initially set to 1). MSA then calculates new reputation metrics for the $(n + 1)^{th}$ reporting interval:

$$R_{n+1}^i = \begin{cases} T_n^i, & \text{if } T_n^i \le R_n^i, \\ (1 - \beta)R_n^i + \beta T_n^i, & \text{otherwise,} \end{cases} \qquad (3)$$

where $\beta \in [0, 1]$. Note the conservative approach—reputation decreases immediately as dictated by diminished trust, but increases somewhat more reluctantly.

7   Preliminary Test Results

Since HMAC protects against injected traffic, we present sample proof-of-concept tests of the 2nd- and 3rd-tier security modules i.e., foiling forging and ruffling attacks. A small-scale PI testbed is shown in Fig. 4. Three IIPS virtual nodes named Node1, Node2 and Node3 host LSAs; a fourth one hosts MSA. They are controlled by a Xen virtualization engine [21] and communicate over IPv6 using SNMPv3.

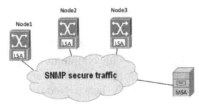

Fig. 4. IIPS testbed emulating a small-scale PI

In the experiments, the focus was on the cooperation of the security mechanisms rather than on the feasibility of specific attacks. Therefore, SREs were only derived from ip6table firewall logs, which were checked for symptoms of forging attacks, and from HMAC data and received traffic volume, which were checked for symptoms of injection and ruffling attacks. In the former case, severity and probability values were adjusted to produce adequate response to the attacks, whereas in the latter, they were calculated based according to Section 5. The reporting interval was 15 s.

In the first scenario (Fig. 5), Node2 starts attacking Node3 at time T_0. LAD at Node3 classifies this as an attack with probability 0.8 and severity 0.9. LSA at Node3 then reports to MSA the trust metric of Node2. As a result, Node2's global trust metric decreases instantly to 55% of the maximum, and remains so until time T_1, when Node2 also attacks Node1. This is detected by LAD at Node1 and causes Node2's global trust metric to drop to about 10%. Since Node2 keeps attacking, its trust metric remains low. Meanwhile, Node1 starts a short-term attack. At time T_2, the now distrusted Node2 reports to MSA an attack from Node1, but this report has minimal influence upon Node1's trust metric. However, when both Node2 and Node3 report an attack from Node1 at time T_3, Node1's trust metric decreases rapidly. This is because Node3's trust (hence, also reputation) metric remains at the maximum and MSA now weights reports about Node1's attacks much higher. When Node1's short-term attack is over, its trust and reputation metrics start increasing.

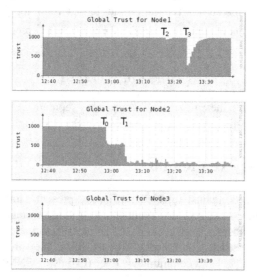

Fig. 5. Global trust for Node1..3 vs. time under Node1 and Node 2's attacks

In Fig. 6a, between times T_0 and T_1, Node1 floods Node3 with IIPS-PDUs performing an nmap scanning attack (with symptoms similar to a DoS attack). LAD at Node3 correctly classifies this as an attack with severity 1 and probability 1. MSA receives repeated reports from Node3, hence Node1's reputation metric decreases instantly to about 62%.

In Fig. 6b, Node1 performs a *sophisticated* scanning attack: after each connection termination it pauses for 1000 ms by executing `nmap -6 --scan-delay 1000 Node3`. LAD at Node3 reports the attack severity 0.1 and probability 0.05. MSA again receives repeated reports, so Node1's reputation and trust metrics decrease, throughout the attack averaging 64% and ranging from 62% to (momentarily) 92%.

In Fig. 6c, Node1 tries a pause duration of 1500 ms (a *moderate* scanning attack). LAD at Node3 detects an attack of severity 0.1 and probability 0.5. The global trust metrics throughout the attack average 71% and range from 65% to 93%, behaving steadily most of the time. (A *lazy* scanning attack with pause durations of 3000 ms does not change the chart visibly; in this case, Node1's global trust metric average rises to 85%, reflecting the limited impact of the attack.)

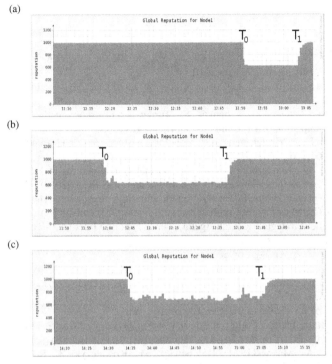

Fig. 6. Global trust for Node1 vs. time under scanning; (a) ordinary, (b) sophisticated, (c) moderate

8   Conclusion

We have proposed a low-level security architecture for a Future Internet system called IIPS, where several Parallel Internets share a common physical transmission infrastructure via link and node virtualization. Security threats have been pointed out that arise from physical link sharing by IIPS and non-IIPS users, as well as from traffic possibly originated at compromised virtual nodes. This calls for security measures different in nature from those addressed by classical security attributes such as data confidentiality, authentication or non-repudiation. A case has been made for a three-tier security architecture featuring HMAC, anomaly detection, and virtual node reputation and trust evaluation mechanisms. Sample test results, obtained from a small-scale Parallel Internet with a repertoire of nodal misbehavior, have been discussed and demonstrated to create adequate response to Level 2 security threats. Future work will focus on fine-tuning of the key LAD and MSA parameters and testing the proposed architecture against a broader scope of low-level attacks.

Acknowledgments. Work supported in part by the European Regional Development Fund Grant POIG.01.01.02-00-045/09-00 Future Internet Engineering. The work of J. Konorski is supported in part by the Air Force Office of Scientific Research, Air Force Material Command, USAF, under Grant FA 8655-11-1-3076.

References

1. Burakowski, W., Tarasiuk, H., Beben, A.: System IIP for supporting "Parallel Internets (Networks)". FIA meeting, Ghent 2010,
   `http://fi-ghent.fiweek.eu/files/2010/12/1535-4-System-IIP-FIA-Ghent-ver1.pdf`
2. Anderson, T., Peterson, L., Shenker, S., Turner, J.: Overcoming the Internet impasse through virtualization. IEEE Computer 38(4), 34–41 (2005)
3. Fernandes, N.C.: Virtual networks: isolation, performance, and trends. Annales des Telecomm. 66(5-6), 339–355 (2011)
4. Campanella, M., Maglaris, V., Potts, M.: Virtual Infrastructures in Future Internet. In: Tselentis, G., et al. (eds.) Towards the Future Internet. IOS Press (2010)
5. Gavras, A., et al.: Future Internet Research and Experimentation: The FIRE Initiative. ACM SIGCOMM Computer Communication Review 37(3) (July 2007)
6. Future Internet-Strategic Research Agenda, ver. 1.1, Future Internet X-ETP Group (2010)
7. `http://www.syssec-project.eu/`
8. `http://www.4ward-project.eu`
9. `http://www.sail-project.eu/wp-content/uploads/2011/08/SAIL_DB1_v1_0_final-Public.pdf`
10. `http://www.effectsplus.eu`
11. `http://initiative.future-internet.eu`
12. European Future Internet Portal, `http://www.future-internet.eu`
13. `http://fipedia.org/fipedia/index.php?title=Category:Security`
14. Flizikowski, A., Majewski, M., Hołubowicz, M., Kowalczyk, Z., Romano, S.P.: The INTERSECTION Framework: Applied Security for Heterogeneous Networks. J. of Telecomm. and Information Technology (January 2011)
15. New Generation Network Architecture: AKARI Conceptual Design, `http://akari-project.nict.go.jp/eng/index2.html`
16. Castrucci, M., Delli Priscoli, F., Pietrabissa, A., Suraci, V.: A Cognitive Future Internet Architecture. In: Domingue, J., Galis, A., Gavras, A., Zahariadis, T., Lambert, D., Cleary, F., Daras, P., Krco, S., Müller, H., Li, M.-S., Schaffers, H., Lotz, V., Alvarez, F., Stiller, B., Karnouskos, S., Avessta, S., Nilsson, M. (eds.) Future Internet Assembly. LNCS, vol. 6656, pp. 91–102. Springer, Heidelberg (2011)
17. Kelly, S., Frankel, S.: Using HMAC-SHA-256, HMAC-SHA-384, and HMAC-SHA-512 with IPsec. Proposed standard (with errata), Internet Engineering Task Force (May 2007)
18. `http://www.netfpga.org/`
19. Burgess, M.: Two Dimensional Time-Series for Anomaly Detection and Regulation in Adaptive Systems. In: Feridun, M., Kropf, P.G., Babin, G. (eds.) DSOM 2002. LNCS, vol. 2506, pp. 169–180. Springer, Heidelberg (2002)
20. Agrawal, R., Srikant, R.: Fast algorithm for mining association rules. In: Bocca, J.B., Jarke, M., Zaniolo, C. (eds.) Proc. 20th Int. Conf. on Very Large Databases, pp. 487–499 (1994)
21. Egi, N., et al.: Evaluating Xen for router virtualization. In: Proc. Int. Conf. on Computer Communications and Networks, ICCCN 2007, pp. 1256–1261 (August 2007)

Experimental DRM Model Using Mobile Code and White-Box Encryption

Stefan-Vladimir Ghita, Victor-Valeriu Patriciu, and Ion Bica

Computer Science Department, Military Technical Academy
Bucharest, 050141, Romania
st.ghita@gmail.com

Abstract. Due to severe DRM failures and the urgent demand for a better solution to solve the existing DRM systems vulnerabilities, this paper discusses the current DRM status, stressing system security objectives and requirements. Based on the analysis of the developed DRM solutions and emerging state of the art DRM technologies, this paper attempts to account for the causes of DRM failures and proposes a novel DRM security paradigm. We present an experimental DRM architectural rework aiming to cope with the existing limitations and weaknesses by using novel technological breakthroughs.

Keywords: DRM architecture, mobile agent, white-box-encryption.

1   Introduction

Given the necessity of developing the content delivery business over the Internet, great efforts have been made to create a better secure environment to employ DRM. In spite of that important leading companies in the industry have given up investing in such technologies demanding for better secured solutions. In this paper we presents the main reasons of DRM weaknesses and propose a novel security paradigm for the DRM ecosystem.

The paper consists of six parts. The introduction makes a presentation of DRM systems, followed by the motivation for our work. The third part describes briefly the important novel technological breakthroughs in the DRM area. The fourth part is a proposal of system redesigning based on the previously presented new tendencies and considerations explained in the motivation section. In the fifth part we submit our experimental simulation in which we assay our proposed model. The paper ends with a consistent part of conclusions.

In a former article [1] we determined and proposed a common base architecture for DRM. From a generic perspective, any DRM ecosystem consists mainly of four major actors: the Content Provider (CP) representing the creator and legal owner of the content, the Distribution System (DS) which promotes and sells digitalized content, the Licensing Service (LS) which is responsible for delivering user rights and the Client (C) that pays user fees and consumes the product.

In addition to the existing standards and drafts [2], [3], [4], many important published proposals [5], [6] use Public Key Infrastructure (PKI) for implementing the mechanisms required for an effective protection of DRM functionalities.

S.M. Thampi et al. (Eds.): SNDS 2012, CCIS 335, pp. 293–303, 2012.

Notations	
K	symmetric secret key
IDc	Content identifier
K_A^{Pu}	public key of A
K_A^{Pr}	private key of A
CERT_A	digital certificate of A
K(M)	encryption of message M using key K (symmetric or asymmetric depending of the K type)
M1 ‖ M2	messages concatenation
URE	User Rights Expression
VER(CERT_A)	certificate validation
A-> B:M	message M is sent from A to B
A:	action taken by A

According to these standards and published proposals, the functional scenarios in a DRM enabled system generally operate as follows:

1. CP creates and packages the content using authoring applications and tools that incorporate DRM technologies such as watermarking and encryption.

2. At this phase, illustrated in Figure 1, CP generates content and content protection metadata, such as presentation information or cryptographic keys, and supplies them to LS in order to be used in the licensing operations. Also, after finalizing content preparation, CP provides it to DS in order to be published and made available for distribution.

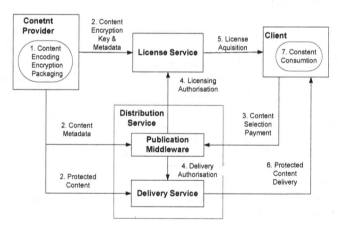

Fig. 1. DRM - functional architecture

3. According to [2], after selecting his desired content, C sends a signed content request (1).

$$C \rightarrow DS: \; CERT\_C \parallel K_C^{Pr}(IDc) \qquad (1)$$

4. Following client authentication and payment, *DS* notifies both *LS* and the delivery service (2), authorizing content delivery and licensing.

$$DS\text{-} > LS : CERT \_ DS \parallel CERT \_ C \parallel K_{LS}^{Pu}(K_D^{Pr}(IDc)) \tag{2}$$

5. Licensing: after certificates validation for *DS* and *C* (3) and licensing request signature verification (4), *LS* issues the license for *C* (5). The license object contains user rights expression and all the necessary cryptographic information for content consumption.

In order not only to remain confidential and integral, but also to provide non-repudiation, the license object needs to be first encrypted with licensing authority private key and secondly with client public key (6).

$$LS: \ VER(CERT\_DS), \ VER(CERT\_C) \tag{3}$$

$$LS: IDc = K_{DS}^{Pu}(K_{DS}^{Pr}(IDc)) \tag{4}$$

$$L = URE \ \parallel K_S^{IDm} \tag{5}$$

$$LS \text{-} > C: \ K_C^{Pu}(K_{LS}^{Pr}(L)) \tag{6}$$

User Rights Expressions (URE), commonly expressed using two industry standards [7] and [8], determine allowed/denied user actions.

6. After acquiring the license from LS, C can pursue with the license interpretation, validation and utilization (7). Content consumption can be achieved only after C validates L (meaning LS signature verification) and decrypts K_S^{IDm} .

$$C: L' = K_C^{Pr}(L*) = K_C^{Pr}(K_C^{Pu}(L*)) = L* = K_{LS}^{Pr}(L)$$
$$L = K_{LS}^{Pu}(L') = K_{LS}^{Pu}(K_{LS}^{Pr}(L)) \tag{7}$$

where L* = received license, L'= decrypted license

Because some previously described messages between DRM actors are signed using PKI, these signatures can be useful for providing non-repudiation of these operations.

7. Finally, after both license and protected content are obtained, content consumption can be accomplished.

From the security perspective this phase is by far the most critical one. Special measures are needed on the client platform while content is being decrypted and rendered. In this standard approach client security leaks can compromise all protection measures that have already been applied.

2   Motivation

One major disadvantage of standard DRM approach is it's PKI centric nature: every DRM interaction must be backed by a PKI operation in order to successfully complete the DRM system flow. From the service perspective this is a mandatory feature in order to deliver service trust, but from the user side it is almost impossible to realize from a practical point of view.

DRM enforcement commonly invokes use of a sealed box client; outside this box the security of any clear content is impossible to guarantee [12]. No matter what cryptographic protection mechanisms are applied, if content decryption artifacts (keys, algorithms) can be extracted and reused to clear ciphered content, the protection efforts is useless.

Starting from this paradigm, it is trivial to conclude that in fully open software environments the goal of DRM is impossible to achieve. This context led to the conclusion of DRM futility if the sealed box condition is not satisfied and some important companies involved in multimedia industry gave up engaging DRM technology. In our opinion the security problems of DRM need a proper reconsideration. In comparison with physical locks, DRM technologies are necessary to prevent intellectual property from being stolen and, also like physical locks, digital locks are important because they provide a clear border definition between what is permitted and what is not. Also, DRM has been proven to be very useful for building business required features, like parental controls for IPTV applications or time/features limited trials to let legitimate users try software products before buying them.

Based on such arguments, the present paper proposes a change in evaluation of DRM security requirements and objectives and proposes an innovative DRM rework which aims to cope with legacy DRM issues by taking advantage of available cutting edge technologies.

3   Cutting Edge DRM Research

Many significant efforts have been made to counter previously presented DRM weaknesses. Hereinafter, we provide only a brief introduction of those efforts we consider valuable for this topic.

3.1   White-Box Encryption

As we previously explained, one major security issue concerns sensitive information (secret, private or confidential) in untrusted software environments. Current cryptographic chippers, like RSA, AES, etc were not designed to protect the secret against execution environment. In fact, in the standard cryptography the endpoints are considered trusted and provide methods for comunications security.

To deal with this challenge, a newer cryptographic technology called White-Box Encryption (WBE) has emerged. The underlying principle of WBE shows that instead of having the secrets as inputs for algorithms they are merged together into an algorithm containing itself the secret. The idea of WBE is to generate customized symmetric cryptographic software for each encryption/decryption operation.

Unfortunatly, published adjustments of AES [9] and DES [10] to achieve WBE have proved that current cipher constructions have fundamental weaknesses in white box implementation [11] and furher design efforts are needed.

3.2   Mobile Agents and DRM

To solve the limitation and weaknesses presented in the previous paragraph, [14] suggests a mobile agent and time limited black-box [15] approach for designing the DRM architecture. In [14] the DRM agent is created together with the content in mobile agent technology and migrates to the client platform to grant usage rights and enforce DRM functions.

We consider that introduction of mobile agents within the DRM architecture is a driving initiative especially because it's flexibility benefits. In other words, mobile agents can be extremely useful when solution wants to keep it's obscurity on the implementation.

Sadly, paper [14] only provide some general messaging protocol between content provider, licensing system and mobile agents deployed for rights management and neither further architectural design nor technological background.

4   Proposed Model

Our proposal is based on the following architectural key features:

1. *Clients no* longer *need PKI certification*, but only a compliant environment.

2. *Impossibility of cryptographic keys recovery* inside the client environment: keep content decryption as obscure as possible inside the client host.

3. *On-line stream based content consumption*: due to the fact that multimedia is commonly consumed using Internet connected devices, we considerer that on-line connectivity is a benefic feature for security model design.

4. *Mobile-Agent based DRM client*: the client DRM component will be assembled only at runtime through mobile code technologies. It will move autonomously between the system entities (DS, C and LS), having its sensitive elements (like decryption bytecode) injected as described in the following paragraphs.

Starting from the above principles, we designed our system with mobile code capabilities. Before beginning any DRM transaction, the client agent implementation should be provided by the CP. This initial state of the agent contains no sensitive modules and only usual code to fulfill the itinerary and validation of the client platform. After initialization, the agent will move from DS to C upon content request and between C and LS in the means of licensing operations. At the end of this journey the DRM client will have all DRM artifacts (decryption bytecode and user rights) injected into its structure. After finishing content consumption the DRM agent will destroy all the critical components from client machine and leave the execution state.

Notations	
*	all notation introduced by previous paragraphs
A	mobile DRM agent
AID	identification of the client Agent
ML	mobile license (the mobile code which will give user access to the content)
Cont/pCont	clear Content/protected Content
H	cryptographic hash function

As shown in Figure 2, our proposal comprises the following DRM workflow:

1. *Content encryption, DRM agent implementation and user rights definition.* To take advantage of previously introduced technologies we engage WBE as a method of content protection. On this DRM start-up phase CP will produce the encryption/decryption bytecodes used for content protection and also the license for content consumption.

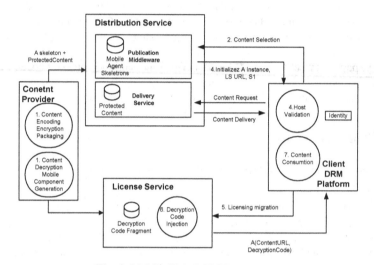

Fig. 2. Mobile Code DRM Ecosystem

Generated DRM agent is delivered to *DS* to be later initialized and it migrates according to the currently presented protocol. Also, after protecting *Cont*, *pCont* is made available to *DS* together with the corresponding license identification information (1).

$$CP\text{->}DS: pCont, A, hl=H(ML) \qquad (8)$$

At this phase content decryption compiled fragment *ML* is provided to *LS* along with the agent identification *H(A)* (2). The decryption bytecode will be used later by *LS* to be injected into the DRM agent on client licensing process.

$$CP\text{->}LS: ML, ha=H(A) \qquad (9)$$

2. *When C selects his desired content, C generates a content request to DS.*
In order to protect clients from fake *DS*, service authentication is involved requiring DS to be PKI certified.

$$C: VER(CERT\_DS) \qquad (10)$$

3. *Based on C request, DS instantiates A and sets the itinerary for A.* At this moment *A* has knowledge of his *AID*, *LS* address, and the signature of *DS* for *LS* (4), used by *LS* both to authenticate *DS* and also to identify the license to be issued for *C*. This information can be useful also for DRM transaction accountability.

$$S1 = K_{LS}^{Pub}(K_{DS}^{Pr}(AID \| hl)) \tag{11}$$

4. *Client host validation.* At agent's first arrival on the client DRM platform it performs a security evaluation of the container, such as suggested in [15] and then migrates to *LS* for carrying out the licensing operation. In case of validation failure various security measures can be imagined such as immediate leave or *DS* alert of possible fraud.

5. *License Request.* Because license acquisition is a sensitive operation, it is mandatory for *LS* to have a PKI certificate so that the operation can support secure service trust delivery.

6. After finalizing agent validation based on *ha* received in protocol setup phase (1) and licensing process (usually a commercial operation), *LS* installs/injects *ML* to *A* which receives with this all the artifacts needed for content consumption. After that, *A* can migrate back to the client in order to complete license acquisition journey. Additionally to *ML*, a license signature (5) is also delivered to *A* in order to serve *DS* for content delivery authorization.

$$S2 = K_{DS}^{Pub}(K_{LS}^{Pr}(AID \| hl)) \tag{12}$$

7. After all the pieces needed for content consumption are obtained and *A* has returned to the client host environment, the client DRM agent requests access to the protected content from *DS* while delivering *S2* in order to prove therewith successful licensing. When content consumption completes, before leaving the execution, the DRM agent destroys both *ML* and all other sensitive and private information.

5   Experimental Simulation

5.1   Implementation

In our experiment we have used JADE framework [13] and Java programming for implementing both server side components (DS, LS) and the DRM agent (as shown in Figure 3). The diagram below illustrates the class hierarchy tree and the most important classes used from the JADE framework.

In this experiment LS and DS components were implemented as JADE agents acting as described in the above protocol based on message reception triggers.

For the ease of the experiment we used the JADE messaging API for both message exchanges but also for passing the license objects to be injected to the DRM client agent. When `mobileDRMAgent` is instantiated by the `DistributionService` agent it will wait for `jade.core.ACLMessage` that contains information about LS location to be stored and used in the itinerary. After the agent arrives on the LS container it will send `ACLMessage` to the `LicenseService` agent setting in the content of this message his instance of `jade.core.AID` to be used for agent identification.

After a simulated authentication and authorization of the licensing request, the `LicenseService` agent will respond with a `MobileLicense` object to be used by `mobileDRMAgent`. Following the proposed protocol, this object is stored and the client agent is able to migrate back to the client platform.

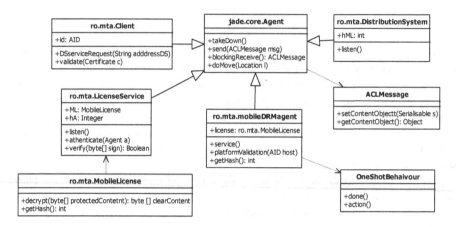

Fig. 3. Proposed DRM system class diagram

Having the license installed, the `mobileDRMAgent` can make the final request to the `DistributionService` for content delivery. Upon service request reception the `DistributionService` will validate the request and deliver the protected content.

Given the fact that WBE is in its early days and no open implementation is available in Java language, we simulated WBE behavior by using a `Serializable` AES wrapper which initializes the chipper on the `readObject` taking the secret from a `Serializable` private attribute.

5.2   Analysis

The aim our experiment was not only to prove the feasibility of our concept but also to create an environment were vulnerabilities can be analyzed. By carefully examining our protocol it is obvious that the most critical part (in terms of content security) happens in the last two steps of the protocol where the DRM agent has the license object installed and migrates back to the client environment.

In addition to the present proposal a important question steel needs to be addressed: what stops clients from cloning/dumping the mobile DRM agent for later illegal usage. The answer to this question can be given based on the fact that to the DRM agent there can be added more security checks through methods like [16], [17] and by creating tight dependency between the legal licensed client and the license object comprised in the agent. This coupling can serve as an instrument to discourage and track such actions.

As [18], [19] and [20] prove, obfuscation is a precious technique to protect software programs tampering. Even if it does not guarantee that obfuscated code is unintelligible nor modifiable it provides a powerful mechanisms creating extremely complicated code for an attacker to identify sensitive data and code.

In our experiment we considered that `MobileLicense.class`, containing the reference to client (`AID`) and our simulated WBE implementation is well suitable as tracking information usable for linking the client with the mobile license. Obfuscating this class by using tools like [21] or [22] just before licensing injection make its bytecode harder to alter or remove the security trace that binds every license object to his legal owner.

6   Conclusions

As anticipated in the motivation section, absolute security for DRM pragmatic implementations remains a desired objective. From our point of view DRM solutions should be relatively secure against adversary threats and carefully balanced between protection requirements and costs. In our opinion dismissing not DRM technology but DRM fundamental means of existence is an undesired option. The application of a protocol similar to the proposed one can relatively secure DRM enabled systems with low cost implementation and important security benefits.

From the security perspective, it can be easily observed that *client authentication and authorization* is covered only by the LS through its implemented payment mechanisms and no digital certificate is required for the client device. We propose PKI certification only for server side components in order to provide *service authentication* and service operation *non-reputation*.

Being a primordial security concern of any DRM solution, *content confidentiality*, is the central security objective. Because of the sealed box exclusive requirement in the traditional DRM approach, we propose an innovative rework of the DRM architecture in such way that neither content decryption key nor license usage rights are directly accessible to a possible malicious host.

Another aspect of the proposed model is that it can be invoked only for on line content consumption which may represent also, in some situations, a source of limitation. No license is installed on the client machine and every time the client needs to consume DRM protected content he needs system connectivity with the server side components.

By comparing our model with standard existing systems, as shown in Table 1, it can be noticed that this approach creates a prerequisite framework for building sophisticated DRM solutions to solve weaknesses and vulnerabilities of   former DRMs.

Table 1. Proposed model assessment compared to standard system

	Legacy DRM	**Proposed approach**
Environmental support	Sealed box: commonly involving temper resistant hardware	Fully opened software
Server Side Authentication	PKI oriented	PKI oriented
Client Side Authentication & Authorisation	PKI oriented	Not the client but the operations based on payment tools
Non Repudiation	Base on PKI signed messages	Using server side operations tracking
License Confidentiality	Guaranteed for sealed box client platforms	No guaranteed. Provides powerful mechanisms for building complex security framework
License Resiliance	Yes: license can be stored on client device	No: designed only for on-line content consumption model
Practicability	Only if sealed box condition is satisfied	Adds more flexibility to content protection mechanisms by allowing dynamic changes of system entities

Our protocol design is based on standard DRM protocols and can be further developed. Also, various scenarios can be imagined starting from this protocol skeleton such as periodically licensing exchange or fraud investigation and audit agents.

References

1. Patriviu, V., Bica, I., Togan, M., Ghita, S.: A Generalized DRM Architectural Framework. In: Advances in Electrical and Computer Engineering, pp. 43–48 (2011) ISSN: 1582-7445
2. OMA-DRM 2.0, Open Mobile Alliance Digital Rights Management (2012), http://www.openmobilealliance.org
3. IETF DRM procedings Working Group, http://www.ietf.org/, MPEG-4 IPMP-x, Specific DRM solution by the MPEG-4 (2012), http://www.mpeg.org
4. ISMA Cryp 2.0, Internet Media Streaming Alliance Encryption & Authentication Specification 2.0 (2012), http://www.isma.tv/spec-request.html
5. Arnab, A., Hutchison, A.: A Requirement Analysis of Enterprise DRM Systems. In: ISSA, Johannesburg, South Africa (2005)
6. Liu, Q., Safavi-Naini, R., Sheppard, N.P.: Digital rights management for content distribution. In: ACSW 2003, Proceedings of the First Australasian Information Security Workshop (2003)
7. OMA-ODRL 2.0, Open Mobile Alliance Open Digital Rights Language, http://odrl.net/
8. XrML 2.0, eXtensible Rights Markup Language (2012), http://www.xrml.org
9. Billet, O., Gilbert, H., Ech-Chatbi, C.: Cryptanalysis of a White Box AES Implementation. In: Handschuh, H., Hasan, M.A. (eds.) SAC 2004. LNCS, vol. 3357, pp. 227–240. Springer, Heidelberg (2004)
10. Wyseur, B., Michiels, W., Gorissen, P., Preneel, B.: Cryptanalysis of White-Box DES Implementations with Arbitrary External Encodings. In: Adams, C., Miri, A., Wiener, M. (eds.) SAC 2007. LNCS, vol. 4876, pp. 264–277. Springer, Heidelberg (2007)
11. Michiels, W., Gorissen, P., Hollmann, H.D.L.: Cryptanalysis of a Generic Class of White-Box Implementations. In: Avanzi, R.M., Keliher, L., Sica, F. (eds.) SAC 2008. LNCS, vol. 5381, pp. 414–428. Springer, Heidelberg (2009)
12. Bruce, S.: Crypto-Gram blog post, The Futility of Digital Copy Prevention (2001), http://www.schneier.com/crypto-gram-0105.html#3
13. JADE 4.1.1, Java Agent DEvelopment Framework (2012), http://jade.tilab.com/
14. Ping, L., Zhengding, L., Fuhao, Z., Hefei, L.: A DRM System Based on Mobile Agent for Digital Rights Redistribution. Wuhan University Journal of Natural Sciences 13(4), 475–480 (2008), doi:10.1007/s11859-008-0419-3
15. Hohl, F.: Time Limited Blackbox Security: Protecting Mobile Agents From Malicious Hosts. In: Vigna, G. (ed.) Mobile Agents and Security. LNCS, vol. 1419, pp. 92–113. Springer, Heidelberg (1998)
16. Ametller, J., Robles, S., Ortega-Ruiz, J.A.: Self Protected Mobile Agents. In: Proceedings of the Third International Joint Conference on Autonomous Agents and Multiagent Systems, AAMAS 2004, NY, USA, pp. 362–367 (2004) ISBN: 1-58113-864-4
17. Basit, H., Pugliesi, S., Smyth, W., Turpin, A., Jarzabek, S.: Efficient Token Based Clone Detection with Flexible Tokenization. In: ESEC/FSE, pp. 513–515 (2007)

18. Barak, B., Goldreich, O., Impagliazzo, R., Rudich, S., Sahai, A., Vadhan, S., Yang, K.: On the (Im)possibility of Obfuscating Programs. In: Kilian, J. (ed.) CRYPTO 2001. LNCS, vol. 2139, pp. 1–18. Springer, Heidelberg (2001)
19. Collberg, C.S., Thomborson, C.: Watermarking, tamper-proffing, and obfuscation: tools for software protection. IEEE Transactions on Software Engineering 28(8), 735–746 (2002)
20. Armoogum, S., Asvin, C.: Obfuscation Techniques for Mobile Agent code confidentiality. Journal of Information & Systems Management 1(1), 83–94 (2011) ISSN: 0976-2930
21. DashO Java Obfuscator (2012),
    http://www.preemptive.com/products/dasho/
22. KlassMaster Java Obfuscator (2012), http://www.zelix.com/klassmaster/

Towards a Secure, Transparent and Privacy-Preserving DRM System

Dheerendra Mishra and Sourav Mukhopadhyay

Department of Mathematics
Indian Institute of Technology
Kharagpur–721302, India
{dheerendra,sourav}@maths.iitkgp.ernet.in

Abstract. The Internet based digital content distribution mechanism is both a blessing and a curse. It provides efficient content distribution infrastructure. However, it creates the threat of content copying and re-distribution. Digital rights management (DRM) system tries to ensure the digital content protection. Although, DRM systems are facing the challenges to facilitate security, privacy, and accountability together so that copyright protection with correctness of content sell can be ensured without violating the consumer's privacy. In this paper, we propose a key management scheme. It manages secure and transparent key distribution and achieves privacy. In addition, proposed framework support accountability parameters, which helps to identify the malicious user.

Keywords: Digital rights management, Key management, Privacy.

1 Introduction

The greatest advancement in research and technology in the field of communication, computing, and consumer electronics has introduced Internet as an efficient mechanism of digital data transfer between remote consumers. It facilitates the easy access of digital content (e-books, music, movies, software, etc.) at low cost. However, it has some drawbacks. The digital contents can be easily copied and redistributed without any deterioration in the quality of content over the network. Therefore, rights holders require a system, which can regulate the content distribution and ensue copyright protection. One of such a mechanism is digital rights management (DRM). It has been developed to ensure the copyright protection [9].

DRM broadly refers to a set of policies, techniques and tools which tries to ensure the authorize access of digital content [14]. It is all about digitally managing the rights of all involve entities. It controls the access of contents using digital license [10]. To enforce legitimate content consumption, the system verifies consumer authenticity (verification of personal data such as credit card information, banking account details, delivery details, email id, etc.) and tracks content consumption. In addition to this, the system tracks consumer's preferences and personal information to analyze consumer content consumption information by

S.M. Thampi et al. (Eds.): SNDS 2012, CCIS 335, pp. 304–313, 2012.

which it can conclude the trend. This analysis helps to increases the competence of business. Since, privacy is not needed for copyright protection. As a result, in DRM enforcement consumer's privacy is usually overlooked or poorly considered. These systems carry various new threats to the personal privacy and elevate the serious privacy concern. Although, privacy in our context may be defined as the rights of consumers to determine, when, how, and to what extent information is collected about them during the course of the digital business transaction; and also the right to choose when, how, and to what extent their personal information is made available to others [8]. However, the maximization of privacy protection for their consumers gives significant commercial benefits where these benefits may be resorting to enhance the public image of the merchant that leads to an increase in the consumer ratio and making many more individuals comfortable to take part in digital business.

Hwang et al. [7] proposed a multilevel content distribution system that presents secure and transparent content key distribution mechanism but fails to achieve privacy. Sachan et al. [12] described a multiparty multilevel (MPML) DRM architecture that accommodates distributors at multiple levels. It maintains a flexible content distribution mechanism, which makes rights violation detection possible in the system. It also protects privacy during rights violation detection but fails to protect privacy during license acquisition. The schemes [2–4] present secure key management in multi-distributor DRM system but do not protect privacy. Thomas et al. [15] that presents a secure content delivery system for MPML DRM architecture and also provide a privacy protection mechanism during protected content download but cannot hide the consumer preferences during license acquisition. There are schemes [5, 6, 16, 17] that provide an efficient privacy protection mechanism. However, they do not provide secure and transplant key management mechanism, where [6] and [16] do not support accountability parameters, i.e., fail to catch the traitor responsible for constraints violation in the DRM system. The key objective of DRM is to provide secure and transparent content distribution mechanism, which does not violate consumer privacy and achieves transparency and accountability. A DRM system should provide a unified strategy where right holders allow controlling their intellectual property rights without violating consumer's privacy.

Our Contribution: In this paper, we propose a unified strategy that gives secure key management with privacy and transparency. The proposed key management mechanism is based on secret sharing scheme, where no party has a complete share of the decryption key. This mechanism protects the key not only from purchasers but also from other principals such as the distributor and the license server such that encrypted digital content can only be decrypted by the consumer who has acquired valid license. Proposed framework ensures the correctness of royalty flow with the help of license distribution statistics. In addition, privacy protection mechanism hides consumer's preferences from the involve parties. Here, privacy is achieved by making content identity anonymous for the license server and distributor.

The rest of the paper is originated as follows. Next section recalls the definition of secret sharing scheme and present notation. Section 3 introduces proposed unified strategy. In section 4, we analyze the scheme. Finally, we conclude in Section 5.

2   Preliminaries

2.1   Secret Sharing Scheme

Blackley [1] and Shamir [13] introduced the concept of secret sharing. Where, Secret sharing refers to method for distributing a secret amongst the involve parties such that each of them gets a share of the secret. The fundamental idea of a (t, n) threshold scheme is to divide the shared secret into n parties in such a way that the secret cannot be retrieved unless t authorized shares are collected. This scheme is mainly used to protect the secret from diverse attacks. The basic concept of this scheme is to allocate partial information about the secret such that authorized subset of shareholders can retrieve the secret.

2.2   Notation

- Each protocol requires the following roles: consumer C, license server L, system owner O, distributor D, Packager P.
- For digital content M, identity of M is id_M, for entity U, identity of entity is ID_U, public key of entity is PK_U, Private key of entity is SK_U, and symmetric key is S.
- Signature generation on message Y using key SK is $\sigma_Y = \mathsf{sig}(Y|SK)$.
- Public key encryption of plaintext PT using key PK is $E_{\mathsf{pub}}(\mathsf{PT}|\mathsf{PK})$.
- Public key decryption of ciphertext CT using key SK is $D_{\mathsf{pub}}(\mathsf{CT}|\mathsf{SK})$.
- Symmetric key encryption of plaintext PT using key S is $E_{\mathsf{sym}}(\mathsf{PT}|S)$.
- Symmetric key decryption of ciphertext CT using key S is $D_{\mathsf{sym}}(\mathsf{CT}|S)$.

3   Proposed Framework

Our multiparty multilevel DRM system basic architecture is similar to the two level distributor system [3], which follows the general DRM system that involves the content provider, clearing house, and distributor. Proposed system accommodates more then one distributor and arranges the distributors in a hierarchical order. Parties involved in our DRM model are:

- Owner O
- Multiple levels of distributors $D_{i,j}$, $1 \leq i \leq k$, $1 \leq j \leq n_i$ where $D_{i,j}$ represents the j-th distributor at the i-th level
- License server L
- consumer C

The owner appoints the distributors at level-1 geographically. Each distributor at level-1 further appoints some sub-distributors in his domain according to system requirement. The total number of content distribution levels may depend upon the diversity of the region to be explored and density of DRM consumers. System owner provides the protected digital contents to the distributors of level-1, level-1 to level-2 and so forth. All involved distributors in the system provide the protected content for free download to the consumer C, where C is mobile and move from one region to another. C can download encrypted content from its preferred distributor, say $D_{i,j}$, which might be location wise nearest to C or offer some promotions/discounts on the price. System works under the following assumption.

- Every party have an authorized public private key pair.
- O handles the consumer's registration with the help of registration authority and assigns a unique registration identity ID_C to C.
- System issues the license only for the authorized and registered consumers where consumer's authenticity verification is done by the distributor.
- License server receives the payment and generates the license with the help of distributor key share to C.

3.1   Content Packing

Let the system have mn distributors $D_{i,j}, \forall 1 \leq i \leq n, 1 \leq j \leq m$ and r contents $M_1, M_2, \cdots, M_r$ with content identity $\mathsf{id}_{M_1}, \mathsf{id}_{M_2}, \cdots, \mathsf{id}_{M_r}$.

- O provides the unprotected content to P. P generates the symmetric keys $K_1, K_2, \cdots, K_r$ and encrypts all the content $M_1, M_2, \cdots, M_r$ using symmetric keys $K_1, K_2, \cdots, K_r$ and gets

$$E_{sym}(M_i|K_i), \forall M_i, 1 \leq i \leq r.$$

- P generates a symmetric key S and encrypts content identities $\mathsf{id}_{M_1}, \mathsf{id}_{M_2}, \cdots, \mathsf{id}_{M_r}$ using symmetric key encryption algorithm, obtains $E_{\mathsf{sym}}(\mathsf{id}_{M_1}|S)$, $E_{\mathsf{sym}}(\mathsf{id}_{M_2}|S), \cdots, E_{\mathsf{sym}}(\mathsf{id}_{M_r}|S)$.

Packager encrypts the all content identities using same key S while to protect digital contents it usages unique keys for each content. Packager sends a pair of protected content with their encrypted identities $((E_{\mathsf{sym}}(M_i|K_i), E_{\mathsf{sym}}(\mathsf{id}_{M_i}|S))$, $i = 1, 2, \cdots, r)$ and content information to the distributors. Distributors keep this protected content over media servers and display content details over their website. Here, protected contents are identified by their encrypted identities.

3.2   Key Delivery

Once the encryption of content is over, packager takes the following stapes.

1. P selects a second degree polynomial $h(x) = a_0 + a_1 x + a_2 x^2 \in Z_p[x]$, where $a_0, a_1, a_2 \in Z_p$, $a_0 = K$, and Z_p is a finite field of order p such that p is a large prime number.

2. P computes $h(x_i) \in Z_p[x]$, for $i = 1, 2, 3$ and generates the key shares
   $t_1 = ((x_1, h(x_1)), (x_2, h(x_2)))$, $t_2 = ((x_2, h(x_2)), (x_3, h(x_3)))$, and
   $t_3 = ((x_1, h(x_1)), (x_3, h(x_3)))$.
3. P creates the tuples of encrypted content's identities and key shares and gets
   $T_1 = (t_1, E_{\mathsf{sym}}(\mathsf{id}_M|S))$, $T_2 = (t_2, E_{\mathsf{sym}}(\mathsf{id}_M|S))$, and $T_3 = (t_3, E_{\mathsf{sym}}(\mathsf{id}_M|S))$.
   P sends T_1 and T_2 to the distributors $D_{i,j}$, $1 \leq i \leq k$, $1 \leq j \leq n_i$ and
   the license server respectively through a secure channel. License server and
   distributors store their key share corresponding to their encrypted identities.
4. P submits key share T_3 to the owner. Owner stores this key share at a secure
   place.

3.3 Name Mapping Information Acquisition

Involved principals, license server and distributors identifies the content key by
content encrypted identities. Therefore, license server/distributor can entertains
the license request if it comes corresponding to content encrypted identity instead of content original identity. Fig. 1 shows the pictorial representation of
the mechanism by which consumer achieves the name mapping between content
identity and content encrypted identity.

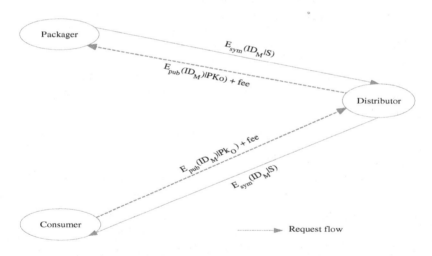

Fig. 1. Information flow during encrypted content identity information acquisition

To know the name mapping between content identity and content encrypted
identity, consumer takes the following steps:

1. Consumer C selects some distributor D within nearest reach to him, which
   can provide him flexible and quick services. C visits D's website, selects some
   content M, gets content identity id_M and encrypts it with the owner's public
   key PK_O and gets $E_{\mathsf{pub}}(\mathsf{id}_M|\mathsf{PK}_O)$. C submits his name mapping request with
   $E_{\mathsf{pub}}(\mathsf{id}_M|\mathsf{PK}_O)$ and fee to D.

2. D forwards C's request with fee to the Packager P without disclosing any information about C.

3. P decrypts $E_{\mathsf{pub}}(\mathsf{id}_M|\mathsf{PK}_O)$ using his private key SK_O and gets the requested content identity as follows:

$$D_{\mathsf{pub}}(E_{\mathsf{pub}}(\mathsf{id}_M|\mathsf{PK}_O)|\mathsf{SK}_O) = \mathsf{id}_M$$

4. P encrypts id_M using symmetric key S and sends $E_{\mathsf{sym}}(\mathsf{id}_M|S)$ to D. Finally, D forwards packager's message to the C.

Distributor plays the role of a middle man that exchanges the message between two parties (consumer and owner). The message is exchanged in a way that the consumer remains anonymous for the packager and consumer's request remains anonymous to the distributor. During message exchange, both incoming and outgoing messages are encrypted with owner's key. It restricts the distributor to retrieve any short of information about consumer's request.

3.4   Anonymous Content Download and License Acquisition

The name mapping (mapping between content encrypted identity and content original identity) provides sufficient knowledge to the consumer such that he can know what he/she has to ask to achieve the content of his/her choice from the distributor/license server and what content he/she should download from the media server to complete his requirement. Fig. 2 shows the pictorial representation of content download and license accusation process.

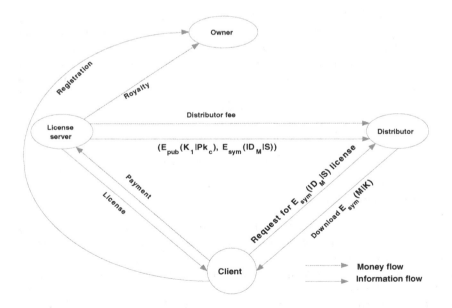

Fig. 2. License acquisition in DRM

Content Download: Protected contents are available on media server and these protected contents are identified only by their encrypted identities rather then content original identity. The consumer acquires encrypted contents' identity information as discussed in section 3.3 and with the help of encrypted content identity $E_{\text{sym}}(\text{id}_M|S)$ information, downloads protected content $E_{\text{sym}}(M|K)$.

License Acquisition: License server issues the license only for registered and authorized consumers. C selects some distributor D and submits his/her license request to D with identity $E_{\text{sym}}(\text{id}_M|S)$. D verifies the consumer's authenticity. If verification success then the process is as follows.

1. D computes $Y_D = E_{\text{pub}}(t_1|\text{PK}_C)$ using consumer's public Key PK_C and generates its signature $\sigma_{Y_D} = \text{sig}(Y_D|\text{SK}_D)$ using its own private key SK_D and sends $(Y_D, \sigma_{Y_D}, ID_C, E_{\text{sym}}(\text{id}_M|S))$ to L through a secure channel.

2. L on receiving the message, it verifies the signature of D (σ_{Y_D}) on Y_D using distributor's public key PK_D. If verification succeeds then L moves forward otherwise rejects the request.

3. On receiving the payment, L computes $Y_L = E_{\text{pub}}(t_2|\text{PK}_C)$ using consumer's public Key PK_C, generates its signature $\sigma_{(Y_D,Y_L)} = \text{sig}((Y_D,Y_L)|\text{SK}_L)$ using its private key SK_L, issues the license which contains $((Y_D,Y_L),\sigma_{(Y_D,Y_L)})$ together with rights and constraints. L issues a unique license for every request.

4. L encrypts C's identity ID_C with its public key PK_L and associates this encrypted consumer's identity $E_{\text{pub}}(\text{ID}_C|\text{PK}_L)$ with the license instead of consumer original identity ID_C. L sends the license to C through a secure channel.

5. C analyzes the license and verifies the L's signature using L's public key. If verification succeeds, C decrypts Y_D and Y_L using his own private key SK_C and extracts the key shares $t_1 = ((x_1, h(x_1)), (x_2, h(x_2)))$ and $t_2 = ((x_2, h(x_2)), (x_3, h(x_3)))$. Since these share form authorized subset so h(x) can be reconstructed with the Lagrange interpolating polynomial as follows:

$$h(x) = \sum_{i=x_1}^{x_3} h(i) \prod_{j=x_1, j\neq i}^{x_3} \frac{x-j}{i-j} \quad (mod\ p)$$

After reconstruction of $h(x)$, consumer recover secret key $K = h(0)$.

3.5 Consumer's Privacy during Rights Violation Detection

Rights violation may cause a huge loss for e-commerce. Therefore, monitoring of content consumption is needed to detect rights violation. Monitoring server analyzes log files of content consumption to catch the traitor. See, e.g., [11]. It is easy to get consumer information and his/her content consumptions details during log collection from consumers' machine because license associates the identity of the consumer. A curious operator may disclose some information about consumers' preference for his personal benefit that a consumer may not want.

In this proposed system, license server associates consumer's encrypted identity $E_{\mathsf{pub}}(\mathsf{ID}_C|\mathsf{PK}_L)$ instead of original identity ID_C with the license. This encrypted consumer's identity gives no information about the consumer. However, system can catch the violation in the system as follows.

- When owner detects rights violation, he retrieves associated encrypted identity $E_{\mathsf{pub}}(\mathsf{ID}_C|\mathsf{PK}_L)$ from the license and sends it to the license server.
- License server decrypts $E_{\mathsf{pub}}(\mathsf{ID}_C|\mathsf{PK}_L)$ using its private key SK_L and get ID_C, as follows.

$$D_{\mathsf{pub}}(E_{\mathsf{pub}}(\mathsf{ID}_C|\mathsf{PK}_L)|\mathsf{SK}_L) = \mathsf{ID}_C.$$

- License server provides consumer identity ID_C to the owner.
- Owner add this malicious user to his revocation list and also inform to all the distributors about this revoked user.

This mechanism supports violation detection without disclosing any information about authorized consumers.

4   Analysis

The proposed Key management scheme is designed to address following security issues.

- *Preventing insider attacks:* No party has a complete secret key share. It prevents unintended parties from achieving the secret key with the help of an insider.
- *Minimizing outsider attacks:* Attacker must compromise license server and one of the distributor to obtain complete authorized key shares.
- *Transparent:* Owner collects the key distribution statistics from both license server and distributor and with the help of usages license data monitors the correctness of royalty flow.

Proposed key management system is able to provide the services in case of distributor and license server failure with the help of owner's key share. It allows the content key to be protected from the distributor as well as license server. Only the consumer who has authorized shares of the key can play the content. Proposed system also gives some strong privacy protection mechanism under all scenarios.

- *Encrypted Content identity acquisition:* Customer gets encrypted content identity information from original content identity without trusting over any third party. The distributor only knows *who is requesting* and owner only knows *What is requesting*. This incomplete information makes a consumer request anonymous.
- *Content download:* It is easy to track the consumer during content streaming or download from media server. However, anonymity of contents identity hides the content information that what exactly consumer is downloading. There is also no need to establish anonymous communication from consumer to achieve anonymity. This mechanism reduce the effort from consumer side.

- *License acquisition:* License server and distributors identify the content by their encrypted identity instead of original identity. When consumer makes license request, he sends content encrypted identity with the license request to the distributor, which gives no information about the original content identity.
- *Payment:* Payment or price of items do not reveals items category because system does not keep the price of all items distinct and allows the same price for two different category items. In case, if some price category have less items then by adding some dummy items, secrecy can be provided.
- *Authentication:* System issues the license only to authorized consumers. Distributor verifies the authenticity of consumer and this verification disclose consumer's identity but the anonymity of content identity hides consumer's selection.
- *Violation Detection:* Proposed system allows violation detection but hides the consumer identity during consumer log analysis by associating the consumer's encrypted identity with the license instead of original identity. Monitoring authority can achieve encrypted identity of consumer during tracking and this mechanism keeps consumer anonymous.

5   Conclusion

We proposed a key management scheme for DRM system, which is based (t, m)-threshold secret sharing scheme. The advantage of this scheme is that it needs no trust distributor or license server in the DRM system. here, encrypted digital content can only be decrypted by the consumer who has a valid license. Proposed system privacy protection mechanism, which is based on anonymity of contents' identity, conceals consumer's preferences. In addition, proposed scheme supports accountability parameters.

References

1. Blaklly, G.R.: Safeguarding cryptographic keys. In: Proceedings of the National Computer Conference, vol. 48, pp. 313–317 (1979)
2. Dutta, R., Mukhopadhyay, S., Dowling, T.: Key management in multi-distributor based DRM system with mobile clients using IBE. In: Second International Conference on the Applications of Digital Information and Web Technologies, ICADIWT 2009, pp. 597–602 (2009)
3. Dutta, R., Mishra, D., Mukhopadhyay, S.: Vector Space Access Structure and ID Based Distributed DRM Key Management. In: Abraham, A., Mauri, J.L., Buford, J.F., Suzuki, J., Thampi, S.M. (eds.) ACC 2011, Part IV. CCIS, vol. 193, pp. 223–232. Springer, Heidelberg (2011)
4. Dutta, R., Mishra, D., Mukhopadhyay, S.: Access Policy Based Key Management in Multi-level Multi-distributor DRM Architecture. In: Joye, M., Mukhopadhyay, D., Tunstall, M. (eds.) InfoSecHiComNet 2011. LNCS, vol. 7011, pp. 57–71. Springer, Heidelberg (2011)

5. Mishra, D., Mukhopadhyay, S.: Privacy rights management in multiparty multilevel DRM system. In: Proceedings of the International Conference on Advances in Computing, Communications and Informatics, pp. 625–631 (2012)
6. Feng, M., Zhu, B.: A DRM system protecting consumer privacy. In: 5th IEEE Consumer Communications and Networking Conference, CCNC 2008, pp. 1075–1079 (2008)
7. Hwang, S.O., Yoon, K.S., Jun, K.P., Lee, K.H.: Modeling and implementation of digital rights. Journal of Systems and Software 73(3), 533–549 (2004)
8. Katsikas, S.K., Lopez, J., Pernul, G.: Trust, Privacy and Security in E-Business: Requirements and Solutions. In: Bozanis, P., Houstis, E.N. (eds.) PCI 2005. LNCS, vol. 3746, pp. 548–558. Springer, Heidelberg (2005)
9. Liu, Q., Safavi-Naini, R., Sheppard, N.P.: Digital Rights Management for Content Distribution. In: Proceedings of Australasian Information Security Workshop Conference on ACSW Frontiers, pp. 49–58 (2003)
10. Rosset, V., Filippin, C.V., Westphall, C.M.: A DRM Architecture to Distribute and Protect Digital Content Using Digital Licenses. In: Telecommunications 2005, pp. 422–427 (2005)
11. Sachan, A., Emmanuel, S.: DRM violation detection using consumer logs analysis. In: IEEE International Conference on Multimedia and Expo., ICME 2011, pp. 1–6 (2011)
12. Sachan, A., Emmanuel, S., Das, A., Kankanhalli, M.S.: Privacy Preserving Multiparty Multilevel DRM Architecture. In: IEEE Consumer Communications and Networking Conference, pp. 1–5 (2009)
13. Shamir, A.: How to Share a Secret. Communications of the ACM 22(11), 612–613 (1979)
14. Subramanya, S.R., Yi, B.K.: Digital rights management. IEEE Potentials 25(2), 31–34 (2006)
15. Thomas, T., Emmanuel, S., Das, A., Kankanhalli, M.S.: Secure multimedia content delivery with multiparty multilevel DRM architecture. In: Proceedings of the 18th International Workshop on Network and Operating Systems Support for Digital Audio and Video, pp. 85–90. ACM (2009)
16. Win, L.L., Thomas, T., Emmanuel, S.: A privacy preserving content distribution mechanism for DRM without trusted third parties. In: IEEE International Conference on Multimedia and Expo., ICME 2011, pp. 1–6 (2011)
17. Yao, J., Lee, S., Nam, S.: Privacy preserving DRM solution with content classification and superdistribution. In: Consumer Communications and Networking Conference, CCNC 2009, pp. 1–5 (2009)

Time Based Constrained Object Identification in a Dynamic Social Network

M.T. Chitra[1], R. Priya[1], and Elizabeth Sherly[2]

[1] University of Kerala, Thiruvananthapuram, Kerala, India
{chitra.mt,priyanil2007}@gmail.com
[2] Indian Institute of Information Technology and Management – Kerala,
Thiruvananthapuram, India
sherly@iiitmk.ac.in

Abstract. Social networking has become an ubiquitous part of communication in this modern era. Categorization in dynamic social network is very challenging because of the key feature of social networks – *continual change*. A typical social network grows exponentially over time, as new activities and interactions evolve rapidly. The dynamic social networks are efficient in modeling the behavior of any real life interactions. In this paper, two algorithms are considered, of which one helps to identify the exact community to which a new node belongs. The second algorithm uses a rule based approach to identify the exact community which satisfies a set of constraints. The social network is conceived as a weighted directed graph consisting of a set of nodes, edges , node weights and edge weights. The node weights are computed based on the node rank algorithm and the edge weights based on the people rank algorithm. In the proposed algorithms, the dynamic attributes of the nodes and time-based constraints play a crucial role in the identification of categories in the social network. The main objective of the algorithm is to obtain an optimal community network with high accuracy by using a heuristic approach. This approach helps to categorize a newly added node or entity to one or more communities dynamically.

Keywords: community detection, dynamic constraints, rule based, node rank, people rank.

1 Introduction

A social network which deals with theoretical construct used to study relationships between individuals, groups, organizations or even societies. The links in the social network represents the interactions between the nodes. The social interactions can be any common feature, the people in the network share, like interest for music or profession or locality. As these features and the structure tend to change with respect to time, it results in a dynamic behaviour. The links through which any social unit connects represent the convergence of the various social contacts of that unit. Identification of a unit sharing common features is very challenging because of the dynamic feature of the social network.

S.M. Thampi et al. (Eds.): SNDS 2012, CCIS 335, pp. 314–322, 2012.

Dynamic social networks are capable of modeling enormous amount of problems occurring in the real world. Much of the research initiatives conducted in social networks mainly concentrate on exploring the static aspects of social networks. But, a typical social network grows exponentially as time evolves, therefore a study of dynamic network is of great demand. The time factor plays a crucial role for tracking and updating the changes in a dynamic social network.

In this work, the behaviour of a social network with time-based constraints either as the network at different snapshots of time or based on the overall interactions of the network for a particular period of time is considered. The nodes in the social network are treated as real world entities or objects with certain characteristics and constraints. Based on these characteristics, the nodes are tagged. The computation of edge weight is based on the static and temporal constraints satisfied by the nodes in the network. Identification of constrained objects in the dynamic social networks requires considerable amount of effort and time.

The rest of the paper is organized as follows: Section II discusses the preliminaries and problem definition. Section III discusses the objective function and the proposed algorithm. Section IV shows the experimental results of our approach on various real world datasets. In section V, a discussion about related work and finally a conclusion of the work in Section VI.

2   Preliminaries and Problem Definition

In this work, social network is conceived as a directed weighted graph with nodes as people and edges as the interaction between people. Edges in the dynamic social networks are often bidirectional, which is formed with a mutual agreement. Each node in the network is associated with a set of static as well as dynamic attributes. The static attributes are defined on the basis of certain priori-defined constraints which are extracted from the characteristics of nodes. There are certain dynamic attributes, which are subjective to change in accordance with the interest of the users. The nodes in the social network are tagged based on these attributes. In order to identify the betweenness of the nodes in a community or group, the edges are assigned weights based on the edge rank algorithm.

The network is a directed weighted graph $G_t (V_t , E_t)$ where V_t is the nodes within that network at time t and E_t represents the relationship between these nodes at time t. G_t represents a snapshot of the social network at time t. $G_t'(V_t' , E_t')$ represents a snapshot at time t'. $G_t' = G_t \cup \Delta G_t$, where ΔG_t represents the changes incorporated into the network over time t'- t. A tag is associated with each node,V_t represented as $<V_t, d(V_t)>$. $d(V_t)$ is computed based on the static and dynamic attributes of the node Vt. Edge weight $E_w(V_i ,V_j)'$ represents the similarities between the nodes V_i and V_j at time t.

3   Objective Function and Proposed Algorithm

The main objective of this work is to identify the exact community to which a particular node belongs to in a dynamic social network. The work also considers the fact that the users can be a part of one or more communities at a time. The dynamic attributes of the nodes and time-based constraints play a crucial role in the identification of categories in the social network.

The objective function can be defined as a set S

$$S=\{V_t \,/\, dom[d(V_t)] = C_i\} \quad \forall \ i=1,...,m \,. \tag{1}$$

where C_i is the set static and dynamic constraints searched for in the social network and m is the maximum number of constraints searched for.

The behavior of the network at time t+1 can be given as

$$G(t+1) = w \times G(t) + R(t,t+1) \,. \tag{2}$$

where w is the weights associated with the social network at time t and R is the random changes incorporated in the network over the time period (t,t+1).

Edge weight $E_w(V_i,V_j)^t$ between the nodes V_i and V_j at time t can be represented as

$$E_w(V_i,V_j)^t = dom[d(V_i)] \quad \cap \quad dom[d(V_j)] \quad \forall \ V_i,V_j \ \boxed{\in} \ V_t \,. \tag{3}$$

3.1   Proposed Algorithm

In this paper, two algorithms are considered, of which one helps to identify the exact community to which a new node belongs.

ALGORITHM 1. To identify the exact community to which a new node belongs.

```
Input: Given G_t(V_t,E_t) and C(c_1,c_2,...,c_m) where c_1,...,c_m
represents the set of static(SC) as well as dynamic
constraints(DC)such that V_t satisfies c_1,...,c_m and the
new node V_new with its Static(S) and dynamic(D)
characteristics.
Output: The new node V_new is assigned to the exact
community W_t.
begin
Step 1: for each V_new such that V_new ∉ V_t, do Steps 2 to
14.
Step 2: tag V_new based on the inputs, S and D.
Step 3: while all V_t(S_t) not traversed do
            Extract the subset  S_t from G_t such that
            tag[V_t (S_t )] = tag[ V_new]_t
Step 4: end while
Step 5: if dom[d(V_t)]=dom[d(V_new)] ∀ V_t ∈ S_t, then
```

```
Step 6: if((per(dom[d(V_t)]>=per(dom[d(V_new)] -  5)
        &&(per(dom[d(V_t)]<=per(dom[d(V_new)]  + 5))
            add V_t to the new working set, Z_t at time t.
Step 7: if DC(V_t)= D(V_new) ∀ V_t in G_t as per Algorithm 2,
then
        add V_t to the working set, W_t at time t.
Step 8: The set W_t U Z_t defines the "People You May
Know" list [PYMK], defined as  X_t
Step 9: Calculate E_w(x_t,V_new) ∀ x_t ∈ X_t.
Step 10: PYMK is ordered based on E_w(x_t,V_new), such that
it ranges from max(E_w)... min( E_w).
Step 11: Select friends manually from the PMYK list.
Step 12: Repeat Step 13 for each time change Δt.
Step 13: Update counter for each x_t in X_t defined as
            <x_t, k(x_t)>
Step 14: Friends List = {x_t / k(x_t) ranges from
            [max(<x_t ,k(x_t)> ... min(<x_i, k(x_i)>]}
end
```

The second algorithm uses a rule based approach to identify the exact community which satisfies a set of constraints.

ALGORITHM 2. To identify the exact community which satisfies a set of dynamic constraints.

```
Input: Dynamic Constraints (Dc), G_t(V_t,E_t) and Dc(V_t).
Output:The community W_t.

begin
Step 1: while all V_t in G_t not traversed do
Step 2:    if D_c = D_c(V_t) then
Step 3:       add V_t to the resulting community W_t.
Step 4:       else if Tr(D_c)= Tr(D_c(V_t)) or
                    Sy(D_c)= Sy(D_c(V_t))
              then go to Step 3.
Step 5:       end if
Step 6: end while
end
```

4   Experimental Results

To simulate the algorithms, an online social network is considered. Here the user is insisted to provide his/her details to be the part of the network community. The user has options to provide his personal, professional and other interests. There are certain fields that are mandatory. For instance, if the user adds his employment details, he must specify the period of employment also. A tag is associated with each characteristic the user is giving. Prediction of period of study in University and School is done on the basis of the period of employment provided along with the employer details.

To test algorithm1, *Identifying the exact community to which a new node belongs*, we considered a new node V_{new} with the following characteristics:

Employer	IIITM-K , Technopark, Trivandrum [2010-Present]
University	University of Kerala, 2004
Interest/other	Music

The tag(V_{new}) = <eud>; where e represents employer, u for university and d for any dynamic constraint. As per the algorithm, we need to identify the community to which the node belongs. We considered a priliminary graph with 20 nodes. The new node will be added as the last node, i.e., $V_{new} = V_{21}$.

Let tag(V_t) in G_t be as given in Table 1:

Table 1. The tagset of nodes in Graph G

Vt	tag(Vt)	Vt	tag(Vt)
V1	<eu>	V11	<d>
V2	<ec>	V12	<esd>
V3	<eh>	V13	<ud>
V4	<eud>	V14	<hd>
V5	<ud>	V15	<csd>
V6	<ehd>	V16	<ehu>
V7	<chsd>	V17	<euchsd>
V8	<sch>	V18	<uch>
V9	<scd>	V19	<sud>
V10	<ecd>	V20	<esud>

where e stands for employer, s stands for schooling, u for university, c for current city, h for hometown, and d for any dynamic characteristic provided by the user when entering the social network.

After matching the static attributes of the tagset of V_t given in Table 1 with that of V_{new} , the resultant set is given in Table 2.

Now, after comparing the domain of V_{new} with the domain of each V_t in G_t given in Table2, and considering the period of employment and study the resultant set obtained is given in Table 3.

Table 2. Resultant set obtained after matching the tagset of V_t with V_{new}

Vt	tag(Vt)	domain(Vt)
V1	<eu>	<IIITM-K[2004-2005], University of Kerala[2003]>
V2	<ec>	<IIIT- B[2005-2008], Trivandrum>
V3	<eh>	<IIITM-K[2008-Present], Trivandrum>
V4	<eud>	<IIITM-K[2001-2002], University of Kerala[2000], Music>
V5	<ud>	<CUSAT[2010-Present], Melody>
V6	<ehd>	<DCE[2011-Present], Kollam, Kathakali>
V10	<ecd>	<ReporterTV[2010-2011], Ernakulam, Drawing>
V12	<esd>	<IIITM-K[2002-2004], St.Thomas[1998], Dance>
V13	<ud>	<University of Kerala[1970], Karnatic Vocal>
V16	<ehu>	<IIITM-K[2002-2004], Trivandrum, University of Kerala[1998]>
V17	<euchsd>	<VSSC[2002-Present], University of Calicut, Trivandrum, Kollam, St.Josephs, Painting>
V18	<uch>	<University of Kerala[1990], Trivandrum, Malappuram>
V19	<sud>	<St Marys[2000], University of Kerala[2004], Gazals>
V20	<esud>	<CDAC[1970-2000], Govt HSS[1962], Kannur University[1968], Agriculture>

Table 3. PYMK List based on static constraints

Vt	tag(Vt)	domain(Vt)
V4	<eud>	<IIITM-K[2001-2002], University of Kerala[2000], Music>
V1	<eu>	<IIITM-K[2004-2005], University of Kerala[2003]>
V3	<eh>	<IIITM-K[2008-Present], Trivandrum>
V19	<sud>	<St Marys[2000], University of Kerala[2004], Gazals>

All the nodes of Table 1 with dynamic constraints not present in PYMK are stored in the Table 4 shown below.

Table 4. List of nodes with <d> which are not in PYMK (Table 3)

Vt	tag(Vt)	domain(Vt)
V5	<ud>	<CUSAT[2010-Present], Melody>
V6	<ehd>	<DCE[2011-Present], Kollam, Kathakali>
V7	<chsd>	<Ernakulam, Kottayam, St Theresa[1998], Melody>
V9	<scd>	<Govt HSS[2000], Trivandrum, Singer>
V10	<ecd>	<ReporterTV[2010-2011], Ernakulam, Drawing>
V11	<d>	<Pop Music>

Table 4. (*continued*)

V14	<hd>	<Kasargod, Oil Painting>
V12	<esd>	<IIITM-K[2002-2004], St.Thomas[1998], Dance>
V13	<ud>	<University of Kerala[1970], Karnatic Vocal>
V15	<csd>	<Bangalore, Loyola[2000], Software Programmer>
V17	<euchsd>	<VSSC[2002-Present], University of Calicut, Trivandrum, Kollam,St.Josephs, Painting>
V20	<esud>	<CDAC[1970-2000], Govt HSS[1962], Kannur University[1968],Agriculture>

The dynamic constraint is matched as per the rule-based methodology proposed in the algorithm2. The domain value of the dynamic attribute of each V_t of Table 4 is matched with that of V_{new} to form Table 5.

Table 5. PYMK List based on dynamic constraints

Vt	tag(Vt)	domain(Vt)
V5	<ud>	<CUSAT[2010-Present], Melody>
V7	<chsd>	<Ernakulam, Kottayam, St Theresa[1998], Melody>
V9	<scd>	<Govt HSS[2000], Trivandrum, Singer>
V11	<d>	<Pop Music>
V13	<ud>	<University of Kerala[1970], Karnatic Vocal>

The final output in the PYMK list is obtained by combining the tables satisfying the static as well as dynamic constraints.

Table 6. The final output in the PYMK list

Vt	tag(Vt)	Vt	tag(Vt)
V4	<eud>	V13	<ud>
V1	<eu>	V19	<sud>
V3	<eh>	V9	<scd>
V21	<eud>	V5	<ud>
V7	<chsd>	V11	<d>

The counter attached with each node V_t defines the depth of intimacy between the node V21 and V_t The friends' list will be prioritized based on the intimacy values. The social network so formed can be graphically represented as shown in Fig 1.

However, Facebook also provides results for the above scenario, but a more appropriate identification of the community cannot be achieved since period of employment and period of study is not considered as criteria of searching in its algorithm. Hence the resultant graph looks like that shown in Fig 2.

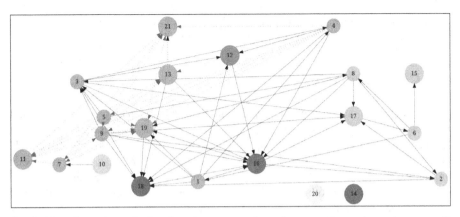

Fig. 1. The directed graph showing the connectedness between the nodes and community detection based on static(solid lines) and dynamic constraints(dotted lines)

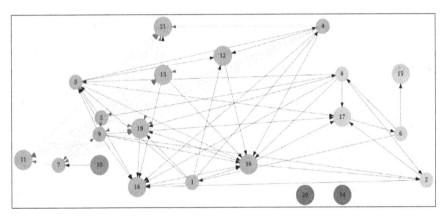

Fig. 2. The directed graph showing the connectedness between the nodes and community detection based on Facebook Social Network

Thus the proposed algorithm of *community detection* and *community identification of a new node entering the social network* becomes more optimistic.

5   Related Work

Community detection on static networks has attracted a lot of attentions and many efficient methods have been proposed on this type of networks. An algorithm [1] is proposed for the identification of the exact community satisfying the static constraints. QCA, an adaptive algorithm [2] for detecting and tracing community structures in dynamic social networks where changes are introduced frequently is also proposed. An evolutionary multimode clustering algorithm [3] is proposed to find community evolution in dynamic multimode networks. An optimization problem of finding community structure from the sequence of arbitrary graphs is formulated in paper [4]. In the paper [5], a new mathematical and computational framework that enables analysis of dynamic social networks is proposed.

6   Conclusion

In this paper, a social network problem based on dynamic constraints and optimization techniques has been explored. Real-world data is used to generate a suitable benchmarking test for comparing different algorithms mainly Facebook. Efficient result is seen in the proposed algorithm for identification of the exact community of people satisfying a set of dynamic constraints. Also, categories can be duration, which is not in other networks including face book. Hence the resultant list obtained becomes more optimistic. Also new categories evolve as the characteristics of the nodes changes.   Further study of more realistic dynamic social network categorization poses an interesting direction for future research, especially considering prediction of the category of nodes on the basis of the mutual characteristics and more dynamic input on a huge network with millions of nodes.

References

1. Priya, R., Chitra, M.T., Elizabeth, S.: Catergorization of Social Networks based on Multiplicity Constraints. International Journal of Computer Science Issues IJCSI 9(2(2)) (March 2012)
2. Nguyen, N.P., Dinh, T.N., Xuan, Y., Thai, M.T.: ZIB Adaptive Algorithms for Detecting Community Structure in Dynamic Social Networks. In: Proceedings of the IEEE Conference on Computer Communication, INFOCOM (2011)
3. Tang, L., Liu, H., Zhang, J., Nazeri, Z.: Community Evolution in Dynamic Multimode Networks. In: Proc. of 14th ACM SIGKDD International Conference on Knowledge Discovery and Data Mining, KDD 2008, pp. 677–685 (2008)
4. Tantipathananandh, C., Berger-Wolf, T.Y.: Finding Communities in Dynamic Social Networks. In: 11th IEEE International Conference on Data Mining, ICDM, pp. 1236–1241 (2011)
5. Berger-Wolf, T.Y., Saia, J.: A framework for analysis of Dynamic Social Networks. In: Proc. of 12th ACM SIGKDD International Conference on Knowledge Discovery and Data Mining, KDD 2006, pp. 523–528 (2006)

A New Approach towards Segmentation for Breaking CAPTCHA

Anjali Avinash Chandavale [1] and A. Sapkal[2]

[1] Member IEEE
anjali.chandavale@mitpune.edu.in
[2] LMIETE
ams.extc@coep.ac.in

Abstract. CAPTCHAs (Completely Automated Public Turing test to tell Computers and Humans Apart) are widespread security measures on the World Wide Web that prevent automated programs from abusing online services. CAPTCHAs are designed to be easy for humans but hard for machines. Academic research into CAPTCHAs takes the form of a friendly 'arms race', with some researchers acting as 'malicious users' that try to attack and defeat the latest CAPTCHA systems automatically. Defeating a CAPTCHA requires two procedures: segmentation and recognition. Recent research shows that the problem of segmentation is much harder than recognition. The efforts to break the CAPTCHA determine its strength & thus in turn help the researcher to build stronger CAPTCHA. In order to test the strength of a particular CAPTCHA, in this paper, we have developed a universal algorithm that measures one of the parameters to measure strength of CAPTCHA. The proposed algorithm can adapt to various cases for segmenting characters from CAPTCHA image. The said algorithm is inspired from projection value of characters, concept of snake game and typical patterns of touching the characters. Experimental results prove that the proposed algorithm has improved correct segmentation rates giving accuracy of 85%.

Keywords: CAPTCHA, segmentation, recognition.

1 Introduction

As the internet increases in terms of size and in terms of available services, people gain more convenience but also face new challenges. Free services on the internet may be abused by automated computer programs (often referred to as scripts or bots – here, we use bot). Such bots may be intended to broadcast junk emails, post advertisements, or ask the server to respond at a very high frequency. All these forms of misuse will decrease the usefulness of Internet services. To prevent such abuses, it is very important to design an automatic system to differentiate between the messages of legitimate human users and non-legitimate computer bots. The Completely Automated Public Turing test to tell Computers and Humans Apart (CAPTCHA) was created to address these needs [5]. The purpose of a CAPTCHA is to separate computer programs from people automatically, using a computer-based test.

S.M. Thampi et al. (Eds.): SNDS 2012, CCIS 335, pp. 323–335, 2012.
© Springer-Verlag Berlin Heidelberg 2012

The typical CAPTCHA user interface consists of two parts: a character image with noise, and an input text box. The CAPTCHA system will ask the user to type the characters shown in the image. However, the CAPTCHA system will contain wrapped shapes of the various characters in the image, along with some arcs or lines to confuse and prevent automated computer recognition of the characters. Fig. 1 shows an example drawn from the MSN CAPTCHA system. Basically, an automated bot cannot answer the question until there is a character recognition technique available that can understand the constituent characters of a given CAPTCHA. On the other hand, humans generally have much better natural abilities when faced with the task of character recognition in a noisy environment, so humans can usually answer these questions in a better manner with least inconvenience. Academic research into CAPTCHAs takes the form of a friendly 'arms race', with some researchers acting as 'malicious users' that try to attack and defeat the latest CAPTCHA systems automatically, e.g. [11][14][15], while other researchers seek to design new defensive CAPTCHA techniques in response to known or anticipated attacks. When designing defensive CAPTCHA techniques, a good CAPTCHA system should consider both computer security and human-friendliness. In practice, balancing these two needs in opposition to one another is very difficult. In considering the design principles of well-known CAPTCHA systems, we see that many well-known websites such as MSN, Yahoo, Google, Badongo, RapidShare and Youtube are employing user interfaces. Each website employs different heuristics to prevent malicious users. Badongo uses colored lines to clutter the image, and Youtube uses colored blocks; whereas RapidShare uses smaller colored characters as image noise to increase the security. MSN and Yahoo do not use colored character as noise. Instead, they use straight and curved lines as image clutter to confuse the defeating program. Although the security of these CAPTCHAs is increased by these heuristics, human-friendliness of them is decreased accordingly; many researchers are trying to find other useable principles which will help human users to pass a CAPTCHA test more easily, while still presenting difficulties to automated programs. While focusing towards the task of attacking a CAPTCHA, we observed two main procedures namely segmentation and recognition. The segmentation procedure requires identification of the correct positions for each character and the recognition procedure identifies which character is in each position. In recent research, [6] shows "segmentation" is a much more difficult problem than "recognition" since machine learning algorithms can efficiently solve the recognition problem, but currently we have no effective general algorithm to solve the segmentation problem caused by these added clutters. Chellapilla's algorithm [11] uses the image opening and labeling technique to design a segmentation algorithm. When the difference of width between clutters and characters is very noticeable, it is able to separate the noise from characters effectively. However, when the difference is not so noticeable, this algorithm will either be unable to eliminate noise, or it may break the characters when attempting to remove image noise. Therefore, this paper proposes an efficient segmentation algorithm for breaking CAPTCHA based on projection value of characters and concept of snake game along with style of touching of characters, resulting into a novel and useful contribution to the field of CAPTCHA analysis. The rest of this paper is organized as follows. Section 2 illustrates the related work where as the importance of segmentation in measuring strength of CAPTCHA along with Projection based segmentation algorithm and Snake segmentation algorithm is mentioned in Section 3. Section 4 presents the proposed segmentation algorithm. Section 5 covers experimental results and Section 6 provides research conclusions.

2   Related Work

Chellapilla and Simard [11] attempted to break a number of visual CAPTCHAs taken from the web (including those used in Yahoo and Google/Gmail) with machine learning algorithms. However, their success rates were low, ranging from merely 4.89% to 66.2 An attack on an unnamed simple CAPTCHA scheme with neural networks was discussed at [12], and it achieved a success rate of around 66%.PWNtcha is an excellent web page that aims to "demonstrate the inefficiency of many captcha implementations" .It comments briefly on the weaknesses of a dozen visual CAPTCHAs. These schemes were claimed to be broken with a success rate ranging from 49% to100%. However, no technical detail was publicly available (and probably as a consequence, at a prominent place of this web page, a disclaimer was included that it was not" a hoax, a fraud or a troll"). More distantly related (inspirit) is work by Naccache and Whelan [13] on decrypting words that were blotted out in declassified US intelligence documents, although it was not about CAPTCHAs as such. The limitations of defending against bots with CAPTCHAs (including protocol-level attacks) were discussed in [6] [7] [15]. A recent survey on CAPTCHAs research can be found in [10].

3   The Role of Segmentation in Measuring Strength of CAPTCHA

As per our previous work [17], the strength of a CAPTCHA depends on number of times it can be defeated and is determined by level of noise, length of string of characters present in an image and speed of breaking.

Noise: Noise or distortion has a clear impact on the strength of CAPTCHA, since human users would find it difficult or impossible to recognize over-distorted characters. For this a system will have to allow multiple attempts for each user. Typically a new challenge is used for each attempt. This will not only annoy users, but also lowers the security of the system by a factor of the number of allowed attempts.

Fig. 1. Example of CAPTCHA

Readability of CAPTCHA can be largely determined by what distortion methods are used and how much distortion is applied to texts.

Character selection, length and its recognition rate: In a CAPTCHA of a given length, the number of permitted symbols determines its maximum possible strength. The number of correctly guessed characters by system determine character recognition rate.

Response Time: how long does it take for a bot to pass the test? One of the ways to judge the strength of a CAPTCHA is to estimate the time and computing power required for cracking.

To extract the above mentioned parameters, it is necessary to break the CAPTCHA. Usually the system of CAPTCHA breaking has three stages, namely preprocessing, segmentation and character recognition. The level and type of noise, length of CAPTCHA is determined by preprocessing and segmentation stage respectively. Finally Response time can be found once the characters are recognized properly by CAPTCHA breaking system.

Character segmentation is an operation that decomposes an image of a sequence of characters into sub images of individual symbols. It is one of the decision processes in character recognition system. The segmentation step requires answering a simply posed question: "What constitutes a character?" The many researchers and developers who have tried to provide an algorithmic answer to this question find themselves in a Catch-22 situation. A character is a pattern that resembles one of the symbols the system is designed to recognize. But to determine such a resemblance the pattern must be segmented from the document image. Each stage depends on the other, and in complex cases it is paradoxical to seek a pattern that will match member of the system's recognition alphabet of symbols without incorporating detailed knowledge of the structure of those symbols into the process. Furthermore, the segmentation decision is not a local decision, independent of previous and subsequent decisions. Producing a good match to a library symbol is necessary, but not sufficient, for reliable recognition. That is, a poor match on a later pattern can cast doubt on the correctness of the current segmentation/recognition result. Even a series of satisfactory pattern matches can be judged incorrect if contextual requirements on the system output are not satisfied. For example, the letter sequence "cl" can often closely resemble a "d," but usually such a choice will not constitute a contextually valid result. Thus, it is seen that the segmentation decision is interdependent with local decisions regarding shape similarity, and with global decisions regarding contextual acceptability. This sentence summarizes the refinement of character segmentation processes in the past 40 years or so. As mentioned in the previous paragraphs, CAPTCHA systems have wide variations in style of embedding characters in image, in the sense that the characters can be disconnected, overlapped and connected as shown in fig.5. It is hard to attack all CAPTCHA tests by a single segmentation algorithm. Some CAPTCHAs which employ noise lines to make segmentation harder still allow excess spacing between characters. This allows an attacker to perform a rough slicing attack using either Color filling segmentation algorithm [17] or Projection based segmentation algorithm [2]. But CAPTCHA image as shown in fig.1 is difficult to break due to harder segmentation process. The refinement in character segmentation process will help to find total number of characters in CAPTCHA thus in turn will help to determine strength of CAPTCHA.

3.1   Projection Based Segmentation Algorithm

Huang et al. defines projection based segmentation algorithm as projecting the image data onto the X-axis. In practice, this is implemented by summing the number of non-white pixels in each column of the image parallel to the Y-axis [2]. Huang et al. algorithm extracts the characters from given image in four steps as enumerated below where characters are segmented depending on static threshold value (refer to Fig. 2).

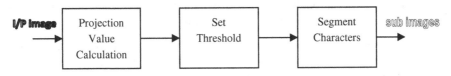

Fig. 2. Projection based segmentation

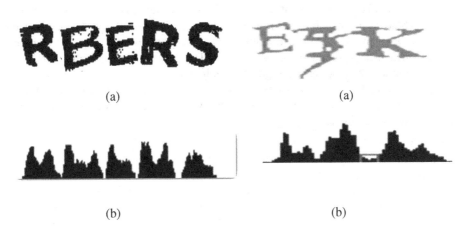

(a)   (a)

(b)   (b)

Fig. 3. a) Original image   b) Projection image

1. The projection value of each column is calculated by summing the number of black pixels in each column of the image.
2. The maximum projection value is equal to the maximum number of black pixels in any column.
3. Calculate the threshold value depending on maximum projection Value.
4. Find those columns where the number of black pixels is less than threshold value. Mark them as a segmentation line.
5. Repeat step 4 till entire image is scanned.

The projection value will be always zero for columns wherever there are gaps between characters or it will have minimum value wherever characters will be connected with thin arcs as shown in Fig. 3. Due to this fact the Projection based technique is significant only for the images having such type of characters (Fig. 3) where as for connected (Fig.6a) or overlapped (Fig. 6c) characters it splits an image into several sub images, which may contain one or more characters.

3.2   Snake Segmentation Algorithm

The snake segmentation algorithm was inspired by the popular "snake" game, which is supported in most mobile phones [1]. In this game, a player moves a growing snake on the screen, and tries to avoid collisions between the snake and dynamic blocks. In this algorithm, a snake represents a line that separates the characters in an image. It starts at the top line of the image and ends at the bottom. The snake can move in four directions: Up, Right, Left and Down, and it can touch foreground pixels of the image, but never cuts through them. The basis for snake segmentation algorithm is vertical segmentation algorithm, which works as follows:

1) The background color of an image is defined as the top-left pixel's color value where as foreground color is any pixel of a different color value.

2) Identifying the first segmentation line: The image is mapped into a coordinate system, in which the top-left pixel has coordinates (0, 0), the top-right pixel (image width, 0) and the bottom-left pixel (0, image height). Starting from point (0, 0), a vertical "slicing" process traverse pixels from top to bottom and then from left to right. This process stops once a pixel with a non-background color is detected. The X co-ordinate of this pixel, x1, defines the first vertical segmentation line X =x1-1

3) The next segmentation line is found by continuing vertical slicing process from (x1+1, 0), until it detects another vertical line that does not contain any foreground pixels.

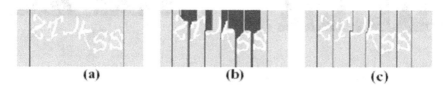

Fig. 4. Snake Segmentation. a) Pre-processing: finding the first and last segmentation lines. b) Before segment finalizing. (c) After segment finalizing.

4) Vertical slicing continues from a pixel to the right of the previous segmentation line. However, the next vertical line that does not contain any foreground pixel is not necessarily the next Segmentation line. It could be a redundant segmentation line, which is ignored by algorithm. Therefore, only when the vertical slicing process cuts through the next letter, the next vertical line that does not contain any foreground pixels is the next segmentation line.

Step 4 repeats until the algorithm determines the last segmentation line (after which, the vertical slicing will not find any foreground pixels).

The first step of the snake segmentation is to preprocess an image to obtain the first and last segmentation lines, as illustrated in Fig 4(a). Next step scans the image vertically from left to right to detect the foreground using the concept of snake game.

The snake moves in downward direction until it detects a foreground pixel. Once a foreground pixel is detected, it moves in other directions. Once the snake reaches the bottom of image, the path traversed by the snake is nothing but the segmentation line. There could be multiple snakes between two segments, see Fig 4(b), where for example the red block between 'K' and 'S' were in fact a set of snake lines that touched each other. Therefore, the last step is to finalize the segments. Fig 4(c) shows the finalized segments of a challenge, one for which vertical segmentation would fail to segment overlapping letters T, J and K. The snake segmentation algorithm gives satisfactory results in case of disconnected and overlapped characters; however it fails for connected characters due to the ability of snake to touch foreground pixels of the image but never cuts through them.

4   Proposed Segmentation Algorithm

4.1   Modified Projection Based Segmentation Algorithm

As seen from previous section, the projection based segmentation algorithm splits image having either connected or overlapped characters into sub images which may have more than one characters. Taking into consideration the fact that generally CAPTCHA images have more than four characters, we have modified projection based segmentation algorithm as shown in Fig. 5, where the threshold changes dynamically. The basic approach for the modified algorithm is as stated below:

1. Calculate projection value of each column by summing number of black pixels.
2. Initially consider threshold value as zero.
3. Scan the image and make segments with respect to current threshold.
4. If number of segments is greater than four, stop.
5. Else find the next minimum count of the black pixels in a column and set threshold to that value.
6. Repeat from step 3.
7. Calculate the width of properly segmented characters.
8. If width of any segmented characters is greater than width as calculated in step 7, then cut the segment in 2 halves.
9. Repeat step 8 till the width of all segmented characters is equal.

Modified projection based segmentation algorithm gives accuracy of 80% for even number of connected characters in a segment.

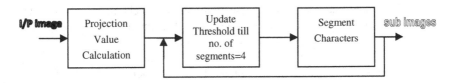

Fig. 5. Modified projection based segmentation

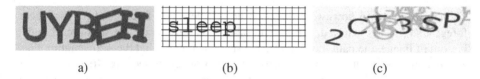

Fig. 6. CAPTCHA having a) Connected b) Disconnected c) Overlapped Characters (T is above C)

Table 1. Style of Touching

Category	Type	Style of touching	Examples
Single-touching	1		*59 33*
	2		*24 02*
	3		*23 52*
	4		*40 00*
Multiple-touching	5		*78 38*

4.2   Proposed Algorithm

Modified projection based algorithm divides a segment of image into two halves but unable to separate odd number of characters. To overcome such limitation, the basic approach of proposed algorithm depends on window of an approximate size (the size of the average individual character plus a small fuzz factor for wrapping). In said window, it checks for continuous connectivity points at the same level at which the characters are connected at offsets from the edge of the window and then reduces, wherever possible. Then it segments the character depending on style of touching of characters as shown in table 1 [3]. The flow chart of the proposed algorithm is shown in Fig 7 and explained as follows:

1) Divide the original image into sub images which may contain one or more than one character depending on projection value of characters by applying method as described in section 2.1.
2) Apply the snake segmentation approach to sub image as described in section 2.2, so as to find continuous connectivity points the characters are connected by determining topmost black pixel for each column from the edge of the window and then reducing, wherever possible.
3) If continuous connectivity points follow style of touching of type 1, 2, 4, and 5 from top of image as shown in table 1, then segment sub image. Similarly

segment characters having style of touching of type 1, 2, 3, and 5 from bottom of sub image as shown in table 1, by determining bottommost pixel for each column from the edge of the window and then reducing, wherever possible.

4) Compare the width of segmented characters with average size of individual segmented characters.. If width of segmented characters is equal to properly segmented characters then store the segment (now segmented sub image contains only one character). Else go to step 5. Accept next sub image.

5) Repeat steps 2, 3 and 4.

The criteria we use to set the threshold value are to segment original image into sub images without cutting any of characters present in it. A small value is restrictive leading to under segmentation, in the sense that overlapped characters are not segmented.   A large value results in creation of sub images and breaking of characters. We arrived at 15% of maximum projection value as a threshold, the one that gives the best results. The size of window is decided by size of individual characters which in turn depends on percentage of total black pixel density in an image. The value of parameters like threshold and window is not derived from any theoretical expressions but it is supported by results obtained from hundreds of images.

5   Performance Analysis

The proposed algorithm is tested on 275 images of different kinds, sizes, and noise levels obtained from Various social web sites like MSN, Yahoo and Google. The set of data is classified into three categories as disconnected characters CAPTCHA, Connected Characters CAPTCHA and Overlapped CAPTCHA. The accuracy of segmentation in these experimental results is based upon the numbers of characters in different images For example; every image in the MSN system has 8 characters. If the algorithm can segment 40 characters from 10 images, the accuracy will be 40/ (10*8) = 0.5, or 50%. Fig. 8 shows the comparison of the proposed algorithm with snake segmentation and projection based algorithm. The segmentation accuracy of the proposed algorithm for breaking CAPTCHA testifies that it can be applied for a wide range of different CAPTCHAs. The proposed algorithm gives approximately 98% accuracy for the disconnected and overlapped characters where as for connected characters the results are improved by 42% as compared to projection based segmentation algorithm resulting in 85% accuracy.   Modified projection based algorithm shows 78% accuracy for even number of connected characters. Fig.9 shows result of projection based segmentation algorithm for connected characters. Fig. 10 represents result of snake segmentation algorithm for overlapped characters. Fig. 11 gives Graphical User Interface (GUI) representation of proposed algorithm used for breaking CAPTCHA.

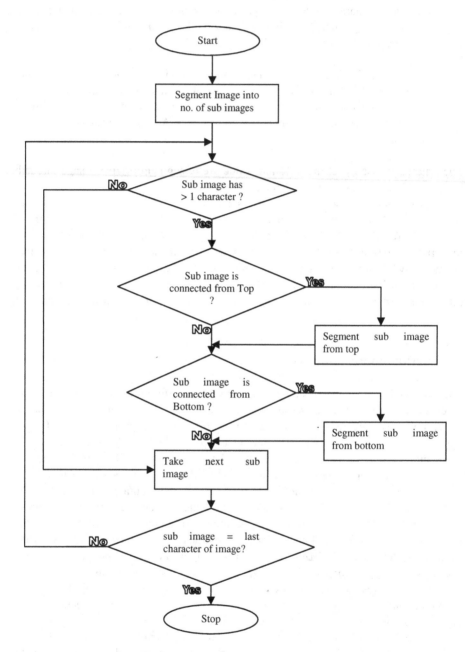

Fig. 7. Proposed segmentation algorithm

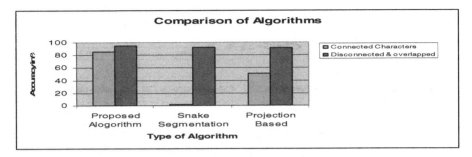

Fig. 8. Comparison of Segmentation Algorithms

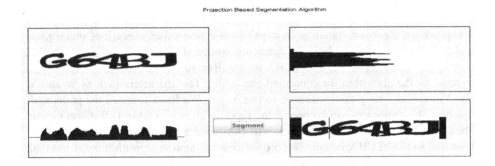

Fig. 9. Projection based segmentation algorithm

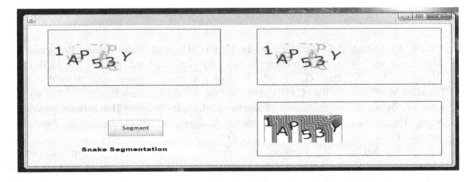

Fig. 10. Snake segmentation algorithm

Fig. 11. GUI representation of proposed algorithm

6   Conclusion

The proposed algorithm based on concept of projection value, concept of snake game and typical patterns of touching the characters, successfully segments disconnected & overlapped characters from CAPTCHA image. But, said this, there is always a need to improve the algorithm for connected characters. The characters such as W and M and Y and V do not give the desired results as yet. We have assumed the patterns of touching the characters can be one of the types as shown in table 1. We don't claim about the only existence of these patterns. But these are common styles of touching observed in CAPTCHA image. The proposed segmentation algorithm helps to break CAPTCHA & thus in turn helps to measure strength of CAPTCHA.

Acknowledgement. The authors would like to thank the referees for their helpful comments. This research is supported by University of Pune.

References

1. Yan, J., El Ahmad, A.S.: Breaking Visual CAPTCHAs with Naïve Pattern Recognition Algorithms. In: 23rd Annual Computer Security Applications Conf., pp. 279–291 (2007)
2. Huang, S., Lee, Y., Bell, G., Ou, Z.: A Projection-based Segmentation Algorithm for Breaking MSN and YAHOO CAPTCHAs. In: Proc. World Congress Eng., vol. 1 (2008)
3. Chen, Y., Wang, Y.: Segmentation of Single- or Multiple-Touching Handwritten Numeral String Using Background and Foreground Analysis. IEEE Trans. Pattern Analysis Machine Intelligence 22(11), 1304–1317 (2000)
4. Simard, P., Szeliski, R., Benaloh, J., Couvreur, J., Calinov, I.: Using Character Recognition and Segmentation to Tell Computers from Humans. In: Int'l Conference on Document Analysis and Recogntion, ICDAR (2003)
5. Von Ahn, L., Blum, M., Langford, J.: Telling Humans and Computer Apart Automatically. CACM 47(2) (2004)
6. Baird, H.S., Moll, M.A., Wang, S.Y.: ScatterType: A Legible but Hard-to-Segment CAPTCHA. In: Eighth International Conference on Document Analysis and Recognition, pp. 935–939 (August 2005)

7. Chew, M., Baird, H.S.: BaffleText: a human interactive proof. In: Proceedings of 10th IS&T/SPIE Document Recognition & Retrieval Conference, San Jose, CA, USA (2003)
8. Yan, J.: Bot, Cyborg and Automated Turing Test. In: Christianson, B., Crispo, B., Malcolm, J.A., Roe, M. (eds.) Security Protocols. LNCS, vol. 5087, pp. 198–201. Springer, Heidelberg (2009)
9. Coates, A.L., Baird, H.S., Fateman, R.J.: PessimalPrint: A Reverse Turing Test. Int'l. J. on Document Analysis & Recognition 5, 158–163 (2003)
10. Pope, C., Kaur, K.: Is It Human or Computer? Defending E-Commerce with CAPTCHA. IEEE IT Professional, 43–49 (March 2005)
11. Chellapilla, K., Simard, P.: Using Machine Learning to Break Visual Human Interaction Proofs (HIPs). In: Advances in Neural Information Processing Systems 17, Neural Information Processing Systems (NIPS). MIT Press (2004)
12. Converse, T.: CAPTCHA Generation as a Web Service. In: Baird, H.S., Lopresti, D.P. (eds.) HIP 2005. LNCS, vol. 3517, pp. 82–96. Springer, Heidelberg (2005)
13. Naccache, D., Whelan, C.: 9/11: Who alerted the CIA (And Other Secret Secrets). Rump session, Eurocrypt (2004)
14. Mori, G., Malik, J.: Recognising Objects in Adversarial Clutter: Breaking a Visual CAPTCHA. In: IEEE Conference on Computer Vision and Pattern Recognition, CVPR 2003, vol. 1, pp. 134–141 (June 2003)
15. Moy, G., Jones, N., Harkless, C., Potter, R.: Distortion Estimation Techniques in Solving Visual CAPTCHAs. In: IEEE Conference on Computer Vision and Pattern Recognition, CVPR 2004, vol. 2, pp. 23–28 (June 2004)
16. Casey, R.G., Lecolinet, E.: A Survey of Methods and Strategies in character segmentation. IEEE Trans. Pattern Analysis Machine Intelligence 18(7), 690–707 (1996)
17. Chandavale, A.A., Sapkal, A.M., Jalnekar, R.M.: A framework to analyze security of Text based CAPTCHA. Int. Journal of Forensics and Computer Application 1(27), 127–133 (2010)

A Similarity Model to Estimate Attack Strategy Based on Intentions Analysis for Network Forensics

Aman Jantan, Mohammad Rasmi, Mohd Izham Ibrahim, and Azri H.A. Rahman

School of Computer Sciences, University Sciences Malaysia
Penang, 11800, Malaysia
aman@cs.usm.my, mr77mr@hotmail.com,
{izham5205,azrihafiz.arahman}@gmail.com

Abstract. Attack analysis acts as a center of gravity in network forensics to resolve the cyber crime cases. Nowadays, the cyber crime strategies have increasingly become more complicated in the digital world. This paper proposes a new model to estimate the similar attack strategy with others. The model uses a cosine similarity method, and it depends on the attack of intention analysis as an effected factor to identify the similar attack strategy. The probability values of accuracy detection of attack intention conducted from the Attack Intention Analysis (AIA) algorithm. The experiments were performed on a virtual cyber crime case to evaluate the proposed model. From the similarity of attack strategy observation, the proposed model can reduce the time and processing cost of a decision-making at investigation phase. In addition, the attack intention maximizes the accuracy of similar attack strategy estimation.

Keywords: attack analysis, attack strategy, cyber crimes, intention similarity, network forensics.

1   Introduction

Nowadays, many organizations face a lot of legal cases and security incidents in their digital environment online and offline. However, they spend more resources on analyzing attacks to their system rather than the detection and prevention solution. The main reason that an organization does not refer cyber crimes for legal action is the lack of useful evidence and insufficient information to prosecute as reported in [1]. Consequently, the network forensics plays an important role in the attack analysis process.

Network forensic techniques enable investigators to trace the attackers. The ultimate goal of these techniques is to provide sufficient evidence to prosecute the perpetrator of the crime as described by [3, 5, 6]. In general, network forensics involves monitoring network traffic and determine if there is an anomaly in the traffic and ascertaining, whether it indicates an attack. If an attack is detected, then the nature of the attack is also determined.

The variety of data sources, data granularity, anti-forensics, data integrity, data as legal evidence and privacy issues are some examples of the network forensics

S.M. Thampi et al. (Eds.): SNDS 2012, CCIS 335, pp. 336–346, 2012.

challenges [2, 4, 7-13]. Evidence analysis constitutes a major challenge for many people who are working in network forensics [4]. Therefore, during the investigation phase, it becomes more complex and difficult to define the attack and apprehend the perpetrator. Attack intentions analysis by identifying the similar attack strategy plays a major rule to analyze evidence in network forensics.

Attack intention analysis support investigators in bringing a close criminal cases with greater accuracy as mentioned in [13, 14]. On the other hand, identifying the attack strategy makes it easier for network forensic investigators to draw a possible comprehensive frame of the criminal case. Moreover, analyzing attack intentions and strategy is very important to accelerate the decision–making processes required for apprehending the perpetrator.

This paper proposes a model to estimate the similarity of the attack strategy with a pre-defined strategies for network forensics. The model based on attack intentions analysis as a new vector in the similarity attack strategy metrics in order to increase the weight of the estimated similarity values. The proposed model uses the cosine similarity as a distance-based similarity measure (Metric Axioms) to show the strength of the relationship between the new attack evidence and pre-defined evidences.

This paper is structured as follows: Section II will present a related work of network forensics analysis, attack intention and attack strategy. The proposed model will describe and define all its components in Section III. Section IV describes the experiments done using a virtual cyber criminal case. Section V gives results and analysis while the Section VI contains the conclusion and a discussion of further work required.

2   Related Works

Security analysis aims to recognize attack plans. In fact, attack plan analysis aims to reconstruct the scenario to find the attack intentions and strategy using a graph algorithm with methods for intrusive intention recognition as used in [15]. Attack recognition is a significant research area in artificial intelligence. It is still in progress in the network security domain and as such intention analysis has become an important research topic [15, 16]. As an example, the main behavioral intentions of an intruder (such as DoS on the web server on a host, gain root privilege of a host, and compromise database on a host) could be observed through time observation; launch host; target host; and rules such as intruder preconditions, network preconditions, intruder effects and network effects [17].

Attack intention is realized when it is able to identify the goal of this attack as mentioned in [15]. Even for a human expert, it is difficult to find a method of intrusion [8], which make the prediction of the attack goal more complex. Hence, the attack intention as well as the attack analysis is still the main challenge in network forensics [2, 16, 18, 19].

The main technique of constructing and analyzing attack strategy is by using an alert correlation method. The alert correlation method used several techniques to analyze the attack strategy such as a complex alerts correlation rules, hard-coded domain knowledge, low-level constructing attack scenarios [20-26]. However, the alert correlation method used to improve the intrusion prevention and/or detection system in advance to minimize the intrusion risks. Furthermore, the techniques depends on this method have difficulty in implementation and limited capabilities of detecting new attack strategies [8, 17, 18, 20-22].

In reality, the similarity measurements could improve the quality of attack analysis results. These results minimize the efforts , and in addition, the duration time and processing cost of decision-making in the investigation phase of network forensics [27]. The similarity methods that are based on distance, feature, or probabilistic measurements often used in alert correlation method, which depends on the similarity of the attack attributes [18, 27, 28]. The proposed model in this paper uses the cosine similarity as a distance-based similarity measure (Metric Axioms) to show the strength of the relationship between the new attack evidence with others. Furthermore, the proposed model uses the probability of detection accuracy values of attack intention as an effected factor with the attack evidence to estimate the similar attack strategy. The probability values conducted from Attack Intention Analysis (AIA) algorithm as introduced by [13].

3   Attack Intention Process Model

Prediction of attack intentions depends on the nature of attack, which had been detected with its evidence. Detecting attacks depends on many security sensors and detection system products (either, commercial or non-commercial security products, such as IDS or sniffer). Knowing that, a specific attack that occurs depends on the accuracy ratio for these products. We believe the current proposed process model in this research that the attack was defined and detected with an acceptable degree of accuracy.

This section is divided into two parts, the first part is to prepare the similarity attack intentions which depend on the attack intention analysis model as described in [14] and AIA algorithm [13]. The second part presents the proposed model to estimate the similarity of the attack strategy depending on the similarity of the attack intentions.

A.   Preparing the Similarity Attack Intention

Similarity attack intentions identifies the intentions of a new attack and estimates the similar intentions with previous ones. A similarity metric for attack intentions will be generated to determine similar intentions. At the beginning, the attack intentions will identify the current attack. A similarity metric for attack intentions will be generated in the next step to determine a similar intentions. Finally, it will select intentions based on the similarity of attack intention between the new attack and previous attacks. Also, it uses a predefined attack evidence depository, which consists previous intentions.

The network tools, such as Wireshark, WinPcap will be used for monitoring and capturing the network traffic. Moreover the Snort will be used as a Network Intrusion Detection System (NIDS). In the first step, the network traffic will be captured, which it will normally produce a huge volume of alerts and security data. A copy of the captured data will be analyzed in the next step to identify attack alerts in advance to collect all the possible evidence of the new attack. Hence, all possible attack intentions, which are related to the new attack, will be prepared.

Attack intention probability for each possible intention will be computed using the AIA algorithm [13]. The attack intentions similarity metric will be generated via association between the intention probability values with a relevant attack group. Finally, the similarity attack intentions metric will select the closest match to the attack intentions of the new attack.

Accordingly, the similarity attack intentions metric aims to estimate the similarity of intentions for a new attack with others. It defines a set of attacks named $\{PA\}$ contains all of past attacks, where $PA=\{A_1, A_2, A_3, \dots, A_n\}$ which n is the integer number. For each attack, there is a set of evidence name $\{AE\}$ detected during analysis of the attack where $AE=\{E_0, E_1, E_2, \dots, E_i\}$, which i is the integer number. Another set name $\{AI\}$ will define the contains of all attack intentions for all predefined attacks, where $AI=\{I_1, I_2, I_3, \dots, I_n\}$, which n is the integer number. Each attack intention or more from the set $\{AI\}$ relevant with one attack or more from the predefined attacks set $\{PA\}$. That means the relation between set $\{AI\}$ and set $\{PA\}$ is many-to-many.

The probability value will be assigned for each attack intention of the set $\{AI\}$ using AIA algorithm [13]. Suppose that there is a new attack name A_k where it belongs to the $\{PA\}$ set, this attack has a set of intentions name $\{A_kI_x\}$, which is a subset of $\{AI\}$ and $x>=1$. The similarity attack intentions metric tries to estimate the similarity between the new attack intentions with others. Firstly, it will find all attacks which have one or more of the attack intention from the subset of $\{A_kI_x\}$. It computes the sum of all the probability value of attack intentions for one attack, which is relevant and similar to the A_k intentions. The similarity of attack intention computed as The total probability value of attack intentions divided by the total number of the similar intentions of a specific attack, as follows:

$$SimA_nI(A_k) = \frac{\sum_{1,I_x \in A_kI_x}^{n} A_nI_x}{r}, for\ all\ A_n, A_k \in \{PA\}\ and\ x,k,r \in \{0..n\}, where\ x\ k,r \geq 1 \quad (1)$$

Where k is the integer number of new attack; n is the integer number to determine a predefined attack number; x is the integer number to determine the relevant intentions with attack n; and r is the total number of the A_kI_x intentions. From the (1) the intentions similarity metric will be generated. However, to find the similarity of attack intention for the new attack A_K with the others, we select the maximum similarity attack intention value from the intentions similarity metric, as follows:

$$SimAI(A_k) = Max(SimA_nI(A_k)), for\ all\ A_n, A_k \in \{PA\}\ and\ k \in \{0..n\}, where\ k \geq 1 \quad (2)$$

Where the value of n presents the maximum similar attack number, which is the closest with new one A_k.

B.   Similarity Attack Strategy Model Based on Intentions

This section presents a model to estimate the similarity attack strategy depending on attack intentions, which is generated by the similarity attack intention analysis process as described in the previous section. The new model aims to estimate the similarity of attack strategy for a new attack with others. The proposed model contains three components as shown in Fig. 1.

The first component aims to classify attack strategy with new addition factor, which is an attack intention. The second component to generate a similarity metric contains all possible strategy that is similar to the new attack strategy. Finally, the third component estimates the similarity of attack strategy based on the maximum similar attack evidence weight after adding analyzed attack intentions. The three components are described as follows:

1) Classify Attack Strategy: In this component, the predefined attacks {PA} and attack evidence {AE} sets should be identified at the beginning. The similarity attack intentions metric for the new attack name A_k is symbolized as $(SimA_nI(A_k))$, which produced the next component and added as a new vector to the similarity attack evidence vectors. This addition will affect the weight of the similarity value for the new attack A_k with others. Therefore, it is given as a set of priority value of n attack evidence (PA_nAE); and a group of n attack evidence A_nG. Each priority value of attack evidence (PA_nAE) is classified into one attack evidence group (A_nG) through classifier function $C(PA_nAE)$, where (PA_nAE) is the domain of $C(PA_nAE_i)$, and (A_nG) is the co domain/target of $C(PA_nAE)$, i.e. $A_nG=C(PA_nAE)$. In the expression $C(PA_nAE_i)$, (PA_nAE_i) is the argument, and $C(PA_nAE_i)$ is the value, where n denotes an attack number and i evidence identity. Each attacks evidence pointed out the similarity of the new attack A_k strategy vectors defined based on the classification evidence function $C(PA_nAE)$, as follows:

$$C(PA_nAE) = \{(PA_nAE_0, PA_nG_1),(PA_nAE_1, PA_nG_2)... \tag{3}$$
$$PA_nAE_i, PA_nG_{i+1})\}, for\ all\ n\ and\ i \in \{0..n\}, where\ n \geq 1\ and\ i \geq 0$$

The attack evidence point (PA_nAE_i, PA_nG_{i+1}) means that every attack evidence has a priority value (PA_nAE_i) assigned from the predefined attack evidence priority database and classified into one attack evidence group (PA_nG_{i+1}) through the classifier function $(C(PA_nAE))$. After that, the distance between the new attack A_k evidence and the other predefined attack evidence, which have the same classification group, will be calculated using Euclidean distance $(Euc(A_kE_i, A_dE_i))$.

2) Generate Attack Strategy Similarity Metric: The cosine similarity function $Sim(A_kE_i, A_dE_i)$ used to generate a similarity metric between the new attack A_k with other attacks evidence which have the same group. It is computed by product of the new attack A_k evidence with other $(A_kE_i) \cdot (A_dE_i)$, which presented as vectors, divided by the Euclidean distance between (A_kE_i) and (A_dE_i) $(Euc(A_kE_i, A_dE_i))$.

The ratio resulting from this equation presents the cosine angle between the attack evidence and intention classifier vectors, with value between 0 (cosine(90)=0) which means, it is completely unrelated to a specific evidence group, and 1(cosine(0)=1), which means it is completely related.

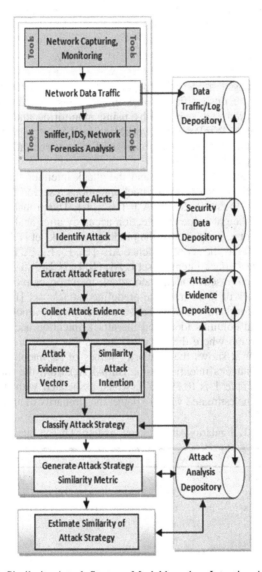

Fig. 1. Similarity Attack Strategy Model based on Intention Analysis

3) Estimate Similarity of Attack Strategy: In this component, each predefined attack has a weight introduce the closeness ratio with the new attack A_k. The weight will be calculated by summing up all the similarity attack evidence with the new attack

A_k (SimA$_d$AE$_i$ (A_k)), added to the similarity of attack intentions with the new attack A_k (SimA$_d$I(A_k)). The result will be divided by the number of evidence plus one for attack intentions factor.

The maximum weight A_d from the set of predefined attacks {PA}, which is distinguished by the attack number (d), will be a candidate to be a closeness ratio of the similarity attack strategy with the new attack A_k (SimAS(A_k)).

4   Experiments

To evaluate the proposed model, this paper will use a virtual cyber criminal case which is caused by the unspecific network attack. This case detects from network traffic which is captured and analyzed by using monitoring and analyzing network tools such as Wireshark, WinPcap, NetworkMiner and Snort as a Network Detection System (NIDS). In addition, this tool is also used to construct all possible evidences associated with the cyber criminal case.

Assumed that this attack named A_6, and the attack intentions analyzed using AIA algorithm and detected as a set of three attack intentions reserved for A_6I_x set, where x presents the number of intention. So the $A_6I=\{I_2, I_4, I_5\}$. The probability values for each intention presents the height value of detection accuracy after analyzing process and it equal (0.67) for each one. Suppose that the predefined attack set is AP=$\{A_1, A_2, A_3, A_4, A_5\}$, which each attack has the set of evidence AE=$\{E_0, E_1, E_2, E_3, E_4, E_5, E_6, E_7, E_8, E_9, E_{10}\}$, and the predefined attack intention set is AI=$\{I_1, I_2, I_3, I_4, I_5, I_6, I_7, I_8, I_9, I_{10}\}$.

According to the proposed model, each attack intention or more from set {AI} is relevant with one attack or more from the predefined attacks set {PA}. The probability of each attack intentions presented in Table 1 as a metric, which is the intersection between the rows and columns identified the attack intention accuracy probability of decoction accuracy value where the (0) value means that there are no intention of the same type. In addition it shows the similarity values of A_6 intention with others. The maximum similarity attacks intention value SimAI(A_6) from the intentions similarity metric as shown in Table 1 is (0.396667), which associated with the attack A_4. This value could increase the estimated value to detect the similarity of attack strategy.

Table 1. Similarity Attack Intention Metric Of The Attack A_6

	A_1	A_2	A_3	A_4	A_5
I_1	0.53	0	0.46	0	0.62
I_2	0	0.25	0.36	0	0.25
I_3	0.35	0	0	0.52	0
I_4	0	0.42	0	0.65	0
I_5	0.45	0	0.41	0.54	0.44
I_6	0	0	0	0.31	0
I_7	0	0.62	0.23	0	0
I_8	0.35	0	0	0.26	0
I_9	0	0.26	0.35	0	0.33
I_{10}	0	0.25	0.45	0	0.45

Applying the classifier function to the attack A_6, assume that the $C(PA_6AE)=\{(3,1), (5,2), (6,3), (2,4), (3,5), (1,6), (3,7), 5,8), (6,9), (7,10)\}$ is used to estimate the similarity of evidence to the predefined attack set $\{AP\}$ evidence in order to generate the similarity metric. In reality, the proposed model manipulates with an uncertain evidence, so the similarity metric contains a match similarity evidence value that are completely related evidence with attack A_6. Table 2 shows the similarity metric between attack A_6 with other attacks evidences which have the same group, and also the similarity of attack intentions with others.

Table 2. Similarity Attack Strategy Metric of the Attack A_6

	A_1	A_2	A_3	A_4	A_5
A_6E_0	0	0	1	1	0
A_6E_1	0	0	0	0	0
A_6E_2	0	1	0	1	1
A_6E_3	1	0	0	0	0
A_6E_4	0	0	0	0	0
A_6E_5	0	1	1	0	0
A_6E_6	0	0	0	0	0
A_6E_7	0	0	1	1	0
A_6E_8	0	0	0	0	0
A_6E_9	1	0	0	1	0
A_6E_{10}	0	0	0	0	1
$SimAI(A_6)$	0.15	0.223333	0.256667	0.396667	0.23

5   Results and Analysis

The advantage of similarity attack strategy based on an attack intention model where the similarities of attack strategy are based on an important and effected factor. This factor is the intention of the attack, which is generated after the process of analyzing attack evidence and predicted intention. In other words, the model exploits the data that have been analyzed before, and linked the results of factor analysis in order to find a similar strategy to new the attack.

As a result, the maximum weight of similar attacks A_6 strategy $(SimAS(A_6))$, which is conducted from the metric of similarity attack strategy go to attack A_4 from the set of predefined attacks $\{PA\}$ with the value (0.366389) as shown in Fig. 2. That means, the attack A_4 will be a stated to be the closest ratio of the similarity attack strategy with the new attack A_6. Moreover, the Figure shows the strength of the relationship between the attack intention and the estimated value of similar attack strategy. The relation shows that the attack intention effect to identify more accurate estimation values for similar attack strategy.

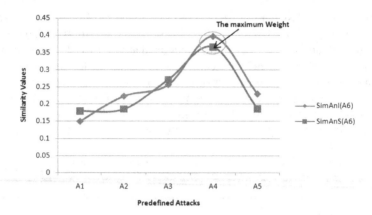

Fig. 2. The Maximum Weight of Similar Attacks (A6) Strategy

6   Conclusions and Future Work

Attack strategy is a necessity factor needs to be analyzed in network forensics attack analysis phase to identify the methodology of the attacker. This paper proposes a new model to estimate the similar attack strategy based on the probability of detection accuracy of attack intentions. The estimated probability values with similarity of attack evidence values need to be combined together to estimate the similar attack strategy with the predefined attack strategy. The results prove that the attack intention analysis increases the accuracy of estimation values of similarity attack strategy with other.

The current network forensics investigation process, which acts as a reactive approach is time consuming, costly and an error-prone process to apprehend the real perpetrator. Future research should manipulate the network forensics process in a proactive way. Furthermore, the phases of network forensics must be a comprehensive and satisfied with the integrity constraints in advance to enhance the quality of incident response decision-making.

Acknowledgments. This work was supported by RU Grant No.1001/PKOMP/ 817048, School of Computer Science, Universiti Sains Malaysia, Penang, Malaysia.

References

1. CERT, CSO, and U.S.S. Service, 2011 CyberSecurity Watch Survey. Software Engineering Institute CERT Program at Carnegie Mellon University and Deloitte (2011)
2. Pilli, E.S., Joshi, R.C., Niyogi, R.: Network forensic frameworks: Survey and research challenges. Digital Investigation 7(1-2), 14–27 (2010)
3. Palmer, G.: A Road Map for Digital Forensic Research. Report from DFRWS 2001, F.D.F.R. Workshop Utica, New York, pp. 27–30 (2001)

4. Almulhem, A.: Network forensics: Notions and challenges. In: 2009 IEEE International Symposium on Signal Processing and Information Technology, ISSPIT (2009)
5. Yasinsac, A., Manzano, Y.: Honeytraps, a network forensic tool. In: Proceedings of the Sixth Multi-Conference on Systemics, Florida, USA (2002)
6. Shin, Y.-D.: New Model for Cyber Crime Investigation Procedure. JNIT: Journal of Next Generation Information Technology 2(2), 1–7 (2011)
7. Casey, E.: Case study: Network intrusion investigation - lessons in forensic preparation. Digital Investigation 2(4), 254–260 (2005)
8. Huang, M.-Y., Jasper, R.J., Wicks, T.M.: A large scale distributed intrusion detection framework based on attack strategy analysis. Computer Networks 31(23-24), 2465–2475 (1999)
9. Rogers, M.K., Seigfried, K.: The future of computer forensics: a needs analysis survey. Computers & Security 23(1), 12–16 (2004)
10. Saptarshi, G., Gautam, K., Niloy, G.: Spammers' networks within online social networks: a case-study on Twitter. In: Proceedings of the 20th International Conference Companion on World Wide Web. ACM, Hyderabad (2011)
11. Rasmi, M., Jantan, A.: A Model for NFAA-Network Forensics Attack Analysis. In: 3rd International Conference on Computer Engineering and Technology, ICCET 2011. ASME Press (2011)
12. Kamal, D., Bassil, M.: The anti-forensics challenge. In: Proceedings of the 2011 International Conference on Intelligent Semantic Web-Services and Applications. ACM, Amman (2011)
13. Rasmi, M., Jantan, A.: AIA: Attack Intention Analysis Algorithm Based on D-S Theory with Causal Technique for Network Forensics - A Case Study. International Journal of Digital Content Technology and its Applications 5(9), 230–237 (2011)
14. Rasmi, M., Jantan, A.: Attack Intention Analysis Model for Network Forensics. In: Zain, J.M., Wan Mohd, W.M.b., El-Qawasmeh, E. (eds.) ICSECS 2011, Part II. CCIS, vol. 180, pp. 403–411. Springer, Heidelberg (2011)
15. Peng, W., Yao, S., Chen, J.: Recognizing Intrusive Intention and Assessing Threat Based on Attack Path Analysis. In: International Conference on Multimedia Information Networking and Security, MINES 2009 (2009)
16. Qin, X., Lee, W.: Attack plan recognition and prediction using causal networks. In: 20th Annual Computer Security Applications Conference (2004)
17. Wang, Z., Peng, W.: An Intrusive Intention Recognition Model Based on Network Security States Graph. In: 5th International Conference on Wireless Communications, Networking and Mobile Computing, WiCom 2009 (2009)
18. Wei, W., Thomas, E.D.: A Graph Based Approach Toward Network Forensics Analysis. ACM Trans. Inf. Syst. Secur. 12(1), 1–33 (2008)
19. Wu, P., Zhigang, W., Junhua, C.: Research on Attack Intention Recognition Based on Graphical Model. In: Fifth International Conference on Information Assurance and Security, IAS 2009 (2009)
20. Zhu, B., Ghorbani, A.A.: Alert Correlation For Extracting Attack Strategies. International Journal of Network Security 3(3), 244–258 (2006)
21. Peng, W., et al.: Recognizing Intrusive Intention Based on Dynamic Bayesian Networks. In: International Symposium on Information Engineering and Electronic Commerce, IEEC 2009 (2009)
22. Bolzoni, D., Etalle, S., Hartel, P.H.: Panacea: Automating Attack Classification for Anomaly-Based Network Intrusion Detection Systems. In: Kirda, E., Jha, S., Balzarotti, D. (eds.) RAID 2009. LNCS, vol. 5758, pp. 1–20. Springer, Heidelberg (2009)

23. Wang, L., Li, Z.-T., Fan, J.: Learning attack strategies through attack sequence mining method. In: International Conference on Communication Technology, ICCT 2006 (2006)

24. Wang, L., Liu, A., Jajodia, S.: Using attack graphs for correlating, hypothesizing, and predicting intrusion alerts. Computer Communications 29(15), 2917–2933 (2006)

25. Wang, L., et al.: A novel algorithm SF for mining attack scenarios model. In: IEEE International Conference on e-Business Engineering, ICEBE 2006 (2006)

26. Nashat, M., Maya, I.C., Ahmad, F.: Filtering intrusion detection alarms. Cluster Computing 13(1), 19–29 (2010)

27. Zaka, B.: Theory and Applications of Similarity Detection Techniques. In: Institute for Information Systems and Computer Media, IICM, p. 171. Graz University of Technology, Graz (2009)

28. Peng, N., Dingbang, X.: Learning attack strategies from intrusion alerts. In: Proceedings of the 10th ACM Conference on Computer and Communications Security. ACM, Washington, D.C. (2003)

Stationary Wavelet Transformation
Based Self-recovery of Blind-Watermark from
Electrocardiogram Signal in Wireless Telecardiology

Nilanjan Dey[1], Anamitra Bardhan Roy[2], Achintya Das[3],
and Sheli Sinha Chaudhuri[4]

[1] Dept. of IT, JIS College of Engineering, Kalyani, West Bengal, India
[2] Dept. of CSE, JIS College of Engineering, Kalyani, West Bengal, India
[3] ECE Department, Kalyani Govt. Engineering College, Kalyani, West Bengal, India
[4] ETCE Department, Jadavpur University, Kolkata, India
dey.nilanjan@ymail.com, greatanamitra@yahoo.co.in,
achintya.das123@gmail.com, shelism@rediffmail.com

Abstract. At present, considerable amount of work has been done in tele-monitoring that involves transmission of biomedical signals through wireless media. Exchange of bio-signals between hospitals requires efficient and reliable transmission. Watermarking is added "ownership" information in multimedia content to prove authenticity, verify signal integrity, and achieve control over the copy process. The ECG signal is a sensitive diagnostic tool that is used to detect various cardio-vascular diseases by measuring and recording the electrical activity of the heart in exquisite detail. This paper proposes a method of binary watermark embedding into the Electrocardiogram (ECG) signal and a self recovery based watermark extraction mechanism using Stationary Wavelet Transformation (SWT), Spread-Spectrum and quantization. In this approach, the generated watermarked signal having an acceptable level of imperceptibility and distortion is compared to the original ECG signal. Finally, a comparative study of detected P-QRS-T components is done to measure the diagnostic value change as an effect of watermarking. In this approach the generated watermarked ECG signal having an acceptable level of imperceptibility and distortion is compared to the Original ECG signal based on Peak Signal to Noise Ratio (PSNR) and correlation value.

Keywords: ECG, Stationary Wavelet Transformation (SWT), P- QRS-T Components, Quantization, Spread- Spectrum.

1 Introduction

Doctors and medical practitioners often exchange medical signal in various diagnostic centers for mutual availability of diagnostic and therapeutic case studies. The communication of medical data through signals requires authentication and security. Embedding of watermarks in signals can cause distortion in the signals. As the signals convey information required for detection of diseases, hence any kind of distortion

S.M. Thampi et al. (Eds.): SNDS 2012, CCIS 335, pp. 347–357, 2012.
© Springer-Verlag Berlin Heidelberg 2012

can result in erroneous diagnosis. Embedding of watermark [1, 2, 3] in ECG signal causes compromise with the diagnostic value of medical signal. Achieving medical watermarking is a challenging task.

An ECG signal is composed of successive repetition of 'PQRST' in monotony. In the beginning, a crest is generated from the linear signal to form the 'P' wave. The declining linear wave soon gets a downward deflection labeled as 'Q' wave. A sudden upright deflection can be observed just beyond the Q wave to form a high cone i.e. the 'R' wave. On its decline a slight downward deflection is the 'S' wave. A noticeable hinge after the 'S' wave is known as 'T' wave that marks the end of a segment of the ECG signal. [4]

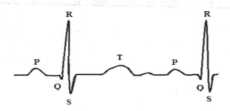

Fig. 1. P, QRS, T Components

Watermarking is the process of embedding data into a 1-D or 2-D signal for security purpose. Blind watermarking scheme does not require the original signal or any other data. Watermark insertion is done by using an embedding algorithm and a pseudo-random key. Blind-watermarking provides a scope for the authentication of the original signal or to provide patient information (Electronic Patient Report).

In 2-D signal processing, watermarking schemes can be classified either as Spatial Domain or as Transformed Domain. Least Significant Bit (LSB) [5] insertion is a very simple and common approach to embed information in an image in special domain. The limitation of this approach is vulnerable to every slight image manipulation. Converting image from one format to another format and back could destroy information hidden in LSBs. Watermarked image can be easily detected by statistical analysis like histogram analysis. This technique involves replacing N number of least significant bit of each pixel of a container image with the data of a watermark. Watermark is destroyed as the value of N increases. In frequency domain analysis data can be kept secret by using Discrete Cosine Transformation (DCT) [6, 7]. Main limitation of this approach is blocking artifact. DCT pixels are grouped into 8x8 blocks that are each transformed into 64 DCT coefficients. A modification of a single DCT co-efficient will affect all 64-image pixels in that block. One of the modern techniques of watermarking is Discrete Wavelet Transformation (DWT) approach [8, 9]. In this approach the imperceptibility and distortion of the watermarked 2-D signal is acceptable. Proposed watermarking method deals with a stationary wavelet transformation based blind-watermark technique where the pseudo-random key for the embedding process is generated from the signal itself.

The extraction mechanism of the watermark is self-recoverable. A comparative study of detected P, QRS and T components is done to measure the diagnostic value changes as an effect of watermarking.

2   Methodology

2.1   Stationary Wavelet Transformation

The wavelet transform describes a multi-resolution decomposition process in terms of expansion of an image into a set of wavelet basis functions. Discrete Wavelet Transformation (DWT) has its own excellent space frequency localization property. Application of DWT in 2D signals corresponds to 2D filter image processing in each dimension. The input image is divided into 4 non-overlapping multi-resolution sub-bands by the filters, namely LL_1 (Approximation coefficients), LH_1 (vertical details), HL_1 (horizontal details) and HH_1 (diagonal details). The sub-band (LL_1) is processed further to obtain the next coarser scale of wavelet coefficients, until some final scale "N" is reached. When "N" is reached, 3N+1 sub-bands are obtained consisting of the multi-resolution sub-bands. Which are LL_X and LH_X, HL_X and HH_X where "X" ranges from 1 to "N". Generally, most of the image energy is stored in the LL_X sub-band.

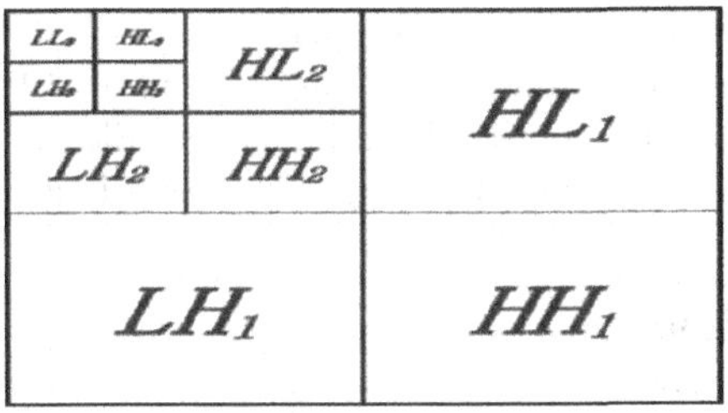

Fig. 2. Three phase decomposition using DWT

Stationary Wavelet Transform (SWT) [13] is the modification of Discrete Wavelet Transform to make it translation-invariant in nature that does not decimate coefficients at every transformation level. Translation-invariance is achieved by removing the downsamplers and upsamplers in the DWT and upsampling the filter coefficients by a factor of $2^{(j-1)}$ in the jth level of the algorithm. It is an inherently redundant scheme as the output of each level contains the same number of samples as the input. So for decomposition of N level there is a redundancy of N in the wavelet coefficients. This algorithm, proposed by Holdschneider is also known as "algorithme à trous" which refers to inserting zeroes in the filters.

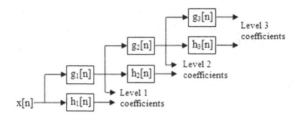

Fig. 3. Three phase decomposition using DWT

Haar wavelet is not continuous, and therefore not differentiable. This property can however be an advantage for the analysis of signals with sudden transitions.

2.2   Signal Denoising

Artificially added random noise [10] in the signal is removed by thresholding of the SWT coefficients up to level 2 using sym 4 wavelet function. As a thresholding method, a soft global threshold δ of an estimated value given by the following Eq. is used.

$$\delta = \sigma \sqrt{2 \log L}$$

where the noise is Gaussian with standard deviation σ of the SWT coefficients and L is the number of samples of the processed signal.

Thresholding can be either soft or hard. In soft and hard thresholding, the entire signal values zeroes out if the signal values are smaller than δ. In case of soft thresholding the subtraction of δ from the signal values is larger than δ.

3   Proposed Method

3.1   Processing ECG Signal for Watermarking

ECG signal is read and the length is calculated followed by the detection of the P, Q, R, S and T components [11].

Watermark Embedding

Watermark embedding process is explained in Figure 4.

Step 1.   ECG signal is converted into a largest possible square 2-D signal followed by decomposition into four sub bands (Ca_1, Ch_1, Cv_1 and Cd_1) using SWT.

Step 2. Ca_1 is further decomposed into four sub bands (Ca_2, Ch_2, Cv_2 and Cd_2) using SWT.

Step 3.   A binary watermarked image is converted into 1D Vector.

Step 4.   The absolute value of approximation coefficient of the ECG Signal is rounded off.

Step 5.   The rounded off values are quantized into steps as specified by partition vector (partitioned into three segments) and encoded based on the codebook vector [-1, 0, 1].

Step 6.   Quantized values are converted into 2D matrix.

Step 7.   Random permutation is applied twice on the quantized matrix to generate two different pseudo-random sequences (PN_Sequence1, PN_Sequence2).

Step 8. Ch_1 and Cv_1 sub bands are modified followed by the modification of Cd_2 accordingly by PN_Sequence1 and PN_Sequence2 depending upon the content of the secret 1D image vector to be embedded.

Step 9.   Four sub bands of the 2nd level SWT decomposed 2D signal including modified sub bands are combined using Inverse Stationary Wavelet Transform (ISWT).

Step 10. Four sub bands of the 1st level SWT decomposed 2D signal including generated resultant 2D signal are combined to generate the Watermarked 2D signal using ISWT.

Step 11. Watermarked 2D signal is reshaped into 1D signal.

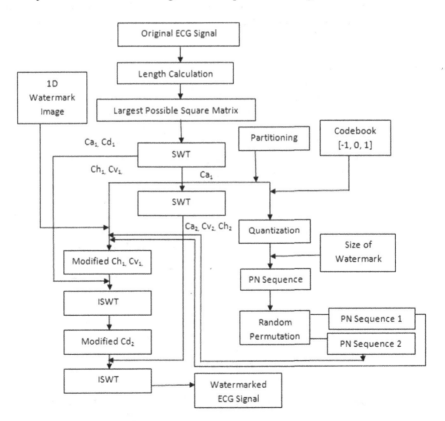

Fig. 4. Watermark Embedding Process

Watermark Extraction

Watermark extraction process is explained in Figure 5.

Step 1.   The watermarked ECG signal is converted into a largest possible square 2-D signal followed by decomposition into four sub bands (Ca_1, Ch_1, Cv_1 and Cd_1) using SWT.

Step 2. Cd_1 is further decomposed into four sub bands (Ca_2, Ch_2, Cv_2 and Cd_2) using SWT.

Step 3.   The absolute value of approximation coefficient (Ca_1) of the watermarked ECG Signal is rounded off.

Step 4.   The rounded off values are quantized into steps as specified by partition vector (partitioned into three segments) and encoded based on the codebook vector [-1, 0, 1].

Step 5.   Only the size of the watermark image is sent to the intended receiver via a secret communication channel.

Step 6.   Watermark image can be recovered from the Ch_2, Cv_2 components of the watermarked 2D signal after 2nd level SWT decomposition using correlation function and knowing the size of the modified ECG signal.

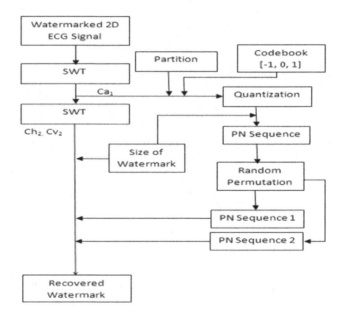

Fig. 5. Watermark Extraction Process

3.2   P, QRS and T Components Detection from Watermarked ECG Signal

P, QRS and T components detection from Watermarked ECG Signal is explained in Figure 6.

Step 1. 2-D watermarked ECG Signal is reshaped into 1-D signal.

Step 2. Signal denoising using soft thresholding method.

Step 3. P, QRS and T components peaks are detected from the denoised ECG signal based on our proposed P, QRS and T components detection method.

Step 4. The time intervals are again calculated considering the positions of two consecutive same-labeled peaks.

Step 5. A comparative study is done for the two consecutive 'R'-peaks and other peaks intervals between original and watermarked ECG signal.

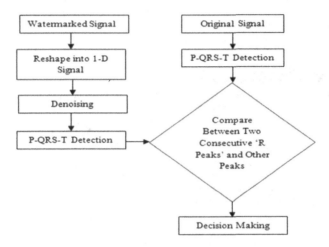

Fig. 6. Comparison between P, QRS and T components Detection from Original ECG Signal and Watermarked signal

4   Result and Discussion

MATLAB 7.0.1 Software is extensively used for the study of the ECG watermarking embedding and extraction process. Concerned images obtained in the result are shown in Fig. 7.

The sample ECG signal analyzed in this method as test cases are rendered by Suraha Nursing Home, Kolkata.

4.1   Peak Signal to Noise Ratio (PSNR)

It measures the quality of a watermarked signal. This performance metric is used to determine perceptual transparency of the watermarked signal with respect to original signal:

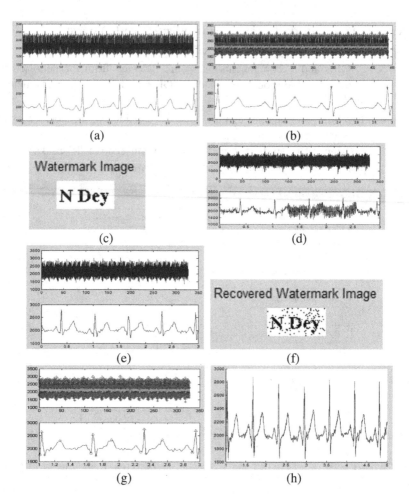

Fig. 7. (a) Original ECG signal(200 sec. long), (b) Plot of ECG signal with P-QRS-T, (c) Original Watermark Image, (d) Recovered Watermarked Signal, (e) Recovered Watermarked De-noised Signal, (f) Recovered Watermark Image, (g) Detected P,QRS and T Components after Watermark Extraction, (h) Overlay of original and de-noised watermarked ECG signal

$$\text{PSNR} = \frac{MN max_{x,y} P_{x,y}^2}{\sum x.y \ (P_{x,y} - \bar{P}_{x,y})^2} \tag{1}$$

where, M and N are number of rows and columns in the input signal, $P_{x,y}$ is the original signal and $\bar{P}_{x,y}$ is the watermarked signal

PSNR between the original signal and watermarked signal is 24.7424 as shown in Table 1.

Table 1. PSNR Value

Original ECG Signal vs. Watermarked Signal	PSNR
	24.7424

4.2   Correlation Coefficient

After secret image embedding process, the similarity of original signal x and watermarked signal x' is measured by the Standard Correlation Coefficient (c) as follows:

$$C = \frac{\sum_{m}\sum_{n}(x_{mn} - x')(y_{mn} - y')}{\sqrt{\left(\sum_{m}\sum_{n}(x_{mn} - x')^2\right)\left(\sum_{m}\sum_{n}(y_{mn} - y')^2\right)}} \tag{2}$$

where y and y' are the discrete wavelet transforms of x and x'.

Correlation (corr2) between watermark image and the recovered watermark image is shown in the Table 2.

Table 2. Correlation Value

Correlation between original Watermark image and recovered Watermark Image	0.8108

It is observed that the extracted watermark is of good visual quality and the method is best suitable for copyright protection technique.

Table 3. Average R-R Interval Before and After Watermarking

Interval	Total no. of Interval	Average Interval Before Watermarking	Average Interval After Watermarking
R-R	10	0.631	0.6400

R-R interval is the inverse of the heart rate.
Heart Rate=60/Avg. R-R Interval (Beats-per-minute)

Table 4. Heart Rate Before and After Watermarking

Heart Rate Before Watermarking	Heart Rate After Watermarking
95.08	93.75

Heart rate almost remains unaffected even after applying watermark.

Cardiac output can be defined as the blood ejection from the left or right ventricle into the aorta or pulmonary trunk per minute.

Cardiac Output = Heart Rate * Stroke Volume

where, Stroke Volume is defined as the amount of blood pumped by each ventricle with each heartbeat (Average 70ml. per beat for the adult at rest).

Stroke Volume is the difference between end diastolic volume and end systolic volume [12].

Cardiac output remains unchanged as an effect of watermarking.

Table 5. Average Q-T Intervals, QT_C intervals of Two Consecutive Peaks Before and After Watermarking and Average QRS Duration in seconds before and after watermarking

Sl. No.	Interval	Total no. of Interval	Time Intervals Before Watermarking	Time Intervals after Watermarking
1	Q-T	10	0.255	0.2600
2	QTc	10	0.317512131	0.3250
3	QRS	10	0.055	0.0600

5   Conclusion

Since the application of wavelet transformation in electro cardiology is relatively a new field of research, many methodological aspects (choice of the mother wavelet, values of the scale parameters) of the wavelet technique requires further investigations in order to improve the clinical worth of medical signal processing technique. Imperative clinical utility is drawn from the innovative application of wavelet transformation in electro cardiology.

Proposed technique of Self-recovery based blind-Watermarking Technique is useful in telecardiology applications for authentication of the source of the information. In this present work, due to watermark embedding a negligible change occurs in the original ECG signal which generates some imperceptibility of ECG data. However, owing to strong security aspects this small amount of imperceptibility is acceptable. The values of correlation and PSNR are very much encouraging regarding the accuracy of the recovered image and quality of reconstruction of the ECG signal, respectively. The major advantage of this approach is self-authentication technique that eliminates the cumbersome process of adjoining the session key or its transfer from sender to receiver end. This has reduced the hazardous complexity resulting in imperious telecardiology scope for much better and successful treatment.

References

1. Rey, C., Dugelay, J.-L.: A Survey of Watermarking Algorithms for Image Authentication. EURASIP Journal on Applied Signal Processing 2002(6), 613–621 (2002)
2. Voyatzis, G., Nikolaidis, N., Pitas, I.: Digital watermarking: an overview. In: Theodoridis, S., et al. (eds.) Signal Processing IX, Theories and Applications: Proceedings of Eusipco 1998, Ninth European Signal Processing Conference, Rhodes, Greece, Patras, September 8-11, pp. 9–12. Typorama Editions (1998)
3. Potdar, V., Han, S., Chang, E.: A survey of digital image watermarking techniques. In: Proceeding of 3rd IEEE-International Conference on Industrial Informatics, Frontier Technologies for the Future of Industry and Business, Perth, WA, August 10, pp. 709–716 (2005)
4. Sharma, P., Kaur, L.: Identification of Cardiac Arrhythmias using ECG. Int. J. Computer Technology & Applications 3(1), 293–297
5. Chan, C.K., Cheng, L.M.: Hiding data in image by simple LSB substitution. Pattern Recognition 37, 469–474 (2003)
6. Hernández, J.R., Amado, M., Pérez-González, F.: DCT-Domain Watermarking Techniques for Still Images: Detector Performance Analysis and a New Structure. IEEE Transactions on Image Processing 9(1) (January 2000)
7. Tao, B., Dickinson, B.: Adaptive watermarking in the DCT domain. In: ICCASP 1997, Munich, Germany, pp. 2985–2988 (April 1997)
8. Anumol, T.J., Karthigaikumar, P.: DWT based Invisible Image Watermarking Algorithm for Color Images. IJCA Special Issue on "Computational Science - New Dimensions & Perspectives" NCCSE (2011)
9. Mei, J., Li, S., Tan, X.: A Digital Watermarking Algorithm Based on DCT and DWT. In: Proceedings of the 2009 International Symposium on Web Information Systems and Applications (WISA 2009), Nanchang, P. R. China, May 22-24, pp. 104–107 (2009)
10. Hôšťálková, E., Procházka, A.: Wavelet Signal and Image Denoising
11. Mukhopadhyay, S., Biswas, S., Roy, A.B., Dey, N.: Wavelet Based QRS Complex Detection of ECG Signal. International Journal of Engineering Research and Applications (IJERA) 2(3), 2361–2365 (2012) ISSN: 2248-9622
12. http://www.physiol.med.uu.nl/interactivephysiology/ipweb/misc/assignmentfiles/cardiovascular/Cardiac_Output.pdf
13. http://en.wikipedia.org/wiki/Stationary_wavelet_transform

eCloudIDS – Design Roadmap for the Architecture of Next-Generation Hybrid Two-Tier Expert Engine-Based IDS for Cloud Computing Environment

Madhan Kumar Srinivasan[1], K Sarukesi[2], Ashima Keshava[1], and P. Revathy[1]

[1] Infosys Limited,
Mysore, India
{madhankrs,ashimakeshava,revamadhankr}@gmail.com
[2] Hindustan University,
Chennai, India
vc@hindustanuniv.ac.in

Abstract. Cloud computing is a new hype and a buzz word in today's business computing world due to its pay-as-you-use model. Organizations are at the edge of a computing revolution which can change the way traditional enterprise IT is run currently. Even with all its benefits, medium to large businesses fear migrating to this computing paradigm because of the security nightmares associated with it. Organizations fear loss of control over their own data and are apprehensive about the cloud vendors' security measures for the same. This paper describes the design roadmap for the architecture of eCloudIDS, a next-generation security system with innovative hybrid two-tier expert engines, namely uX-Engine (tier-1) and sX-Engine (tier-2), approach for cloud computing environment. eCloudIDS architecture uses both supervised and unsupervised machine learning techniques from artificial intelligence cradle which can ease some of the contemporary urgent security threats present in today's cloud computing environment.

Keywords: eCloudIDS, uX-Engine, sX-Engine, Behavior Analyzer, eCloudIDS C3, Cloud VM/Instance Monitor, CIM, H-log-H, Standard Audit repository, SAR, Special Permission Audit repository, SPAR, Acute Audit Repository, AAR, Warning level Generator, Alert System, two-tier expert engine, state-of-the-art cloud computing security taxonomies.

1   Introduction

Enterprise IT is abuzz with the notion of cloud computing. It is changing the perspective of the business world towards their IT solutions. From renting IT resources such as infrastructure to platforms to software, to ubiquitous on-demand service, cloud computing has simplified all under its ambit. The end-users need not know the details of a specific technology while hosting their applications, as the service is completely managed by the cloud service provider (CSP) [1] [2]. Users can consume services at a rate that is set by their particular needs while paying relatively

S.M. Thampi et al. (Eds.): SNDS 2012, CCIS 335, pp. 358–371, 2012.

cheaper rates and the CSP takes care of all the necessary complex operations on behalf of the user. It provides the complete system which allocates the required resources for execution of user applications and management of the entire system flow. Figure 1, describes the visual representation of the architecture of cloud computing.

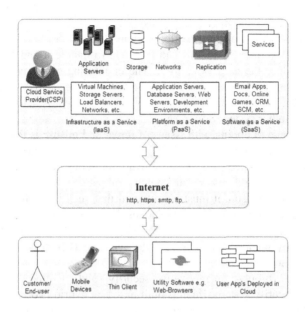

Source: Madhan Kumar Srinivasan, et al.: State-of-the-art Cloud Computing Security Taxonomies – A classification of security challenges in the present cloud computing environment. DOI: 10.1145/2345396.2345474, ACM (2012)[1].

Fig. 1. Cloud Computing Architecture

Additionally, this new model has gathered many proponents because of being labeled as a 'Greener computing alternative' [3]. Analysts say that pooling of resources and facilities can help cut significant costs for a company. In addition, this also has an extremely positive effect on the environment as an AT&T supported study posits [4]. By 2020, the group estimates, large US companies that use cloud computing can achieve annual energy savings of $12.3 billion and annual carbon reductions equivalent to 200 million barrels of oil.

Even though, cloud computing carries with it the charm of a win-win situation for all stakeholders today in the IT scenario, there are many security concerns that are preventing companies from migrating to this modern computing paradigm [1] [5] [6]. It is important to understand and address these security gaps by taking into account the user privacy and sensitivity of data in critical enterprise applications when it gets deployed on cloud, especially in public (and hybrid) cloud environments.

Security of information systems has become a burgeoning issue of concern with respect to present computing needs. We find ourselves paralyzed against not only the growing ways of security breaches from a malicious intruder, but also from insiders with whom there is an implicit code of trust. This has caused a major challenge for system administrators as increasing vulnerabilities need expensive and more complex security mechanisms. The issues of identity theft, unauthorized action in the network, access to information, manipulation of this information, rendering a system unreliable or unusable [7] are still persistent to this day and age. These threats form the basis of all security surveillance and monitoring measures.

A fast action online intrusion detection system (IDS) is the first line of control to detect an intrusion so that provisions can be made to handle it and try to prevent it completely, or reduce the harm done by it. The monitoring of a user's behavior on a host is the first important measure that can be taken up by an IDS. The system can block access to the network, and isolate the system if a threat is detected so as to not let it propagate to other system resources.

A major challenge of coping with issues of threat and misuse is that only the audit trails of an operating system can be of any viable use to the security enforcer. Even after vulnerability is handled, it is essential that continuous monitoring of the system is done and new threats and unwarranted behavioral patterns of a user can be reported immediately. For this reason, it must be assumed that such a monitoring mechanism can generate a report or is alive even after a host has been compromised. Even here a measure of uncertainty exists, where a user's normal behavior and abnormal behavior cannot be correctly mapped. Such issues will need the IDS to be trained based on experience continuously.

In this paper we propose an innovative security solution titled "eCloudIDS" is a next-generation security system which is built based on hybrid two-tier expert engines especially for the public cloud computing environment. More specifically, eCloudIDS is a prototype hybrid security system that will monitor user behavior and sound alerts on intrusions from both inside and outside sources based on artificial intelligence machine learning mechanisms [8] (both supervised and unsupervised). eCloudIDS works efficient towards security threats related to public cloud computing environment; especially with respect to its top three State-of-the-art cloud computing security taxonomies [1] such as logical storage segregation & multi-tenancy security issues (taxonomy #1), identity management issues (taxonomy #2), and insider attacks (taxonomy #3).

2   Related Work

Taking into account the current cloud scenario, multi-tenancy issues are fundamental to cloud computing. CSPs are able to build their network infrastructure that are highly scalable, computationally very efficient and easily rises to serve many customers who share the CSP's infrastructure. This clearly means that tenants share infrastructure resources like hardware, servers, computing power and data storage devices. With SaaS (Software-as-a-service) tenants are sharing the same application, which means their data is likely to be stored in same database and may even share same database table [9]. Due to this, the possibility of access to one's confidential data by other tenants is very high [10]. In order to address this issue, the CSP's should provide proper ways of data isolation and logical segregation [1].

Identity Management part of cloud computing needs to be more secure and reliable. The "pay as you use" model really needs a sophisticated IdM system to take care of the granular provisioning of resources to users. As the identity and access management in traditional systems still face many challenges [11] [12] from various aspects such as security, privacy, provisioning of services it clearly needs to be more secure and sophisticated in case of cloud computing systems. As stated by [13] an IdM module in cloud environment has to manage dynamic composite/ decommissioned machines, control points, virtual device or service identities, etc. IdM, in cloud, should ideally store a VM's (Virtual Machine) details till it is active. Meanwhile, access to its relevant stored data has to be monitored and granted based on the defined access level for that mode as mentioned in the SLA. Traditional IdM is not directly suitable for cloud computing due to these features of cloud. Today's cloud requires dynamic governance of typical IdM issues like provisioning/de-provisioning, lifecycle management, entitlement, synchronization, etc.

One of the main reasons for customers hesitating to deploy their information on cloud is because they lose direct control on their private data. Even though existing CSP's assure that this issue will be taken care of, since the CSPs are outside the circle of trust for enterprises, customers are still apprehensive about the security of their data in the cloud environment. CSP's may not be willing to provide information of their employees who will have access to the client's data and the way of monitoring their access. [1] [5] categorize "Malicious Insider" as one of the top three security threats in the cloud environment. According to an Intel survey's [14] key findings, organizations that have adopted public cloud are facing a higher number of security breaches than they experience with their traditional IT infrastructure. As high as 28 percent of companies, who have migrated to public cloud, have experienced a security breach. Gradually, IT experts concur that this number is higher than what they experienced with their in premises computing. Finally, this report concludes that nearly one-third of the security threats faced by companies come from internal sources. In addition, Verizon 2010 data breach report [15] indicates that there is a 26% increase in the data breaches by malicious insiders accounting to a total of 48% of data breaches being carried out by malicious insiders. Although this number is same for both traditional infrastructure and cloud computing, the consequence of such a breach in a cloud scenario has far greater implications. It can lead to situations like financial impact, brand damage, huge productivity losses, etc. BBC's research report [16] sensitizes that insider attacks are on the rise so even though the cloud provider may be trusted, a cloud administrator could potentially be a rogue.

3   Cloud Security Challenges – Considered and Resolved by eCloudIDS

IT enterprises have significant security concerns about both public and private cloud, but research shows that IT professionals are most concerned about the security of the public cloud [14]. In a public cloud environment, the greatest concern is access control i.e. the control of corporate data and services to only authorized users. Another concern is the lack of control over resources. And the third major concern is inadequate firewalling. This situation brings up the following security concerns to be adequately addressed by CSP.

Security Concern #1: Who retains the data ownership and control ownership?
Security Concern #2: Who maintains the audit records of the data?
Security Concern #3: What is the mechanism in the delivery of this audit record to the customer?
Security Concern #4: As a real owner of the data, does the CSP allow customers to secure and manage access from end-users (customer's client)?

To handle such sensitive situations, CSP must ensure proper data isolation. This isolation is not only concerned with protecting data (& applications) from threats or external penetrations, but also preventing unwanted changes by the CSP employees. Hence, providing security to the user data, which is logically segregated, from any other user (and/or CSP) in terms of unauthorized access/attacks, isolation of data, and maintaining proper compliance & SLAs becomes the order-of-the-day of all cloud computing security concerns.

Our proposed 'eCloudIDS Architecture', a next-generation hybrid two-tier expert engine-based IDS for cloud computing environment, has been designed taking in view of the top three State-of-the-art cloud computing security taxonomies [1] as mentioned below (from #1 to #3). The eCloudIDS takes into account the behavioral patterns of persons accessing the cloud VMs, and also all abnormalities and inconsistencies brought by attackers from CSP's side, hobbyist hackers accessing cloud through Internet, malicious worms, viruses etc.

The security challenges considered and addressed (up to an extent) by eCloudIDS are as follows:

eCloudIDS Resolved Issue #1: Logical storage segregation and multi-tenancy security issues
eCloudIDS Resolved Issue #2: Identity management issues
eCloudIDS Resolved Issue #3: Insider attacks
eCloudIDS Resolved Issue #4: Hacker attacks
eCloudIDS Resolved Issue #5: Signature based attacks caused by Worms, Viruses, Trojans, etc.

4   eCloudIDS Architecture

This section details the eCloudIDS architecture. eCloudIDS is primarily designed based on its two main subsystems namely uX-Engine and sX-Engine. These subsystems are functionally built by unsupervised and supervised machine learning algorithms, respectively. Due to the availability of a wide range of these machine learning techniques, organizations that implement eCloudIDS, can opt for algorithms that are better suited for their business needs. The appropriate selection of these machine learning techniques (single algorithm or combination of algorithms) decides the scope, accuracy and efficiency of eCloudIDS as an end product. Fig. 2 depicts eCloudIDS reference architecture along with its process workflow.

Fundamentally this architecture design is targeted for specific singular VM/Instance (Virtual Machine) on the cloud IaaS infrastructure. Our motive in designing the eCloudIDs architecture was to ensure that the end product of the CSP i.e. the VM, which is resourced to the customers for deployment of applications and data, is secure. For this reason, an IDS for each resourced VM becomes necessary. From the CSPs point of view, based on security the utmost importance must be given to:

1. The underlying infrastructure i.e. cloud infrastructure or IaaS (created on top of CSP's hardware and networking resources)
2. VM's (which are created for the purpose of CSP's customers)

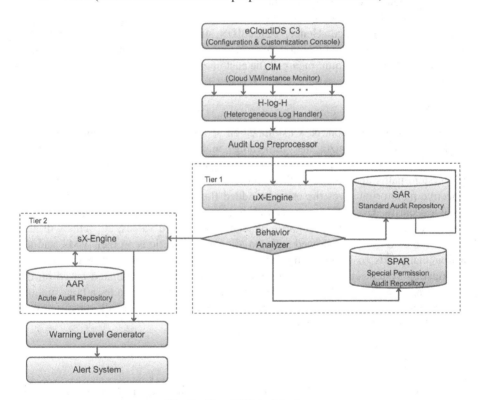

Fig. 2. eCloudIDS Architecture

These must necessarily be secure for a smooth and hassle free operation between the customer and the CSP. For CSPs, infrastructure maintenance is very similar to a company's in premise infrastructure. A CSP need not choose anything new apart from the existing list of security products, digital certificates and mechanisms, as they are known to be strong and developed for in premises security requirements. In addition, a general belief in industry is that the in-premise computing is safer than cloud (which means public cloud). So, this serves as the main reason for companies to look towards private or hybrid cloud computing for their highly secure configurations and less chances of intrusions.

Let us consider the VM further. Once the underlying infrastructure is deployed, CSP can provide services to other companies using a pay-as-you-use model. CSP will segregate his infrastructure logically (but not physically) with the help of virtualization through hypervisors. Hypervisors are software tools which help in deployment and maintenance of virtual machines based on the customers' requirements. Once a VM has been allocated, the customer can deploy their applications and data there. When a VM is up and running, the client and client's end-user's may access the VM/Instance (a running VM is also called an instance) over Internet in general case. As the VM is accessible publically over the Internet it can attract the attention of attackers and hackers.

Taking into account the above facts, it is required that the security of the VM be given utmost importance. Hence, eCloudIDS attempts to provide solution to this scenario. Further, this architecture can be used in handling multiple VM/Instances, based on the business requirements of the customer.

4.1   eCloudIDS C3

eCloudIDS Configuration & Customization Console (C3) subsystem is used to configure and customize the remaining multiple subsystems of eCloudIDS architecture with respect to the user's requirements. C3 allows users to configure the file system paths and databases that need to be monitored by the architecture. This selective monitoring gives the users an added flexibility to decide which data needs greater security. Using C3, users can customize the two-tier subsystems uX-Engine and sX-Engine with suitable algorithms and its associated values, etc. This will also be used to configure the allowed and non-allowed transactions on their VMs, and the action that needs to be taken by the system when tampering of data is found. A notification system or an action based system can then be formulated based on the policies agreed upon by the users. In general, eCloudIDS C3 includes a huge amount of configuration and customization properties and activities in all subsystems of eCloudIDS reference architecture.

4.2   CIM

Cloud VM/Instance Monitor (CIM) subsystem is responsible for observing the actions performed on the user specified virtual machines or instances. It continuously monitors the VM on the user specified application-related directories and files, and database tables as configured in C3. CIM is responsible for monitoring all the activities of both authorized and unauthorized users (hackers) and inform it to H-log-H for immediate recording of each and every activity for the configured VMs. This includes the recording of both normal and anomalous behaviors. CIM might result in heterogeneous audit logs generation based on the nature of item accessed in selected VMs by any subject/user, irrespective of whether it is authorized or unauthorized.

4.3   H-log-H

Heterogeneous Log Handler (H-log-H) subsystem meticulously associates with CIM for recording each and every activity occurred on user configured VMs. Generally, files and directory related logs are managed and maintained by the concerned Operating Systems in their own formats (for example, UbuntuOS and MacOS audit logs are not in the same formats). Similarly, tables and database related logs are managed and maintained by different DBMS utilities with differences in formats (for example, MySQL's and Firebird's audit logs are not in same format). Likewise, depending on the type of and number of applications, tools, databases systems, etc. configured on VM, it produces multiple type of audit logs to H-log-H. After recording these heterogeneous assorted audit logs will be surrendered to Audit Log Preprocessor subsystem by H-log-H subsystem, for further process.

4.4   Audit Log Preprocessor

Audit Log Preprocessor (ALP) subsystem accepts the input from H-log-H, integrated heterogeneous audit logs from multiple types of application, tools, etc. Upon the reception of input, ALP rearranges, processes, and converts unstructured audit logs into structured data. During this conversion, ALP is expected to utilize numerous techniques and mechanisms to handle these dissimilar audit logs. Segregation of these heterogeneous audit logs to the corresponding log handling mechanism will help ALP in better management of huge amount of logs. ALP's processed output (i.e. uniformly formatted structured audit logs) will be given as input to both the two-tier's uX-Engine and sX-Engine. Hence, ALP in eCloudIDS becomes a backbone subsystem which demands utmost accuracy in conversion with extreme computation complexity in implementation.

4.5   eCloudIDS Tier-1

eCloudIDS Tier-1 billets its functionality with two subsystems and its associated audit repositories. The tier as a whole verifies the normalcy of the audits being produced by the user configured VMs.

uX-Engine. It is an unsupervised machine learning-based expert engine subsystem that predominantly focuses on the identification of activities that are allowed on the VM. uX-Engine deals with clustering of event logs that form normal day-to-day transactions on the user configured VMs. In its initial learning stage, it accepts the uniformly formatted structured audit logs as input from ALP, generally through a dry-run of audit logs in VMs (for the period of 10 days, for example). These logs are used during the learning process of the configured unsupervised algorithm (like [8] K-Mean, SOM [17], GHSOM, etc.) to form clusters based on relative feature mapping and similarity in behavior. From these preplanned audit logs clusters uX-Engine learns standard activities with respect to the CIM monitored VMs. After the initial learning, those logs used for learning, will be stored in Standard Audit Repository (SAR) for future references of uX-Engine. Once the VM, has been deployed, all the incoming activities will be monitored by CIM and sent to ALP for preprocessing, through H-log-H subsystem. The preprocessed logs will then be used to verify the learning of the uX-Engine. The audits will be compared against the clusters formed during the initial training. If an audit is not found to be similar to any of the clusters it will be sent to the behavior analyzer for verification. Here it is assumed that an outlier audit can either be an intrusion attack or a normal activity that the uX-Engine has not learned yet. If the audit is found to be normal it is stored in the SAR (collection of normal behavior audit logs).

Behavior Analyzer. Decision making subsystem in eCloudIDS that has abundant amount of responsibility built in it. Behavior Analyzer (BA) has a tightly coupled association with the Cloud IdP (Identity and Access Management Provider) [11] [12] [13] of the specific VMs. This relationship helps BA to take appropriate decisions at important situations during the eCloudIDS process workflow. As described above uX-Engine forwards the outlying, dissimilar audits to Behavior Analyzer subsystem. Based on the uX-Engine's results BA further analyzes the log and classifies it in any of the three categories given below.

Category #1 – Normal Behaviour:
> When a new log settles with existing clusters or when a new log doesn't fit with any of the existing clusters due to the dynamic change in user configurations (for example, if user admin change some configurations at VM but don't update the eCloudIDS C3)

Category #2 – Special Permission Behaviour:
> When a new log doesn't fit with any of the existing clusters and that log's behavioral analysis turn TRUE with the verification of Cloud IdP as exceptions/special permissions/temporary provisioning by admin, etc.

Category #3 – Anomalous Behaviour:
> When a new log doesn't fit with any of the existing clusters and that log's behavioral analysis turn FALSE with Cloud IdP in all cases

As a result, if the monitored audit log(s) are found under the category #1 i.e. Normal Behaviour, then they will be safely sent to the Standard Audit Repository SAR. Those found under the category #2 i.e. Special Permission Behavior are moved into Special Permission Audit Repository (SPAR). Finally, those found under the category #3, i.e. Anomalous Behaviour are directly sent to the eCloudIDS architectures tier-2 subsystem sX-Engine.

Standard Audit Repository (SAR). It is an audit repository that is tightly-coupled with uX-Engine & Behavior Analyzer subsystems. Standard Audit Repository contains the category #1 type logs i.e. Normal behavioral activity logs that have been analyzed and verified using the Behavior Analyzer. SAR stores only those audit logs after the clearance acceptance from Behavior Analyzer. Logs contained in SAR will be fed to the uX-Engine for further learning, this ensures that the uX-Engine is up to date with activity identification on the VM. It will also help in making the uX-Engine, a dynamic learning machine.

Special Permissions Audit Repository (SPAR). It is also an audit repository, which will be tightly-coupled with Behavior Analyzer subsystem of eCloudIDS & Cloud IdP services. Special Permission Audit Repository contains the category #2 type logs i.e. Special Permission Behaviour event logs that are not normal behavior but have passed as acceptable through the behavior analyzer after its verification with Cloud IdP system services. These activities can be of any sort of special permissions on a specific subject/user/object/identity in an organization due to the dynamic nature of business requirement fluctuations from time to time. These kinds of exceptional permissions can be given at almost all the SDLC phases of both in project and in business workflow. Users can customize SPAR to connect it. Warning Level Generator and Alert System subsystems through eCloudIDS C3 console depending upon their requirements. SPAR will not be used in either uX-Engine or sX-Engine; but simply present in the system as repository for auditing and analysis purpose.

4.6   eCloudIDS Tier-2

eCloudIDS Tier-2 encompasses a subsystem with its associated audit repository. This tier is responsible for classifying the outlying event log, which has been provided by the Behavior Analyzer subsystem of eCloudIDS Tier-1, into an appropriate threat pattern. Further, this tier helps the Warning Level Generator and Alert System subsystems in their respective processes.

sX-Engine. It is a supervised machine learning-based expert engine subsystem that principally focuses on accepting the input of eCloudIDS Tier-1 Behavior Analyzer subsystem's category #3 Anomalous Behavior type of outlying audit logs into an appropriate threat pattern classification. sX-Engine involves in pattern recognition and classification based on its training and testing procedures. An important feature/property of sX-Engine is that once the log is categorized as #3, whatever may be the case sX-Engine considers it as Anomalous Behavior and create further processes till this will be informed to concerned stake holders i.e. appropriate customer (Cloud User) and CSP executives. For its training purpose, the corpus contains all feasible and quantifiable collection of host/network-based attacks, virus, worms, vulnerabilities, threats signatures. Considering the fact that creating such a global and vast corpus is a challenging mission, it will require massive human effort. After building a corpus of such immensity, the developing organization can choose a supervised machine learning technique based on their business requirement. And this appropriate selection of suitable algorithm decides the quality and accuracy of sX-Engine's overall execution. Now, sX-Engine will be trained using a selected algorithm, based on our designed ultra-powerful generous corpus which contains all possible anomalous activities, henceforth referred as Acute Audit Repository (AAR). These training phase activities will be accomplished on sX-Engine well before it performs the testing on anomalous behavior. In testing phase, the trained sX-Engine accepts the category #3 Anomalous Behavior type of outlying audit logs as input from Behaviour Analyzer and checks the patterns for classification. Classification will be performed based on the features extracted from the input audit logs and the same will be compared with the AAR corpus logs features. All those events that could not be matched to a class of threats in AAR will undergo a manual inspection so as to assign a new class and will be subsequently used to train the sX-Engine dynamically. After testing, sX-Engine passes the appropriate classification result as feedback to Warning Level Generator subsystem to spawn a suitable warning level. In addition, sX-Engine stores back the input anomalous audit log into AAR with generated warning level information as label.

Acute Audit Repository (AAR). It is an audit repository that is tightly-coupled with sX-Engine subsystem. This is basically a corpus of huge collection of all possible attacks, virus, worms, vulnerabilities and threats signatures. This corpus helps sX-Engine during its training and testing phases. In addition, it stores back the input audit log after the testing along with warning level information label.

4.7   Warning Level Generator

Warning Level Generator (WLG) subsystem takes the feedback given by the sX-Engine and works on it further to classify them under priority warning levels based on the user configuration of eCloudIDS C3. Events that were mapped as an intrusion after classification by sX-Engine will be assigned to a class of threat. Based on the class, the warning level generator will make a decision for the type of alert that needs to be given. This process helps in making the system to not respond to intrusion/attack/anomalous behavior in the same way. WLG involves in segregation of different anomalous behavior under various priority warning levels, for example high-medium-low, or red-blue-green, etc. In other way WLG helps both CU (Cloud User) and CSP in achieving an appropriate SLA process workflow automation.

4.8   Alert System

Alert System (AS) is a subsystem in eCloudIDS which takes care of notifying the concerned stakeholders at the customer side and at the CSP organization. Once a warning level has been generated, the list of concerned stakeholders for the particular level of warning will be notified using this module. For example, if the warning level for the intrusion is found to be low, then only the CSP and CU admins will be notified of the intrusion. For medium and high priority levels, the CU as well as CSP stakeholders will be notified of the intrusion. Based on the AS notification, CSP needs to provide appropriate solution for the intrusion and explanation to CU. This will help maintain transparency between the CU and the CSP at all times.

4.9   Summary and Concluding Benefits – eCloudIDS Architecture

eCloudIDS Architecture is responsible for various security related activities with respect to current cloud computing environment. eCloudIDS performs the following roles to handle the security of an VM/Instance.

eCloudIDS Role #1: VM Monitor
eCloudIDS Role #2: System Auditor
eCloudIDS Role #3: Intrusion Detection System
eCloudIDS Role #4: Behavioral Analyzer
eCloudIDS Role #5: Alert Agent

Various cloud computing security issues addressed and resolved by eCloudIDS architecture are listed in Table 1.

Table 1. eCloudIDS's paybacks to present cloud computing security issues

S. No	Issues Considered & Addressed by eCloudIDS Architecture	eCloudIDS Role(s), Tightly Associated in Resolving the Issue
1	Logical storage segregation and multi-tenancy security issues	Role #1: VM Monitor Role #3: Intrusion Detection System Role #4: Behavioral Analyzer Role #5: Alert Agent
2	Identity management issues	Role #1: VM Monitor Role #2: System Auditor Role #4: Behavioral Analyzer
3	Insider attacks	Role #1: VM Monitor Role #3: Intrusion Detection System Role #4: Behavioral Analyzer Role #5: Alert Agent
4	Hacker attacks	Role #3: Intrusion Detection System Role #4: Behavioral Analyzer Role #5: Alert Agent
5	Signature based attacks caused by Worms, Viruses, Trojans, etc.	Role #3: Intrusion Detection System Role #4: Behavioral Analyzer Role #5: Alert Agent

5   Conclusion

It is proven that cloud computing is growing as a destiny of future enterprise business computing due to its catchy technical and financial benefits. Considering cloud's exposed public nature, it equally attracts the attention of hackers and attackers which intersects more severe security challenges and risks to it. On the other hand, the amounts of investment made by these Cloud Service Providers are also significantly high. At this juncture, unless CSP's take some action in reaching more customers using cloud services by removing these present security issues/vulnerabilities, they will be in serious trouble. Considering all these facts, this paper presents eCloudIDS, a next-generation security system which is built based on hybrid two-tier expert engines especially for the public cloud computing environment. eCloudIDS architecture answers the top three State-of-the-art cloud computing security taxonomies such as logical storage segregation & multi-tenancy security issues (taxonomy #1), identity management issues (taxonomy #2), and insider attacks (taxonomy #3). This architecture can help build greater confidence in medium to large businesses in migrating their applications and databases into public cloud environment. For businesses that value security of information over all else, this system will give adequate reassurance that their data is safe and they can rely on CSPs with greater transparency. The eCloudIDS can utilize a variety of advanced machine learning algorithms for uX-Engine and sX-Engine. The greater the learning capacity, the greater will be the security. With granular auditing and a holistic feature extraction, the system will show better results.

References

1. Madhan, K.S., Sarukesi, K., Rodrigues, P., Saimanoj, M., Revathy, P.: State-of-the-art Cloud Computing Security Taxonomies – A classification of security challenges in the present cloud computing environment. In: ICACCI 2012, pp. 470–476. ACM, India (2012), doi:10.1145/2345396.2345474, ISBN: 978-1-4503-1196-0
2. Mell, P., Grance, T.: The NIST Definition of Cloud Computing. NIST Special Publication 800-145. Technical report, National Institute of Standards and Technology (2011)
3. Cloud Computing and Sustainability: The Environmental Benefits of moving to the Cloud. Technical report, Accenture (2010)
4. Reeve, R.: Building a 21st Century Communications Economy. Technical report, Carbon Disclosure Project in support with AT&T (2011)
5. Security Guidance for Critical Areas of Focus in Cloud Computing V2.1. Technical report, Cloud Security Alliance (2009)
6. Top Threats to Cloud Computing V1.0. Technical report, Cloud Security Alliance (2010)
7. Computer Security Threat Monitoring and Surveillance. Technical report, James P. Anderson Co. (1980)
8. Ghahramani, Z.: Unsupervised Learning. In: Bousquet, O., von Luxburg, U., Rätsch, G. (eds.) Machine Learning 2003. LNCS (LNAI), vol. 3176, pp. 72–112. Springer, Heidelberg (2004)
9. Securing Multi-Tenancy and Cloud Computing. Technical report, Juniper Networks (2012)
10. Li, H., Sedayao, J., Hahn-Steichen, J., Jimison, E., Spence, C., Chahal, S.: Developing an Enterprise Cloud Computing Strategy. Technical report, Intel Corporation (2009)
11. Madhan Kumar, S., Rodrigues, P.: A Roadmap for the Comparison of Identity Management Solutions Based on State-of-the-Art IdM Taxonomies. In: Meghanathan, N., Boumerdassi, S., Chaki, N., Nagamalai, D. (eds.) CNSA 2010. CCIS, vol. 89, pp. 349–358. Springer, Heidelberg (2010)
12. Madhan, K.S., Rodrigues, P.: Analysis on Identity Management Systems with Extended State-of-the-art IdM Taxonomy Factors. International Journal of Ad hoc, Sensor & Ubiquitous Computing 1(4), 62–70 (2010), doi:10.5121/ijasuc.2010.1406
13. Anu, G.: Cloud Computing Identity Management. Technical report, SETLabs Briefings 7(7), 45–55, Infosys Limited (2009)

14. What's Holding Back the Cloud? Technical report, Intel IT Center (2012)
15. Baker, W., Hutton, A.: 2010 Data Breach Investigations Report, A study conducted by the Verizon RISK Team with cooperation from the U.S. Secret Service and the Dutch High Tech Crime Unit. Technical report, Verizon, New Jersey (2010)
16. Shiels, M.: Malicious insider attacks to rise. Technical report, BBC News, Silicon Valley (2009)
17. Srinivasan, M.K., Sarukesi, K., Keshava, A., Revathy, P.: eCloudIDS Tier-1 uX-Engine Subsystem Design and Implementation using Self-Organizing Map (SOM) for Secure Cloud Computing Environment. In: Thampi, S.M., et al. (eds.) SNDS 2012. CCIS, vol. 335, pp. 429–440. Springer, Heidelberg (2012)
18. Keerthi, B., Madhan, K.S., Sarukesi, K., Rodrigues, P.: Implementation of Next-generation Traffic Sign Recognition System with Two-tier Classifier Architecture. In: ACM International Conference on Advances in Communications, Computing and Informatics, ICACCI 2012, pp. 481–487. ACM, India (2012), doi:10.1145/2345396.2345476, ISBN: 978-1-4503-1196-0
19. Balasundaram, K., Srinivasan, M.K., Sarukesi, K.: iReSign-Implementation of Next-Generation Two-Tier Identity Classifier-Based Traffic Sign Recognition System Architecture using Hybrid Region-Based Shape Representation Techniques. In: Thampi, S.M., et al. (eds.) SNDS 2012. CCIS, vol. 335, pp. 407–420. Springer, Heidelberg (2012)

A Comparative Study on Wormhole Attack Prevention Schemes in Mobile Ad-Hoc Network

Subhashis Banerjee and Koushik Majumder

Department of Computer Science & Engineering, West Bengal University of Technology,
Kolkata, India
koushik@ieee.org

Abstract. A Mobile Ad-Hoc Network (MANET) is a self configuring, infrastructure-less network of mobile devices connected by wireless links. Lack of fixed infrastructure, wireless medium, dynamic topology, rapid deployment practices and the hostile environments in which they may be deployed, make MANET vulnerable to a wide range of security attacks and wormhole attack is one of them. During wormhole attack a malicious node captures packets from one location in the network, and tunnels them to another malicious node at a distant point, which replays them locally. In this paper wormhole attacks against various kinds of mobile ad-hoc network routing protocols have been studied in detail. We have classified the well known countermeasures against the wormhole attack according to their detection and prevention techniques, and have also carried out a detailed comparative analysis of these techniques according to their relative advantages and disadvantages.

Keywords: MANETs, Wormhole Attack, Periodic Protocols, On-demand Protocols, Local broadcast protocols.

1 Introduction

A Mobile Ad-hoc Networks (MANET) is a highly challenged network environment due to its special characteristics such as decentralization, dynamic topology and neighbor based routing. This type of network consists of nodes that are organized and maintained in a distributed manner without a fixed infrastructure. These nodes, such as laptop computers, PDAs and wireless phones, have a limited transmission range. Hence, routing is essentially multi-hop in case of mobile ad hoc networks. Since the transmission between two nodes has to rely on relay nodes, many routing protocols [1-4] have been proposed for ad hoc networks. Most of the routing protocols, however, do not consider the security and attack issues because they assume that other nodes are trustable. This lack of security mechanism provides many opportunities for the attackers to conduct attacks on the network. And also, the lack of infrastructure, open nature of wireless communication channels, rapid deployment practices, and the hostile environments in which they may be deployed, make them vulnerable to a wide range of security attacks described in [5-7].

S.M. Thampi et al. (Eds.): SNDS 2012, CCIS 335, pp. 372–384, 2012.

In this paper we investigate a specific type of attack, known as wormhole attack. Such attacks are relatively easy to mount, while being difficult to detect and prevent. During the attack a malicious node captures packets from one location in the network, and tunnels them to another malicious node at a distant point, which replays them locally, this is illustrated in Fig. 1.

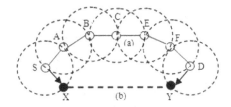

Fig. 1. Wormhole attack in ad hoc networks: (a) Normal link, (b) Wormhole link

In the ad hoc network in Fig. 1, we assume that S, A, B, C, E, F, D are the legitimate nodes and X and Y are the malicious nodes. S can communicate with D using the path S – A – B – C – E – F– D. For conducting the wormhole attack successfully the attacker places the malicious nodes X and Y close to S and D. Then the attacker makes S and D think that they are neighbours by allowing X to capture the packets sent by S and tunnel the packets to Y. Y, further, replays the packets to D. From that point on, S and D use the malicious link for communication. Thus, the attacker is able to successfully mount the wormhole attack on the network.

The remainder of this paper is organized as follows: in section 2 we describe wormhole attack against ad-hoc routing protocols and local broadcast protocols. In section 3, some existing methods for detecting and preventing these attacks have been discussed. In section 4, a comparison study has been done on the different wormhole detection and prevention methods and finally, in section 5 we conclude the paper.

2   The Wormhole Attack in Action

2.1   Wormhole Attack against Routing Protocols

Routing protocols for Ad hoc network are classified into periodic protocols [8-10] and on-demand protocols [11, 12]. In periodic protocols, every node stores the routing paths towards any destination, and to maintain the best network routes, periodically updates the stored routing information by exchanging information with its neighbors. On the other hand in on-demand protocols, a routing path is discovered only when a node wants to send messages to some destination. Wormhole attack can be efficiently launched in both categories of routing protocols in the following ways.

2.1.1   Wormhole Attack on Periodic Protocols
Periodic protocols are based on the concept of distance vector routing algorithm [13]. In this protocol, each node maintains a table containing entries for each possible

destination along with the associated routing cost and the corresponding next hop information towards that destination. All nodes periodically, or when a network change occurs, update their own routing tables by exchanging information with their neighbors.

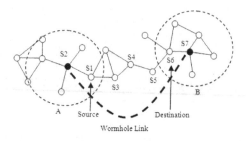

Fig. 2. Wormhole attack on periodic protocol

Consider Fig. 2 which shows a MANET of 19 nodes. In a MANET connection between two nodes si and sj is established if the distance between them is less than the communication range r. Now consider an attacker establishing a wormhole by using a low-latency link between nodes s2 and s7. So, when node s1 broadcasts its routing table, node s6 will hear the broadcast via the wormhole and assume it is two hops away from s1. Accordingly, s6 will update its table entries for node s1, reachable via {s2, s7}.

2.1.2   Wormhole Attack on On-Demand Protocols

A wormhole attack against on-demand routing protocols can result in similar false route establishment due to some fake route reply message broadcasted by the attacker node during the route discovery phase [11,12].

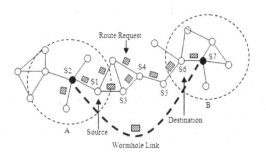

Fig. 3. Wormhole attack on on-demand protocol

For example, in Fig. 3 consider that the attacker establishes a wormhole link between nodes s2 and s7. Also, assume that node s1 wants to send data to node s6. When node s1 broadcasts the route request message, all nodes that hear the message will re-broadcast the request until the destination s6 has been discovered. The attacker nodes s2 and s7 will forward the request via the wormhole link to node s6. Node s6 will select the shortest route via the wormhole link. And then s6 will send a route reply via the wormhole link between nodes s2 and s7 to node s1. At this point, nodes s1 and s6 will establish a route via the wormhole link {s2, s7}.

2.2   Wormhole Attack against Local Broadcast Protocols

In some applications nodes need to communicate some information only within their neighborhood. For example, consider a wireless sensor network which is used for monitoring purpose. The sensor nodes in the network perform monitoring (for example monitoring temperature of a region), and broadcast local measurements to a central node or cluster head. Then the cluster head takes some action (for example turn on the alarm) depending upon the condition estimated by the estimation algorithm. So in such applications, false local information broadcasted by the malicious nodes can lead to significant performance degradation of the estimation algorithms.

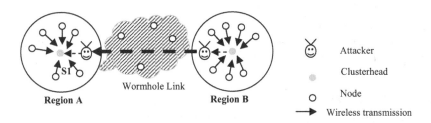

Fig. 4. Wormhole attack on local broadcast protocol

3   Review of the Countermeasures against Wormhole Attack

3.1   Location and Time Based Solutions

3.1.1   Packet Leashes, Temporal [14]
In [14] authors introduced the notion of a Temporal Leashes which ensures that the packet has an upper bound on its lifetime, which restricts the maximum travel distance, since the packet can travel at most at the speed of light. Detection process for wormhole attack by Temporal Leashes can be described as follows:

- When sending a packet at local time t_s, in order to prevent the packet to travel further than distance L, the sender needs to set the packet expiration time to $t_e = t_s + L / c - \Delta$ (All nodes are time synchronized up to a maximum time synchronization error Δ and c is the propagation speed of wireless signal).

- When the receiver gets the packet at local time t_r, it further processes the packet if the temporal leash is not expired (i.e., $t_r < t_e$), otherwise it drops the packet.

3.1.2 Packet Leashes, Geographical [14]

In [14] the authors also gave the notion of Geographical Leashes which ensures that the recipient of the packet is within a certain distance from the sender. Detection process for wormhole attack by Geographical Leashes can be described as follows:

  (i)   When sending a packet, the sending node includes in the packet its own location, p_s, and the time at which it sent the packet, t_s;
  (ii) When receiving a packet, the receiving node compares these values to its own location, p_r, and the time at which it received the packet, t_r.
  (iii) If the clocks of the sender and receiver are synchronized to within $\pm\Delta$, and v is an upper bound on the velocity of any node, then the receiver can compute an upper bound on the distance between the sender and itself, d_{sr}.
  (iv) Given the timestamp t_s in the packet, the local receive time t_r, the maximum relative error in location information δ, and the locations of the receiver p_r and the sender p_s, then d_{sr} can be bounded by $d_{sr} \leq \| p_s - p_r \| + 2v (t_r - t_s + \Delta) + \delta$.

A regular digital signature scheme, e.g., RSA [15], or other authentication technique, can be used to allow a receiver to authenticate the location and timestamp in the received packet.

3.1.3 Packet Leashes, End-to-End (COTA) [16]

The end-to-end wormhole detection mechanism proposed in [16] can detect wormholes on a multi-hop route. The mechanism consists of the following steps:

  (i)   All intermediate nodes will attach their timestamps and positions to the detection packets. But only the destination node can conduct all examining operations.
  (ii) If an intermediate node declares its position P_1 at its clock time t_1, and P_2 at its clock time t_2, then the destination can estimate its average moving speed and examine whether it is lying or not.
        If $\| P1 - P2 \| - \delta / \| t1 - t2 \| + \Delta > V$, then the destination can conclude that the node lies about its position and hence, there is a wormhole in the path.
  (iii) After receiving a detection packet, the destination will check for the following:
        (1) All MAC codes are calculated correctly or not.
        (2) Whether the neighbor nodes are within the direct communication range.

(3) The average moving speed of a node, between its receiving and forwarding the packet, does not exceed V.

(4) The sending and receiving time of the same transmission satisfy $\| t_{recv} - t_{send} \| \leq \Delta + t_{prop}$.

(5) The new <time, position> pair and the previous pairs of the same node do not conflict.

(iv) If many consecutive detection packets are all lost or a wormhole is detected, then the destination node will broadcast a message notifying the source to abort the current route and activate the re-initiation.

3.1.4 End-to-End Detection of Wormhole Attack (EDWA) [17]

EDWA is based on the comparison of estimated shortest path and the actual shortest path. It is used to determine whether there is a wormhole attack for each received route. Based on its own measured position and the receiver's position, the sender estimates the shortest path in terms of hop count. The sender also retrieves the hop count value from the received ROUTE REPLY packet and compares it with the estimated value. This method denotes the estimated hop count of the shortest path as **he** and the value from the ROUTE REPLY packet as **hr**. If the received hop count value is smaller than the estimation, that is **hr < α.he**, the sender predicts a wormhole attack and will mark the corresponding route. Since **he** is the estimated shortest path between the source and the destination, the source node is expecting that all legitimate routes will be at least as long as **α** times the estimation. **α** is a parameter adjustable to the network. In the simulation the authors have used **α= 1**. If some shortest routes have smaller hop count than the estimated value, it is with high probability that the route has gone through a wormhole as a wormhole tends to bring nodes that are far away to be neighbors. Once a wormhole attack is detected, the source node launches wormhole TRACING procedure to identify the two end points of the wormhole and the result is broadcast into the network to warn other nodes. Finally, based on the wormhole detection and identification, the source can select shortest route from a set of legitimate routes.

3.2 Hop-Count Analysis Based Schemes

3.2.1 Multipath Hop-Count Analysis (MHA) [18]

MHA is a simple hop-count analysis based scheme for avoiding wormhole attacks in MANET. MHA uses the observation that the route under the wormhole attack has a smaller hop-count than normal. As a result, users who avoid routes with relatively small hop-counts can avoid most wormhole attacks. MHA has two phases. In the first phase it examines the hop-count values of all routes. Then a safe set of routes is chosen for data transmission. Finally, it randomly transmits packets through safe routes. Even if the wormhole can not be not avoided in some severe cases, it can still minimize the rate of using the route path through the wormhole.

3.2.2   Delay Per Hop Indication (DelPHI) [19]

Delay Per Hop Indication (DelPHI) uses delay as a parameter for detecting wormhole attack in MANET. The detection mechanism uses the delay/hop value for detecting wormhole attacks. The reason is that, under normal situation the delay that a packet experiences in propagating one hop should be similar for each hop along the path. Whereas, under a wormhole attack, the delay for propagating across false neighbors should be unreasonably high since there are in fact many hops between them. Therefore, we observe that if we compare the delay per hop of a legitimate path with the delay per hop of a path that is under wormhole attack, we should find that the delay/hop of the legitimate path is smaller. Hence, if a path has a distinguishable high delay/hop value, it is likely to have been subjected to a wormhole attack.

3.3   Statistics- Based Solutions

3.3.1   Simple Scheme Based on Statistical Analysis (SAM) [20]

N. Song et al. [20] proposed another detection technique for detection of the wormhole attacks called a simple scheme based on statistical analysis (SAM). They mainly considered the relative frequency of each link appearing in the set of all obtained routes and calculated the difference between the most frequently appeared link and the second most frequently appeared link in the set of all obtained routes. The maximum relative frequency and the difference are much higher under wormhole attack than that in normal system. The two values are used together to determine whether the routing protocol is under wormhole attack. The malicious node can be identified by the attack link which has the highest relative frequency. Song's method requires neither special hardware nor any changes to existing routing protocols. In fact, it does not even require aggregation of any special information, as it only uses routing data already available to a node. These factors allow for easy integration of this method into intrusion detection systems.

3.3.2   Neighbor Number Test (NNT) and All Distances Test (ADT) [21]

Two statistical approaches to detect wormhole attack in wireless ad hoc sensor networks have been introduced in [21]. The first one, called Neighbor Number Test is based on a simple assumption that a wormhole will increase the number of neighbors of the nodes (fake neighbors) in its radius. The base station gets neighborhood information from all the sensor nodes, computes the hypothetical distribution of the number of neighbors and uses statistical test to determine if there is a wormhole or not. The second one is called All Distance Test which detects wormhole by computing the distribution of the length of the shortest paths between all pairs of nodes. In these two algorithms, most of the workload is done in the base station to save sensor nodes' resources. However, one of the major drawbacks is that they cannot pinpoint the location of wormhole which is necessary for a successful defense.

4 A Comparative Study of Wormhole Attack Countermeasures

Table 1. Comparative study of different wormhole detection and prevention schemes

	Countermeasure	Advantages	Disadvantages
A L O C A T I O N A N D T I M E B A S E D	1) Packet leashes, temporal	1. A wormhole is detected between two nodes by checking whether the packet has traveled too far by comparing the traveling time and thus detection can be achieved using any packet that is to be transmitted by a node. The network can be checked for the presence of a wormhole in the RREQ phase of routing (in On-Demand routing protocols) itself. There is no need for a separate detection phase for the detection of wormholes. 2. This solution can be categorized with pro-active mitigating solutions for wormhole attack and thus prevent wormhole formation. 3. Is reliable and has a high detection rate.	1. The nodes require tightly synchronized clocks. 2. Special hardware is needed to achieve tight time synchronization between the nodes which makes the set up more complex and costly. 3. Each node requires one to one communication with each of its neighbors. 4. Overheads may increase as the size of the packet is increased due to the use of packet leash. 5. This approach assumes that the packet sending and receiving delay are negligible, but in reality this is impossible. 6. Each node requires predicting the sending time and computing signature while having to timestamp the message with its transmission time. 7. This solution only prevents closed wormholes.
S O L U	2) Packet leashes, geo-graphi-cal	1. Time synchronization can be much looser. 2. Attacker can be caught if it pretends to reside at multiple locations. 3. Geographic leashes have the advantage that they can be used in conjunction with a radio propagation model, thus allowing them to detect tunnels through obstacles.	1. In certain circumstances, bounding the distance between the sender and receiver, d_{sr}, cannot prevent wormhole attacks; for example, when obstacles prevent communication between two nodes that would otherwise be in transmission range, a distance-based scheme would still allow wormholes between the sender and receiver. 2. A network that uses location information to create a geographical leash can control even these kinds of wormholes. To accomplish this,

T I O N S			each node has a radio propagation model. A receiver can verify that every possible location of the sender $(a \delta + v (t_r - t_s + 2\Delta))$ radius around p_s) can reach every possible location of the receiver $(a \delta + v (t_r - t_s + 2\Delta))$ radius around p_r). The use of a radio propagation model with geographic leashes would be extremely expensive. 3. A clever attacker could defeat the entire premise of geographic leashes by cleverly choosing their false locations. 4. Also, the upper bound on the velocity of a node would be difficult to define. 5. This solution only prevents closed wormholes.
3) Packet leashes, end-to-end	1.	It can detect the conflicting information sent by the attacker to different neighbors. 2. Cross packet examination must be adopted by the end-to-end mechanism. 3. The end-to-end mechanism has a weaker requirement on the accuracy of the sending timestamp than packet leashes 4. Every intermediate node attaches two <time, position> pairs and a MAC code to each detection packet. So there is not much computation overhead at the intermediate nodes. And they do not need to store any information.	1. Since the mobile devices have limited resources, the end-to-end mechanism, as a security enhancement, must consider the communication, computation, and storage overhead. 2. A scheme must be designed to prevent the destination node from being overwhelmed by the overhead. 3. The communication overhead includes byte overhead and packet overhead. The byte overhead will increase fast with increasing path length. It does not scale well for long routes. 4. Total computation overhead of destination node for the m packets and l path length will be $O (lm + lm^2)$, and the required storage space will be $O (lm)$.

	4) EDWA	1. All above methods can only detect wormhole or avoid the affection of wormhole attack. But EDWA can effectively identify wormhole using wormhole TRACING. 2. It is a location-based end-to-end wormhole attack detection technique. 3. It can identify the location of the two end points of a hidden wormhole using wormhole TRACING.	1. The communication overhead in EWDA is caused by the wormhole TRACING which involves one TRACING message from the source and one TRACING-RESPONSE message from each intermediate node. 2. The storage overhead is involved in identifying the peak increase of hop count in wormhole TRACING.
B H O P C O U N T A N A L Y S I S B A S E D	5) Multi- path Hop- count Analy- sis (MHA)	1. It is a highly efficient protocol which does not require any special supporting hardware. 2. MHA is designed to use split multipath routes, so the transmitted data is naturally split into separate routes. An attacker on a particular route cannot completely intercept (and subvert) the content.	1. The dynamic information of the packets can still be modified. This issue can be solved by some cryptographic method. 2. There can be some attacks anticipating MHA. For example, attackers may add fake nodes to an intermediate list so the route has a longer distance.
	6) Delay Per Hop Indica- tion (Del- PHI)	1. DelPHI is able to detect both kinds of wormhole attacks - Hidden Attack and Exposed Attack. 2. DelPHI does not require clock synchronization and position information, and it does not require the mobile nodes to be equipped with some special hardware, thus it provides higher power efficiency. 3. DelPHI can achieve higher than 95% in detecting normal path and 90% in detecting wormhole attack, in the absence of background traffic.	1. It cannot pinpoint the location of a wormhole. 2. DelPHI does not work well when all the paths are tunneled. 3. The message overhead of DelPHI is a weak point of it. There is a tradeoff between providing reliability of DelPHI and minimizing the message overhead.

STATISTICS BASED		Advantages	Disadvantages
	7) Simple scheme based on statistical analysis (SAM)	1. SAM is successful at detecting wormhole attacks and locating the malicious nodes. 2. SAM works well under different network topologies and node transmission range. 3. SAM introduce very limited overhead. It only needs the route information collected by route discovery.	1. Statistical analysis is the tool to detect routing anomaly as long as sufficient information of routes is available from multi-path routing. 2. It cannot directly apply to table driven routing algorithms, such as AODV. 3. If a malicious node behaves normally during routing, SAM cannot detect it. 4. SAM assumes that nodes have low mobility compared to the routing period.
	8) NNT and ADT	1. Both mechanisms can detect the wormhole with high accuracy when the radius of the wormhole is comparable to the radio range of the sensors. 2. In terms of false alarms, both algorithms perform reasonably well.	1. Both methods can detect only the presence of a wormhole, but they do not pinpoint its location. 2. Both mechanisms require few base stations, and assume that the base stations have no resource limitations, and they can run complex algorithms.

5   Conclusion and Future Work

Routing protocols in MANET are vulnerable due to the inherent design disadvantages. Many researchers have used diverse techniques to propose different types of detection and prevention mechanisms for wormhole problem. In this paper, we have first summarized the effect of wormhole attack on popular routing protocols in wireless mobile ad hoc networks. Then, we have discussed about some of the works available in the literature in detecting and preventing wormhole attacks. Finally, we have carried out a detailed comparative analysis of these techniques according to their relative advantages and disadvantages.

Therefore, by going through the current research activities, we see that there is still a huge scope of research in the field of wormhole detection and prevention. According to this review work we observed that most of these proposed detection and prevention techniques have suffered from its own weaknesses, e.g. - hardware need, time synchronization, communication overhead or need of statistical data. There is no detection technique that can detect wormhole attack completely. The proposed methods are not sufficient to detect or prevent all types of wormhole attacks. Time synchronization based solutions can only prevent closed wormhole attack. Though statistical analysis based solutions can detect multiple wormhole attacks but they need low mobility network and enough routing information to be available. Also the reliability of hop count based solutions are inversely proportional to the communication overhead.

Therefore, after going through the disadvantages of the various schemes and by analyzing them we find that there is still a huge scope of work towards the development of a new hybrid wormhole detection and prevention scheme which will combine the features of both software driven and hardware driven detection techniques thereby offering the advantages like low communication overhead and eliminating the need for special hardware. The wormhole problem is still an active research area. We hope that this paper will benefit more researchers to realize the current state of art rapidly.

References

1. Perkins, C.E., Belding-Royer, E.M., Das, S.R.: Ad hoc on-demand distance vector (AODV) routing. RFC 3561, The Internet Engineering Task Force, Network Working Group (2003), http://www.ietf.org/rfc/rfc3561.txt
2. Johnson, D.B., Maltz, D.A.: Dynamic source routing in ad hoc wireless networks. In: Imielinski, Korth (eds.) Mobile Computing, vol. 353, pp. 153–181. Kluwer Academic Publishers (1996)
3. Maltz, D.A., Johnson, D.B., Hu, Y.: The dynamic source routing protocol (DSR) for mobile ad hoc networks for IPv4. RFC 4728, The Internet Engineering Task Force, Network Working Group (2007), http://www.ietf.org/rfc/rfc4728.txt
4. Royer, E.M., Toh, C.K.: A Review of Current Routing Protocols for Ad hoc Mobile Wireless Networks. IEEE Personal Communications Magazine, 46–55 (April 1999)
5. Nguyen, H.L., Nguyen, U.T.: A study of different types of attacks on multicast in mobile ad hoc networks. Ad Hoc Networks 6(1), 32–46 (2008)
6. Karmore, P., Bodkhe, S.: A Survey on Intrusion in Ad Hoc Networks and its Detection Measures. International Journal on Computer Science and Engineering, IJCSE (2011)
7. Rai, A.K., Tewari, R.R., Upadhyay, S.K.: Different Types of Attacks on Integrated MANET-Internet Communication. International Journal of Computer Science and Security, IJCSS 4(3) (2010)
8. Boppana, R.V., Konduru, S.: An Adaptive Distance Vector Routing Algorithm for Mobile Ad Hoc Networks. In: Proceedings of INFOCOM, pp. 1753–1762 (April 2001)
9. Murthy, S., Garcia-Luna-Aceves, J.J.: An Efficient Routing Protocol for Wireless Networks. ACM Mobile Networks and App. J., Special Issue on Routing in Mobile Communication Networks, 183–197 (October 1996)
10. Perkins, C.E., Bhagwat, P.: Highly Dynamic Destination-Sequenced Distance-Vector routing (DSDV) for mobile computers. In: Proceedings of the SIGCOMM, pp. 234–244 (August 1994)
11. Johnson, D.B., Maltz, D.A., Broch, J.: The Dynamic Source Routing Protocol for Multihop Wireless Ad Hoc Networks. In: Ad Hoc Networking, ch. 5, pp. 139–172. Addison-Wesley (2001)
12. Perkins, C.E., Royer, E.M.: Ad-Hoc On-Demand Distance Vector Routing. In: Proceedings of WMCSA, pp. 90–100 (February 1999)
13. Bertsekas, D., Gallager, R.: Data Networks, 2nd edn. Prentice Hall, NJ (1992)
14. Hu, Y., Perrig, A., Johnson, D.: Packet Leashes: A Defense against Wormhole Attacks in Wireless Ad Hoc Networks. In: Proceedings of INFOCOM (2004)

15. Rivest, R.L., Shamir, A., Adleman, L.M.: A Method for Obtaining Digital Signatures and Public-Key Cryptosystems. Communications of the ACM 21(2), 120–126 (1978)
16. Weichao, W., Bharat, B., Lu, Y., Wu, X.: Defending against Wormhole Attacks in Mobile Ad Hoc Networks. Wireless Communication and Mobile Computing (2006)
17. Wang, X., Wong, J.: EDWA: End-to-end detection of wormhole attack in wireless Ad hoc networks. International Journal of Information and Computer Security, IJICS (2007)
18. Jen, S., Laih, C., Kuo, W.: A Hop-Count Analysis Scheme for Avoiding Wormhole Attacks in MANET. Sensors 9(6), 5022–5039 (2009)
19. Chiu, H.S., Lui, K.S.: DelPHI: Wormhole Detection Mechanism for Ad Hoc Wireless Networks. In: Proc. of International Symposium on Wireless Pervasive Computing, Phuket, Thailand (2006)
20. Song, N., Qian, L., Li, X.: Detection of wormhole attacks in multi-path routed wireless ad hoc networks: A statistical analysis approach. In: Proceeding of the 19th International Parallel and Distributed Processing Symposium, IPDPS 2005 (2005)
21. Buttyán, L., Dóra, L., Vajda, I.: Statistical Wormhole Detection in Sensor Networks. In: Molva, R., Tsudik, G., Westhoff, D. (eds.) ESAS 2005. LNCS, vol. 3813, pp. 128–141. Springer, Heidelberg (2005)

Management of Routed Wireless M-Bus Networks for Sparsely Populated Large-Scale Smart-Metering Installations

Philipp Digeser, Marco Tubolino, Martin Klemm, and Axel Sikora

University of Applied Sciences Offenburg, Badstrasse 24, D77652 Offenburg, Germany
{pdigeser,mtubolin,mklemm}@stud.hs-offenburg.de,
axel.sikora@hs-offenburg.de

Abstract. If sensor networks are sparsely populated, the installation and the investment for central nodes, like data collectors or gateways, is always a challenge. Collection of data from more sensors than in the direct vicinity can help to alleviate this problem. The basic modes of Wireless M-Bus protocol, which is one of the major contenders for local metrology networks (LMN) in Europe, supports only single-hop star topologies. The Q-mode adds algorithms for routing and for time synchronization. This paper reports on a Work-in-Progress implementation of Wireless M-Bus Q-mode in a model based way employing the real-time operating system TinyOS. Therefore algorithms, management techniques and tools for its use in sparsely populated large-scale smart-metering installations are highlighted.

Keywords: Wireless M-Bus, Q-Mode, Routing, TinyOS, Smart Metering.

1 Introduction

Smart grids implementations rely on smart metering and on Local Metrological Networks (LMNs) which accomplish various requirements regarding adaptability, efficiency, flexibility, sustainability and cost. In order to aggregate these characteristics the Wireless M-Bus protocol, which enjoys wide popularity in Europe, is used and complemented with additional features to meet these demands. The Wireless M-Bus protocol enjoys wide popularity in Europe and other regions. It strives for a reasonable compromise between these requirements and is complemented with additional features. Thus, the Wireless M-Bus protocol according to EN 13757-4 [1] and EN 13757-5 [2] is a major contender for LMNs in smart metering and smart grid applications. For flexibility reasons, it is realized in various different modes (C-, D-, F-, N-, P-, Q-, S- and T-mode), which allow different features and functionalities. One of the latest extensions is the Q-mode, which enables routing within the Wireless M-Bus networks [2]. In addition it can be enhanced by extensions from groups, like Open Metering System (OMS) Group, or national bodies. The aim of the WiMBex project (Remote wireless

S.M. Thampi et al. (Eds.): SNDS 2012, CCIS 335, pp. 385–395, 2012.

water meter reading solution based on the EN 13757 standard, providing high autonomy, interoperability and range) is to add a powerful set of new features to the Wireless M-Bus platforms developed by the consortium SMEs, to enable them to keep pace, and even surpass the needs of the emergent Automatic Water Meter Reading (AWMR) market in Europe, and also to license the developed technology. Thus, it tries to make use of the new standard by implementing and adding state-of-the-art techniques in an embedded system based on Tiny-OS according to a UML model based design. Hereby one of the main objectives is the system optimization for ultra-low energy consumption to ensure long-lasting battery life-time in the range of 5 to 10 years, and even beyond. Therefore an energy harvesting module will be provided and a TDMA energy-aware routing protocol will be implemented to avoid mains powering, which would restrict installation flexibility and would add cost in the context of distributed water metering. This document is organized as follows: Ch. 2 describes state-of-the-art wireless communication protocols used for smart metering, ch. 3 describes the new features given by the Q-Mode, ch. 4 depicts the background of the project, ch. 5 illustrates the approaches employed for the implementation, ch. 6 describes the test procedures, ch. 7 gives a conclusion about current results and finally in ch. 8 the future work is explained.

2   Protocols for Smart Metering

2.1   ZigBee Smart Energy Profile

Various protocols for wireless routed approaches have been defined. Besides the Wireless M-Bus, ZigBee is another widespread option [3]. While the Wireless M-Bus is standardized by an European standard (EN) the independent ZigBee Alliance was founded by a commercial group of currently more than 300 companies. The first standard with regard to smart metering was ratified in 2008 followed by numerous certified products. Currently the new standard ZigBee Smart Metering 2.0 is under development not only by members of the ZigBee Alliance but also it is opened for parties outside the organization. ZigBee currently uses only 2.4 GHz-band, and possibly has the option to also make use of the 868/915 MHz band, which is already envisaged in the baseline IEEE802.15.4 standard. However, the recently opened 169MHz band is not in the scope [4].

2.2   Wireless M-Bus

The M-Bus protocol is a European standard (Communication system for meters and remote reading of meters) [5] [6] for smart metering which was extended by the Wireless M-Bus as an out-of-wire interface in the EN 13757-4 [1] and EN 13757-5 [2]. While different operating modes are defined the present project deals with the Wireless M-Bus Q-mode defined in section 7 of the EN 13757-5. This approach regards among others the implementation of a low-power system whereas radio reception is only enabled in defined timer intervals. Moreover routing is considered

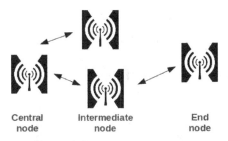

Fig. 1. Routing with central node, intermediate node and end node to establish large-scale communication

by implementing a hierarchical network structure as illustrated in Fig. 1. A central node is responsible for the data collection and several intermediate nodes are used to forward frames to end nodes located outside the ration frequency (RF) coverage of the central node. Thus the coverage of sparsely populated large-scale networks is guaranteed. Moreover to establish connections to any present node in a network a search procedure as well as a network management protocol is defined. Communication operates in the 169 MHz frequency band to enable long distance transmission. In order to avoid data loss an acknowledgement mechanism shall guarantee the successful transmission at each hop.

2.3   Further Protocols

Apart from these protocols, further protocols and their derivatives, are available. However, those still try to find their way from proprietary products to open standards. This is namely Radian, Wavenis [7], and Z-Wave [4]. Practically, all of the protocols follow some kind of layered approach, which is, however, not covering all the layers of the ISO-OSI-reference model. Most of the protocols even define the complete protocol stack from layer 1 through to layer 7, which severely impedes interoperability, as interfaces (service access points, SAPs) are very specific [4] [7].

3   Wireless M-Bus Q-mode Extensions

Wireless-M-Bus N-mode foresees operation in the 169 MHz frequency band and thus ensures long range communication [2]. Since one main objective of this mode is to allow communication in sparsely populated areas, it is promising to combine this mode with the Q-mode extension, which comprises routing functionality. For the support of the Q-mode, an all-new frame structure of the network layer has been developed, which is shown in Fig. 2.

To guarantee utilization of the optimal path regarding signal strength to any node a search procedure is defined in the standard. The corresponding strategy is illustrated in Fig. 3 and based on the signal-to-noise ratio (SNR) of a received frame. This works as stated below:

Nctrl	TID	DA	SA	TTL	SNR	Nodes	Current	Addr. List	App. Data
1 byte	1 byte	7 bytes	7 bytes	1 byte	1 byte	1 byte	1 byte	hops x 2 bytes	n bytes

Fig. 2. Protocol of the network frame

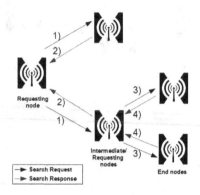

Fig. 3. Search procedure of the network layer

1. The requesting node initiates a search procedure by sending a search request to all nodes within its range.
2. If nodes receiving this search request are not registered yet they respond by sending the SNR of the received frame as a response message.
3. The recently new detected nodes send another search request to all nodes within their range.
4. This procedure continues until all nodes within the range of a network, with a maximum distance of 9 hops or 10 nodes are registered.
5. Conclusively the information about the corresponding addresses and SNR are forwarded to and stored by the central node since this information builds the foundation for a routing process [2].

Reducing energy consumption by implementing a protocol supporting precision timing is realized by adding energy saving (sleep) state. Nodes listen regularly for a wake-up signal sent ahead of a frame on another bit-rate. While normal communication takes place at a bit rate of 4.8 kbps a wake-up signal is sent at a bit rate of 3.12 kpbs. The selection of the relative routing cost is based on the residual node energy [8]. This consists of four main elements: node residual energy, energy for transmission process, energy for receive process, replenishment rate have to be taken into account.

4 Project Background

WiMBex aims to develop a low-cost, low-power and multi-band (169MHz/868MHz) wireless network for automatic water meter reading according to the EN 13757 Wireless M-Bus standard in order to employ its new features. A time-synchronized energy-aware routing protocol based on a Time Division Multiple Access (TDMA) Media Access Control (MAC) scheduling shall be designed and implemented. The WimBex project is financed partly from the European Commission in 7th Framework Program 3. Besides the authors' team two research institutions (Catalonian Research and Innovation Centre, CRIC, Institut fuer Mikro- und Informationstechnik, HSG-IMIT) are involved in the development process [9]. Since up to now the usage of traditional programming techniques are still common in such systems the authors' goal is to develop the system on a model-based structure according to UML employing the generic open source real-time operating system TinyOS.

5 Implementation Approaches

The implementation is accomplished in compliance to the model based approach described in [10]. Within the SyncSen Project [11], a predecessor project of WimBex, several mode implementations and driver functionalities for the DLL are already given on a stable platform. In order to implement the model based design in the existing system the new code is designed with two different strategies as described below.

5.1 Data Link Layer

The data link layer (DLL) is mainly based on sequential programming paradigms since it uses algorithms of the previous modes which are implemented without a model driven architecture in the predecessor project [11]. Therefore the code is described in state charts illustrated according to the current UML standard 2.4.1. An example is illustrated in Fig. 4. Note that the states displayed in Fig. 4 are arranged in a way, that they behave like flow charts. Different than on the network layer no events are used but guards are defined to ensure the proper program flow. The following is implemented so far:

1. The extensions of the Q-mode require a new frame format. The DLL is able to decode and encode a packet and read the DLL relevant information. The remaining parts of the packet are handled as payload and might be passed to network layer based to its content. Furthermore the content is checked according to the EN 13757-5 standard. In case of a wrong CRC checksum the packet will be dropped.
2. The DLL adjusts the radio chip with the corresponding mode settings. To ensure flexibility the DLL is able to support the CC1101 and CC1120 radio chips [12] [13]. The type of radio chip must be determined via pre-compiler settings [2].
3. The Q-mode is added to the existing modes such that each mode is available for transmission. Currently the required mode must be defined before the program compilation due to lack of memory. Later versions will ensure a run-time shift between the different modes.
4. The DLL is able to evaluate the address consisting of hardware address, network address and manufacturer identification. An additional bit configuration enables to define the address type (evaluate_destination_address).

5. In case of direct transmissions the DLL of the receiving node compiles and transmits an acknowledge if desired. This will be done during a defined period T_{wait} in which every node within the RF range waits for further communication to ensure a clear channel. The note which initiates the transmission also switches to the receiving mode for the time period T_{wait} in order to receive the expected acknowledge. After the expiration of the time T_{wait} every node within the RF range is allowed to transmit data. This guarantees equal access times for every node.

6. If a data packet is received an algorithm decides if the packet contains data which has to be processed by the DLL (dll_process).

7. In case of broad- and multicast frames the DLL (dll_forward) forwards the packet and passes the data to the network layer. This part is not implemented yet and a reliable handling of the forwarding process must be determined since it is not defined in the Q-mode standard.

8. Some components of the algorithms set a variable named 'packet_handling'. This variable contains information about the frame type and controls the behavior of the DLL layer regarding the packet. Eventually the variable determines if there is a necessity to send an acknowledge, to push data to the upper layer or to drop the data. If the packet is dropped the error type (wrong address, CRC fail, wrong packet format, etc.) will be stored so that upper layers can access and process this error information.

5.2   Network Layer

The network layer is based on a model based development approach which is not adapted from the SyncSen project [11] and thus has a different structure. The establishment of sequence charts constitutes the communication procedure. State charts are used to define the detailed handling procedure of the network layer [14]. For each state machine a common implementation is applied to maintain a clear structure which can be changed and extended easily.

Fig. 5 and Listing 1 illustrate a sample state chart and its respective implementation. This state machine shows the simplified process of receiving data on the network layer. Depicted are two branches, one for the case of proper data with further processing and one for incorrect data that creates an error message. The state chart has four different states: An idle state, a state to check the received data, one to process the correct data and one to generate an error message. There are two different events shown (i_trig_xxx), one to receive data which is called by the receive event shown in Listing 1 and one that indicates that the data was checked.

The state machine is implemented as a task, a special construct of TinyOS [15]. A scheduler is part of TinyOS which allows to post tasks that are processed one after another and can be interrupted by events. Using this functionality allows to execute different state machines quasi parallel. Since this state machines are event driven there is no polling involved. This means that events (e.g. a receive event) set so-called triggers and post the state machine task afterwards. The state machine depicted in Fig. 5 describes the following steps:

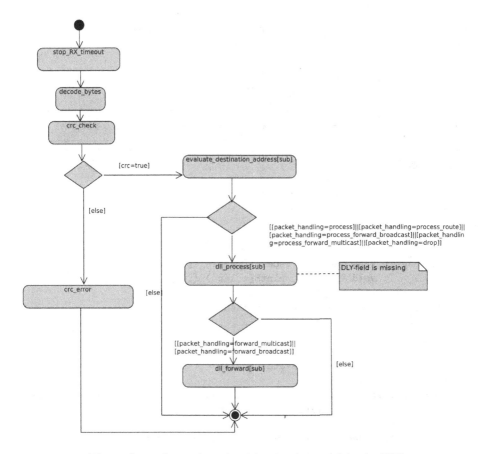

Fig. 4. State chart of an algorithm implemented in the DLL

1. The state machine is in the idle state.
2. The RadioReceive.receive event is called from lower layers.
3. In this event there must be a check if the state machine is already running. It is possible that a second packet is received while the state machine is still processing the first one. In this simple example the second packet is discarded.
4. In case the state machine is not processing a frame the trigger is set and the state machine is posted.
5. When the task is executed the proper case (s_check_data) is chosen corresponding to the trigger.
6. In this state an internal event is generated (i_trig_data_checked_xxx) and the task is posted again.
7. Depending on the case the data is processed or an error message is generated. Since these two states are the last ones they have to set the processing/busy variable to free respectively zero.

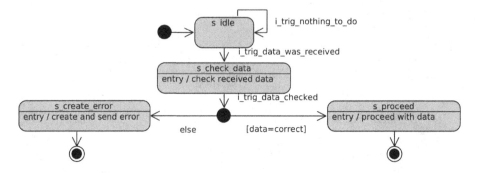

Fig. 5. State chart example of the model based approach for the network layer

```
event message_t *RadioReceive.receive( message_t *msg,
              void *payload, uint8_t len ) {
   i_trigger=i_trig_data_was_received;
   post main_sm(); //start the state machine
   return msg;
}

task void main_sm(){ // main state machine
   switch (i_trigger){
      case i_trig_nothing_to_do: //idle state
         m_state=s_idle; //set actual state for error handling
         break;
      case i_trig_data_was_received: //check data state
         m_state=s_check_data;
         if(data==correct) //check if data is correct and choose branch
            i_trigger=i_trig_data_checked_correct;
         else
            i_trigger=i_trig_data_checked_error;
         post main_sm();
         break;
      case i_trig_data_checked_correct: //s_proceed
         m_state=s_proceed;
         i_trigger=i_trig_nothing_to_do;
         break;
      case i_trig_data_checked_error: //s_create_error
         m_state=s_create_error;
         i_trigger=i_trig_nothing_to_do;
         break;
   }
}
```

Listing 1. Code example for the state chart in fig. 5

5.3   Application Layer

An application layer provides a test environment that is able to transmit several test cases and establish a connection to the PC which evaluates the received results.

6   Testing

In order to test the proper functionality of the implemented state charts unit tests are performed. Based on the corresponding state charts a state transition table is created. Fig. 1 shows such a transition table for the state chart in Fig. 5. All states and the resulting states based on the possible events/guards are

Table 1. State transition table for the state chart shown in Fig. 5

	do_nothing	data_was_recieved	data_checked	
			data=correct	else
s_idle	s_idle	s_check_data	–	–
s_check_data	–	–	s_proceed	s_create_error
s_create_error	–	–	–	–
s_proceed	–	–	–	–

listed. In this case e.g. if an i_data_was_recieved event is fired only in the s_idle state changes shall occur. Based on this table a transition tree is designed as illustrated in Fig. 6. This tree possesses three different paths which at least need to be tested. Also additional error cases are regardéd as e.g. if a an event is fired but a state should remain. The corresponding test frames are stored in

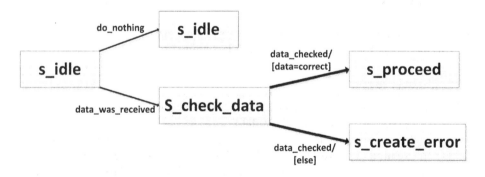

Fig. 6. Transition tree based on state chart in Fig. 5

arrays and sent by one node. The frames received and processed by another node are evaluated. Since TinyOS offers weak debug support for the MSP430 which is used in this project, the serial port is utilized to analyze the behavior of the program and the structure of the received packets. This enables a fast and simple debugging and investigation and errors can be detected easily.

7 Conclusion

Work on the DLL layer which is affected by the SyncSen project has so far resulted in the following:

1. Q-Mode DLL frame structure: The new structure of the Q-Mode DLL frame is implemented and the different address types are evaluated.
2. Radio-chip: The DLL layer can control transmission as well as reception employing the CC1101 or the CC1120 radio-chip.
3. Acknowledgment: Sending/receiving procedure of an acknowledgment is implemented. The mechanism to consider a time window in which an acknowledgement should be received is also regarded.
4. Low power listening: Nodes are in a sleep state and wake up after a certain time interval to check if a wake-up signal is present.

One main objective of the project is to develop a system based on a model driven design applying TinyOS as an open software platform. On the NWL this intend can be realized since there is no earlier basis. UML charts are designed and implemented employing the given means by TinyOS. Therefore the following is done:

1. Q-Mode NWL frame structure: The frame format given by the Q-Mode is implemented and tested.
2. State charts: Required functionality is included in the designed state charts.
3. Routing: A simple routing mechanism according to the SNR of a transmission is implemented and tested.

8 Future Work

In order to complete the design process several steps on the different layers will be conducted by the development team. This comprises

1. DLL
    (a) A delay information needs to be generated indicating the time employed by a node to process a frame. This information will be stored in the DLL frame in a field named "DLY-field".
    (b) A forwarding mechanism for broad- and multicast messages will be implemented. This refers to the fact that these messages carry no network layer information and thus forwarding can be conducted on the DLL layer.
2. NWL:
    (a) Up to now the implementation of routing based on the SNR is not realized. Therefore, routing algorithms and parameterizations are currently being designed, and will be subsequently implemented.
    (b) The search procedure is already designed in state charts but will also be implemented in the next step.

3. APL:
   (a) For the application layer several management services are defined in the standard including for example commands to execute a search procedure.
   (b) To fulfill all requirements additional services will be designed.
   (c) In addition an interface allowing costumers to access the designed services and add costumer services will be implemented.

The unit test procedure described in section 6 will be employed for further implementations. Therefore proper test functions will be designed and an evaluation will be conducted.

References

1. Communication systems for meters and remote reading of meters, Part 4: Wireless meter readout (Radio meter reading for operation in the 868 MHz to 870 MHz SRD band), EN 13757-4
2. Communication systems for meters and remote reading of meters, Part 5: Wireless Relaying, EN 13757-5
3. Kupris, G., Sikora, A.: ZigBee - Datenfunk mit IEEE802.15.4 und ZigBee. Franzis-Verlag Poing (2007) ISBN 978-3-7723-4159-5
4. http://www.z-wavealliance.org/
5. Communication systems for meters and remote reading of meters, Part 2: Physical and link layer, EN 13757-2
6. Communication systems for meters and remote reading of meters, Part 3: Dedicated application layer; EN 13757-3
7. http://www.wavenis-osa.org/
8. Lin, L., Shroff, N.B., Srikant, R.: Asymptotically optimal energy-aware routing for multihop wireless networks with renewable energy sources. IEEE/ACM Trans. Netw. 15(5), 1021–1034 (2007)
9. http://www.wimbex.com/
10. Sikora, A., Digeser, P., Klemm, M., Tubolino, M., Werner, R.: Model Based Development of a TinyOS-based Wireless M-Bus Implementation. In: IEEE International Symposium on Wireless Systems within the Conferences, Intelligent Data Acquisition and Advanced Computing Systems, Offenburg, Germany (September 2012)
11. http://syncsen.cric-projects.com/index.html
12. CC1101 Low-Power Sub-1 GHz RF Transceiver (Rev. G)
13. High Performance RF Transceiver for Narrowband Systems (Rev. C)
14. Bachmeier, S.: Using UML for modeling TinyOS components. University of Stuttgart
15. Levis, P., Sharp, C.: TinyOS Enhancement Proposals 106: Schedulers and Tasks

A Survey of Blackhole Attacks and Countermeasures in Wireless Mobile Ad-hoc Networks

Subhashis Banerjee and Koushik Majumder

Department of Computer Science & Engineering, West Bengal University of Technology,
Kolkata, India
koushik@ieee.org

Abstract. In the next generation of wireless communication systems, there will be a need for the rapid deployment of independent mobile users. Such network scenarios cannot rely on centralized and organized connectivity, and can be conceived as applications of Mobile Ad-Hoc Networks. A MANET is an autonomous collection of mobile users, which is an infrastructure less, self con-figuring network of mobile devices connected by wireless links. Lack of fixed infrastructure, wireless medium, dynamic topology, rapid deployment practices, and the hostile environments in which they may be deployed, make MANET vulnerable to a wide range of security attacks. The Blackhole and its variant Co-operative Blackhole are some of the deadliest security threats in wireless mobile ad hoc networks as they are very difficult to handle due to the ineffec-tiveness of the traditional security mechanisms in case of MANET. In this pa-per, we have reviewed Blackhole and Co-operative Blackhole attacks in Mobile Ad-Hoc networks. An attempt has also been made to thoroughly analyze the various existing schemes against the Blackhole attacks and to find out their ad-vantages and disadvantages.

Keywords: Mobile ad hoc network, Security, Blackhole, Co-operative Blackhole.

1 Introduction

Mobile Ad-hoc Networks (MANETs) are different than the wired networks due to their special characteristics such as *decentralization, dynamic topology* and *neighbor based routing.* This type of network consists of nodes that are organized and main-tained in an autonomous and distributed manner without a fixed infrastructure. These nodes, such as laptop computers, PDAs and wireless phones, have a limited transmis-sion range. Hence, each node has the ability to communicate directly only with another node within its communication range. In case of communication with a node outside its communication radius, cooperation of the intermediate nodes is required. Since the transmission between two nodes has to rely on relay nodes, many routing protocols [1-4] have been proposed for ad hoc networks. However, most of them as-sume that other nodes are trustable and hence they do not consider the security and attack issues. This provides many opportunities for attackers to break the network. Moreover, the open nature of wireless communication channels, the lack of infrastruc-ture, rapid deployment practices, absence of clear entry points and the hostile

S.M. Thampi et al. (Eds.): SNDS 2012, CCIS 335, pp. 396–407, 2012.
© Springer-Verlag Berlin Heidelberg 2012

environments in which they may be deployed, make them vulnerable to a wide range of security attacks described in [5-7].

In this paper we investigate some specific type of attacks, known as Blackhole and Co-operative Blackhole [8-16]. Such attacks are relatively easy to mount, while being difficult to detect and prevent. During the attack a malicious node sends fake routing information, claiming that it has an optimum route and causes other good nodes to route data packets through the malicious one. On the receipt of data packets, the malicious one simply drops them, instead of forwarding to the destination.

The remainder of this paper is organized as follows: in section 2 we describe Blackhole and Co-operative Blackhole attacks against Ad-hoc routing protocols. In section 3 we describe some methods that have been proposed for detecting and preventing these attacks. In section 4 we compare the countermeasures according to their corresponding advantages and disadvantages. Finally, in section 5, we conclude the paper.

2 Blackhole and Co-operative Blackhole Attacks on Routing Protocols

2.1 Single Blackhole Attack [8,9]

In a Single Blackhole attack, a malicious node sends fake routing information, claiming that it has an optimum route and causes other good nodes to route data packets through the malicious one. On the receipt of data packets, the malicious one simply drops them, instead of forwarding to the destination.

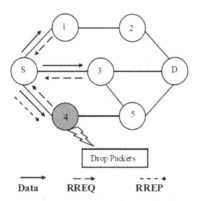

Fig. 1. Single Blackhole Attack

As an example, consider the following scenario in Fig. 1. Here node S is the source node and D is the destination node. Nodes 1 to 5 act as the intermediate nodes. Node 4 acts as the Blackhole. When the source node wishes to transmit a data packet to the destination, it first sends out the RREQ packet to the neighboring nodes. The malicious nodes being part of the network, also receive the RREQ. Since the Blackhole node has the characteristic of responding first to any RREQ, it immediately sends out the RREP. The RREP from the Blackhole node 4 reaches the source node, well ahead of the other RREPs, as it can be seen from the Fig 1. Now on receiving the RREP from node 4, the source starts transmitting the data packets. On the receipt of data packets, node 4 simply drops them, instead of forwarding to the destination. Thus the data packets get lost and hence never reach the intended destination.

2.2   Co-operative Blackhole Attack [10]

In a Co-operative Blackhole attack the malicious nodes act in a group. As an example, consider the following scenario in Fig. 2. Here node S is the source node and D is the destination node. Nodes 1 to 5 act as the intermediate nodes. Node 4 and node 5 act as the Co-operative Blackholes. When the source node wishes to transmit a data packet to the destination, it first sends out the RREQ packet to the neighboring nodes. The malicious nodes being part of the network, also receive the RREQ. Since the Blackhole node has the characteristic of responding first to any RREQ, it immediately sends out the RREP. The RREP from the Blackhole node 4 reaches the source node, well ahead of the other RREPs, as it can be seen from the Fig. 2. Now on receiving the RREP from node 4, the source starts transmitting the data packets. On the receipt of data packets, node 4 simply drops them, instead of forwarding to the destination or node 4 forwards all the data to node 5. Then node 5 simply drops the received packets instead of forwarding to the destination. Thus the data packets get lost and hence never reach the intended destination.

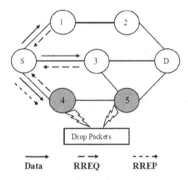

Fig. 2. Co-operative Blackhole Attack

3   Review of the Existing Countermeasures

3.1   Watchdog and Pathrater [9]

S. Marti et al. proposed two methods called Watchdog and Pathrater which can be used for detecting and mitigating routing misbehavior.

Watchdog:
The watchdog method detects misbehaving nodes. Fig. 3 illustrates how the watchdog works. Suppose there exists a path from node S to D through intermediate nodes A, B,

and C. Node A cannot transmit all the way to node C, but it can listen in on node B's traffic. Thus, when A transmits a packet for B to forward to C, A can often tell if B transmits the packet. If encryption is not performed separately for each link, which can be expensive, then A can also tell if B has tampered with the payload or the header. The implementation of watchdog requires maintaining a buffer of recently sent packets and comparing each overheard packet with the packet in the buffer to see if there is a match. If so, the packet in the buffer is removed and forgotten by the watchdog, since it has been forwarded on. If a packet has remained in the buffer for longer than a certain timeout, the watchdog increments a failure tally for the node responsible for forwarding the packet. If the tally exceeds a certain threshold bandwidth, it determines that the node is misbehaving and sends a message to the source notifying it of the misbehaving node.

Fig. 3. When B forwards a packet from S toward D through C, A can overhear B's transmission and can verify that B has attempted to pass the packet to C. The solid line represents the intended direction of the packet sent by B to C, while the dashed line indicates that A is within transmission range of B and can overhear the packet transfer.

Pathrater:
The Pathrater, run by each node in the network, combines knowledge of misbehaving nodes with link reliability data to pick the route most likely to be reliable. Each node maintains a rating for every other node it knows about in the network. It calculates a path metric by averaging the node ratings in the path and chooses the path with the highest metric.

3.2   Collaborative Security Architecture for Blackhole Attack Prevention [10]

A. Patcha et al. proposed a collaborative architecture to detect and exclude malicious nodes that act in groups or alone which is an extension to watchdog design. The algorithm categorizes nodes into two groups called trusted and ordinary. The first few nodes that form a network are trusted nodes. Trusted nodes have previously proved their trustworthiness to other nodes. Watchdog nodes that monitor the network are selected from these trusted nodes. Watchdog nodes are selected for a given period of time according to some criteria such as: 1) node energy, 2) node storage capacity available, 3) node computing power. Watchdog tasks exchange between trusted nodes after a period of time. Two thresholds are maintained in each watchdog node. 1) ACCEPTANCE_THRESHOLD : is a measure of the neighboring node's good behavior and when exceeded as a result of continuous acceptable behavior of packet forwarding over specified period of time qualifies that neighboring node as a trusted node. 2) SUSPECT_THRESHOLD: is used to count maliciousness of one node for packet dropping and after exceeding that limit, enters that node in malicious nodes list and announces that node as a Blackhole node to the network.

3.3   Redundant Route Method and Unique Sequence Number Scheme [11]

M. Al-Shurman et al. proposed two solutions to avoid the Blackhole attacks in MANET. The first solution uses the notation of redundant routes within the routing path for preventing Blackhole attack. The working flow of redundant route mechanism is described briefly as below.

First, the source node sends a ping packet, a RREQ packet, to the destination. The receiver who has a route to the destination will reply to this request, and an acknowledge examination is executed at source node. Then the sender will buffer the RREP packet until there are more than two received RREP packets, and transmit the buffered packets after identifying a safe route. The safe route identification procedure uses the observation that two or more of these routes must have some shared hops. From these shared hops the source node can recognize the safe route to the destination. If there is no shared node appearing in these redundant routes, the sender will wait for another RREP until a route with shared nodes is identified or routing timer is expired. After that, the source node recognizes the safe route from the number of hops or nodes, and prevents the Blackhole attacks.

And the second solution is based on the observation that the next packet sequence number must have higher value than the current packet sequence number. In this solution, every node needs to have two additional small-sized tables. One table stores last packet-sequence-numbers for the last packet sent to every node. The second table is used to keep last packet-sequence-numbers for the last packet received from every node. When packet is arrived or transmitted these tables are updated. When a node receives reply from another node, it checks the last sent and received sequence numbers. If there is any mismatch then an ALARM indicates the existence of Blackhole node.

3.4   Receive Watch and Redirect (REWARD) [12]

It uses the concept of replication for detection and prevention of Blackhole attack. Fig. 4 shows the sequence of multihop transmissions under REWARD. After five transmissions the destination receives two packets with identical data. One packet is received over the path S–>A–>B–>C–>D and another through S–>B–>D. Each node forwards the packet to immediate neighbors, one node forward and one node backward. If a node attempts a Blackhole attack and drops a package, it will be detected by the next node in the path. The watcher waits for a specific time period, sends the packet for changing the path and also broadcasts a SAMBA (suspicious area, mark a black-hole attack) message. The SAMBA message contains the location of the Blackhole node.

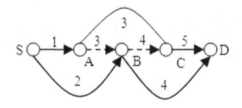

Fig. 4. Two identical packets are sent to the destination

3.5   Local and Co-operative Detection [13]

Proposed mechanism involves both local and co-operative detection to identify any malicious node in the network. The mechanism consists of four security procedures which are invoked sequentially. The security procedures are: (1) Neighborhood data collection, (2) Local anomaly detection, (3) Co-operative anomaly detection, and (4) Global alarm raiser.

(1) *Neighborhood data collection module*: Each node in the network collects the data forwarding information in its neighborhood and stores it in a table known as the Data Routing Information (DRI) table.

(2) *Local anomaly detection module*: This security procedure is invoked by a node when it identifies a suspicious node by examining its DRI table.

(3) *Co-operative anomaly detection module*: The objective of this procedure is to increase the detection reliability by reducing the probability of false detection of local anomaly detection procedure.

(4) *Global alarm raising module*: This procedure is invoked to establish a network wide notification system for sending alarm messages to all the nodes in the network about the grayhole node(s) that has been detected by the co-operative anomaly detection algorithm. It also ensures that the identified malicious node(s) is isolated so that it cannot use any network resources.

3.6   The Distributed and Co-operative Mechanism (DCM) [14]

Chang Wu Yu et al. proposed a collaborative Blackhole attack detection and prevention mechanism called DCM. This is a distributed and co-operative mechanism. In this method the nodes works co-operatively, so that they can analyze, detect, mitigate multiple Blackhole attacks. The DCM consists of four sub-modules which are shown in Fig.5.

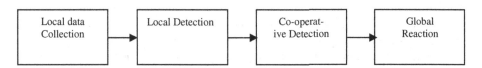

Fig. 5. Sub-modules of DCM

- Local Data Collection:
With the local data collection step, each node in the network is required to evaluate if there is any suspicious node in its neighborhood by collecting information through overhearing packets and using the collected information to construct an estimation table. The estimation table can be used to identify suspicious Blackhole nodes. If a node has not successfully routed any data packets from or through some neighboring node, that particular node may be a potential Blackhole node and needs to be inspected further.

- Local Detection

When a suspicious Blackhole node is identified according to the estimation table in the local data collection phase, the detecting node, referred to as the initial detection node, would initiate the local detection procedure to analyze whether the suspicious one is indeed a malicious Blackhole node.

- Co-operative Detection

Once the local detection procedure has detected a possible Blackhole node, the co-operative detection procedure is activated. The Co-operative detection procedure is initiated by the initial detection node, which proceeds by first broadcasting and notifying all the one hop neighbors of the possible suspicious node to co-operatively participate in the decision process confirming that the node in question is indeed a malicious one.

- Global Reaction

As soon as a confirmed Blackhole node is identified, the fourth procedure - the global reaction is activated to establish a proper notification system to send warnings to the whole network.

3.7   Secure-ZRP (S-ZRP) Protocol [15]

ZRP (Zone Routing Protocol) is a hybrid approach that combines advantages of both proactive and reactive routing protocol. R. Shree et al. proposed a secure version of ZRP called S-ZRP, which can detect and prevent Blackhole attack.

Authors gave the notion of 'bluff probe' packet for detecting Blackhole attack. A 'bluff probe' packet contains the address of destination but in actual this is the address of a nonexistent node. When local communication takes place, at that time, originator node broadcasts this packet. This massage is called bluff probe request packet. This message is received by all direct neighbours. They check their entries in the table and if they are not Blackhole nodes then they will forward the message to the next neighbors. If the malicious node is present in the zone, it will give immediate response to the source node through the intermediate node. As it gives response, the source node catches it as a Blackhole node and blocks the Blackhole node. After this, the source node sends information to the direct neighbours for updating their entries. Therefore we can see that this algorithm provides an efficient approach for detecting and preventing single Blackhole as well as multiple Blackhole attack in a MANET.

3.8   Next Hop Information Scheme [16]

Ping YI et al. proposed this path based scheme for Blackhole and Grayhole detection. In this method a node only observes the next hop behavior in current route path and need not watch every node in the neighbor. For example, consider Fig. 6, where S is the source node, D is the destination node; and A is a Blackhole node. Node S is sending some data packets to node D through the path S->A->B->D. According to this protocol node S only watches node A, which is the next hop.

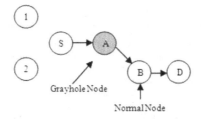

Fig. 6. A path based detection scheme

In this method every node keeps a FwdPktBuffer, which is a packet signature buffer. When a detection node forwards a packet, it adds its signature into its FwdPktBuffer. When the detecting node overhears the action that the next hop forwards the packet, it deletes the signature from the FwdPktBuffer. At a fixed period of time, the detecting node should calculate the overhear rate of its next hop and compare it with a threshold called overhear rate in the Nth period of time, defined as OR(N) = total overheard packet number / total forwarded packet number. And if the forwarding rate of the next hop is lower than the threshold, the detecting node will consider the node as a black or grayhole node. Later, the detecting node would avoid forwarding packets through this suspect node.

4   A Comparative Study of Blackhole Attack Countermeasures

Table 1. Comparative study of different blackhole attack countermeasure schemes

Countermeasure	Advantages	Disadvantages
1) Watchdog and Pathrater	1. This is a simple method, where one node should just listen to its next node in the route. 2. It has the advantage that it can detect misbehavior at the forwarding level and not just the link level.	1. Watchdog's weaknesses are that it can not detect a misbehaving node in the presence of a) ambiguous collisions, b) receiver collisions, c) limited transmission power, d) false misbehavior, e) collusion, and f) partial dropping. 2. Source node depends on the other node's information about one node's misbehavior. 3. During extreme mobility watchdog and Pathrater can double the transmission overhead percentage. 4. This method cannot detect Co-operative Blackhole & Grayhole attack.

Table 1. *(continued)*

2) Collaborative Security Architecture for Blackhole Attack Prevention	1. This method can successfully detect the presence of colluding malicious nodes in the absence of mobility. 2. Decreases monitoring overhead on all the nodes by selecting some trusted nodes for monitoring.	1. The method assumes that there is little or no movement of nodes. 2. If some trusted nodes start to drop packets, like Grayhole attack, then the security of the whole network will be compromised. 3. The method introduced new packet types that significantly increases the network overhead. 4. Though it can successfully detect co-operative Blackhole, it cannot discover a secure path from source to destination.
3) Redundant Route Method and Unique Sequence Number Scheme	1. Redundant Route Method can guarantee to find a safe route to the destination. 2. Unique Sequence Number Scheme provides a fast and reliable way to identify the suspicious reply. And no overhead will be added to the channel.	1. In Redundant Route Method many RREP packets have to be received and processed by the source and after that the safe route can be found. This produces large amount of time delay. 2. Cannot detect Co-operative Blackhole and Grayhole attacks.
4) REWARD	1. It uses the notion of distributed database for detecting Blackhole attacks which also distribute the overhead among the nodes. 2. REWARD allows striking the balance between security capability and lifetime performance. 3. The method has different levels of security which can be set according to the local conditions.	1. REWARD declines the network's vulnerability at the expense of more energy drawn from the batteries of the involved nodes. 2. REWARD is more suitable for dense networks.
5) Local and Co-operative Detection	1. This mechanism can detect malicious grayhole nodes in MANETs, which is very difficult due to their occasional misbehavior. 2. The scheme is efficient in terms of communication overhead.	1. This mechanism will be particularly suitable for routing protocols like AODV, as nodes need to know the information regarding its neighboring nodes only for routing. 2. Overhead due to DRI tables and probe packets.

Table 1. *(continued)*

6) The Distributed and Co-operative Mechanism(DCM)	1. The mechanism is distributed so that it can fit with the ad hoc nature of network, and nodes in the protocol work co-operatively together so that they can analyze, detect, and eliminate possible multiple Blackhole nodes in a more reliable fashion. 2. Distribute the overhead among nodes. 3. This method imposes less overhead, especially when the network is busy.	1. During the co-operative detection procedure, it uses broadcast to notify all the neighbors of the suspicious node, which inevitably increases the network traffic. 2. Cannot detect Grayhole attack.
7) Secure-ZRP (S-ZRP) Protocol	1. Security mechanism has been associated with ZRP protocol. 2. This is only detection technique that is applicable on both proactive and reactive protocol.	1. Cannot detect Grayhole attack. 2. Every node has to maintain valid route table that imposes too much overhead. 3. Also communication overhead for this method is considerably higher.
8) Next Hop Information Scheme	1. In this scheme, each node only depends on itself to detect a black or gray hole. The algorithm does not send out extra control packets so that routing packet overhead remains the same as the standard DSR routing protocol. 2. This method does not require any encryption on the control packets. 3. There is no need to watch all the neighbors' behavior. Only the next hop in the route path should be observed.	1. It suffers from a high false positive probability under high network overload if a constant threshold is used. 2. When collision rate rises, dynamic detection threshold increases as well, so that some gray hole will not be detected. This is an unsolved problem in the adaptive threshold strategy.

5   Conclusion and Future Work

Routing protocols in MANET are vulnerable due to the inherent design disadvantages. Many researchers have used diverse techniques to propose different types of detection and prevention mechanisms for different types of Blackhole attacks. In this paper, we first summarized the effect of Blackhole attack and its variant co-operative Blackhole attack on ad hoc routing protocols. Then, we discussed some of the proposed works for detecting and preventing such attacks. Finally, by analyzing pros and cons of the existing countermeasures, we presented the open research issues in this area.

According to this review work we observed that most of these countermeasures suffer from the following pitfalls:

— In most of the detection techniques, misbehaving node is identified based on the information provided by its neighbours, which is not reliable.
— Some of them impose huge communication overhead, due to some cross checking verification techniques. This wastes the energy drawn from the batteries of the involved nodes.
— Many of them cannot detect the Grayhole attack and also do not take into consideration the high mobility requirement of the network.
— Some of them use some tables for storing routing related information or some information related to suspicious nodes. This also imposes storage overhead on the mobile nodes.

After going through the disadvantages of the various existing Blackhole detection and prevention schemes and by analyzing them we find that there is still a huge scope of work towards the development of a new detection/prevention method which will eliminate the pitfalls described above. The Blackhole problem is still an active research area and we hope that this paper will benefit more researchers to realize the current state of art rapidly.

References

1. Perkins, C.E., Belding-Royer, E.M., Das, S.R.: Ad hoc on-demand distance vector (AODV) routing. RFC 3561, The Internet Engineering Task Force, Network Working Group (2003), http://www.ietf.org/rfc/rfc3561.txt
2. Johnson, D.B., Maltz, D.A.: Dynamic source routing in ad hoc wireless networks. In: Imielinski, Korth (eds.) Mobile Computing, vol. 353, pp. 153–181. Kluwer Academic Publishers (1996)
3. Maltz, D.A., Johnson, D.B., Hu, Y.: The dynamic source routing protocol (DSR) for mobile ad hoc networks for IPv4. RFC 4728, The Internet Engineering Task Force, Network Working Group (2007), http://www.ietf.org/rfc/rfc4728.txt
4. Boppana, R.V., Konduru, S.P.: An adaptive distance vector routing algorithm for mobile ad hoc networks. In: IEEE Computer and communications Societies, INFOCOM, pp. 1753–1762 (2001)
5. Nguyen, H.L., Nguyen, U.T.: A study of different types of attacks on multicast in mobile ad hoc networks. Ad Hoc Networks 6(1), 32–46 (2008)
6. Karmore, P., Bodkhe, S.: A Survey on Intrusion in Ad Hoc Networks and its Detection Measures. International Journal on Computer Science and Engineering, IJCSE (2011)
7. Rai, A.K., Tewari, R.R., Upadhyay, S.K.: Different Types of Attacks on Integrated MANET-Internet Communication. International Journal of Computer Science and Security, IJCSS 4(3) (2010)
8. Deng, H., Li, W., Agrawal, D.P.: Routing Security in Wireless Ad-hoc Networks. IEEE Communications Magazine 40(10), 70–75 (2002), doi:10.1109/MCOM.2002.1039859
9. Marti, S., Giuli, T.J., Lai, K., Baker, M.: Mitigating routing misbehavior in mobile ad hoc networks. In: Proceedings of the 6th Annual International Conference on MOBICOM, Boston, Massachusetts, United States, pp. 255–265 (2000)
10. Patcha, A., Mishra, A.: Collaborative security architecture for Blackhole attack prevention in mobile ad hoc networks. In: Proceedings of the Radio and Wireless Conference, RWCON, VA, USA, pp. 75–78 (2003)

11. Al-Shurman, M., Yoo, S.M., Park, S.: Blackhole Attack in Mobile Ad Hoc Networks. In: Proceedings of the 42nd Annual ACM Southeast Regional Conference, ACM-SE'42, Huntsville, Alabama (April 2004)

12. Karakehayov, Z.: Using REWARD to detect team black-hole attacks in wireless sensor networks. In: Workshop on Real-World Wireless Sensor Networks, REALWSN 2005, Stockholm, Sweden (June 2005)

13. Sen, J., Chandra, M.G., Harihara, S.G., Reddy, H., Balamuralidhar, P.: A mechanism for detection of gray hole attack in mobile ad hoc networks. In: Proceedings of the 6th International Conference on Information, Communications & Signal Processing, Singapore, pp. 1–5 (2007)

14. Yu, C.W., Wu, T.-K., Cheng, R.-H., Chang, S.C.: A Distributed and Cooperative Black Hole Node Detection and Elimination Mechanism for Ad Hoc Networks. In: Washio, T., Zhou, Z.-H., Huang, J.Z., Hu, X., Li, J., Xie, C., He, J., Zou, D., Li, K.-C., Freire, M.M. (eds.) PAKDD 2007. LNCS (LNAI), vol. 4819, pp. 538–549. Springer, Heidelberg (2007)

15. Shree, R., Dwivedi, S.K., Pandey, R.P.: Design Enhancements in ZRP for Detecting Multiple Blackhole Nodes in Mobile Ad Hoc Networks. International Journal of Computer Applications 18(5), 6–10 (2011)

16. Yi, P., Zhu, T., Liu, N., Wu, Y., Li, J.: Cross-layer Detection for Blackhole Attack in Wireless Network. J. Computational Information Systems 10(8), 4101–4109 (2012)

iReSign – Implementation of Next-Generation Two-Tier Identity Classifier-Based Traffic Sign Recognition System Architecture Using Hybrid Region-Based Shape Representation Techniques

Keerthi Balasundaram[1], Madhan Kumar Srinivasan[1], and K. Sarukesi[2]

[1] Infosys Limited,
Mysore, India
{bskeerthi7390, madhankrs}@gmail.com
[2] Hindustan University,
Chennai, India
vc@hindustanuniv.ac.in

Abstract. Today's modern human life-style is in a great uplift with respect to anything and everything. The requirement of road transportation and vehicles is increasing day-by-day which is proportional to the number of accidents happening eventually. At this juncture, building an intelligent vehicle system and other safety driven driver assistance systems have become the order-of-the-day. Despite the fact that considerable research has been carried out in detecting and tracking the traffic signs, still there is a huge lack in pertinent traffic sign recognition systems, especially in countries like India. This paper designates on the implementation of iReSign, next-generation two-tier identity classifier-based traffic sign recognition system architecture using Zernike and GFD algorithms for the future intelligent vehicle systems. Further, this paper details the results and its analysis, which is based on 840 images of 28 distinct traffic signs of India (collected manually). Using Zernike Moments and Generic Fourier Descriptors (GFD) region-based global shape recognition techniques, iReSign produced 78.33%, 90% cross validation accuracy and 77.85%, 91% testing recognition accuracy respectively. Using our new hybrid approach of combining Zernike Moments and GFD, iReSign produced 92% cross validation accuracy and 95% testing recognition accuracy.

Keywords: iReSign, traffic sign recognition, two-tier identity classifier, Zernike moments, GFD, LIBSVM, XPF extraction algorithm, C-CUBE, P-RESIZER, pattern labeller, pixel value generator, feature extractor, identity modeler, identity recognizer.

1   Introduction

Traffic sign boards placed on roadside provides safety information to the vehicle drivers. With traffic volume increasing day by day, many countries has adopted

S.M. Thampi et al. (Eds.): SNDS 2012, CCIS 335, pp. 408–421, 2012.

pictorial sign representations to simplify and standardize their signs to facilitate international travelers. This adoption of pictorial representation was mainly to overcome the barriers created by language differences, and in general to enhance safety in tourism and travel. Such pictorial signs use symbols in place of words and are based on international protocols. Such signs were first developed in Europe and have been adopted by most of the countries in varying degrees. There are various sign conventions being followed across the world. Countries like India, Singapore, Sri Lanka, Egypt, Indonesia, South Africa, etc. follows Vienna convention [1]. The traffic signs in general are being grouped as priority signs, mandatory signs, directions, additional panels, warning or cautionary signs. In India, they are classified into cautionary, information and mandatory signs [2].

In our day to day life, lack of awareness of traffic sign boards and increasing number of vehicles has led to more accidents. Hence there is a need to build a system that will automatically detect the traffic sign boards, recognize and alert the driver thereby assisting him to drive safely. The actual framework of such system involves three major subsystems namely detection, tracking and recognition of the traffic sign boards. There is considerable research being pursued distinctly in the areas of detection, tracking and recognition of the traffic sign boards or at times, together. Considering the existing literature on traffic signs, it is clear that the systems are implemented with respect to very few traffic signs (mostly speed limit signs) [3] [4] [5]. Considerable research has been made for the traffic sign boards in countries like Bangladesh [6], Sweden [4] [5], Japan and China [7] etc., but the research on traffic sign boards in countries like India, Singapore, Sri Lanka, Egypt, Indonesia, South Africa (where Vienna convention is followed) is rare when compared relatively with the other countries. Hence a better system for recognizing the traffic sign is required in these countries.

In [2] we had proposed a generic system architecture, which is now named as iReSign, capable of handling traffic signs of any international conventions. The iReSign is a new generic recognition system which uses two-tier classifier architecture that would be helpful to build a strong recognition component for the intelligent vehicle system and other driver assistance systems. Extending our earlier work, this paper showcases the experimental results of iReSign for Indian traffic signs through selective region-based shape representation technique along with an attempt to a new hybrid approach. The iReSign leverages the LIBSVM tool [8] for implementation purposes.

2   Shape Representation Techniques

2.1   Selection of Shape Representation Techniques

In general, shape representation techniques can be categorized as contour-based and region-based. Contour-based shape representation techniques [9] will exploit only the boundary information of the shape. In region-based techniques, the entire area of the shape is taken into account to obtain the representation of the shape. Due to the nature of traffic signs taking different meaning with the change in their orientation, it is ideal to choose region-based techniques for traffic sign recognition system design. Further, there are two sub-categories in region-based, such as structural and global. As detailed in [2], region-based structural techniques have issues like complex computation and graph matching.

Region-based global methods use moment descriptors to describe the shape that considers the whole image and the representation is a numeric feature that will be used for shape description. These techniques make use of all the pixel information within an image region. Some of the region-based global techniques are Zernike Moments, Generic Fourier Descriptors (GFD), Geometric Moment Invariants, Algebraic Moment Invariants, Orthogonal Moments, Shape Matrix and Grid Methods. Among these techniques, Zernike Moments and GFD exhibit [10] good retrieval accuracy, compact features, low complexity and robust performance and can be used for real time applications. A detailed study on Zernike had also proved that it has reconstruction power compared to other Moments algorithms [11]. Due to simple implementation and performance, we had used Zernike Moments technique for iReSign implementation in our previous research work [2]. In continuation, we chose GFD for iReSign implementation and could able to achieve quantifiable improvements in the retrieval of traffic sign results.

2.2   Zernike Moments

The Zernike moment of order p with repetition q is defined as follows:

$$Z_{pq} = \frac{p+1}{\pi} \sum_X \sum_Y f(x,y) \, W_{pq}(r,\theta) \tag{1}$$

Where,

$$W_{pq}(r,\theta) = R_{pq} e^{iq\theta}$$

$$R_{p,\pm q}(r) = \sum_{k=q, p-|k|=even}^{p} B_{pqk} r^k$$

$$B_{pqk} = \frac{(-1)^{(p-k)/2}((p+k)/2)!}{((p-k)/2)!((q+k)/2)!((k-q)/2)!}$$

Since Zernike polynomial is a complete set of an orthogonal basis, it is also called as orthogonal moments.

2.3   Generic Fourier Descriptor (GFD)

For an input image f(x,y) it is first transformed to a polar image f(r,Θ)

$$PF(\rho, \phi) = \sum_r \sum_i f(r, {}_i) \, exp \left[j2\Pi \left(\frac{r}{R}\rho + \frac{2\Pi i}{T}\phi \right) \right] \qquad (2)$$

Where $r = \sqrt{((x - x_c)^2 + (y - y_c)^2)}$

$\qquad = arc\ tan(y - y_c/x - x_c)$

Here, $x_c = \frac{1}{M}\Sigma_0(N - 1)x$ $\qquad$ and $\qquad$ $y_c = \frac{1}{N}\Sigma_0(M - 1)y$

Where ${}_i = \left(\frac{2\Pi}{T} \right)$

and $0 \leq r \leq R, 0 \leq \rho \leq R, 0 \leq \phi \leq T$

R = radial frequency

T = angular frequency

3   Related Work

Multi-category SVMs for traffic sign recognition and BP algorithm was used by Liu & Zhu [12] for comparing Chinese and Japanese traffic signs. This method had computational complexity to be implemented in real time. In other work [6] with prime focus on Bangladeshi traffic signs, color segmentation and moment invariants were used. Though computational time complexity was improved, robustness was missing in case of signs captured under different kinds of atmospheric and luminance conditions.

Shi, Wu, and Fleyeh proposed a robust model for Swedish traffic signs [4] based on support vector machines. Prominence was given for a very few categories of speed limit signs and traffic signs shades. The results were satisfying; however this method would not be ideal for real time application as only few signs were considered for recognition. In the work [5], Swedish road signs were again subjected for research. In this study the sign borders and pictograms were investigated majorly using Zernike moments and fuzzy ARTMAP technique. In this work, the images were normalized to 36x36 pixels before training using fuzzy ARTMAP. The problem here is time required for pre-computation for normalizing or reducing the image size is an overhead to be implemented in a real time scenario.

In the research work of [7] involving Chinese road signs, Color-Geometric Model was proposed for recognition. The approach here involved color information and shape information and hence addressing the recognition in case of a difference in atmospheric or luminance or climate would be a problem. This is due to the fact that the color of the traffic sign board may change in case of a climatic change while capturing with a camera. Since shape attribute was also focused, addressing the problem of occlusion was not investigated.

Hough transform along with template matching was used for traffic sign recognition in [3]. This paper also purely focused on speed limit signs limiting its usage to a real time system. This approach also lacks efficiency in terms of computational time. Tchebichef moments and support vector machine was proposed in [13]. In this method, the RGB images that were captured by the camera were converted into HSV color space. These images were then applied for recognition. Even in this method only Chinese traffic signs were concentrated. Pixel based approach was often adopted for classification and the traffic signs was determined or recognized by cross-correlation template matching [14] [15]. Gao et al [16] used 49–dimensional feature vectors encoding their local edge orientation and density at the arbitrary fixation points to the corresponding vectors computed for the template sign images [17]. But in this approach, features were manually selected which is not convincing. Bahlmann Et Al. [17] used Bayes classifier. Though only 6% error rate was reported, the work was done for narrow subset of signs only.

Using all the above information as a backbone to this paper we can typically perceive that majority of the research works were focused only on a single semantic category of traffic signs, mostly speed limits. As stated earlier, research on traffic signs in countries like India are rare. One more problem was the complex environment of roads and scenes around traffic sign boards. This is because of the variations in climatic and light conditions; the illumination geometry would be affected. Also some of the existing systems were not invariant to rotational and scaling. Analyzing these constraints and lack of such system in India like countries, we had already proposed a generic architecture [2] in our previous work. The system had addressed the problem of rotational and scaling invariance too. To improve the accuracy of the system, the GFD algorithm [18] is chosen for research in this paper as it produced good results as compared to our previous work [2] involving Zernike moments algorithm. Also the kernel of GFD was quite easy to compute relatively than Zernike moments method. In Zernike the shape was to be normalized into a unit disk to calculate the moments whereas in GFD it was not required. When large scaling was carried out, the spatial distribution changed and using Zernike moments the shape features could be analyzed only in circular direction, but GFD proved strong by examining the shape in radial directions. More importantly when the number of images in training and testing set was increased, GFD proved to be more robust than Zernike moments. Further, the easiness in the implementation of Zernike Moments algorithm combined with the computational strength of GFD made us to attempt a new hybrid approach where both the methods were involved to produce the features of the traffic sign images. This reflected significantly in the testing accuracy of iReSign implementation.

4   iReSign Architecture

Figure 1 depicts 'iReSign' system architecture. This architecture is made up of several components such as traffic sign C-CUBE, PIS, P-RESIZER, pattern labeller, pixel value generator, feature extractor, tier-1 classifier identity modeler and tier-2 classifier identity recognizer. The traffic sign C-CUBE (i.e. CCC) is the corpus configuration console used to configure the traffic sign convention to be used along with other parameters such as the number of traffic signs/classes, number of images per class, number of images for training set, number of images for testing set, labeling parameters etc. The PIS, Preliminary Image Source, selects all the raw images that are to be considered for the final corpus. The P-RESIZER is the preprocessor and resizer that will resize the input images to a constant size, so as to minimize the calculations and the time complexity before the corpus is finalized. Based on the configuration made in the traffic sign C-CUBE, the corpus will be split into training and testing set.

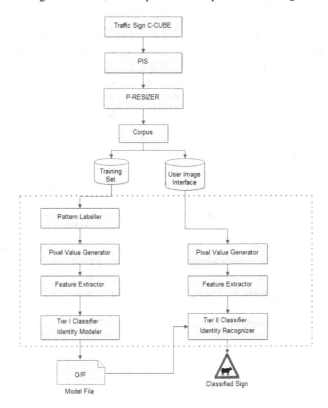

Fig. 1. iReSign – Next-generation two-tier classifier-based traffic sign recognition system architecture

Due to multiple signs being used in the corpus, to distinguish one from the other, a component called pattern labeller is used. Pattern labeller will create a (customizable) unique label per sign in the training set. Pixel value generator component will extract the color intensity value for each pixel and returns the sum of intensities of an image, which has major weightage to form the feature vector. The output of pixel value generator will be fed as input to the feature extractor which calculates the features for that image using a suitable algorithm. The output of feature extractor would be the features in a vector file. This file is compatible to feed to the two-tier classifiers for training and testing respectively. The two-tier classifiers, identity modeler and identity recognizer, executes the core functionality of the iReSign architecture. Identity modeler focuses on training phase of the system where in it accepts the features of the images from the repository and produces a model file containing all the information about the pattern of the input images. This model file will be one of the inputs to the tier-2 classifier identity recognizer. Identity recognizer takes the model file from the tier-1 classifier identity modeler along with the features of a new/testing image and classifies it accordingly.

In training phase, the images pass through the pattern labeller followed by pixel value generator and the feature extractor. The feature extractor will take the calculated pixel intensities of the image from the pixel value generator. Then it will apply a feature selection algorithm using these values, to obtain the features. Using the master file from feature extractor as input, the identity modeler learns them and creates a model file. During the testing phase, the image that is to be tested is passed directly to the pixel value generator, but the output of the feature extractor would be a user image feature file. Using this vector and model files as input, identity recognizer will predict the output by indicating the class of the given user input image.

5   Implementation

To train iReSign architecture we need to design the corpus of the system. Initially, we investigated on those traffic signs that are frequently found in Indian roads. As a result, we identified and finalized upon 28 Indian traffic signs, which in turn used for creating the corpus of the system. A sample image in each class is depicted in Figure 2. These images are taken manually by capturing them using a digital and video cameras. After collecting these images, with the help of our preprocessor subsystem, we obtain the potential area which is necessary for the processing. We randomly captured the traffic signs in various climatic and illumination conditions and fixed the number of images as 50 per each class. These 50 images in each class are used as 30 and 20 for training and testing respectively.

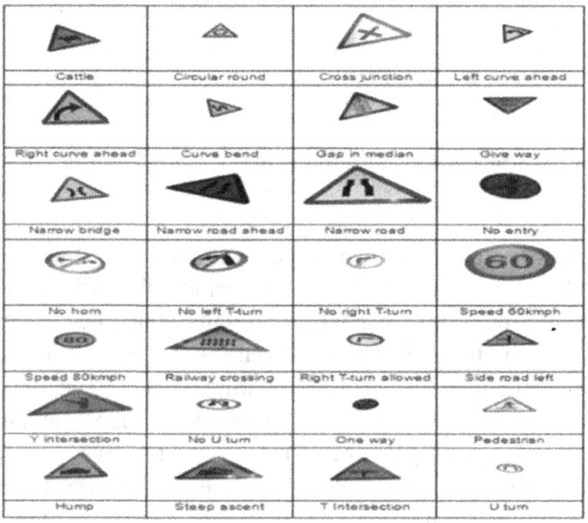

Cattle	Circular round	Cross junction	Left curve ahead
Right curve ahead	Curve bend	Gap in median	Give way
Narrow bridge	Narrow road ahead	Narrow road	No entry
No horn	No left T-turn	No right T-turn	Speed 60kmph
Speed 80kmph	Railway crossing	Right T-turn allowed	Side road left
Y intersection	No U turn	One way	Pedestrian
Hump	Steep ascent	T Intersection	U turn

Fig. 2. Sample traffic signs that were considered

Having created the corpus with rich collection of 28 traffic signs, we implemented the iReSign system (with its core components) using Zernike Moments algorithm. The outcome of this experiment pushed us towards choosing GFD due its computational forte [18]. As expected, this resulted in better performance and accuracy uplift, which inspired us towards merging the benefit of Zernike's ease of implementation and GFD's extraordinary computational capabilities together. That stemmed in our hybrid approach of the above two region-based global shape representation techniques. In this process, first the features are captured using the Zernike Moments algorithm to form a vector file. Then, with the PF Extraction algorithm [2], GFD for the images was acquired and accumulated to form another vector file. A third vector file was formed by combining these two vector files using Extended PF or 'XPF Extraction Algorithm' as shown below. This vector file was exposed to the training and testing phase of iReSign Architecture evidencing good results.

XPF Extraction Algorithm

Input: Traffic sign image

Output: Hybrid Features vectors of the input image

Step 1: *Input image*

Step 2: *Obtain width and height of the image*

Step 3: *Set low threshold value = 245*

  Set high threshold value = 255

Step 4: *For pixels from (0, 0) to (width, height)*

  Step 4a: *Calculate the red, blue and green intensity*

Red → Color of the pixel in RGB value & 0xff0000 >> 16

Green → Color of the pixel in RGB value & 0xff00 >> 8

Blue → Color of the pixel in RGB value & 0xff

  Step 4b: *Intensity of pixel(x, y) is given by*

  *Intensity = 0.299 * red + 0.587 * green + 0.114 * blue*

  Where red, green and blue are respective values calculated in the previous step

  Step 4c: *Store this into data[x][y]*

Step 5: *Calculate HM1(data) and store in a vector file a*

Step 6: *Calculate HM2(data) and store in a vector file b*

Step 7: *Ensemble (vector file a, vector file b)*

Step 8: *Obtain the feature vectors*

---

6   Results and Analysis

The implementation of iReSign (core components) was carried out using the Eclipse IDE 3.4.2 and Java language. This section describes and analyses the obtained results. In training set, we had used the mentioned 28 traffic signs/classes and 30 images in each class. All these images were trained using LIBSVM tool with Zernike Moments and GFD, both individually and combined (for hybrid approach). A set of images in a class that was taken for implementation is been depicted in figure 3.

Fig. 3. Samples from the training set.

6.1   Results

To evaluate the performance of iReSign, many experiments using cross fold validations have been conducted. To check the consistency of the output we have done cross validation which will compute the accuracy rate. The 10-fold cross validation first divides the training set into 10-subset of equal sizes. Then one subset is tested using the classifier trained on the remaining 9 subsets sequentially. For each class it randomly shuffles training set images and divides the images into 10 blocks of 84 images each. For the first run, first 84 images are used as testing data and the remaining images are used for training. In a similar way in the second run the next 84 images are used for testing and the remaining will be used for training. Similarly 10 runs of validation are performed. The parameter values c (cost value) and g (gamma value) differs for each method depending upon the number of features generated. The result of 10-fold cross validation for each run is presented in Table 2.

Table 1. Results of 10-fold cross validation

Runs	Zernike Moments	GFD	Hybrid
1-Run	77.97%	91.78%	92.02%
2-Run	79.28%	90.35%	91.42%
3-Run	79.40%	90.83%	92.50%
4-Run	77.73%	90.35%	92.73%
5-Run	77.85%	91.30%	92.02%
6-Run	77.61%	91.07%	92.26%
7-Run	78.21%	90.23%	92.02%
8-Run	78.09%	91.54%	91.90%
9-Run	78.80%	90.23%	92.61%
10-Run	78.45%	90.71%	91.78%
Average	**78.33%**	**90.83%**	**92.12%**

The following graphs (Fig. 4, 5 and 6) are plotted using gnu plot [19] that shows the accuracy and the parameter values of GFD and hybrid approach training.

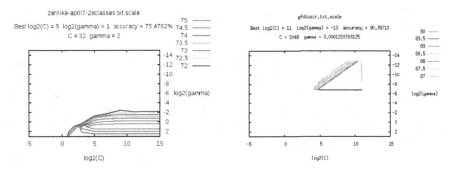

Fig. 4. and **5.** Cross-validation accuracy obtained through a sample run in LIBSVM using Zernike Moments and GFD.

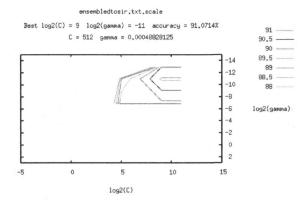

Fig. 6. Cross-validation accuracy obtained through a sample run in LIBSVM using hybrid approach.

6.2   Testing – Analysis

In testing phase, we had used 20 different images per each class of traffic sign that was not used for training. The accuracy obtained by testing is summarized in the table below.

Table 2.   Results of testing phase.

Method Used	Cross Validation Accuracy	Testing Accuracy
Zernike Moments	78.33%	77.85%
GFD	90%	91%
Hybrid	92%	95%

Confusion matrices have been drawn to indicate the number of images that were not classified in each class using individual methods as well as the hybrid method. The rows and columns represent the respective class labels and the number inside the grid represents the classification of the class during the testing phase. For example, the cell [7, 7] represents that about 16 images in class 7 are correctly classified, whereas the cell [7, 2] represents that 4 images from class 7 have been is classified as class 2.

Our experiments with Zernike Moments, GFD and hybrid approach clearly showcases incremental and convincing results on 28 important Indian traffic signs. Our attempt in Zernike and GFD combined hybrid approach results with 95% accuracy. This proves the importance of further research attempts in such hybrid approaches, especially with respect to traffic sign intelligent system design. Our experiment also demonstrates its recognition accuracy of 95% with 28 images, which is considerably an appealing number compared to many other existing systems that included signs such as speed limits and stop signs.

Table 3. Confusion matrix for Zernike Moments

	1	2	3	4	5	6	7	8	9	10	11	12	13	14	15	16	17	18	19	20	21	22	23	24	25	26	27	28
1	17								1										1								1	
2		18													1													1
3	1		14																			4						1
4				20																								
5					20																							
6	2					15		3																				
7		4					16																					
8								13											2								3	2
9									20																			
10				3					2	14	1																	
11											16								2							2		
12	2			1								17																
13													15														2	3
14							3							17														
15															20													
16	1															19												
17	1		2										2				15											
18																		18								1	1	
19								4								3			12									1
20	2	2																		16								
21				4																2	9						2	3
22								2														14						
23		3																						11			4	2
24												2										3	12		3			
25																									20			
26	1	1		3				2																		12		
27	3			4																						2	11	
28				3																								17

Table 4. Confusion matrix for GFD

	1	2	3	4	5	6	7	8	9	10	11	12	13	14	15	16	17	18	19	20	21	22	23	24	25	26	27	28
1	20																											
2		18	1																									1
3			19																						1			
4				19																	1							
5					20																							
6	1					17		1		1																		
7	2		1				17																					
8								17																		3		
9									19																			1
10				1						19																		
11		1									19																	
12												20																
13	1												19															
14														20														
15															20													
16																19		1										
17																	20											
18																		18								1	1	
19								2											19									
20																			1	19								
21								1										1				13					2	3
22																					19					1		
23								1						1									18					
24		1																						16		3		
25																									19			
26	1	1			1			2																		14		1
27	1			1																						1	17	
28	1			1																								18

Table 5. Confusion matrix for hybrid approach.

	1	2	3	4	5	6	7	8	9	10	11	12	13	14	15	16	17	18	19	20	21	22	23	24	25	26	27	28
1	20																											
2		19																										1
3			20																									
4				19																	1							
5					20																							
6	1					18		1																				
7	1	1					18																					
8								18																			2	
9									20																			
10				1						19																		
11											20																	
12												20																
13													20															
14														20														
15															20													
16																20												
17																	20											
18																		20										
19							2												18									
20																				20								
21								1											1		14						2	2
22																						20						
23																							20					
24																								19		1		
25																									20			
26	1	1			1			1																		16		
27	1		2																							1	16	
28			1																									19

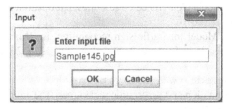
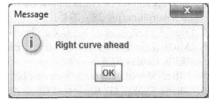

Fig. 7. and **8.** Input and output screens of iReSign system

7   Conclusion

This work demonstrates the implementation of iReSign, next-generation two-tier classifier-based traffic sign recognition system architecture using Generic Fourier Descriptors, a region-based global shape representation technique. In addition, this paper also presents a novel hybrid approach for traffic sign recognition by combing two region-based global shape representation techniques such as Zernike Moments and GFD. This work, specifically, addresses the traffic sign recognition system design for countries like India, Singapore, Sri Lanka, Egypt, Indonesia, South Africa, etc. which follows Vienna convention. Using GFD, the iReSign produced cross validation accuracy as 90% and testing accuracy as 92%, which is superior when compared to our previous Zernike Moments results of 78% and 77% respectively. Our new hybrid approach produced cross validation accuracy as 92% and testing accuracy as 95%. Thus iReSign architecture with the proposed hybrid capability can build the ultimate intelligent vehicle system to create an accident free world.

References

1. Official website of India - Delhi Traffic Police listing signs as per standards,
   `http://www.delhitrafficpolice.nic.in/`
   `traffic-mandatory-signs.html/`
2. Keerthi, B., Madhan, K.S., Sarukesi, K., Rodrigues, P.: Implementation of Next-generation Traffic Sign Recognition System with Two-tier Classifier Architecture. In: International Conference on Advances in Communications, Computing and Informatics, pp. 481–487. ACM, India (2012)
3. Yongping, W., Shimeiping, Tao, W.: A Method of Fast and Robust For Traffic Sign Recognition. In: 5th IEEE International Conference on Image and Graphics, pp. 891–895. IEEE Computer Society, China (2009)
4. Shi, M., Wu, H., Fleyeh, H.: A Robust Model for Traffic Signs recognition based on Support Vector Machines. In: International Congress on Image and Signal Processing, pp. 516–524. IEEE, China (2008)
5. Fleyeh, H., Dougherty, M., Aenugula, D., Baddam, S.: Invariant road sign recognition with Fuzzy ARTMAP and Zernike Moments. In: Intelligent Vehicles Symposium, pp. 31–35. IEEE Intelligent Transportation Systems Society, Istanbul (2007)
6. Hossain, M.S., Hasan, M.M., Ali, M.A., Kabir, M.H., Ali, A.B.M.S.: Automatic detection and recognition of Traffic signs. In: International Conference on Robotics, Automation and Mechatronics, pp. 286–291. IEEE, Singapore (2010)
7. Zhu, S., Liu, L., Lu, X.: Color Geometric Model for traffic sign recognition. In: IMACS Mulitconference on Computational Engineering in Systems Applications, pp. 2028–2032. IEEE, China (2006)
8. LIBSVM tool, `http://www.csie.ntu.edu.tw/cjlin/libsvm/`
9. Zhang, D., Lu, G.: Review of shape representation and description techniques. The Journal of the Pattern Recognition Society 37, 1–19 (2004)
10. Kan, C., Srinath, M.D.: Invariant Character recognition with Zernike and Orthogonal Fourier-Mellin moments. The Journal of the Pattern Recognition Society 35, 143–154 (2002)
11. Kotoulas, L., Dis, A.: Real-time Computation of Zernike Moments. IEEE Transactions on Circuits and System for Video Technology 15, 801–809 (2002)
12. Liu, L., Zhu, S.: Research of Intelligence Classifier for Traffic sign recognition. In: 6th International Conference on ITS Telecommunications, pp. 78–81. IEEE, China (2006)
13. Li, L., Li, J., Sun, J.: Traffic Sign classification based on Support vector machines and Tchebichef Moments. In: The International Conference on Computational Intelligence and Software Engineering, pp. 1–4. IEEE, China (2009)
14. Piccioli, G., De Micheli, E., Campani, M.: A Robust Method for Road Sign Detection and Recognition. In: Eklundh, J.-O. (ed.) ECCV 1994. LNCS, vol. 800, pp. 493–500. Springer, Heidelberg (1994)
15. De la Escalera, A., Armingol, J.M., Pastor, J.M., Rodriguez, F.J.: Visual sign information extraction and identification by deformable models for intelligent vehicles. IEEE Transactions on Intelligent Transportation Systems 5, 57–68 (2004)
16. Gao, X.W., Podladchikova, L., Shaposhnikov, D., Hong, K., Shevtsova, N.: Recognition of traffic signs based on their colour and shape features extracted using human vision models. The Journal on Visual Communication and Image Representation 17, 675–685 (2006)

17. Ruta, A., Li, Y., Liu, X.: Real-time traffic sign recognition from video by class-specific discriminative features. The Journal of the Pattern Recognition Society 43, 416–430 (2010)
18. Zhang, D., Lu, G.: Generic Fourier descriptor for shape-based image retrieval. In: IEEE International Conference on Multimedia and Expo., pp. 425–428. IEEE, Switzerland (2002)
19. GNU plot, http://www.gnuplot.info/

Neural Synchronization by Mutual Learning Using Genetic Approach for Secure Key Generation

S. Santhanalakshmi[1], T.S.B. Sudarshan[1], and Gopal K. Patra[2]

[1] Dept. of CS&E, Amrita Vishwa Vidyapeetham, School of Engineering,
Bangalore Campus Bangalore, India
s_lakshmi@blr.amrita.edu, sudarshan.tsb@gmail.com
[2] Centre for Mathematical Modelling and Computer Simulations,
Council of Scientific and Industrial Research, Bangalore-560037
gkpatra@cmmacs.ernet.in

Abstract. Neural cryptography is a new way to create shared secret key. It is based on synchronization of Tree Parity Machines (TPM) by mutual learning. Two neural networks trained on their mutual output bits synchronize to a state with identical time dependent weights. This has been used for creation of a secure cryptographic secret key using a public channel. In this paper a genetic approach has been used in the field of neural cryptography for synchronizing tree parity machines by mutual learning process. Here a best fit weight vector is found using a genetic algorithm and then the training process is done for the feed forward network. The proposed approach improves the process of synchronization.

Keywords: Tree Parity Machine, Neural Synchronization, Genetic algorithm, Fitness function.

1   Introduction

Cryptography is the science of securing private information from unauthorized access for ensuring data integrity and authentication, and for controlling against   security threats. It describes methods to transmit secret messages between two partners A and B. An opponent E who is able to eaves drop to the communication should not be able to recover the secret message.

In neural cryptography, both the communicating networks receive an identical input vector, generate an output bit and are trained on their mutual output. This leads to a synchronization by mutual learning. The synaptic weights of the two networks relax to a common identical weight vector, which still depends on time.[1,2,3]. Thus, the generated identical weight vectors are shared and used as a secret cryptographic key. In Tree Parity Machines an interesting phenomenon can be observed: two neural networks learning from each other synchronize faster than a third network which is eve dropping and listening to the communication.

In this paper, a genetic algorithm approach is being proposed to find the optimal weight vector for training the TPM.

S.M. Thampi et al. (Eds.): SNDS 2012, CCIS 335, pp. 422–431, 2012.

The paper is organized as follows. Section 2 describes the training of TPM. Generation of secret Keys is explained in section 3. Genetic approach and the algorithm are explained in section 4. Section 5 presents the implementation results and comparison of genetic and random approach . Section 6 describes the way this genetic approach method responds to different security attacks. The final section concludes this work.

2   Tree Parity Machine

A multilayer feed forward neural network so called as Tree Parity Machine (TPM) is shown in Fig.1. The TPM has k hidden units ($1 \leq k \leq K$).Each hidden unit receives N different inputs ($1 \leq j \leq N$) leading to an input of size KxN . Each input take binary values, $X_{kj} = \pm 1$ and weight associated with inputs W_{kj} bounded by [L, -L]. The binary hidden units are denoted by $\sigma_1, \sigma_2, \dots \sigma_k$ and the output bit τ is the product of the state of the hidden units. The communicating partners A and B use a TPM network with K hidden units as stated below.

$$\sigma_i^A = \text{sign}(W_i^A . X_i) ; \quad \sigma_i^B = \text{sign}(W_i^B . X_i) \quad i=1\dots K$$

where, Signum function is defined as,

$$\text{sign}(x) = \begin{cases} 1 & \text{if } x \geq 0, \\ -1 & \text{otherwise} \end{cases}$$

W_i's are N-dimensional vectors of synaptic discrete weights and the X_i's are N-dimensional input vectors given as,

$$W_{i,j}^{A/B} \in \{ -L, -L+1, \dots\dots, L-1, L \}; \quad X_{i,j} \in \{ -1, +1 \}$$

The K hidden bits σ are combined to an output bit τ of each network as follows

$$\tau^A = \Pi(\sigma_i^{A)}; \quad \tau^B = \Pi(\sigma_i^B) \quad i=1\dots K$$

If the output bits of the communicating partners differ then synchronization is achieved by a mutual training process. At each training step the two machines A and B receive identical input vectors X_i.

The training algorithm is :

1. Initialize random weight values
2. Execute these steps until the full synchronization is achieved
    a. Generate random input vector X
    b. Compute the values of the hidden neurons
    c. Compute the value of the output neuron
    d. Compare the values of both tree parity machines
3. Outputs are not same : go to step 2
4. Outputs are same: Update the weights using learning rule.

In this case, only the hidden unit σ_i which is identical to τ changes its weights using the Hebbian learning rule:

$$W_i^+ = W_i + \sigma_i . X_i .\Theta (\sigma_i.\tau).\Theta(\tau^A \tau^B)$$

and the same is applied for the network B. If this training step pushes any component $W_{i,j}$ out of the interval $-L, \dots +L$ the component is replaced by $+L$ or $-L$ correspondingly.

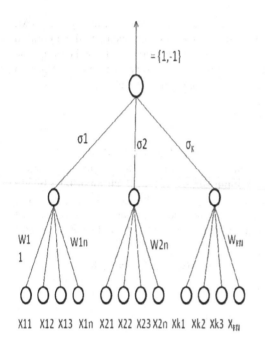

K = no of Hidden Neurons
N = no of Input Neurons
$X_{ij} \in \{-1,+1\}$ –Input to neurons

$W_{ij} \in \{-L,....,O,....,+L\}$ – Weights associated between Input and Hidden unit.

$\sigma_i = Sgn\left(\sum W_{ij} X_{ij}\right)$ – Output Of

　　　　Hidden Neurons.
Signum function returns +1 or -1.

$$\tau = \prod_{i}^{k} \sigma_i$$ –Output of tree parity Machine .it returns +1 or -1

Fig. 1. Tree Parity machine

3   Generation of Secret Keys

Mutual learning of tree parity machines, as explained before, leads to synchronization of the time dependent synaptic weight vectors w_i^A and w_i^B. Both partners start with random weight vectors (3 N random numbers each) and train their weight vectors according to the algorithm. At each training step they receive three common random input vectors x_i.

It turns out that after a relatively short number of training steps all pairs of weight vectors are identical $W_i^A = W_i^B$. The two multilayer networks have identical synaptic weights. Since, according to the learning rule, after synchronization at least one pair of weight vector is changed random walk in weight space for each training step, the synaptic weights are always moving. In fact, it is hard to distinguish this motion form. Therefore the two multilayer networks perform a kind of synchronized random walk in the discrete space of $(2L+1)^{3N}$ points. Synchronization of neural networks can immediately be translated to key generation in cryptography: The common identical weights of the two partners A and B can be used as a key for encryption, either immediately as one-time pad, as a seed for random bit generators or as a key in other encryption algorithms (DES,AES).

Compared to algorithms based on number theory, the neural algorithm has several advantages: First, it is very simple. The training algorithm is essentially a linear filter, which can easily implemented in hardware. Second, the number of calculations to generate the key is low. To generate a key of length N one needs of the order of N computational steps. Third, for every communication, or even for every block of the message, a new key can be generated. No secret information has to be stored for a longer time. But useful keys have to be secure. An attacker E who is recording the communication between A and B should not be able to calculate the secret key.

4   Genetic Approach

Genetic algorithms [4] [5] are based on the real processes of natural selection and survival of the fittest. In biological populations, individuals of every particular species are constantly evolving and adapting to the surrounding environment. Such an adaptation process represents a biological analogy of the mathematical problem of maximizing an objective function, which in the case of Genetic algorithm is referred to as the fitness function.

In genetic algorithms, a set of artificial individuals (models) are used to define a population, and as in the case of biological systems, some genetic information is transmitted from generation to generation by a relatively simple set of combinatorial rules. While this evolution is taking place, the process of natural selection ensures that the fittest individuals are the ones with more probability of transmitting their genetic information. In this way, with the running of time, the individuals and the population are able to get more and more adapted to the environment; even if the environment itself changes with time.

In the evolution of the algorithm, the individuals of a given population interchange their genotypes, according to their fitness values and some probabilistic transition rules, in order to produce a new generation. In this context, the objective function or fitness function provides an artificial selection criterion for giving to the best adapted individuals a higher chance to reproduce.

The genetic algorithm shown in Fig.2, can be described as follows. First, it starts with a certain population of individuals selected at random from the model space. Then, an iterative procedure follows, in which each of its iterations forms three basic steps: selection, crossover and mutation. Finally, the iteration is ended when certain convergence criterion is achieved.

Selection: In this step, individuals are selected for crossover according to their relative fitness with respect to the others in the population. In this way, those individuals whose fitness values are above the population's average fitness will have more chance to reproduce than those whose fitness values are below the average. This selection step is implemented in practice by the creation of a mating pool. In the mating pool, certain number of copies of each individual is placed according to its relative fitness. The use of the mating pool resource enables the use of a uniformly distributed random generator during crossover. However, in more complex system, it is always possible to combine selection and crossover in a single step by using a properly biased random generator.

Crossover: In this step, the genetic material of the individuals in the mating pool is recombined in order to produce a new generation. First, the individuals are picked in pairs from the mating pool. This is done uniformly at random. Then, for each pair, it is decided if crossover is going to be performed or not according to some probability Pc, which is called the crossover rate. If no crossover is required, both individuals are included just as they are in the new generation. On the other hand, if crossover is to be performed, their genotypes are used to generate a new pair of individuals.

In simple crossover, one locus is selected at random dividing the strings in two sections. Then, the alleles in one corresponding pair of sections are interchanged between the strings. In multiple crossovers, more than one locus is selected at random dividing the strings in multiple sections. Then, corresponding non consecutive pairs of sections are swapped.

Mutation: In this step, some random alterations are performed to the genotypes of the individuals in the new generation. This is done according to certain probability Pm, the mutation probability. In general, Pm must be a very small value, such that the order of alterations would be around one in every thousand alleles. For every individual in the population, it is decided if a mutation must occur or not. Then, if it must occur, one locus is selected at random, and the value of its correspondent allele is altered.

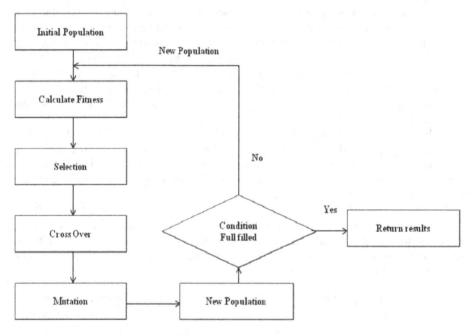

Fig. 2. Genetic Algorithm

4.1   Genetic Algorithm Implementation

Here the weight vector L is taken as 3,4,5,6 for both TPM , the initial population is taken as set of random numbers in the range (-L…L).

Here in this paper an objective function is defined considering a range criterion. The fitness function f(x) is given by:

$$f(x) = \begin{cases} -L & x < -L \\ x^2 & -L \leq x < L \\ L & x \geq L \end{cases}$$

The fitness value for each string in the population is calculated. Based on the fitness value, the most fitted strings from the population are selected using Roulette Wheel selection method. On the selected string crossover and mutation are performed based on the Crossover rate (Pc) and Mutation rate (Pm). This completes one cycle of GA process. If the termination condition is met, the iteration is stopped and the new population generated will be considered as the optimal solution. Then Fig.3. shows how new optimal weights generated by GA are used in the TPM network for mutual learning by both the parties.

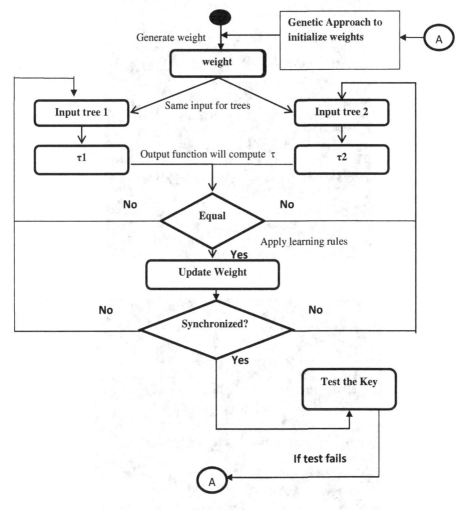

Fig. 3. GA in TPM

5   Results

Implementation of the above algorithm has been carried out in C. For different L values say 3, 4, 5, 6 the algorithm is implemented using random weights and genetic weights. The observed result is shown in the Table 1.Fig.4. shows the result without using the genetic approach i.e., the simple neural key exchange protocol using random weights. Here the simple rand function is used for generating the random weights, and then neural key exchange protocol is applied to generate key.

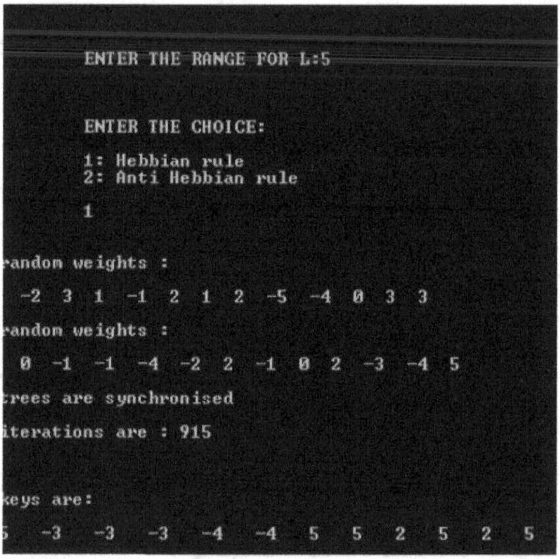

Fig. 4. key generation using random weights

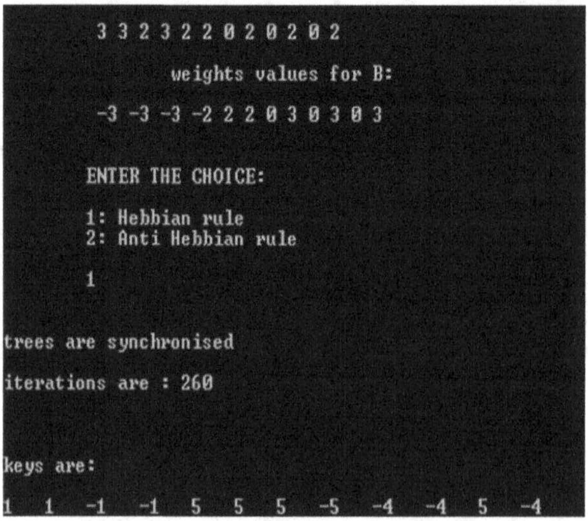

Fig. 5. key generation using genetic weights

After applying genetic algorithm a best fit weight vector is obtained for both A and B. With this, the network is trained. It has been noted that, by performing genetic algorithm, the synchronization time has got reduced   (i.e. it takes only less number of iterations to get synchronized). Fig,5. shows the final key obtained using genetic approach.

The final key obtained is tested for randomness, which is a probabilistic property.

Once the key generated passes all these random tests, [6] it can be used for encryption purposes. If any of the tests fail, process has to be repeated, until a random sequence is obtained. Result is compared with number of iteration and time taken for different range of weights. Table 1 show that number of iterations taken by neural network for synchronization is very less when GA weights are used as compared to Random weights.

Table 1. Average number of iterations with different weight range using Random and Genetic weights obtained over 10^2 samples

For Weight range	No. Of Iterations	
	Using Random weights	*Using Genetic weights*
3	350	150
4	547	263
5	923	300
6	1185	650

The algorithm complexity, $O(MN^2)$ which is higher than the random approach as compared to genetic algorithm . Even though the complexity is high, the use of genetic approach will be more secure and powerful when it is used for stream of key generation. And also the use of genetic approach takes less number of iteration for the network to synchronize. Table 1. shows the average number of iterations taken to generate the key using random weights and genetic weights respectively. The experimentations conducted suggest that the genetic algorithm approach reduces the number of iteration by nearly 50% as compared to random weight approach.

6   Security Attacks

Here primarily Brute Force and Protocol Specific Attack has been considered.

In Brute force method the attacker has to test all possible keys. Therefore for a 48 bit key 2^{48} possibilities will have to be checked. Therefore the likelihood for obtaining key is very less.

In Protocol Specific Attack, the attacker has to learn with his own TPM. Then the attacker tries to synchronize his TPM with the two parties. Three situations could occur

- Output(A) ≠ Output(B): No party updates its weights
- Output(A) = Output(B) = Output(E): All the three parties update weights in their tree parity machines.
- Output(A) = Output(B) ≠ Output(E): Parties A and B update their tree parity machines, but the attacker can not

It has been shown in [7] that synchronization of two parties is faster than learning by the attacker. The security of the system can be improved by increasing the synaptic depth. In fact, numerical simulations as well as analytic calculations show that an attacker E will synchronize with A and B after some learning time. Now using the proposed algorithm, it is observed that although A & B synchronize in 500-600 iterations, but the attacker is not able to learn even after 10,000 iterations. This observation leads to conclude that Genetic approach in neural cryptography method will be less prone to attacks.

This is not an exhaustive analysis of all possible attacks. There are some more complicated attacks like majority flipping attack [8], which has successfully broken, the basic neural cryptography. The current modification is being analyzed against this attack. The purpose of this work is to see whether the use of genetic algorithms can fasten the process of synchronization of genuine parties in comparison to the attacker, so that many attacks, which are generally successful due to lengthy synchronization process, can be avoided. More analysis is being done in order to establish the advantage of this implementation over others.

7   Conclusion

The TPM's were successfully synchronized using the genetic approach. And the neural network was able to synchronize faster because of the best optimal weights obtained from genetic process. From the existing literature it can be said that, neural cryptography is the first algorithm for key generation over public channels, which are not based on number theory. It has several advantages over known protocols: It is fast and simple and for each message a new key can be used and no information is stored permanently. Thus Neural cryptography promises to revolutionize secure communication by providing security based on neural networks assisting the current state of   mathematical algorithms or computing technology.Therefore, genetic approach in neural cryptography may lead to novel applications in future.

References

1. Kinzel, W., Kanter, I.: Neural Cryptography. cond mat/0208453 (2002)
2. Rosen-Zvi, M., Kanter, I., Kinzel, W.: Cryptography based on Neural Networks: Analytical Results, cond- mat/0202350 (2002)
3. Kanter, I., Kinzel, W., Kanter, E.: Secure Exchange of Information by Synchronization of Neural Networks. Europhys. Letter 57, 141–147 (2002)
4. Goldberg, D.E.: Genetic Algorithms in Search, Optimization and Machine Learning. Addison-Wesley

5. Konar, A.: Computational Intelligence. Principles, Techniques and Applications. Springer, Heidelberg (2005)
6. Rukhin, A., Soto, J., Nechvatal, J., Smid, M., Barker, E., Leigh, S., Levenson, M., Vangel, M., Banks, D., Heckert, A., Dray, J., Vo, S.: A Statistical test suite for random and pseudorandom number generators for Cryptographic Applications
7. Klein, E., Mislovathy, R., Kanter, I., Ruttor, A., Kinzel, W.: Synchronization of Neural Networks by Mutual Learning and its Application to Cryptography. In: Advances in Neural Information Processing Systems, vol. 17, pp. 689–696. MIT Press, Cambridge (2005)
8. Klimov, A., Mityagin, A., Shamir, A.: Analysis of Neural Cryptography. In: Zheng, Y. (ed.) ASIACRYPT 2002. LNCS, vol. 2501, pp. 288–298. Springer, Heidelberg (2002)

eCloudIDS Tier-1 uX-Engine Subsystem Design and Implementation Using Self-Organizing Map (SOM) for Secure Cloud Computing Environment

Madhan Kumar Srinivasan[1], K Sarukesi[2], Ashima Keshava[1], and P. Revathy[1]

[1] Infosys Limited,
Mysore, India
{madhankrs,ashimakeshava,revamadhankr}@gmail.com
[2] Hindustan University,
Chennai, India
vc@hindustanuniv.ac.in

Abstract. Cloud computing is becoming more influential as a technical-cum-business model in the present scenario of enterprise business computing. It attracts the customers with its glossy catchphrase 'pay-as-you-use'. Even after knowing all its benefits, many organizations ranging from medium to large businesses fear migrating to this computing paradigm because of the security issues associated with it. The reason being, today's business computing world breathes solely on users and their data which require sophisticated mechanisms to protect it against theft and misuse. Subsequently, due to the public and multi-tenancy nature of cloud, the security threats and the velocity of consequences are higher in cloud, than in in-premises computing. eCloudIDS a next-generation security system designed with innovative hybrid two-tier expert engines, namely uX-Engine (tier-1) and sX-Engine (tier-2), is considered as a most suitable security solution for cloud computing environments; precisely public cloud. This paper deals with the design and implementation of our proposed eCloudIDS architecture's Tier-1 uX-Engine Subsystem using one of the unsupervised machine learning techniques named Self-Organizing Map (SOM). This experiment was conducted on the setup with 6 machines which had Ubuntu 10.04 LTS 64-bit LTS Desktop edition as native operating system, CloudStack 3.0.0 as IaaS platform, XenServer 6.0 as virtualization host, and all systems with statically allocated IP addresses. This paper travels through the phases and footprints involved in the implementation of proposed eCloudIDS Tier-1 uX-Engine subsystem architecture using SOM. Further, our implemented system showcases the detection performance rate as 89% with minimal false alarm rates, which is considerably substantial for an unsupervised machine learning implementation.

Keywords: eCloudIDS, uX-Engine, Self-Organizing map, SOM, sX-Engine, Instance-M, CloudStack, XenServer, Behavior Analyzer, eCloudIDS C3, Cloud VM/Instance Monitor, CIM, H-log-H, Standard Audit repository, SAR, Special Permission Audit repository, SPAR, Acute Audit Repository, AAR, Warning level Generator, Alert System, two-tier expert engine, state-of-the-art cloud computing security taxonomies.

S.M. Thampi et al. (Eds.): SNDS 2012, CCIS 335, pp. 432–443, 2012.

1   Introduction

Cloud computing is rapidly becoming an influential technical-cum-business model in the present scenario of enterprise business computing. It attracts the customers with its glossy catchphrase 'pay-as-you-use'. While cloud computing reduces the overall business cost, it also offers the ultimate computing revolution which is changing the way of traditional IT's each and every functionalities today. Cloud computing has simplified all the pieces of business by renting IT resources, on-demand service etc. CSP plays an important role in cloud computing as this service is maintained by them. The end users or the customers need not know the technology used because the service is maintained by the CSP [1]. Customers can pay only for the resources used thereby ending up paying cheaper rates. Figure 1 depicts the representation of cloud computing architecture.

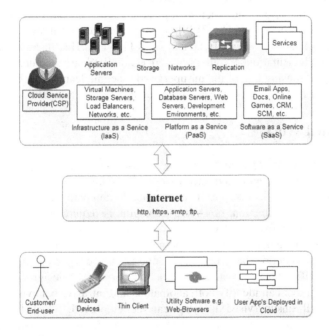

Source: Madhan Kumar Srinivasan, et al.: State-of-the-art Cloud Computing Security Taxonomies – A classification of security challenges in the present cloud computing environment. DOI: 10.1145/2345396.2345474, ACM (2012) [1].

Fig. 1. Cloud Computing Architecture

In addition, this model is largely being supported because of "Greener computing alternative" label [2]. Even after knowing all its benefits, many organizations ranging from medium to large businesses fear migrating to this computing paradigm because of the security hallucinations associated with it [1] [3] [4] [5] [6]. So it becomes an important step in understanding and addressing these security gaps through significant consideration towards user privacy, sensitivity of data etc.

Security aspect has become a main concern in today's computing world. We find ourselves trapped against the rising security breaches from a malicious intruder as well as from organization (insiders) with whom there is code of trust. Today's business computing world breathes solely on users and their data which require sophisticated mechanisms to protect it against theft and misuse. Security measures that monitor any sort of data handling is the order of the day in both traditional as well as cloud computing environments. Considerably, due to the public and multi-tenancy nature of cloud, the security threats and the velocity of consequences are higher in cloud, than in-premises computing.

eCloudIDS [3] is a next-generation security system designed with innovative hybrid two-tier expert engines, namely uX-Engine (tier-1) and sX-Engine (tier-2), is considered as a most suitable security solution for cloud computing environments; precisely public cloud. eCloudIDS answers the top three State-of-the-art cloud computing security taxonomies such as logical storage segregation & multi-tenancy security issues (taxonomy #1) [1] [7] [8], identity management issues (taxonomy #2) [1] [9] [10], and insider attacks (taxonomy #3) [1] [11]. This paper deals with the design and implementation of our proposed eCloudIDS architecture's Tier-1 uX-Engine Subsystem using one of the unsupervised machine learning techniques named Self-Organizing Map (SOM) for secure cloud computing environment.

2   Related Work

Intrusion detection can be used to identify misuse as well as anomalies. In misuse detection the detection engine is trained to identify the known patterns of attack and a database of known attacks needs to be maintained to compare with incoming activity patterns. In anomaly detection, however, the engine is required to search something unusual and deviating from the baseline activity. For this, unlabeled data is used so as to enable the engine to detect unknown and new intrusion patterns.

Hence, neural networks have become a popular choice for problems that concern clustering, classification and patterning. For the purpose of designing an intrusion detection system that can identify both anomalous and intrusive behaviors, supervised learning as well unsupervised learning can be employed. Trusted unsupervised learning algorithm to detect anomalies and unusual patterns are K-means clustering, self-organizing maps (SOM), growing hierarchical SOM (GHSOM), etc. Based on literature survey it has been observed that SOM is a popular choice for an unsupervised learning algorithm.

In [14] SOM algorithm is used to create a topological map of known attacks for forensic analysis of suspicious network traffic. SOM is used to create an abstraction of the attacks while preserving the topological relationships. Here, SOM is used both as a post-mortem tool for analysis of known attacks but also to identify and analyze new attacks.

In [15], Patole et al. used Self-Organizing Maps (SOM) to cluster normal and intrusive activity from the patterns in the network traffic. A packet sniffer was employed to collect different network packets to collect information on downloading, port scanning, surfing, etc. The results of the experiment were represented on the map and were clustered as normal behavior on one part of the map and intrusion on the other part. The advantages of SOM are manifold. It does not need prior supervision during the training to identify specific attack signatures and clusters similar data perfectly.

In [16] and [17] SOM is used as a clustering tool for network data. The implementation primarily focused on Denial-Of-Service (DOS) attacks by collecting data about regular IP addresses that accessed the network and corresponding network traffic. Even here unsupervised learning algorithm SOM was used as opposed to other algorithms for its various merits.

In [18], self-organizing map is used to give visual representation to network traffic as well as to give meaningful clustering technique. The authors used SOM for clustering of data and then used a multi-layered perceptron for detection of the attack.

Literature on IDSs is rife with the implementation of SOM and has posed many merits of this algorithm. SOM as an algorithm is easy to understand, maintains topology of data while clustering, works on non-linear data-set and has excellent capability to visualize high dimensional data onto 1 or 2 dimensional space, making it unique for dimensionality reduction [15].

In our previous work [3], we have given the design roadmap for eCloudIDS architecture, which uses both supervised and unsupervised machine learning techniques from artificial intelligence domain. This system is considered as a most suitable security solution for cloud computing environments; precisely public cloud. In this paper, based on the explored facts, we have implemented the eCloudIDS architecture's Tier-1 uX-Engine subsystem by incorporating the merits of SOM in clustering behavioral data in the cloud environment. This implementation witnessed the considerably acceptable accuracy as a result.

3   eCloudIDS Architecture

Figure 2 shows eCloudIDS Architecture discussed briefly in our preceding paper [3], which utilizes machine learning to identify anomalies or security breaches that might occur in the cloud ecosystem. The architecture contains various components as shown in Figure 2.

eCloudIDS is a hybrid two-tier expert engine-based IDS architecture. Tier-1 uses unsupervised machine learning algorithm in uX-Engine subsystem whereas Tier-2 uses supervised algorithm in sX-Engine subsystem. The eCloudIDS Configuration & Customization Console (C3) subsystem is used to configure and customize the remaining multiple subsystems of eCloudIDS architecture with respect to the user's requirements. Cloud VM/Instance Monitor (CIM) subsystem is responsible for observing the actions performed on the user specified virtual machines or instances. It continuously monitors the VM on the user specified application-related directories and files. CIM is responsible for monitoring all the activities of both authorized and unauthorized users (hackers) and inform it to H-log-H for immediate recording. Heterogeneous Log Handler (H-log-H) subsystem is responsible for recording each and every activity occurred on user configured VMs.

Audit Log Preprocessor (ALP) subsystem accepts the input from H-log-H, integrated heterogeneous audit logs from multiple types of application, tools, etc. Upon the reception of input, ALP rearranges, processes, and converts unstructured audit logs into structured data. ALP utilizes feature extraction techniques to extract useful features from the structured data and then feeds these features to uX-Engine.

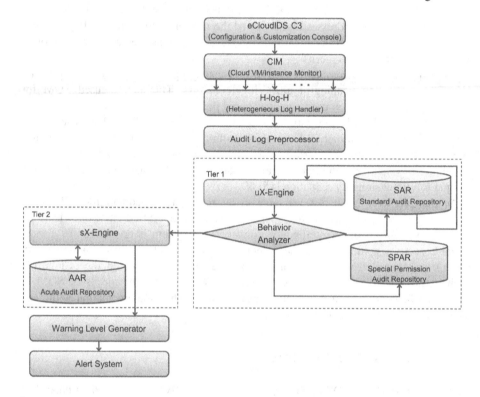

Source: Madhan Kumar Srinivasan, et al.: eCloudIDS – Design Roadmap for the Architecture of Next-generation Hybrid Two-tier Expert Engine-based IDS for Cloud Computing Environment. Springer-Verlag Berlin Heidelberg (2012) [3].

Fig. 2. eCloudIDS Architecture

uX-Engine is an unsupervised expert engine that finds anomaly in the activities being carried out on the VM. Behaviour Analyzer (BA) module will analyze the outlying and abnormal log activities as indicated by the uX-Engine with the organization's policies set in the C3 console. BA categories the audit logs into normal, special permission, and anomalous behaviors. If the abnormality is verified to be acceptable based on organizational policies, the log is sent to Standard Audit Repository (SAR). If the company mandates special permissions that may be temporary the audit is placed in the Special Permission Audit Repository (SPAR). However, if the abnormality is verified as an intrusion, the Behavior Analyzer sends it to the sX-Engine to classify the intrusion threat.

The sX-Engine uses supervised machine learning algorithm [19] [20] to classify the outlying activities produced by the uX-Engine and verified by the Behavior Analyzer. Acute Audit Repository (AAR) stores all the outlying events classification and is used to train sX-Engine continuously. It will be trained to classify class of threat based on incongruous user behavior, to identify threats caused due to viruses, Trojans, worms, etc. The Warning Level Generator subsystem is used to generate the level of warning and is configured by the user at eCloudIDS C3. It gives priority to the intrusions and correspondingly generates the alert level. Alert System subsystem will finally takes care about sounding the alarm as per the warning level of the threat detected.

It is clear from the architecture shown that the backbone of the eCloudIDS rests on the uX-Engine and the sX-Engine subsystems. These together form the core components that drive the function of detecting and identifying the intrusion patterns.

4   Implementation Progress

This implementation was performed on the setup which had Ubuntu 10.04 64-bit LTS Desktop edition as native operating system, CloudStack 3.0.0 [21] as IaaS platform, XenServer 6.0 [22] as virtualization host, and all systems with statically allocated IP addresses. Due to its vastness and the computational complexity, the implementation of the eCloudIDS architecture was taken up in two parallel phases. After the successful deployment of Cloud (IaaS) platform using CloudStack 3.0.0 and Citrix XenServer 6.0 hypervisor, we have created few VMs with varying requirements. One of the Cloud VM was installed with Ubuntu 10.04 32-bit LTS edition (henceforth referred as Instance-M). Instance-M was later configured with a model Java application deployed with few MySQL database tables. This cloud Instance-M has been used for all the further experimental purpose of this study. In the first phase, we have created the CIM subsystem which keeps monitor all the activities performed on cloud Instance-M. When CIM identifies an activity with respect to file system present in Instance-M, H-log-H will immediately records it. In this process, audits logs were maintained for all read/write operations carried on the files. The logs produced by the H-log-H were directed onto CloudStack Dashboard's Events tab [21].

In the second phase, the Audit Log preprocessor (ALP) was implemented which worked on the logs produced by cloud VM Instance-M. The ALP was used to gather the OS audit logs which are enabled using Zeitgeist Framework which is the default logger for Ubuntu 10.04 32-bit LTS edition. For the gathered logs feature extraction techniques were implemented so as to produce inputs for the learning phase of the uX-Engine. In this paper, we will focus on the Phase-2 implementation of the eCloudIDS uX-Engine subsystem.

5   Self-Organizing Maps

As mentioned above, SOM is a competitive learning network that can be used to visualize high dimensional data in one or two dimensional space. It is a popular choice for pattern recognition and clustering problems. The structure of a SOM consists of nodes or neurons that have been organized in a plane that we call a map or lattice.

Each neuron has the exact dimensions of the input data. The neurons are randomly initialized .The training of these neurons is on a competitive basis, i.e. 'Winner Takes All'. When an input vector is presented to the neuron map, the neuron weight vector that is closest to the input vector is termed as the Best matching Unit (BMU). The neurons in the neighborhood of the BMU are then adjusted to make them similar to the BMU. As more inputs are fed into the network, the neurons form clusters that are representative of inputs. Each cluster is formed by neurons that share similar values which are also significantly different from the values of neurons from other clusters. The training process of self-organizing maps has been summarized below:

1. The neuron weight vector wi are initialized to small values where i=1,2,3..m and m is the number of nodes Nt in the map.
2. A random input is chosen from the input set and the Euclidean distance is found from all the neurons. The neuron k which has minimum distance from the input is taken as winning neuron or the Best Matching Unit.

$$\| w_k - x \| = \min \| w_i - x \| \ , \quad i \in Nt \tag{1}$$

3. The weights of all the Nr neurons within the neighborhood radius η of neuron k are updated i.e. the value of the neurons are moved closer to the value of the BMU. The updating of weights is controlled by the learning rate σ which decreases over time.

$$w_i\,(t+1) := w_i(t) + \sigma \cdot \eta\,(i,\,k) \cdot (x - w_i(t)) \tag{2}$$

4. This process is continued until the specified number of iterations is reached and the network is said to have converged. Both the neighborhood radius and the learning rate decrease with subsequent iteration.

After the network as "learned", the map looks like a topologically ordered representation of data.

6   eCloudIDS Tier-1 uX-Engine – Design and Implementation

The uX-Engine has been implemented in Java and the software has been mounted on Instance-M Ubuntu 10.04 32-bit LTS OS platform. As mentioned above, the CIM module has been implemented separately. For the purpose of generating the audit logs for the uX-Engine's initial learning process we have enabled Ubuntu's default logger, Zeitgeist Framework. This framework keeps the logs of all user activities that are being carried out in a session using the 4 log files, such as System Log file, Authorization Log file, Daemon Log file, and Recently-Used-Files Log file. These log files will results in getting authorization logs (i.e. sign in/sign out logs), background processes logs, applications logs, and finally recent activities logs performed on files, etc. As and when the customer/end-user accesses the system, logs will be generated.

These logs are not always in the same format i.e. they can be in XML or text format. H-log-H is realized through a parser, which is employed to bring together all such logs into one format and send it to the Audit Log Preprocessor (ALP). The ALP is designed as a data preprocessor that will extract features from the audits and convert it into numerical data that will be used in the learning process of SOM for uX-Engine implementation. For this experimental purpose, we had executed the dry-run on Instance-M for 5 days i.e. CIM and H-log-H were continually deployed on Instance-M to monitor and gather audit logs for continuous 5 days. During this dry-run period, we performed only the normal/authorized behavior on Instance-M. This was required to prepare the Standard Audit Repository (SAR) with only category #1 Normal Behavior audit logs for the purpose of uX-Engine' learning process.

6.1 Feature Extraction

The SOM uX-Engine uses the features extracted by the ALP. These features are extracted from gathered Instance-M system logs that are produced by H-log-H subsystem. We have extracted 10 features and opted for an explicit representation of time in the data space. Extracted features are listed below.

1. Time of event
2. Start time of event
3. Duration of event
4. Event concerning (file, application, session)
5. User activity (modified, created, visited, accessed)
6. Event severity (INFO, WARN, DEBUG, FATAL, ERROR)
7. Frequency of the event
8. Workspace path of the users

Features that comprised of numerals were given as such, and logs with features 4, 5, 6 were assigned numerical symbols i.e. file=1, application=2, session=3, etc. and similarly with user activity and event severity. The workspace path was converted to base64 which provided unique numbers to it.

6.2 uX-Engine Learning

To extract the features the collection of Instance-M's dry-run audit logs (of only normal activities) were used. After initializing the dry-run, once adequate logs have been generated by H-log-H, the audits are passed through the ALP. The ALP processed feature vectors are given to uX-Engine for learning. The uX-Engine is configured to use the SOM algorithm to cluster the audit logs. This SOM configured uX-Engine was made learned using the features that were extracted by the ALP.

After the learning process, the uX-Engine will have the clustered audit logs that have been topologically represented. The learning process on the uX-Engine has rendered it to take the shape of the learning dataset. This allows it to identify those data points that are dissimilar to the data-set it represents. Hence, now it can differentiate between normal behavior that it has learnt and the abnormal behavior that will be presented to it.

6.3   Cluster Threshold Resolving

The obtained clusters were recorded and the learning was applied for logs that contained both normal and anomalous behavior. For the testing portion we devised the following algorithm:

1.   Mean μ_k for all the k-clusters was computed.
2.   The standard deviation from mean of all the neurons within a cluster was computed and the maximum was chosen as threshold r_k for k^{th} cluster.

$$r_k = \max \| \mu_k - w_{k\,i} \| \tag{3}$$

3.   The Euclidean distance between the test input and the mean of all clusters of computed and compared with the threshold value for all clusters.

$$\| \mu_k - x_i \| <= r_k \tag{4}$$

4.   If the distance was within the threshold of any cluster, the input was considered a normal behavior, otherwise if the input was beyond the threshold of all clusters it was taken as an anomalous behavior.

The system can be made online as the convergence time of SOM has been recorded to 4 milliseconds. H-log-H subsystem parser will run continuously and collect data from the logs and send it to the ALP.

7   Results

uX-Engine learning result and the visualization of cluster formation is shown in Fig. 3. This output was generated using our Instance-M's dry-run audit logs on SOM algorithm implementation of uX-Engine. After the learning, the learning was applied on the day to day logs generated by Instance-M. These logs contained both anomalous and normal activity data. After inspection of the results and its statistical analysis we have come to the performance measure of the SOM uX-Engine module as tabulated in Table 1. On examination of the anomalies detected it was found that, the uX-Engine was able to detect anomalies pertaining to user login time. Also, the algorithm was able to identify when a user changed their workspace folders. In addition to this, based on the frequency of access to files/applications, we could detect when a user was carrying out an 'abnormal' activity.

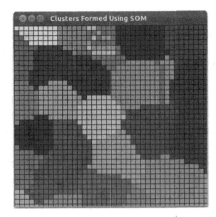

Fig. 3. uX-Engine SOM Cluster Visualization using Instance-M's Dry-run Audit Logs

The analysis of the result has shown that the uX-Engine has shown detection of intrusion for instances where user was performing normal activities. This constitutes to a small percentage of 9% and can be due to the lack of adequate learning logs to define normal behavior. It was also seen that a minute fraction of logs (almost 2%) were not detected as intrusions at all when we injected it into the system. These intrusions were in general those activities that were too similar to the normal behavior as learned by the uX-Engine.

Table 1. eCloudIDS Tier-1 uX-Engine SOM Implementation Performance Result

Detection Rate	False Negative Rate	False Positive Rate
89%	2%	9%

Further, our implemented SOM uX-Engine showcases the detection performance rate as 89%, which is considerably substantial for an unsupervised machine learning implementation. The system detects anomalies but has been seen to give false negatives and false positive in some experimental runs. To get enhanced detection rate, SOM needs still better feature extraction. Currently we are trying to implement a improve feature extraction algorithm, which is targeted to give better results for SOM uX-Engine.

8   Conclusion

eCloudIDS architecture targets at offering security assurance for companies which value the security of their data over everything else in public and hybrid cloud computing environments. This paper explores the internal design details and implementation steps for eCloudIDS architecture's Tier-1 uX-Engine subsystem. eCloudIDS at its core uses VM/Instance-based IDS which is considered the most promising technology for security in cloud computing environment. The key task in the architecture is identifying intrusion attacks that are broadly taken as anomaly as well as misuse detection in the VM environment. This architecture utilizes Self-Organizing Maps (SOM) in its uX-Engine which detects intrusion based on anomalies by clustering the audits. The access to applications and files under workspaces will account for normal behavior, but access outside the workspace or trying to get root privileges can be noted by the system. This will greatly help in identifying malicious insiders within an organization. Our implementation of uX-Engine using SOM returns in 89% as the performance detection rate, which is likely to be better result at this initial stage of eCloudIDS employment. The greater the learning capacity, the greater will be the security. With granular auditing and a holistic feature extraction, the system will show better results.

References

1. Madhan, K.S., Sarukesi, K., Rodrigues, P., Saimanoj, M., Revathy, P.: State-of-the-art Cloud Computing Security Taxonomies – A classification of security challenges in the present cloud computing environment. In: ICACCI 2012, pp. 470–476. ACM, India (2012), doi:10.1145/2345396.2345474, ISBN: 978-1-4503-1196-0
2. Cloud Computing and Sustainability: The Environmental Benefits of moving to the Cloud. Technical report, Accenture (2010)
3. Srinivasan, M.K., Sarukesi, K., Keshava, A., Revathy, P.: eCloudIDS – Design Roadmap for the Architecture of Next-Generation Hybrid Two-Tier Expert Engine-Based IDS for Cloud Computing Environment. In: Thampi, S.M., et al. (eds.) SNDS 2012. CCIS, vol. 335, pp. 357–370. Springer, Heidelberg (2012)
4. Security Guidance for Critical Areas of Focus in Cloud Computing V2.1. Technical report, Cloud Security Alliance (2009)
5. Top Threats to Cloud Computing V1.0. Technical report, Cloud Security Alliance (2010)
6. What's Holding Back the Cloud? Technical report, Intel IT Center (2012)
7. Securing Multi-Tenancy and Cloud Computing. Technical report, Juniper Networks (2012)
8. Li, H., Sedayao, J., Hahn-Steichen, J., Jimison, E., Spence, C., Chahal, S.: Developing an Enterprise Cloud Computing Strategy. Technical report, Intel Corporation (2009)
9. Madhan Kumar, S., Rodrigues, P.: A Roadmap for the Comparison of Identity Management Solutions Based on State-of-the-Art IdM Taxonomies. In: Meghanathan, N., Boumerdassi, S., Chaki, N., Nagamalai, D. (eds.) CNSA 2010. CCIS, vol. 89, pp. 349–358. Springer, Heidelberg (2010)
10. Madhan, K.S., Rodrigues, P.: Analysis on Identity Management Systems with Extended State-of-the-art IdM Taxonomy Factors. International Journal of Ad hoc, Sensor & Ubiquitous Computing 1(4), 62–70 (2010), doi:10.5121/ijasuc.2010.1406
11. Shiels, M.: Malicious insider attacks to rise. Technical report, BBC News (2009)
12. Mell, P., Grance, T.: The NIST Definition of Cloud Computing. NIST Special Publication 800-145. Technical report, National Institute of Standards and Technology (2011)
13. Ghahramani, Z.: Unsupervised Learning. In: Bousquet, O., von Luxburg, U., Rätsch, G. (eds.) Machine Learning 2003. LNCS (LNAI), vol. 3176, pp. 72–112. Springer, Heidelberg (2004)

14. Kayacik, H.G., Zincir-Heywood, A.N., Heywood, M.I.: A Hierarchical SOM based Intrusion Detection System. Journal of Engineering Applications of Artificial Intelligence 20(4), 439–451 (2007), doi:10.1016/j.engappai.2006.09.005
15. Patole, V.A., Pachghare, V.K., Kulkarni, P.: Self-Organizing Maps to Build Intrusion Detection System. Intl. Journal of Computer Applications, 1–4 (2010)
16. Khaled, L., Rao, V.: NSOM – A Real-Time Network-Based Intrusion Detection System Using Self-Organizing Maps. University of California. Technical report. Davis (2002)
17. Zanero, S.: Improving Self-Organizing Map Performance for Network Intrusion Detection. In: SDM 2005 Workshop on Clustering High Dimensional Data and its Applications (2005)
18. Bivens, A., Palagiri, C., Smith, R., Szymanski, B., Embrechts, M.: Network-based Intrusion Detection using Neural Networks. In: Intelligent Engineering Systems through Artificial Neural Networks, ANNIE 2002, New York, vol. 12, pp. 579–584 (2002)
19. Keerthi, B., Madhan, K.S., Sarukesi, K., Rodrigues, P.: Implementation of Next-generation Traffic Sign Recognition System with Two-tier Classifier Architecture. In: ACM ICACCI 2012, pp. 481–487. ACM, India (2012), doi:10.1145/2345396.2345476
20. Balasundaram, K., Srinivasan, M.K., Sarukesi, K.: iReSign-Implementation of Next-Generation Two-Tier Identity Classifier-Based Traffic Sign Recognition System Architecture using Hybrid Region-Based Shape Representation Techniques. In: Thampi, S.M., et al. (eds.) SNDS 2012. CCIS, vol. 335, pp. 407–420. Springer, Heidelberg (2012)
21. CloudStack 3.0.0 Release Notes. Technical report. Citrix Systems, Inc. (2012)
22. XenServer 6.0 Release Notes. Technical report. Citrix Systems, Inc. (2012)

Implementation of MD6

Ananya Chowdhury and Utpal Kumar Ray

Department of Information Technology, Jadavpur University
Salt Lake Campus, Salt Lake City, Block-LB, Plot No.8, Sector-III, Kolkata: 700098,
West Bengal, India
chowdhury.ananya@gmail.com, utpal_ray@yahoo.com

Abstract. Distributed Computing and Network Communication has revolutionized the face of modern computing. But this includes serious security concerns like verifying the integrity and authenticity of the transmitted data. The sender and the receiver communicating over an insecure channel essentially require a method by which the information transmitted by the sender can be easily authenticated by the receiver as "unmodified" (authentic). Techniques such as Encryption can protect against passive attacks like eavesdropping but for active attack like falsification of data, Message Authentication Code (MAC) is needed. A modern technique that relies on a related family of functions called Hash Functions provides message authentication. Cryptographic Hash Functions have many applications such as Digital Signatures, Time Stamping Methods and File Modification Detection Methods. MD6 is one such modern well-known cryptographic hash function. In the subsequent sections we shall analyze the software implementation of MD6 and its performance in various scenarios.

Keywords: Message Authentication Code (MAC), Avalanche Effect, Message Digest, Modification Detection Code (MDC), Hash Function, Keyed Hash Function, Un-keyed Hash Function, Merkle Tree Structure, Compression Function, Random Oracle (RO).

1   Introduction

A cryptographic hash function [1][6] is an algorithm that takes an arbitrary block of data as input and returns a fixed-size bit string, the "hash value" as output. The hash function is designed in such a way that a change (accidental or intentional) to the data will (with very high probability) change the hash value. This phenomenon of small change(s) in the source input drastically changing the output is known as "Avalanche Effect". The data to be encoded is often called the "message," and the hash value is sometimes called the "Message Digest" or simply "Digests". One such hash function is MD5. But it is not collision resistant and thus not suitable for applications like SSL Certificates or Digital Signatures that rely on this property. For all these reasons Ron Rivest and his team at MIT started working on MD6. MD6 hash algorithm, proposed by Ronald Rivest, is a provably secure, efficient, simple, robust, flexible hash algorithm enabling immense parallelism by using Merkle Tree-like structure. It allows parallel computation of hashes for very long inputs at ease.

S.M. Thampi et al. (Eds.): SNDS 2012, CCIS 335, pp. 444–455, 2012.

This algorithm hence has a potential of exploiting the high speed of future processors with tens and thousands of cores instead of the conventional uni-core or dual-core systems and providing an impressive performance enhancement. Thus MD6 seems to have a bright future ahead.

2   Message Authentication and Hash Function

A message, file or a document is said to be authentic when it satisfies all the following conditions [1]:

- ❖ The contents of the message are not being altered.
- ❖ The source of the message is authentic.
- ❖ The message has arrived in time (i.e. it not artificially delayed or replayed).
- ❖ The message is in correct sequence relative to the sender and the receiver.

Authentication can be of 2 types [1]:

- ❖ Authentication using Conventional Encryption,
- ❖ Authentication without Message Encryption (using Hash Function).

2.1   Authentication without Message Encryption (using Hash Function)

This method does not rely on encryption but on a related family of functions called hash functions. This is specifically useful in the following scenarios [1]

- ❖ When the same message is broadcast to a large number of recipients.
- ❖ An exchange of information in which one side (sender or receiver) is experiencing a heavy load and so cannot afford to perform encryption for authentication.

2.2   Hash Function and Its Properties

A hash function H, is a transformation that takes a variable-size input "m" and returns a fixed-size string, which is called the" hash value" or "message digest" of n bits(say).Hash Functions have the following 6 important properties [1][2].

- ❖ H can be applied to a block of data of any size.
- ❖ H produces a fixed length output.
- ❖ H(x) is relatively easy to compute for any given value of x, making both hardware and software implementations practical.
- ❖ For any given code m, it is computationally infeasible to find x such that H(x) = m. This implies that for a given fixed size output value; it must be computationally infeasible to find the input data to the function that generated that value. This is known as **"One Way Property or First Pre-image Property"**.
- ❖ For any given block x, it is computationally infeasible to find y! = x with H(y) = H(x). This is known as **"Second Pre-image Resistant Property"**. Given a fixed input value, second pre-image resistance implies that it should

be infeasible to find another input value that results in the same hash as the first input value. It is also known as **"Weak-Collision Resistance Property"**.

❖ It is computationally infeasible to find a pair (x, y) such that H(x) = H(y). This sixth property is known as **"Strong Collision Resistant Property"**. It means that it must be computationally infeasible to find two differing input values which hash to the same output value.

The first five properties guarantee that an alternative message hashing to the same value as a given message cannot be found. The hash function that satisfies the first five properties in the list is referred to as a weak hash function. If the sixth property is also satisfied then the hash function is known as a strong hash function. The sixth property protects against a sophisticated class of attacks known as Birthday Attack.

2.3   Different Types of Hash Function

❖ **Simple Hash:** The input (message, file, etc.) is viewed as a sequence of n-bit blocks. The input is processed one block at a time in an iterative fashion to produce an n-bit hash function .One of the simplest hash functions is the bit-by-bit exclusive OR (XOR) of every block. This can be expressed as follows:

$C_i = b_{i1} \oplus bi2 \oplus ... \oplus b_{im}$ 1

Where,

C_i = ith bit of the hash code, where 1<=i<=n m = number of n-bit blocks in the input

b_{ij} = ith bit in jth block

$\oplus$ = XOR operation

This operation produces a simple parity for each bit position and is known as a longitudinal redundancy check.

❖ **Iterated Hash Function:** Iterated hash function was first proposed by Merkle [1979] and is the structure of most hash functions in use today including MD6.The hash function takes an input message and partitions it into L fixed-sized blocks of b bits each. If necessary, the final block is padded to b bits. The final block also includes the value of the total length of the input to the hash function. A typical hash function involves repeated use of a compression function, f that takes two inputs (an n-bit input from the previous step, called the chaining variable, and a b-bit block) and produces an n-bit output. At the start of hashing, the chaining variable has an initial value that is specified as part of the algorithm. The final value of the chaining variable is the hash value, often, b > n and hence the term compression. The hash function can be summarized as follows:

$CVo = IV$ = initial n-bit value.....................................2

$CVi = f (CVi-1, Yi-1)$..3

Where 1<=i<=L

$H (M) = CVL$..4

The input to the hash function is a message M, consisting of blocks Y0, Y1 ...YL-1.
Thus if the compression function is collision resistant, then so is the resultant iterated
hash function.

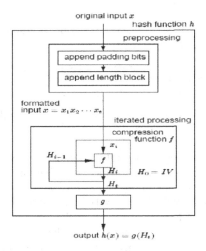

Fig. 1. The figure shows the working principle of an Iterated Hash Function which accepts the
"original input x" fed to the hash function *"h"*.

- ❖ **Keyed Hash and Un-keyed Hash:** Hash functions can be split into two
  classes: Un-keyed [6] Hash Functions, whose specification dictates a single
  input parameter (a message); and Keyed Hash [6] Functions, whose
  specification dictates two distinct inputs, a message and a secret key.
- ❖ **MDC and MAC:** A Modification Detection Code (MDC) is a message
  digest that can prove the integrity of the message. It is also known as
  Message Integrity Code or MIC. A Message Authentication Code (MAC)
  ensures the integrity of the message and the data origin authentication. The
  difference between an MDC and a MAC is that the second includes a secret
  between sender and receiver i.e. the key.

3   Mode of Operation, Specification and Compression Function of MD6

MD6 [2] is thus simple, robust MAC algorithm that uses Merkle's Tree-like structure
for enabling sufficient parallelism. It follows the structure of a 4-ary tree. It is capable
of operating both in as sequential as well as a tree-based mode. It can be keyed or un-
keyed .It can accept input message of bit length 2^64 which is large enough to suit
increased data communication requirements. It can produce hash digest of any length
between 1 to512.

MD6 [2] is resistant to Differential Cryptanalysis, Linear Cryptanalysis, SAT
Solver's Attack, Cut and Paste Attack and Multi-Collision Attack. In addition is

computationally infeasible to break the preimage resistance and collision resistance properties of MD6.

3.1   Mode of Operation of MD6

There are primarily 2 modes of operations of MD6 - Hierarchical Mode of Operation [2] and Sequential Mode of Operation [2].

❖   **Hierarchical Mode of Operation:** This is the tree-based standard mode of operation of MD6 [2]. But the disadvantage is it requires storage at least proportional to the height of the tree. Since some very small devices may not have sufficient storage available, MD6 provides a height-limiting parameter L. When the height reaches L + 1, MD6 switches from the Parallel Compression Operator (PAR) to the Sequential Compression Operator (SEQ). The MD6 mode of operation is thus optionally parameterized by the integer L, 0<=L<=64, which allows a smooth transition from the default tree-based hierarchical mode of operation (for large L) down to an iterative mode of operation (for L = 0).When L = 0, MD6 works in a manner similar to that of the well-known Merkle-Damgard method. MD6 makes up to L "parallel" passes over the data, each one reducing the size of the data by a factor of four, and then performs (if necessary) a single sequential pass to finish up. The default value of L is 64 and the default MD6 is fully tree-based/hierarchical/parallel. This tree structure works in bottom-up, level by level manner. Thus the leaf nodes in the Merkle Tree run the compression function which takes successive blocks of input and compress it down to a chaining value. These chaining values are then fed into a parent node, which uses the same compression function to produce its own chaining value, and so on up to the root node. Thus due to the tree structure, the function is highly parallelizable, and scales almost linearly with the number of CPU cores available. With a single core, it is not super-fast. MD6-256 on a 64-bit CPU is 77 MB/sec and MD6-512 is 49 MB/sec. But the performance drastically improves with the increasing number of cores. We shall provide a detailed discussion and illustration on this in the subsequent sections.

Fig. 2. Hierarchical Mode of Operation of MD6 [2]

❖   **Sequential Mode of Operation:** Fig. 3 describes the Sequential Mode [2] of operation of MD6 (where L= 0). The computation proceeds from left to right only. Here level 1 represents processing by SEQ.The hash function output is produced by the rightmost node on level 1. This is similar to standard Merkle-Damgard processing. The white circle at the left on level 1 is the 1024-bit all-zero initialization vector for the sequential computation at that level. Each node has four 1024-bit inputs: one from the left, and three from below.

Fig. 3. Sequential Mode of Operation of MD6 [2]

❖ **Merkle Structure followed by MD6:** This structure is followed by MD6 for an intermediate value of L (L = 1). Here the computation proceeds from bottom to top and left to right; level 2 represents processing by SEQ. The hash function output is produced by the rightmost node on level 2. The white circle at the left on level 2 is the all-zero initialization vector for the sequential computation at that level. Where:

- Q - a constant vector of length q = 15 words. (Giving an approximation to the fractional part of the square root of 6)
- K - A "key" of length k = 8 words containing a supplied key of "keylen" bytes. (Serving as salt, tag, tweak, secret key etc.)
- U - A one-word "unique node ID".
- V - A one-word "control word".
- B – A data block of length b = 64 words

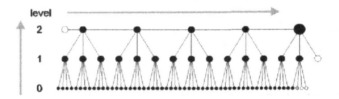

Fig. 4. Sequential Mode of Operation of MD6 [2]

3.2   MD6 Specification and Compression Function

❖ MD6 Specification: MD6 has 2 mandatory inputs while the other 3 inputs to MD6 are optional

- M - Message to be hashed (mandatory).
- d - Message digest length desired, in bits (mandatory).
- K - Key value (optional).
- L - Mode control (optional).
- r - Number of rounds (optional).

The only mandatory inputs are the message M to be hashed and the desired message digest length d. Optional inputs have default values if any value is not supplied.

❖ **MD6 Compression Function:** A hash function is typically constructed from a "Compression Function" [2] which maps fixed-length inputs to shorter fixed length outputs. A mode of operation then specifies how the compression function can be used repeatedly to hash inputs of arbitrary nonnegative lengths to outputs of fixed lengths. The compression function f takes as input an array N of length n = 89 words. It outputs an array C of length c = 16 words. Here f is described as having a single 89-word input N, although it may also be viewed as having a 25-word "auxiliary" input (Q‖K‖U‖V) followed by a 64-word "data" input block B. Where

- Q - a constant vector of length q = 15 words.
- K - a "key" (serving as salt, tag, tweak, secret key, etc.) of length k = 8 words containing a supplied key of "keylen" bytes.
- U- a one-word "unique node ID".
- V- a one-word "control word".

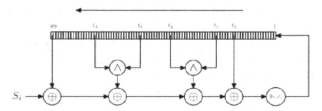

Fig. 5. Compression Function of MD6 [2]

❖ **Output of MD6**: The output of MD6 is a bit string D of exactly d bits in length. $D = H_{d, K, L, r}(M)$.

Table 1. Comparison of MD5 and MD6

Sr. No	Featutes	MD5	MD6
1.	Initial Input Length	$0 <= m < = 2^{64}$	$0 <= m < = 2^{64}$
2.	No. of Rounds	4	Variable(Default for Un-keyed=40+[d/4], for Keyed=max(80, 40+[d/4]))
3.	Structure	Merkle Damgard	Merkle Tree
4.	Length of the Digest(in bits)	128	$0 < d <= 512$
5.	Can be implemented in machine having word size(s) in bits	32	targeted for 64 but can run on 8, 32
6.	Internal chaining values for the Compression Function(in bits)	128	1024
7.	Input Data Block(in words)	16	64

4   Security Aspects of MD6

❖ MD6 Compression Function: After 11 rounds it is in-differentiable from Random Oracle (RO).

❖ Collision Resistance, Preimage Resistance, Second Preimage Resistance provided.

❖ MD6: Resistant against Differential and Linear Cryptanalysis.

❖ Combats general Algebraic Attacks and SAT Solver's Attack.

❖ Mode of operation of Hash Function is secured due to the secured compression function.

❖ Wide pipe Strategy: Multi-Collision Attack is defeated.

❖ Secure against Length-Extension Attack and Cut-Paste Attack.

5   Performance Analysis of MD6

This section describes in details the inputs, outputs, experimental results and graphical analysis of implementation of MD6 under various conditions. Our chief objective is to show the performance improvement that the parallel processing brings about.

All the experiments are performed on the following hardware and software platform and the experimental results are recorded with the best possible precision and accuracy under the laboratory experimental setup.

❖ Hardware Configuration:
   - Intel(R) Core(TM) 2 Quad CPU
   - Q8400 @2.66GHz
   - 2.65GHz, 3.24GB of RAM
   - Physical Address Extension

❖ Operating System:
   - Fedora release 11(Leonidas)

❖ Software Configuration:
   - Language Used : C
   - Compiler: gcc (GCC) 4.4.0 20090506(Red Hat 4.4.0-4)

5.1   Test Results for Single Thread Implementations

Here "L" is the mode of control of MD6 which is an optional input to the Hash Function. When $L = 0$, the mode of operation is purely sequential and when $L = 64$, the mode of operation is purely hierarchical (tree based/parallel). Fig6.clearly shows that for varying rage of input (1MB, 10MB, 100MB and 1000MB) the time taken in hierarchical mode ($L = 64$) is either equal to or greater than the time taken in sequential mode ($L = 0$). Ideally, when $L = 64$ the performance of MD6 must be better than when $L = 0$. But when $L = 64$, the performance decreases to a certain extent due to the additional processing overhead incurred in hierarchical mode.

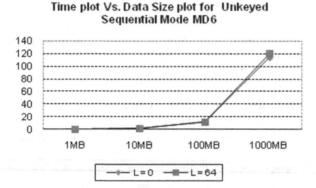

Fig. 6. Time vs. Data Size Plot for Un-keyed Sequential Mode MD6 with, L = 0 and L = 64, r = 168, d = 512

5.2   Test Results for Single Processor and Multiple Thread Implementations

We know that a Tree based MD6 or Hierarchical MD6 provides a scope for huge parallelism. Fig 7.shows as the no. of threads increases the time taken by the Hash Function to execute also increases owing to the additional processing overhead.

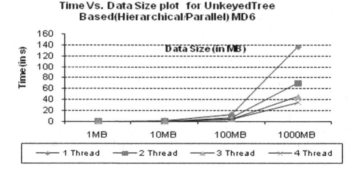

Fig. 7. Time vs. Data Size Plot for Un-keyed Tree Based (Hierarchical/Parallel) MD6 with, L = 64, r =168, d=512 and k = 0

5.3   Test Results for No. of Processors vs. Time

Fig.8. shows the behavior of parallel MD6 for 4 different size inputs (1MB, 10MB, and 100MBand 1000 MB). Here we can see as the size of the data increases (for 1000MB) the performance of MD6 increases (as seen in the graph as the execution time decreases). Thus MD6 has a huge potential of performance improvement for substantially larger inputs in a multiprocessor environment.

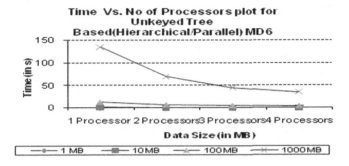

Fig. 8. Time vs. No. of Processors Plot for Unkeyed Tree Based (Hierarchical/Parallel)MD6 with, L = 64, r =168, d=512 and k = 0

5.4   Test Results for No. of Processors vs. Speedup

Fig.9 shows the speedup attained by using multiple processors. Speedup is given by dividing time taken by sequential implementation by that of parallel implementation. It is actually a representation of how much effective the multithreaded approach can be. **Speedup=Tseq/Tpar**, where Tseq and Tpar are time needed for sequential and parallel implementation respectively.

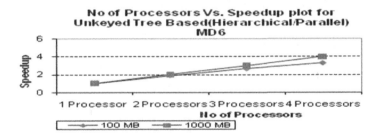

Fig. 9. Speedup vs. No of Processors Plot for Unkeyed Tree Based (Hierarchical/Parallel) with, L=64, r=168, d=512

Theoretically its value should be 4 for implementation using 4 processors and we see in the Fig.9. that it is really very close to the desired result.

The slight deviations seen in Fig.9 for 100MB input and 1000MB input(for 1,2 and 3 processor systems) is mostly due to the thread creation and maintenance overhead compared to the input size. So we infer that to fully exploit the parallelism input size must be big and the coding must support more parallelism.

5.5   Test Results for No. of Processors vs. Efficiency

Efficiency=Speedup/No of Processors
Ideally the value of Efficiency is 1 but practically it sinks below the desired mark as no of processors increases. Fig.10 follows the same trend. We can see in Fig.10 that the ideal value of efficiency i.e. 1 is achieved for larger input such as 1000MB.

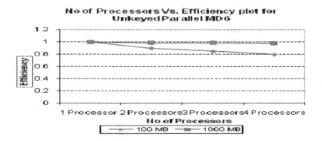

Fig. 10. Efficiency vs. No of Processors Plot for Parallel MD6 with, L=64, r=168, d=512 and k = 0

5.6   Test Results for Variation of No. of Rounds

The variation in number of rounds affects the time needed for MD6 implementation. Since this is a user provided specification (optional), it can be freely varied to optimize trade-off between time taken and security constraints. Each compression function implements the specified number of rounds. Hence lesser the number of rounds, lesser is the time taken. As a matter of fact number of rounds can vary between 1 to 168.Fig. 11 shows the result.

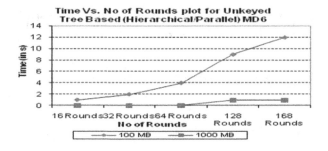

Fig. 11. Time vs. Number of Rounds Plot for Tree-Based MD6 with, L=64, d=512 and k = 0

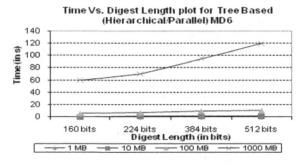

Fig. 12. Time vs. Digest Length Plot for Tree-Based MD6 with, L=64

5.7   Test Results for Variation of Digest Length

Although digest length has nothing to do with the time required for computing MD6 hash digest but it has a direct effect on the no of rounds that is specified for the compression function.

Number of Rounds=40+floor (digest length/4)
So lesser the number of bits in hash digest (unless otherwise stated by user) number of rounds gets lessened accordingly and thus the time required to compute the hash digest is also reduced. Fig.12 shows the time vs. digest length plot for variation data input sizes and with L=64.

6   Conclusion

Thus from the above discussion we can conclude that MD6 is simple, robust, flexible, efficient hash algorithm. It can act as an un-keyed as well as secure, keyed hash function producing hash digests of various lengths like 160,224,384,512 etc. The mode to be used solely depends on the security requirements of the user. It accepts data size up to (2^64 - 1) bits. It acts both as MDC and MAC It follows Merkle's tree structure forming a 4-ary tree and hence enabling parallelism and exploiting the increased speed, storage and processing capacities of modern computers especially in a parallel processing environment to its fullest. Apart from scaling well for multi core and parallel processors, it can switch to a traditional, iterative, sequential Merkle-Damgard mode of operation requiring minimal memory, thus marking a balance between parallelism and memory requirements.

Interestingly, MD6 shows better performance for a substantially larger input in a parallel processing environment. This makes the hash function MD6 one of the most suitable candidates for multi-core processor architecture.

Acknowledgments. With great pleasure we would like to express our heartfelt gratitude to all the staff-members of Department of Information Technology, Jadavpur University, for the help and cooperation.

References

1. Stallings, W.: Cryptography and Network Security (Principles and Practices), 5th edn., p. 624, pp. 638–640, 642–644
2. Rivest, R.L., Agre, B., Bailey, D.V., Crutchfield, C., Dodis, Y., Elliott, K., Khan, F.A., Krishnamurthy, J., Lin, Y., Reyzin, L., Shen, E., Sukha, J., Sutherland, D., Tromer, E., Yin, Y.L.: The MD6 hash function: A proposal to NIST for SHA-3 (2008)
3. Christopher Yale Crutchfield, B.S.: Electrical Engineering and Computer Science (2006)
4. Heilman, E.: Restoring the Differential Resistance of MD6 (2001), http://eprint.iacr.org/2011/374
5. Schneier on Security, http://www.schneier.com/blog/archives/2009/07/md6.html
6. Bellare, M., Canetti, R., Krawczyk, H.: Keying Hash Functions for Message Authentication

Location Estimation of Mobile
in GSM and CDMA Networks

Adapa Tataram and Alwyn Roshan Pais

Department of Computer Science & Engineering
National Institute of Technology, Karnataka, Surathkal
Mangalore, India
{adapaltataram,alwyn.pais}@gmail.com

Abstract. In this Paper, we present the design and implementation of location estimation tool that provides the location of mobile for a known mobile number. During emergency, persons who are in deep trouble should be located concisely and accurately due to the critical importance. With any tracing mechanism of least delay, culprits could be caught by authorities. In such kind of scenarios, our location estimation tool detects the location of the person carrying the mobile. This tool works at either Base Station Controller (BSC) or Mobile Switching Centre (MSC) at mobile network side. Location estimation tool works based on neighbor BTS and serving cells signal strength information. At MSC, Signal strength values are to be collected from signal dump file of mobile number. Tool gives the location of a mobile as latitude, longitude values on Google maps in different cases.

Keywords: GSM architecture, CDMA architecture, Base Transceiver Station (BTS), Base Station Controller (BSC), Mobile Switching Centre (MSC).

1   Introduction

There are so many websites available to give the location of a mobile for a given mobile number. But the result of those websites are not up to the mark, at most they will give good result as location of serving BTS. Theoretically BTS can cover a maximum of 70 KM diameter range, but in practical it can cover up to 25 KM range based on remoteness of the area. Even we know the location of BTS, it is very difficult to find out correct location of mobile within that 25 KM diameter range of area. We have designed location estimation tool which gives the exact location of mobile in the wide range covered by BTS.

Location estimation tool gathers neighbour BTS signal strengths information, base station identity code (BSIC), location area identity (LAI), cell Id (CID) and frequency values from signal dump file of a given mobile number. Location estimation tool uses hata model to calculate distance (BTS to mobile) from signal strength. This tool uses Google map API to give location of mobile as point on Google map with longitude and latitude values. We present design and implementation of our tool in GSM environment [1], [2], [3], [4] here, but the same design and algorithms can be used for CDMA network [6], [7] also. Location estimation tool has been designed in three different cases based on information in input signal file [5], [13].

S.M. Thampi et al. (Eds.): SNDS 2012, CCIS 335, pp. 456–465, 2012.

2   Literature Study

Mobile Networks have always been an area of research. Location finding of a mobile is an important issue under which so much research work is going on. The following are some of the related research work [8], [9], [10], [11] carried out to find the location of a mobile.

Karim Y. Kabalan, Jinane I. Mounsef addressed the problem of determining the position of GSM cellular mobiles in a cost- efficient way, i.e. without any change in the infrastructure or the handset [10]. It uses the signal strength technique as a major tool to solve the mobile location problem. James Caffery, Gordon Stuber investigated subscriber radio location techniques for code-division multiple-access (CDMA) cellular networks [11]. Two methods are considered for radio location: measured times of arrival (ToA) and angles of arrival (AoA). The ToA measurements are obtained from the code tracking loop in the CDMA receiver, and the AoA measurements at a base station (BS) are assumed to be made with an antenna array.

Christopher Drane, Malcolm Macnaughtan, and Craig Scott have proposed methods for positioning GSM telephones [8]. They have examined the ability to derive position information from GSM signals, based on their May 1996 achievement of accurate position measurements using GSM. They also explained about self-positioning, remote positioning and indirect positioning techniques.

From the above literature survey, we understood that we do not have any software that gives the location of mobile without adding any extra hardware either at network side or at mobile side. We have designed such software which is a network based positioning tool, to give the location of mobile.

3   Methodology

Location estimation tool has to work in three different cases based on the information in input signal file. In all the cases, we have used hata model empirical formulae to get the distance of mobile from BTS with the help of BTS BCCH signal strength (RxLev) and some other factors like tower height, antenna gain, transmission power etc. This model is being considered for use by ITU-R in the IMT-2000 standards activities.

According to Hata model [12], pathloss is given by

ΔP (dB) = 69.55 + 26.19 * $\log_{10}fc$ - 13.82 * $\log_{10}hBTS$ - a(hms) + (44.9-6.55 * $\log_{10}hBTS$) * $\log_{10}d$.

Where fc is carrier frequency, hBTS is height of BTS in meters, d is distance between ms and BTS in km, a(hms) is correction factor to compensates the antenna variations of the ms, and is given by

a(hms) = (1.1 * $\log_{10}fc$ - 0.7) * hms - (1.56 * $\log_{10}fc$ - 0.8) in small or medium sized cities,

a(hms) = 3.2 * $(\log_{10}(11.75 * hms))^2$ - 4.97 in large cities.

Generally path loss ΔP can be obtained as follows,

ΔP = transmitter power – RxLev + 110.5 + antenna gain.

Hence distance can be obtained as

$d = 10(\Delta P - (69.55 + 26.19 * \log_{10}fc - 13.82 * \log_{10}hBTS - a(hms)))$ $/ (44.9 - 6.55 * \log_{10}hBTS)$.

The design of the tool can be explained well by algorithms designed in all the cases.

3.1   Number of BTS Signal Strength Values > 2

In this case more than two Base Transceiver Stations (BTS) are available in the nearby neighborhood location of the mobile. Hence MSC will have the received signal strength information from each BTS for the corresponding mobile. This information at MSC is used to detect the exact location of the mobile. The algorithm for the same is given below.

Algorithm: Location estimation of mobile.

Input: Signal dump file of a given mobile number in xml format which has the rxlev information of at least 3 BTS.

Output: Location of a mobile in Google maps with latitude and longitude values.

Procedure

1. Identify the serving BTS based on the BSIC value obtained by parsing the given input file. Treat serving BTS as currentBTS
2. Locate the currentBTS position on the map with its latitude and longitude values.
3. Calculate the distance between MS and currentBTS with the help of hata model using rxlev value and required parameters of currentBTS.
4. Draw the circle around the currentBTS with obtained distance in step3 as radius. This circle will be the locus of our location.
5. Repeat from step2 for all uncovered neighbour BTS as currentBTS.
6. Finally the intersection point of all the circles will be the location of MS.

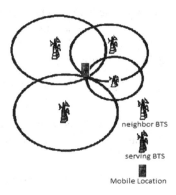

Fig. 1. Location estimation of mobile in more than two BTS signals strength values case

As discussed in algorithm, the process involved in this case is shown in Fig. 1.

3.2   Number of BTS Signal Strength Values = 2

In this case exactly two Base Transceiver Stations (BTS) are available in the nearby neighborhood location of the mobile. Hence MSC will have exactly two received signals strength information of each BTS for the corresponding mobile. This information is used to detect the exact location of the mobile. The algorithm for the same is given below.

Algorithm: Location estimation of mobile.

Input: Signal dump file of a given mobile number in xml format which has the rxlev information of exactly 2 BTS.

Output: Location of a mobile in Google maps with latitude and longitude values.

Procedure

1. Identify the serving BTS based on the BSIC value obtained by parsing the given input file. Treat serving BTS as currentBTS.
2. Locate the currentBTS position on the map with its latitude and longitude values.
3. Calculate the distance between MS and currentBTS with the help of hata model using rxlev value and required parameters of currentBTS.
4. Draw the circle around the currentBTS with obtained distance in step3 as radius. This circle will be the locus of our location.
5. Identify the sector based on the BCCH carrier frequency corresponding to currentBTS rxlev value. Now only that sector part of the circle will be the locus of location.
6. Identify the neighbour BTS which has rxlev information in input file. Treat neighbour BTS as current BTS and repeat process from step2.
7. Now those two sectors either intersect at one point or at two points. If two sectors intersect at two points go to step 9.
8. The intersection point of two sectors will be the location of a mobile.
9. Here to find the location among two locations, we need to apply CellSignalInfo_VirtualBTS algorithm.

As discussed in algorithm if two loci intersect at only one point then that point will be the location of MS. If two loci have two intersection points, we have to apply CellSignalInfo_VirtualBTS algorithm to find out correct location of mobile. Fig. 2 shows possible scenarios in this case. Figure 2(a) shows two sectors intersect at only one point, so the intersection point is location of mobile. Figure 2(b) shows two sectors intersect at two points, so location will be any one of these two intersecting points.

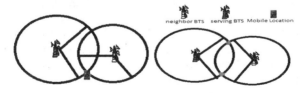

Fig. 2. Two possible scenarios in exactly two BTS signal strength values case

3.2.1   CellSignalInfo_VirtualBTS Algorithm

This algorithm is mainly used to find the exact location among two locations that are obtained by previous algorithm.

Each BTS have three or more cells, and each cell covers one sector. Hence input file may have different rxlev for each cell in a single BTS.

Algorithm: CellSignalInfo_VirtualBTS

Input: Signal dump file which is such that after Location estimation in Two BTS RxLev case, we end up with two sectors intersecting at two points.

Output: Location of a mobile in Google maps with latitude and longitude values.

Procedure

1. Identify the serving BTS based on the BSIC value obtained by parsing the given input file.
2. Check whether any of two BTS has more than one cell rxlev information or not. If yes follow the steps, otherwise go to step 5.
3. If serving BTS has 2 cells rxlev information (1serving+1neighbor cell) the location of the mobile will be the location which is nearer to the neighbor cell for which rxlev information is available.
4. If serving BTS has 3 cells rxlev information (1serving+2neighbor cells) the location of the mobile will be the location which is nearer to the neighbor cell for which rxlev value is high.
5. As shown in Fig. 3 , virtually move the serving BTS (if this transformation is first time)/ new BTS (second time onwards) from "**a**" to "**e**" by 100 meters (movement "l") in 60^0 to the edges of sector **abc**. This is technically called transformation of BTS from old BTS location (a) to new BTS location (e). Draw the new sector **efg** at new BTS location (e).
6. Edges of new sector **efg** cut the sector **abc** arc at two points (**h** and **i**) as shown in Fig. 3. The distance (**eh** or **ei**) from any one of these points to new BTS is calculated as distance d (between MS and BTS) – movement l (how much distance new BTS moved from original BTS) /2 + small distance (in most of the times negligible). Name this distance as deciding_length.
7. Predict RxLev value of mobile station from new BTS (Virtually) location. For prediction we have used series of RxLev values those are measured by mobile station at regular intervals from original BTS.
8. From the predicted RxLev value calculate distance between new BTS and MS. If this distance is less than deciding_length (**eh** or **ei**), then we can say mobile is inside the edges (**eh** or **ei**) of new sector. Hence we can eliminate two regions (**bh** or **ic**) on original sector arc which are outside the new BTS edges. In this case we have to go back to the step5 (to move BTS further by 100 meters virtually). This cycle stops when if condition fails or we end up with the inside original sector arc length of less than 200 meters.
9. If that distance is more than deciding_length, then we can say mobile is outside the edges of new sector. In this case we end up with two regions (**bh** or **ic**) of length nearly 100 meters.
10. So finally either we end up with two regions of length 100 meters or one region of length less than 200 meters. We have already obtained two locations from earlier algorithm. Among these two obtained locations, the location which is inside any one of these two regions (if we end up with two) or the location which is inside the region (if we end up with one) is the original location of the mobile.

3.3   Number of BTS Signal Strength Values = 1

In this case only one BTS is available in the nearby neighborhood location of the mobile. Hence MSC will have only serving BTS signal strength information. This information is used to detect the exact location of the mobile. Following algorithm is the basic algorithm that our tool follows before apply the BTS replacement procedure. The output of the algorithm will be sector arc as a locus of the location of a mobile. Further improvement in location will be done based on BTS replacement procedure and CellSignalInfo_FermatPointReplace algorithm.

Algorithm: Location estimation of mobile.

Input: Signal dump file of a given mobile number in xml format which has the rxlev information of only serving BTS.

Output: Sector arc as Locus of the location of a GSM mobile in Google maps.

Procedure
1. Identify the serving BTS based on the BSIC value obtained by parsing the given input file.
2. Locate the BTS position on the map with its latitude and longitude values.
3. Calculate the distance between MS and BTS with the help of hata model using rxlev value and required parameters of BTS.
4. Draw the circle around the BTS with obtained distance in step3 as radius. This circle will be the locus of our location.
5. Identify the sector based on the BCCH carrier frequency corresponding to serving BTS rxlev value. Now only that sector part of the circle will be the locus of location.

3.3.1   BTS Replacement Procedure

Here to get more accurate point of location, we will assume transformation on the location of BTS from "a" to "e" (we will move BTS for 100 meters in 600 to the both sector edges ab and ac as in Fig. 3). Edges of new sector efg cut the sector abc arc of old one at two points "h" and "i". If we are able to calculate the distance between MS and BTS after replacement, we can eliminate unwanted location from previous obtained location by comparing the distances as in algorithm CellSignalInfo_VirtualBTS. By moving BTS further and further we will eliminate unwanted sector area. Fig. 3 shows proposed method to reduce the arc length to give minimum possible location of the mobile as discussed above. So after apply the above method we have possibility to end up with two scenarios. Either we end up with two locations or with only one location (near to 100 meters). If we end up with one region of length less than 200 meters that will be the final location of the mobile, otherwise we need to apply

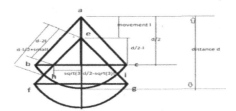

Fig. 3. Proposed method to reduce arc length for getting minimum range of accurate location

CellSignalInfo_FermatPointReplace algorithm to find out correct location among two regions of length 100 meters.

3.3.2   CellSignalInfo_FermatPointReplace Algorithm

This algorithm is mainly used to find the exact location among two locations that are obtained by BTS replacement procedure.

Algorithm: CellSignalInfo_FermatPointReplace.

Input: Signal dump file which is such that after BTS replacement procedure we end up with two regions of length 100 meters.

Output: Location of a mobile in Google maps with latitude and longitude values.

Procedure

1. Identify the serving BTS based on the BSIC value obtained by parsing the given input file.
2. Check whether serving BTS has more than one cell rxlev information (including serving cell). If yes follow the steps, otherwise go to step 5.
3. If serving BTS has 2 cells rxlev information (1serving+1neighbor cell) the location of the mobile will be the location which is nearer to the neighbor cell for which rxlev information is available.
4. If serving BTS has 3 cells rxlev information (1serving+2neighbor cells) the location of the mobile will be the location which is nearer to the neighbor cell for which rxlev value is high compared with other neighbor cell.
5. Find out the fermat point of the triangle formed with new BTS and the two points where the new BTS edges meet the old sector region. If the angle between two edges is 120^0, the fermat point will be new BTS location itself.
6. Replace fermat point for some distance say 80meters with an angle of 330^0. After replacement triangle tilts such that one vertex is in one of the locations, other vertex will go outside and that will be in omitted region. We are able to calculate rxlev values at the vertex which is in considerable region, if those rxlev values are giving considerable results then the location where vertex of the tilted triangle is there will be the final location of the mobile.
7. To find out rxlev values do the following. Calculate distance from original BTS location to replaced fermat point. Based on that distance calculate rxlev of MS at fermat point.
8. Also calculate the distance between replaced fermat point and point where new BTS edge cuts the old sector. Calculate rxlev from obtained distance. This time calculation of rxlev slightly depends on direction also (one of the variable in path loss calculation depends on the direction).
9. If these two obtained rxlev values are approximately equal then location will be the location where vertex of the tilted triangle is there, otherwise other location will be the position of the mobile station.

4   Results

There are three different cases to be considered to give the location of a mobile. Here we present some of the results obtained in all the cases. We also show comparison of our results with GPS system in all cases.

4.1   Number of BTS Signal Strength Values > 2

We have created sample signal dump file from our lab (lab coordinates are 13.011287, 74.79232). This signal dump file has shown three neighbour BTS signal strength values. We have used our tool to calculate the location of mobile by giving this signal file as input. Our tool has applied "More than one neighbour BTS signal strength value availability" case and given output coordinates as 13.013877, 74.791891.   There was 290 meters error in distance compared with original location. We have also taken values from GPS installed mobile, the coordinates obtained from that mobile are 13.0215852, 74.792406. GPS itself is saying, it will give location of mobile with an accuracy of 2500 meters range. But practically our tool will not give more than 550 meters error in distance. This is possible, because we are comparing the obtained distance (from serving BTS to MS) with TA value (of serving BTS). Table 1 explains the comparison of errors in original location by our software and GPS system.

Table 1. Error comparison table in three BTS case

	Co ordinates	Error (in meters) from original location
Original location	13.011287,74.79232	0
Location Obtained from our tool	13.013877,74.791891	290
Location obtained from GPS system	13.0215852,74.79240	1145

The output of location estimation tool in this case is shown in Fig. 4. Output is shown as location of a mobile with latitude, longitude values in Google map.

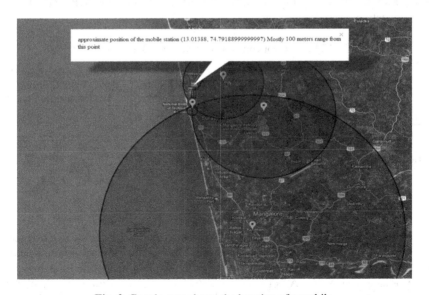

Fig. 3. Google map shows the location of a mobile

4.2   Number of BTS signal strength values = 2

We have modified the sample signal dump file which we have created from our lab, such that it has only one neighbour BTS signal strength value (we have removed other two neighbour BTS signal strength values manually). We have given this modified sample file as input to our tool. By following "Exactly one neighbour BTS signal strength value availability" case our tool has given coordinates as 13.013980536, 74.79227122. Table 2 shows error comparison table of locations given by our tool and GPS system with original location.

Table 2. Error comparison table in two BTS case

	Co ordinates	Error (in meters) from original location
Original location	13.011287,74.79232	0
Location Obtained from our tool	13.013980,74.7922712	299.5
Location obtained from GPS system	13.0215852,74.79240	1145

4.3   Number of BTS Signal Strength Values = 1

We have modified the sample signal dump file which we have created from our lab; such that it has only serving BTS signal strength value (we have removed neighbour BTS signal strength values manually). We have given this modified sample file as input to our tool. By following "No neighbour BTS signal strength value availability" case our tool has given coordinates as 13.0085741, 74.79586000708969. Table 3 shows error comparison table of locations given our tool and GPS system with original location.

Table 3. Error comparison table in one BTS case

	Co ordinates	Error (in meters) from original location
Original location	13.011287,74.79232	0
Location Obtained from our tool	13.008574,74.79586	487.9
Location obtained from GPS system	13.0215852,74.79240	1145

5   Conclusion and Future Work

Finding location of a mobile is an interesting area under which so much research work has been carried out and is still going on. Our location estimation tool is the first tool that works at network side, to give the exact location of mobile by using signal file information at MSC. As our tool is network based positioning tool, it works irrespective of mobile station model. If mobile got signal from even a single BTS, it is possible for our tool to locate that mobile provided we knew the mobile number. In India GPS is giving mobile location with an accuracy of 2500 meters range. At any case our tool will not give error more than 550 meters range in location; this is possible because we are using TA values for comparison of distances. We do not require any extra hardware either at network or at mobile side, to make our tool working. Our tool is a light weighted program which requires connections with BTS information (BTS tower location, height, transmission power) providing databases. With our software we are successful to give exact location of the mobile in all the cases.

We have designed our tool in GSM network; it will work in all the cases in GSM. But whatever the techniques and algorithms used for GSM can be used for CDMA also. The only difference is we will read signal strength values based on BCCH channel in GSM, we have to get signal strength from pilot channel in case of CDMA. Due to unavailability of CDMA signal files, we haven't implemented our tool on CDMA network. As a future work we can extend the functionality of our tool for CDMA network as well.

References

1. Eberspacher, J., Vogel, H.J.: GSM Switching, Services and Protocols, 2nd edn. John wiley & Sons Ltd. (2001)
2. Heine, G.: GSM Networks: Protocols, Terminology, and Implementation. Artech House, Inc., Norwood (1999)
3. Yousef, P.: GSM-Security: a Survey and Evaluation of the current situation. Master's thesis, Linkoping Institute of Technology (2004)
4. Schreiber, F.A., Falleni, M.L.: Analysis of Data Transmission Performance over a GSM Cellular Network. In: Proceedings of the Thirtieth Hawaii International Conference on System Sciences (1997)
5. Broek, F.V.D.: Catching and Understanding GSM-Signals. Computer Science thesis, Radboud University, Nijmegen (2010)
6. CDMA Forward and Reverse Channels, http://www.wirelessapplications.com/wireless/services/lostFound/images/CDMA_Channels_Final.pdf
7. Code Division Multiple Access, http://en.wikipedia.org/wiki/Code_division_multiple_access
8. Drane, C., Macnaughtan, M.: Positioning GSM Telephones. IEEE Communications Magazine, 46–59 (1998)
9. Lin, D.B., Juang, R.T., Lin, H.P.: Mobile Location Estimation and Tracking for GSM Systems. In: 15th IEEE International Symposium on Personal, Indoor and Mobile Radio Communications, PIMRC (2004)
10. Kabalan, K.Y., Mounsef, J.L.: Mobile Location in GSM Using Signal Strength Technique. In: 10th IEEE International Conference on Electronics, Circuits and Systems, ICECS (2003)
11. Caffery, J., Stuber, G.L.: Subscriber Location in CDMA Cellular Networks. IEEE Transactions on Vehicular Technology 47(2) (1998)
12. Hata Model, http://en.wikipedia.org/wiki/Hata_Model
13. Signal file information, https://svn.berlin.ccc.de/projects/airprobe/wiki/tracelog

An Adaptive Distributed Intrusion Detection System for Cloud Computing Framework

Deepa Krishnan and Madhumita Chatterjee

Pillai's Institute of Information Technology,New Panvel,Mumbai, India
deepa@pointingarrow.com, madhumita@it.iitb.ac.in

Abstract. Cloud Computing is the recent buzz word in computing which has enormous potential to revolutionize the IT industry. Cloud opened up new computing scenarios coupled with many significant benefits, however they also turned to become new avenues of attacks and exploits. This paper proposes a unique Distributed Intrusion Detection System (DIDS) based on a novel combination of two variant trends in intrusion detection-the behavior based and knowledge based intrusion detection mechanisms. The behavior based approach facilitates improved detection in the dynamic cloud environment and the knowledge based approach supports the detection scheme with its definitive rule base. The functionality of both these approaches has been improved by the addition of an adaptive approach which helps to significantly assist in lowering the false positives. In addition to this, another novel and the striking advantage of the proposed detection scheme is the alert clustering and analyzing facility thereby helping all cooperating nodes in detecting false alarms from any malicious nodes. DOS attacks in one node can be sent as alerts to help other cooperating nodes in updating themselves about new attack patterns leading to early detection and prevention of attacks. This scheme collectively helps to make the underlying cloud infrastructure more immune to attacks and continue to provide services to users.

Keywords: Cloud Computing, Distributed Intrusion Detection System, Knowledge-based and Behavior-based, Adaptive nature.

1   Introduction

Cloud is the most remarkable computing paradigm in the evolution of IT. The potential impact of cloud computing is amazing as it allows users to access applications that actually reside at a location other than our computer or other Internet-connected device; most often it will be a distant datacenter. But this promising area of IT is also prone to almost all the security attacks that a conventional network environment has. Some of the attacks jerking the foundation of the cloud technology are flooding or Denial of service attacks, authentication based attacks, side channel attacks [1] and malware attacks. Most of these arise due to the weakness in the protection mechanisms used. As it is seen, a Cloud is inherently a multi-tenant infrastructure, so an attack against a single customer is actually an attack against all

S.M. Thampi et al. (Eds.): SNDS 2012, CCIS 335, pp. 466–473, 2012.
© Springer-Verlag Berlin Heidelberg 2012

customers in that Cloud or at least a significant proportion of those customers. This is because they are sharing not only common network infrastructure but also a common computing infrastructure. Hence the potential for damage is extremely high and in light of this Cloud service providers need to ensure that they have proper security controls installed well in place.

Among the various security controls, Intrusion detection systems (IDS) are an essential component of defense measures protecting computer systems and network against harm or abuse [2]. In general, IDS collects network traffic, analyzes these traffic, and makes response or alerts the network if there is an intrusion taking place. Thus, the aim of the IDS is to alert or notify the system that some malicious activities have taken place.

According to the method of the collection of intrusion data, all the intrusion detection systems can be classified into two types: host-based and network-based IDSs. Host-based intrusion detection systems (HIDSs) analyze audit data collected by an operating system about the actions performed by users and applications; while network-based intrusion detection systems (NIDSs) analyze data collected from network packets.

Based on the way in which the attack is detected, there are two types of intrusion detection systems: knowledge-based or signature based and anomaly based or behavior based. The behavior-based method dictates how to compare recent user actions to the usual or the standard behavior where as the signature based approach monitors the ongoing network traffic and various activities against a known rule set. Both of the above approaches have their own pros and cons thus a combined approach would be preferable.

However we should also remember the intricacies in the deployment of the IDS and the way in which it can perform intrusion. The ability to perform Intrusion Detection in the cloud is heavily dependent on the model of cloud computing that is being used. In cloud computing, three kinds of services are provided: Software as a Service (SaaS) systems [3] , Infrastructure as a Service (IaaS) providers, and Platform as a Service (PaaS). When SaaS is used, the responsibility to perform intrusion detection relies on the cloud provider and similarly in PaaS the installation of an IDS and monitoring for an intrusion is again the responsibility of the service provider. However when IaaS is used the customer has the flexibility in the deployment of the IDS.

Another significant point of concern about the use of IDS in cloud is whether single IDS installed either at the customer or provider is capable enough to detect and notify the attacks. The Cloud infrastructure has massive amount of data and traffic hence the IDS must be robust and reliable to handle such a traffic flow. The traditional host based and network based IDSs are not efficient enough to detect the sophisticated and distributed attacks. Thus it is worthy to rely on a distributed IDS installed on various key points in the cloud. This motivated us to think on the distributed approach of IDS and the various ways in which the existing approaches can be improved.

A distributed IDS [4](DIDS) consists of multiple Intrusion Detection Systems (IDS), all of which communicate with each other, or with a central server that facilitates advanced network monitoring, incident analysis, and instant attack data.

In this paper we propose a Distributed Intrusion detection mechanism for Cloud Computing using a behavior-based and signature-based approach. A key feature of our approach is the ability to detect false alarms from malicious nodes and the adaptability to changing network scenarios thereby being able to considerably reduce the false positives. It also helps in updating the cooperating nodes about new attack patterns which helps in early detection of attacks.

The remainder of this paper is organized as follows: Related work in this field is discussed in section 2, where we have tried to bring out a comparative study of various researches and work in this direction. In section 3 the proposed scheme is discussed in detail and in section 4 the relative merits of our scheme is outlined, followed by conclusion and future scope in Section 5.

2   Related Work

Several efforts have been made in the area of Intrusion Detection systems for Cloud Computing environment, but many attacks still prevail. In [5], the authors discuss an implementation of IDS in Cloud environment which is responsible for monitoring the utilization of resources for the virtual machine using data acquired from virtual machine monitors. All monitoring operations are done outside the virtual machines so the attacker cannot modify the system in case of a breach. However, some intrusions such as an authorized abnormal activity will be detected as an intrusion which can significantly degrade the performance of the IDS.

On the other hand, [6] researchers like Chi-Chun Lo, Chun-Chieh Huang and Joy Ku have brought out the co-operative intrusion detection model for the grid and cloud computing in which the IDS are distributed among the nodes of the grid and alert other nodes when an attack occurs. Indeed, this approach made a giant leap over other models for the same as this helps other nodes in avoiding the same attacks from occuring. This system also helps in preventing single point of failure since the IDSs are distributed across the cloud.

Another important work which can be considered as an enhancement to the above work is done by Westphal and his team where they have proposed Grid and Cloud Computing Intrusion Detection System (GCCIDS) [7] which is designed to cover the attacks that network- and host-based systems cannot detect. Their proposed method used the integration of knowledge and behavior analysis to detect specific intrusions. However, the proposed prototype cannot discover new types of attacks or create an attack database which can be adaptively updated according to changing network conditions. We have attempted to bridge the above gaps and have added other crucial and pertinent features for a cloud IDS in our work.

Another related work which has made a remarkable contribution is the multi-threaded NIDS approach. In [8], the authors proposed an efficient model that used multithreading technique for improving the performance in the cloud computing environment to handle large number of data packet flows. The researchers have conducted experiments to perform the performance evaluation of their proposed method relative to the single thread approach. They have used parameters like processing time and execution for their comparative study.

The work of Guangsen Zhang and Parkar [9] in the area of DDOS detection in network environment have provided us key insights for our thoughts. In the proposed approach, "Cooperative Defence against DDoS Attacks" DDoS defence systems are deployed in the network to detect DDoS attacks independently. A gossip based communication mechanism is used to exchange information about network attacks between these independent detection nodes to aggregate information about the overall network attacks observed. Using the aggregated information, the individual defence nodes have approximate information about global network attacks and can stop them more effectively and accurately. This work has led us to the idea that a cooperative defense approach can also be extended for the DDOS mitigation.

In view of all the above works and some of its inherent drawbacks, we have proposed an integrated IDS which combines the features of behavior based IDS and knowledge based IDS and integrates it with the cloud. The highlight of our proposed method over other methods is that they can reduce false positives to a significant extent and also verify the authenticity of a newly received alert before adding to the rule base.

3   Proposed Scheme for Intrusion Detection

3.1   Overview of the Scheme

The proposed scheme uses a distributed approach in intrusion detection combining a knowledge based system and behavioral based scheme. This is in turn supplemented by an innovative feature termed as a surveillance agent in our paper which helps in bringing out the adaptive nature in IDS functionality. The knowledge base component of our scheme has the knowledge regarding the previous attack signatures which forms the definitive rule base against which all attempts of access can be matched. On the other hand, Behavior-based intrusion component creates a model of normal or valid behavior extracted from reference systems collected by various means. An intrusion can be detected in this scheme by observing a deviation from normal or expected behavior of the system or the users. Along with these two approaches which works in a scheme which can be rightly called a hybrid model of IDS, a surveillance agent also works hand in hand which continuously monitors the node behaviors so that an adaptive line of detection is done. This is explained in more detail in the architectural description of the proposed scheme.

The IDSs are distributed in the cloud framework and every node will be monitored by the respective IDS installed in them. When a potential attack is detected by an IDS, it issues alerts to other nodes in the framework. In this way every node updates attack patterns which are set as rules within themselves and also helps in updating other nodes also about new attack patterns. Thus the effectiveness of the proposed system is boosted by the coordinated alert mechanism from peer cloud nodes.

3.2   Architecture and Working of the Proposed Scheme

The architecture of proposed distributed IDS can be best described with the help of its components viz IDS service Agent, Alert Agent and Storage Agent. They communicate among each other and with the peer nodes as shown in Fig.1.

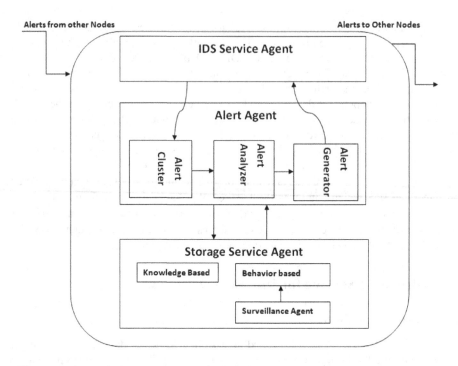

Fig. 1. Architectural diagram of proposed DIDS showing various agents and its components

The details of the different modules of the DIDS are given below:

A. IDS Service Agent

The IDS Service agent monitors connection requests and resources of the node. It also facilitates communication with other nodes. The IDS service agent maintains logs of various user requests and services. When a new access request comes, it consults the Alert Agent and Storage Agent to detect whether it is an intrusion or an authorized access request.

B. Alert Agent

The functioning of the alert agent can be best described using its components which are as follows:

a) Alert Cluster: This module collects alerts that are sent by other IDSs when they are suffering from severe attacks. Each IDS in every node exchanges their alerts and upon receiving an alert it passes this to alert analyzer. Alerts sent to other nodes are organized in a format which helps other nodes in formulating rule bases to update their knowledge base.

b) Alert Analyzer: Alert Analyzer analyses the incoming alerts to evaluate the trustworthiness of the alerts. When a new alert is received at a node the alert analyzer will keep the alert in observation and analysis stage, till a decision is taken regarding whether to accept it for new rule formation. The receiver nodes arrive at a decision based on two parameters:

• Previous acquaintance and trust about the sender.
• A majority function.

If the receiver is having the sender listed among its trusted peers, the alert will be passed to the new rule formation stage and eventually would get added to its rule base. If the alert is from a new node it executes a majority function described as follows;

Let number of IDSs sending the same alert messages = NIDSA
Let Number of IDSs in the cloud computing = NIDSC
If NIDSA / NIDSC > 0.5 then: the alert analyzer detects it as a legitimate alert and passes the message to IDS service agent and storage agent.

c) Alert Generator: Alert Generator initiates new outgoing alert when new attack is detected by respective IDS in a node. IDS Service Agent facilitates in issuing outgoing alerts to other nodes.

C. Storage Agent

This module holds the attack rules that the IDS Service must analyze. It is implemented as a combination of knowledge-based and behavior-based storage agent and is supported by the use of one more crucial component called surveillance agent. This component plays a key role in the effective implementation of the adaptive feature of our proposed approach.

a) Behavior based: Behavior based approach uses the technique of studying the normal behavior of the system in terms of network traffic, logged in users, IP connections. We focus here on identifying user behavioral patterns and deviations from such patterns. A template of existing normal behavior is formulated and stored in the behavior based component of the storage service agent. Every node notes the deviation from the expected behavior and detects the malicious activities. The approach of detecting the attack with statistics of usage and behavior can sometimes lead to more false alarms. The functionality of the behavior based agent is supplemented by the usage of the surveillance agent. The functionality of this agent is described as follows: Surveillance agent has been implemented as part of the storage service agent. This agent is pre-configured with the various observed normal values of parameters like number of users connected, log in time of users, bandwidth utilization, incoming and outgoing traffic flow, various connected ports, protocols and IP addresses used in incoming received requests. With the normal values set, the agent runs in the back ground and then observes continuously the values of these parameters. Any abnormal spurge in the values of any of these parameters can be noted and can be monitored further in a quarantine manner, so that its aberration can be confirmed as a changed normal behavior or a purely abnormal activity. If the observed deviation is a part of a recent genuine modification of the system configuration then the template of the expected behavior in the behavior based storage service agent is updated.

b) Knowledge based: Knowledge based intrusion detection is the most often applied technique in this field because it results in a low false alarm rate and high positive rates. This is also called signature-based as attack patterns are stored as signatures or rules. Thus every access patterns are compared against these rules to detect an attack. Using this behavior-based approach, a malicious behavior can be detected and can be added as a rule to the knowledge-based storage agent.

As described in the overview of the proposed approach the combined working of the knowledge based and behavior based schemes with support of the surveillance agent significantly improves the performance of the IDS scheme.

3.3   Deployment

Our proposed scheme can be deployed on the virtual network and the Virtual machine as it facilitates homogenous and compatible communication mechanisms between various nodes. This would allow us to monitor and analyze communications between VMs, between host system and VM and within the virtual network. This method of IDS installation can be very effective as it helps in effective detection both in the VM host and the virtual network so that majority of traffic and activity are under check. The network administrators can wisely choose to install the IDS in various critical choke points of the virtual network in a way that it facilitates easier exchange of the alerts among the peer nodes.

4   Relative Merits of Proposed Approach

The proposed scheme for intrusion detection combines the inherent advantages of the both behavior based and a knowledge based approaches for IDS. The behavior based scheme in its native form has a disadvantage of generating lot of false alarms which can significantly deteriorate the performance of the scheme. However our approach has successfully mitigated this drawback with the introduction of the surveillance agent and adaptively updating the behavioral parameters. Thus, in short our system will learn to detect an unusual authorized activity as normal and will not generate false alarms thus bringing down false positives. The behavior based module supported by the surveillance agent offers an adaptive capability to consider a changed normal behavior of a system as an expected behavior by carefully examining the behavior change for its non malicious nature.

As it is a hybrid scheme, this approach also gets the advantages of signature based detection. Our scheme has an alert analyzer component which ensures the trust worthiness of alerts received at every node so that fake alerts are not added to the rule base. In addition to this, due to cooperative alert exchanging the proposed method also has the benefit of knowledge about new attack patterns detected in other nodes so that any attack of its kind can be avoided.

5   Conclusion and Future Work

In this paper we propose a distributed cooperative intrusion detection system for cloud computing network in which IDSs are distributed in every node. This scheme detects new alerts using behavior based learning techniques and known alerts using knowledge based system. DOS attacks in other nodes are sent as alerts to other cooperating nodes to help them know about the new attack patterns. By co-operating among the cloud nodes an early detection and prevention is implemented. This scheme using its adaptive approach can also bring down the number of false alarms. We are doing our experimentations with CloudSim simulator integrated with Snort IDS.

As a future scope we could further revise the adaptive approach by including expert system based techniques. We would also envision the development of the scheme by incorporating data mining techniques and decision trees as databases of attack patterns grow. This can be done by matching patterns extracted from a simple audit set with those referred to warehoused unknown attacks. With data mining it is easy to correlate data related to alarms with mined audit data, thereby considerably reducing the rate of false alarms, thus our scheme can be improved further.

References

1. Zunnurhain, K., Vrbsky, S.V.: Security Attacks in Clouds. In: CloudCom 2010 (2010)
2. Kazienko, P., Dorosz, P.: Intrusion Detection Systems (IDS) Part2-Classification, methods, techniques (July 23, 2004), http://www.windowsecurity.com/articles/ids-part2-Classification-methods-techniques.html
3. Cox, P.: Intrusion detection in a cloud computing environment, http://www.searchcloudcom-putingtarget.com/tip/Intrusion-detection-in-a-cloud-computing-environment
4. Einwechter, N.: An introduction to Intrusion Detection System, http://www.symantec.com/connect/articles/introduction-distributed-intrusion-detection-systems
5. Nikolai, J.: Detecting Unauthorized usage in a cloud using Tenant, http://www.homepages.dsu.edu/malladis/teach/717/Papers/nikolai.pdf
6. Lo, C.-C., Huang, C.-C., Ku, J.: A cooperative intrusion detection system framework for cloud computing networks, 1530-2016/10,2010 IEEE
7. Vieira, K., Schulter, A., Westphall, C.B., Westphall, C.M.: Intrusion Detection for Grid and Cloud Computing, 1520-9202/10,2010 IEEE
8. Gul, I., Hussain, M.: Distributed Cloud Intrusion Detection Model. International Journal of Advanced Science and Technology 34, 71–82 (2011)
9. Zhang, G., Parashar, M.: Cooperative Defence against DDOS Attacks. Journal of Research and Practice in Information Technology 38(1) (February 2006)

Biologically Inspired Computer Security System: The Way Ahead

Praneet Saurabh[1], Bhupendra Verma[1], and Sanjeev Sharma[2]

[1] Department of Computer Science and Engineering, TIT, Bhopal, M.P, India
[2] Department of Information Technology, SoIT, UTD, RGPV, M.P, India
praneetsaurabh@gmail.com, bk_verma3@rediffmail.com,
sanjeev@rgtu.net

Abstract. Last two decades have witnessed tremendous growth of internet and it acts as a centrifugal force for a whole new array of applications and services which drives the e- business/ commerce globally. Millions of application has been designed to reach out to the end-user to provide necessary information. The users who are participating in various activities over internet are exposed to public network which is vulnerable to the ever growing threats like never before due to the fascination and value of information/ transaction involved. So concern about security of computer systems is justifiable, and to overcome/ prevent these threats has resulted in the development of various security concepts and products such as Firewalls, Intrusion Detection Systems (IDS) and Intrusion Prevention Systems (IPS). Lately it has been witnessed that there lies a huge potential in biological algorithms and methods to solve complex real world problems, we just need to relate and model the solution based on these biological theories. This paper critically reviews the information that is available on the internet as one has to spend a considerable amount of time to search it, also it explores the possibilities of development of a biologically inspired computer security system to overcome the ever growing complex security challenges.

Keywords:-Computer Security, IDS, IPS, HIS.

1   Introduction.

Definition of "Computer Security" is not easy as difficulty lies in a definition that should be broad enough to be valid regardless of the system being described, yet specific enough to describe what Computer Security really is. In a generic sense, security is "freedom from risk or danger."[3, 5] In the context of computer science, security is the prevention of, or protection against [1],

   (I) Access to information by unauthorized recipients, and
   (II) Intentional but unauthorized destruction or alteration of that information.

Computer security is frequently associated with the perspective of three keywords which are:

S.M. Thampi et al. (Eds.): SNDS 2012, CCIS 335, pp. 474–484, 2012.

- **Confidentiality** -- Ensuring that information is not accessed by unauthorized persons.
- **Integrity** -- Ensuring that information is not altered by unauthorized persons in a way that is not detectable by authorized users.
- **Authentication** -- Ensuring that users are the persons they claim to be.

The reliance of the world's infrastructure on computer systems is immense as computers and is used in every domains of life [4,8] and participation can be through any of the methods such as electronic communication, e-commerce over the Internet [1, 4]. Networks and the number of users are increasing all the time leading to the introduction of more naive users [5, 7]. Some of them are unknowingly causing many security gaps which can be explored to take advantage to get inside the target network [7]. All the information sent or shared on the public network so the potential chances of misuse is enormous as it is exposed to unauthorized "hackers" also [5,6]. Its pervasiveness makes "Network/ Computer Security" an issue of great importance and value since it has become a necessity in the digital age [6, 7]. All these points indicate and highlight the challenges and the need for the development of a computer security system [5, 6, 8] which will be competent for the highly dynamic, unorganized, imperfect, uncontrolled and open network environments.

AIS (Artificial immune System) [14, 15] are modeled after HIS (Human Immune System) which enables every organism to survive from the various threats posed by the environment. Immunity is the mechanism that is used by the body for its protection from different environmental threats. The way the human body reacts to these different threats and attacks encourages the researchers to model computer security system after Human Immune System as its survives under very demanding circumstances efficiently[16,17].

Swarm Intelligence and optimization is a machine-learning technique loosely inspired by birds flocking in search of food. It consists of a number of particles (birds) that collectively move on the search space in search of the global optimum [18]. Some Intrusion Detection techniques have already been proposed using swarm behavior metaphors because these paradigms can adapt seamlessly to today's complex computing environments and provide a solution to the badly needed adaptability requirement of computer security using the self organizing principle [23].

Ant colony optimization (ACO) takes inspiration from the behavior of ants. These ants deposit pheromone on the ground in order to mark some favorable path that should be followed by other members of the colony [22]. ACO algorithms are not guaranteed to find the shortest path in complex, high-dimensional graphs, theyfind the satisfactory solutions with relatively little computation.

Section 2 highlights the background information of computer security, Section 3 contains literature about currently available tools, Section 4 explores the perspective of a biologically inspired security system, and Section 5 concludes the discussion.

2   Background Information

Attacks, intrusions identified at the user level as classified by Harmer et al. [3, 5, 8, 20] are as:

(1) **Misuse/abuse:** unauthorized activities by authorized users.
(2) **Reconnaissance:** findings of systems and services that may be exploitable.
(3) **Penetration attempt:** unauthorized activity to gain access to computing resources.
(4) **Penetration:** successful access to computing resources by unauthorized users.
(5) **Trojanization:** presence and activity of unauthorized processes.
(6) **Denial of service:** an attack that obstructs legitimate access to computing.

A cyber-attack [1, 2] is an attempt to get inside the system without formal permission, on the basis of activity attacks can be categorized into:

(1) **Passive:** which is aimed at gaining access to penetrate the system without compromising IT resources.
(2) **Active:** which results in an unauthorized state change of IT resources.

In terms of the user access, attacks are categorized [2,5] as:

(1) **Internal,** coming from own enterprise's employees or their business partners or customers.
(2) **External,** coming from outside, frequently via the Internet.

Security arsenal and awareness of threat is growing with each passing day but the threat perception has neither been eliminated nor mitigated. Motives of these crimes are changing from mere fun and bragging to high financial gains, information gathering for information warfare and terrorism. CSI survey 2009 [4] reported big jumps in incidence of financial fraud (19.5 percent, over 12 per-cent last year); malware infection (64.3 percent over 50 percent last year); denials of service (29.2 percent, over 21 percent last year), password sniffing (17.3 percent, over 9 percent last year); and Web site defacement (13.5 percent over 6 percent last year). A primary reason for this increase is that the network protocols and Internet were never developed with security in mind. Additionally, building absolutely secure systems of this magnitude is unlikely anyway due to the complexity of these systems and likelihood of human errors in implementing these systems. The increase in dependence on computer systems and the corresponding risks and threats has revolutionized computer security technologies. Due to these risks and we need new concepts and paradigms to be developed and adopted to look after the security concerns.

3   Current Available Tools

3.1   Firewalls

These are the first-line of defense for any network and is responsible to permit, deny or proxy data to a computer network [1,2]. Packet filter firewalls worked on the principle of inspecting the "packets" which is transferred between the source and destination on the network [5]. Second-generation firewalls are called Circuit level firewalls worked up to transport layer of the OSI model. These worked on the principle of maintaining records of the entire are passing through the firewall and then tried to find whether a packet is the start of a new connection, a part of an existing connection, or is an invalid packet [3]. An application firewall is the third generation of firewall, it covers all the seven layers. It inspects all the packets for malicious content, and then based on the definition it restrict or prevent the spread of any malicious content to the network [10].

Firewalls are not always effective against the numerous intrusion attempts. Since the Firewalls are deployed for a network which monitors the incoming traffic to the network but it fails to addresses the attacks which comes or launched from within the organization [5,6]. It also does not have a proactive approach to counter any new threat [10].

3.2   Intrusion Detection System (IDS)

Intrusion detection System can be defined as the tools, methods, and resources to help identify, assess, and report unauthorized or unapproved network activity [1, 10, 12]. It works on the principle of the principle that the behavior of the intruder will be different from that of a legitimate user that can be quantified. Preprocessing, Analysis, Response and Refinement are the key phases of IDS [5]. Based on its deployment it can be have three categories [10,12] which are as:

A. Host-based intrusion-detection system (HIDS): Deployed on the host it scans all the host activity within the secure data base and check that the event occurred matches with the malicious event or not.

B. Network-based intrusion-detection system (NIDS): Deployed on the host it is inline with the network, it analyzes the network packets that are looking for attacks. It receives all the packets by taps or port mirroring, then it reconstructs the streams of traffic to analyze them for patterns of malicious behavior.

C. Hybrids of the two: A hybrid IDS combines a HIDS, which monitors events occurring on the host system, with a NIDS, which monitors network traffic.

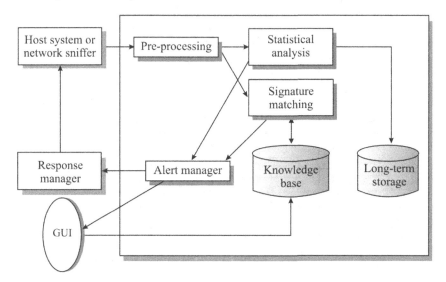

Fig. 1. Block Diagram of IDS

There are two basic classifications of intrusion detection techniques:

A. **Misuse detection:** It is also called Rule-Based Detection or signature detection technique. This technique is based on what's wrong. It contains the attack patterns (or "signatures") [10,11] and match them against the audit data stream, for evidence of known attacks.

B. **Anomaly based detection**: It is also referred as profile-based detection; the basic assumption of anomaly detection is that attacks will be different from normal behavior [10, 11]. This detection technique compares desired behavior of users and the applications with the actual ones by creating and maintaining a profile system that flags any events that strays from the normal pattern and passes this information on to output routines [1,3].

Intrusion detection systems have its own problems, such as false positives, operational issues in high-speed   environments, and the difficulty of detecting unknown threats. In addition, intrusion prevention is still in its infancy. Most of the problems with intrusion detection are caused by improper implementation and misunderstanding of what the technology can and cannot do[12]. It also fails to provide adequate protection due to the fact that they cannot detect and respond to all intrusions in real-time [8].

3.3   Intrusion Prevention System (IPS)

These are proactive defense mechanisms [7, 9] which sits inline on the network and monitors the traffic, if it detects malicious packets within normal network traffic then takes measures to stop the intrusions by blocking the incoming traffic automatically before it does any damage rather than simply raising an alert as, or after the malicious code has been delivered.[3,9]

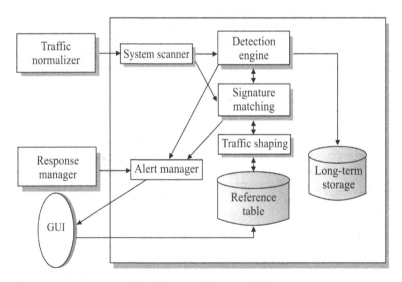

Fig. 2. Block Diagram of IPS

Based on its deployment it can be classified into of two types [7,9]:

A. Host based Intrusion Prevention System (HIPS): It monitors data streams and the environment specific to a particular application, relies on agents installed directly on the system that needs to be protected [7,9].

B. Network based Intrusion Prevention System (NIPS): User actions should correspond to actions in a predefined knowledge base as it sits inline so all the packets have to pass through it [7]. Therefore the moment a suspicious packet has been detected it takes proactive measures and that packed is stopped or contained [9].

An IPS also generates false positives that can create serious problems if automated responses are used, it becomes expensive, also these are slow in reaction time and consume lots of recourses [7, 9]. All the current solutions for network security are based on static methods that collect, analyze and extract evidences after attacks. Lack ofself-learning and self-adapting abilities contribute in failure of detecting unknown and new attacks [10].

All these solutions still face the challenges of inherent system flaws, OS bugs, and social engineering attacks. All the system which currently looks after the network/ computer security lacks in addressing the additional and advanced requirements such as false positive, single point solution, reactive approach to tackle threat, distributedness and robustness and thus performance suffers heavily on these parameters.Based on the review of the current prevailing security solutions the requirements of a computer security system that have been identified are as:

4 Biological Perspective in Computer Security

4.1 Artificial Immune System

AIS are a computational systems inspired by the principles and processes of the biological immune system [14, 15]. The biological immune system is a robust, complex, adaptive system which defends the body from foreign pathogens. It is able to categorize all cells (or molecules) within the body as self-cells or non-self-cells. It does this with the help of a distributed task force that has the intelligence to take action from a local and also a global perspective using its network of chemical messengers for communication [16].

Human immune system has the ability to detect foreign substances and to responds properly. It is distributed, fault tolerant and has the capability to distinguish own body cells from foreign substances which is also referred as self/non-self discrimination. Immune system is constituted by central lymphoid whose purpose is to generate and mature immune cells, bone marrow and thymus do the task and peripheral lymphoid organ which facilitates the interaction between lymphocytes and antigen. Thymus procedures mature T cells, beneficial T- cells are kept whereas the remaining ones are discarded and then released into blood stream to perform different immunological functions [16].

4.1.1 Negative Selection Algorithm

Negative selection provides tolerance for self cells and it deals with the immune system's ability to detect unknown antigens while not reacting to the self-cells

[13,20]. A lot of variations of negative selection algorithms have been frequently proposed, but the crux remains the same [15,16] is to build self profile once it has been built, non self patterns are randomly generated. If the random pattern matches a self pattern then it is removed, otherwise it becomes a detector pattern and monitors newly arriving patterns.Forrest [17] was the first to apply the idea of negative selection, Detectors, inspired by T-cells, represented in binary strings. A detector string match an antigen string if the two strings shared the same characters in an uninterrupted stretch of r bits; this is known as the r-contiguous bits matching rule. If the detector matches any new pattern, then it has detected an anomaly and becomes a memory cell which is stored for future attacks.

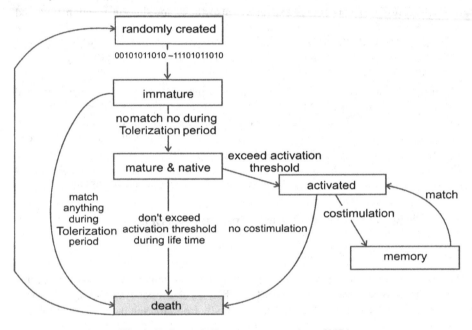

Fig. 3. Hofmeyr & Forrest representation of NSA

Zhang et al [24] proposed a novel distributed intrusion detection model based on immune agents (IA-DIDM) which is inspired by Negative Selection paradigm lymphocyte's working in the BIS.The system by Okamoto and Ishida [25] focused on anomaly detection in user behavior. Immunity based anomaly detection system with a new mechanism of diversity generation is discussed inspired by the mechanism of positive and negative selection in the thymus. Negative Selection algorithm proposed by Forrest et. al. [15] has been improved with mutation by Zhongmin et al. [26], in design of agent for detecting and analyzing data in intrusion detection based on immune principle.

4.1.2 Clonal Selection Theory

Clonal selection theory elucidates the proliferation of immune cells when activated in the presence of an antigen. Detection of an antigen by lymphocyte can be viewed as a random event as it is selected from a large repertoire of lymphocyte receptors. Once activated these lymphocytes proliferates through the process called cloning. The main properties of clonal selection are:

- Elimination of self-reacting clones.
- Proliferation and differentiation of mature lymphocytes through antigenic simulation.
- Restriction of one pattern to one differentiated cell and retention of this pattern by clonal descendants.
- Generation of new random genetic changes subsequently expressed as diverse antibody patterns by a form of accelerated somatic mutation.

4.1.3 Immune Network Theory

The "immune network (IN) theory" was proposed by Niels K. Jerne [16] makes an effort to describe the mechanism of formation of immune memory. The concept hypothesized that the immune system acts as a regulated network of antibodies and anti-antibodies, which is called an "idiotypic network," which recognizes one another. Aickelin et al. [27] introduced client/server architecture which can be used to implement AIS algorithms. The libtissue client provides input to the algorithms.

4.1.4 Danger Theory

Self in Danger Theory model is considered as harmless to which the body develops tolerance, many a times the immune system becomes tolerant to antigens that are not same as self, but to those which do not pose any danger.[27] In DT, the immune response is determined by the presence or absence of alarm signals these signals trigger an immune reaction and in response APCs are activated.

According to Matzinger in (1994) [16], the immune system is activated on receipt of molecular signals, which indicate damage (or stress) to the body rather than by pattern matching of "nonself" versus "self." She states that our bodies are never completely tolerant. As long as the thymus and bone marrow are producing new B and T cells, there will be a few new circulating self-reactive lymphocytes.

The distressed cells and tissues transmit danger signals, which results in capturing antigens by antigen-presenting cells (APCs) such as macrophages, APCs then travel to the local lymph node and present the antigen to lymphocytes [27].

Table 1. Modelling of Immunological terms in Computational Models

Immunological Terms	Computational Modelling Terms
T cells, B cells, and antibodies	Detectors, clusters, classifiers, and strings
Self-cells, self-molecules, and immune cells	Positive samples, training data, and patterns
Antigens, pathogens, and epitopes	Incoming data, verifying data samples, and test data
String-matching rule Complementary rule and other rules	Distance and similarity measures Affinity measure in the shape–space

4.2   Swarm Intelligence

Swarm Intelligence (SI) is another example of the powerful phenomenon of learning and adaptation observed in many natural systems (social insects and birds). A swarm is defined as a "set of (mobile) agents which are liable to communicate directly or indirectly with each other [15]. Particle swarm optimization (PSO) is a machine-learning technique loosely inspired by birds flocking in search of food[20]. Particle swarm optimization has been used with success in several do-mains ranging from regulation of power plants to the class of traveling salesman problems proposed by Kennedy and Eberhart [21]. Swarm optimization searches the problem space in parallel with a population of candidate solutions. In Foukia and Hassas [18] and Foukia [19] a mobile agent based Intrusion Detection and Response System (IDRS) is proposed using the AIS and SI approaches.

4.3   Ant Colony Optimization

Ant colony optimization (ACO) is another family of optimization algorithms, these algorithms were originally conceived to find the shortest route in traveling salesman problems. In ACO several ants travel across the edges that connect the nodes of a graph while depositing virtual pheromones. Genetic Algorithm & Optimization Ants that travel on the shortest path will be able to make more return trips and deposit more pheromones in a given amount of time. Consequently, that path will attract more ants in a positive feedback loop. A major advantage of ACO over other algorithms for path finding is that virtual ants discover and maintain several short paths in addition to the best one.

5   Conclusion

It has been quite a substantial amount of time from the first theory has been proposed as an Intrusion Detection System inspired by the Human Immune System. Combination & fusion of the concepts of biological algorithms will lead and foster the development of Computer security solutions that will be very efficient counter the challenges posed in imperfect, uncontrolled and open scenario. The resulting computer security system will beDistributed, Multilayered, Diverse, Disposable, Autonomous, Adaptive, and have self-learning, self-configuringcapabilities. The resulting CSS will address the problems that remained unanswered by the various different security solutions; also research on immune inspired techniques in the future may follow many directions. One of these may be unified architecture that will mimic natural defense mechanisms by integrating a set of heterogeneous immune components. Despite the successes of AIS in modeling many techniques, still there remain some issues that are unaddressed. Self-configuration mechanism needs to be introduced as many a time security system unnecessarily consumes resources. The most important limitation of the analogy is that it is not concerned of protecting secrets, privacy, or other issues of confidentiality, this needs to be addressed and lastly we should must keep in mind how to apply our knowledge of immunology to overcome the problems in computer security.

References

[1] Marin, A.G.: Network Security Basics, Security and Privacy, pp. 68–72. IEEE (2005)

[2] Bishop, M.: Computer Security Art and Science. Pearson Education (2003)

[3] Zhang, X.: Intrusion Prevention System Design. In: Computer and Information Technology, pp. 386–390 (2004)

[4] Robert, R.: CSI Computer Crime & Security Survey 2010 (2011)

[5] Zafar, F.M., Naheed, F., Ahmad, Z., Anwar, M.M.: Network Security: A Survey of Modern Approaches. The Nucleus 45(1-2), 11–31 (2008)

[6] Bishop, M.: An Overview of Computer Viruses in a Research Environment. In: 4th DPMA, IEEE, ACM Computer Virus and Security Conference, pp. 154–163 (1997)

[7] Guillen, E.: Weakness and Strength Analysis over Network-Based Intrusion Prevention & Prevention Systems. Communications, 1–5 (2009)

[8] Krause, M., Tipton, F.H.: Handbook of Information Security, Management. CRC Press LLC (2006) ISBN: 0849399475

[9] Carter, E.: Intrusion Prevention Fundamentals: an introduction to network attack mitigation with IPS. Cisco Press (2006)

[10] Endorf, C., Schultz, E., Mellander, J.: Intrusion Detection & Prevention. McGraw-Hill (2004)

[11] Denning, E.D.: An Intrusion-Detection Model. IEEE Transactions on Software Engineering SE-13(2), 222–232 (1987)

[12] Mukerjee, B., Heberlein, T.L., Levitt, N.K.: Network Intrusion Detection. IEEE Network, 26–41 (1994)

[13] de Castro, L., Timmis, J.: Artificial Immune Systems as a Novel Soft Computing Paradigm. Soft Computing, Journal 7(7), 526–544 (2003)

[14] Dasgupta, D., Forrest, S.: An Anomaly Detection Algorithm Inspired by the Immune System. In: Artificial Immune Systems & their Applications, ch. 14, pp. 262–277. Springer-Verlag, Inc. (January 1999)

[15] Forrest, S., Hofmeyr, S., Somayaji, A.: Computer Immunology. Communications of the ACM 40(10), 88–96 (1997)

[16] de Castro, L., Zuben, F.: Artificial Immune Systems: Part I – Basic Theory and Applications. TR – DCA 01/99 (1999)

[17] Forrest, S., Hofmeyr, A.S., Somayaji, A., Longstaff: Sense of self for Unix processes. In: Proceedings of the 1996, IEEE Symposium on Security and Privacy, pp. 120–128 (1996)

[18] Foukia, N., Hassas, S.: Managing Computer Networks Security Through Self-Organization: A Complex System Perspective. In: Di Marzo Serugendo, G., Karageorgos, A., Rana, O.F., Zambonelli, F. (eds.) ESOA 2003. LNCS (LNAI), vol. 2977, pp. 124–138. Springer, Heidelberg (2004)

[19] Foukia, N.: IDReAM: Intrusion Detection and Response Executed with Agent Mobility. In: Brueckner, S.A., Di Marzo Serugendo, G., Karageorgos, A., Nagpal, R. (eds.) ESOA 2005. LNCS (LNAI), vol. 3464, pp. 227–239. Springer, Heidelberg (2005)

[20] Paul, H.K., Paul, W.D., Gregg, G.H., Gary, L.B.: An artificial immune system architecture for computer security applications. IEEE Transactions on Evolutionary Computation 6(3), 252–280 (2002)

[21] Kennedy, J., Eberhart, R.C.: Swarm Intelligence. Morgan Kaufmann, San Francisco (2001)

[22] Birattari, Dorigo, M., Stutzle, T.: Ant colony optimization. IEEE Computational Intelligence Magazine 1(4), 28–39 (2006)

[23] Kennedy, J., Eberhart, R.C.: Particle swarm optimization. In: IEEE International Conference on Neural Networks, pp. 1942–1948. IEEE Press, NJ (1995)

[24] Zhang, Z., Luo, W., Wang, X.: Designing abstract immune mobile agents for distributed intrusion detection. In: Proceedings of the International Conference on Neural Networks and Brain, ICNN&B 2005, Beijing, vol. (2), pp. 748–753 (2005)

[25] Ishida, Y.: The Next Generation of Immunity-Based Systems: From Specific Recognition to Computational Intelligence. In: Fulcher, J., Jain, L.C. (eds.) Computational Intelligence: A Compendium. SCI, vol. 115, pp. 1091–1121. Springer, Heidelberg (2008)

[26] Zhongmin, C., Yu, W., Baowen, X.: The algorithm design of agent for detecting and analyzing data in intrusion detection based on immune principle. In: Proceedings of the International Conference on Wireless Communications, Networking and Mobile Computing, Shanghai, pp. 1779–1783 (2007)

[27] Aickelin, U., Greensmith, J., Twycross, J.: Immune System Approaches to Intrusion Detection – A Review. In: Nicosia, G., Cutello, V., Bentley, P.J., Timmis, J. (eds.) ICARIS 2004. LNCS, vol. 3239, pp. 316–329. Springer, Heidelberg (2004)

A Comparative Analysis of the Ant Based Systems for QoS Routing in MANET

Debajit Sensarma and Koushik Majumder

Department of Computer Science & Engineering, West Bengal University of Technology,
Kolkata, India
koushik@ieee.org

Abstract. The huge growth of mobile and handheld devices has immensely popularized the ad hoc networks, which do not require any wired infrastructure for intercommunication. The nodes of mobile ad hoc network operate as the routers as well as the end hosts. The communication occurs in single hop and multi-hop paths. Due to explosive growth of mobile devices, the user's desires for real time applications are increasing day by day providing the new challenges in the design of protocols for mobile ad hoc networks. Support for quality of service (QoS) like delay, bandwidth, energy, hop-count etc. are necessary to face the challenges and to enable real time applications for Mobile Ad hoc network. In particular, it is important that the routing protocols incorporate the QoS metrics in route finding and maintenance to support the end-to-end QoS. In this paper we have studied the issues and challenges involved with the existing QoS-aware routing schemes and the use of biologically inspired ant colony optimization technique for QoS-aware routing in MANET. In addition to this, we have carried out a thorough comparison study of the existing ant colony based QoS-aware routing schemes in order to analyze the strengths and weaknesses of these schemes. Finally the future scope, which is inferred from the comparison study of existing protocols have been discussed.

Keywords: Mobile ad-hoc network, Ant colony optimization, QoS Routing.

1 Introduction

Routing in MANET is a Dynamic Optimization Problem as the search space changes over time. Due to the time varying nature of the topology of the networks, traditional routing techniques such as distance-vector and link-state algorithms that are used in fixed networks, cannot be directly applied to mobile Ad hoc networks. Centralized algorithms have scalability problems, static algorithms have trouble keeping up-to-date with network changes, and other distributed and dynamic algorithms have oscillations and stability problems. Ant based routing provides a promising alternative to these approaches. Ant-based routing utilizes mobile software agents (Ants) for network management. These agents are autonomous entities, both proactive and

S.M. Thampi et al. (Eds.): SNDS 2012, CCIS 335, pp. 485–496, 2012.

reactive, and have the capability to adapt, cooperate and move from one location to the other in the MANET.

Ant colony [1-9] provides a number of advantages [10] due to the use of mobile agents and stigmergy (a form of indirect communication used by ants in nature to coordinate their problem-solving activities). It provides scalability, i.e. the population of the agents can be adapted according to the network size. It is fault tolerant, i.e. it does not rely on a centralized control mechanism. Therefore, loss of a few nodes or links does not result in catastrophic failure. Besides this, it provides adaptation, where agents can change, die or reproduce according to the network changes. Speed is achieved, because change in network can be propagated very fast. Agent acts independently of other network layers, so it gives modularity. Also, little or no human supervision is required. So, it provides autonomy. Lastly, it provides parallelism, i.e. agents operate inherently in parallel. These properties make Ant Colony very attractive for MANET. However, one of the biggest difficulties with ant colony algorithms applied in network routing area is that multiple constraints often make the routing problem intractable [11].

The rest of this paper is organized as follows. In section 2, the issues and difficulties for QoS support in MANET has been discussed. Ant colony optimization is described in brief in section 3. Section 4 presents a review of the existing works on ant colony based QoS routing in MANET. We have done a comparative study of these existing schemes in section 5. Finally in section 6, after analyzing the weaknesses of the existing schemes, we present the future scope of research and conclude the paper.

2   QoS Support in MANETs - Issues and Difficulties

Quality of service issues play a very important role for multimedia and real time applications. To achieve better efficiency, some attributes such as delay, bandwidth, probability of packet loss, energy, jitter etc are necessary to be taken into account for routing in MANET and for providing uninterrupted communication between the source and the destination. These are called QoS metrics. There are many difficulties with QoS-aware routing in MANET. These issues are described as follows.

Unpredictable and Unreliable Wireless Channel: MANET is unpredictable as well as unreliable. Here packet collision can occur, signal can fade, interference can occur and multi-path cancellation may exist. These make the measurements of delay, bandwidth unpredictable. A node in the path may be malicious in a MANET and finding malicious nodes in a MANET is a very difficult problem.

Lack of Centralized Control: The ad-hoc network can be formed spontaneously at anywhere any time and the topology can change dynamically. The ad hoc network has no centralized control mechanism. It operates in completely distributed manner. This increases the algorithm's overhead and complexity as QoS requirements have to be considered for the real time and multimedia applications.

Node Mobility: Node mobility creates dynamic topology. The nodes move independently and randomly and the topology information is not fixed. It must be updated frequently to allow the proper delivery of data packets to the destination.

Heterogeneous Nature of MANET: The data rates of links in MANET are not same. If a node with high data rate forwards more traffic to a node with low data rate, then there is chance of congestion, which leads to queuing delay in routers. So, hop by hop congestion control is necessary.

Limited Battery Life: Mobile devices have finite battery sources. So, the QoS routing must consider the battery power and the rate of battery consumption as a QoS constraint and all the QoS routing must be power-aware and power-efficient.

Security: Security is a very important attribute in case of MANET. Without security many unauthorized access can occur and it may violate QoS negotiation.

3   Ant Colony Optimization

The ant colony optimization (ACO) meta-heuristic is a generic problem representation and it adopts real ant's foraging behavior. Ants initially start random walk when multiple paths exist between nest to food. They lay a chemical substance called pheromone during their food searching trip as well as their return trip to the nest. Pheromone serves as route mark, which the ants follow. Newer ants will take that path which has higher pheromone concentration and also the pheromone concentration of that path will increase by the time. This is an autocatalytic effect and this helps the solution to be emerging quickly [1].

Figure 1 illustrates the behavior of ants. A set of ants moves along a straight line from their nest S to a food source D (Figure 1a). At a given moment, an obstacle is put across this way so that side (A) is longer than side (B) (Figure 1b). Now, the ants have to decide which direction they will take: either A or B. The first ones will choose a random direction and will deposit pheromone along their way. The ants taking the way SBD (or DBS), will arrive at the end of the obstacle (depositing more pheromone on their way) before those that take the way SAD (or DAS). So, pheromone intensity of route SBD becomes greater than that of route SAD. Hence, the ants choose the path SBD (Figure 1c).

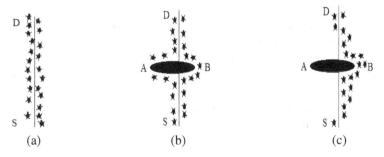

(a)   (b)   (c)

Fig. 1. Behavior of ants for searching the food from S to D

In most cases, an artificial ant will deposit a quantity of pheromone represented by $\Delta\tau_{i,j}$ only after completing their route and not in an incremental way during their advancement. This quantity of pheromone is a function of the found route quality. Pheromone is a volatile substance. An ant changes the amount of pheromone on the path (i, j) when moving from node i to node j as follows:

$$\tau_{i,j} = \sigma.\tau_{i,j} + \Delta\tau_{i,j} \tag{1}$$

Where σ is the pheromone evaporation factor. It must be lower than 1 to avoid pheromone accumulation and premature convergence. At one point i , an ant chooses the point j (i.e. to follow the path (i, j)) according to the following probability:

$$P_{i,j} = \frac{(\tau_{ij})^{\alpha}.(\eta_{ij})^{\beta}}{\sum_{i,k\in C}(\tau_{ik})^{\alpha}.(\eta_{ik})^{\beta}} \tag{2}$$

Where, $\tau_{i,j}$: is the pheromone intensity on path (i, j).
$\eta_{i,j}$: is the ant's visibility field on path (i, j)(an ant assumes that there is food at the end of this path).
α and β : are the parameters which control the relative importance of the pheromone intensity compared to ant's visibility field.
C: represents the set of possible paths starting from point i ((i,k) is a path of C).

4   Review of Existing Works

4.1   Ant Colony Based QoS Routing Algorithm for Mobile Ad Hoc Networks [1]

P.Deepalakshmi, Dr.S.Radhakrishnan proposed an on-demand QoS routing algorithm. This algorithm is highly adaptive in nature and mainly reduces the end to end delay in high mobility cases.

This is a good routing scheme when node mobility is high. Here in route discovery the minimum QoS requirements in terms of bandwidth, delay and hop count are considered. But the other QoS constraints i.e. other network layer or link layer metrics like energy, jitter, link stability etc. are not considered here. Furthermore, here link failure is not handled properly. One disadvantage of TCP is that, it treats the link failure as congestion in the network. This phenomenon is not taken into account here. MANETs are heterogeneous in nature, so data rates are different for each link. Thus, when the source node sends Route_Request_Ant to all its neighbors, it does not take the data rate into account. Hence, flow control between the nodes is not considered here which might cause congestion in the network. Nodes in MANET communicate with each other through a shared medium. Thus, packet collision can occur in

MANET. As a result, packet loss rate is increased, which degrades the throughput. Moreover, interference of channel is not considered separately and admission control is not taken into account which is useful for proper resource utilization.

4.2 Route Failure Management Technique for Ant Based Routing in MANET [2]

S.B.Wankhade, M.S.Ali proposed this on demand routing algorithm. This algorithm is inspired by the ant colony routing algorithm. Route failure management is the main key of this algorithm. Authors have shown that it has good maintenance scheme and it supports good packet delivery ratio (PDR) with less packet drop and can achieve less delay in comparison with ANTHOCNET.

In this technique, at the time of route discovery, only delay, bandwidth, hop count, PDR are taken into account but other network layer metrics or link layer metrics like throughput, jitter, node buffer size etc. are not taken into consideration. Here, in route updation phase, multiple routes are found and in maintenance phase, fuzzy logic is used to find Link Stability Coefficient. So, a small overhead is involved with route updation in some time interval. Furthermore, here flow control is not handled explicitly, so when source generates HANT it does not takes into account the data rate of the link in heterogeneous MANET. Packet collision and channel interference also are not considered. The computation of fuzzy logic in the node may cause premature death to the nodes due to the limited energy of the nodes. For real time and multimedia communication only improvement of packet delivery ratio is not sufficient, because end to end delay, processing delay at each node and also other QoS constraints affects the throughput.

4.3 Ant Colony Based Routing for Mobile Ad-Hoc Networks towards Improved Quality of Services [3]

B. Roy, S. Banik, P. Dey, S. Sanyal and N. Chaki proposed this new QoS on-demand routing algorithm for mobile ad hoc network. This algorithm is based on link state routing and supports multimedia communication with both reactive and proactive components.

As it is a hybrid technique, so there is a significant amount of overhead involved. Furthermore, it only considers the QoS metrics like delay, bandwidth, but other network layer or link layer metrics are not taken into account. Here the individual nodes require more power and they have greater overhead for processing and storing. As here proactive strategy is used for continuous monitoring of the path, overhead is increased. In this work, packet loss rate is not taken into account, which is extremely necessary for multimedia applications. As it uses proactive procedure, so, the resources may not be utilized properly. This affects the admission control.

4.4   Ant Based Dynamic Source Routing Protocol to Support Multiple Quality of Service (QoS) Metrics in Mobile Ad Hoc Networks [4]

R. Asokan, A. M. Natarajan and C. Venkatesh have proposed this method. Here the QoS requirements such as delay, jitter and energy are taken into account. It performs well in route discovery phase with dynamically changing topology and produces better throughput with low delay variance.

This algorithm performs well in case of dynamically changing topology. But it considers only some of the network layer metrics like delay, jitter, energy and throughput. But, only these constraints are not sufficient for real time applications as other network layer or MAC layer metrics are also necessary. In this routing protocol the packet header size is increased with increasing route length due to its source routing nature. Consequently, the routing overhead is also increased. Again flooding of route request may potentially reach all nodes in the network, so bandwidth wastage increases and efficiency degrades. Besides this, it is a collision and contention prone routing protocol. Thus, packet delivery ratio decreases, congestion increases and throughput also become very poor in case of multimedia communication.

4.5   An Optimized Ant Colony Algorithm Based on the Gradual Changing Orientation Factor for Multi-constraint QoS Routing [5]

Hua Wang, Zhao Shi, Anfeng Ge, Chaoying Yu have proposed this method. This concept deals with the problem of QoS routing by adding an orientation heuristic factor to the conventional ant colony algorithm, which enables the ant to get rid of the blindness at the initial stage of path searching. The ant in the modified algorithm not only makes use of the previous search findings, but also reduces the misguiding effect of pheromones on the irrelevant paths, thus overcoming the problem of slow convergence. This algorithm modifies the ant colony optimization algorithm by adding gradual changing orientation factor and applies this to solve multi constraint QoS-aware routing problem.

It is a very complex routing algorithm which involves the complex calculation of the gradual changing orientation factor. Here route failure problem in TCP is not taken care of. Congestion is only taken into account in terms of packet delivery ratio. The most important is the node processing power, as this protocol requires complex calculations. But it does not take into account the individual nodes energy to obtain optimal energy. Furthermore, flow control of the heterogeneous MANET is not considered separately here. Admission control in terms of resource utilization is not stated and also contention, collision and interference are not considered. Therefore, it is not sufficient for achieving better throughput for real time applications.

4.6   Ant Colony Optimization for Routing in Mobile Ad-Hoc Networks [6]

S. Kanan, T. Kalaikumaran, S. Kartik and V. P. Arunachalam proposed this method. It is a multi agent ant based routing algorithm for MANET. This is a new technique which increases the connectivity of the nodes during high node mobility and for this the QoS constraints like delay is decreased and packet delivery ratio (PDR) is increased.

It mainly focuses on the node mobility by only supporting QoS requirements like delay, PDR etc. which is not sufficient for multimedia application. Other network and link layer metrics have to be considered. There are various other issues. This algorithm uses both proactive and reactive routing. Paths are monitored always, so the overhead is increased in routing. It does not take into account the heterogeneous MANET behavior, where the data rate of each link can be different, so flow control is necessary, which is not noticed here. Consequently, there is a lack of Congestion control. Moreover, in MAC layer as nodes communicate through the shared medium, hence, there is a chance of collision, contention and interference. These problems are not taken into account in this algorithm. Furthermore admission control is not tackled properly for better throughput and efficiency.

4.7   The Efficient Ant Routing Protocol for MANET [7]

Srinivas Sethi and Siba K.Udgata proposed this novel meta-heuristic on-demand routing protocol Ant-E, using the Blocking Expanding Ring Search (Blocking-ERS) to control the overhead and local retransmission for improving the reliability in terms of packet delivery ratio (PDR). This algorithm offers improved efficiency, robustness and reliability by using blocking-ERS and local retransmission by reducing the QoS constraints like end to end delay, packet delivery ratio (PDR).

This is an efficient routing technique in terms of route discovery, but it only considers the QoS requirements – delay and PDR, which cannot give better throughput without considering the other network layer or MAC layer QoS metrics. Besides this, it does not use proactive routing and if route failure occurs, then source need to reinitiate the route discovery procedure, which is a time consuming procedure. Congestion control is taken care of in terms of PDR, but flow control is not taken into account, which can increase congestion in the link and degrade the network performance. Here, admission control is also not handled properly. Besides this, the problem of TCP where link failure is treated as congestion, is not overcome properly.

4.8   Multipath Dynamic Source Routing with Cost and Ant Colony Optimization for MANETS [8]

It is a concept to support the reliability as a QoS metric through multipath routing. The Enhanced Multipath Dynamic Source Routing (EMP-DSR) is improved with fuzzy cost mechanism. Here the QoS constraints like bandwidth, hop count, delay and energy are considered during route discovery process. The system provides the user choice-based route discovery.

As this is a multi-path routing, it supports the dynamic topology and it is highly adaptive. But it only takes care of the QoS constraints such as delay, energy and bandwidth, whereas other metrics of network layer or link layer are not considered. Here route failure problem in TCP is not taken care of. Fuzzy logic is used as improvement in routing protocol, but implementing fuzzy logic requires more processing delay in the nodes. The most important is the node processing power, as this protocol requires complex calculations. Moreover, flow control of the heterogeneous MANET is not considered separately and admission control in terms of resource utilization is not stated. So, it is not sufficient for achieving better throughput for real time applications.

4.9   An Ant Colony-Based Multi Objective Quality of Service Routing for Mobile Ad Hoc Networks [9]

P. Deepalakshmi and S. asundaram Radhakrishnan proposed AMQR, an ant-based multi-objective on-demand QoS routing algorithm for mobile ad hoc network. Here QoS metrics like delay, bandwidth and hop count are considered during route discovery. Link failure can be detected quickly as node uses updated view of the network with positive and negative feedback.

As it is a multi-path routing algorithm, therefore, it supports node mobility in a better way. The main drawback of this approach is, at the time of route discovery, it only considers delay, throughput and jitter as the QoS metrics but other network layer or MAC layer metrics are not considered for achieving more stable route and high throughput. Furthermore, congestion issues like flow control in the network are not considered and packets may be lost due to the absence of proper flow control mechanism. Also, admission control and resource utilization are not taken into account. Lastly, the MAC layer collision is not considered, which causes the degradation of efficiency of the network.

5   Comparative Study of the Existing Schemes

MANET is dynamic in nature and its topology is not fixed. So, for supporting real time or multimedia applications, demand of QoS-aware routing is increasing. Hence, the routing algorithms have to support all possible QoS constraints for achieving better throughput. But this increases the overhead of the routing protocols. It is very hard to manage or balance all the constraints. Algorithm [1] is highly adaptive and it performs well in the high mobility cases. In comparison, algorithm [9] also guarantees good performance in the high mobility cases along with positive and negative feedback and randomness in routing. Thus, in addition, it ensures quick link failure prediction, although they both use same QoS metrics. Algorithm [1] and algorithm [8] both are highly adaptive, but the plus point of algorithm [8] is that, node energy is considered here and fuzzy logic is used for route selection and cost estimation of the route. Algorithms [6, 7] consider PDR as QoS metric but do not take into account the hop count and bandwidth. Algorithm [2] uses fuzzy logic for link failure management but does not take into consideration the energy of the nodes. Whereas algorithm [7] uses fuzzy logic in route discovery phase and additionally considers individual node energy for increased network lifetime. On the other hand, in algorithm [9] link failure

Table 1. Use of different QoS metrics by the existing ANT based QoS routing schemes

ROUTING PROTOCOLS	End to End delay	Bandwidth	Packet Delivery Ratio	Energy	Jitter	Hop Count	Link expiration time	Throughput
Ant Colony Based QoS Routing Algorithm for Mobile Ad Hoc Networks	✓	✓				✓		
Route Failure Management Technique for Ant Based Routing in MANET	✓	✓	✓			✓		
Ant Colony based Routing for Mobile Ad-Hoc Networks towards Improved Quality of Services	✓	✓					✓	
Ant Based Dynamic Source Routing Protocol to Support Multiple Quality of Service (QoS) Metrics in Mobile Ad Hoc Networks	✓			✓	✓			✓
An Optimized Ant Colony Algorithm based on the Gradual Changing Orientation Factor for Multi-constraint QoS Routing	✓	✓	✓			✓		
Ant Colony Optimization for Routing in Mobile Ad-Hoc Networks	✓		✓					
The Efficient Ant Routing Protocol for MANET	✓		✓					
Multipath Dynamic Source Routing with Cost and Ant Colony Optimization for MANETS	✓	✓		✓		✓		
An Ant Colony-based Multi Objective Quality of Service Routing for Mobile Ad hoc Networks	✓	✓	✓		✓	✓		

is detected quickly by using the positive feedback, negative feedback and randomness. Algorithm [3] uses optimized link state routing and basically maintains stable route between source and the destinations. It considers link expiration time which is a very important parameter that the other algorithms do not consider. Algorithm [4] is based on ADSR and it considers throughput. But in case of this approach, packet header size increases with the route length as source routing is used and bandwidth is lost due to flooding. Other algorithms do not suffer from this problem. Also this algorithm is more contention and collision prone in comparison to other algorithms. Algorithm [5] is based on ACO meta-heuristics like other algorithms but the difference is that it calculates gradual changing orientation factor which guarantees the quick convergence. But here greater node processing capacity is required and for this, energy of nodes plays a vital role. But the energy metric is not taken into account here like algorithm [4, 8]. Algorithm [6] and algorithm [7] both consider the metric delay and PDR. Algorithm [6] emphasizes only on node mobility and connectivity of dynamic MANET whereas algorithm [7] emphasizes on reliability, robustness and efficiency by using blocking-ERS. They both do not consider the other QoS metrics which are necessary for the real time communication. Algorithm [8] is multi-path DSR based on fuzzy logic. Here energy is taken into account for optimizing the power and path is selected based on cost factor, which is different from the other algorithms. But other QoS metrics are not considered here in comparison to the other routing algorithms. Lastly, algorithm [9] is nearly the same as algorithm [1] except that it guarantees quick discovery of link failure but here also the other necessary QoS constraints are not considered.

6   Conclusion and Future Work

Algorithm [1] is suitable for high node mobility scenario. But it uses only bandwidth, delay and hop count as the QoS constraints which are not sufficient for real time and multimedia communication. So, other QoS constraints can be incorporated into this algorithm to make it more efficient. Besides this, as TCP considers link failure as congestion, therefore, it is a big problem to distinguish between congestion and link failure. Hence, we need to introduce a new mechanism to avoid this problem. MANETs are heterogeneous in nature, i.e. data rate cannot remain same for all the links. Thus, if a high data rate node forwards more traffic to a low data rate node, there is a chance of congestion. This increases queuing delay which needs to be avoided. Hence, proper flow control is necessary. In order to handle this, data rate, buffer queuing delay, link quality and MAC overhead can be taken into consideration. The node buffer space is another important factor which plays a vital role for congestion control in the network, because if a node's buffer in an active routing path is overflowed by the packets then packet loss increases, which degrades the throughput of the network. Hence, this also needs to be taken into consideration. Besides this, link stability can be considered, because for multimedia communication, a stable connection is necessary. In addition to this, other network layer, link layer and MAC layer metrics can be taken into account to avoid packet collision, contention and interference problem. Along with this, a proper admission control facility can be incorporated to enhance resource utilization.

Algorithm [2] emphasizes link failure management and fuzzy logic is used to maintain the path. Here congestion control is tackled with the metric PDR, but it alone is not sufficient for better throughput. Data rate, buffer queuing delay, node buffer space etc. can be incorporated within this algorithm for better flow control. In this approach, nodes need high processing power; therefore, energy metric can be incorporated to optimize the power for increased system lifetime. In addition to this, other network layer and MAC layer metrics can be added to avoid collision, contention and interference. Admission control must also be taken into account.

Algorithm [3] is a hybrid routing algorithm. Here a stable path is always maintained considering the metrics delay, bandwidth and link expiration time. But these are not sufficient for achieving better throughput and efficiency. So, other network layer and link layer metrics need to be incorporated. For example, in order to control congestion - node buffer space and queuing delay can be considered. Proper flow control mechanism is also necessary due to the heterogeneous nature of the network. Besides this, the MAC layer problems like channel contention, packet collision and interference need to be tackled.

Algorithm [4] is an on demand routing algorithm based on DSR. Here delay, energy, jitter and throughput are taken into account. But, only these constraints are not sufficient for better efficiency. So, other metrics need to be incorporated. The problem with DSR is that here flooding is used and consequently the bandwidth wastage increases, so, some mechanism to control the flooding should be incorporated. Besides this, the protocol is collision and contention prone. Hence, some of the MAC layer metrics can be considered here to reduce the problems. Link failure management can be made better and congestion and flow control mechanism can be incorporated considering PDR, buffer space etc.

Algorithm [5] is based on ACO and it calculates gradual changing orientation factor to achieve quick convergence. It considers delay, bandwidth, jitter and packet delivery ratio (PDR) as QoS metrics. For better congestion control and flow control, metrics like data rate, buffer space and queuing delay can be considered. Link failure management also needs to be made better. Admission control can be improved and other network layer or MAC layer metrics can be included to tackle the problems of MAC layer and for achieving better throughput.

Algorithm [6] emphasizes on the connectivity of the nodes in high mobility cases. As a result, the overhead increases. Here, only delay and PDR are considered but these are not sufficient and other network and MAC layer metrics need to be included to avoid the MAC layer collision, contention and interference problem. Energy of individual nodes have to be considered because this algorithm has high overhead of performing five steps. Congestion can be controlled using the PDR but other metrics like the buffer space of node and data rate can be incorporated also for better flow control. Proper resource utilization also needs to be ensured.

Algorithm [7] uses blocking-ERS to increase efficiency, reliability and throughput. It only considers end to end delay and PDR as QoS constraints. But the problems of congestion control, flow control and admission control need to be considered here by incorporating other QoS metrics. Besides this, link failure management can be improved by tackling the drawback of TCP. MAC layer problems also can be avoided by including the MAC layer metrics in this protocol.

Algorithm [8] is a multi-path routing algorithm. Route discovery of this algorithm is based on fuzzy cost estimation and here delay, bandwidth, energy and hop count are taken into account as the QoS metrics. Links are continuously updated according to the dynamic topology and in case of high mobility scenarios, the routing overhead increases due to its multi-path nature. This problem can be tackled by using reactive mechanism. Here link failure management can be improved also by using fuzzy logic and congestion can be controlled by considering PDR, node buffer size, data rate etc. which also controls the flow of packets in the network. Resource utilization can be handled properly by incorporating admission control.

Algorithm [9] is a multi-path routing algorithm which considers only delay, bandwidth and hop count and here link failure is detected very quickly. But like algorithm [1] it has some deficiencies which can be avoided by considering the other QoS metrics of network and link layers, improving congestion control, flow control, admission control and by controlling the MAC layer problems of contention, collision and interference.

In this paper, we present a review of the current research related to the provision of QoS in an ad hoc networking environment. We discuss issues involved in providing QoS in an ad hoc network. From the above discussion regarding the existing and recent works, we can conclude that although, many techniques have been proposed based on ant systems for QoS routing in ad hoc network, still, there are many weaknesses in the above mentioned schemes. Therefore, further research needs to be done in order to eliminate these weaknesses and for designing a new and more efficient QoS based routing algorithm for MANET.

References

1. Deepalakshmi, P., Radhakrishnan, S.: Ant Colony Based QoS Routing Algorithm for Mobile Ad Hoc Networks. International Journal of Recent Trends in Engineering 1(1), 459–462 (2009)
2. Wankhade, S.B., Ali, M.S.: Route Failure Management Technique for Ant Based Routing in MANET. International Journal of Scientific & Engineering Research 2(9) (2011)
3. Roy, B., Banik, S., Dey, P., Sanyal, S., Chaki, N.: Ant Colony based Routing for Mobile Ad-Hoc Networks towards Improved Quality of Services. Journal of Emerging Trends in Computing and Information Sciences 3(1) (2012)
4. Asokan, R., Natarajan, A.M., Venkatesh, C.: Ant Based Dynamic Source Routing Protocol to Support Multiple Quality of Service (QoS) Metrics in Mobile Ad Hoc Networks. International Journal of Computer Science and Security 2(3) (2008)
5. Wang, H., Shi, Z., Ge, A., Yu, C.: An optimized ant colony algorithm based on the gradual changing orientation factor for multi-constraint QoS routing. Computer Communications (2008)
6. Kannan, S., Kalaikumaran, T., Karthik, S., Arunachalam, V.P.: Ant Colony Optimization for Routing in Mobile Ad-Hoc Networks. International Journal of Soft Computing 5(6), 223–228 (2010)
7. Sethi, S., Udgata, S.K.: The Efficient Ant Routing Protocol for MANET. International Journal on Computer Science and Engineering 02(07), 2414–2420 (2010)
8. Sarala, P., Kalaiselvi, D.: Multipath Dynamic Source Routing with Cost and Ant Colony Optimization for MANETS. International Journal of Applied Engineering Research 1(1) (2010)
9. Deepalakshmi, P., Radhakrishnan, S.: An ant colony-based multi objective quality of service routing for mobile ad hoc networks. EURASIP Journal on Wireless Communications and Networking (2011)
10. Kassabalidis, I., El-Sharkawi, M.A., Marks, R.J., Arabshahi, P., Gray, A.A.: Swarm Intelligence for Routing in Communication Networks. In: IEEE Globecom (2002)
11. Mirabedini, S.J., Teshnehlab, M., Shenasa, M.H., Movaghar, A., Rahmani, A.M.: AFAR: Adaptive fuzzy ant based routing for communication networks. Journal of Zhejiang University Science A 9(12), 1666–1675 (2008)

Efficient Weighted *i*nnovative Routing Protocol (EW*i*RP) to Balance Load in Mobile Ad Hoc Networks (MANETs): Simulation and Feasibility Analysis

Nitin Goel[1], Shruti Sangwan[2], and Ajay Jangra[2]

[1] Associate-Solutions, Decimal Technologies Pvt. Ltd., Gurgaon, Haryana, India
[2] CSE Department, UIET, Kurukshetra University, Kurukshetra, Haryana, India
`{goelnitin0887,ssshrutisangwan8}@gmail.com,`
`er_jangra@yahoo.co.in`

Abstract. Mobile Ad Hoc Networks (MANETs) are vulnerable to having their optimality in variety of operations and calculations, compromised by various challenges. After an analysis on MANET routing, a load balancing and resource aware routing protocol is proposed which evaluates the routes with node's residual energy, load information and computes delay along multiple paths for different service classes of the network? In this paper the evaluation results are presented that demonstrate the operation of Efficient Weighted *i*nnovative Routing Protocol (EW*i*RP) in mobile ad hoc environments. Simulations with EW*i*RP over AODV (single path) and MAODV (multipath), shows that the proposed scheme has a potential to improve performance significantly with respect to the aggregated throughput, jitter, end to end delay and delivery ratio. The proposed EW*i*RP algorithm intended for a variety of scenarios without much control overhead as the simulation study is performed by taking 25 and 50 nodes over different grid areas.

Keywords: Mobile Ad-hoc Networks (MANETs), Load Balancing, EW*i*RP, Clustering, Authentication.

1 Introduction to MANETs

Advances in mobile processing platforms, small sized equipments and wireless technologies have stimulated mobile ad-hoc NETworks (MANET) where without the requirement of a statically deployed network infrastructure, MANET units can autonomously organize in a peer-to-peer mode. These special features of MANET bring great opportunities together with severe challenges like routing efficiency, trustworthiness, security, effective resource utilization being the primary challenges to be met. In such environments, it is desirable to adopt a routing scheme which can dynamically disperse traffic load, provide security and efficient routing to the network by effectively utilizing the network vital resources.

With this insight, our protocol has put emphasis on three factors: First is, the malicious, selfish and unauthenticated entities violate the protocols and disrupt the communication either actively or passively. To avoid such scenarios the identity of a

S.M. Thampi et al. (Eds.): SNDS 2012, CCIS 335, pp. 497–506, 2012.

node must be verified before allowing it to participate in the network operations. Secondly, to support diverse applications, it is an absolute essentiality for mobile ad hoc networks to have a quality of service mechanism, efficient resource usage and utilization of the available limited amount of energy in deploying the network in the most efficient way .The network performance might be improved if the network is clustered more proficiently by grouping together nodes that are in close proximity via efficient clustering scheme. Thirdly, the lifetime of a network is a key design factor of mobile ad-hoc networks (MANETs). To prolong the lifetime of MANETs, there is a requirement to attain the tradeoff of minimizing the energy consumption and load balancing. [1,2,4]

2   Related Work

Efficient Weighted innovative Routing Protocol (EW*i*RP) begins with search for multiple paths in the view of balancing load, by effectively using the bandwidth of the connections through *Bw_Req* and *Bw_avl* fields in routing packets. The EW*i*RP_RnR table reduces the overhead and stores this bandwidth information at a node. The allocation and reservation mechanism imparts QoS to the overall scheme. The preference and quality of all the feasible paths b/w a source and destination pair is computed using time delay (TD_P), residual energy (RE_P) and network interface queue status ($NIQS_P$) along a path P, as the basic parameters, which makes the overall approach, a weighted approach. The weight of a path will be high if the nodes on it possess high energy, cause lesser delay and have larger queue space available. The various concepts, i.e. the effect of type of data entering the network on path selection, switch to secondary paths when primary degrades, EW*i*RP_RnR table at nodes give an advanced view of MANET routing. [1,3,13]

2.1   EWiRP Packets and RnR Table [3]:

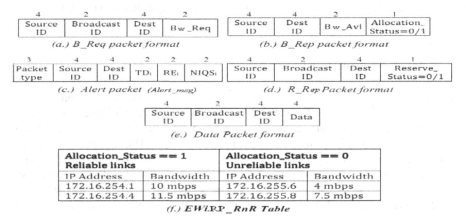

(f.) EWiRP_RnR Table

Fig. 1. (a-e) The packets used to establish paths and for communication between source and destination. (f.) RnR table to be maintained at every node, to store the available bandwidths of nodes in vicinity and categorize them as reliable (R) and unreliable (nR).

2.2   EWiRP (Efficient Weighted *i*nnovative Routing Protocol): Proposed Protocol [3]

```
1) Source node broadcasts B_Req with Bw_Req=B to neighbors j
2) For every j,
   if (Bj>=B+λ)  //set λ according to network parameters//
     a.) Compute avg(MIN_B, MAX_B)
     b.) Set allocate_B= avg(MIN_B, MAX_B)
     c.) Unicast B_Rep with allocate_status==1 and Bw_Avl=Bj

   else, Unicast B_Rep with allocate_status==0 and Bw_Avl=Bj
3) Source node forwards Alert_msg to selected links
4) if (DestID==D)
   then        goto 5
   else        goto 1 // intermediate node will act as source//
5) Wait for period k, receive all Alert_msg
     a.)   Compute weight, Wp
     b.)   Maintain Priority_queue
     c.)   for every p ∈ Priority_queue, generate R_Rep
     d.)   Update the Priority_queue
6) if   (Error msg||(Df<0))
            Select the next path p ∈ Priority_queue
     else   Continue sending data along primary path
```

Multiple feasible paths with acceptable weight values will be stored in a *Priority_queue* at destination, according to their preference (higher the weight, high will be the preference). Degradation factor (*Df*) is used as a path evaluator, to estimate worth or quality of the active path. So the source node will opt for a secondary path if primary breaks or degrades. A node effectively utilizes the link bandwidth by using the links as per the available and required link bandwidth instead of selecting the paths randomly. EWiRP_RnR Table guarantees the optimum use of bandwidth and ensures efficient use of node's energy by selecting the most pertinent link for communication. Whenever a request for a path arises, it carries its bandwidth requirement with it. [1,3]

2.3   EWiRP (Efficient Weighted *innovative* Routing Protocol): Process

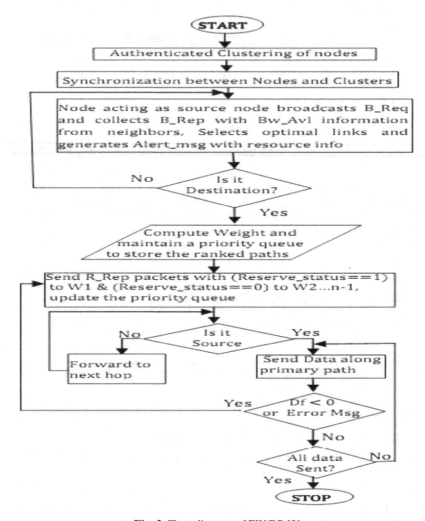

Fig. 2. Flow diagram of EWiRP [3]

3   Simulation

Efficient Weighted innovative Routing Protocol (EWiRP) is simulated on Network Simulator II (NS2), version 2.34 over Linux Operating System. To analyze the feasibility of EWiRP for all possible MANETs environments, it is simulated under two network scenarios, one network consists of 25 nodes and other consists of 50 nodes. Protocols used for both networks scenario are AODV (single path) and MAODV (multipath) with grid areas for each scenario are 1000*500 and 1000*1000.

Fig. 3 shows the simulated network scenario of EWiRP consists of 25 nodes under grid area 1000*500. This network illustrates how formation of clusters can be done;

process of packets sent, received and dropped; formation of multipath along with clusters on the bases of calculated weight for each path with mobility of nodes.

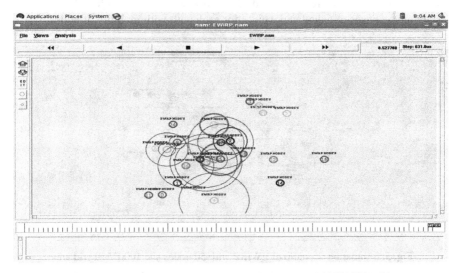

Fig. 3. Simulation Scenario of EW*i*RP with 25 nodes and 1000*500 grid area

Fig. 4 shows the simulated network scenario of EW*i*RP consists of 25 nodes under grid area 1000*1000. This network illustrates how formation of clusters can be done; process of packets sent, received and dropped; formation of multipath along with clusters on the bases of calculated weight for each path with mobility of nodes.

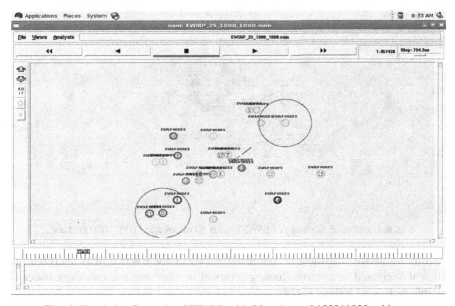

Fig. 4. Simulation Scenario of EW*i*RP with 25 nodes and 1000*1000 grid area

Fig. 5 shows the simulated network scenario of EWiRP consists of 50 nodes under grid area 1000*500. This network illustrates how formation of clusters can be done; process of packets sent, received and dropped; formation of multipath along with clusters on the bases of calculated weight for each path with mobility of nodes.

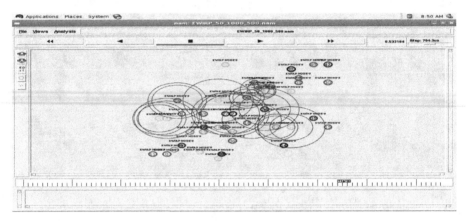

Fig. 5. Simulation Scenario of EWiRP with 50 nodes and 1000*500 grid area

Fig. 6 shows the simulated network scenario of EWiRP consists of 50 nodes under grid area 1000*1000. This network illustrates how formation of clusters can be done; process of packets sent, received and dropped; formation of multipath along with clusters on the bases of calculated weight for each path with mobility of nodes.

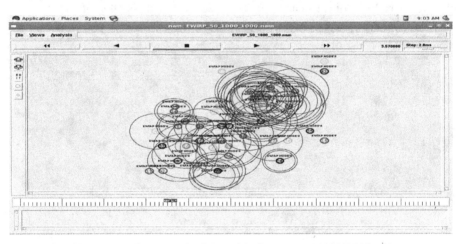

Fig. 6. Simulation Scenario of EWiRP with 50 nodes and 1000*1000 grid area

From the above snapshots of simulated networks for EWiRP, it is analyzed that Efficient Weighted innovative Routing protocol is adaptable and can work under all possible mobile ad hoc networks.

4   Results and Important Findings

Results calculation and evaluation of EW*i*RP is done by taking some network parameters i.e. throughput, jitter, packets sent and packets drop and after introducing clustering, authentication and load balancing scheme in EW*i*RP, it is analyzed that EW*i*RP gives optimal results in the form all network parameters discussed above.

Graph 1 shows results of network parameters (Throughput, Jitter, Packets sent and Packets drop) for the network of 25 nodes with 1000*500 grid area.

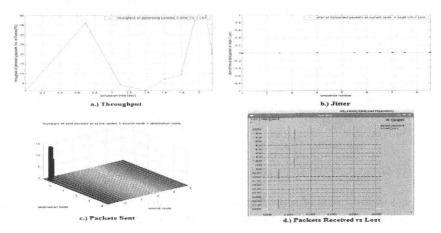

Graph 1. Results for the network of 25 nodes with 1000*500 grid area

Graph 2 shows results of network parameters (Throughput, Jitter, Packets sent and Packets drop) for the network of 25 nodes with 1000*1000 grid area.

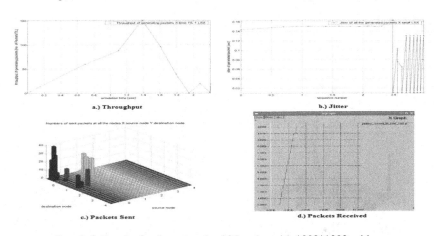

Graph 2. Results for the network of 25 nodes with 1000*1000 grid area

Graph 3 shows results of network parameters (Throughput, Jitter, Packets sent and Packets drop) for the network of 50 nodes with 1000*500 grid area.

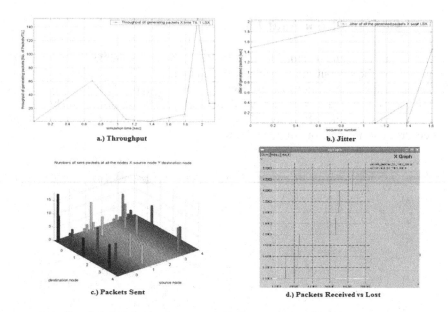

a.) Throughput

b.) Jitter

c.) Packets Sent

d.) Packets Received vs Lost

Graph 3. Results for the network of 50 nodes with 1000*500 grid area

Graph 4 shows results of network parameters (Throughput, Jitter, Packets sent and Packets drop) for the network of 50 nodes with 1000*1000 grid area.

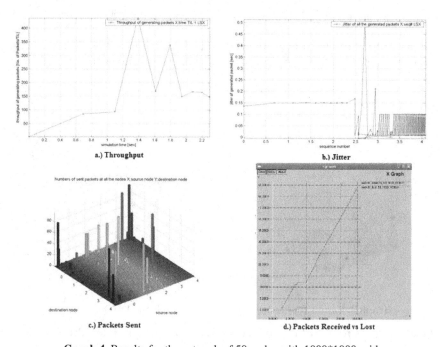

a.) Throughput

b.) Jitter

c.) Packets Sent

d.) Packets Received vs Lost

Graph 4. Results for the network of 50 nodes with 1000*1000 grid area

5   Conclusion

In this paper we presented and discussed a simulation study of proposed load balancing mechanism called EW*i*RP, which applies adaptive load balancing to utilize network resource more efficiently and minimizes congestion. EW*i*RP can co-operate with different routing protocols i.e. with single path (AODV) as well as with multipath (MAODV). The simulation results show that performance gains are significant in terms of aggregated throughput, jitter, end to end delay and delivery ratio which considerably prove the routing strength and optimality of EW*i*RP in MANETs. The proposed protocol is load, energy and delays aware, so can evenly distribute traffic, minimizes delay and improves node lifetime. To evaluate the validity of the proposed protocol it is implemented with AODV and MAODV. From the simulation results obtained, EW*i*RP yields robustness, availability and reliability that best suit any scalable and dynamic mobile ad hoc environment.

6   Future Scope

Under Water Mobile Networks could be an area where the deployment of mobile ad hoc networks will set new trends in technology. Till now, the research in the field of mobile ad hoc networks (MANETs) has mainly focused on wireless medium in air wave only. The study of wireless communication underwater poses several challenges. The future approach will be to study those factors like error rates, collision interference, bandwidth constraints, and power limitations which pose new challenges in network control.

Mobile ad-hoc networks can use mobile routers to provide Internet connectivity to mobile ad-hoc users. So, *Access to Internet through* EW*i*RP is the future area of research, especially in the design of higher level protocols for routing and in implementing applications with quality of service requirements and to implement test studies. Ensuring security in MANETs require the *Study/Detection of all the Unknown Threats.* The deployment of such networks in different environments and identifying different, undetected attacks gives a scope for future work.

References

[1] Jangra, A., Goel, N., Priyanka: Efficient Power Saving Adaptive Routing Protocol (EPSAR) for MANETs using AODV and DSDV: Simulation and Feasibility Analysis, 978-0-7695-4498-4/11© 2011 IEEE, doi 10.1109/IPTC.2011.13

[2] Caballero-Gil, P., Caballero-Gil, C., Molina-Gil, J., Quesada-Arencibia, A.: A Simulation Study of New Security Schemes in Mobile Ad-Hoc NETworks. In: Moreno Díaz, R., Pichler, F., Quesada Arencibia, A. (eds.) EUROCAST 2007. LNCS, vol. 4739, pp. 73–81. Springer, Heidelberg (2007)

[3] Goel, N., Sangwan, S., Jangra, A.: Efficient Weighted innovative Routing Protocol (EW*i*RP) to Balance Load in Mobile Ad Hoc Networks (MANETs). In: ICAESM 2012, Chennai, India, ISBN: 978-81-909042-2-3 ©2012, IEEE

[4] Chatterjee, N., Potluri, A., Negi, A.: A Self-Organising Approach to MANET Clustering

[5] Tekaya, M., Tabbane, N., Tabbane, S.: Multipath Routing Mechanism and Load balancing in Ad hoc networks, 978-1-4244-7042-6/10 ©2010 IEEE

[6] Saghir, M., Wan, T.-C., Budiarto, R.: Load Balancing QoS Multicast Routing Protocol in Mobile Ad Hoc Networks. In: Cho, K., Jacquet, P. (eds.) AINTEC 2005. LNCS, vol. 3837, pp. 83–97. Springer, Heidelberg (2005)

[7] Chen, X., Jones, H.M., Jayalath, A.D.S.: Congestion-Aware Routing Protocol for Mobile Ad Hoc Networks, 1-4244-0264-6/07 ©2010 IEEE

[8] Sangwan, S., Goel, N., Jangra, A.: Robust Authenticated Clustering Strategies for Mobile Ad hoc Networks (MANETs). IJARCS 2(4), 160–164 (2011)

[9] Bannack, A., Albini, L.C.P.: Investigating the Load Balance of Multipath Routing to Increase the Lifetime of a MANET, 978-1-4244-1708-7/08 ©2008 IEEE

[10] Clin, Y., Wen, Y.Y., Ang, H.Y., Gwee, C.L.: A Routing Protocol with Energy and Traffic Balance Awareness in Wireless Ad hoc Networks, 1-4244-0983-7/07 ©2007 IEEE

[11] Siva Kumar, P., Duraiswamy, K.: A QoS Routing Protocol for Mobile Ad hoc Networks based on the Load Distribution, 978-1-4244-5967-4/10 ©2010 IEEE

[12] Xu, J., Zhu, X.C.: A Load-Balancing and Energy-Aware Routing Protocol for MANET Accessing Internet. In: Eighth IEEE International Conference (2009)

[13] Rani, A., Dave, M.: Weighted Load Balanced Routing Protocol for MANET, 978-1-4244-3805-1/08 ©2008 IEEE

[14] Rong, B., Kadoch, M.: Achieve load Balancing and Avoid Bandwidth Fragmentation in MANET QoS routing, 0-7803-8886-0/05 ©2005 IEEE

Author Index

Abidi, Amine 85
Abraham, Jobin 110
Achuthan, Krishnasree 168
Aggarwal, Alok 240
Aiello, Maurizio 195
Akira, Ailton Shinoda 23
Amberker, B.B. 11, 135
Anitha, Ramalingam 272
Araújo, Nelcileno 23
Asawa, Krishna 205
Ashok, Aravind 168
Ayed, Ghazi Ben 85

Balan, C. 225
Balasundaram, Keerthi 408
Banerjee, Subhashis 372, 396
Baruntar, Sudhanshu 35
Bhargava, Bharat 23
Bica, Ion 293
Bouffard, Guillaume 185

Cabaj, Krzysztof 283
Cambiaso, Enrico 195
Chandavale, Anjali Avinash 97, 323
Chatterjee, Madhumita 466
Chaudhuri, Sheli Sinha 347
Chelliah, Balan 234
Chitra, M.T. 314
Chowdhury, Ananya 444

Darji, Monika 54
Das, Achintya 347
Das, Ashok Kumar 1
Das, Sanjoy 147
Deepthi, T.R. 225
de Oliveira, Ruy 23
Dey, Nilanjan 347
Digeser, Philipp 385
Dija, S. 225

Ferreira, Ed' Wilson Tavares 23

Geetha, Angelina 252
Ghita, Stefan-Vladimir 293
Goel, Himanshu 205

Goel, Nitin 497
Goswami, Adrijit 1

Hemalatha, M. 157
Hidhaya, S. Fouzul 252

Ibrahim, Mohd Izham 336

Jangra, Ajay 497
Jantan, Aman 336
Jayanna, H.S. 127
John, Jinu Elizabeth 75

Kamoun, Farouk 85
Keshava, Ashima 358, 432
Klemm, Martin 385
Kolaczek, Grzegorz 283
Konorski, Jerzy 283
Kotulski, Zbigniew 283
Krishnan, Deepa 466
Kumar, Adarsh 240

Lanet, Jean-Louis 185
Lobiyal, Daya Krishan 147
Luthra, Ankit 205

Mahalingam, P.R. 264
Majumder, Koushik 372, 396, 485
Manghat, Srikumar 117
Mattam, Manjunath 45
Mishra, Dheerendra 304
Mishra, Prashant Kumar 35
Mukhopadhyay, Sourav 304
Muthulakshmi, Angamuthu 272

Nagaraja, B.G. 127
Nallusamy, Rajarathnam 178
Nascimento, Valtemir 23

Odelu, Vanga 1

Pacyna, Piotr 283
Pais, Alwyn Roshan 456
Papaleo, Gianluca 195
Patra, Gopal K. 422
Patriciu, Victor-Valeriu 293
Paul, Varghese 110

Poornachandran, Prabaharan   75, 168,
    215
Princy, Krishnan   272
Priya, R.   314
Purushothama, B.R.   11, 135

Rahman, Azri H.A.   336
Rasmi, Mohammad   336
Raso Mattos, Lucas Rodrigo   178
Raw, Ram Shringar   147
Ray, Utpal Kumar   444
Razafindralambo, Tiana   185
Remya Ajai, A.S.   75, 215
Revathy, P.   358, 432
Rohini, S.   272
Roy, Anamitra Bardhan   347

Sahoo, Debasish   64
Sangwan, Shruti   497
Santhanalakshmi, S.   422
Sapkal, A.   97, 323
Sarukesi, K.   358, 408, 432
Saurabh, Praneet   474
Sensarma, Debajit   485
Shabana, P.   234

Sharma, Sambhav   205
Sharma, Sanjeev   474
Sherly, Elizabeth   314
Shirisha, Kusuma   135
Sikora, Axel   385
Singh, Kunwar   35
Srinivasan, Madhan Kumar   358, 408,
    432
Sruthi, P.V.   215
Sudarshan, T.S.B.   422
Szalachowski, Pawel   283

Tataram, Adapa   456
Thampi, Bhagyalekshmy N.   185
Thomas, K.L.   225, 234
Tiwari, Harshvardhan   205
Tripathy, Somanath   64
Trivedi, Bhushan   54
Tubolino, Marco   385

Varadharajan, Vijayaraghavan   178
Vasanthi, V.   157
Verma, Bhupendra   474
Vidyadharan, Divya S.   234